DICTIONARY
OF TRANSLATED
NAMES AND TITLES

Also by Adrian Room

Dictionary of Cryptic Crossword Clues
Dictionary of Trade Name Origins
Naming Names: A Book of Pseudonyms and Name Changes
Room's Classical Dictionary: The Origins of the Names of Characters in Classical Mythology
Room's Dictionary of Confusibles
Room's Dictionary of Distinguishables
Place-Name Changes Since 1900: A World Gazetteer
Dictionary of Confusing Words and Meanings

DICTIONARY OF TRANSLATED NAMES AND TITLES

Adrian Room

ROUTLEDGE & KEGAN PAUL
LONDON, BOSTON AND HENLEY

First published in 1986
by Routledge and Kegan Paul plc

14 Leicester Square, London WC2H 7PH, England

9 Park Street, Boston, Mass. 02108, USA and

Broadway House, Newtown Road,
Henley on Thames, Oxon RG9 1EN, England

Set in Times
by Hope Services, Abingdon, Oxon
and printed in Great Britain
by The Thetford Press
Thetford, Norfolk

Library of Congress Cataloging in Publication Data

Room, Adrian.
Dictionary of translated names and titles.

English, French, German, Italian, Spanish, and Russian.
Bibliography: p.
Includes index.
1. Arts—Names—Dictionaries—Polyglot. 2. Titles
of works of art—Dictionaries—Polyglot. I. Title.
NX80.R66   1985   700′.3   84-26244

ISBN 0–7100–9953–3

CONTENTS

INTRODUCTION

The Englishman, in spite of his traditionally insular attitude to life and languages, is nevertheless well aware that many of his native cultural products do travel abroad, and that there is a corresponding inflow of plays, novels, films, operas and other artistic creations from foreign countries to Britain. Shakespeare, thus, has long gained international status, and his plays, or derivative works based on them, are seen, heard or read in countries round the world, from Paris to Pekin, Bonn to Buenos Aires. In more recent times, Frenchmen have enjoyed Agatha Christie, Germans responded to Conan Doyle, Italians appreciated Bernard Shaw, Spaniards laughed at Peter Sellers, and Russians empathised with Thomas Hardy and even Kipling. On a reciprocal basis, Englishmen themselves have become familiar, however painfully, with the works of Molière, Mozart, Masaccio, Cervantes and Tolstoy, and in the twentieth century have emoted more readily to the cinematic art of Truffaut, Fassbinder, Antonioni, Buñuel and Eisenstein.

Like their cultural products, and despite their island ties, the English do also go abroad, and there, in alien and apparently unspeakable tongues, they encounter a multitude of foreign names and titles. They discover, for example, that Dunkirk (such an English-sounding name) is Dunkerque in its native France, that Brussels, of homely sprouts associations, is either Bruxelles or Brussel, that in Italy all roads apparently lead to Roma, not Rome, and that, landing at Moscow's main airport, the Soviet capital is apparently known to its indigenous population as MOCKBA, a name suggesting a new synthetic type of chocolate. On street billboards and in local newspapers they furthermore find Shakespeare's *Comme il vous plaira* in production at a Paris theatre, a rerun of the film *Vom Winde verweht* at a Hanover (or Hannover) cinema, and a performance of Britten's opera *Il giro di vite* on at a famous Milan (or Milano) opera-house.

Vom Winde verweht . . . Why yes, that must be *Gone With the Wind*, and presumably *Comme il vous plaira*, suggesting 's'il vous plaît', must be *As You Like It*. But *Il giro di vite*? Not so readily (perhaps with the tactful aid of an Italian friend) does it become apparent that this is not an opera about some kind of bank account or a cycle race but actually *The Turn of the Screw*, based on the novel by Henry James.

Such linguistic traumas may well result in further speculation. If *that's* the French for *As You Like It*, what would *The Merry Wives of Windsor* be? If *that's* the

German for *Gone With the Wind*, how can one discover if *One Flew Over the Cuckoo's Nest* is on anywhere locally? If *that's* what Italians call *The Turn of the Screw*, why do they themselves produce so many operas with untranslated titles (*La Traviata, Il Trovatore, Così fan tutte, Cavalleria rusticana*)? What do *they* all mean, come to that?

The aim of this present dictionary is to supply the answers. In fact, the aim is to do considerably more than this, since the book gives not only the traditional or agreed translations of over 4000 English names and titles into five different foreign languages (French, German, Italian, Spanish, Russian, as being the most common European languages traditionally encountered by English speakers), but also translations from each of these five languages into English. (The latter is done by means of a separate cross-index section at the end of the book; see page 295.)

True, some of the larger bilingual dictionaries do give a selection of common names and their translations, often tucked away in an appendix, but there has not been – until now – a single-volume dictionary devoted entirely to names and titles in different languages. The intention, therefore, is to fill a long-felt gap, and provide a handy reference book that will guide not only the travelling Englishman in his daily linguistic encounters, but also a wide range of writers, readers, students (especially of languages), teachers (likewise), journalists, tourists, holiday-makers and businessmen, among others. The book, too, may well appeal to language-lovers and aspiring or actual 'culture vultures' of all kinds, from the self-confessed amateur or 'ham' to the professional.

Perhaps the really original contribution of the work is its large number of translated *titles* (as distinct from mere geographical or personal names). Here will be found a wide selection of the titles of literary works (novels, plays, poems, and so on) as well as of films and works of art (paintings, sculptures, architectural monuments and the like). The literary works themselves range, via the books of the Bible and other religious writings, from the classics of Greek and Roman writers to modern fiction, and the 'artistic' titles embrace not only films and the fine and applied arts but musical works (operas, ballets, symphonies, for example) and more miscellaneous creations such as the Bayeux Tapestry (really a name, more than a title) and Cleopatra's Needle (more a nickname).

For ease of reference, all true titles in the dictionary are printed in italics, with the exception of the Russian titles which, as is customary in that language, are given in quotes.

The *names* in the dictionary cover not only geographical and personal names (places and people) but also historical events (wars, battles, pacts, revolutions) and international organisations such as the United Nations and the World Health Fund. Personal names cover not only well-known historical characters, including those known by nicknames (Eric the Red, Charles Martel), but also biblical personages, mythological characters, saints, popes, fictional characters (Man Friday) and semi-mythical persons such as Robin Hood and King Arthur. There are also a good representation of astronomical names, whether or not based on the characters of classical mythology, as many of them are.

When it comes to geographical names, the scope is virtually worldwide, as indeed it needs to be. So here are the names of almost all the countries of the world, with the capitals of most of them, as well as major provinces and territories, islands, towns and cities, oceans, seas, lakes, straits, rivers, canals, mountains, hills, and historic regions such as Cochinchina, Normandy and Sudetenland.

A special appendix (page 000) gives the traditional and multilingual equivalents of over seventy first names (Christian names).

Other types of name and title can be best discovered by examining the entries themselves, where it will also be found that much additional information in the form of authorship, dates, geographical location and grammatical guidance is additionally provided. (For more precise details concerning the entries and their arrangement, see the second section of this Introduction, p. xiii).

The hazards of determining the foreign equivalent of a familiar name or title are legion, and the 'expert' is unduly susceptible to error, even howler. This particularly applies to the rendering of an ambiguous or apparently (as it stands) untranslatable title. Aldous Huxley, for example, delighted in such baffling titles for his novels as *Crome Yellow* (*sic*, not 'Chrome'), *Point Counter Point, Antic Hay* (suggesting a harvest-time rough-and-tumble) and *Eyeless in Gaza*. How is one to translate these in any satisfactory or meaningful manner? Then Cronin's *Hatter's Castle* and even Shakespeare's *The Taming of the Shrew* are titles potentially tricky for the translator. The first (translated *El castillo de Hatter* in a solid Spanish reference work) relates not to a man called Hatter but to a man who is a hatter by trade; the second, despite childhood visions to the contrary, concerns a sharp-tongued, bad-tempered woman, not a rogue rodent. (The 'shrew', Katharina, is eventually 'tamed' by Petruchio – and over three centuries later was to become the heroine of the much more unambiguous Cole Porter musical, *Kiss Me, Kate*.)

The Spanish slip mentioned was not the only one encountered in the course of research for the dictionary. Among others noted were (again Spanish) *El pueblo de Blacksmith* ('The Village of Blacksmith') for Longfellow's *The Village Blacksmith*, German *Die Mühle am Fluß* ('The Mill on the River', admittedly an apt alternative) for George Eliot's *The Mill on the Floss*, Spanish *Obsesión* ('Obsession') for Jane Austen's *Persuasion*, German *Der Rodney-Stein* ('The Rodney Stone') for Conan Doyle's *Rodney Stone* (the name is that of the central character and narrator of the story), and Russian *Ovechka ledi Karoliny* ('Lady Caroline's Lamb') for Robert Bolt's film of 1972, *Lady Caroline Lamb*. It will be noted that in almost all these cases the snare lay in a proper name, as it did in one German rendering of Anne Brontë's *The Tenant of Wildfell Hall* as *Der Pächter von Wildfall Hall*. 'Wildfall', suggesting to a German 'wild ruin', is an understandable subconscious 'correction' of an English house name.

On the whole, 'world classic' titles, such as those of Shakespeare's plays, have come to acquire a standard accepted version in a non-native language. Thus, almost invariably, *All's Well That Ends Well* is rendered in French as *Tout est bien qui finit bien*, in German, more succinctly, as *Ende gut, alles gut*, in Italian, more wordily, as *Tutto è bene quel che finisce bene*, in Spanish, more originally, as *A buen fin no hay mal principio* (literally, 'To a good end there is no bad beginning'), and Russian *Konets – delu venets* (literally, 'The end is the crown to the affair'). I said 'almost invariably', since even with established works, of international repute, different translated titles can exist. For example *Twelfth Night*, to cite Shakespeare yet again, is known to Italians as both (literally) *La dodicesima notte* or (to reflect the special festive sense of the title) *La notte dell'Epifania*. This instability of title works the other way round, too, especially when several versions of a work exist, so that Molière's play *Le Médecin malgré lui* has been billed and produced in England both as *The Doctor in Spite of Himself* and *The Reluctant Doctor*, and the same great dramatist's *Le Bourgeois Gentilhomme* has emerged in English not only as *The Would-Be Gentleman* but also as *The Prodigious Snob* and even *The Proper Gent*. What's more, there would be nothing to stop me or you producing yet another version of the play and calling it *The Nouveau Riche* or even *The Jumped-up Jack* if we so chose. What I have had to do consistently here is select the title that has become, as far as can be established, the most widely accepted.

I only regret that the already considerable size of the volume has made it impossible to give a literal translation of the foreign versions of an English title where they noticeably differ from the original. Most, of course, are straightforward and direct renderings: one need only come up with the foreign-language equivalent of 'The boy dressed in blue' or 'The boy wearing blue clothes', for example, to translate Gainsborough's *Blue Boy*. When it comes to the more complex or obscure Aldous Huxley type of title, however, one may frequently find something quite different to the original. Somerset Maugham's *Cakes and Ale* (entry 586), for example, is translated literally only by the Russians: the French prefer 'The Round of Love' (or even 'The Round-Dance of Love), the Germans choose 'His First Wife' as their title, the Italians go for 'The Skeleton in the Cupboard', and the Spanish, like the French, plump more romantically for 'Captive of Love'. In some cases, the translated version is not only as appropriate as the English but somehow even an improvement. Who can resist the charms of the evocative French *Les Hauts de Hurlevent* ('The Heights of Howlwind') to render *Wuthering Heights*? Even the German *Sieben gegen Theben* has a poetic lilt that the English title of Aeschylus' *Seven Against Thebes* somehow lacks (or, if one dare say so, even the original Greek *Hepta epi Thebas*).

However, since the user of the dictionary will presumably have some knowledge of languages, or interest in them, he or she will doubtless be able to discover further surprises unaided – such as the brief *Bunbury* to provide the German title for Wilde's punning *The Importance of Being Earnest*, or *Cocktail für eine Leiche* ('Cocktails for a Corpse', almost as effective in English) for Hitchcock's film *Rope*.

Some titles will be seen to be identical in all languages. This can happen for one of two reasons.

First, many musical works, notably operas and ballets, have come to retain not only in English but also internationally the title in their original language. This especially occurs when the title is either difficult to translate accurately without resorting to paraphrase or is acceptably brief and memorable. A familiar example is Mozart's *Così fan tutte*, which Italian title is the preferred one in English-speaking lands as well as France, Germany, Spain and many other European countries. The title literally means 'Thus do all', with the last word grammatically feminine (the masculine would be *tutti*), and so meaning 'all women'. So one possible English version might be 'That's What Women Are' or, perhaps more effectively, 'All Women Are Like That'. The latter is the version I have selected for the title's entry in the book, although other readers may prefer some other equivalent (such as 'That's Women For You!'). However, for whatever reason, the opera is usually known and billed under its Italian title, and this fact is reflected in its entry.

Second, and conversely, many English-language works keep their English title in foreign countries. This in particular applies to American (and later British) musicals, as well as recent films, so that *My Fair Lady*, *West Side Story*, *E.T.* and *The Shining* are the titles under which these productions are advertised and performed in most European cities, as well as in their native United States or Britain.

The single exception to this monolinguistic principle is the Russian, since Russian titles are invariably translated wherever possible, even of modern works. Thus *Così fan tutte* in Russian is usually known as *Vse oni takovy* ('They are all like that'), and *My Fair Lady*, which has been performed in the Soviet Union with no small success, is habitually rendered *Moya prekrasnaya ledi*. If *The Shining* ever materialises in Moscow, it will be as *Siyanie*.

Before proceeding to an account of the mechanics of the entries, it may be worth stating what is apparently the obvious: that many of the 'other-language' equivalents are not strictly speaking translations but traditional versions, even transliterations, usually adapted to the speech-sounds and grammatical demands of the language concerned. This particularly applies to geographical and personal names, where the principle is, in short, that the older the name, the more likely it will be that a distinctive 'own language' version of it exists. This can be seen, for example, in the names of many countries, where *Norway*, say, has settled to its French version of *Norvège*, German *Norwegen*, Italian *Norvegia*, Spanish *Noruega*, and Russian *Norvegiya*, each of these representing the native variant of the name of the Scandinavian country whose sea was the 'northern way' for (who else?) the Norsemen in days of old. Similarly, Thucydides, the Greek historian of the fifth century BC, has come to have his name adapted in these same European languages, respectively, as *Thucydide*, *Thukydides*, *Tucidide*, *Tucídides* and *Fukidid*. Each country here had to provide its own solution for coping with the initial Greek letter theta ('th').

Similar to the untranslated Italian opera titles are those of many English literary works, notably when they consist of a proper name. This, of course, is not usually translatable, so is left as it is (with an appropriate transliteration into Cyrillic in the case of Russian). Among such titles are those of names of people (*Jane Eyre*) and places (*Middlemarch*). They are included here in the dictionary not simply to occupy valuable space but to indicate that such titles *are* the same in all languages (with perhaps the smallest variation in spelling, or the addition of an accent), and also to give the accepted Russian transliteration of the name. Such titles, however, are certainly in a minority. They cannot be ignored or omitted, though, since they are among the most familiar of the 'world classics'.

This finally leads to a second statement of the obvious: that the 4000-plus names and titles included in the book are only one individualistic selection of the hundreds of thousands of names that exist. The selection may even be subjective in places. Even so, I have aimed to cover as wide a spectrum as possible and to incorporate a large number of well-known names and familiar (and important) titles – together with some that may perhaps be less well-known. And if at least one reader finds this selection useful or entertaining, I shall be more than compensated for the long and sometimes difficult hours needed to compile and check it.

ARRANGEMENT AND CONTENT
OF ENTRIES

The entries are arranged under their English alphabetical order, with the English (GB) name or title followed by its equivalents in French (F), German (D), Italian (I), Spanish (E), and Russian (SU), these abbreviations being, for convenience, those of the respective countries' International Vehicle Registrations.

As mentioned earlier, all titles are printed in *italics* except for the Russian, which are in quotes. This means that all the other entries not in italics are regarded as names. Books of the Bible, however, are not italicised as titles.

In the case of a title, the English entry will normally be followed by (in brackets) the name of the author (director, artist, sculptor, etc.) together with the date(s) of the work's creation or first performance, as appropriate. The date itself may be precise, as a year, or more general, as a century. (See separate section on dates below.) The title given is usually the traditional short one, so we thus have Dickens's *Pickwick Papers*, not *The Posthumous Papers of the Pickwick Club*, which is the work's longer and more formal title, and Kubrick's film *Doctor Strangelove*, not its extended title of *Doctor Strangelove, or, How I Learned to Stop Worrying and Love the Bomb*. The reader is thus, with only the slightest twinge of regret, spared Peter Brook's *The Persecution and Assassination of Jean-Paul Marat as performed by the inmates of the Asylum of Charenton under the Direction of the Marquis de Sade*, in all six languages, but referred instead to his *Marat/Sade*.

The author's name is repeated for the Russian entry, but not for the other languages unless it is significantly different from the English.

If the title was originally in a language that is not one of the six dealt with in the book, it will be added in square brackets after the English. This applies, for example, to the original Greek or Latin of a classical work, or, say, the Norwegian title of an Ibsen play or the Danish title of an Andersen fairy tale. In cases where, as mentioned earlier, the work is traditionally known internationally in its language of origin, as many Italian operas, the literal translation of the title will also be given after the English. The same applies for an English-language work that was given a foreign title, perhaps a Latin one, by its author, as Newman's *Apologia Pro Vita Sua*, or Carlyle's *Sartor Resartus*.

In the case of a name, additional information may be given in brackets as follows:

(a) the country in which a geographical place is located, or the town or city in which a building or other architectural monument is found;

(b) the dates or century in which a historical character lived (see section on dates below);

(c) an abbreviation indicating the name's category (mythological, biblical, historical, astronomical, etc.) or, in the case of a person, his or her status (saint, ruler, etc.);

(d) the abbreviation traditionally used for the name of an organisation, such as UNO for the United Nations Organisation, or for the name of a country, such as USSR for the Soviet Union. The abbreviation USA may be used either geographically or historically to indicate the United States. (This particular abbreviation is used for all languages except Russian, since it is now virtually international.)

For a list of abbreviations used in each language, see page xvii.

In some cases, a name is both that of a person or place, and that of a literary or other artistic work. Where this occurs, the name, although subsequently also a title, is *not* printed in italics, but an indication is given after the English (and also the Russian) entry that the name had a secondary use. This usually appears by means of a plus sign in a formula such as 'Hippolytus (myth. + Euripides)', meaning that the mythological character Hippolytus had his name used by Euripides as the title of a play. It will be appreciated, I am sure, that it has not been possible to include all such derivative titles, since for most mythological and biblical characters someone, somewhere, has written a work or painted a picture or composed a musical piece using their name as a title, and such artistic 'spin-offs', however interesting, would really require a reference book of their own. Even so, some of the more important or better known 'name-titles' are nevertheless given.

As a grammatical aid, the definite article is added before a name where it is commonly used, as with the names of many countries in French, for example. This also serves to indicate the gender of the name. It does not follow, of course, that the name will always be so preceded, and the finer points of grammatical usage of the article are not dealt with here! However, where the article does not in itself indicate the grammatical gender of the name, this may be added in brackets. An example would be 'l'Indochine (f.)' in French, to show that this name is feminine. A similar system is also used for Russian geographical names that end in a soft sign. (See entry 2312, for example, where the gender of the Russian name of Marseille is supplied.)

Otherwise all foreign-language entries will have their correct accents or diacritics, and the Russian entries will have their stress indicated, as is usual in dictionaries. (Russian names with an alternative stress have two stress marks, as in entry 298.)

Most other devices, such as the cross-referring of one alternative title to another (for example, *Sir Charles Grandison→History of Sir Charles Grandison*), are self-explanatory. The aim has been to make the information consistent, and easily accessible.

ACKNOWLEDGMENTS

Although the overall responsibility for the accuracy of the entries and their arrangement must remain mine, I would like to acknowledge the assistance of a number of people at various points in the compilation of the dictionary.

First, both chronologically and 'loadwise', I would like to thank Diana Simmance, who not only typed most of the main entries, in all the different languages (excepting the Russian), but also gamely undertook research ventures and checking projects in various libraries. She was a great morale booster at a time when I was initially taking on the whole work single-handed.

Almost all the film titles, again in the different languages (but again excepting the Russian), were researched and provided by Sally Hibbin and Susan Leonard, using the facilities of the British Film Institute. My thanks to both of them for their efficiency and enthusiasm.

When it came to the cross-indexing, in each of the different languages, I was very glad to have the help of further assistants, as follows: Clémence Hills, who alphabetised all the French entries, Elisabeth Brun, who took on the German, Angela Jarvis, who dealt similarly with both the Italian and Spanish, and Graham Message, who efficiently sorted all the Russian entries.

There is no doubt that without the help of these people I would have found it difficult to meet the publisher's deadline. Thanks to them, the whole project and compilation was completed on schedule.

Adrian Room
Petersfield, Hampshire

DATES

For a title, such as a novel or the first production of a play, the date is normally given as a year, for example '*Above the Rocks* (Pereda, 1895)'. In a few cases, the date is given as a century, in Roman figures. This mostly applies to classical works, for example '*Annals* (Tacitus, II)' means that Tacitus wrote his *Annals* some time in the second century AD – we don't know exactly when.

An approximate year, or even century, is printed in italics, so that for example '*Brandenburg Concertos* (Bach, *1721*)' means that Bach wrote these concertos some time about the year 1721.

For a name, usually that of a person, dates are given in the normal way, with years of birth and death, so that 'Anne of Austria (1601–66)', for example, means that Anne of Austria was born in 1601 and died in 1666, while 'Anne Boleyn (*1507*–36)' means that she was born in approximately the year 1507 (we don't know for sure) and died in 1536 (beheaded when still not yet 30, by order of her husband Henry VIII, on a charge of adultery).

Most dates will be AD, but BC ones are indicated either by means of a minus sign, for example '*Oedipus at Colonus* (Sophocles, −401)', or, when a person's birth and death years are given, by the second date being lower than the first, for example 'Julius Caesar (100–44)' meaning that Caesar was born in 100 BC and died in 44 BC. In one or two cases, a person was born BC but died AD. Here his dates will be given as follows: 'Livy (−59–+17)', meaning that Livy was born in 59 BC but died in 17 AD. Such 'straddle' dates are rare, however.

Where a person's name is followed by no dates, this means that there was more than one person of the name. For example, there was not only the Roman emperor Augustus but also various European rulers of the same name (the so-called Electors of Saxony). Many kings and popes, of course, also had identical names, and so mostly their dates will not be given.

On the whole, century dates, in Roman figures, will mostly be given for early events and historical characters, such as 'Punic Wars (III–II)', meaning that the Punic Wars began in the third century BC and finished in the second, and 'Lawrence (saint, III)', meaning that St Lawrence lived some time in the third century AD.

Overall, however, the dates are really a bonus, and the prime aim of the dictionary is to give the different versions of the name or title. Too much date detail must not therefore be expected in the entries.

ABBREVIATIONS/ABRÉVIATIONS/ ABKÜRZUNGEN/ABBREVIAZIONI/ ABREVIATURAS/СОКРАЩЕНИЯ

(GB)   astron.   astronomy
       Bib.   Bible
       hist.   history
       myth.   mythology
       rel.   religion
       USA   United States of America

(F)   astron.   astronomie
       Bib.   Bible
       f.   féminin
       hist.   histoire
       m.   masculin
       myth.   mythologie
       relig.   religion
       USA   United States of America ('États-Unis d'Amérique')

(D)   Astron.   Astronomie
       Bib.   Bibel
       Gesch.   Geschichte
       Herr.   Herrscher
       myth.   mythologischer Name, mythologische Person
       relig.   religiöser Name, Name in Religion
       USA   United States of America ('Vereinigte Staaten')

(I)   astron.   astronomia
       Bib.   Bibbia
       mit.   mitologia
       relig.   religione
       st.   storia
       USA   United States of America ('Stati Uniti d'America')

(E)   astron.   astronomía
       Bib.   Biblia
       hist.   historia

	mit.	mitología
	relig.	religión
	sob.	sobrano/a
	USA	United States of America ('EE. UU.')
(SU)	астр.	астрономия
	библ.	библеизм
	ж.	женский род
	иск.	искусство
	ист.	история
	м.	мужской род
	миф.	мифология
	прав.	правитель
	рел.	религия
	св.	святой, –ая
	США	Соединённые Штаты Америки

A

1 GB Aachen (Germany)
    F Aix-la-Chapelle (Allemagne)
    D Aachen (Deutschland)
    I Aquisgrana (Germania)
    E Aquisgrán (Alemania)
    SU Áхен (Гермáния)

2 GB Aaron (Bib.)
    F Aaron (Bib.)
    D Aron (Bib.)
    I Aronne (Bib.)
    E Aarón (Bib.)
    SU Аарóн (библ.)

3 GB *Abbot, The* (Scott, 1820)
    F *L'Abbé*
    D *Der Abt*
    I *L'abate*
    E *El monasterio*
    SU «Аббáт» (Скотт)

4 GB *Abduction from the Seraglio, The* (Mozart, 1782)
    F *L'Enlèvement au sérail*
    D *Die Entführung aus dem Serail*
    I *Il ratto dal serraglio*
    E *El rapto del serrallo*
    SU «Похищéние из серáля» (Мóцарт)

5 GB Abel (Bib.)
    F Abel (Bib.)
    D Abel (Bib.)
    I Abele (Bib)
    E Abel (Bib.)
    SU Áвель (библ.)

6 GB Abigail (Bib.)
    F Abigaïl (Bib.)
    D Abigal (Bib.)
    I Abigail (Bib.)
    E Abigaíl (Bib.)
    SU Авигéя (библ.)

7 GB Abominable Snowman, the
    F l'abominable homme des neiges
    D der Schneemensch
    I l'abbominabile uomo delle neve
    E el abominable hombre de las nievas
    SU «снéжный человéк»

8 GB *Above the Rocks* (Pereda, 1895)
    F *Dans les montagnes*
    D *Hoch oben auf den Felsen*
    I *Su per la montagna*
    E *Peñas arriba*
    SU «Над скáлами» (Перéда)

9 GB Abraham (Bib.)
    F Abraham (Bib.)
    D Abraham (Bib.)
    I Abramo (Bib.)
    E Abraham (Bib.)
    SU Авраáм (библ.)

10 GB Abruzzi (Italy)
    F les Abruzzes (m.) (Italie)
    D die Abruzzen (Italien)
    I Abruzzo (Italia)
    E los Abruzos (Italia)
    SU Абрýцци (Итáлия)

11 GB Absalom (Bib.)
    F Absalon (Bib.)
    D Absalom (Bib.)
    I Assalonne (Bib.)
    E Absalón (Bib.)
    SU Авессаллóм (библ.)

12 GB *Absalom, Absalom!* (Faulkner, 1936)
    F *Absalon, Absalon!*
    D *Absalom, Absalom!*
    I *Assalonne! Assalonne!*
    E *¡Absalón, Absalón!*
    SU «Авессалóм, Авессалóм!» (Фóлкнер)

13   GB   *Absalom and Achitopel* (Dryden, 1681)
   F   *Absalon et Achitophel*
   D   *Absalom und Achitophel*
   I   *Absalom e Achitophel*
   E   *Absalón y Aquitafel*
   SU   «Авессалóм и Ахитофéль» (Дрáйден)

14   GB   Abyssinia (hist.)
   F   l`Abyssinie (f.) (hist.)
   D   Abessinien (Gesch.)
   I   l`Abissinia (hist.)
   E   Abisinia (hist.)
   SU   Абиссúния (ист.)

15   GB   Academus (myth.)
   F   Académos (myth.)
   D   Akademos (myth.)
   I   Academo (mit.)
   E   Academos (mit.)
   SU   Акадéм (миф.)

16   GB   *Ace in the Hole* (Wilder, 1951)
   F   *Le Gouffre aux chimères*
   D   *Reporter des Satans*
   I   *L'asso nella manica*
   E   *El gran carnaval*
   SU   «Карнавáл» (Уáйлдер)

17   GB   Achaea (Greece)
   F   l`Achaïe (f.) (Grèce)
   D   Achaia (Griechenland)
   I   l`Acaia (Grecia)
   E   Acaya (Grecia)
   SU   Ахáйя (Грéция)

18   GB   *Acharnians, The [Acharneis]*
    (Aristophanes, −425)
   F   *Les Acharniens* (Aristophane)
   D   *Die Dörfler von Acharnai*
    (Aristophanes)
   I   *Gli acarnesi* (Aristofane)
   E   *Los Acarneos* (Aristófanes)
   SU   «Ахáрняне» (Аристофáн)

19   GB   Achelous (myth.)
   F   Achéloos (myth.)
   D   Acheloos (myth.)
   I   Acheloo (mit.)
   E   Aqueloo (mit.)
   SU   Ахелоóс (миф.)

20   GB   Acheron (myth.)
   F   Achéron (myth.)
   D   Acheron (myth.)
   I   Acheronte (mit.)
   E   Aqueronte (mit.)
   SU   Ахерóн (миф.)

21   GB   Achilles (myth.)
   F   Achille (myth.)
   D   Achilles (myth.)
   I   Achille (mit.)
   E   Aquiles (mit.)
   SU   Ахúлл (миф.)

22   GB   Acis and Galatea (myth., + Handel,
    1718–20)
   F   Acis et Galatée (myth.)
   D   Acis und Galatea (myth.)
   I   Aci e Galatea (mit.)
   E   Acis y Galatea (mit.)
   SU   Акúд и Галатéя (миф., + Гéндель)

23   GB   Acre (Israel)
   F   Acre (Israël)
   D   Akka (Israel)
   I   Akko (Israele)
   E   Acre (Israel)
   SU   Áкка (Изрáиль)

24   GB   Acropolis, the (Athens)
   F   l`Acropole (f.) (Athènes)
   D   die Akropolis (Athen)
   I   l`Acropoli (Atene)
   E   el Acrópolis (Atenas)
   SU   Акрóполь (м.) (Афúны)

25   GB   *Across the River and Into the Trees*
    (Hemingway, 1950)
   F   *Par-delà la rivière et parmi les arbres*
   D   *Über dem Fluß und in die Wälder*
   I   *Al di là dal fiume e tra gli alberi*
   E   *Al otro lado del río y entre los árboles*
   SU   «За рекóй, в тенú дерéвьев»
    (Хемингуэ́й)

26   GB   Actaeon (myth.)
   F   Actéon (myth.)
   D   Aktäon (myth.)
   I   Atteone (mit.)
   E   Acteón (mit.)
   SU   Актеóн (миф.)

27   GB   Acts of the Apostles, the (Bib.)
   F   les Actes des Apôtres (Bib.)
   D   die Apostelgeschichte (Bib.)
   I   gli Atti degli apostoli (Bib.)
   E   los Hechos de los Apóstoles (Bib.)
   SU   «Дея́ния апóстолов» (библ.)

28   GB   Adam (Bib.)
   F   Adam (Bib.)
   D   Adam (Bib.)
   I   Adamo (Bib.)
   E   Adán (Bib.)
   SU   Адáм (библ.)

29 GB *Adam Bede* (Eliot, 1859)
    F *Adam Bede*
    D *Adam Bede*
    I *Adam Bede*
    E *Adam Bede*
    SU «Áдам Бид» (Э́лиот)

30 GB Adelaide (Australia)
    F Adélaïde (Australie)
    D Adelaide (Australien)
    I Adelaide (Australia)
    E Adelaida (Australia)
    SU Аделайда (Австрáлия)

31 GB Admetus (myth.)
    F Admète (myth.)
    D Admetos (myth.)
    I Admeto (mit.
    E Admeto (mit.)
    SU Адмéт (миф.)

32 GB *Admirable Crichton, The* (Barrie, 1902)
    F *L'Admirable Crichton*
    D *Der vortreffliche Crichton*
    I *L'incomparabile Crichton*
    E *El admirable Crichton*
    SU «Восхити́тельный Кра́йтон» (Бáрри)

33 GB *Admirable Crichton, The* (*Male and Female*, USA), (De Mille, 1919)
    F *L'Admirable Crichton*
    D *Zustände wie im Paradies*
    I *Maschio e femmina*
    E *Macho y hembra*
    SU «Самцы́ и сáмки» (Де Милль)

34 GB Admiralty Islands, the
    F les îles de l'Amirauté
    D die Admiraltäts-Inseln
    I le isole dell'Ammiragliato
    E las islas del Almirantazgo
    SU островá Адмиралтéйства

35 GB *Adolphe* (Constant, 1815)
    F *Adolphe*
    D *Adolphe*
    I *Adolfo*
    E *Adolfo*
    SU «Адóльф» (Констáн де Ребéк)

36 GB *Adonais* (Shelley, 1821)
    F *Adonaïs*
    D *Adonais*
    I *Adonais*
    E *Adonais*
    SU «Адонаис» (Шéлли)

37 GB Adonis (myth.)
    F Adonis (myth.)
    D Adonis (myth.)
    I Adone (mit.)
    E Adonis (mit.)
    SU Адони́с (миф.)

38 GB *Adoration of the Lamb, The* (Van Eyck, 1432)
    F *L'Adoration de l'Agneau mystique*
    D der *Genter Altar*
    I il *Polittico dell'Agnello mistico*
    E *El cordero místico*
    SU «Поклонéние áгнцу» (Ван Эйк)

39 GB *Adoration of the Magi, The* (art)
    F *L'Adoration des Rois mages* (art)
    D *Die Verehrung der Magier* (Kunst)
    I *Adorazione dei Magi* (arte)
    E *Adoración de los Reyes Magos* (arte)
    SU «Поклонéние волхвóв» (иск.)

40 GB Adrastus (myth.)
    F Adraste (myth.)
    D Adrastos (myth.)
    I Arasto (mit.)
    E Adrasto (mit.)
    SU Адрáст (миф.)

41 GB Adrian (saint, pope)
    F Adrien (saint, pape)
    D Hadrian (Heiliger, Papst)
    I Adriano (santo, papa)
    E Adriano (santo, papa)
    SU Адриáн (св., пáпа ри́мский)

42 GB Adrianopolis (hist., = Edirne)
    F Andrinople (hist.)
    D Adrianopel (Gesch.)
    I Adrianopoli (st.)
    E Andrinópolos (hist.)
    SU Адрианóполь (м.) (ист., = Эди́рне)

43 GB Adriatic Sea, the
    F la mer Adriatique
    D das Adriatische Meer
    I il mare Adriatico
    E el mar Adriatico
    SU Адриати́ческое мóре

44 GB Advent (rel.)
    F l'Avent (m.) (relig.)
    D der Advent (relig.)
    I l'avvento (relig.)
    E el Adviento (relig.)
    SU рождéственский пост (рел.)

45 GB *Adventures of Augie March, The*
         (Bellow, 1953)
     F   *Les Aventures d'Augie March*
     D   *Die Abenteuer des Augie March*
     I   *Le avventure di Augie March*
     E   *Las aventuras de Augie March*
     SU «Приключе́ния О́ги Ма́рча» (Бе́ллоу)

46 GB *Adventures of Caleb Williams, The*
         (Godwin, 1794)
     F   *Les Aventures de Caleb Williams*
     D   *Caleb Williams, oder Die Dinge, wie sie
         sind*
     I   *Le avventure di Caleb Williams*
     E   *Las aventuras de Caleb Williams*
     SU «Ве́щи, как они́ есть, и́ли Приключе́ния
         Ка́леба Ви́льямса» (Го́двин)

47 GB *Adventures of Harry Richmond, The*
         (Meredith, 1871)
     F   *Les Aventures de Harry Richmond*
     D   *Die Abenteuer des Harry Richmond*
     I   *Le avventure di Harry Richmond*
     E   *Las aventuras de Harry Richmond*
     SU «Приключе́ния Га́рри Ри́чмонда»
         (Ме́редит)

48 GB *Adventures of Huckleberry Finn, The*
         (Twain, 1884)
     F   *Les Aventures de Huckleberry Finn*
     D   *Huckleberry Finns Abenteuer*
     I   *Le avventure di Huckleberry Finn*
     E   *Las aventuras de Huckleberry Finn*
     SU «Приключе́ния Ге́кльберри Фи́нна»
         (Твен)

49 GB *Adventures of Peregrine Pickle*, The
         (Smollett, 1751)
     F   *Les Aventures de Peregrine Pickle*
     D   *Peregrine Pickles Abenteuer*
     I   *Le avventure di Peregrine Pickle*
     E   *Las aventuras de Peregrine Pickle*
     SU «Приключе́ния Пе́регрина Пи́кля»
         (Смо́ллетт)

50 GB *Adventures of Pinocchio, The* (Collodi,
         1883)
     F   *Les Aventures de Pinocchio*
     D   *Pinocchios Abenteuer*
     I   *Le avventure di Pinocchio*
     E   *Las aventuras de Pinocho*
     SU «Приключе́ния Пино́ккио» (Колло́ди)

51 GB *Adventures of Roderick Random, The*
         (Smollett, 1748)
     F   *Les Aventures de Roderick Random*
     D   *Roderick Randoms Abenteuer*
     I   *Le avventure di Roderick Random*
     E   *Las aventuras de Roderick Random*
     SU «Приключе́ния Ро́дрика Рэ́ндома»
         (Смо́ллетт)

52 GB *Adventures of Sherlock Homes, The*
         (Doyle, 1891)
     F   *Les Aventures de Sherlock Holmes*
     D   *Sherlock Holmes' Abenteuer*
     I   *Le avventure di Sherlock Holmes*
     E   *Las aventuras de Sherlock Holmes*
     SU «Приключе́ния Шё́рлока Хо́лмса»
         (Дойл)

53 GB *Adventures of Telemachus, The*
         (Fénelon, 1699)
     F   *Les Aventures de Télémaque*
     D   *Telemachs Abenteuer*
     I   *Le avventure di Telemaco*
     E   *Las aventuras de Telémaco*
     SU «Приключе́ния Телема́ка» (Фенело́н)

54 GB *Adventures of Tom Sawyer, The* (Twain,
         1876)
     F   *Les Aventures de Tom Sawyer*
     D   *Tom Sawyers Abenteuer*
     I   *Le avventure di Tom Sawyer*
     E   *Las aventuras de Tom Sawyer*
     SU «Приключе́ния То́ма Со́йера» (Твен)

55 GB Aeacus (myth.)
     F   Éaque (myth.)
     D   Äakus (myth.)
     I   Eaco (mit.)
     E   Éaco (mit.)
     SU Эа́к (миф.)

56 GB Aegean Sea, the
     F   la mer Égée
     D   das Ägäische Meer
     I   il mare Egeo
     E   el mar Egeo
     SU Эге́йское мо́ре

57 GB Aeneas (myth.)
     F   Énée (myth.)
     D   Äneas (myth.)
     I   Enea (mit.)
     E   Eneas (mit.)
     SU Эне́й (миф.)

58 GB *Aeneid*, the (Virgil, −19)
 F l'*Énéide* (f.) (Virgile)
 D die *Äneide* (Vergil)
 I l'*Eneide* (Virgilio)
 E la *Eneida* (Virgilio)
 SU «Энеи́да» (Верги́лий)

 GB Aeolian Islands →Lipari Islands

59 GB Aeolus (myth.)
 F Éole (myth.)
 D Äolus (myth.)
 I Eolo (mit.)
 E Eolo (mit.)
 SU Эо́л (миф.)

60 GB Aeschylus (525–456)
 F Eschyle
 D Äschylus
 I Eschilo
 E Esquilo
 SU Эсхи́л

61 GB Aesop (−V)
 F Ésope
 D Äsop
 I Esopo
 E Esopo
 SU Эзо́п

62 GB Aesop's *Fables*
 F les *Fables d'Ésope*
 D die äsopischen Fabeln
 I le favole di Esopo
 E las *Fabulas de Esopo*
 SU «Эзо́повы ба́сни»

63 GB *Aethiopica*, the (Heliodorus, III)
 F les *Éthiopiques* (Héliodore)
 D die *Aithiopika* (Heliodoros)
 I le *Etiopiche* (Eliodoro)
 E las *Etiópicas* (Heliodoro)
 SU «Эфио́пская по́весть» (Гелиодо́р)

64 GB *Affair, The* (Snow, 1959)
 F *L'Affaire*
 D *Die Affäre*
 I *L'affare*
 E *El asunto*
 SU «Де́ло» (Сно́у)

65 GB Afghanistan
 F l'Afghanistan (m.)
 D Afghanistan
 I l'Afghanistan
 E Afganistán
 SU Афганиста́н

66 GB Africa
 F l'Afrique (f.)
 D Afrika
 I l'Africa
 E África
 SU А́фрика

67 GB *Africa* (Petrarch, 1338–43)
 F *Africa* (Pétrarque)
 D *Africa* (Petrarca)
 I *Africa* (Petrarca)
 E *África* (Petrarca)
 SU «А́фрика» (Петра́рка)

68 GB *African Queen, The* (Huston, 1951)
 F *La Reine Africaine*
 D *African Queen*
 I *La regina d'Africa*
 E *La reina de África*
 SU «Африка́нская короле́ва» (Хью́стон)

69 GB *African Woman, The* (Meyerbeer, 1865)
 F *L'Africaine*
 D *Die Afrikanerin*
 I *L'Africana*
 E *La africana*
 SU «Африка́нка» (Мейербе́р)

70 GB *After Many a Summer* (Huxley, 1939)
 F *Jouvence*
 D *Nach vielen Sommern*
 I *Dopo molte estati*
 E *Viejo muere el cisne*
 SU «По́сле мно́гих лет умира́ет ле́бедь» (Ха́ксли)

71 GB *Afternoon of a Faun, The* (Mallarmé, 1876)
 F *L'Après-midi d'un faune*
 D *Der Nachmittag eines Fauns*
 I *Il pomeriggio di un fauno*
 E *La siesta de un fauno*
 SU «Послеполу́дня фа́вна» (Малларме́)

72 GB Agamemnon (myth.)
 F Agamemnon (myth.)
 D Agamemnon (myth.)
 I Agamennone (mit.)
 E Agamenón (mit.)
 SU Агаме́мнон (миф.)

73 GB Agatha (saint) (III)
 F Agathe (sainte)
 D Agathe (Heilige)
 I Agata (santa)
 E Agata (santa)
 SU Ага́та (св.)

74 GB Agincourt (France)
F Azincourt (France)
D Azincourt (Frankreich)
I Azincourt (Francia)
E Azincourt (Francia)
SU Азенку́р (Фра́нция)

75 GB Agnes (saint) (III)
F Agnès (sainte)
D Agnes (Heilige)
I Agnese (santa)
E Ines (santa)
SU Агне́сса (св.)

76 GB *Agnes Grey* (Brontë, 1847)
F *Agnes Grey*
D *Agnes Grey*
I *Agnes Grey*
E *Agnes Grey*
SU «А́гнес Грей» (Бро́нте)

77 GB Agricola (37–93)
F Agricola
D Agricola
I Agricola
E Agrícola
SU Агри́кола

78 GB Agrippa (I)
F Agrippa
D Agrippa
I Agrippa
E Agripa
SU Агри́ппа

79 GB Agrippina (I)
F Agrippine
D Agrippina
I Agrippina
E Agripina
SU Агриппи́на

80 GB Ahab (Bib.)
F Achab (Bib.)
D Ahab (Bib.)
I Acab (Bib.)
E Acab (Bib.)
SU Аха́в (библ.)

81 GB *Aida* (Verdi, 1871)
F *Aïda*
D *Aida*
I *Aida*
E *Aida*
SU «Аи́да» (Ве́рди)

82 GB Ajax (myth. + Sophocles, −V)
F Ajax (myth. + Sophocle)
D Ajax (myth., + Sophokles)
I Aiace (mit., + Sofocle)
E Áyax (mit. + Sófocles)
SU Ая́кс (миф., + Софо́кл)

83 GB *Aladdin or the Wonderful Lamp*
(*Thousand and One Nights*)
F *Aladin ou la Lampe Merveilleuse* (*Mille et une nuits*)
D *Aladin, oder Die wunderbare Lampe* (*Tausendundeine Nacht*)
I *Aladino, o La lampada meravigliosa* (*Mille e una notte*)
E *Aladino o La lámpara maravillosa* (*Mil y una noches*)
SU «Ала́дин и волше́бная ла́мпа» («Ты́сяча и одна́ ночь»)

84 GB Alaska (USA)
F l'Alaska (m.) (USA)
D Alaska (USA)
I l'Alaska (USA)
E Alaska (USA)
SU Аля́ска (США)

85 GB Albania
F l'Albanie (f.)
D Albanien
I l'Albania
E Albania
SU Алба́ния

86 GB Albert (sovereign)
F Albert (souverain)
D Albert (Herr.)
I Alberto (sovrano)
E Alberto (sob.)
SU Альбе́рт (прав.)

87 GB Alberta (Canada)
F l'Alberta (f.) (Canada)
D Alberta (Kanada)
I l'Alberta (Canada)
E Alberta (Canadá)
SU Альбе́рта (Кана́да)

88 GB Albert Canal, the (Belgium)
F le canal Albert (Belge)
D der Albert-Kanal (Belgien)
I il canale Alberto (Belgio)
E el canal Alberto (Bélgica)
SU А́льберт-кана́л (Бе́льгия)

89 GB Alcestis (myth.)
F Alceste (myth.)
D Alkeste (myth.)
I Alcesti (mit.)
E Alcestes (mit.)
SU Альцéста (миф.)

90 GB *Alchemist, The* (Jonson, 1610)
F *L'Alchimiste*
D *Der Alchemist*
I *L'alchimista*
E *El alquimista*
SU «Алхи́мик» (Джóнсон)

91 GB Alcibiades (*450*–404)
F Alcibiade
D Alkibiades
I Alcibiade
E Alcibíades
SU Алкивиáд

92 GB Alcmaeon (myth.)
F Alcméon (myth.)
D Alkmäon (myth.)
I Alcmeone (mit.)
E Alcmeón (mit.)
SU Алкмеóн (миф.)

93 GB Alcmene (myth.)
F Alcmène (myth.)
D Alkmene (myth.)
I Alcmena (mit.)
E Alcmena (mit.)
SU Алкмéна (миф.)

94 GB Alcuin (735–804)
F Alcuin
D Alkuin
I Alcuino
E Alcuino
SU Áлкуин

95 GB Alderney (Channel Islands)
F Aurigny (îles Anglo-Normandes)
D Alderney (Kanalinseln)
I Alderney (isole Normanne)
E Alderney (islas Anglonormandas)
SU Óлдерни (Нормáндские островá)

96 GB Alessandria (Italy)
F Alessandria (Italie)
D Alexandria (Italien)
I Alessandria (Italia)
E Alejandría (Italia)
SU Алессáндрия (Итáлия)

97 GB Aleutian Islands, the
F les îles Aléoutiennes
D die Alëuten
I le isole Aleutine
E las islas Aleutianas
SU Алеýтские островá

98 GB Alexander (saint, pope, sovereign)
F Alexandre (saint, papa, souverain)
D Alexander (Heiliger, Papst, Herr.)
I Alessandro (santo, papa, sovrano)
E Alejandro (santo, papa, sob.)
SU Алексáндр (св., пáпа ри́мский, прав.)

99 GB Alexander Nevsky (1220–63)
(+Eisenstein, 1938)
F Alexandre Nevski
D Alexander Newskij
I Alessandro Nevskij
E Alejandro Nevski
SU Алексáндр Нéвский (+ Эйзенштéйн)

100 GB Alexander the Great (356–323)
F Alexandre le Grand
D Alexander der Große
I Alessandro Magno
E Alejandro Magno
SU Алексáндр Македóнский

101 GB Alexandretta (=Iskenderun, Turkey)
F Alexandretta (Turquie)
D Alexandrette (Turkei)
I Alessandretta (Turchia)
E Alejandreta (Turquía)
SU Александрéтта (= Искендерóн, Тýрция)

102 GB Alexandria (Egypt)
F Alexandrie (Égypte)
D Alexandria (Ägypten)
I Alessandria (Egitto)
E Alejandría (Egipto)
SU Александри́я (Еги́пет)

103 GB Alexis (sovereign)
F Alexis (souverain)
D Alixis (Herr.)
I Alesso (sovrano)
E Alejo (sob.)
SU Алексéй (прав.)

104 GB Alfonso (sovereign)
F Alphonse (souverain)
D Alfons (Herr.)
I Alfonso (sovrano)
E Alfonso (sob.)
SU Альфóнс (прав.)

105 GB Alfonso the Wise (1221–84)
    F Alphonse le Sage
    D Alfons der Weise
    I Alfonso il Saggio
    E Alfonso el Sabio
    SU Альфóнс Мýдрый

106 GB Alfred the Great (*849–899*)
    F Alfred le Grand
    D Alfred der Große
    I Alfredo il Grande
    E Alfredo Magno
    SU Альфрéд Велúкий

107 GB Algeria
    F l'Algérie (f.)
    D Algerien
    I l'Algeria
    E Argelia
    SU Алжúр

108 GB Algiers (Algeria)
    F Alger (Algérie)
    D Algier (Algerien)
    I Algeri (Algeria)
    E Argel (Argelia)
    SU Алжúр (Алжúр)

109 GB Alhambra, the (Granada, Spain)
    F l'Alhambra (Grenade, Espagne)
    D die Alhambra (Granada, Spanien)
    I l'Alhambra (Granada, Spagna)
    E la Alhambra (Granada, España)
    SU Альгáмбра (Гранáда, Испáния)

110 GB *Ali Baba and the Forty Thieves*
       (*Thousand and One Nights*)
    F *Ali Baba et les Quarante Voleurs* (*Mille*
       et une nuits)
    D *Ali Baba und die vierzig Räuber*
       (*Tausendundeine Nacht*)
    I *Ali Baba e i quaranta ladri* (*Mille e una*
       notte)
    E *Alí Babá y los cuarenta ladrones* (*Mil y*
       una noches)
    SU «Алú Бабá и Сóрок разбóйников»
       («Тысяча и однá ночь»)

111 GB *Alice Doesn't Live Here Any More*
       (Scorsese, 1974)
    F *Alice n'est plus ici*
    D *Alic lebt nicht mehr hier*
    I *Alice non abita più qui*
    E *Alicia ya no vive aquí*
    SU «Алúсы здесь бóльше нет»
       (Скорсéсе)

112 GB *Alice in Wonderland* (Carroll, 1865)
    F *Alice au pays des merveilles*
    D *Alice im Wunderland*
    I *Alice nel paese delle meraviglie*
    E *Alicia en el país de las maravillas*
    SU «Алúса в странé чудéс» (Кэрролл)

113 GB *All About Eve* (Mankiewicz, 1950)
    F *Ève*
    D *Alles über Eva*
    I *Eva contro Eva*
    E *Eva al desnudo*
    SU «Éва как онá есть» (Манкéвич)

114 GB Allah (rel.)
    F Allah (relig.)
    D Allah (relig.)
    I Allah (relig.)
    E Alá (relig.)
    SU Аллáх (рел.)

115 GB *All for Love* (Dryden, 1678)
    F *Tout pour l'amour*
    D *Alles für Liebe*
    I *Tutto per amore*
    E *Todo por amor*
    SU «Всё для любвú» (Дрáйден)

116 GB *All God's Chillun Got Wings* (O'Neill,
       1924)
    F *Tous les enfants du Bon Dieu ont des*
       ailes
    D *Alle Kinder Gottes haben Flügel*
    I *Tutti i figli di Dio hanno le ali*
    E *Todos los hijos de Dios tienen alas*
    SU «У всех детéй гóспода бóга есть
       крылья» (О'Нúл)

117 GB *All Men are Enemies* (Aldington, 1933)
    F *Tous les hommes sont des ennemis*
    D *Alle Männer sind Feinde*
    I *Tutti gli uomini sono nemici*
    E *Todos los hombres son enemigos*
    SU «Все люди – вรагú» (Óлдингтон)

118 GB *All My Sons* (Miller, 1947)
    F *Tous mes fils*
    D *Alle meine Söhne*
    I *Erano tutti miei figli*
    E *Todos son mis hijos*
    SU «Все мои сыновья» (Мúллер)

119   GB   *All Quiet on the Western Front*
             (Remarque, 1927)
      F   *À l'ouest rien de nouveau*
      D   *Im Westen nichts Neues*
      I   *All'Ovest niente di nuovo*
      E   *Sin novedad en el fronte*
      SU   «На Западном фронте без
             переме́н» (Рема́рк)

120   GB   All Saints' Day (rel.)
      F   la Toussaint (relig.)
      D   das Allerheiligen (relig.)
      I   l'Ognissanti (relig.)
      E   el Día de Todos los Santos (relig.)
      SU   день всех святы́х (рел.)

121   GB   All Souls' Day (rel.)
      F   le jour des Morts (relig.)
      D   das Allerseelen (relig.)
      I   il giorno dei morti (relig.)
      E   el Día de las Ánimas (relig.)
      SU   день всех душ (рел.)

122   GB   *All's Well That Ends Well*
             (Shakespeare, 1600)
      F   *Tout est bien qui finit bien*
      D   *Ende gut, alles gut*
      I   *Tutto è bene quel che finisce bene*
      E   *A buen fin no hay mal principio*
      SU   «Коне́ц – де́лу вене́ц» (Шекспи́р)

123   GB   *All the King's Men* (Warren, 1946)
      F   *Les Fous du roi*
      D   *Der Gouverneur*
      I   *Tutti gli uomini del re*
      E   *Todos los hombres del rey*
      SU   «Вся короле́вская рать» (Уо́ррен)

124   GB   *All the President's Men* (Pakula, 1976)
      F   *Les Hommes du président*
      D   *Die Unbestechlichen*
      I   *Tutti gli uomini del presidente*
      E   *Todos los hombres del presidente*
      SU   «Лю́ди президе́нта» (Паку́ла)

125   GB   *Almagest*, the (Ptolemy, II)
      F   l'*Almageste* Ptolémée)
      D   die *Almagest* (Ptolemäus)
      I   l'*Almagesto* (Tolomeo)
      E   el *Almagesto* (Ptolomeo)
      SU   «Альмаге́ст» (Птолеме́й)

126   GB   *Almayer's Folly* (Conrad, 1895)
      F   *La Folie-Almayer*
      D   *Almayers Wahn*
      I   *La follia di Almayer*
      E   *La locura de Almayer*
      SU   «Капри́з Óлмейера» (Кóнрад)

127   GB   Alps, the
      F   les Alpes (f.)
      D   die Alpen
      I   le Alpi
      E   los Alpes
      SU   Áльпы (ж.)

128   GB   Alsace (France)
      F   l'Alsace (f.) (France)
      D   Elsaß (Frankrcich)
      I   l'Alsazia (Francia)
      E   Alsacia (Francia)
      SU   Эльзáс (Фрáнция)

129   GB   Alsace-Lorraine (France/Germany)
      F   l'Alsace-Lorraine (f.)
             (France/Allemagne)
      D   Elsaß-Lothringen
             (Frankreich/Deutschland)
      I   l'Alsazia-Lorena (Francia/Germania)
      E   Alsacia Lorena (Francia/Alemania)
      SU   Эльзáс-Лотари́нгия
             (Фрáнция/Гермáния)

130   GB   *Alton Locke* (Kingsley, 1850)
      F   *Alton Locke*
      D   *Alton Locke*
      I   *Alton Locke*
      E   *Alton Locke*
      SU   «Óлтон Локк» (Ки́нгсли)

131   GB   *Amahl and the Night Visitors* (Menotti,
             1951)
      F   *Amahl et les visiteurs nocturnes*
      D   *Amahl und die Gäste der Nacht*
      I   *Amahl o gli ospiti notturni*
      E   *Amahl y los Reyes Magos*
      SU   «Амáль и ночны́е гóсти» (Менóтти)

132   GB   Amalekites, the (Bib.)
      F   les Amalécites (Bib.)
      D   die Amalekiter (Bib.)
      I   gli Amaleciti (Bib.)
      E   los amalecitas (Bib.)
      SU   амаликитя́не (библ.)

133   GB   Amalthaea (myth.)
      F   Amalthée (myth.)
      D   Amalthea (myth.)
      I   Amaltea (mit.)
      E   Amaltea (mit.)
      SU   Амальтéя (миф.)

134   GB   *Amarcord* (Fellini, 1973)
      F   *Amarcord*
      D   *Amarcord*
      I   *Amarcord*
      E   *Amarcord*
      SU   «Амаркóрд» (Фелли́ни)

135 GB   Amazon (River), the
   F   l'Amazone (f.)
   D   der Amazonas
   I   il Rio delle Amazzoni
   E   el Amazonas
   SU   Амазóнка

136 GB   Amazons, the (myth.)
   F   les Amazones (myth.)
   D   die Amazonen (myth.)
   I   le amazzoni (mit.)
   E   las Amazonas (mit.)
   SU   амазóнки (миф.)

137 GB   *Ambassadors, The* (James, 1903)
   F   *Les Ambassadeurs*
   D   *Die Gesandten*
   I   *Gli ambasciatori*
   E   *Los embajadores*
   SU   «Послы́» (Джеймс)

138 GB   Ambrose (saint) (339–397)
   F   Ambroise (saint)
   D   Ambrosius (Heiliger)
   I   Ambrogio (santo)
   E   Ambrosio (santo)
   SU   Амврóсий (св.)

139 GB   *Amelia* (Fielding, 1751)
   F   *Amélie*
   D   *Amelia*
   I   *Amelia*
   E   *Amelia*
   SU   «Амéлия» (Фи́лдинг)

140 GB   America
   F   l'Amérique (f.)
   D   Amerika
   I   l'America
   E   América
   SU   Амéрика

141 GB   *America, America* (Kazan, 1964)
   F   *America, America*
   D   *Die Unbezwingbaren*
   I   *America, America*
   E   *América, América*
   SU   «Амéрика, Амéрика!» (Кáзан)

142 GB   *American, The* (James, 1877)
   F   *L'Américain*
   D   *Der Amerikaner*
   I   *L'americano*
   E   *El americano*
   SU   «Американец» (Джеймс)

143 GB   American Civil War, the (1861–5)
   F   la guerre de Sécession
   D   der Sezessionskrieg
   I   la guerra di secessione
   E   la guerra de Secesión
   SU   Американская гражданская войнá

144 GB   *American in Paris, An* (Minnelli, 1951)
   F   *Un Américain à Paris*
   D   *Ein Amerikaner in Paris*
   I   *Americano a Parigi*
   E   *Un americano en París*
   SU   «Американец в Пари́же» (Миннéлли)

   GB   American Revolution→
        Independence, War of

145 GB   *American Tragedy, An* (Dreiser, 1925)
   F   *Une tragédie américaine*
   D   *Eine amerikanische Tragödie*
   I   *Una tragedia americana*
   E   *Una tragedia americana*
   SU   «Американская трагéдия» (Дрáйзер)

   GB   American War of Independence→
        Independence, War of

146 GB   Ammonites, the (Bib.)
   F   les Ammonites (Bib.)
   D   die Ammoniter (Bib.)
   I   gli ammoniti (Bib.)
   E   los amonitas (Bib.)
   SU   аммони́ты (библ.)

147 GB   *Amok* (Zweig, 1923)
   F   *Amok*
   D   *Amok*
   I   *Amok*
   E   *Amok*
   SU   «Áмок» (Цвейг)

148 GB   *Amoretti* (Spenser, 1591–1)
   F   *Amoretti*
   D   *Amoretti*
   I   *Amoretti*
   E   *Amoretti*
   SU   «Аморéтти» (Спéнсер)

149 GB   Amos (Bib.)
   F   Amos (Bib.)
   D   Amos (Bib.)
   I   Amos (Bib.)
   E   Amós (Bib.)
   SU   Амóс (библ.)

150   GB   Amphitrite (myth.)
       F   Amphitrite (myth.)
       D   Amphitrite (myth.)
       I   Anfitrite (mit.)
       E   Anfitrite (mit.)
       SU   Амфитри́та (миф.)

151   GB   Amphitryon (myth. + Molière, 1668)
       F   Amphitryon (myth.)
       D   Amphitryon (myth.)
       I   Anfitrione (mit.)
       E   Anfitrión (mit.)
       SU   Амфитрио́н (миф., + Молье́р)

152   GB   *Amphitryon 38* (Giraudoux, 1929)
       F   *Amphitryon 38*
       D   *Amphitryon 38*
       I   *Anfitrione 38*
       E   *Anfitrión 38*
       SU   «Амфитрио́н 38» (Жироду́)

153   GB   Anabaptists, the (rel.)
       F   les anabaptistes (relig.)
       D   die Wiedertäufer (relig.)
       I   gli anabattisti (relig.)
       E   los anabaptistas (relig.)
       SU   анабапти́сты (рел.)

154   GB   *Anabasis*, the [*The Expedition*]
            (Xenophon, −370)
       F   l'*Anabase* (f.) (Xénophon)
       D   die *Anabasis* (Xenophon)
       I   l'*Anabasi* (Senofonte)
       E   la *Anábasis* (Jenofonte)
       SU   «Ана́басис» (Ксенофо́н)

155   GB   Anacreon (*563–478*)
       F   Anacréon
       D   Anakreon
       I   Anacreonte
       E   Anacreonte
       SU   Анакрео́нт

156   GB   Ananias (Bib.)
       F   Ananias (Bib.)
       D   Ananias (Bib.)
       I   Anania (Bib.)
       E   Ananías (Bib.)
       SU   Ана́ния (библ.)

157   GB   Anatolia (hist.)
       F   l'Anatolie (f.) (hist.)
       D   Anatolien (Gesch.)
       I   l'Anatolia (st.)
       E   Anatolia (hist.)
       SU   Анато́лия (ист.)

158   GB   *Anatomy Lesson* (Rembrandt, 1632)
       F   *Leçon d'anatomie*
       D   die *Anatomie des Dr. Tulp*
       I   *Lezione d'anatomia*
       E   *Lección de anatomía*
       SU   «Уро́к анато́мии до́ктора Тю́лпа
             (Ре́мбрандт)

159   GB   *Anatomy of Melancholy, The* (Burton,
            1621)
       F   *L'Anatomie de la mélancolie*
       D   *Die Schwermut der Liebe*
       I   *Anatomia della malincolia*
       E   *Anatomía de la melancolía*
       SU   «Анато́мия меланхо́лии» (Бёртон)

160   GB   Anaxagoras (*500–428*)
       F   Anaxagore
       D   Anaxagoras
       I   Anassagora
       E   Anaxágoras
       SU   Анаксаго́р

161   GB   Anaximander (*610–546*)
       F   Anaximandre
       D   Anaximander
       I   Anassimandro
       E   Anaximandro
       SU   Анаксима́ндр

162   GB   Anaximenes (*586–528*)
       F   Anaximène
       D   Anaximenes
       I   Anassimene
       E   Anaxímenes
       SU   Анаксиме́н

163   GB   Anchises (myth.)
       F   Anchise (myth.)
       D   Anchises (myth.)
       I   Anchise (mit.)
       E   Anquises (mit.)
       SU   Анхи́з (миф.)

       GB   *Ancient Mariner, Rime of the*→*Rime of
            the Ancient Mariner*

164   GB   Andalusia (Spain)
       F   l'Andalousie (f.) (Espagne)
       D   Andalusien (Spanien)
       I   l'Andalusia (Spagna)
       E   Andalucía (España)
       SU   Андалу́сия (Испа́ния)

165 GB Andes, the
F les Andes (f.)
D die Anden
I le Ande
E los Andes
SU Áнды (ж.)

166 GB Andorra
F l'Andorre (f.)
D Andorra
I l'Andorra
E Andorra
SU Андóрра

GB *And Quiet Flows the Don→Silent Don, The*

167 GB Andrea del Sarto (1486–1531)
F Andrea del Sarto
D Andrea del Sarto
I Andrea del Sarto
E Andrea del Sarto
SU Андрéа дель Сáрто

168 GB Andrew (saint, sovereign)
F André (saint, souverain)
D Andreas (Heiliger, Herr.)
I Andrea (santo, sovrano)
E Andrés (santo, sob.)
SU Андрéй (св., прав.)

169 GB *Andrian Girl, The [Andria]* (Terence, −160)
F *L'Andrienne* (Térence)
D *Das Mädchen von Andros* (Terentius)
I *La donna di Andro* (Terenzio)
E *Andria* (Terencio)
SU «Дéвушка с Áндроса» (Терéнций)

170 GB Androcles (I)
F Androclès
D Androcles
I Androclo
E Androcles
SU Андрóкл

171 GB *Androcles and the Lion* (Shaw, 1912)
F *Androclès et le lion*
D *Androcles und der Löwe*
I *Androclo e il leone*
E *Androcles y el león*
SU «Андрóкл и лев» (Шóу)

172 GB Andromache (myth., + Euripides, −426; Racine, 1667)
F Andromaque (myth., + Euripide, Racine)
D Andromache (myth., + Euripides, Racine)
I Andromaca (mit., + Euripide, Racine)
E Andrómaca (mit., + Eurípides, Racine)
SU Андромáха (миф., + Еврипи́д, Раси́н)

173 GB Andromeda (myth., astron.)
F Andromède (myth., astron.)
D Andromeda (myth., Astron.)
I Andromeda (mit., astr.)
E Andrómeda (mit., astr.)
SU Андромéда (миф., астр.)

174 GB *And Suddenly It's Evening* (Quasimodo, 1942)
F *Et tout à coup, c'est le soir*
D *Und es ist gleich Abend*
I *Ed è subito sera*
E *Y de pronto, la tarde*
SU «А вдруг – вéчер» (Квази́модо)

175 GB Angelico, Fra (*1395–1455*)
F Fra Angelico
D Fra Angelico
I Beato Angelico
E Fra Angélico
SU Анджéлико

176 GB *Angel Pavement* (Priestley, 1930)
F *Ruelle de l'ange*
D *Engelsgasse*
I *La via dell'angelo*
E *El callejón del ángel*
SU «У́лица Áнгела» (При́стли)

177 GB *Angelus, The* (Millet, 1858)
F *L'Angelus*
D *Das Abendgebet*
I *L'Angelus*
E *El Ángelus*
SU «Áнжелюс» (Миллé)

178 GB Angles, the (hist.)
F les Angles (hist.)
D die Angeln (Gesch.)
I gli angli (st.)
E los anglos (hist.)
SU áнглы (ист.)

179 GB *Anglo-Saxon Attitudes* (Wilson, 1956)
F *Attitudes anglo-saxonnes*
D *Späte Entdeckungen*
I *Prima che sia tardi*
E *Actitudes anglosajonas*
SU «Англосаксо́нские по́зы» (Уи́лсон)

180 GB Anglo-Saxons, the (hist.)
F les Anglo-Saxons (hist.)
D die Angelsachsen (Gesch.)
I gli anglosassoni (st.)
E los anglosajones (hist.)
SU англоса́ксы (ист.)

181 GB Angoulême (France)
F Angoulême (France)
D Angoulême (Frankreich)
I Angoulême (Francia)
E Angulema (Francia)
SU Ангуле́м (Фра́нция)

182 GB Angry Young Men, the (*1957–1965*)
F les "jeunes gens en colère"
D die "zornigen jungen Männer"
I i "giovani arrabbiati"
E los "jóvenes airados"
SU «рассе́рженные молоды́е лю́ди»

183 GB *Animal Farm* (Orwell, 1946)
F *La République des animaux*
D *Farm der Tiere*
I *La fattoria degli animali*
E *Rebelión en la granja*
SU «Фе́рма живо́тных» (О́руэлл)

184 GB Anjou (France)
F l'Anjou (m.) (France)
D Anjou (Frankreich)
I l'Angio (Francia)
E Anjeo (Francia)
SU Анжу́ (Фра́нция)

185 GB *Anna and the King of Siam* (Cromwell, 1946)
F *Anna et le Roi de Siam*
D *Anna und der König von Siam*
I *Anna e il Re del Siam*
E *Ana y el Rey de Siam*
SU «А́нна и король Сиа́ма» (Кро́мвель)

186 GB *Anna Karenina* (Tolstoy, 1876–7)
F *Anna Karénine* (Tolstoï)
D *Anna Karenina* (Tolstoj)
I *Anna Karenina* (Tolstoj)
E *Ana Karenina* (Tolstoi)
SU «А́нна Каре́нина» (Толсто́й)

187 GB *Annals*, the [*Annales*] (Tacitus, II)
F les *Annales* (Tacite)
D die *Annalen* (Tacitus)
I gli *Annali* (Tacito)
E los *Anales* (Tácito)
SU «Анна́лы» (Та́цит)

188 GB *Anna of the Five Towns* (Bennett, 1902)
F *Anna des cinq villes*
D *Anna aus den fünf Städten*
I *Anna delle cinque città*
E *Ana de Cinco Villas*
SU «А́нна из пяти́ городо́в» (Бе́ннетт)

189 GB Anne (saint, sovereign)
F Anne (sainte, souveraine)
D Anna (Heilige, Herr.)
I Anna (santa, sovrana)
E Ana (santa, sob.)
SU А́нна (св., прав.)

190 GB Anne Boleyn (*1507–36*)
F Anne Boleyn
D Anna Boleyn
I Anna Bolena
E Ana Bolena
SU А́нна Боле́йн

191 GB Anne of Austria (1601–66)
F Anne d'Autriche
D Anna von Österreich
I Anna d'Austria
E Ana de Austria
SU А́нна Австри́йская

192 GB Anne of Cleves (1515–57)
F Anne de Clèves
D Anna von Kleve
I Anna di Clèves
E Ana de Cleves
SU А́нна Кле́вская

193 GB Annunciation, the (rel.)
F l'Annonciation (f.) (relig.)
D die Verkündigung (relig.)
I l'Annunciazione (relig.)
E la Anunciación (relig.)
SU благове́щение (рел.)

194 GB *Ann Veronica* (Wells, 1909)
F *Anne-Véronique*
D *Ann Veronica*
I *Ann Veronica*
E *Ana Verónica*
SU «А́нна-Веро́ника» (Уэ́ллс)

195 GB   Antarctica
      F   l'Antarctique (f.)
      D   das Südpolargebiet
      I   l'Antartide
      E   la Antártida
      SU   Антáрктика

196 GB   Antarctic Ocean, the
      F   l'océan Glacial Antarctique
      D   das Südliche Eismeer
      I   il mare Glaciale Antartico
      E   el océano Glacial Antártico
      SU   Ю́жный океáн

197 GB   Anthony (saint)
      F   Antoine (saint)
      D   Antonius (Heiliger)
      I   Antonio (santo)
      E   Antonio (santo)
      SU   Антóний (св.)

198 GB   Anthony of Padua (saint, 1195–1231)
      F   Antoine de Padoue (saint)
      D   Antonius von Padua (Heiliger)
      I   Antonio da Padova (santo)
      E   Antonio de Padua (santo)
      SU   Антóний Падуáнский (св.)

199 GB   *Antic Hay* (Huxley, 1923)
      F   *Antic Hay*
      D   *Phantastisches Heu*
      I   *Passo di danza*
      E   *Danza fantástica*
      SU   «Шутовскóй хоровóд» (Хáксли)

200 GB   Antichrist (rel.)
      F   Antéchrist (relig.)
      D   der Antichrist (relig.)
      I   Anticristo (relig.)
      E   Anticristo (relig.)
      SU   Антихрúст (рел.)

201 GB   Antigone (myth., + Sophocles, −442, Anouilh, 1942)
      F   Antigone (myth., + Sophocle, Anouilh)
      D   Antigone (myth., + Sophokles, Anouilh)
      I   Antigone (mit., + Sofocle, Anouilh)
      E   Antígona (mit., + Sófocles, Anouilh)
      SU   Антигóна (миф., + Софóкл, Анýй)

202 GB   Antilles, the
      F   les Antilles (f.)
      D   die Antillen
      I   le Antille
      E   las Antillas
      SU   Антúльские островá

203 GB   Antioch (Bib.)
      F   Antioche (Bib.)
      D   Antiochia (Bib.)
      I   Antiochia (Bib.)
      E   Antioquía (Bib.)
      SU   Антиóх (библ.)

204 GB   Antipodes Islands, the
      F   les iles Antipodes
      D   die Antipoden
      I   le isole Antipode
      E   las islas Antipodas
      SU   островá Антипóдов

205 GB   *Antiquary, The* (Scott, 1816)
      F   *L'Antiquaire*
      D   *Der Altertümler*
      I   *L'antiquario*
      E   *El anticuario*
      SU   «Антиквáрий» (Скотт)

206 GB   *Antony and Cleopatra* (Shakespeare, 1606)
      F   *Antoine et Cléopâtre*
      D   *Antonius und Kleopatra*
      I   *Antonio e Cleopatra*
      E   *Antonio y Cleopatra*
      SU   «Антóний и Клеопáтра» (Шекспúр)

207 GB   Antwerp (Belgium)
      F   Anvers (Belge)
      D   Antwerpen (Belgien)
      I   Anversa (Belgio)
      E   Amberes (Bélgica)
      SU   Антвéрпен (Бéльгия)

208 GB   *Apartment, The* (Wilder, 1960)
      F   *La Garçonnière*
      D   *Das Appartement*
      I   *L'appartamento*
      E   *El apartamento*
      SU   «Квартúра» (Уáйлдер)

209 GB   Apennines, the (Italy)
      F   les Apennins (m.) (Italie)
      D   die Apenninen (Italien)
      I   gli Appennini (Italia)
      E   los Apeninos (Italia)
      SU   Апеннúны (ж.) (Итáлия)

210 GB   Aphrodite (myth.)
      F   Aphrodite (myth.)
      D   Aphrodite (myth.)
      I   Afrodite (mit.)
      E   Afrodita (mit.)
      SU   Афродúта (миф.)

211 GB Apocrypha, the (Bib.)
     F   les Apocryphes (m.)(Bib.)
     D   die Apokryphen (Bib.)
     I   gli apocrifi (Bib.)·
     E   los libros apócrifos (Bib.)
     SU Апо́крифы (м.) (библ.)

212 GB Apollo (myth.)
     F   Apollon (myth.)
     D   Apollo (myth.)
     I   Apollo (mit.)
     E   Apolo (mit.)
     SU Аполло́н (миф.)

213 GB Apollodorus (300–260)
     F   Apollodore
     D   Apollodoros
     I   Apollodoro
     E   Apolodoro
     SU Аполлодо́р

214 GB Apollonius (−III)
     F   Apollonios
     D   Apollonius
     I   Apollonio
     E   Apolonio
     SU Аполло́ний

215 GB *Apologia pro Vita Sua* ["A Justification
         of His Life"] (Newman, 1864)
     F   *Apologia pro vita sua*
     D   *Verteidigung seines Lebens*
     I   *Apologia pro vita sua*
     E   *Apología pro vita sua*
     SU «Оправда́ние свое́й жи́зни»
         (Нью́мен)

216 GB *Apology* [*Apologia Sokratous*] (Plato,
         −399)
     F   *Apologie* (Platon)
     D   *Verteidigungsrede des Sokrates*
         (Platon)
     I   *Apologia di Socrate* (Platone)
     E   *Apología de Sócrates* (Platón)
     SU «Аполо́гия Сокра́та» (Плато́н)

217 GB Apostles' Creed, the (rel.)
     F   le Symbole des Apôtres (relig.)
     D   das Apostolische Glaubensbekenntnis
         (relig.)
     I   il Credo apostolico (relig.)
     E   el Símbolo de los Apóstoles (relig.)
     SU апо́стольский си́мвол ве́ры (рел.)

218 GB *Apotheosis of Venice, The* (Veronese,
         1578–85)
     F   *Le Triomphe de Venise* (Véronèse)
     D   die *Apotheose Venedigs* (Veronese)
     I   il *Trionfo di Venezia* (Veronese)
     E   *El triunfo de Venecia* (Veronés)
     SU «Триу́мф Вене́ции» (Вероне́зе)

219 GB Appalachian Mountains, the
     F   les Appalaches (m.)
     D   die Appalachen
     I   i monti Appalachi
     E   los Apalaches
     SU Аппала́чи (м.)

220 GB Appian Way, the (Italy)
     F   la voie Appienne (Italie)
     D   die Appische Straße (Italien)
     I   la via Appia (Italia)
     E   la vía Apia (Italia)
     SU А́ппиева доро́га (Ита́лия)

221 GB *Apple Cart, The* (Shaw, 1929)
     F   *La Charrette de pommes*
     D   *Der Kaiser von Amerika*
     I   *Il carretto delle mele*
     E   *La carreta de las manzanas*
     SU «Теле́жка с я́блоками» (Шо́у)

222 GB *Appointment in Samarra* (O'Hara,
         1934)
     F   *Rendez-vous à Samara*
     D   *Treffpunkt in Samarra*
     I   *Appuntamento a Samarra*
     E   *Cita en Samarra*
     SU «Свида́ние в Сама́рре» (О'Ха́ра)

223 GB Apuleius (II)
     F   Apulée
     D   Apuleius
     I   Apuleio
     E   Apuleyo
     SU Апуле́й

224 GB Apulia (Puglia) (Italy)
     F   la Pouille (Italie)
     D   Apulien (Italien)
     I   la Puglia (Italia)
     E   Pulla (Italia)
     SU Апу́лия (Ита́лия)

225 GB Aquarius (astron.)
     F   le Verseau (astron.)
     D   der Wassermann (Astron.)
     I   Acquario (astr.)
     E   el Acuario (astr.)
     SU Водоле́й (астр.)

226 GB Aquitaine (France)
F l'Aquitaine (f.) (France)
D Aquitanien (Frankreich)
I l'Aquitania (Francia)
E Aquitania (Francia)
SU Аквита́ния (Фра́нция)

227 GB *Arabesques* (Gogol, 1835)
F *Arabesques*
D *Arabesken*
I *Arabeschi*
E *Arabescos*
SU «Арабе́ски» (Го́голь)

228 GB Arabia
F l'Arabie (f.)
D Arabien
I l'Arabia
E Arabia
SU Ара́вия

229 GB Arabian Desert, the (Egypt)
F le Désert arabique (Égypte)
D die Arabische Wüste (Ägypten)
I il deserto Orientale (Egitto)
E el desierto de Arabia (Egipto)
SU Арави́йская пусты́ня (Еги́пет)

GB *Arabian Nights*, the→*Thousand and One Nights*

230 GB Arab Republic of Egypt, the (ARE)
F la République Arabe d'Egypte (RAE)
D die Arabische Republik von Ägypten (ARÄ)
I la Repubblica Araba Egitto (RAE)
E la República Árabe de Egipto (RAE)
SU Ара́бская Респу́блика Еги́пет (АРЕ)

231 GB Arachne (myth.)
F Arachné (myth.)
D Arachne (myth.)
I Aracne (mit.)
E Aracné (mit.)
SU Ара́хна (миф.)

232 GB Aragon (Spain)
F l'Aragon (m.) (Espagne)
D Aragonien (Spanien)
I l'Aragona (Spagna)
E Aragón (España)
SU Араго́н (Испа́ния)

233 GB Aral Sea, the (USSR)
F la mer d'Aral (URSS)
D die Aral-See (UdSSR)
I el lago Aral (URSS)
E el mar de Aral (URSS)
SU Ара́льское мо́ре (СССР)

234 GB Ararat, Mount (Turkey)
F le mont Ararat (Turquie)
D Ararat (Türkei)
I Ararat (Turchia)
E Ararat (Turquía)
SU Арара́т (Ту́рция)

235 GB Arcadia (Greece)
F l'Arcadie (f.) (Grèce)
D Arkadien (Griechenland)
I l'Arcadia (Grecia)
E Arcadia (Grecia)
SU Арка́дия (Гре́ция)

236 GB Arc de Triomphe, the [Triumphal Arch] (Paris)
F l'Arc de triomphe (Paris)
D das Arc de Triomphe (Paris)
I l'Arco di Trionfo (Parigi)
E el Arco de Triunfo (París)
SU Триумфа́льная а́рка (Пари́ж)

237 GB Archangel (Arkhangelsk) (USSR)
F Arkhangelsk (URSS)
D Archangelsk (UdSSR)
I Arcangelo (URSS)
E Arcángel (URSS)
SU Арха́нгельск (СССР)

238 GB Archimedes (287–212)
F Archimède
D Archimedes
I Archimede
E Arquímedes
SU Архиме́д

239 GB Arctic Ocean, the
F l'océan (Glacial) Arctique
D das Nördliche Eismeer
I il mare Glaciale Artico
E el océano Ártico
SU Се́верный Ледови́тый океа́н

240 GB Arctic (Regions), the
F l'Arctique (f.)
D das Nordpolargebiet
I le regioni artiche
E las regiones árticas
SU А́рктика

241 GB Arcturus (astron.)
F Arcturus (astron.)
D Arktur (Astron.)
I Arturo (astr.)
E Arcturo (astr.)
SU Аркту́р (астр.)

242 GB Ardennes, the (Europe)
F les Ardennes (f.) (Europe)
D die Ardennen (Europa)
I le Ardenne (Europa)
E las Ardenas (Europa)
SU Ардéнны (ж.) (Еврóпа)

243 GB *Areopagitica* (Milton, 1644)
F *Areopagitica*
D *Areopagitica*
I *Areopagitica*
E *Areopagitica*
SU «Ареопагѝтика» (Мѝльтон)

244 GB Areopagus, the (Athens)
F l'Aréopage (m.) (Athènes)
D der Areopag (Athen)
I l'Areopago (Atene)
E el Areópago (Atenas)
SU Ареопáг (Афѝны)

245 GB Ares (myth., astron.)
F Arès (myth., astron.)
D Ares (myth., Astron.)
I Ares (mit., astr.)
E Ares (mit., astr.)
SU Арéс (миф., астр.)

246 GB Arethusa (myth.)
F Aréthuse (myth.)
D Arethusa (myth.)
I Aretusa (mit.)
E Aretusa (mit.)
SU Аретýса (миф.)

247 GB Argentina
F l'Argentine (f.)
D Argentinien
I l'Argentina
E la Argentina
SU Аргентѝна

248 GB Argonauts, the (myth.)
F les Argonautes (m.) (myth.)
D die Argonauten (myth.)
I gli Argonauti (mit.)
E los Argonautas (mit.)
SU аргонáвты (миф.)

249 GB Argus (myth.)
F Argus (myth.)
D Argus (myth.)
I Argo (mit.)
E Argos (mit.)
SU Áргус (миф.)

250 GB Ariadne (myth.)
F Ariane (myth.)
D Ariadne (myth.)
I Arianna (mit.)
E Ariadna (mit.)
SU Ариáдна (миф.)

251 GB *Ariadne and Bluebeard* (Dukas, 1907)
F *Ariane et Barbe-Bleue*
D *Ariane und Blaubart*
I *Arianna e Barbablù*
E *Ariane y Barbe-Bleue*
SU «Ариáдна и Сѝняя Бородá» (Дюкá)

252 GB *Ariadne on Naxos* (Strauss, 1912)
F *Ariane à Naxos*
D *Ariadne auf Naxos*
I *Arianna a Nasso*
E *Ariadna a Naxos*
SU «Ариáдна на Нáксосе» (Штрáус)

253 GB Aries (astron.)
F le Bélier (astron.)
D der Widder (Astron.)
I Ariete (astr.)
E Aries (astr.)
SU Óвен (астр.)

254 GB Arion (myth., astron.)
F Arion (myth., astron.)
D Arion (myth., Astron.)
I Arione (mit., astr.)
E Arión (mit., astr.)
SU Арióн (миф., астр.)

255 GB Aristarchus (−II)
F Aristarque
D Aristarch
I Aristarco
E Aristarco
SU Аристáрх

256 GB Aristides (530–468)
F Aristide
D Aristides
I Aristide
E Aristides
SU Аристѝд

257 GB Aristophanes (445–*380*)
F Aristophane
D Aristophanes
I Aristofano
E Aristófanes
SU Аристофáн

258 GB   Aristotle (384–322)
F   Aristote
D   Aristoteles
I   Aristotele
E   Aristóteles
SU   Аристóтель

259 GB   Arius (256–336)
F   Arius
D   Arius
I   Ario
E   Ario
SU   Áрий

    GB   Armada, Spanish→Spanish Armada

260 GB   *Armance* (Stendhal, 1823)
F   *Armance*
D   *Armance*
I   *Armance*
E   *Armanica*
SU   «Армáнс» (Стендáль)

261 GB   Armenia (USSR)
F   l'Arménie (f.) (URSS)
D   Armenien (UdSSR)
I   l'Armenia (URSS)
E   Armenia (URSS)
SU   Армéния (СССР)

262 GB   *Arms and the Man* (Shaw, 1894)
F   *Le Héros et le soldat*
D   *Helden*
I   *Le armi e l'uomo*
E   *Las armas y el hombre*
SU   «Орýжие и человéк» (Шóу)

263 GB   *Around the World in Eighty Days* (Verne, 1873)
F   *Le Tour du monde en quatre-vingts jours*
D   *Die Reise um die Welt in achtzig Tagen*
I   *Il giro del mondo in ottanta giorni*
E   *La vuelta al mundo en ochenta días*
SU   «Вокрýг свéта в вóсемьдесят дней» (Верн)

264 GB   *Arrowsmith* (Lewis, 1925)
F   *Arrowsmith*
D   *Dr. med. Arrowsmith*
I   *Arrowsmith*
E   *El doctor Arrowsmith*
SU   «Э́роусмит» (Льюис)

265 GB   *Arsenic and Old Lace* (Capra, 1944)
F   *Arsenic et vieilles dentelles*
D   *Arsen und Spitzenhäubchen*
I   *Arsenico e vecchi merletti*
E   *Arsénico por compasión*
SU   «Мышья́к и стáрые кружевá» (Кáпра)

266 GB   *Artamenus, or the Great Cyrus* (Scudéry, 1649–53)
F   *Artamène, ou le Grand Cyrus*
D   *Artamenus*
I   *Il Grande Ciro*
E   *El gran Ciro*
SU   «Артамéн, и́ли Кир Вели́кий» (Скюдери́)

267 GB   Artaxerxes (king)
F   Artaxerxès (roi)
D   Artaxerxes (König)
I   Artaserse (re)
E   Artajerjes (rey)
SU   Артаксéркс (царь)

268 GB   Artemis (myth.)
F   Artémis (myth.)
D   Artemis (myth.)
I   Artemide (mit.)
E   Artemisa (mit.)
SU   Артеми́да (миф.)

269 GB   Arthur (?VI)
F   Arthur
D   Artus
I   Artù
E   Arturo
SU   Артýр

270 GB   *Art of Love, The* [*Ars amatoria*] (Ovid, −I)
F   *L'Art d'aimer* (Ovide)
D   *Das Lehrbuch der Liebe* (Ovidius)
I   *L'arte amatoria* (Ovidio)
E   *Arte de amar* (Ovidio)
SU   «Наýка любви́» (Ови́дий)

271 GB   *Art of Poetry, The* [*Ars poetica*] (Horace, −I)
F   *Art poétique* (Horace)
D   *Von der Dichtkunst* (Horaz)
I   *Arte poetica* (Orazio)
E   *Arte poética* (Horacio)
SU   «Наýка поэ́зии» (Горáций)

272 GB   *Art of the Fugue, the* (Bach, 1751)
F   *L'Art de la fugue*
D   *Die Kunst der Fuge*
I   *L'arte della fuga*
E   *El arte de la fuga*
SU   «Искýсство фýги» (Бах)

273 GB Ascension, the (rel.)
    F l'Ascension (f.) (relig.)
    D die Himmelfahrt Christi (relig.)
    I l'Ascensione (relig.)
    E la Ascensión (relig.)
    SU вознесéние (рел.)

274 GB Ascension Island
    F l'île de l'Ascension
    D Ascension
    I Ascensione
    E la isla de la Ascensión
    SU óстров Вознесéния

275 GB *Ascent of F6, The* (Auden + Isherwood, 1936)
    F *La Montée de F6*
    D *Der Aufstieg von F6*
    I *L'ascesa di F6*
    E *La subida de F6*
    SU «Восхождéние на Ф-6» (Óден/Йшервуд)

276 GB Asclepius (myth.)
    F Asclépios (myth.)
    D Asklepios (myth.)
    I Asclepio (mit.)
    E Asclepio (mit.)
    SU Асклéпий (миф.)

277 GB Asher (Bib.)
    F Aser (Bib.)
    D Aser (Bib.)
    I Aser (Bib.)
    E Aser (Bib.)
    SU Асúр (библ.)

278 GB Ash Wednesday (rel., + Eliot, 1930)
    F le mercredi des Cendres (relig.)
    D der Aschermittwoch (relig.)
    I il giorno delle Ceneri (relig.)
    E el miércoles de Ceniza (relig.)
    SU пéпельная средá (рел., +Элиот)

279 GB Asia
    F l'Asie (f.)
    D Asien
    I l'Asia
    E Asia
    SU Áзия

280 GB Asia Minor (hist.)
    F l'Asie Mineure (hist.)
    D Kleinasien (Gesch.)
    I l'Asia Minore (st.)
    E Asia Menor (hist.)
    SU Мáлая Áзия (ист.)

281 GB *As I Lay Dying* (Faulkner, 1930)
    F *Tandis que j'agonise*
    D *Als ich im Sterben lag*
    I *Mentre io agonizzo*
    E *Mientras yo agonizo*
    SU «На смéртном одрé» (Фóлкнер)

282 GB *Asphalt Jungle, The* (Huston, 1950)
    F *Quand la ville dort*
    D *Asphalt-Dschungel*
    I *Giungla d'asfalto*
    E *La jungla de asfalto*
    SU «Асфáльтовые джýнгли» (Хьюстон)

283 GB Assisi (Italy)
    F Assise (Italie)
    D Assisi (Italien)
    I Assisi (Italia)
    E Asís (Italia)
    SU Ассúзи (Итáлия)

284 GB Association of South-East Asian Nations, the (ASEAN)
    F l'Association des nations de l'Asie du Sud-Est (ASEAN)
    D die Vereinigung südostasiatischen Staaten (ASEAN)
    I l'Associazione delle nazioni dell'Asia sudorientale (ASEAN)
    E la Asociación de las naciones de Asia sudoriental (ASEAN)
    SU Ассоциáция госудáрств Юго-Востóчной Áзии (АСЕÁН)

285 GB Assumption, the (rel.)
    F l'Assomption (f.) (relig.)
    D die Mariä Himmelfahrt (relig.)
    I l'Assunzione (relig.)
    E la Asunción (relig.)
    SU успéние (рел.)

286 GB Assyria (hist.)
    F l'Assyrie (f.) (hist.)
    D Assyrien (Gesch.)
    I l'Assiria (st.)
    E Asiria (hist.)
    SU Ассúрия (ист.)

287 GB *Astrophel and Stella* (Sidney, 1591)
    F *Astrophel et Stella*
    D *Astrophel und Stella*
    I *Astrophel e Stella*
    E *Astrofel y Stella*
    SU «Астрóфель и Стéлла» (Сúдни)

288 GB Asturias, the (Spain)
    F les Asturies (f.) (Espagne)
    D die Asturien (Spanien)
    I le Asturie (Spagna)
    E las Asturias (España)
    SU Асту́рия (Испа́ния)

289 GB *As You Like It* (Shakespeare, 1599)
    F *Comme il vous plaira*
    D *Wie es euch gefällt*
    I *Come vi piace*
    E *Como gustéis*
    SU «Как вам э́то понра́вится» (Шекспи́р)

290 GB *Athalia* (Racine, 1691)
    F *Athalie*
    D *Athalie*
    I *Atalia*
    E *Atalía*
    SU «Ата́лия» (Раси́н)

291 GB Athanasius (saint, *293–373*)
    F Athanase (saint)
    D Athanasius (Heiliger)
    I Atanasio (santo)
    E Atanasio (santo)
    SU Афана́сий (св.)

292 GB *Atheist's Tragedy, The* (Tourneur, 1611)
    F *La Tragédie de l'athée*
    D *Die Tragödie des Atheisten*
    I *La tragedia dell'ateo*
    E *La tragedia del ateo*
    SU «Траге́дия атеи́ста» (Те́рнер)

293 GB Athena (Athene) (myth.)
    F Athéna (myth.)
    D Athene (myth.)
    I Atena (mit.)
    E Atenea (mit.)
    SU Афи́на (миф.)

294 GB Athens (Greece)
    F Athènes (f.) (Grèce)
    D Athen (Griechenland)
    I Atene (Grecia)
    E Atenas (Grecia)
    SU Афи́ны (ж.) (Гре́ция)

295 GB Atlantic Ocean, the
    F l'océan Atlantique
    D der Atlantische Ozean
    I l'oceano Atlantico
    E el océano Atlántico
    SU Атланти́ческий океа́н

296 GB Atlantis (myth.)
    F l'Atlantide (f.) (myth.)
    D Atlantis (myth.)
    I l'Atlantide (mit.)
    E Atlántida (mit.)
    SU Атланти́да (миф.)

297 GB Atlas (myth.)
    F Atlas (myth.)
    D Atlas (myth.)
    I Atlante (mit.)
    E Atlas (mit.)
    SU А́тлас (миф.)

298 GB Atlas Mountains, the
    F l'Atlas (m.)
    D das Atlasgebirge
    I l'Atlante
    E el Atlas
    SU А́тла́с

299 GB Atreus (myth.)
    F Atrée (myth.)
    D Atreus (myth.)
    I Atreo (mit.)
    E Atreo (mit.)
    SU Атре́й (миф.)

300 GB *Atta Troll* (Heine, 1843)
    F *Atta Troll*
    D *Atta Troll*
    I *Atta Troll*
    E *Atta Troll*
    SU «А́тта Тролль» (Ге́йне)

301 GB Attica (Greece)
    F l'Attique (f.) (Grèce)
    D Attika (Griechenland)
    I l'Attica (Grecia)
    E Ática (Grecia)
    SU А́ттика (Гре́ция)

302 GB Attila (V, + Corneille, 1667)
    F Attila
    D Attila
    I Attila
    E Atila
    SU Атти́ла (+ Корне́ль)

303 GB Augustine (saint) (354–430)
    F Augustin (saint)
    D Augustinus (Heiliger)
    I Agostino (santo)
    E Agustín (santo)
    SU Августи́н (св.)

304 GB *August 1914* (Solzhenitsyn, 1971)
 F *Août 14* (Soljenitsyne)
 D *August 1914* (Solschenizyn)
 I *Agosto 1914* (Solženicyn)
 E *Agosto 1914* (Soljenitsin)
 SU «Áвгуст 1914 гóда» (Солженúцын)

305 GB Augustus (emperor, sovereign)
 F Auguste (empereur, souverain)
 D Augustus (Kaiser, Herr.)
 I Augusto (imperatore, sovrano)
 E Augusto (emperador, sob.)
 SU Áвгуст (импepáтор, прав.)

306 GB Aurelian (215–275)
 F Aurélien
 D Aurelianus
 I Aureliano
 E Aureliano
 SU Аврелиáн

307 GB Aurora (myth.)
 F Aurore (myth.)
 D Aurora (myth.)
 I Aurora (mit.)
 E Aurora (mit.)
 SU Аврóра (миф.)

308 GB Australasia
 F l'Australasie (f.)
 D Australasien
 I l'Australasia
 E Australasia
 SU Австралáзия

309 GB Australia
 F l'Australie (f.)
 D Australien
 I l'Australia
 E Australia
 SU Австрáлия

310 GB Australian Capital Territory
   (Australia)
 F le Territoire de la capitale fédérale
   (Australie)
 D der Bundesbezirk (Australien)
 I l'Australian Capital Territory
   (Australia)
 E el Australian Capital Territory
   (Australia)
 SU Австралúйская столúчная
   территóрия (Австрáлия)

311 GB Austria
 F l'Autriche
 D Österreich
 I l'Austria
 E Austria
 SU Áвстрия

312 GB Austrian Succession, War of the
   (1740–8)
 F la guerre de la Succession d'Autriche
 D der Österreichische Erbfolgekrieg
 I la guerra di successione austriaca
 E la Guerra de Sucesión de Austria
 SU войнá за австрúйское наслéдство

313 GB Autolycus (myth.)
 F Autolycos (myth.)
 D Autolykos (myth.)
 I Autolico (mit.)
 E Autólico (mit.)
 SU Автóлик (миф.)

314 GB Auvergne, the (France)
 F l'Auvergne (f.) (France)
 D Auvergne (Frankreich)
 I l'Alvernia (Francia)
 E Auvernia (Francia)
 SU Овéрнь (ж.) (Фрáнция)

315 GB Aventine Hill, the (Rome)
 F le mont Aventin (Rome)
 D der Aventinische Hügel (Rom)
 I l'Aventino (Roma)
 E el Monte Aventino (Roma)
 SU Авентúн (Рим)

316 GB Avicenna (*980–1037*)
 F Avicenne
 D Avicenna
 I Avicenna
 E Avicena
 SU Авицéнна

317 GB Avignon (France)
 F Avignon (France)
 D Avignon (Frankreich)
 I Avignone (Francia)
 E Aviñón (Francia)
 SU Авиньóн (Фрáнция)

318 GB *Avventura, L'* [*The Adventure*]
   (Antonioni, 1959)
 F *L'Aventure*
 D *Die mit der Liebe spielen*
 I *L'avventura*
 E *La aventura*
 SU «Приключéние» (Антониóни)

319 GB *Awakening of Spring, The* (Wedekind, 1891)
  F *L'Éveil du printemps*
  D *Frühlings Erwachen*
  I *Risveglio di primavera*
  E *Despertar de primavera*
  SU «Пробуждéние весны́» (Вéдекинд)

320 GB Azerbaijan (Azerbaydzhan) (USSR)
  F l'Azerbaïdjan (URSS)
  D Aserbeidschan (UdSSR)
  I l'Azerbaigian (URSS)
  E Azerbaidján (URSS)
  SU Азербайджáн (СССР)

321 GB Azores, the
  F les Açores (f.)
  D die Azoren
  I le Azzorre
  E las islas Azores
  SU Азóрские островá

322 GB Aztecs, the (hist.)
  F les Aztèques (hist.)
  D die Azteken (Gesch.)
  I gli aztechi (st.)
  E los aztecas (hist.)
  SU ацтéки (ист.)

B

323 GB *Babbitt* (Lewis, 1922)
    F *Babbitt*
    D *Babbitt*
    I *Babbitt*
    E *Babbitt*
    SU «Бэ́ббит» (Лью́ис)

324 GB Babel, the Tower of (Bib.)
    F la tour de Babel (Bib.)
    D der Babylonische Turm (Bib.)
    I la torre di Babele (Bib.)
    E la torre de Babel (Bib.)
    SU вавило́нская ба́шня (библ.)

325 GB *Baby Doll* (Kazan, 1956)
    F *La Poupée de chair*
    D *Baby Doll*
    I *Baby Doll – la bambola viva*
    E *Baby Doll*
    SU «Жива́я ку́колка» (Ка́зан)

326 GB Babylon (Bib.)
    F Babylone (f.) (Bib.)
    D Babylon (Bib.)
    I Babele (Bib.)
    E Babilonia (Bib.)
    SU Вавило́н (библ.)

327 GB Bacchae, the (myth., + Euripides, 405–6)
    F les Bacchantes (myth., + Euripide)
    D die Bakchen (myth., + Euripides)
    I le Baccanti (mit., + Euripide)
    E las Bacantes (mit., + Eurípides)
    SU вакха́нки (миф., + Еврипи́д)

328 GB Bacchus (myth.)
    F Bacchus (myth.)
    D Bacchus (myth.)
    I Bacco (mit.)
    E Baco (mit.)
    SU Вакх (миф.)

329 GB Bactria (hist.)
    F la Bactriane (f.) (hist.)
    D Baktrien (Gesch.)
    I la Battriana (st.)
    E Bactriana (hist.)
    SU Ба́ктрия (ист.)

330 GB *Bad and the Beautiful, The* (Minnelli, 1952)
    F *Les Ensorcelés*
    D *Die Stadt der Illusionen*
    I *Il bruto e la bella*
    E *Cautivos del mal*
    SU «Очаро́ванные» (Минне́лли)

331 GB *Bad Day at Black Rock* (Sturges, 1955)
    F *Un homme est passé*
    D *Stadt in Angst*
    I *Giorno maledetto*
    E *Conspiración de silencio*
    SU «Взволно́ванный го́род» (Стёрджес)

332 GB Baghdad (Iraq)
    F Bagdad (Iraq)
    D Bagdad (Irak)
    I Baghdad (Iraq)
    E Bagdad (Iraq)
    SU Багда́д (Ира́к)

333 GB Bahamas, the
    F les Bahamas (f.)
    D die Bahama-Inseln
    I le Bahama
    E las Bahamas
    SU Бага́мские острова́

334 GB Bahrain
    F les îles Bahreïn
    D die Bahrein-Inseln
    I Bahrein
    E Bahrein
    SU Бахре́йн

335 GB *Baker's Wife, The* (Pagnol, 1938)
     F   *La Femme du boulanger*
     D   *Des anderen Weib*
     I   *La moglie del fornaio*
     E   *El pan y el perdón*
     SU «Пекарша» (Паньоль)

336 GB Balaam (Bib.)
     F   Balaam (Bib.)
     D   Bileam (Bib.)
     I   Balaam (Bib.)
     E   Balaam (Bib.)
     SU Валаам (библ.)

337 GB *Bald Primadonna, The* (Ionesco, 1950)
     F   *La Cantatrice chauve*
     D   *Die kahle Sängerin*
     I   *La cantatrice calva*
     E   *La cantante calva*
     SU «Лысая певица» (Ионеско)

338 GB Baldwin (sovereign)
     F   Baudouin (souverain)
     D   Balduin (Herr.)
     I   Baldovino (sovrano)
     E   Baldovino (sob.)
     SU Балдуин (прав.)

339 GB Balearic Islands, the
     F   les îles Baléares
     D   die Balearen
     I   le Baleari
     E   las Baleares
     SU Балеарские острова

340 GB Balkan Peninsula, the
     F   la péninsule balkanique
     D   die Balkanhalbinsel
     I   la penisola balcanica
     E   la península de los Balcanes
     SU Балканский полуостров

341 GB Balkans, the (Bulgaria)
     F   les Balkans (Bulgarie)
     D   der Balkan (Bulgarien)
     I   i Balcani (Bulgaria)
     E   los Balcanes (Bulgaria)
     SU Балканские горы (Болгария)

342 GB *Ballad of a Soldier* (Chukhrai, 1959)
     F   *Ballade d'un soldat*
     D   *Ballade vom Soldaten*
     I   *Ballata di un soldato*
     E   *La balada del soldado*
     SU «Баллада о солдате» (Чухрай)

343 GB *Ballad of Dead Ladies, The* (Villon, 1461)
     F   *Ballade des dames du temps jadis*
     D   *Ballade der Damen aus alten Zeiten*
     I   *Ballata delle dame del tempo che fu*
     E   *Balada de las damas de antaño*
     SU «О дамах минувших времён» (Вийон)

344 GB *Ballad of Peckham Rye, The* (Spark, 1960)
     F   *La Ballade de Peckham Rye*
     D   *Die Ballade von Peckham Rye*
     I   *La ballata di Peckham Rye*
     E   *La balada de Peckham Rye*
     SU «Баллада о предместье» (Спарк)

345 GB *Ballad of Reading Gaol, The* (Wilde, 1898)
     F   *La Ballade de la géole de Reading*
     D   *Die Ballade vom Zuchthaus zu Reading*
     I   *La ballata del carcere di Reading*
     E   *La balada de la cárcel de Reading*
     SU «Баллада Рédингской тюрьмы» (Уайльд)

346 GB *Ballad of the Hanged, The* (Villon, 1463)
     F   *Ballade des pendus*
     D   *Die Ballade der Erhängten*
     I   *Ballata degli impiccati*
     E   *Balada de los ahorcados*
     SU «Баллада повешенных» (Вийон)

347 GB Ballets Russes, the [Russian Ballets] (1909–29)
     F   les Ballets russes
     D   das Russische Ballett
     I   i Balletti Russi
     E   los Ballets rusos
     SU Русский балет

348 GB *Ball of Fat* (Maupassant, 1880)
     F   *Boule de suif*
     D   *Fettklößchen*
     I   *Palla di sego*
     E   *Bola de sebo*
     SU «Бочонок» (Мопассан)

349 GB Balthasar (Bib.)
     F   Balthazar (Bib.)
     D   Balthasar (Bib.)
     I   Baldassarre (Bib.)
     E   Baltasar (Bib.)
     SU Валтасар (библ.)

350 GB Baltic Sea, the
F la mer Baltique
D die Ostsee
I il mare Baltico
E el mar Báltico
SU Балти́йское мо́ре

351 GB Bangladesh
F le Bangladesh
D Bangladesh
I il Bangladesh
E el Bangladesh
SU Бангладе́ш

352 GB *Bank Holiday* (Reed, 1938)
F *Bank Holiday*
D *Bankfeiertag*
I *Fiamme di passione*
E *El amor manda*
SU «Пра́здник ба́нковских слу́жащих»
(Рид)

353 GB Bank of England, the (London)
F la Banque d'Angleterre (Londres)
D die Bank von England (London)
I la banca d'Inghilterra (Londra)
E el banco de Inglaterra (Londres)
SU Англи́йский банк (Ло́ндон)

354 GB Bantus, the
F les Bantous
D die Bantus
I i bantu
E los bantúes
SU ба́нту

355 GB Baptists, the (rel.)
F les baptistes (relig.)
D die Baptisten (relig.)
I i battisti (relig.)
E los bautistas (relig.)
SU бапти́сты (рел.)

356 GB Barabbas (Bib., + Lagerkvist, 1950)
F Barabbas (Bib.)
D Barrabas (Bib.)
I Barabba (Bib.)
E Barrabás (Bib.)
SU Вара́вва (библ., + Ла́герквист)

357 GB *Bar at the Folies-Bergère* (Manet, 1881)
F *Bar aux Folies-Bergère*
D *Eine Bar in Folies-Bergère*
I *Il bar alle Folies-Bergère*
E *Bar del Folies Bergère*
SU «Бар ,,Фоли́-Берже́р"» (Мане́)

358 GB Barbados
F la Barbade
D Barbados
I Barbados
E Barbados
SU Барба́дос

359 GB Barbarossa (XVI)
F Barberousse
D Barbarossa
I Barbarossa
E Barbarroja
SU Барбаро́сса

360 GB *Barber of Bagdad, The* (Cornelius, 1858)
F *Le Barbier de Bagdad*
D *Der Barbier von Bagdad*
I *Il barbiere di Bagdad*
E *El barbero de Bagdad*
SU «Багда́дский цирю́льник» (Корне́лиус)

361 GB *Barber of Seville, The* (Beaumarchais, 1775; Rossini, 1816)
F *Le Barbier de Séville*
D *Der Barbier von Sevilla*
I *Il barbiere di Siviglia*
E *El barbero de Sevilla*
SU «Севи́льский цирю́льник» (Бомарше́, Росси́ни)

362 GB Barcelona (Spain)
F Barcelone (Espagne)
D Barcelona (Spanien)
I Barcellona (Spagna)
E Barcelona (España)
SU Барсело́на (Испа́ния)

363 GB *Barchester Towers* (Trollope, 1857)
F *Les Tours de Barchester*
D *Barchester Towers*
I *Le torri di Barchester*
E *Las torres de Barchester*
SU «Барче́стерские ба́шни» (Тро́ллоп)

364 GB Barents Sea, the
F la mer de Barents
D die Barents-See
I il mare di Barents
E el mar de Barents
SU Ба́ренцево мо́ре

365 GB Barmecides, the (VIII)
F les Barmécides
D die Barmakiden
I i Barmecidi
E los Barmécidas
SU Бармаки́ды

366 GB Barnabas (Bib.)
F Barnabé (Bib.)
D Barnabas (Bib.)
I Barnaba (Bib.)
E Bernabé (Bib.)
SU Варна́ва (библ.)

367 GB *Barnaby Rudge* (Dickens, 1841)
F *Barnaby Rudge*
D *Barnaby Rudge*
I *Barnaby Rudge*
E *Barnaby Rudge*
SU «Ба́рнаби Редж» (Ди́ккенс)

368 GB *Barrack-Room Ballads* (Kipling, 1892)
F *Chansons de la chambrée*
D *Balladen aus dem Biwak*
I *Ballate di caserma*
E *Baladas del cuartel*
SU «Пе́сни каза́рмы» (Ки́плинг)

369 GB *Bartered Bride, The* [*Prodaná nevěsta*] (Smetana, 1866)
F *La Fiancée vendue*
D *Die verkaufte Braut*
I *La sposa venduta*
E *La novia vendida*
SU «Про́данная неве́ста» (Сме́тана)

370 GB Bartholomew (Bib.)
F Barthélemy (Bib.)
D Bartholomäus (Bib.)
I Bartolomeo (Bib.)
E Bartolomé (Bib.)
SU Варфоломе́й (библ.)

371 GB Baruch (Bib.)
F Baruch (Bib.)
D Baruch (Bib.)
I Baruc (Bib.)
E Baruc (Bib.)
SU Ва́рух (библ.)

372 GB Basel (Basle) (Switzerland)
F Bâle (f.) (Suisse)
D Basel (Schweiz)
I Basilea (Svizzera)
E Basilea (Suiza)
SU Ба́зель (м.) (Швейца́рия)

373 GB Basil (saint)
F Basile (saint)
D Basilius (Heiliger)
I Basilio (santo)
E Basilio (santo)
SU Васи́лий (св.)

374 GB Basque Country, the (Spain)
F les provinces basques (Espagne)
D die Baskischen Provinzen (Spanien)
I le Province Basche (Spagna)
E Las Provincias Vascongadas (España)
SU Страна́ Ба́сков (Испа́ния)

375 GB Basques, the (Spain)
F les Basques (Espagne)
D die Basken (Spanien)
I i baschi (Spagna)
E los vascos (España)
SU ба́ски (Испа́ния)

376 GB Bastille, the (Paris)
F la Bastille (Paris)
D die Bastille (Paris)
I la Bastiglia (Parigi)
E la Bastilla (París)
SU Басти́лия (Пари́ж)

377 GB *Bat, The* (Strauss, 1874)
F *La Chauve-souris*
D *Die Fledermaus*
I *Il pipistrello*
E *El murciélago*
SU «Лету́чая мышь» (Штра́ус)

378 GB Bathsheba (Bib.)
F Bethsabée (Bib.)
D Bathseba (Bib.)
I Bethsabea (Bib.)
E Betsabé (Bib.)
SU Вирса́вия (библ.)

GB Battle of . . .   →   . . . , Battle of

379 GB *Battle of the Books, The* (Swift, 1697)
F *La Bataille des livres*
D *Die Bücherschlacht*
I *La battaglia dei libri*
E *La batalla de los libros*
SU «Би́тва книг» (Свифт)

380 GB *Battleship "Potemkin", The* (Eisenstein, 1925)
F *Le Cuirassé "Potemkine"*
D *Der Panzerkreuzer Potemkin*
I *La corazzata Potëmkin*
E *El acorazado Potemkin*
SU «Бронено́сец ,,Потёмкин''» (Эйзенште́йн)

381 GB Bavaria (Germany)
F la Bavière (Allemagne)
D Bayern (Deutschland)
I la Baviera (Germania)
E Baviera (Alemania)
SU Бава́рия (Герма́ния)

382 GB Bayeux Tapestry, the
F   la tapisserie de la reine Mathilde
D   der Bayeux-Teppich
I   l'arazzo di Bayeux
E   la tapicería de Bayeux
SU «Ковёр из Байё»

GB Bay of . . . → . . . , Bay of

383 GB Bayonne (France)
F   Bayonne (France)
D   Bayonne (Frankreich)
I   Bayonne (Francia)
E   Bayona (Francia)
SU Байонна (Франция)

384 GB Beatitudes, the (Bib.)
F   les Béatitudes (f.) (Bib.)
D   die Seligpreisungen (Bib.)
I   le Beatitudini (Bib.)
E   las Bienaventuranzas (Bib.)
SU заповеди блаженства (библ.)

385 GB *Beatrice and Benedict* (Berlioz, 1862)
F   *Béatrice et Bénédict*
D   *Beatrice und Benedict*
I   *Beatrice e Benedetto*
E   *Beatriz y Benito*
SU «Беатриче и Бенедикт» (Берлиоз)

386 GB *Beauchamp's Career* (Meredith, 1876)
F   *La Carrière de Beauchamp*
D   *Beauchamps Laufbahn*
I   *La carriera di Beauchamp*
E   *La carrera de Beauchamp*
SU «Карьера Бичема» (Мередит)

387 GB *Beautiful and the Damned, The*
    (Fitzgerald, 1922)
F   *La Belle et Damnée*
D   *Die Schönen und Verdammten*
I   *I belli e i dannati*
E   *Los malditos y los bellos*
SU «Прекрасные н обречённые»
    (Фицджеральд)

388 GB *Beautiful Miller Girl, The* (Schubert,
    1823)
F   *La Belle Meunière*
D   *Die schöne Müllerin*
I   *La bella mugnaia*
E   *La bella molinera*
SU «Прекрасная мельничиха» (Шуберт)

389 GB *Beauty and the Beast*
F   *La Belle et la Bête*
D   *Die Schöne und das Tier*
I   *La Bellezza e la Bestia*
E   *La Bella y la Bestia*
SU «Красавица и чудовище»

390 GB *Beaux' Stratagem, The* (Farquhar,
    1707)
F   *Le Stratagème des petits-maîtres*
D   *Des Stutzers List*
I   *Lo stratagemma dei bellimbusti*
E   *La estratagema de los petimetres*
SU «Хитрый план щёголей» (Фаркер)

391 GB *Beaver Coat, The* (Hauptmann, 1893)
F   *La Pelisse de castor*
D   *Der Biberpelz*
I   *La pelliccia di castoro*
E   *La piel de castor*
SU «Бобровая шуба» (Гауптман)

392 GB *Becket, or the Honour of God*
    (Anouilh, 1959)
F   *Becket ou l'Honneur de Dieu*
D   *Becket oder die Ehre Gottes*
I   *Becket e il suo re*
E   *Tomás Beckett*
SU «Беккет, или Честь божья» (Ануй)

393 GB *Bed Bug, The* (Mayakovsky, 1929)
F   *La Punaise* (Maïakovski)
D   *Die Wanze* (Majakowskij)
I   *La cimice* (Majakovskij)
E   *La pulga* (Mayakovsky)
SU «Клоп» (Маяковский)

GB Bede, the Venerable→Venerable Bede

394 GB Beelzebub (Bib.)
F   Belzébuth (Bib.)
D   Beelzebub (Bib.)
I   Belzebú (Bib.)
E   Belcebú (Bib.)
SU Вельзевул (библ.)

395 GB Beersheba (Bib.)
F   Beersheba (Bib.)
D   Beerscheba (Bib.)
I   Bersabea (Bib.)
E   Beersheba (Bib.)
SU Вирсавия (библ.)

396 GB *Beggar's Opera, The* (Gay, 1728)
F   *L'Opéra du gueux*
D   *Die Bettleroper*
I   *L'opera del mendicante*
E   *La ópera de los mendigos*
SU «Опера нищих» (Гей)

397 GB *Begum's Fortune, The* (Verne, 1879)
  F *Les Cinq Cents Millions de la bégum*
  D *Die fünfhundert Millionen der Begum*
  I *I cinquecento milioni della begum*
  E *Los quinientos millones de la begún*
  SU «500 миллио́нов Бегу́мы» (Верн)

398 GB *Being and Nothingness* (Sartre, 1943)
  F *L'Être et le Néant*
  D *Das Sein und das Nichts*
  I *L'essere e il nulla*
  E *El ser y la nada*
  SU «Бытие́ и ничто́» (Сартр)

399 GB *Being and Time* (Heidegger, 1927)
  F *L'Être et le Temps*
  D *Sein und Zeit*
  I *Essere e tempo*
  E *Ser y tiempo*
  SU «Бытие́ и вре́мя» (Ха́йдеггер)

400 GB Beirut (Lebanon)
  F Beyrouth (Liban)
  D Beirut (Libanon)
  I Beirut (Libano)
  E Beirut (Líbano)
  SU Бейру́т (Лива́н)

  GB *Bel-Ami*→*Fine Friend*

401 GB Belgian Congo, the (hist.)
  F le Congo belge (hist.)
  D Belgisch-Kongo (Gesch.)
  I il Congo Belga (st.)
  E el Congo Belga (hist.)
  SU Бельги́йское Ко́нго (ист.)

402 GB Belgium
  F la Belgique
  D Belgien
  I il Belgio
  E Bélgica
  SU Бе́льгия

403 GB Belgrade (Yugoslavia)
  F Belgrade (Yougoslavie)
  D Belgrad (Jugoslawien)
  I Belgrado (Iugoslavia)
  E Belgrado (Yugoslavia)
  SU Белгра́д (Югосла́вия)

404 GB Belisarius (505–565)
  F Bélisaire
  D Belisar
  I Belisario
  E Belisario
  SU Велиса́рий

405 GB Belize
  F le Belize
  D Belize
  I il Belize
  E Belice
  SU Бели́з

406 GB *Bell, The* (Murdoch, 1958)
  F *La Cloche*
  D *Die Wasser der Sünde*
  I *La campana*
  E *La campana*
  SU «Ко́локол» (Мёрдок)

407 GB *Bella* (Giraudoux, 1926)
  F *Bella*
  D *Bella*
  I *Bella*
  E *Bella*
  SU «Бе́лла» (Жироду́)

408 GB *Belle Dame Sans Merci, La* ["The
      Pitiless Beauty"] (Keats, 1819)
  F *La Belle Dame sans merci*
  D *Die mitleidlose Schöne*
  I *La bella dama senza pietà*
  E *La hermosa dama sin piedad*
  SU «Безжа́лостная краса́вица» (Китс)

409 GB *Belle de Jour* [*Beauty of the Day*]
      (Buñuel, 1967)
  F *Belle de jour*
  D *Schöne des Tages*
  I *Bella di giorno*
  E *Belle de jour*
  SU «Дневна́я краса́вица» (Бюнюэ́ль)

410 GB *Belle Jardinière, La* [*The Lovely Lady
      Gardener*] (Raphael, 1507)
  F *La Belle Jardinière* (Raphaël)
  D *Madonna mit Kind und Johannes*
      (Raffael)
  I *La bella giardiniera* (Raffaello)
  E *La bella jardinera* (Rafael)
  SU «Прекра́сная садо́вница» (Рафаэ́ль
      Са́нти)

411 GB Bellerophon (myth.)
  F Bellérophon (myth.)
  D Bellerophontes (myth.)
  I Bellerofonte (mit.)
  E Belerofonte (mit.)
  SU Беллерофо́нт (миф.)

412 GB *Belles de Nuit, Les* [*Beauties of the Night*] (Clair, 1952)
F *Les Belles de nuit*
D *Die Schönen der Nacht*
I *Le belle della notte*
E *Mujeres soñades*
SU «Ночны́е краса́вицы» (Клер)

413 GB *Bells, The* (Poe, 1849)
F *Les Cloches*
D *Die Glocken*
I *Le campane*
E *Las campanas*
SU «Колокола́» (По)

414 GB *Belly of Paris, The* (Zola, 1873)
F *Le Ventre de Paris*
D *Der Bauch von Paris*
I *Il ventre di Parigi*
E *El vientre de París*
SU «Чре́во Пари́жа» (Золя́)

415 GB Belorussia (USSR)
F la Biélorussie (URSS)
D Bjelorußland (UdSSR)
I la Bielorussia (URSS)
E Bielorrusia (URSS)
SU Белору́ссия (СССР)

416 GB Benedict (saint, pope)
F Benoît (saint, pape)
D Benedikt (Heiliger, Papst)
I Benedetto (santo, papa)
E Benedicto (santo, papa)
SU Бенеди́кт (св., папа ри́мский)

417 GB Benedictines, the (rel.)
F les Bénédictins (relig.)
D die Benediktiner (relig.)
I i benedittini (relig.)
E los Benedictinos (relig.)
SU бенедикти́нцы (рел.)

418 GB Bengal
F le Bengale
D Bengalen
I il Bengala
E Bengala
SU Бенга́лия

419 GB Benjamin (Bib.)
F Benjamin (Bib.)
D Benjamin (Bib.)
I Beniamino (Bib.)
E Benjamín (Bib.)
SU Вениами́н (библ.)

420 GB *Benvenuto Cellini* (Berlioz, 1838)
F *Benvenuto Cellini*
D *Benvenuto Cellini*
I *Benvenuto Cellini*
E *Benvenuto Cellini*
SU «Бенвену́то Челли́ни» (Берлио́з)

421 GB Berenice (Bib., + Racine, 1670)
F Bérénice (Bib.)
D Berenike (Bib.)
I Berenice (Bib.)
E Berenice (Bib.)
SU Верени́ка (библ., + Раси́н)

422 GB Berlin (Germany)
F Berlin (Allemagne)
D Berlin (Deutschland)
I Berlino (Germania)
E Berlín (Alemania)
SU Берли́н (Герма́ния)

423 GB Bermuda
F les îles Bermudes
D Bermuda
I le Bermude
E las islas Bermudas
SU Берму́да

424 GB Bernard (saint)
F Bernard (saint)
D Bernhard (Heiliger)
I Bernardo (santo)
E Bernardo (santo)
SU Берна́рд (св.)

425 GB Bern(e) (Switzerland)
F Berne (Suisse)
D Bern (Schweiz)
I Berna (Svizzera)
E Berna (Suiza)
SU Берн (Швейца́рия)

426 GB Besançon (France)
F Besançon (France)
D Besançon (Frankreich)
I Besançon (Francia)
E Besanzón (Francia)
SU Безансо́н (Фра́нция)

427 GB Bessarabia
F la Bessarabie
D Bessarabien
I la Bessarabia
E Besarabia
SU Бессара́бия

428 GB *Best Judge is the King, The* (Lope de
       Vega, 1620–3)
      F   *Le meilleur alcade est le roi*
      D   *Der beste Richter ist der König*
      I   *Il miglior giudice è il re*
      E   *El mejor alcalde, el rey*
      SU «Лу́чший алька́льд – коро́ль» (Ве́га
          Ка́рпьо)

429 GB *Best Years of Our Lives, The* (Wyler,
       1946)
      F   *Les Plus Belles Années de notre vie*
      D   *Die besten Jahre unseres Lebens*
      I   *I migliori anni della nostra vita*
      E   *Los mejores años de nuestra vida*
      SU «Лу́чшие го́ды на́шей жи́зни»
          (Уа́йлер)

430 GB *Bête Humaine, La* [*The Human
       Animal*] (Renoir, 1938)
      F   *La Bête humaine*
      D   *Bestie Mensch*
      I   *L'angelo del male*
      E   *La bête humaine*
      SU «Челове́к-зверь» (Ренуа́р)

431 GB Bethany (Bib.)
      F   Béthanie (Bib.)
      D   Bethanien (Bib.)
      I   Betania (Bib.)
      E   Betania (Bib.)
      SU Вифа́ния (библ.)

432 GB Bethel (Bib.)
      F   Béthel (Bib.)
      D   Bethel (Bib.)
      I   Betel (Bib.)
      E   Betel (Bib.)
      SU Вефи́ль (м.) (библ.)

433 GB Bethlehem (Bib.)
      F   Bethléem (Bib.)
      D   Bethlehem (Bib.)
      I   Betlemme (Bib.)
      E   Belén (Bib.)
      SU Вифлее́м (библ.)

434 GB *Betrothed, The* (Manzoni, 1827)
      F   *Les Fiancés*
      D   *Die Verlobten*
      I   *I promessi sposi*
      E   *Los novios*
      SU «Обручённые» (Мандзо́ни)

435 GB *Between the Acts* (Woolf, 1941)
      F   *Entre les actes*
      D   *Zwischen den Akten*
      I   *Fra un'azione e l'altra*
      E   *Entre actos*
      SU «Ме́жду де́йствиями» (Вулф)

436 GB *Beyond a Reasonable Doubt* (Lang,
       1956)
      F   *L'Invraisemblable Vérité*
      D   *Jenseits allen Zweifels*
      I   *L'alibi era perfetto*
      E   *Más allá de la duda*
      SU «Вне вся́ких сомне́ний» (Ланг)

437 GB *Beyond Good and Evil* (Nietzsche,
       1886)
      F   *Par-delà le bien et le mal*
      D   *Jenseits von Gut und Böse*
      I   *Al di là del bene e del male*
      E   *Más allá del bien y del mal*
      SU «По ту сто́рону добра́ и зла» (Ни́цше)

438 GB *Beyond Our Strength* [*Over ævne*]
       (Bjørnson, 1883)
      F   *Au-dessus des forces humaines*
      D   *Über die Kraft*
      I   *Oltre le forze umane*
      E   *Más allá de las fuerzas humanas*
      SU «Свы́ше на́ших сил» (Бьёрнсон)

439 GB *Beyond the Horizon* (O'Neill, 1920)
      F   *Derrière l'horizon*
      D   *Jenseits des Horizonts*
      I   *Al di là dell'orizzonte*
      E   *Más allá del horizonte*
      SU «За горизо́нтом» (О'Ни́л)

440 GB Bhutan
      F   le Bhoutan
      D   Bhutan
      I   il Bhutan
      E   Bután
      SU Бута́н

441 GB Bible, the
      F   la Bible
      D   die Bibel
      I   la Bibbia
      E   la Biblia
      SU Би́блия

442 GB *Bicycle Thieves, The* (De Sica, 1948)
      F   *Les Voleurs de bicyclette*
      D   *Fahrraddiebe*
      I   *Ladri di biciclette*
      E   *Ladrón de bicicletas*
      SU «Похити́тели велосипе́дов» (Де Си́ка)

443 GB *Big Heat, The* (Lang, 1953)
F *Règlements de comptes*
D *Heißes Eisen*
I *Il grande caldo*
E *Los sobornados*
SU «Большáя жарá» (Ланг)

444 GB *Big Money, The* (Dos Passos, 1936)
F *La Grosse Galette*
D *Die Hochfinanz*
I *Un mucchio di quattrini*
E *La gran moneda*
SU «Большúе дéньги» (Дос Пáссос)

445 GB *Big Sleep, The* (Hawks, 1946)
F *Le Grand Sommeil*
D *Der tiefe Schlaf*
I *Il grande sonno*
E *El sueño eterno*
SU «Вéчный сон» (Хокс)

446 GB Bill of Rights, the (1689)
F la Déclaration des droits
D die Freiheitsurkunde
I il Bill of Rights
E la Declaración de Derechos
SU «Билль о правáх»

447 GB *Billy Budd* (Melville, 1924)
F *Billy Budd*
D *Billy Budd*
I *Billy Budd*
E *Billy Budd*
SU «Бúлли Бад» (Мéлвилл)

448 GB *Billy the Kid* (Vidor, 1930)
F *Billy le kid*
D *Der letzte Bandit*
I *Billy the kid*
E *Billy, el niño*
SU «Бúлли – бандúт» (Вúдор)

449 GB *Bird, The* (Michelet, 1856)
F *L'Oiseau*
D *Der Vogel*
I *L'uccello*
E *El pájaro*
SU «Птúца» (Мишлé)

450 GB *Birds, The* (Hitchcock, 1963)
F *Les Oiseaux*
D *Die Vögel*
I *Gli uccelli*
E *Los pájaros*
SU «Птúцы» (Хúчкок)

451 GB *Birds, The* [*Ornithes*] (Aristophanes, −414)
F *Les Oiseaux* (Aristophane)
D *Die Vögel* (Aristophanes)
I *Gli uccelli* (Aristofane)
E *Las aves* (Aristófanes)
SU «Птúцы» (Аристофáн)

452 GB *Birthday Party, The* (Pinter, 1959)
F *L'Anniversaire*
D *Die Geburtstagfeier*
I *Il compleanno*
E *Tea Party*
SU «Именúны» (Пúнтер)

453 GB *Birth of a Nation, The* (Griffith, 1915)
F *Naissance d'une nation*
D *Die Geburt einer Nation*
I *Nascita di una nazione*
E *El nacimiento de una nación*
SU «Рождéние нáции» (Грúффит)

454 GB *Birth of Venus, The* (Botticelli, XV)
F *La Naissance de Vénus*
D *Die Geburt der Venus*
I *La nascita di Venere*
E *El nacimiento de Venus*
SU «Рождéние Венéры» (Боттичéлли)

455 GB Biscay, the Bay of
F le golfe de Gascogne
D der Golf von Biscaya
I il golfo di Biscaglia
E el golfo de Vizcaya
SU Бискáйский залúв

456 GB Bizerte (Bizerta) (Tunisia)
F Bizerte (Tunisie)
D Biserta (Tunesien)
I Biserta (Tunisia)
E Bizerta (Túnez)
SU Бизéрта (Тунúс)

457 GB *Black Arrow, The* (Stevenson, 1888)
F *La Flèche noire*
D *Der schwarze Pfeil*
I *La freccia nera*
E *Las fleches negras*
SU «Чёрная стрелá» (Стúвенсон)

458 GB *Blackboard Jungle, The* (Brooks, 1955)
F *Graine de violence*
D *Die Saat der Gewalt*
I *Il seme della violenza*
E *Semilla de maldad*
SU «Семенá насúлия» (Брукс)

459 GB Black Death, the (XIV)
    F la Peste Noire
    D der Schwarze Tod
    I la peste nera
    E la peste negra
    SU «Чёрная смерть»

460 GB Black Forest, the (Germany)
    F la Forêt-Noire (Allemagne)
    D der Schwarzwald (Deutschland)
    I la Selva Nera (Germania)
    E la Selva Negra (Alemania)
    SU Шва́рцвальд (Герма́ния)

461 GB *Black Gold* (Tolstoy, 1931)
    F *L'Or noir* (Tolstoï)
    D *Das schwarze Gold* (Tolstoj)
    I *L'oro nero* (Tolstoj)
    E *El oro negro* (Tolstoi)
    SU «Чёрное зо́лото» (Толсто́й)

462 GB Black Prince, the (= Edward, 1330–76)
    F le Prince Noir (= Edouard)
    D der Schwarze Prinz (= Eduard)
    I il Principe Nero (= Edoardo)
    E el Príncipe Negro (= Eduardo)
    SU Чёрный принц (= Эду́ард)

463 GB Black Sea, the
    F la mer Noire
    D das Schwarze Meer
    I il mare Nero
    E el mar Negro
    SU Чёрное мо́ре

464 GB *Bleak House* (Dickens, 1853)
    F *Bleak House*
    D *Bleak-Haus*
    I *Casa desolata*
    E *La casa desolada*
    SU «Холо́дный дом» (Ди́ккенс)

465 GB Blenheim, the Battle of (1704)
    F la bataille de Blenheim
    D die Schlacht bei Höchstädt
    I la battaglia di Blenheim
    E la batalla de Blenheim
    SU сраже́ние при Го́хштедте

466 GB Blessed Virgin (Mary), the (rel.)
    F la Sainte Vierge (Marie) (relig.)
    D die Heilige Jungfrau (Maria) (relig.)
    I la Santissima Vergine (Maria) (relig.)
    E la Santísima Virgen (María) (relig.)
    SU пресвята́я де́ва (Мари́я) (рел.)

467 GB *Blind Musician, The* (Korolenko, 1886)
    F *Le Musicien aveugle*
    D *Der blinde Musiker*
    I *Il musicista cieco*
    E *El músico ciego*
    SU «Слепо́й музыка́нт» (Короле́нко)

468 GB *Blithe Spirit* (Coward, 1941)
    F *L'esprit s'amuse*
    D *Vergnügter Geist*
    I *Spirito allegro*
    E *Un espíritu burlón*
    SU «Дух весёлый» (Ко́уард)

469 GB *Blithe Spirit* (Lean, 1945)
    F *L'esprit s'amuse*
    D *Geisterkomödie*
    I *Spirito allegro*
    E *Un espíritu burlón*
    SU «Дух весёлый» (Лин)

470 GB *Blood and Sand* (Blasco Ibáñez, 1909)
    F *Arènes sanglantes*
    D *Die blutige Arena*
    I *Sangue e arena*
    E *Sangre y arena*
    SU «Кровь и песо́к» (Бла́ско Иба́ньес)

471 GB *Blood and Sand* (Niblo, 1922)
    F *Sang et arène*
    D *König der Toreros*
    I *Sangue e arena*
    E *Sangre y arena*
    SU «Кровь и песо́к» (Ни́бло)

472 GB *Blood of the Others, The* (Beauvoir, 1944)
    F *Le Sang des autres*
    D *Das Blut der anderen*
    I *Il sangue degli altri*
    E *La sangre de los otros*
    SU «Чужа́я кровь» (Бовуа́р)

473 GB *Blood Wedding* (Lorca, 1933)
    F *Noces de sang*
    D *Bluthochzeit*
    I *Nozze di sangue*
    E *Bodas de sangre*
    SU «Крова́вая сва́дьба» (Гарси́а Ло́рка)

474 GB Bloody Mary (= Mary I, 1516–58)
    F Marie la Sanglante (= Marie I)
    D Maria die Blutige (= Maria I)
    I Maria la Sanguinaria (= Maria I)
    E María la Sanguinaria (= María I)
    SU Крова́вая Мари́я (= Мари́я I)

475 GB *Blow-up* (Antonioni, 1966)
 F *Blow up*
 D *Blow up*
 I *Blow up*
 E *Blow up*
 SU «Бло́у ап» (Антонио́ни)

476 GB *Blue Angel, The* (Sternberg, 1930)
 F *L'Ange bleu*
 D *Der blaue Engel*
 I *L'angelo azzurro*
 E *El ángel azul*
 SU «Голубо́й а́нгел» (Штэ́рнберг)

477 GB *Bluebeard* (Perrault, 1697)
 F *Barbe-Bleue*
 D *Blaubart*
 I *Barbablù*
 E *Barba azul*
 SU «Си́няя Борода́» (Перро́)

478 GB *Blue Bird, The* (Maeterlinck, 1905)
 F *L'Oiseau bleu*
 D *Der blaue Vogel*
 I *L'uccello azzurro*
 E *El pájaro azul*
 SU «Си́няя пти́ца» (Ме́терли́нк)

479 GB *Blue Boy, The* (Gainsborough, 1779)
 F *Garçon en bleu*
 D *Knabe in blau*
 I *Ragazzo vestito di azzurro*
 E *Niño vestido de azul*
 SU «Голубо́й ма́льчик» (Ге́йнсборо)

480 GB *Blue Danube, The* (Strauss, 1867)
 F *Le Beau Danube bleu*
 D *An der schönen blauen Donau*
 I *Sul bel Danubio blu*
 E *El Danubio azul*
 SU «На прекра́сном голубо́м Дуна́е» (Штра́ус)

481 GB *Blue Lamp, The* (Dearden, 1950)
 F *La Lampe bleue*
 D *Die blaue Lampe*
 I *I giovani uccidono*
 E *El farol azul*
 SU «Си́няя ла́мпа» (Ди́рден)

482 GB Blue Mountains, the (Australia)
 F les Montagnes Bleues (Australie)
 D die Blauen Berge (Australien)
 I i Monti Azzurri (Australia)
 E los Montes Azules (Australia)
 SU Голубы́е го́ры (Австра́лия)

483 GB Blue Nile, the
 F le Nil Bleu
 D der Blaue Nil
 I il Nilo Azzurro
 E el Nilo Azul
 SU Голубо́й Нил

484 GB Boccaccio (1313–75)
 F Boccàce
 D Boccaccio
 I Boccaccio
 E Boccaccio
 SU Бокка́ччо

485 GB Boeotia (Greece)
 F la Béotie (Grèce)
 D Böotien (Griechenland)
 I la Beozia (Grecia)
 E Beocia (Grecia)
 SU Бео́тия (Гре́ция)

486 GB Boer War, the (1899–1902)
 F la guerre des Boers
 D der Burenkrieg
 I la guerra anglo-boera
 E la guerra dos Boers
 SU А́нгло-бу́рская война́

487 GB Bohemia (hist.)
 F la Bohème (hist.)
 D Böhmen (Gesch.)
 I la Boemia (st.)
 E Bohemia (hist.)
 SU Боге́мия (ист.)

488 GB *Bohemian Girl, The* (Puccini, 1896)
 F *La Bohème*
 D *La Bohème*
 I *La Bohème*
 E *La Bohème*
 SU «Боге́ма» (Пуччи́ни)

489 GB *Bolero* (Ravel, 1928)
 F *Boléro*
 D *Bolero*
 I *Bolero*
 E *Bolero*
 SU «Болеро́» (Раве́ль)

490 GB Bolivia
 F la Bolivie
 D Bolivien
 I la Bolivia
 E Bolivia
 SU Боли́вия

491 GB Bologna (Italy)
    F Bologne (Italie)
    D Bologna (Italien)
    I Bologna (Italia)
    E Bolonia (Italia)
    SU Болóнья (Итáлия)

492 GB Bolsheviks, the (hist.)
    F les bolcheviks (hist.)
    D die Bolschewiken (Gesch.)
    I i bolscevichi (st.)
    E los bolcheviques (hist.)
    SU большевикú (ист.)

493 GB Bonaventure (saint)
    F Bonaventure (saint)
    D Bonaventura (Heiliger)
    I Bonaventura (santo)
    E Buenaventura (santo)
    SU Бонавентúра (св.)

494 GB Boniface (saint, pope)
    F Boniface (saint, pape)
    D Bonifatius (Heiliger, Papst)
    I Bonifacio (santo, papa)
    E Bonifacio (santo, papa)
    SU Бонифáций (св., пáпа рúмский)

495 GB *Bonjour Tristesse [Good Morning, Sadness]* (Sagan, 1954)
    F *Bonjour tristesse*
    D *Bonjour tristesse*
    I *Buongiorno, tristezza*
    E *Bonjour tristesse*
    SU «Здрáвствуй, грусть» (Сагáн)

496 GB *Bonnie and Clyde* (Penn, 1967)
    F *Bonnie et Clyde*
    D *Bonnie und Clyde*
    I *Gangster Story*
    E *Bonnie y Clyde*
    SU «Бóнни и Клайд» (Пенн)

    GB Book of . . . (Bib.)→ . . . , Book of

497 GB *Book of Hours, The* (Rilke, 1905)
    F *Le Livre d'heures*
    D *Das Stundenbuch*
    I *Il libro d'ore*
    E *El libro de horas*
    SU «Часослóв» (Рúльке)

498 GB *Book of Pictures, The* (Rilke, 1902)
    F *Le Livre des images*
    D *Buch der Bilder*
    I *Libro delle immagini*
    E *Libro de imágenes*
    SU «Кнúга óбразов» (Рúльке)

499 GB *Book of Snobs, The* (Thackeray, 1848)
    F *Le Livre des snobs*
    D *Das Snob-Buch*
    I *Il libro degli snob*
    E *El libro de los snobs*
    SU «Кнúга снóбов» (Тéккерей)

500 GB *Book of Songs* (Heine, 1927)
    F *Le Livre des chants*
    D *Buch der Lieder*
    I *Libro dei canti*
    E *Libro de canciones*
    SU «Кнúга пéсен» (Гéйне)

501 GB *Book of the Dead*, the (?–XX)
    F *Le Livre des Morts*
    D das *Buch der Toden*
    I *Il libro dei morti*
    E el *Libro de los muertos*
    SU «Кнúга мёртвых»

502 GB Boötes (astron.)
    F le Bouvier (astron.)
    D Bootes (Astron.)
    I Boote (astr.)
    E el Boyero (astr.)
    SU Волопáс (астр.)

503 GB Bordeaux (France)
    F Bordeaux (France)
    D Bordeaux (Frankreich)
    I Bordeaux (Francia)
    E Burdeos (Francia)
    SU Бордó (Фрáнция)

504 GB Boreas (myth.)
    F Borée (myth.)
    D Boreas (myth.)
    I Borea (mit.)
    E Bóreas (mit.)
    SU Борéй (миф.)

505 GB *Boris Godunov* (Pushkin, 1825; Mussorgsky, 1869)
    F *Boris Godounov* (Pouchkine, Moussorgski)
    D *Boris Godunow* (Puschkin, Mussorgskij)
    I *Boris Godunov* (Puškin, Musorgskij)
    E *Boris Godunov* (Puschkin, Mussorgski)
    SU «Борúс Годунóв» (Пýшкин, Мýсоргский)

506 GB *Born Free* (Adamson, 1960)
   F *Vivre libre*
   D *Freigeboren, die Königin der Wildnis*
   I *Nata libera*
   E *Nacida libre*
   SU «Рождённая на во́ле» (А́дамсон)

507 GB Bosnia and Hercegovina (Yugoslavia)
   F la Bosnie-Herzégovine (Yougoslavie)
   D Bosnien und Herzegowina
      (Jugoslawien)
   I la Bosnia-Erzegovina (Iugoslavia)
   E Bosnia y Herzegovina (Yugoslavia)
   SU Бо́сния и Герцегови́на (Югосла́вия)

508 GB Bosporus (Bosphorus), the
   F le Bosphore
   D der Bosporus
   I il Bosforo
   E el Bósforo
   SU Боспо́р

509 GB Boston Tea Party, the (1773)
   F le "thé de Boston"
   D der Teesturm von Boston
   I il "tè di Boston"
   E el "té de Boston"
   SU «Босто́нское чаепи́тие»

510 GB Bothnia, the Gulf of
   F le golfe de Botnie
   D der Bottnische Meerbusen
   I il golfo di Botnia
   E el golfo de Botnia
   SU Ботни́ческий зали́в

511 GB Bourbons, the (house)
   F les Bourbons (maison)
   D die Bourbon (Herrschergeschlecht)
   I i Borbone (casata)
   E los Borbones (casa)
   SU Бурбо́ны (дина́стия)

512 GB Boxer Rebellion, the (1900)
   F la révolte des Boxers
   D der Boxeraufstand
   I la rivolta dei boxers
   E la rebelión dos Boxers
   SU Боксёркое восста́ние

513 GB *Boy Captain, The* (Verne, 1878)
   F *Un capitaine de quinze ans*
   D *Ein Kapitän von fünfzehn Jahren*
   I *Capitano di quindici anni*
   E *Un capitán de quince años*
   SU «Пятнадцатиле́тний капита́н» (Верн)

   GB Boy Scouts → Scouts

514 GB *Boy's Magic Horn, The* (Brentano +
      Arnim, 1805–8; Mahler, 1888–96)
   F *Le Cor merveilleux*
   D *Des Knaben Wunderhorn*
   I *La cornucopia del fanciullo*
   E *El cuerno mágico del muchacho*
   SU «Волше́бный рог ма́льчика»
      (Брента́но/А́рним, Ма́лер)

515 GB Brabant (Belgium)
   F Brabant (Belge)
   D Brabant (Belgien)
   I Brabante (Belgio)
   E Brabante (Bélgica)
   SU Браба́нт (Бе́льгия)

516 GB *Braggart Warrior, The* [*Miles gloriosus*]
      (Plautus, −II)
   F *Le Soldat fanfaron* (Plaute)
   D *Der prahlende Soldat* (Plautus)
   I *Il soldato spaccone* (Plauto)
   E *El soldado fanfarrón* (Plauto)
   SU «Хвастли́вый во́ин» (Плавт)

517 GB Brahma (rel.)
   F Brahma (relig.)
   D Brahma (relig.)
   I Brahma (relig.)
   E Brahma (relig.)
   SU Бра́хма (рел.)

518 GB *Brand* (Ibsen, 1865)
   F *Brand*
   D *Brand*
   I *Brand*
   E *Brand*
   SU «Бранд» (И́бсен)

519 GB Brandenburg (Germany)
   F Brandebourg (Allemagne)
   D Brandenburg (Deutschland)
   I Brandeburgo (Germania)
   E Brandeburgo (Alemania)
   SU Бранденбу́рг (Герма́ния)

520 GB *Brandenburg Concertos*, the (Bach,
      1721)
   F les *Concertos brandebourgeois*
   D die *Brandenburgischen Konzerte*
   I i *Concerti brandeburghesi*
   E los *Conciertos de Brandeburgo*
   SU «Бранденбу́ргские конце́рты» (Бах)

521 GB Brandenburg Gate, the (Berlin)
   F la porte de Brandebourg (Berlin)
   D das Brandenburger Tor (Berlin)
   I la porta di Brandeburgo (Berlino)
   E la puerta de Brandeburgo (Berlín)
   SU Бранденбу́ргские воро́та (Берли́н)

522 GB Braunschweig (Brunswick) (Germany)
    F Brunswick (Allemagne)
    D Braunschweig (Deutschland)
    I Braunschweig (Germania)
    E Brunswick (Alemania)
    SU Бра́уншвейг (Герма́ния)

523 GB *Brave New World* (Huxley, 1932)
    F *Le Meilleur des Mondes*
    D *Wackere neue Welt*
    I *Il mondo nuovo*
    E *Un mundo feliz*
    SU «Прекра́сный но́вый мир» (Ха́ксли)

524 GB Brazil
    F le Brésil
    D Brasilien
    I il Brasile
    E el Brasil
    SU Брази́лия

525 GB *Breakfast at Tiffany's* (Edwards, 1961)
    F *Diamants sur canapé*
    D *Frühstück bei Tiffany*
    I *Colazione da Tiffany*
    E *Desayuno con diamantes*
    SU «За́втрак у Ти́ффани» (Э́двардс)

526 GB *Breathless* (Godard, 1959)
    F *À bout de souffle*
    D *Außer Atem*
    I *Fino all'ultimo respiro*
    E *Al final de la escapada*
    SU «На после́днем дыха́нии» (Года́р)

527 GB Bremen (Germany)
    F Brême (Allemagne)
    D Bremen (Deutschland)
    I Brema (Germania)
    E Brema (Alemania)
    SU Бре́мен (Герма́ния)

528 GB *Bride of Lammermoor, The* (Scott, 1819)
    F *La Fiancée de Lammermoor*
    D *Die Braut von Lammermoor*
    I *La sposa di Lammermoor*
    E *Lucía de Lammermoor*
    SU «Ламмерму́рская неве́ста» (Скотт)

529 GB *Brideshead Revisited* (Waugh, 1945)
    F *Retour à Brideshead*
    D *Wiedersehen mit Brideshead*
    I *Ritorno a Brideshead*
    E *Regreso a Brideshead*
    SU «Возвраще́ние в Бра́йдсхед» (Во)

530 GB *Bridge of San Luis Rey, The* (Wilder, 1927)
    F *Le Pont de San Luis Rey*
    D *Die Brücke von San Luis Rey*
    I *Il ponte di San Luis Rey*
    E *El puente de San Luis Rey*
    SU «Мост короля́ Людо́вика Свято́го» (Уа́йлдер)

531 GB Bridge of Sighs, the (Venice)
    F le pont des Soupirs (Venise)
    D die Seufzerbrücke (Venedig)
    I il ponte dei Sospiri (Venezia)
    E el puente dos Suspiros (Venecia)
    SU «мост вздо́хов» (Вене́ция)

532 GB *Bridge on the River Kwai, The* (Lean, 1957)
    F *Le Pont de la rivière Kwaï*
    D *Die Brücke am Kwai*
    I *Il ponte sul fiume Kwai*
    E *El puente sobre el río Kwai*
    SU «Мост че́рез ре́ку Квай» (Лин)

533 GB *Bridge Too Far, A* (Attenborough, 1977)
    F *Un pont trop loin*
    D *Die Brücke von Arnheim*
    I *Quell'ultimo ponte*
    E *Un puente lejano*
    SU «А́рнемский мост» (А́ттенборо)

534 GB *Brief Encounter* (Lean, 1946)
    F *Brève Rencontre*
    D *Begegnung*
    I *Breve incontro*
    E *Breve encuentro*
    SU «Коро́ткая встре́ча» (Лин)

535 GB *Brighton Rock* (Greene, 1938)
    F *Le Rocher de Brighton*
    D *Der Abgrund des Lebens*
    I *La rocca di Brighton*
    E *La roca de Brighton*
    SU «Бра́йтонская скала́» (Грин)

536 GB Bristol Channel, the (England)
    F le canal de Bristol (Angleterre)
    D der Bristolkanal (England)
    I il canale di Bristol (Inghilterra)
    E el canal de Bristol (Inglaterra)
    SU Бристо́льский зали́в (А́нглия)

537 GB Britain (= Great Britain)
    F l'Angleterre (f.) (= Grande Bretagne)
    D England (= Großbritannien)
    I l'Inghilterra (= Gran Bretagna)
    E Inglaterra (= Gran Bretaña)
    SU Брита́ния (= Великобрита́ния)

538 GB Britain (hist.)
   F la Bretagne (hist.)
   D Britannien (Gesch.)
   I la Britannia (st.)
   E Britania (hist.)
   SU Брита́ния (ист.)

539 GB Britain, the Battle of (1940–1)
   F la bataille (aérienne) de
       Grande-Bretagne
   D die Luftoffensive gegen
       Großbritannien
   I la battaglia d'Inghilterra
   E la batalla (aérea) de Inglaterra
   SU «Би́тва за А́нглию»

540 GB Britannicus (41–55, + Racine, 1669)
   F Britannicus
   D Britannicus
   I Britannico
   E Británico
   SU Брита́ник (+ Раси́н)

541 GB British Columbia (Canada)
   F la Colombie britannique (Canada)
   D Britisch-Columbia (Kanada)
   I la Columbia Britannica (Canada)
   E Colombia Británica (Canadá)
   SU Брита́нская Колу́мбия (Кана́да)

542 GB British Empire, the (hist.)
   F l'Empire britannique (hist.)
   D das Britische Reich (Gesch.)
   I l'impero britannico (st.)
   E el Imperio Británico (hist.)
   SU брита́нская импе́рия (ист.)

543 GB British Honduras (hist.)
   F le Honduras britannique (hist.)
   D Britisch-Honduras (Gesch.)
   I l'Honduras Britannico (st.)
   E Honduras Británica (hist.)
   SU Брита́нский Гондура́с (ист.)

544 GB British Isles, the
   F les îles Britanniques
   D die britischen Inseln
   I le isole Britanniche
   E las Islas Británicas
   SU Брита́нские острова́

545 GB British Museum, the (London)
   F le British Museum (Londres)
   D das Britische Museum (London)
   I il British Museum (Londra)
   E el British Museum (Londres)
   SU Брита́нский музе́й (Ло́ндон)

546 GB Britons (Ancient Britons), the (hist.)
   F les Bretons (hist.)
   D die Briten (Gesch.)
   I i britanni (st.)
   E los britanos (hist.)
   SU бри́тты (ист.)

547 GB Brittany (France)
   F la Bretagne (France)
   D die Bretagne (Frankreich)
   I la Bretagna (Francia)
   E Bretaña (Francia)
   SU Брета́нь (ж.) (Фра́нция)

548 GB *Broken Heart, The* (Ford, 1633)
   F *Le Coeur brisé*
   D *Das gebrochene Herz*
   I *Il cuore spezzato*
   E *Corazón roto*
   SU «Разби́тое се́рдце» (Форд)

549 GB Bronze Age, the (hist.)
   F l'âge du bronze (hist.)
   D das Bronzezeitalter (Gesch.)
   I l'età del bronzo (st.)
   E la Edad del Bronce (hist.)
   SU бро́нзовый век (ист.)

550 GB *Bronze Horseman, The* (Pushkin, 1833)
   F *Le Cavalier de bronze* (Pouchkine)
   D *Der eherne Reiter* (Puschkin)
   I *Il cavaliere di bronzo* (Puškin)
   E *El jinete de bronce* (Puschkin)
   SU «Ме́дный вса́дник» (Пу́шкин)

551 GB *Brothers, The* [*Adelphoe*] (Terence, −160)
   F *Les Frères* (Térence)
   D *Die Brüder* (Terentius)
   I *I fratelli* (Terenzio)
   E *Los hermanos* (Terencio)
   SU «Бра́тья» (Тере́нций)

552 GB *Brothers Karamazov, The* (Dostoievsky, 1879–80)
   F *Les Frères Karamazov* (Dostoïevski)
   D *Die Brüder Karamasow* (Dostojewskij)
   I *I fratelli Karamazov* (Dostoevskij)
   E *Los hermanos Karamazov* (Dostoievski)
   SU «Бра́тья Карама́зовы» (Достое́вский)

553 GB Bruges (Brugge) (Belgium)
   F Bruges (Belge)
   D Brügge (Belgien)
   I Bruges (Belgio)
   E Brujas (Bélgica)
   SU Брю́гге (Бе́льгия)

554 GB Brunei
     F   Brunei
     D   Brunei
     I   Brunei
     E   Brunei
     SU Бруне́й

     GB Brunswick→Braunschweig

555 GB Brussels (Belgium)
     F   Bruxelles (Belge)
     D   Brüssel (Belgien)
     I   Bruxelles (Belgio)
     E   Bruselas (Bélgica)
     SU Брюссе́ль (м.) (Бе́льгия)

556 GB Brutus (Roman name)
     F   Brutus (nom romain)
     D   Brutus (Römername)
     I   Bruto (nome romano)
     E   Bruto (nombre romano)
     SU Брут (древнери́мское и́мя)

557 GB Bucharest (Romania)
     F   Bucarest (Roumanie)
     D   Bukarest (Rumänien)
     I   Bucarest (Romania)
     E   Bucarest (Rumania)
     SU Бухаре́ст (Румы́ния)

558 GB *Bucolics*, the [*Bucolica*] (Virgil, 42–39)
     F   les *Bucoliques* (f.) (Virgile)
     D   die *Bukoliken* (Vergil)
     I   le *Bucoliche* (Virgilio)
     E   las *Bucólicas* (Virgilio)
     SU «Буко́лики» (ж.) (Верги́лий)

559 GB Budapest (Hungary)
     F   Budapest (Hongrie)
     D   Budapest (Ungarn)
     I   Budapest (Ungheria)
     E   Budapest (Hungría)
     SU Будапе́шт (Ве́нгрия)

560 GB *Buddenbrooks* (Mann, 1901)
     F   *Les Buddenbrooks*
     D   *Buddenbrooks*
     I   *I Buddenbrook*
     E   *Los Buddenbrooks*
     SU «Бу́дденброки» (Манн)

561 GB Buddha (−VI)
     F   Bouddha
     D   Buddha
     I   Buddha
     E   Buda
     SU Бу́дда

562 GB Buenos Aires (Argentina)
     F   Buenos Aires (Argentine)
     D   Buenos Aires (Argentinien)
     I   Buenos Aires (Argentina)
     E   Buenos Aires (Argentina)
     SU Буэ́нос-А́йрес (Аргенти́на)

563 GB Buffalo Bill (1846–1917)
     F   Buffalo Bill
     D   Buffalo Bill
     I   Buffalo Bill
     E   Búfalo Bill
     SU Бу́ффало Билл

564 GB Bulgaria
     F   la Bulgarie
     D   Bulgarien
     I   la Bulgaria
     E   Bulgaria
     SU Болга́рия

565 GB *Bullfighters, The* (Montherlant, 1926)
     F   *Les Bestiaires*
     D   *Tiermenschen*
     I   *I gladiatori*
     E   *Los bestiarios*
     SU «Бести́арии» (Монтерла́н)

566 GB *Burghers of Calais, The* (Rodin, 1895)
     F   *Les Bourgeois de Calais*
     D   *Die Bürger von Calais*
     I   *I borghesi di Calais*
     E   *Los burgueses de Calais*
     SU «Гра́ждане Кале́» (Роде́н)

567 GB Burgundy (France)
     F   la Bourgogne (France)
     D   Burgund (Frankreich)
     I   la Borgogna (Francia)
     E   Borgoña (Francia)
     SU Бургу́ндия (Фра́нция)

568 GB *Burial of Count Orgaz, The* (El Greco, 1586)
     F   *L'Enterrement du comte d'Orgaz*
     D   *Begräbnis des Grafen Orgaz*
     I   *L'entierro del conte d'Orgaz*
     E   *Entierro del Conde de Orgaz*
     SU «Погребе́ние гра́фа О́ргаса» (Эль Гре́ко)

569 GB Burma
     F   la Birmanie
     D   Birma
     I   la Birmania
     E   Birmania
     SU Би́рма

570	GB	Bushmen, the (Africa)
	F	les Bockimans (Afrique)
	D	die Buschmänner (Afrika)
	I	i boscimani (Africa)
	E	los bosquimanos (África)
	SU	бушме́ны (А́фрика)

571	GB	*Butch Cassidy and the Sundance Kid* (Hill, 1969)
	F	*Butch Cassidy et le kid*
	D	*Zwei Banditen*
	I	*Butch Cassidy*
	E	*Dos hombres y un destino*
	SU	«Два челове́ка, одна́ судьба́» (Хилл)

572	GB	*Butterfield 8* (O'Hara, 1935)
	F	*Glória*
	D	*Butterfield 8*
	I	*Butterfield 8*
	E	*Butterfield 8*
	SU	«Ба́ттерфилд 8» (О'Ха́ра)

573	GB	Byzantine Empire, the (395–1453)
	F	l'Empire byzantin
	D	das Byzantinische Reich
	I	l'impero bizantino
	E	el Imperio Bizantino
	SU	Византи́я

574	GB	Byzantium (hist.)
	F	la Byzance (hist.)
	D	Byzanz (Gesch.)
	I	Bizanzio (st.)
	E	Bizancio (hist.)
	SU	Виза́нтий (ист.)

C

575	GB	*Cabaret* (Fosse, 1972)
	F	*Cabaret*
	D	*Cabaret*
	I	*Cabaret*
	E	*Cabaret*
	SU	«Кабаре́» (Фосс)

576	GB	*Cabin, The* (Blasco Ibáñez, 1898)
	F	*Terres maudites*
	D	*Die Scholle*
	I	*Ah, il pane*
	E	*La barraca*
	SU	«Ху́тор» (Бла́ско Иба́ньес)

577	GB	*Cabinet of Dr Caligari, The* (Wiene, 1919)
	F	*Le Cabinet du docteur Caligari*
	D	*Das Kabinett des Dr. Caligari*
	I	*Il gabinetto del dottor Caligari*
	E	*El gabinete del doctor Caligari*
	SU	«Кабине́т до́ктора Калига́ри» (Ви́не)

578	GB	Cacus (myth.)
	F	Cacus (myth.)
	D	Cacus (myth.)
	I	Caco (mit.)
	E	Caco (mit.)
	SU	Как (миф.)

579	GB	Cadiz (Spain)
	F	Cadix (Espagne)
	D	Cadiz (Spanien)
	I	Cadice (Spagna)
	E	Cádiz (España)
	SU	Ка́дис (Испа́ния)

580	GB	Cadmus (myth.)
	F	Cadmos (myth.)
	D	Cadmus (myth.)
	I	Cadmo (mit.)
	E	Cadmo (mit.)
	SU	Кадм (миф.)

	GB	Caesar, Julius→Julius Caesar

581	GB	*Caesar and Cleopatra* (Shaw, 1906)
	F	*César et Cléopâtre*
	D	*Cäsar und Kleopatra*
	I	*Cesare e Cleopatra*
	E	*César y Cleopatra*
	SU	«Це́зарь и Клеопа́тра» (Шо́у)

582	GB	Caiaphas (Bib.)
	F	Caïphe (Bib.)
	D	Kaiphas (Bib.)
	I	Caifa (Bib.)
	E	Caifás (Bib.)
	SU	Каиафа́ (библ.)

583	GB	Cain (Bib.)
	F	Caïn (Bib.)
	D	Kain (Bib.)
	I	Caino (Bib.)
	E	Caín (Bib.)
	SU	Ка́ин (библ.)

584	GB	*Caine Mutiny, The* (Dmytryk, 1954)
	F	*Ouragan sur le Caine*
	D	*Die Caine war ihr Schicksal*
	I	*L'ammutinamento del Caine*
	E	*El motín del Caine*
	SU	«Мяте́ж на ,,Ка́ине"» (Дми́трик)

585	GB	Cairo (Egypt)
	F	le Caire (Égypte)
	D	Kairo (Ägypten)
	I	Il Cairo (Egitto)
	E	El Cairo (Egipto)
	SU	Каи́р (Еги́пет)

586	GB	*Cakes and Ale* (Maugham, 1930)
	F	*La Ronde de l'amour*
	D	*Seine erste Frau*
	I	*Lo scheletro nella credenza*
	E	*Cautiva de amor*
	SU	«Пря́ники и эль» (Мо́эм)

587 GB Calabria (Italy)
F la Calabre (Italie)
D Kalabrien (Italien)
I la Calabria (Italia)
E Calabria (Italia)
SU Кала́брия (Ита́лия)

588 GB Calcutta (India)
F Calcutta (Inde)
D Calcutta (Indien)
I Calcutta (India)
E Calcuta (India)
SU Калькýтта (Йндия)

589 GB California (USA)
F la Californie (USA)
D Kalifornien (USA)
I la California (USA)
E California (USA)
SU Калифóрния (США)

590 GB Caligula (12–41)
F Caligula
D Caligula
I Caligola
E Calígula
SU Кали́гула

591 GB *Caliph of Bagdad, The* (Boïeldieu, 1800)
F *Le Calife de Bagdad*
D *Der Kalif von Bagdad*
I *Il califfo di Bagdad*
E *El califa de Bagdad*
SU «Кали́ф Багда́дский» (Буальдьё)

592 GB Callimachus (*310–240*)
F Callimaque
D Kallimachos
I Callimaco
E Calímaco
SU Каллима́х

593 GB Calliope (myth.)
F Calliope (myth.)
D Kalliope (myth.)
I Calliope (mit.)
E Calíope (mit.)
SU Каллиóпа (миф.)

594 GB *Call of the Wild* (London, 1903)
F *L'Appel de la forêt*
D *Ruf der Wildnis*
I *Il richiamo della foresta*
E *La llamada de la selva*
SU «Зов предкóв» (Лóндон)

595 GB Calvary (Bib.)
F le Calvaire (Bib.)
D der Kalvarienberg (Bib.)
I il Calvario (Bib.)
E el Calvario (Bib.)
SU Голгóфа (библ.)

596 GB Calvin (1509–64)
F Calvin
D Calvin
I Calvino
E Calvino
SU Кальви́н

597 GB Calypso (myth.)
F Calypso (myth.)
D Kalypso (myth.)
I Calipso (mit.)
E Calipso (mit.)
SU Калипсó (миф.)

598 GB Cambodia
F le Cambodge
D Kambodscha
I la Cambogia
E Camboya
SU Камбóджа

599 GB Cameroon
F le Cameroun
D Kamerun
I il Camerun
E el Camerún
SU Камерýн

600 GB Campagna de Roma (Roman Campagna), the (Italy)
F la Campagne Romaine (Italie)
D die Campagna di Roma (Italien)
I la Campagna Romana (Italia)
E la Campiña Romana (Italia)
SU Ри́мская Кампа́нья (Ита́лия)

601 GB Campania (Italy)
F la Campanie (Italie)
D Kampanien (Italien)
I la Campania (Italia)
E Campania (Italia)
SU Кампа́ния (Ита́лия)

602 GB Cana (of Galilee) (Bib.)
F Cana (de Galilée) (Bib.)
D Kana (in Galiläa) (Bib.)
I Cana (della Galilea) (Bib.)
E Caná (de Galilea) (Bib.)
SU Ка́на (Галилéйская) (библ.)

603 GB Canada
    F le Canada
    D Kanada
    I il Canada
    E el Canadá
    SU Кана́да

    GB Canal Zone→Panama Canal Zone

604 GB Canary Islands, the
    F les îles Canaries
    D die Kanarischen Inseln
    I le Canarie
    E las islas Canarias
    SU Кана́рские острова́

605 GB Cancer (astron.)
    F le Cancer (astron.)
    D der Krebs (Astron.)
    I il Cancro (astr.)
    E Cáncer (astr.)
    SU Рак (астр.)

606 GB *Cancer Ward* (Solzhenitsyn, 1968)
    F *Le Pavillon des cancéreux*
      (Soljenitsyne)
    D *Krebsstation* (Solschenizyn)
    I *Divisione Cancro* (Solženicyn)
    E *Pabellón de cancerosos* (Soljenitsyn)
    SU «Ра́ковый ко́рпус» (Солжени́цын)

607 GB *Candida* (Shaw, 1903)
    F *Candide*
    D *Candide*
    I *Candida*
    E *Cándida*
    SU «Ка́ндида» (Шо́у)

608 GB *Candide* (Voltaire, 1759)
    F *Candide*
    D *Candide*
    I *Candido*
    E *Cándido*
    SU «Канди́д» (Вольте́р)

609 GB Candlemas (rel.)
    F la Chandeleur (relig.)
    D die (Mariä) Lichtmaß (relig.)
    I la Candelora (relig.)
    E la Candelaria (relig.)
    SU сре́тение (рел.)

610 GB *Candlestick, The* (Musset, 1835)
    F *Le Chandelier*
    D *Der Leuchter*
    I *Il candeliere*
    E *El candelero*
    SU «Подсве́чник» (Мюссе́)

611 GB Canis Major (astron.)
    F le Grand Chien (astron.)
    D der Große Hund (Astron.)
    I il Cane Maggiore (astr.)
    E el Can Mayor (astr.)
    SU Большо́й Пёс (астр.)

612 GB Canis Minor (astron.)
    F le Petit Chien (astron.)
    D der Kleine Hund (Astron.)
    I il Cane Minore (astr.)
    E el Can Menor (astr.)
    SU Ма́лый Пёс (астр.)

613 GB *Cannery Row* (Steinbeck, 1945)
    F *Rue de la Sardine*
    D *Die Straße der Ölsardinen*
    I *Vicolo Cannery*
    E *Los arrabales de Cannery*
    SU «Консе́рвный ряд» (Сте́йнбек)

614 GB Cannes (France)
    F Cannes (France)
    D Cannes (Frankreich)
    I Cannes (Francia)
    E Cannes (Francia)
    SU Канн (Фра́нция)

615 GB Cantabrian Mountains, the (Spain)
    F les monts Cantabriques (Espagne)
    D das Kantabrische Gebirge (Spanien)
    I i monti Cantabrici (Spagna)
    E la Cordillera Cantábrica (España)
    SU Кантабри́йские го́ры (Испа́ния)

616 GB Canterbury (England)
    F Canterbury (Angleterre)
    D Canterbury (England)
    I Canterbury (Inghilterra)
    E Cantorbery (Inglaterra)
    SU Ке́нтербери (А́нглия)

617 GB *Canterbury Tales, The* (Chaucer,
      1387–1400)
    F *Les Contes de Cantorbéry*
    D *Die Canterbury Geschichten*
    I *I racconti di Canterbury*
    E *Los cuentos de Cantorbery*
    SU «Кентербери́йские расска́зы» (Чо́сер)

618 GB Canute (Cnut) (*995–1035*)
    F Knud
    D Knut
    I Canuto
    E Canuto
    SU Кнуд

619 GB Cape Horn
F le cap Horn
D Kap Hoorn
I il capo Horn
E el cabo de Hornos
SU мыс Горн

620 GB Cape of Good Hope, the
F le cap de Bonne Espérance
D das Kap der Guten Hoffnung
I il capo di Buona Speranza
E el cabo de Buena Esperanza
SU мыс Дóброй Надéжды

621 GB Cape Province (South Africa)
F la province du Cap (Afrique du Sud)
D die Kapprovinz (Südafrika)
I la Provincia del Capo (Africa del Sud)
E la Provincia del Cabo (África del Sur)
SU Кáпская провúнция (Ю́жная Áфрика)

622 GB Capernaum (Bib.)
F Capharnaüm (Bib.)
D Kapernaum (Bib.)
I Cafarnao (Bib.)
E Cafarnaum (Bib.)
SU Капéрнаум (библ.)

623 GB Cape Town (South Africa)
F Le Cap (Afrique du Sud)
D Kapstadt (Südafrika)
I Città del Capo (Africa del Sud)
E El Cabo (África del Sur)
SU Кейптáун (Ю́жная Áфрика)

624 GB Cape Verde Islands, the
F les îles du Cap Vert
D die Kapverdischen Inseln
I le isole del Capo Verde
E las islas del Cabo Verde
SU островá Зелёного Мы́са

625 GB *Capital* (Marx, 1867, 1885, 1894)
F *Le Capital*
D *Das Kapital*
I *Il capitale*
E *El capital*
SU «Капитáл» (Маркс)

626 GB Capitol, the (Rome, Washington)
F le Capitole (Rome, Washington)
D das Kapitol (Rom, Washington)
I il Capitolium (Roma), il Capitol (Washington)
E el Capitolio (Roma, Washington)
SU Капитóлий (Рим, Вашингтóн)

627 GB Capitoline Hill, the (Rome)
F le mont Capitolin (Rome)
D der Kapitolinische Hügel (Rom)
I il Campidoglio (Roma)
E el monte Capitolino (Roma)
SU Капитóлий (Рим)

628 GB Capricorn (astron.)
F le Capricorne (astron.)
D der Steinbock (Astron.)
I il Capricorno (astr.)
E Capricornio (astr.)
SU Козерóг (астр.)

629 GB *Captain Brassbound's Conversion* (Shaw, 1900)
F *La Conversion du capitaine Brassbound*
D *Kapitän Brassbounds Bekehrung*
I *La conversione del capitano Brassbound*
E *La conversión del capitán Brassbound*
SU «Обращéние капитáна Брáсбаунда» (Шóу)

630 GB *Captain Fracasse* (Gautier, 1863)
F *Le Capitaine Fracasse*
D *Kapitän Fracasse*
I *Capitan Fracassa*
E *El capitán Fracasse*
SU «Капитáн Фракáсс» (Готьé)

631 GB *Captain of Köpenick, The* (Zuckmayer, 1931)
F *Capitaine Köpenick*
D *Der Hauptmann von Köpenick*
I *Il capitano di Köpenick*
E *El capitán de Köpenick*
SU «Капитáн из Кёпеника» (Цýкмайер)

632 GB *Captain's Daughter, The* (Pushkin, 1836)
F *La Fille du capitaine* (Pouchkine)
D *Die Hauptmannstochter* (Puschkin)
I *La figlia del capitano* (Puškin)
E *La hija del capitán* (Puschkin)
SU «Капитáнская дóчка» (Пýшкин)

633 GB *Captain Worse* [*Skipper Worse*] (Kielland, 1882)
F *Capitaine Worse*
D *Schiffer Worse*
I *Il capitano Worse*
E *El capitán Worse*
SU «Шкúпер Вóрше» (Хьéлланн)

634 GB   Capuchins, the (rel.)
F   les capucins (relig.)
D   die Kapuziner (relig.)
I   i cappuccini (relig.)
E   los Capuchinos (relig.)
SU   капуци́ны (рел.)

635 GB   Caravaggio (1573–1610)
F   le Caravage
D   Caravaggio
I   il Caravaggio
E   el Caravaggio
SU   Карава́джо

636 GB   Carbonari, the (hist.)
F   les carbonari (hist.)
D   die Karbonari (Gesch.)
I   i Carbonari (st.)
E   los Carbonarios (hist.)
SU   карбона́рии (ист.)

637 GB   Caracassonne (France)
F   Caracassonne (France)
D   Caracassonne (Frankreich)
I   Caracassonne (Francia)
E   Caracasona (Francia)
SU   Каркассо́нн (Фра́нция)

638 GB   *Caretaker, The* (Pinter, 1960)
F   *Le Gardien*
D   *Der Hausmeister*
I   *Il guardiano*
E   *El vigilante*
SU   «Сто́рож» (Пи́нтер)

639 GB   Caribbean Sea, the
F   la mer des Antilles
D   das Karibische Meer
I   il mare Caribico
E   el mar Caribe
SU   Кари́бское мо́ре

640 GB   Carmel, Mount (Bib.)
F   le mont Carmel (Bib.)
D   Karmel (Bib.)
I   il monte Carmelo (Bib.)
E   el Monte Carmelo (Bib.)
SU   гора́ Ка́рмил (библ.)

641 GB   Carmelites, the (rel.)
F   les carmes (relig.)
D   die Karmeliter (relig.)
I   i carmelitani (relig.)
E   los Carmelitas (relig.)
SU   кармели́ты (рел.)

642 GB   *Carmen* (Mérimée, 1845; Bizet 1875)
F   *Carmen*
D   *Carmen*
I   *Carmen*
E   *Carmen*
SU   «Ка́рмен» (Мериме́, Бизе́)

643 GB   *Carmina Burana* [*Songs from the Benediktbeuern Monastery*] (Orff, 1935)
F   *Carmina burana*
D   *Carmina burana*
I   *Carmina burana*
E   *Carmina burana*
SU   «Карми́на бура́на» (Орф)

644 GB   *Carnaval* (Schumann, 1835)
F   *Carnaval*
D   *Karneval*
I   *Carnaval*
E   *Carnaval*
SU   «Карнава́л» (Шу́ман)

645 GB   *Carnet de Bal, Un* [*A Dance Programme*] (Duvivier, 1937)
F   *Un carnet de bal*
D   *Spiel der Erinnerung*
I   *Carnet di ballo*
E   *Carnet de baile*
SU   «Ба́льная записна́я кни́жка» (Дювивье́)

646 GB   *Carnival in Flanders* (Feyder, 1935)
F   *La Kermesse héroïque*
D   *Die klugen Frauen*
I   *La kermesse eroica*
E   *La kermese heroica*
SU   «Геро́йческая керме́сса» (Фейде́р)

647 GB   Caroline Islands, the
F   les îles Carolines
D   die Karolinen
I   le isole Caroline
E   las islas Carolinas
SU   Кароли́нские острова́

648 GB   Carolingians, the (hist.)
F   les Carolingiens (hist.)
D   die Karolinger (Gesch.)
I   i Carolingi (st.)
E   los carolingios (hist.)
SU   кароли́нги (ист.)

649 GB   Carpathian Mountains, the (Europe)
F   les monts Carpates (Europe)
D   die Karpaten (Europa)
I   i Carpazi (Europe)
E   los Cá́rpatos (Europe)
SU   Карпа́ты (ж.) (Евро́па)

650 GB Carthage (Tunisia)
    F Carthage (Tunisie)
    D Karthago (Tunesien)
    I Cartagine (Tunisia)
    E Cartago (Túnez)
    SU Карфаге́н (Туни́с)

651 GB Carthusians, the (rel.)
    F les chartreux (relig.)
    D die Kartäuser (relig.)
    I i certosini (relig.)
    E los Cartujos (relig.)
    SU картезиа́нцы (рел.)

652 GB *Case of Sergeant Grischa, The* (Zweig, 1928)
    F *Le Cas du sergent Grischa*
    D *Der Streit um den Sergeanten Grischa*
    I *La questione del sergente Grischa*
    E *El sargento Grischa*
    SU «Спор об у́нтере Гри́ше» (Цвейг)

653 GB Caspian Sea, the (USSR)
    F la mer Caspienne (URSS)
    D das Kaspische Meer (UdSSR)
    I il mare Caspio (URSS)
    E el mar Caspio (URSS)
    SU Каспи́йское мо́ре (СССР)

654 GB Cassandra (myth.)
    F Cassandre (myth.)
    D Kassandra (myth.)
    I Cassandra (mit.)
    E Casandra (mit.)
    SU Касса́ндра (миф.)

655 GB Cassiopeia (astron.)
    F Cassiopée (astron.)
    D Kassiopeia (Astron.)
    I Cassiopea (astr.)
    E Casiopea (astr.)
    SU Кассиопе́я (астр.)

656 GB Cassius (Roman name)
    F Cassius (nom romain)
    D Cassius (Römername)
    I Cassio (nome romano)
    E Casio (nombre romano)
    SU Ка́ссий (древнери́мское и́мя)

657 GB Castile (Spain)
    F la Castille (Espagne)
    D Kastilien (Spanien)
    I la Castiglia (Spagna)
    E Castilla (España)
    SU Касти́лия (Испа́ния)

658 GB *Castle, The* (Kafka, 1926)
    F *Le Château*
    D *Das Schloß*
    I *Il castello*
    E *El castillo*
    SU «За́мок» (Ка́фка)

659 GB *Castle in Sweden, A* (Sagan, 1960)
    F *Un château en Suède*
    D *Ein Schloß in Schweden*
    I *Un castello in Svezia*
    E *Castillo en Suecia*
    SU «За́мок в Шве́ции» (Сага́н)

660 GB *Castle of Indolence, The* (Thomson, 1748)
    F *Le Château de l'indolence*
    D *Das Schloß der Trägheit*
    I *Il castello dell'indolenza*
    E *El castillo de la indolencia*
    SU «За́мок лени́вости» (То́мсон)

661 GB *Castle of Otranto, The* (Walpole, 1764)
    F *Le Château d'Otrante*
    D *Die Burg von Otranto*
    I *Il castello d'Otranto*
    E *El castillo de Otranto*
    SU «За́мок Отра́нто» (Уо́лпол)

662 GB Castor and Pollux (myth., astron., + Rameau, 1737)
    F Castor et Pollux (myth., astron.)
    D Castor und Pollux (myth., Astron.)
    I Castore e Polluce (mit., astr.)
    E Cástor y Pólux (mit., astr.)
    SU Ка́стор и По́ллукс (миф., астр., + Рамо́)

663 GB Catalonia (Spain)
    F la Catalogne (Espagne)
    D Katalonien (Spanien)
    I la Catalogna (Spagna)
    E Cataluña (España)
    SU Катало́ния (Испа́ния)

664 GB *Cat and Mouse* (Grass, 1961)
    F *Le Chat et la Souris*
    D *Katz und Maus*
    I *Gatto e topo*
    E *El Gato y el ratón*
    SU «Ко́шка и мышь» (Грасс)

665 GB Catania (Sicily)
    F Catane (Sicile)
    D Catania (Sizilien)
    I Catania (Sicilia)
    E Catania (Sicilia)
    SU Ката́ния (Сици́лия)

666 GB   *Cat Ballou* (Silverstein, 1965)
    F   *Cat Ballou*
    D   *Cat Ballou – Hängen sollst Du in Wyoming*
    I   *Cat Ballou*
    E   *La ingenua explosiva*
    SU   «Кэт Баллу́» (Си́лверстайн)

667 GB   *Catcher in the Rye, The* (Salinger, 1951)
    F   *L'Attrape-coeurs*
    D   *Der Fänger im Roggen*
    I   *Il giovane Holden*
    E   *El cazador oculto*
    SU   «Над про́пастью во ржи» (Сэ́линджер)

668 GB   *Cathedral, The* (Walpole, 1922)
    F   *La Cathédrale*
    D   *Die Kathedrale*
    I   *La cattedrale*
    E   *La catedral*
    SU   «Собо́р» (Уо́лпол)

669 GB   Catherine the Great (1729–96)
    F   Catherine la Grande
    D   Katharina die zweite
    I   Caterina la Grande
    E   Catalina la Grande
    SU   Екатери́на II

670 GB   Catherine de Médicis (1519–89)
    F   Catherine de Médicis
    D   Katharina von Medici
    I   Caterina de' Medici
    E   Catalina de Médicis
    SU   Екатери́на Ме́дичи

671 GB   Catherine of Aragon (1485–1536)
    F   Catherine d'Aragon
    D   Katharina von Aragon
    I   Caterina d'Aragona
    E   Catalina de Aragón
    SU   Екатери́на Араго́нская

672 GB   Catherine of Siena (saint) (1347–80)
    F   Catherine de Sienne (sainte)
    D   Katharina von Siena (Heilige)
    I   Caterina da Siena (santa)
    E   Catalina de Siena (santa)
    SU   Екатери́на Сие́нская (св.)

673 GB   *Catiline's War* [*Bellum Catilinae*] (Sallust, 43–42)
    F   *La Conjuration de Catilina* (Salluste)
    D   *Die Verschwörung des Catilina* (Sallustius)
    I   *La congiura di Catilina* (Sallustio)
    E   *La conjuración de Catilina* (Salustio)
    SU   «О за́говоре Катили́ны» (Саллю́стий)

674 GB   Cato (234–149; 95–46)
    F   Caton
    D   Cato
    I   Catone
    E   Catón
    SU   Като́н

675 GB   *Cat on a Hot Tin Roof* (Williams, 1955)
    F   *La Chatte sur un toit brûlant*
    D   *Die Katze auf dem heißen Blechdach*
    I   *La gatta sul tetto che scotta*
    E   *La gata sobre el tejado de zinc*
    SU   «Ко́шка на раскалённой кры́ше» (Уи́льямс)

676 GB   *Catriona* (Stevenson, 1893)
    F   *Catriona*
    D   *Catriona*
    I   *Catriona*
    E   *Catriona*
    SU   «Катрио́на» (Сти́венсон)

677 GB   Catullus (*87–54*)
    F   Catulle
    D   Catullus
    I   Catullo
    E   Catulo
    SU   Кату́лл

678 GB   *Caucasian Chalk Circle, The* (Brecht, 1948)
    F   *Le Cercle de craie caucasien*
    D   *Der Kaukasische Kreidekreis*
    I   *Il cerchio di gesso del Caucaso*
    E   *El círculo de tiza caucasiano*
    SU   «Кавка́зскнй меловой круг» (Брехт)

679 GB   Caucasus, the
    F   le Caucase
    D   der Kaukasus
    I   il Caucaso
    E   el Cáucaso
    SU   Кавка́з

680 GB *Cavalier of the Rose, The* (Strauss, 1911)
F *Le Chevalier à la rose*
D *Der Rosenkavalier*
I *Il cavaliere della rosa*
E *El caballero de la rosa*
SU «Кавале́р роз» (Штра́ус)

681 GB *Cavalleria Rusticana [Rustic Chivalry]* (Mascagni, 1894)
F *Cavelleria rusticana*
D *Cavalleria rusticana*
I *Cavalleria rusticana*
E *Caballería rusticana*
SU «Се́льская честь» (Маска́ньи)

682 GB *Cavalry Officer, The* (Géricault, 1812)
F *Officier de chasseur à cheval chargeant*
D *Reiteroffizier in der Schlacht*
I *L'ufficiale dei cacciatori a cavallo*
E *Oficial de caballería*
SU «Офице́р ко́нных егере́й» (Жерико́)

683 GB Cayman Islands, the (West Indies)
F les îles Caïmans (Antilles)
D die Caymaninseln (Westindien)
I le isole Cayman (Antille)
E las islas Caimanes (Antilles)
SU Кайма́новы острова́ (Вест-И́ндия)

684 GB Cecilia (saint) (II)
F Cécile (sainte)
D Cäcilia (Heilige)
I Cecilia (santa)
E Cecilia (santa)
SU Цеци́лия (св.)

685 GB *Celebrated Jumping Frog, The* (Twain, 1867)
F *La Célèbre Grenouille sauteuse*
D *Der berühmte Springfrosch*
I *La famosa rana saltatrice*
E *La célebre rana saltadora*
SU «Знамени́тая ска́чущая лягу́шка» (Твен)

686 GB Celts, the (hist.)
F les Celtes (hist.)
D die Kelten (Gesch.)
I i celti (st.)
E los Celtas (hist.)
SU ке́льты (ист.)

687 GB *Cenerentola [Cinderella]* (Rossini, 1817)
F *Cendrillon*
D *Cenerentola*
I *Cenerentola*
E *La Cenicienta*
SU «Зо́лушка» (Росси́ни)

688 GB Centaurs, the (myth.)
F les Centaures (myth.)
D die Kentauren (myth.)
I i centauri (mit.)
E los centauros (mit.)
SU кента́вры (миф.)

689 GB Centaur(us) (astron.)
F le Centaure (astron.)
D der Zentaur (Astron.)
I il Centauro (astr.)
E Centauro (astr.)
SU Цента́вр (астр.)

690 GB Central African Republic, the
F la République Centrafricaine
D die Centralafrikanische Republik
I la Repubblica Centrafricana
E la República Centroafricana
SU Центральноафрика́нская респу́блика

691 GB Central America
F l'Amérique centrale
D Mittelamerika
I l'America centrale
E América Central
SU Центра́льная Аме́рика

692 GB Cepheus (myth.)
F Céphée (myth.)
D Cepheus (myth.)
I Cefeo (mit.)
E Cefeo (mit.)
SU Цефе́й (миф.)

693 GB Cerberus (myth.)
F Cerbère (myth.)
D Zerberus (myth.)
I Cerbero (mit.)
E Cerbero (mit.)
SU Це́рбер (миф.)

694 GB Ceres (myth.)
Г Cérès (myth.)
D Ceres (myth.)
I Cerere (mit.)
E Ceres (mit.)
SU Цере́ра (миф.)

695 GB *Certain Smile, A* (Sagan, 1956)
F   *Un certain sourire*
D   *Ein gewisses Lächeln*
I   *Un certo sorriso*
E   *Una cierta sonrisa*
SU «Подобие улыбки» (Саган)

696 GB Cetus (astron.)
F   la Baleine (astron.)
D   der Walfisch (Astron.)
I   la Balena (astr.)
E   la Ballena (astr.)
SU Кит (астр.)

697 GB Ceylon (hist.)
F   le Ceylon (hist.)
D   Ceylon (Gesch.)
I   il Ceylon (st.)
E   Ceilán (hist.)
SU Цейлóн (ист.)

698 GB Chad
F   le Tchad
D   Tschad
I   il Ciad
E   el Chad
SU Чад

699 GB Chaldea (Bib.)
F   la Chaldée (Bib.)
D   Chaldäa (Bib.)
I   la Caldea (Bib.)
E   Caldea (Bib.)
SU Халдéя (библ.)

700 GB Champagne (France)
F   la Champagne (France)
D   die Champagne (Frankreich)
I   la Champagne (Francia)
E   Champaña (Francia)
SU Шампáнь (ж.) (Фрáнция)

701 GB Champ-de-Mars, the (Paris)
F   le Champ-de-Mars (Paris)
D   der Marsfeld (Paris)
I   lo Champ de Mars (Parigi)
E   el Campo de Marte (París)
SU Мáрсово пóле (Парúж)

702 GB Champs-Elysées, the (Paris)
F   les Champs-Elysées (Paris)
D   die Champs Elysees (Paris)
I   i Campi Elisi (Parigi)
E   los Campos Elísios (París)
SU Елисéйские поля (Парúж)

703 GB *Changeling, The* (Middleton +
Rowley, 1623)
F   *L'Enfant échangé*
D   *Der Wechselbalg*
I   *Il bambino scambiato*
E   *El niño cambiado*
SU «Подменённый ребёнок»
(Мúдльтон/Рóули)

704 GB Channel Islands, the
F   les îles Anglo-Normandes
D   die Kanalinseln
I   le isole Normanne
E   las islas Anglonormandas
SU Нормáндские островá

705 GB *Chanticleer* (Rostand, 1910)
F   *Chantecler*
D   *Chantecler*
I   *Chantecler*
E   *Chantecler*
SU «Шантеклéр» (Ростáн)

706 GB *Characters* [*Charaktēres*]
(Theophrastus, −III)
F   *Caractères* (Théophraste)
D   *Charaktere* (Theophrastos)
I   *Caratteri* (Teofrasto)
E   *Caracteres* (Teofrasto)
SU «Харáктеры» (Теофрáст)

707 GB *Chariots of Fire* (Hudson, 1981)
F   *Les Chariots de feu*
D   *Die Stunde des Siegers*
I   *Momenti di gloria*
E   *Carros de fuego*
SU «Квадрúги огня» (Хáдсон)

708 GB Charlemagne (*742*–814)
F   Charlemagne
D   Karl der Große
I   Carlo Magno
E   Carlomagno
SU Кáрл Велúкий

709 GB Charles (saint, sovereign)
F   Charles (saint, souverain)
D   Karl (Heiliger, Herr.)
I   Carlo (santo, sovrano)
E   Carlos (santo, sob.)
SU Карл (св., прав.)

710 GB Charles d'Anjou (1226–85)
F   Charles d'Anjou
D   Karl von Anjou
I   Carlo d'Angio
E   Carlos de Anjeo
SU Карл Анжýйский

711 GB   Charles Martel (688–741)
    F   Charles Martel
    D   Karl Martell
    I   Carlo Martello
    E   Carlos Martel
    SU   Карл Мартéлл

712 GB   Charles the Bold (1433–77)
    F   Charles le Téméraire
    D   Karl der Kühne
    I   Carlo il Temerario
    E   Carlos el Temerario
    SU   Карл Смéлый

713 GB   Charon (myth.)
    F   Charon (myth.)
    D   Charon (myth.)
    I   Caronte (mit.)
    E   Caronte (mit.)
    SU   Харóн (миф.)

714 GB   *Charterhouse of Parma, The* (Stendhal, 1839)
    F   *La Chartreuse de Parme*
    D   *Die Kartause von Parma*
    I   *La certosa di Parma*
    E   *La cartuja de Parma*
    SU   «Пáрмская обúтель» (Стендáль)

715 GB   *Chaste Maid in Cheapside, A* (Middleton, 1630)
    F   *Une chaste jeune fille à Cheapside*
    D   *Eine Keusche in Cheapside*
    I   *Una casta fanciulla a Cheapside*
    E   *Una linda muchacha de Cheapside*
    SU   «Непорóчная дéвушка в Чúпсайде» (Мúдльтон)

716 GB   *Chatterton* (Vigny, 1835)
    F   *Chatterton*
    D   *Chatterton*
    I   *Chatterton*
    E   *Chatterton*
    SU   «Чáттертон» (Виньú)

717 GB   *Cheaper by the Dozen* (Lang, 1950)
    F   *Treize à la douzaine*
    D   *Im Dutzend billiger*
    I   *Dodici lo chiamano papà*
    E   *Trece por docena*
    SU   «За дюжину - со скúдкой» (Ланг)

718 GB   Cherbourg (France)
    F   Cherbourg (France)
    D   Cherbourg (Frankreich)
    I   Cherbourg (Francia)
    E   Cherburgo (Francia)
    SU   Шербýр (Фрáнция)

719 GB   *Cherry Orchard, The* (Chekhov, 1904)
    F   *La Cerisaie* (Tchekhov)
    D   *Der Kirschgarten* (Tschechow)
    I   *Il giardino dei ciliegi* (Čechov)
    E   *El jardín de los cerezos* (Chejov)
    SU   «Вишнёвый сад» (Чéхов)

720 GB   *Chien Andalou, Un* [*An Andalusian Dog*] (Buñuel, 1928)
    F   *Un chien andalou*
    D   *Ein andalusischer Hund*
    I   *Un chien andalou*
    E   *Un perro andaluz*
    SU   «Андалýзский пёс» (Бюнюэ́ль)

721 GB   *Childe Harold's Pilgrimage* (Byron, 1812–18)
    F   *Le Pèlerinage de Childe Harold*
    D   *Ritter Harolds Pilgerfahrt*
    I   *Il pellegrinaggio del giovane Aroldo*
    E   *La peregrinación de Childe Harold*
    SU   «Палóмничество Чайльд Гарóльда» (Бáйрон)

722 GB   *Childhood* (Gorky, 1913–13)
    F   *Ma vie d'enfant* (Gorki)
    D   *Meine Kindheit* (Gorkij)
    I   *Infanzia* (Gor'kij)
    E   *Mi infancia* (Gorki)
    SU   «Дéтство» (Гóркий)

723 GB   *Childhood, Boyhood, Youth* (Tolstoy, 1852, 1854, 1857)
    F   *Enfance, Adolescence, Jeunesse* (Tolstoï)
    D   *Kindheit, Knabenjahre, Jünglingszeit* (Tolstoj)
    I   *Infanzia, Adolescenza, Giovinezza* (Tolstoj)
    E   *Infancia, Adolescencia, Juventud* (Tolstoi)
    SU   «Дéтство», «Óтрочество», «Юность» (Толстóй)

724 GB   *Child is Waiting, A* (Kramer, 1963)
    F   *Un enfant attend*
    D   *Ein Kind wartet*
    I   *Gli esclusi*
    E   *Ángeles sin paraíso*
    SU   «Ждёт ребёнок» (Крéймер)

725 GB   *Children of Captain Grant, The* (Verne, 1867–8)
    F   *Les Enfants du capitaine Grant*
    D   *Die Kinder des Kapitän Grant*
    I   *I figli del capitano Grant*
    E   *Los hijos del capitán Grant*
    SU   «Дéти капитáна Грáнта» (Верн)

726   GB   Chile
  F   le Chili
  D   Chile
  I   il Cile
  E   Chile
  SU   Чили

727   GB   Chimera, the (myth.)
  F   la Chimère (myth.)
  D   die Chimäre (myth.)
  I   la Chimera (mit.)
  E   Quimera (mit.)
  SU   Химéра (миф.)

728   GB   China
  F   la Chine
  D   China
  I   la Cina
  E   China
  SU   Китáй

  GB   China Sea→South China Sea

729   GB   Chinese People's Republic, the
  F   la République populaire de China
   (RPC)
  D   die Volksrepublik China (VRC)
  I   la Repubblica Popolare Cinese (RPC)
  E   la República Popular de China (RPC)
  SU   Китáйская Нарóдная Респýблика
   (KHP)

730   GB   Chiron (myth.)
  F   Chiron (myth.)
  D   Chiron (myth.)
  I   Chirone (mit.)
  E   Quirón (mit.)
  SU   Хирóн (миф.)

731   GB   Christ (Bib.)
  F   le Christ (Bib.)
  D   Christus (Bib.)
  I   il Cristo (Bib.)
  I   Cristo (Bib.)
  SU   Христóс (библ.)

732   GB   *Christ and St. Thomas* (Verrocchio,
   1476–83)
  F   *Incrédulité de saint Thomas*
  D   *Christus und Thomas*
  I   *Incredulità di Santo Tommaso*
  E   *Cristo y Santo Tomás*
  SU   «Невéрие Фомы́» (Веррóккьо)

733   GB   Christian Science (rel.)
  F   la Science chrétienne (relig.)
  D   das Christian Science (relig.)
  I   la Scienza cristiana (relig.)
  E   la Ciencia Cristiana (relig.)
  SU   «Христиáнская наýка» (рел.)

734   GB   Christmas (rel.)
  F   le Noël (relig.)
  D   die Weihnacht(en) (relig.)
  I   (la) Natale (relig.)
  E   la Navidad (relig.)
  SU   рождествó [Христóво] (рел.)

735   GB   *Christmas Books, The* (Dickens, 1852)
  F   *Les Contes de Noël*
  D   *Weihnachtserzählungen*
  I   *Racconti di Natale*
  E   *Cuentos de Navidad*
  SU   «Рождéственские пóвести» (Дńккенс)

736   GB   *Christmas Carol, A* (Dickens, 1843)
  F   *Chanson de Noël*
  D   *Ein Weihnachtslied*
  I   *Canzone di Natale*
  E   *Canción de Navidad*
  SU   «Рождéственская пéсня» (Дńккенс)

737   GB   Christmas Island
  F   l'île Christmas
  D   (die) Weihnachtsinsel
  I   l'isola Christmas
  E   la isla Christmas
  SU   óстров Рождествá

738   GB   Christopher (saint) (III)
  F   Christophe (saint)
  D   Christoph (Heiliger)
  I   Cristoforo (santo)
  E   Cristóbal (santo)
  SU   Христофóр (св.)

739   GB   Christopher Columbus (1451–1506)
  F   Christophe Colomb
  D   Christoph Kolumbus
  I   Cristoforo Colombo
  E   Cristóbal Colón
  SU   Христофóр Колýмб

740   GB   *Christ Recrucified* [*O Christos*
   xanastravronete] (Kazantzakis, 1950)
  F   *Le Christ recrucifié*
  D   *Griechische Passion*
  I   *Cristo di nuovo in croce*
  E   *Cristo de nuevo crucificado*
  SU   «Христá распинáют вновь»
   (Казандзáкис)

741   GB   *Christ Stopped at Eboli* (Levi, 1945)
      F   *Le Christ s'est arrêté à Eboli*
      D   *Christus kam nur bis Eboli*
      I   *Cristo si è fermato a Eboli*
      E   *Cristo se paró en Eboli*
      SU   «Христо́с останови́лся в Эболи»
           (Ле́ви)

742   GB   Chronicles (Bib.)
      F   les Chroniques (Bib.)
      D   die Bücher der Chronika (Bib.)
      I   le Cronache (Bib.)
      E   los Libros de las Crónicas (Bib.)
      SU   «Паралипомено́н» (библ.)

      GB   Chrysostom→John Chrysostom

743   GB   Church of England, the
      F   l'Église anglicane
      D   die anglikanische Kirche
      I   la chiesa anglicana
      E   la Iglesia Anglicana
      SU   англика́нская це́рковь

744   GB   Cicero (106–43)
      F   Cicéron
      D   Cicero
      I   Cicerone
      E   Cicerón
      SU   Цицеро́н

745   GB   Cid, El (1026–99)
      F   le Cid
      D   Cid (Campeador)
      I   Cid Campeador
      E   el Cid (Campeador)
      SU   Сид Кампеадо́р

746   GB   *Cid, Le* (Corneille, *1637*)
      F   *Le Cid*
      D   *Le Cid*
      I   *Il Cid*
      E   *El Cid*
      SU   «Сид» (Корне́ль)

747   GB   *Cinderella* (Perrault, 1697)
      F   *Cendrillon*
      D   *Aschenbrödel*
      I   *Cenerentola*
      E   *Cenicienta*
      SU   «Зо́лушка» (Перро́)

748   GB   *Cinq-Mars* (Vigny, 1826)
      F   *Cinq-Mars*
      D   *Cinq-Mars*
      I   *Cinque-marzo*
      E   *Cinq-Mars*
      SU   «Сен-Ма́р» (Виньи́)

749   GB   Circe (myth.)
      F   Circé (myth.)
      D   Circe (myth.)
      I   Circe (mit.)
      E   Circe (mit.)
      SU   Цирце́я (миф.)

750   GB   Cistercians, the (rel.)
      F   les cisterciens (relig.)
      D   die Zisterzienser (relig.)
      I   i cisterciensi (relig.)
      E   los Cistercienses (relig.)
      SU   цистерциа́нцы (рел.)

751   GB   *Citadel, The* (Cronin, 1937)
      F   *La Citadelle*
      D   *Die Zitadelle*
      I   *La cittadella*
      E   *La ciudadela*
      SU   «Цитаде́ль» (Кро́нин)

752   GB   Cîteaux (France)
      F   Cîteaux (France)
      D   Cîteaux (Frankreich)
      I   Cîteaux (Francia)
      E   Cister (Francia)
      SU   Сито́ (Фра́нция)

753   GB   *Citizen Kane* (Welles, 1941)
      F   *Le Citoyen Kane*
      D   *Citizen Kane*
      I   *Quarto potere*
      E   *Ciudadano Kane*
      SU   «Граждани́н Кейн» (Уэ́ллс)

754   GB   *City Lights* (Chaplin, 1931)
      F   *Les Lumières de la ville*
      D   *Lichter der Großstadt*
      I   *Luci della città*
      E   *Luces de la ciudad*
      SU   «Огни́ большо́го го́рода» (Ча́плин)

755   GB   *City of God, The* [*De civitate Dei*]
           (Augustine, 413–424)
      F   *La Cité de Dieu* (Augustin)
      D   *Der Gottesstaat* (Augustinus)
      I   *De civitate Dei* (Agostino)
      E   *La ciudad de Dios* (Agustín)
      SU   «О гра́де бо́жием» (Августи́н)

756   GB   Clairvaux (France)
      F   Clairvaux (France)
      D   Clairvaux (Frankreich)
      I   Clairvaux (Francia)
      E   Claraval (Francia)
      SU   Клерво́ (Фра́нция)

757 GB *Clarissa Harlowe* (Richardson, 1747–8)
 F *Clarissa Harlowe*
 D *Clarissa*
 I *Clarissa*
 E *Clarisa Harlowe*
 SU «Кларисса» (Ричардсон)

758 GB Claudius (I)
 F Claudius
 D Claudius
 I Claudio
 E Claudio
 SU Клавдий

759 GB *Claudius the God and his Wife Messalina* (Graves, 1934)
 F *Claude le Dieu*
 D *Claudius, Kaiser und Gott*
 I *Il divo Claudio*
 E *Claudio, el dios, y su esposa Mesalina*
 SU «Клавдий - бог» (Грейвс)

760 GB *Clavigo* (Goethe, 1774)
 F *Clavigo*
 D *Clavigo*
 I *Clavigo*
 E *Clavijo*
 SU «Клавиго» (Гёте)

761 GB *Clayhanger* (Bennett, 1910)
 F *Clayhanger*
 D *Clayhanger*
 I *Clayhanger*
 E *Clayhanger*
 SU «Клёйхенгер» (Беннетт)

762 GB *Clemency of Titus, The* (Mozart, 1791)
 F *La Clémence de Titus*
 D *La clemenza di Tito*
 I *La clemenza di Tito*
 E *La clemenza di Tito*
 SU «Милосéрдие Тита» (Моцарт)

763 GB Clement (pope)
 F Clément (pape)
 D Klemens (Papst)
 I Clemente (papa)
 E Clemente (papa)
 SU Климéнт (пáпа римский)

764 GB Cleopatra (69–30)
 F Cléopâtre
 D Kleopatra
 I Cleopatra
 E Cleopatra
 SU Клеопáтра

765 GB Cleopatra's Needle (London, New York)
 F l'obélisque de Cléopâtre (Londres, New-York)
 D der Obelisk der Kleopatra (London, New-York)
 I l'obelisco di Cleopatra (Londra, New York)
 E el obelisco de Cleopatra (Londres, Nueva York)
 SU «Иглá Клеопáтры» (Лóндон, Нью-Йóрк)

766 GB Clio (myth.)
 F Clio (myth.)
 D Klio (myth.)
 I Clio (mit.)
 E Clío (mit.)
 SU Клиó (миф.)

767 GB *Clockwork Orange, A* (Burgess, 1962)
 F *Une orange mécanique*
 D *Uhrwerk Orange*
 I *Un'arancia a orologeria*
 E *La naranja mecánica*
 SU «Заводнóй апельсин» (Бёрджесс)

768 GB *Clockwork Orange, A* (Kubrick, 1971)
 F *Orange mécanique*
 D *Uhrwerk Orange*
 I *Arancia meccanica*
 E *Una naranja con mecanismo de reloj*
 SU «Механический апельсин» (Кубрик)

769 GB *Cloister and the Hearth, The* (Reade, 1861)
 F *Le Cloître et le foyer*
 D *Kloster und Herd*
 I *Il chiostro e il focolare*
 E *El claustro y el hogar*
 SU «Монастырь и камин» (Рид)

770 GB *Closed Garden, The* (Green, 1927)
 F *Adrienne Mesurat*
 D *Adrienne Mesurat*
 I *Adriana Mesurat*
 E *Adriana Mesurat*
 SU «Адриáна Мезюрá» (Грин)

771 GB *Close Encounters of the Third Kind* (Spielberg, 1977)
 F *Rencontres du troisième type*
 D *Unheimliche Begegnung der dritten Art*
 I *Incontri ravvicinati del terzo tipo*
 E *Encuentros íntimos de tercera clase*
 SU «Близкие встрéчи трéтьего типа» (Спилберг)

772 GB *Clouds, The [Nephelai]* (Aristophanes,
          −423)
     F *Les Nuées* (Aristophane)
     D *Die Wolken* (Aristophanes)
     I *Le nuvole* (Aristofane)
     E *Las nubes* (Aristófanes)
     SU «Облакá» (Аристофáн)

773 GB Clovis (*466–511*)
     F Clovis
     D Chlodwig
     I Clodoveo
     E Clodoveo
     SU Хлóдвиг

774 GB Cluniacs, the (rel.)
     F les clunisiens (relig.)
     D die Kluniazenser (relig.)
     I i cluniacensi (relig.)
     E los cluniacenses (relig.)
     SU клюнúйцы (рел.)

775 GB Clytemnestra (myth.)
     F Clytemnestre (myth.)
     D Klytämnestra (myth.)
     I Clitennestra (mit.)
     E Clitemnestra (mit.)
     SU Клитемнéстра (миф.)

776 GB Cochin China (hist.)
     F la Cochinchine (hist.)
     D Kotschinchina (Gesch.)
     I la Cocincina (st.)
     E Cochinchina (hist.)
     SU Кохинхúна (ист.)

777 GB *Cocktail Party, The* (Eliot, 1949)
     F *Cocktail-Party*
     D *Die Cocktail Party*
     I *Cocktail Party*
     E *Cocktail Party*
     SU «Коктéйль» (Элиот)

778 GB *Coiners, The* (Gide, 1926)
     F *Les Faux-Monnayeurs*
     D *Die Falschmünzer*
     I *I falsari*
     E *Los monederos falsos*
     SU «Фальшивомонéтчики» (Жид)

779 GB Cologne (Germany)
     F Cologne (Allemagne)
     D Köln (Deutschland)
     I Colonia (Germania)
     E Colonia (Alemania)
     SU Кёльн (Гермáния)

780 GB *Colomba* (Mérimée, 1840)
     F *Colomba*
     D *Colomba*
     I *Colomba*
     E *Colomba*
     SU «Колóмба» (Меримé)

781 GB Colombia
     F la Colombia
     D Kolumbien
     I la Colombia
     E Colombia
     SU Колýмбия

782 GB *Colonel Chabert* (Balzac, 1832)
     F *Le Colonel Chabert*
     D *Oberst Chabert*
     I *Il colonnello Chabert*
     E *El coronel Chabert*
     SU «Полкóвник Шабéр» (Бальзáк)

783 GB *Colonel's Daughter, The* (Aldington,
          1931)
     F *La Fille du colonel*
     D *Die Tochter des Obersten*
     I *La figlia del colonnello*
     E *La hija del coronel*
     SU «Дочь полкóвника» (Óлдингтон)

784 GB Colosseum, the (Rome)
     F le Colisée (Rome)
     D das Kolosseum (Rom)
     I il Colosseo (Roma)
     E el Coliseo (Roma)
     SU Колизéй (Рим)

785 GB Colossians, the Epistle of Paul to the
          (Bib.)
     F l'Épître de Saint Paul aux Colossiens
          (Bib.)
     D der Kolosserbrief (Bib.)
     I la lettera di Paulo ai Colossesi (Bib.)
     E la Epístola de San Pablo a los colosios
          (Bib.)
     SU «Послáние к Колоссянам» (библ.)

786 GB Colossus of Rhodes, the
     F le Colosse de Rhodes
     D der Koloß von Rhodos
     I il Colosso di Rodi
     E el Coloso de Rodas
     SU Колóсс Родóсский

     GB Columbus, Christopher→Christopher
          Columbus

787   GB   *Comedy of Errors, The* (Shakespeare,
            1592–3)
      F   *La Comédie des erreurs*
      D   *Die Komödie der Irrungen*
      I   *La commedia degli equivoci*
      E   *La comedia de las equivocaciones*
      SU   «Комéдия ошúбок» (Шекспúр)

788   GB   *Commentaries on the Civil War* [*De
            bello civili*] (Caesar, −45)
      F   *Commentaires de la guerre civile*
            (César)
      D   *Bürgerkrieg* (Caesar)
      I   *Della guerra civile* (Cesare)
      E   *De la guerra civil* (César)
      SU   «Запúски о граждáнской войне»
            (Цéзарь)

789   GB   Common Market, the
      F   le marché commun
      D   der gemeinsame Markt
      I   il mercato comuno
      E   el mercado común
      SU   óбщий рýнок

790   GB   *Common Sense* (Paine, 1776)
      F   *Le Sens commun*
      D   *Common Sense*
      I   *Senso comune*
      E   *El sentido común*
      SU   «Здрáвый смысл» (Пейн)

      GB   Commons, House of→House of
            Commons

791   GB   *Communist Manifesto, The* (Marx +
            Engels, 1848)
      F   *Le Manifeste du parti communiste*
      D   *Das Kommunistische Manifest*
      I   *Il Manifesto del partito comunista*
      E   *El Manifiesto del Partido Comunista*
      SU   «Манифéст Коммунистúческой пáртии»
            (Маркс/Энгельс)

792   GB   Comoro Islands, the
      F   les Comores (f.)
      D   die Komoren
      I   le Comore
      E   las Comores
      SU   Комóрские островá

793   GB   *Comus* (Milton, 1634)
      F   *Comus*
      D   *Comus*
      I   *Comus*
      E   *Comus*
      SU   «Кóмус» (Мúльтон)

794   GB   *Concept of Dread, The* [*Begrebet
            Angest*] (Kierkegaard, 1844)
      F   *Le Concept d'angoisse*
      D   *Der Begriff der Angst*
      I   *Il concetto dell'angoscia*
      E   *Concepto de la angustia*
      SU   «Поня́тие мýки» (Кьéркегор)

795   GB   Conciergerie, the (Paris)
      F   la Conciergerie (Paris)
      D   die Conciergerie (Paris)
      I   la Conciergerie (Parigi)
      E   la Conserjería (París)
      SU   Консьержерú (Парúж)

796   GB   Concorde, the Place de la, (Paris)
      F   la place de la Concorde (Paris)
      D   die Place de la Concorde (Paris)
      I   la piazza della Concordia (Parigi)
      E   la Plaza de la Concordia (París)
      SU   плóщадь Соглáсия (Парúж)

797   GB   *Condemned for Lack of Faith* (Tirso de
            Molina, 1634)
      F   *Le Damné par manque de confiance*
      D   *Der Kleinmütige*
      I   *Il condannato per mancanza di fede*
      E   *El condenado por desconfiado*
      SU   «Осуждённый за недостáток вéры»
            (Тúрсо де Молúна)

798   GB   Confederation of the Rhine, the (1806
            −13)
      F   la Confédération du Rhin
      D   der Rheinbund
      I   la confederazione del Reno
      E   la confederación del Rin
      SU   Рéйнский сою́з

799   GB   *Confession, A* (Tolstoy, 1879–81)
      F   *Confession* (Tolstoï)
      D   *Beichte* (Tolstoi)
      I   *Confessione* (Tolstoj)
      E   *Confesión* (Tolstoi)
      SU   «Úсповедь» (Толстóй)

800   GB   *Confessions* (Augustine, *400*;
            Rousseau, 1766–70)
      F   *Les Confessions* (Augustin)
      D   *Die Bekentnisse* (Augustinus)
      I   *Le confessioni* (Agostino)
      E   *Las confesiones* (Agustín)
      SU   «Úсповедь» (Августúн, Руссó)

801 GB *Confessions of a Child of the Century,*
     The (Musset, 1836)
F   *La Confession d'un enfant du siècle*
D   *Beichte eines Kindes seiner Zeit*
I   *Le confessioni di un figlio del secolo*
E   *Confesión de un hijo del siglo*
SU «Исповедь сына века» (Мюссе)

802 GB *Confessions of a Fool* (Strindberg,
     1888)
F   *Le Plaidoyer d'un fou*
D   *Beichte eines Toren*
I   *La confessione di un pazzo*
E   *Alegato de un loco*
SU «Исповедь безумца» (Стриндберг)

803 GB *Confessions of a Lover, The* (Prévost,
     1891)
F   *La Confession d'un amant*
D   *Die Beichte eines Liebhabers*
I   *La confessione di un amante*
E   *La confesión de un amante*
SU «Исповедь любовника» (Прево)

804 GB *Confessions of an English Opium Eater*
     (De Quincey, 1822)
F   *Confessions d'un mangeur d'opium*
D   *Bekentnisse eines englischen*
     Opiumessers
I   *Confessioni di un mangiatore d'oppio*
E   *Confesiones de un fumador de opio*
SU «Исповедь англичанина опиомана»
     (Де Куинси)

805 GB *Confessions of Felix Krull, Confidence*
     Man, The (Mann, 1954)
F   *Les Confessions du chevalier*
     d'industrie Felix Krull
D   *Die Bekentnisse des Hochstaplers Felix*
     Krull
I   *Confessioni del cavaliere d'industria*
     Felix Krull
E   *Confesiones del aventurero Félix Krull*
SU «Исповедь Феликса Крюлла,
     мошенника» (Манн)

806 GB *Confidential Clerk, The* (Eliot, 1954)
F   *L'Employé de confiance*
D   *Der Privatsekretär*
I   *L'impiegato di fiducia*
E   *El hombre de confianza*
SU «Личный секретарь» (Элиот)

807 GB Confucius (551–479)
F   Confucius
D   Konfutse
I   Confucio
E   Confucio
SU Конфуций

808 GB Congo
D   le Congo
F   Kongo
I   il Congo
E   el Congo
SU Конго

809 GB *Connecticut Yankee in King Arthur's*
     Court, A (Twain, 1889)
F   *Un Yankee à la cour du roi Arthur*
D   *Ein Yankee an König Artus' Hof*
I   *Uno yankee del Connecticut alla corte*
     di re Artù
E   *Un yanqui en la corte del rey Artús*
SU «Янки из Коннектикута при дворе
     короля Артура» (Твен)

810 GB *Conquerors, The* (Malraux, 1928)
F   *Les Conquérants*
D   *Die Eroberer*
I   *I conquistatori*
E   *Los conquistadores*
SU «Завоеватели» (Мальро)

811 GB *Conquest of Happiness, The* (Russell,
     1930)
F   *La Conquête du bonheur*
D   *Die Eroberung des Glücks*
I   *La conquista della felicità*
E   *La conquista de la felicidad*
SU «Победа счастья» (Рассел)

812 GB *Considerations on the Greatness and*
     Decadence of the Romans
     (Montesquieu, 1734)
F   *Considérations sur les causes de la*
     grandeur des Romains et de leur
     décadence
D   *Betrachtungen über Größe und Verfall*
     der Römer
I   *Considerazioni sulle cause della*
     grandezza dei romani e della loro
     decadenza
E   *Consideraciones sobre la grandeza y la*
     decadencia de los romanos
SU «Размышления о причинах величия
     и падения римлян» (Монтескьё)

813 GB *Consolation of Philosophy, The* [*De*
     consolatione philosophiae] (Boethius,
     524)
F   *La Consolation de la philosophie*
     (Boèce)
D   *Trost der Philosophie* (Boëthius)
I   *De consolatione philosophiae* (Boezio)
E   *De la consolación de la filosofía*
     (Boecio)
SU «Утешение философское» (Боэций)

814 GB *Conspiracy of the Fiescos in Genoa,*
   The (Schiller, 1783)
   F *La Conjuration de Fiesque*
   D *Die Verschwörung des Fiesko zu*
   Genua
   I *La congiura dei Fiesco*
   E *La conjuración de Fiesco*
   SU «Заговор Фиéско в Гéнуе» (Шúллер)

815 GB Constance, Lake (Europe)
   F le lac de Constance (Europe)
   D der Bodensee (Europe)
   I il lago di Costanza (Europa)
   E el lago Constanza (Europa)
   SU Бóденское óзеро (Еврóпа)

816 GB Constantine (pope, emperor,
   sovereign)
   F Constantin (pape, empereur,
   souverain)
   D Konstantin (Papst, Kaiser, Herr.)
   I Costantino (papa, imperatore,
   sovrano)
   E Constantino (papa, emperador, sob.)
   SU Константúн (пáпа рúмский,
   императóр, прав.)

817 GB Constantine the Great (288–337)
   F Constantin le Grand
   D Konstantin der Große
   I Costantino il Grande
   E Constantino el Grande
   SU Константúн Велúкий

818 GB Constantinople (hist., = Istanbul)
   F Constantinople (hist., = Istanbul)
   D Konstantinopel (Gesch., = Istanbul)
   I Costantinopoli (st., = Istanbul)
   E Constantinopla (hist., = Estambul)
   SU Константинóполь (м.) (= Стамбýл)

819 GB *Constant Tin Soldier, The* [*Den*
   standhaftige tinsoldat] (Andersen,
   1838)
   F *L'Intrépide Soldat de plomb*
   D *Der standhafte Zinnsoldat*
   I *L'intrepido soldatino di stagno*
   E *El soldadito de plomo*
   SU «Стóйкий оловя́нный солдáтик»
   (Áндерсен)

820 GB Constanza (Romania)
   F Constantza (Roumanie)
   D Konstanza (Rumänien)
   I Costanza (Romania)
   E Constantza (Rumania)
   SU Констáнца (Румы́ния)

821 GB *Consuelo* (Sand, 1842)
   F *Consuelo*
   D *Consuelo*
   I *Consuelo*
   E *Consuelo*
   SU «Консуэ́ло» (Санд)

822 GB *Consul, The* (Menotti, 1950)
   F *Le Consul*
   D *Der Konsul*
   I *Il console*
   E *El cónsul*
   SU «Кóнсул» (Менóтти)

823 GB *Contemplations* (Hugo, 1856)
   F *Les Contemplations*
   D *Betrachtungen*
   I *Contemplazioni*
   E *Las contemplaciones*
   SU «Размышлéния» (Гюгó)

824 GB *Conversations on the Plurality of*
   Worlds (Fontenelle, 1686)
   F *Entretiens sur la pluralité des mondes*
   D *Unterhaltungen über die Vielheit der*
   Welten
   I *Conversazioni sulla pluralità dei mondi*
   E *Diálogos sobre la pluralidad de los*
   mundos
   SU «Бесéды о мнóжественности мирóв»
   (Фонтенéль)

825 GB Copenhagen (Denmark)
   F Copenhague (f.) (Danemark)
   D Kopenhagen (Dänemark)
   I Copenaghen (Danimarca)
   E Copenhague (Dinamarca)
   SU Копенгáген (Дáния)

826 GB Copernicus (1473–1543)
   F Copernic
   D Coppernicus
   I Copernico
   E Copérnico
   SU Копéрник

827 GB Copts, the (hist.)
   F les coptes (hist.)
   D die Kopten (Gesch.)
   I i copti (st.)
   E los coptos (hist.)
   SU кóпты (ист.)

828 GB Coral Sea, the
   F la mer de Corail
   D das Korallenmeer
   I il mare dei Coralli
   E el mar del Coral
   SU Корáлловое мóре

829 GB Cordova (Cordoba) (Spain)
F Cordoue (f.) (Espagne)
D Cordoba (Spanien)
I Cordoba (Spagna)
E Córdoba (España)
SU Кóрдова (Испáния)

830 GB Corfu
F Corfou
D Korfu
I Corfu
E Corfú
SU Кóрфу

831 GB *Corinne* (Staël, 1807)
F *Corinne*
D *Corinne*
I *Corinna*
E *Corinna*
SU «Корúнна» (Сталь)

832 GB Corinth (Greece)
F Corinthe (f.) (Grèce)
D Korinth (Griechenland)
I Corinto (Grecia)
E Corinto (Grecia)
SU Корúнф (Грéция)

833 GB Corinthians, the Epistle of Paul to the (Bib.)
Г l'Épître de Saint Paul aux Corinthiens (Bib.)
D der Korintherbrief (Bib.)
I le lettere di Paolo ai Corinti (Bib.)
E la Epístola de San Pablo a los Corintios (Bib.)
SU «Послáние к Коринфия́нам» (библ.)

834 GB *Coriolanus* (Shakespeare, 1607–8; Beethoven, 1807)
F *Coriolan*
D *Coriolanus*
I *Coriolano*
E *Coriolano*
SU «Кориолáн» (Шекспúр, Бетхóвен)

835 GB Cornwall (England)
F le Cornwall (Angleterre)
D Cornwall (England)
I la Cornovaglia (Inghilterra)
E el Cornualles (Inglaterra)
SU Кóрнуолл (Áнглия)

836 GB *Coronation of the Virgin, The* (Fra Angelico, *1432*)
F *Le Couronnement de la Vierge* (Fra Angelico
D *Die Marienkrönung* (Fra Angelico)
I *La coronazione della Vergine* (Beato Angelico)
E *La coronación de la Virgen* (Fra Angélico)
SU «Коронова́ние Мари́и» (Анджéлико)

837 GB Corpus Christi (rel.)
F la Fête-Dieu (relig.)
D der Fronleichnam (relig.)
I il Corpus Domini (relig.)
E el Corpus (relig.)
SU прáздник тéла Христóва (рел.)

838 GB Correggio (1494–1534)
F le Corrège
D Correggio
I il Correggio
E el Correggio
SU Коррéджо

839 GB *Corridors of Power, The* (Snow, 1964)
F *Les Couloirs du pouvoir*
D *Korridore der Macht*
I *I corridoi del potere*
E *Los pasillos del poder*
SU «Коридóры влáсти» (Снóу)

840 GB Corsica
F la Corse
D Korsika
I la Corsica
E Córcega
SU Кóрсика

841 GB *Così fan tutte* [*All Women Are Like That*] (Mozart, 1790)
F *Così fan tutte*
D *Così fan tutte*
I *Così fan tutte*
E *Così fan tutte*
SU «Все они́ таковы́» (Мóцарт)

842 GB Corunna (La Coruña) (Spain)
F la Corogne (Espagne)
D La Coruña (Spanien)
I La Coruña (Spagna)
E La Coruña (España)
SU Ла-Корýнья (Испáния)

843 GB *Cossacks, The* (Tolstoy, 1863)
     F   *Les Cosaques* (Tolstoï)
     D   *Die Kosaken* (Tolstoj)
     I   *I cosacchi* (Tolstoj)
     E   *Los cosacos* (Tolstoi)
     SU «Казаки́» (Толсто́й)

844 GB Costa Blanca, the [White Coast]
         (Spain)
     F   la Costa Blanca (Espagna)
     D   die Costa Blanca (Spanien)
     I   la Costa Blanca (Spagna)
     E   la Costa Blanca (España)
     SU Ко́ста Бла́нка (Испа́ния)

845 GB Costa Brava, the [Wild Coast] (Spain)
     F   la Costa Brava (Espagne)
     D   die Costa Brava (Spanien)
     I   la Costa Brava (Spagna)
     E   la Costa Brava (España)
     SU Ко́ста Бра́ва (Испа́ния)

846 GB Costa del Sol, the [Sunny Coast]
         (Spain)
     F   la Costa del Sol (Espagna)
     D   die Costa del Sol (Spanien)
     I   la Costa del Sol (Spagna)
     E   la Costa del Sol (España)
     SU Ко́ста-дель-со́ль (Испа́ния)

847 GB Costa Rica
     F   le Costa Rica
     D   Costa Rica
     I   il Costa Rica
     E   Costa Rica
     SU Ко́ста-Ри́ка

848 GB Costa Smeralda, the [Emerald Coast]
         (Sardinia)
     F   la Costa Smeralda (Sardaigne)
     D   die Costa Smeralda (Sardinien)
     I   la Costa Smeralda (Sardegna)
     E   la Costa Smeralda (Cerdeña)
     SU Ко́ста Смера́льда (Сарди́ния)

     GB Côte d'Azur [Azure Coast]→French
         Riviera

849 GB Council for Mutual Economic
         Assistance (CMEA), the (Comecon)
     F   le Conseil d'assistance économique
         mutuelle (Comecon)
     D   der Rat für gegenseitige
         Wirtschaftshilfe (RGW)
     I   il Consiglio di aiuto economico
         reciproco (Comecon)
     E   el Consejo de ayuda económica mutua
         (Comecon)
     SU Сове́т Экономи́ческой Взаимопо́мощи
         (СЭВ)

850 GB Council of Europe, the
     F   le Conseil d'Europe
     D   der Europa-Rat
     I   il Consiglio d'Europa
     E   el Consejo de Europa
     SU Европе́йский сове́т

     GB Council of Trent→Trent, Council of

851 GB Counter-Reformation, the
         (XVI–XVII)
     F   la Contre-Réforme
     D   die Gegenreformation
     I   la controriforma
     E   la Contrareforma
     SU контрреформа́ция

852 GB *Countess Cathleen, The* (Yeats, 1893)
     F   *La Comtesse Cathleen*
     D   *Gräfin Cathleen*
     I   *La contessa Cathleen*
     E   *La condesa Catalina*
     SU «Графи́ня Кэ́тлин» (Йитс)

853 GB *Count of Luxembourg, The* (Lehar,
         1908)
     F   *Le Comte de Luxembourg*
     D   *Der Graf von Luxemburg*
     I   *Il conte di Lussemburgo*
     E   *El conde de Luxemburgo*
     SU «Граф Люксембу́рг» (Лега́р)

854 GB *Count of Monte-Cristo, The* (Dumas,
         1844)
     F   *Le Comte de Monte-Cristo*
     D   *Der Graf von Monte-Cristo*
     I   *Il conte di Montecristo*
     E   *El conde de Montecristo*
     SU «Граф Мо́нте-Кри́сто» (Дюма́)

855 GB *Count Orgel Opens the Ball* (Radiguet, 1924)
    F *Le Bal du comte d'Orgel*
    D *Der Ball des Comte d'Orgel*
    I *Il ballo del conte d'Orgel*
    E *El baile del Conde de Orgel*
    SU «Бал гра́фа д'Оржéля» (Радигé)

856 GB *Country Wife, The* (Wycherley, 1673)
    F *La Femme de province*
    D *Das Landmädchen*
    I *La moglie di campagna*
    E *La provinciana*
    SU «Деревéнская женá» (Уи́черли)

857 GB *Course in General Linguistics* (Saussure, 1916)
    F *Cours de linguistique générale*
    D *Grundfragen der allgemeinen Sprachwissenschaft*
    I *Corso di linguistica generale*
    E *Curso de linguística general*
    SU «Курс óбщей лингви́стики» (Соссю́р)

858 GB *Courtier, The* (Castiglione, 1528)
    F *Le Parfait Courtisan*
    D *Der Hofmann*
    I *Il cortegiano*
    E *El cortesano*
    SU «Придвóрный» (Кастильóне)

859 GB Courtrai (Belgium)
    F Courtrai (Belge)
    D Kortrijk (Belgien)
    I Courtrai (Belgio)
    E Courtrai (Bélgica)
    SU Кóртрейк (Бéльгия)

860 GB *Courtship of Miles Standish, The* (Longfellow, 1863)
    F *Miles Standish*
    D *Die Werbung des Miles Standish*
    I *Il corteggiamento di Miles Standish*
    E *Las bodas de Miles Standish*
    SU «Сватовствó Мáйлза Стéндиша» (Лонгфéлло)

861 GB *Cousin Betty* (Balzac, 1846)
    F *La Cousine Bette*
    D *Tante Lisbeth*
    I *La cugina Betta*
    E *La prima Bette*
    SU «Кузи́на Бéтта» (Бальзáк)

862 GB *Cousin Pons* (Balzac, 1847)
    F *Le Cousin Pons*
    D *Vetter Pons*
    I *Il cugino Pons*
    E *El primo Pons*
    SU «Кузéн Понс» (Бальзáк)

863 GB *Cranes Are Flying, The* (Kalatozov, 1957)
    F *Quant passent les cigognes*
    D *Wohin die Kraniche ziehen*
    I *Quando passono le gru*
    E *Cuando vuelan las cigüeñas*
    SU «Летя́т журавли́» (Калатóзов)

864 GB Cranford (Gaskell, 1853)
    F *Cranford*
    D *Cranford*
    I *Cranford*
    E *Cranford*
    SU «Крéнфорд» (Гáскелл)

865 GB *Creation, The* (Haydn, 1798)
    F *La Création*
    D *Die Schöpfung*
    I *La creazione*
    E *La creación*
    SU «Сотворéние ми́ра» (Гайдн)

866 GB *Creditors, The* [*Creditörer*] (Strindberg, 1898)
    F *Les Créanciers*
    D *Die Gläubiger*
    I *Creditori*
    E *Débito y crédito*
    SU «Кредитóры» (Стри́ндберг)

867 GB Creon (myth.)
    F Créon (myth.)
    D Kreon (myth.)
    I Creonte (mit.)
    E Creón (mit.)
    SU Креóнт (миф.)

868 GB Crete
    F la Crète
    D Kreta
    I Creta
    E Creta
    SU Крит

869 GB *Cricket on the Hearth, The* (Dickens, 1845)
    F *Le Grillon du foyer*
    D *Das Heimchen am Herd*
    I *Il grillo del focolare*
    E *El grillo del hogar*
    SU «Сверчóк на ками́не» (Ди́ккенс)

870 GB Crimea, the (USSR)
 F la Crimée (URSS)
 D die Krim (UdSSR)
 I Crimea (URSS)
 E Crimea (URSS)
 SU Крым (СССР)

871 GB *Crime and Punishment* (Dostoievsky, 1866)
 F *Crime et châtiment* (Dostoïveski)
 D *Schuld und Sühne* (Dostojewskij)
 I *Delitto i castigo* (Dostoevskij)
 E *Crimen y castigo* (Dostoievski)
 SU «Преступле́ние и наказа́ние» (Достое́вский)

872 GB Crimean War, the (1854–6)
 F la guerre de Crimée
 D der Krimkrieg
 I la guerra di Crimea
 E la guerra de Crimea
 SU Кры́мская война́

873 GB *Crime of Sylvestre Bonnard, The* (France, 1881)
 F *Le Crime de Sylvestre Bonnard*
 D *Das Verbrechen des Sylvestre Bonnard*
 I *Il delitto di Sylvestre Bonnard*
 E *El crimen de Sylvestre Bonnard*
 SU «Преступле́ние Сильве́стра Бонна́ра» (Франс)

874 GB *Crime on Goat Island* (Betti, 1950)
 F *L'Île des chèvres*
 D *Verbrechen auf der Ziegeninsel*
 I *Delitto all'isola delle Capre*
 E *Delito en la isla de las cabras*
 SU «Преступле́ние на ко́зьем о́строве» (Бе́тти)

875 GB *Crisis of European Conscience, The* (Hazard, 1935–40)
 F *La Crise de la conscience européenne*
 D *Die Krise des europäischen Geistes*
 I *La crisi della coscienza europea*
 E *La crisis de la conciencia europea*
 SU «Кри́зис европе́йской со́вести» (Аза́р)

876 GB *Critic, The* (Sheridan, 1779)
 F *Le Critique*
 D *Der Kritiker*
 I *Il critico*
 E *El crítico*
 SU «Кри́тик» (Ше́ридан)

877 GB *Critique of Judgement* (Kant, 1790)
 F *Critique de la faculté de juger*
 D *Kritik der Urteilskraft*
 I *Critica del giudizio*
 E *Crítica del juicio*
 SU «Кри́тика спосо́бности сужде́ния» (Кант)

878 GB *Critique of Practical Reason* (Kant, 1788)
 F *Critique de la raison pratique*
 D *Kritik der praktischen Vernunft*
 I *Critica della ragion pratica*
 E *Crítica de la razón prática*
 SU «Кри́тика практи́ческого ра́зума» (Кант)

879 GB *Critique of Pure Reason* (Kant, 1781)
 F *Critique de la raison pure*
 D *Kritik der reinen Vernunft*
 I *Critica della ragion pura*
 E *Crítica de la razón pura*
 SU «Кри́тика чи́стого ра́зума» (Кант)

880 GB *Crito* [*Kriton*] (Plato, −IV)
 F *Criton* (Platon)
 D *Kriton* (Platon)
 I *Critone* (Platone)
 E *Critón* (Platón)
 SU «Крито́н» (Плато́н)

881 GB Croatia (Yugoslavia)
 F la Croatie (Yougoslavie)
 D Kroatien (Iugoslawien)
 I la Croazia (Iugoslavia)
 E Croacia (Yugoslavia)
 SU Хорва́тия (Югосла́вия)

882 GB Croesus (−VI)
 F Crésus
 D Krösus
 I Creso
 E Creso
 SU Крёз

883 GB *Crome Yellow* (Huxley, 1921)
 F *Jaune de chrome*
 D *Chromgelb*
 I *Giallo cromo*
 E *Los escándalos de Crome*
 SU «Жёлтый Кром» (Ха́ксли)

884 GB Cromwell (Hugo, 1827)
 F *Cromwell*
 D *Cromwell*
 I *Cromwell*
 E *Cromwell*
 SU «Кро́мвель» (Гюго́)

885 GB Cronos (myth.)
F Cronos (myth.)
D Kronos (myth.)
I Crono (mit.)
E Cronos (mit.)
SU Кро́нос (миф.)

886 GB *Crossfire* (Dmytryk, 1947)
F *Feux croisés*
D *Im Kreuzfeuer*
I *Odio implacabile*
E *Encrucijada de odios*
SU «Перекрёстный ого́нь» (Дми́трик)

887 GB *Crowd Roars, The* (Hawks, 1932)
F *La foule hurle*
D *Der Schrei der Menge*
I *L'urlo della folla*
E *Avidez de tragedia*
SU «Толпа́ ревёт» (Хокс)

888 GB *Crucible, The* (Miller, 1953)
F *Les Sorcières de Salem*
D *Hexenjagd*
I *Il crogiuolo*
E *Las brujas de Salem*
SU «Суро́вое испыта́ние» (Ми́ллер)

889 GB Crusades, the (XI–XIII)
F les croisades
D die Kreuzzüge
I le crociate
E las cruzadas
SU кресто́вые похо́ды

890 GB Cuba
F Cuba
D Kuba
I Cuba
E Cuba
SU Ку́ба

891 GB *Cunning Little Vixen, The* [*Příhody Lišky Bystroušky*] (Janáček, 1924)
F *Le Rusé Petit Renard*
D *Das schlaue Füchslein*
I *La volpe astuta*
E *La zorra astuta*
SU «Лиси́чка-плуто́вка» (Яна́чек)

892 GB Cupid (myth.)
F Cupidon (myth.)
D Kupido (myth.)
I Cupido (mit.)
E Cupido (mit.)
SU Купидо́н (миф.)

893 GB *Cuttlefish Bones* (Montale, 1925)
F *Os de seiche*
D *Tintenfischknochen*
I *Ossi di seppia*
E *Huesos de sepia*
SU «Ра́ковины карака́тицы» (Монта́ле)

894 GB Cybele (myth.)
F Cybèle (myth.)
G Kybele (myth.)
I Cibele (mit.)
E Cibeles (mit.)
SU Кибе́ла (миф.)

895 GB Cyclops (myth.)
F le Cyclope (myth.)
D der Zyklop (myth.)
I il ciclope (mit.)
E el cíclope (mit.)
SU кикло́п (миф.)

896 GB Cygnus (astron.)
F le Cygne (astron.)
D der Schwan (Astron.)
I il Cigno (astron.)
E el Cisne (astron.)
SU Ле́бедь (астр.)

897 GB *Cymbeline* (Shakespeare, 1610)
F *Cymbeline*
D *Cymbeline*
I *Cimbelino*
E *Cimbelino*
SU «Цимбели́н» (Шекспи́р)

898 GB Cyprus
F Chypre (f.)
D Zypern
I Cipro
E Chipre
SU Кипр

899 GB *Cyrano de Bergerac* (Rostand, 1897; Alfano, 1936)
F *Cyrano de Bergerac*
D *Cyrano von Bergerac*
I *Cirano di Bergerac*
E *Cyrano de Bergerac*
SU «Сирано́ де Бержера́к» (Роста́н, Альфа́но)

900 GB Cyril (saint)
F Cyrille (saint)
D Kyrill (Heiliger)
I Cirillo (santo)
E Cirilo (santo)
SU Кири́лл (св.)

901 GB   *Cyropedia, The* [*Kyrou paideia*] [*The Education of Cyrus*] (Xenophon, −IV)
    F   *La Cyropédie* (Xénophon)
    D   *Die Erziehung des Kyros* (Xenophon)
    I   *La Ciropedia* (Senofonte)
    E   *La Ciropedia* (Jenofonte)
    SU «Киропе́дия» (Ксенофо́нт)

902 GB   Cyrus the Great (*558–528*)
    F   Cyrus le Grand
    D   Cyrus der Älte
    I   Ciro il Grande
    E   Ciro el Grande
    SU Кир Бели́кий

903 GB   Czechoslovakia
    F   la Tchécoslovaquie
    D   die Tschechoslowakei
    I   la Cecoslovacchia
    E   Checoslovaquia
    SU Чехослова́кия

D

904 GB Dacia (Europe, hist.)
  F la Dacie (Europe, hist.)
  D Dakien (Europa, Gesch.)
  I la Dacia (Europa, st.)
  E Dacia (Europa, hist.)
  SU Дáкия (Еврóпа, ист.)

905 GB Daedalus (myth.)
  F Dédale (myth.)
  D Dädalus (myth.)
  I Dedalo (mit.)
  E Dédalo (mit.)
  SU Дедáл (миф.)

906 GB Dahomey (hist.)
  F le Dahomey (hist.)
  D Dahomey (Gesch.)
  I il Dahomey (st.)
  E Dahomey (hist.)
  SU Дагомéя (ист.)

907 GB Dalmatia (Yugoslavia)
  F la Dalmatie (Yougoslavie)
  D Dalmatien (Jugoslawien)
  I la Dalmazia (Iugoslavia)
  E Dalmacia (Yugoslavia)
  SU Далмáция (Югослáвия)

908 GB Damascus (Bib.)
  F Damas (Bib.)
  D Damaskus (Bib.)
  I Damasco (Bib.)
  E Damasco (Bib.)
  SU Дамáск (библ.)

909 GB *Damnation of Faust, The* (Berlioz, 1846)
  F *La Damnation de Faust*
  D *Fausts Verdammnis*
  I *La dannazione di Faust*
  E *La condenación de Fausto*
  SU «Осуждéние Фáуста» (Берлиóз)

910 GB Damocles (−IV)
  F Damoclès
  D Damokles
  I Damocle
  E Damocles
  SU Дамóкл

911 GB Danaë (myth.)
  F Danaé (myth.)
  D Danaë (myth.)
  I Danae (mit.)
  E Dánae (mit.)
  SU Данáя (миф.)

912 GB *Dance of Death [Dödsdansen]* (Strindberg, 1901)
  F *La Danse de mort*
  D *Totentanz*
  I *Danza macabra*
  E *Danza macabra*
  SU «Пля́ска смéрти» (Стри́ндберг)

913 GB *Dangerous Acquaintances* (Laclos, 1782)
  F *Les Liaisons dangereuses*
  D *Gefährliche Liebschaften*
  I *Le relazioni pericolose*
  E *Las amistades peligrosas*
  SU «Опáсные свя́зи» (Лаклó)

914 GB *Dangerous Corner* (Priestley, 1932)
  F *Virage dangereux*
  D *Wenn . . . ?*
  I *Angolo pericoloso*
  E *Curva peligrosa*
  SU «Опáсный поворóт» (При́стли)

915 GB *Dangling Man* (Bellow, 1944)
  F *L'Homme de Buridan*
  D *Mann in der Schwebe*
  I *L'uomo in bilico*
  E *Hombre en suspenso*
  SU «Праздношатáющийся» (Бéллоу)

916 GB Daniel (Bib.)
    F   Daniel (Bib.)
    D   Daniel (Bib.)
    I   Daniele (Bib.)
    E   Daniel (Bib.)
    SU Дании́л (библ.)

917 GB *Daniel Deronda* (Eliot, 1874–6)
    F   *Daniel Deronda*
    D   *Daniel Deronda*
    I   *Daniel Deronda*
    E   *Daniel Deronda*
    SU «Даниэ́ль Деро́нда» (Э́лиот)

918 GB *Danton's Death* (Büchner, 1835)
    F   *Mort de Danton*
    D   *Dantons Tod*
    I   *La morte di Danton*
    E   *La muerte de Danton*
    SU «Смерть Данто́на» (Бю́хнер)

919 GB Danube (River), the (Europe)
    F   le Danube (Europe)
    D   die Donau (Europa)
    I   il Danubio (Europa)
    E   el Danubio (Europa)
    SU Дуна́й (Евро́па)

920 GB Daphne (myth.)
    F   Daphné (myth.)
    D   Daphne (myth.)
    I   Dafne (mit.)
    E   Dafne (mit.)
    SU Да́фна (миф.)

921 GB *Daphnis and Chloe* (Ravel, 1912)
    F   *Daphnis et Chloé*
    D   *Daphnis und Chloë*
    I   *Dafni e Cloe*
    E   *Dafnis y Cloe*
    SU «Да́фнис и Хло́я» (Раве́ль)

922 GB Dardanelles, the (Turkey)
    F   les Dardenelles (f.) (Turquie)
    D   die Dardanellen (Türkei)
    I   i Dardanelli (Turchia)
    E   los Dardanelos (Turquía)
    SU Дардане́ллы (ж.) (Ту́рция)

923 GB Darius (king)
    F   Darios (roi)
    D   Darius (König)
    I   Dario (re)
    E   Darío (rey)
    SU Да́рий (царь)

924 GB *Dark Journey, The* (Green, 1929)
    F   *Léviathan*
    D   *Leviathan*
    I   *Léviathan*
    E   *Léviathan*
    SU «Левиафа́н» (Грин)

925 GB *Darkness at Noon* (Koestler, 1940)
    F   *Le Zéro et l'Infini*
    D   *Sonnenfinisternis*
    I   *Buio a mezzogiorno*
    E   *El cero y el infinito*
    SU «Со́лнечное затме́ние» (Кёстлер)

926 GB *Daughter of the Regiment, The*
         (Donizetti, 1840)
    F   *La fille du régiment*
    D   *Die Regimentstochter*
    I   *La figlia del reggimento*
    E   *La hija del regimiento*
    SU «Дочь полка́» (Донице́тти)

927 GB Dauphiné (France)
    F   le Dauphiné (France)
    D   Dauphiné (Frankreich)
    I   il Delfinato (Francia)
    E   el Delfinado (Francia)
    SU Дофине́ (Фра́нция)

928 GB David (Bib., saint, sovereign)
    F   David (Bib., saint, souverain)
    D   David (Bib., Heiliger, Herr.)
    I   Davide (Bib., santo, sovrano)
    E   David (Bib., santo, sob.)
    SU Дави́д (библ., св., прав.)

929 GB *David Copperfield* (Dickens, 1850)
    F   *David Copperfield*
    D   *David Copperfield*
    I   *David Copperfield*
    E   *David Copperfield*
    SU «Дэ́вид Ко́пперфилд» (Ди́ккенс)

930 GB *Day of the Locust, The* (West, 1939;
         Schlesinger, 1975)
    F   *Le Jour du fléau*
    D   *Der Tag der Heuschrecke*
    I   *Il giorno della locusta*
    E   *El día de la langosta*
    SU «День саранчи́» (Уэ́ст, Шле́зингер)

931 GB *Day of Wrath [Vredens Dag]* (Dreyer)
    F   *Jour de colère*
    D   *Dies irae*
    I   *Dies irae*
    E   *Días de ira*
    SU «День гне́ва» (Дре́йер)

932 GB *Dead Christ* (Holbein, 1521)
    F   *Christ mort*
    D   *Toter Christus*
    I   *Cristo morto*
    E   *Cristo muerto*
    SU «Мёртвый Христо́с» (Хо́льбейн)

933 GB Dead Sea, the
    F   la mer Morte
    D   das Tote Meer
    I   il mare Morto
    E   el mar Muerto
    SU Мёртвое мо́ре

934 GB Dead Sea Scrolls, the
    F   les manuscrits de la mer Morte
    D   die Schriftrollen von Qumrân
    I   i manoscritti di Qumran
    E   los manuscritos del mar Muerto
    SU ру́кописи Мёртвого мо́ря

935 GB *Dead Souls* (Gogol, 1842)
    F   *Les Âmes mortes*
    D   *Die toten Seelen*
    I   *Le anime morte*
    E   *Las almas muertas*
    SU «Мёртвые ду́ши» (Го́голь)

936 GB *Death and the Maiden* (Schubert, 1824)
    F   *La Jeune Fille et la Mort*
    D   *Der Tod und das Mädchen*
    I   *La morte e la fanciulla*
    E   *La muerte y la doncella*
    SU «Смерть и де́вушка» (Шу́берт)

937 GB *Death and Transfiguration* (Strauss, 1889)
    F   *Mort et Transfiguration*
    D   *Tod und Verklärung*
    I   *Morte e trasfigurazione*
    E   *Muerte y transfiguración*
    SU «Смерть и просветле́ние» (Штра́ус)

938 GB *Death in the Afternoon* (Hemingway, 1932)
    F   *Mort dans l'après-midi*
    D   *Tod am Nachmittag*
    I   *Morte nel pomeriggio*
    E   *Muerte en el atardecer*
    SU «Смерть по́сле полу́дня» (Хемингуэ́й)

939 GB *Death in Venice* (Mann, 1912)
    F   *La Mort à Venise*
    D   *Der Tod in Venedig*
    I   *La morte a Venezia*
    E   *Muerte en Venecia*
    SU «Смерть в Вене́ции» (Манн)

940 GB *Death of a Hero* (Aldington, 1929)
    F   *Mort d'un héros*
    D   *Heldentod*
    I   *Morte di un eroe*
    E   *Muerte del héroe*
    SU «Смерть геро́я» (О́лдингтон)

941 GB *Death of a Salesman* (Miller, 1949)
    F   *Mort d'un commis voyageur*
    D   *Tod des Handlungsreisenden*
    I   *Morte di un commesso viaggiatore*
    E   *La muerte de un viajante*
    SU «Смерть коммивояжёра» (Ми́ллер)

942 GB *Death of Ivan Ilyitch, The* (Tolstoy, 1884)
    F   *La Mort d'Ivan Ilitch* (Tolstoï)
    D   *Der Tod des Iwan Iljitsch* (Tolstoj)
    I   *La morte di Ivan Il'ič* (Tolstoj)
    E   *La muerte de Iván Iljich* (Tolstoi)
    SU «Смерть Ива́на Ильича́» (Толсто́й)

943 GB *Death of the Gods* (Merezhkovsky, 1896)
    F   *La Mort des dieux* (Merejkovski)
    D   *Julian Apostata* (Mereshkowskij)
    I   *Giuliano l'Apostata, o la morte degli dei* (Merežkovskij)
    E   *La muerte de los dioses* (Merejkovski)
    SU «Юлиа́н Отсту́пник, и́ли Смерть бого́в» (Мережко́вский)

944 GB *Death of Wolfe, The* (West, 1771)
    F   *La Mort du général Wolfe*
    D   *Der Tod des Generals Wolfe*
    I   *La morte del generale Wolfe*
    E   *La muerte del general Wolfe*
    SU «Смерть генера́ла Ву́лфа» (Уэ́ст)

945 GB *Deaths and Entrances* (Thomas, 1946)
    F   *Morts et entrées*
    D   *Tode und Tore*
    I   *Morti e ammissioni*
    E   *Muertes e ingresos*
    SU «Сме́рти и вхо́ды» (То́мас)

946 GB Death Valley (USA)
    F   la Vallée de la Mort (USA)
    D   Death Valley (USA)
    I   la Valle della Morte (USA)
    E   el valle de la Muerte (USA)
    SU Доли́на Сме́рти (США)

947 GB Deborah (Bib.)
    F   Déborah (Bib.)
    D   Debora (Bib.)
    I   Debora (Bib.)
    E   Débora (Bib.)
    SU Дебо́ра (библ.)

948 GB   *Decameron, the* (Boccaccio, 1348–53)
    F   le *Décameron* (Boccace)
    D   das *Dekameron* (Boccaccio)
    I   il *Decameron* (Boccaccio)
    E   el *Decamerón* (Boccaccio)
    SU «Декамеро́н» (Бокка́ччо)

949 GB   Declaration of Human Rights, the
          (1948)
    F   la Déclaration internationale des droits
        de l'homme
    D   die Allgemeine Deklaration der
        Menschenrechten
    I   la Dichiarazione dei diritti dell'uomo
    E   la Declaración Universal de los
        Derechos del Hombre
    SU Деклара́ция прав челове́ка

950 GB   Declaration of Independence, the
          (1776)
    F   la Déclaration d'indépendance
    D   die Unabhängigkeitserklärung
    I   la Dichiarazione di indipendenza
    E   la Declaración de la Independencia
    SU Деклара́ция незави́симости

951 GB   Declaration of the Rights of Man, the
          (1789)
    F   la Déclaration des droits de l'homme et
        du citoyen
    D   die Menschenrechtserklärung
    I   la Dichiarazione dei diritti dell'uomo e
        del cittadino
    E   la Declaración de los Derechos del
        Hombre y del Ciudadano
    SU Деклара́ция прав челове́ка и
        граждани́на

952 GB   *Decline and Fall* (Waugh, 1928)
    F   *Le Déclin et la chute*
    D   *Auf der schiefen Ebene*
    I   *Declino e caduta*
    E   *Decadencia y caída*
    SU «Упа́док и крах» (Во)

953 GB   *Decline and Fall of the Roman Empire,*
          The (Gibbon, 1776–88)
    F   *Histoire de la décadence et de la chute*
        de l'Empire romain
    D   *Geschichte von dem Niedergang und*
        Fall des Römischen Reiches
    I   *Storia della decadenza e caduta*
        dell'impero romano
    E   *Historia de la decadencia y caída del*
        Imperio Romano
    SU «Исто́рия упа́дка и разруше́ния
        Ри́мской импе́рии» (Ги́ббон)

954 GB   *Decline of the West* (Spengler, 1918)
    F   *Déclin de l'Occident*
    D   *Der Untergang des Abendlandes*
    I   *Il tramonto dell'Occidente*
    E   *La decadencia del Occidente*
    SU «Зака́т Евро́пы» (Шпе́нглер)

955 GB   *Deer Hunter, The* (Cimino, 1978)
    F   *Voyage au bout de l'enfer*
    D   *Die durch die Hölle gehen*
    I   *Il cacciatore*
    E   *El cazador de ciervos*
    SU «Охо́тник на оле́ней» (Си́мино)

956 GB   *Deerslayer, The* (Cooper, 1841)
    F   *Le Tueur de daims*
    D   *Der Wildtöter*
    I   *L'uccisore di cervi*
    E   *El matador de ciervos*
    SU «Зверобо́й» (Ку́пер)

957 GB   Defenestration of Prague, the (1618)
    F   la Défenestration de Prague
    D   der Prager Fenstersturz
    I   la defenestrazione di Praga
    E   la Defenestración de Praga
    SU Дефенстра́ция Пра́ги

958 GB   *Dehumanisation of Art, The* (Ortega y
          Gasset, 1925)
    F   *La Déshumanisation de l'art*
    D   *Die Vertreibung des Menschen aus der*
        Kunst
    I   *La disumanizzazione dell'arte*
    E   *La deshumanización del arte*
    SU «Дегуманиза́ция иску́сства»
        (Орте́га-и-Гасе́т)

959 GB   *Deirdre* (Yeats, 1907)
    F   *Deirdre*
    D   *Deirdre*
    I   *Deirdre*
    E   *Deirdre*
    SU «Де́йрдре» (Йитс)

960 GB   *Deirdre of the Sorrows* (Synge, 1910)
    F   *Deirdre des douleurs*
    D   *Deirdre – Tochter der Klagen*
    I   *Deirdre l'addolorata*
    E   *Deirdre de los dolores*
    SU «Де́йрдре – дочь печа́лей» (Синг)

961 GB   Delilah (Bib.)
    F   Dalila (Bib.)
    D   Delila (Bib.)
    I   Delila (Bib.)
    E   Dalila (Bib.)
    SU Дали́ла (библ.)

962 GB Delphi (Greece)
   F Delphes (f.) (Grèce)
   D Delphi (Griechenland)
   I Delfi (Grecia)
   E Delfos (Grecia)
   SU Дéльфы (ж.) (Грéция)

963 GB *Delphine* (Staël, 1802)
   F *Delphine*
   D *Delphine*
   I *Delfina*
   E *Delfina*
   SU «Дельфи́на» (Сталь)

964 GB Demeter (myth.)
   F Déméter (myth.)
   D Demeter (myth.)
   I Demetra (mit.)
   E Deméter (mit.)
   SU Деме́тра (миф.)

965 GB Demetrius (sovereign)
   F Démétrios (souverain)
   D Demetrius (Herr.)
   I Demetrio (sovrano)
   E Demetrio (sob.)
   SU Деме́трий (прав.)

966 GB Democratic Party, the
   F le parti démocratique
   D die Democratic Party
   I il partito democratico
   E el Partido Democrático
   SU Демократи́ческая па́ртия

967 GB Democritus (*460–370*)
   F Démocrite
   D Demokritos
   I Democrito
   E Demócrito
   SU Демокри́т

968 GB *Demoiselles d'Avignon, Les* [*The Girls of Avignon*] (Picasso, 1907)
   F *Les Demoiselles d'Avignon*
   D *Mädchen*
   I *Les demoiselles d'Avignon*
   E *Las muchachas de Avignon*
   SU «Авиньо́нские де́вушки» (Пика́ссо)

969 GB *Demon, The* (Lermontov, 1838)
   F *Le Démon*
   D *Der Dämon*
   I *Il demone*
   E *El demonio*
   SU «Демо́н» (Ле́рмонтов)

970 GB Demosthenes (384–322)
   F Démosthène
   D Demosthenes
   I Demostene
   E Demóstenes
   SU Демосфéн

971 GB Denmark
   F le Danemark
   D Dänemark
   I la Danimarca
   E Dinamarca
   SU Дáния

972 GB *Deposition from the Cross*, the (art)
   F la *Déposition de la Croix* (art)
   D die *Kreuzabnahme* (Kunst)
   I la *Deposizione della Croce* (arte)
   E el *Descendimiento de la Cruz* (arte)
   SU «Сня́тие с креста́» (иск.)

973 GB Descartes (1596–1650)
   F Descartes
   D Descartes
   I Cartesio
   E Descartes
   SU Дека́рт

974 GB *Deserted Village, The* (Goldsmith, 1770)
   F *Le Village abandonné*
   D *Das verlassene Dorf*
   I *Il villaggio abbandonato*
   E *La aldea abandonada*
   SU «Поки́нутая дере́вня» (Го́лдсмит)

975 GB *Desert Song, The* (del Ruth, 1929)
   F *Le Chant du désert*
   D *Liebeslied der Wüste*
   I *Il canto del deserto*
   E *El canto del desierto*
   SU «Пе́сня пусты́ни» (дель Рут)

976 GB *Desire Under the Elms* (O'Neill, 1924)
   F *Le Désir sous les ormes*
   D *Gier unter Ulmen*
   I *Desiderio sotto gli olmi*
   E *El deseo bajo los olmos*
   SU «Стра́сти под вя́зами» (О'Ни́л)

977 GB *Destinies* (Vigny, 1864)
   F *Destinées*
   D *Die Geschicke*
   I *I destini*
   E *Los destinos*
   SU «Су́дьбы» (Виньи́)

978 GB *Destiny of a Man* (Bondarchuk, 1959)
   F   *Destin d'un homme*
   D   *Menschenschicksal*
   I   *Destino di un uomo*
   E   *El destino de un hombre*
   SU «Судьба́ челове́ка» (Бондарчу́к)

979 GB Deuteronomy (Bib.)
   F   Deutéronome (Bib.)
   D   Deuteronomium (Bib.)
   I   Deuteronomio (Bib.)
   E   Deuteronomio (Bib.)
   SU «Второзако́ние» (библ.)

980 GB *Devil in the Flesh, The* (Radiguet, 1923)
   F   *Le Diable au corps*
   D   *Den Teufel in Leib*
   I   *Il diavolo in corpo*
   E   *El diablo en el cuerpo*
   SU «Дья́вол во плоти́» (Радиге́)

   GB *Devils, The→Possessed, The*

981 GB *Devil's Disciple, The* (Shaw, 1896)
   F   *Le Disciple du diable*
   D   *Der Teufelsschüler*
   I   *Il discepolo del diavolo*
   E   *El discípulo del diablo*
   SU «Учени́к дья́вола» (Шо́у)

982 GB *Devil's Elixirs, The* (Hoffmann, 1816)
   F   *Les Élixirs du diable*
   D   *Die Elixiere des Teufels*
   I   *Gli elisir del diavolo*
   E   *El elixir del diablo*
   SU «Эликси́р дья́вола» (Го́фман)

983 GB Devil's Island (French Guiana)
   F   l'Île du Diable (Guyane française)
   D   Teufelsinsel (Französisch-Guayana)
   I   l'isola del Diavolo (Guayana Francese)
   E   la isla del Diablo (Guayana Francesa)
   SU о́стров Дья́вола (Францу́зская Гвиа́на)

984 GB *Devil's Pool, The* (Sand, 1846)
   F   *La Mare au diable*
   D   *Der Teufelssumpf*
   I   *La pozza del diavolo*
   E   *La charca del diablo*
   SU «Чёртова лу́жа» (Санд)

985 GB *Devil upon Two Sticks, The* (Lesage, 1707)
   F   *Le Diable boiteux*
   D   *Dèr hinkende Teufel*
   I   *Il diavolo zoppo*
   E   *El diablo cojuelo*
   SU «Хромо́й бес» (Леса́ж)

986 GB *Dharma Bums, The* (Kerouac, 1958)
   F   *Les Clochards célestes*
   D   *Gammler, Zen und hohe Berge*
   I   *I vagabondi del Dharma*
   E   *Los vagabundos del Dharma*
   SU «Бродя́ги Дха́рмы» (Керуа́к)

987 GB *Dialogues of the Dead* (Fontenelle, 1685)
   F   *Dialogues des morts*
   D   *Totengespräche*
   I   *Dialoghi dei morti*
   E   *Diálogos de los muertos*
   SU «Диало́ги мёртвых» (Фонтене́ль)

988 GB *Dialogues of the Dead, The* [*Nekrikoi dialogoi*] (Lucian, II)
   F   *Les Dialogues des morts* (Lucien)
   D   *Die Totengespräche* (Lukianos)
   I   *I dialoghi dei morti* (Luciano)
   E   *Los diálogos de los muertos* (Luciano)
   SU «Разгово́ры мёртвых» (Лукиа́н)

989 GB *Dialogues of the Gods* [*Theon dialogoi*] (Lucian, II)
   F   *Dialogues des dieux* (Lucien)
   D   *Göttergespräche* (Lukianos)
   I   *Dialoghi degli dei* (Luciano)
   E   *Diálogos de los dioses* (Luciano)
   SU «Разгово́ры бого́в» (Лукиа́н)

990 GB Diana (myth.)
   F   Diane (myth.)
   D   Diana (myth.)
   I   Diana (mit.)
   E   Diana (mit.)
   SU Диа́на (миф.)

991 GB *Diary of a Chambermaid, The* (Renoir, 1945)
   F   *Le Journal d'une femme de chambre*
   D   *Das Tagebuch einer Kammerzofe*
   I   *Il diario di una cameriera*
   E   *Memorias de una doncella*
   SU «Дневни́к горни́чной» (Ренуа́р)

992 GB *Diary of a Country Priest, The* (Bernanos, 1936)
   F   *Journal d'un curé de campagne*
   D   *Tagebuch eines Landpfarrers*
   I   *Diario di un parroco di campagna*
   E   *Diario de un cura rural*
   SU «Дневни́к се́льского свяще́нника» (Бернано́с)

993 GB   *Diary of a Writer* (Dostoievsky, 1873–81)
F   *Journal d'un écrivain* (Dostoïevski)
D   *Tagebuch eines Schriftstellers* (Dostojewskij)
I   *Diario di uno scrittore* (Dostoevskij)
E   *Diario de un escritor* (Dostoievski)
SU   «Дневни́к писа́теля» (Достое́вский)

994 GB   *Diary of My Times, A* (Bernanos, 1938)
F   *Les Grands Cimetières sous la lune*
D   *Die großen Friedhöfe unter dem Mond*
I   *I grandi cimiteri sotto la luna*
E   *Los grandes cementerios bajo la luna*
SU   «Больши́е кла́дбища под луно́й» (Бернано́с)

995 GB   *Dice Box, The* (Jacob, 1917)
F   *Le Cornet à dés*
D   *Der Würfelbecher*
I   *Il bussolotto per dadi*
E   *El cubilete de dados*
SU   «Коро́бочка для косте́й» (Жако́б)

996 GB   *Dictionary of the English Language, A* (Johnson, 1747–55)
F   *Dictionnaire de la langue anglaise*
D   *Wörterbuch der englischen Sprache*
I   *Dizionario della lingua inglese*
E   *Diccionario de la lengua inglesa*
SU   «Слова́рь англи́йского языка́» (Джо́нсон)

997 GB   *Dido* (myth.)
F   *Didon* (myth.)
D   *Dido* (myth.)
I   *Didone* (mit.)
E   *Dido* (mit.)
SU   Дидо́на (миф.)

998 GB   *Dido and Aeneas* (Purcell, *1689*)
F   *Didon et Énée*
D   *Dido und Äneas*
I   *Didone e Enea*
E   *Dido y Eneas*
SU   «Дидо́на и Эне́й» (Пёрселл)

999 GB   *Diocletian* (245–316)
F   *Dioclétien*
D   *Diokletianus*
I   *Diocleziano*
E   *Diocleciano*
SU   Диоклетиа́н

1000 GB   Diogenes (−IV)
F   Diogène
D   Diogenes
I   Diogene
E   Diógenes
SU   Диоге́н

1001 GB   Dionysius (saint, III)
F   Dionysos (saint)
D   Dionysius (Heiliger)
I   Dionisio (santo)
E   Dionisio (santo)
SU   Диони́сий (св.)

1002 GB   Dionysus (myth.)
F   Dionysos (myth.)
D   Dionysos (myth.)
I   Dionisio (mit.)
E   Dionisio (mit.)
SU   Диони́с (миф.)

1003 GB   Directory, the (France, 1795–9)
F   le Directoire (France)
D   das Direktorium (Frankreich)
I   il direttorio (Francia)
E   el Directorio (Francia)
SU   Директо́рия (Фра́нция)

1004 GB   *Dirty Hands* (Sartre, 1948)
F   *Les Mains sales*
D   *Die schmutzigen Hände*
I   *Le mani sporche*
E   *Las manos sucias*
SU   «Гря́зные ру́ки» (Сартр)

1005 GB   *Disasters of War, The* (Goya, 1810–20)
F   *Désastres de la guerre*
D   *Greuel des Krieges*
I   *Disastri della guerra*
E   *Los desastres de la guerra*
SU   «Бе́дствия войны́» (Го́йя)

1006 GB   *Discourse on Man, A* (Voltaire, 1738)
F   *Discours sur l'homme*
D   *Abhandlung über den Mensch*
I   *Discorsi in versi sull'uomo*
E   *Discurso sobre el hombre*
SU   «Рассужде́ние в стиха́х о челове́ке» (Вольте́р)

1007 GB   *Discourse on Method* (Descartes, 1637)
F   *Discours de la méthode* (Descartes)
D   *Abhandlung über die Methode* (Descartes)
I   *Discorso sul metodo* (Cartesio)
E   *Discurso del método* (Descartes)
SU   «Рассужде́ние о ме́тоде» (Дека́рт)

1008 GB *Discourse on the Origin and Basis of Inequality Among Men* (Rousseau, 1754)
  F *Discours sur l'origine de l'inégalité parmi les hommes*
  D *Über die Ungleichheit in der Gesellschaft*
  I *Discorso sull'origine dell'ineguaglianza tra gli uomini*
  E *Sobre el origen de la desigualdad entre los hombres*
  SU «Рассужде́ние о нача́ле и основа́нии нера́венства ме́жду людьми́» (Руссо́)

1009 GB *Discourse on Voluntary Servitude, A* (La Boëtie, 1576)
  F *Discours de la servitude volontaire*
  D *Abhandlung über die freiwillige Knechtschaft*
  I *Discorso della servitù volontaria*
  E *Discurso sobre la servidumbre*
  SU «Рассужде́ние о доброво́льном ра́бстве» (Ла Боэси́)

1010 GB *Discreet Charm of the Bourgeoisie, The* (Buñuel, 1972)
  F *Le Charme discret de la bourgeoisie*
  D *Der diskrete Charme der Bourgeoisie*
  I *I fascino discreto della borghesia*
  E *El encanto discreto de la burguesía*
  SU «Скро́мное очарова́ние буржуази́и» (Бюнюэ́ль)

1011 GB *Divine Comedy, The* (Dante, 1307–21)
  F *La Divine Comédie* (Dante Alighieri)
  D *Die Göttliche Komödie* (Dante Alighieri)
  I *La Divina Commedia* (Dante Alighieri)
  E *La Divina Comedia* (Dante Alighieri)
  SU «Боже́ственная коме́дия» (Да́нте)

1012 GB *Divine Precepts, The* [*Divinae institutiones*] (Lactantius, IV)
  F *Institutions divines* (Lactance)
  D *Unterweisung in der christlichen Lehre* (Lactantius)
  I *Istituzioni divine* (Lattanzio)
  E *Los siete libros de las instituciones divinas* (Lactancio)
  SU «Боже́ственные наставле́ния» (Лакта́нций)

1013 GB *Divorce Italian Style* (Germi, 1962)
  F *Divorce à l'italienne*
  D *Scheidung auf italienisch*
  I *Divorzio all'italiana*
  E *Divorcio a la italiana*
  SU «Разво́д по-италья́нски» (Дже́рми)

1014 GB Djibouti
  F Djibouti
  D Dschibuti
  I Gibuti
  E Jibuti
  SU Джибу́ти

1015 GB Dnieper (River), the (USSR)
  F le Dnieper (URSS)
  D der Dnjepr (UdSSR)
  I il Dnepr (URSS)
  E el Dniéper (URSS)
  SU Днепр (СССР)

1016 GB Dniester (River), the (USSR)
  F le Dniestr (URSS)
  D der Dnjestr (UdSSR)
  I il Dnestr (URSS)
  E el Dniéster (URSS)
  SU Днестр (СССР)

1017 GB *Doctor Faustus* (Mann, 1947)
  F *Le Docteur Faustus*
  D *Doktor Faustus*
  I *Dottor Faustus*
  E *Doctor Faustus*
  SU «До́ктор Фа́устус» (Манн)

  GB *Doctor Faustus* (Marlowe)→ *Tragical History of Doctor Faustus, The*

1018 GB *Doctor in Spite of Himself, The* (Molière, 1666; Gounod, 1858)
  F *Le Médecin malgré lui*
  D *Der Arzt wider Willen*
  I *Il medico per forza*
  E *El médico a palos*
  SU «Ле́карь понево́ле» (Молье́р, Гуно́)

  GB *Dr Jekyll and Mr Hyde*→ *Strange Case of Dr Jekyll and Mr Hyde, The*

1019 GB *Doctor Love* (Molière, 1665)
  F *L'Amour médecin*
  D *Die Liebe als Arzt*
  I *L'amore medico*
  E *El amor médico*
  SU «Любо́вь-ле́карь» (Молье́р)

1020 GB *Doctor's Dilemma, The* (Shaw, 1906)
  F *Le Dilemma du docteur*
  D *Der Arzt am Scheideweg*
  I *Il dilemma del dottore*
  E *El dilema del doctor*
  SU «Диле́мма врача́» (Шо́у)

1021 GB   *Doctor Strangelove* (Kubrick, 1964)
     F   *Docteur Folamour*
     D   *Dr. Seltsam*
     I   *Il dottor Stranamore*
     E   *¿Teléfono rojo? volamos hacia Moscú*
     SU «Дóктор Стрéйнджлав» (Кýбрик)

1022 GB   *Doctor Zhivago* (Pasternak, 1957)
     F   *Le Docteur Jivago*
     D   *Doktor Schiwago*
     I   *Il dottor Živago*
     E   *El doctor Jivago*
     SU «Дóктор Живáго» (Пастернáк)

1023 GB   Dodecanese, the (Greece)
     F   le Dodécanèse (Grèce)
     D   das Dodekanes (Griechenland)
     I   il Dodecaneso Grecia
     E   el Dodecaneso (Grecia)
     SU Додеканéс (Грéция)

1024 GB   *Dodsworth* (Lewis, 1929)
     F   *Dodsworth*
     D   *Dodsworth*
     I   *Dodsworth*
     E   *Dodsworth*
     SU «Дóдсворт» (Льюис)

1025 GB   *Dog Years, The* (Grass, 1963)
     F   *Les Années de chien*
     D   *Hundejahre*
     I   *Anni di cani*
     E   *Años de perro*
     SU «Собáчьи гóды» (Грасс)

1026 GB   *Doll's House, A* [*Et dukkehjem*] (Ibsen, 1879)
     F   *Maison de poupée*
     D   *Nora oder Ein Puppenheim*
     I   *Casa di bambola*
     E   *Casa de muñecas*
     SU «Кýкольный дом» (Йбсен)

1027 GB   *Dombey and Son* (Dickens, 1848)
     F   *Dombey et fils*
     D   *Dombey und Sohn*
     I   *Dombey e figlio*
     E   *Dombey e hijo*
     SU «Дóмби и сын» (Дúккенс)

1028 GB   Domesday Book, the (1086)
     F   le Domesday-Book
     D   das Reichsgrundbuch
     I   il Domesday Book
     E   el Domesday Book
     SU «Кнúга стрáшного судá»

1029 GB   Dominic (saint, 1170–1222)
     F   Dominique (saint)
     D   Dominikus (Heiliger)
     I   Domenico (santo)
     E   Domingo (santo)
     SU Домúник (св.)

1030 GB   Dominica (West Indies)
     F   la Dominique (Antilles)
     D   Dominica (Westindien)
     I   la Dominica (Antille)
     E   Dominica (Antillas)
     SU Доминúка (Вест-Úндия)

1031 GB   Dominican Republic, the (West Indies)
     F   la république Dominicaine (Antilles)
     D   die Dominikanische Republik (Westindien)
     I   la Repubblica Dominicana (Antille)
     E   la República Dominicana (Antillas)
     SU Доминикáнская Респýблика (Вест-Úндия)

1032 GB   Dominicans, the (rel.)
     F   les Dominicains (relig.)
     D   die Dominikaner (relig.)
     I   i domenicani (relig.)
     E   los Dominicos (relig.)
     SU доминикáнцы (рел.)

1033 GB   Domitian (51–96)
     F   Domitien
     D   Domitianus
     I   Domiziano
     E   Domiciano
     SU Домициáн

1034 GB   *Don Carlos* (Schiller, 1787; Verdi, 1867)
     F   *Don Carlos*
     D   *Don Karlos*
     I   *Don Carlos*
     E   *Don Carlos*
     SU «Дон Кáрлос» (Шúллер, Вéрди)

1035 GB   *Don Gil Green Trousers* (Tirso de Molina, 1615)
     F   *Don Gil aux chausses vertes*
     D   *Don Gil mit den grünen Hosen*
     I   *Don Gil dalle calze verdi*
     E   *Don Gil de las calzas verdes*
     SU «Дон Хиль зелёные штаны́» (Тúрсо де Молúна)

1036 GB *Don Giovanni* [*Don Juan*] (Mozart,
  1787)
 F *Don Giovanni*
 D *Don Giovanni*
 I *Don Giovanni*
 E *Don Juan*
 SU «Дон Жуа́н» (Мо́царт)

1037 GB *Don Juan* (Byron, 1819–24)
 F *Don Juan*
 D *Don Juan*
 I *Don Giovanni*
 E *Don Juan*
 SU «Дон Хуа́н» (Ба́йрон)

1038 GB *Don Quixote* (Cervantes, 1805, 1815)
 F *Don Quichotte* (Cervantès)
 D *Don Quijote* (Cervantes)
 I *Don Chisciotte* (Cervantes Saavedra)
 E *Don Quijote* (Cervantes)
 SU «Дон Кихо́т» (Серва́нтес)

1039 GB Dordogne (France)
 F Dordogne (France)
 D Dordogne (Frankreich)
 I Dordogne (Francia)
 E Dordoña (Francia)
 SU Дордо́нь (ж.) (Фра́нция)

1040 GB *Double, The* (Dostoievsky, 1846)
 F *Le Sosie* (Dostoïveski)
 D *Der Doppelgänger* (Dostojewskij)
 I *Il sosia* (Dostoewskij)
 E *El doble* (Dostoievski)
 SU «Двойни́к» (Достое́вский)

1041 GB *Double Indemnity* (Wilder, 1944)
 F *Assurance sur la mort*
 D *Frau ohne Gewissen*
 I *La fiamma del peccato*
 E *Perdición*
 SU «Страхова́ние сме́рти» (Уа́йлдер)

1042 GB Dover (England)
 F Douvres (Angleterre)
 D Dover (England)
 I Dover (Inghilterra)
 E Dover (Inglaterra)
 SU Дувр (А́нглия)

1043 GB Dover, the Strait(s) of
 F le pas de Calais
 D die Straße von Dover
 I il paso di Calais
 E el estrecho de Calais
 SU проли́в Па-де-Кале́

1044 GB *Down and Out in Paris and London*
  (Orwell, 1933)
 F *La Vache enragée*
 D *Erledigt in Paris und London*
 I *Miseria a Parigi e Londra*
 E *Sin blanca en París y Londres*
 SU «Разорённый в Пари́же и
  Ло́ндоне» (О́руэлл)

1045 GB *Down There* (Huysmans, 1891)
 F *Là-bas*
 D *Da unten*
 I *Laggiù*
 E *Más allá*
 SU «Там, внизу́» (Гюисма́нс)

1046 GB *Do You Like Brahms?* (Sagan, 1959)
 F *Aimez-vous Brahms?*
 D *Lieben Sie Brahms?*
 I *Le piace Brahms?*
 E *¿Usted guste Brahms?*
 SU «Лю́бите ли вы Бра́мса?» (Сага́н)

1047 GB Draco(n) (−VII)
 F Dracon
 D Drakon
 I Dracone
 E Dracón
 SU Драко́нт

1048 GB Drakensberg Mountains, the (South
  Africa)
 F les montagnes Drakensberg (Afrique
  du Sud)
 D die Drakensberge (Südafrika)
 I i monti dei Draghi (Africa del Sud)
 E las montañas Drakensberg (África del
  Sur)
 SU Драко́новы го́ры (Ю́жная А́фрика)

1049 GB *Dram Shop, The* (Zola, 1877)
 F *L'Assommoir*
 D *Die Kneipe zum Totschläger*
 I *L'ammazzatoio*
 E *La taberna*
 SU «Западня́» (Золя́)

1050 GB *Dreamer, The* (Green, 1934)
 F *Le Visionnaire*
 D *Der Geisterseher*
 I *Il visionario*
 E *El visionario*
 SU «Мечта́тель» (Грин)

1051 GB *Dream of Gerontius, A* (Newman, 1865; Elgar, 1900)
F *Le Songe de Gerontius*
D *Der Traum des Gerontius*
I *Il sogno di Geronzio*
E *El sueño de Gerontius*
SU «Сновиде́ние Геро́нтиуса» (Нью́мен, Э́лгар)

1052 GB Dresden (Germany)
F Dresde (Allemagne)
D Dresden (Deutschland)
I Dresda (Germania)
E Dresde (Alemania)
SU Дре́зден (Герма́ния)

1053 GB Druids, the (rel., hist.)
F les druides (relig., hist.)
D die Druiden (relig., Gesch.)
I i druidi (relig., st.)
E los druidas (relig., hist.)
SU дру́иды (рел., ист.)

1054 GB *Drunken Boat, The* (Rimbaud, 1871)
F *Le Bateau ivre*
D *Das trunkene Schiff*
I *Il battello ebbro*
E *El barco ebrio*
SU «Пья́ный кора́бль» (Рембо́)

1055 GB Dublin (Ireland)
F Dublin (Irlande)
D Dublin (Irland)
I Dublino (Irlanda)
E Dublín (Irlanda)
SU Ду́блин (Ирла́ндия)

1056 GB *Dubliners* (Joyce, 1914)
F *Gens de Dublin*
D *Dublin*
I *Dublinesi*
E *Gentes de Dublín*
SU «Ду́блинцы» (Джойс)

1057 GB Dubrovnik (Yugoslavia)
F Dubrovnik (Yougoslavie)
D Dubrovnik (Jugoslawien)
I Ragusa (Iugoslavia)
E Dubrovnik (Yugoslavia)
SU Дубро́вник (Югосла́вия)

1058 GD *Duchess of Malfi, The* (Webster, 1613)
F *La Duchesse de Malfy*
D *Die Herzogin von Malfy*
I *La duchessa di Amalfi*
E *La duquesa de Malfy*
SU «Герцоги́ня Ама́льфи» (Уэ́бстер)

1059 GB *Duel, The* (Kuprin, 1905)
F *Le Duel*
D *Das Duell*
I *Il duello*
E *El duelo*
SU «Поеди́нок» (Купри́н)

1060 GB *Duel in the Sun* (Vidor, 1946)
F *Duel au soleil*
D *Duell in der Sonne*
I *Duello al sole*
E *Duelo al sol*
SU «Поеди́нок на со́лнце» (Ви́дор)

1061 GB *Duino Elegies* (Rilke, 1912–15)
F *Élégies à Duino*
D *Duineser Elegien*
I *Elegie Duinesi*
E *Elegías del Duino*
SU «Ду́инские эле́гии» (Ри́льке)

1062 GB *Duke Bluebeard's Castle* (Bartók, 1918)
F *Château de Barbe-Bleue*
D *Herzog Blaubarts Burg*
I *Il castello di Barbablù*
E *El castillo de Barba Azul*
SU «За́мок ге́рцога Си́няя Борода́» (Ба́рток)

1063 GB *Dunciad, The* (Pope, 1728)
F *La Dunciade*
D *Das Lied vom Dummkopf*
I *La zucconeide*
E *La dunciada*
SU «Дунсиа́да» (Поп)

1064 GB Dunkirk (France)
F Dunkerque (France)
D Dünkirchen (Frankreich)
I Dunkerque (Francia)
E Dunkerque (Francia)
SU Дюнке́рк (Фра́нция)

1065 GB Duns Scotus (*1266*–1308)
F Duns Scot
D Duns Scotus
I Duns Scoto
E Duns Escoto
SU Дунс Скот

1066 GB Dürer (1471–1528)
F Dürer
D Dürer
I Dürer
E Durero
SU Дю́рер

1067 GB Dutch East Indies, the (hist.)
     F   les Indes orientales hollandaises (hist.)
     D   Niederländisch-Ostindien (Gesch.)
     I   le Indie Orientali Olandesi (st.)
     E   las Indias Orientales Holandesas (hist.)
     SU Голла́ндская Ост-Йндия (ист.)

1068 GB *Dwarf, The* [*Dvärgen*] (Lagerkvist, 1945)
     F   *Le Nain*
     D   *Der Zwerg*
     I   *Il nano*
     E   *El enano*
     SU «Ка́рлик» (Ла́герквист)

1069 GB *Dynasts, The* (Hardy, 1904–8)
     F   *Les Dynastes*
     D   *Die Herrscher*
     I   *I dinasti*
     E   *Los dinastas*
     SU «Дина́сты» (Ха́рди)

E

1070 GB   *Eagle and the Serpent, The* (Guzmán, 1928)
     F   *L'Aigle et le serpent*
     D   *Adler und Schlange*
     I   *L'aquila e il serpente*
     E   *El águila y la serpiente*
     SU   «Орёл и змея́ (Гусма́н)

1071 GB   *Earth is Round, The* (Salacrou, 1938)
     F   *La Terre est ronde*
     D   *Die Erde ist rund*
     I   *La terra è rotonda*
     E   *La tierra es redonda*
     SU   «Земля́ кругла́» (Салакру́)

1072 GB   East Africa
     F   l'Afrique orientale
     D   Ostafrika
     I   l'Africa orientale
     E   el África oriental
     SU   Восто́чная А́фрика

1073 GB   East Berlin (Germany)
     F   Berlin-Est (Allemagne)
     D   Ostberlin (Deutschland)
     I   Berlino Est (Germania)
     E   Berlín Este (Alemania)
     SU   Восто́чный Берли́н (Герма́ния)

1074 GB   Easter (rel.)
     F   Pâques (relig.)
     D   das Ostern (relig.)
     I   la Pasqua (relig.)
     E   la Pascua (relig.)
     SU   па́сха (рел.)

1075 GB   Easter Island
     F   l'île de Pâques
     D   Osterinsel
     I   l'isola di Pasqua
     E   la isla de Pascua
     SU   о́стров Па́схи

1076 GB   East Falkland (Falkland Islands)
     F   Falkland orientale (îles Falklands)
     D   Ostfalkland (Falklandinseln)
     I   Falkland Orientale (isole Falkland)
     E   Soledad (Malvinas)
     SU   Восто́чный Фолкле́нд (Фолкле́ндские острова́)

1077 GB   East India Company, the (hist.)
     F   la Compagnie des Indes orientales (hist.)
     D   die Ostindische Kompanie (Gesch.)
     I   la Compagnia delle Indie orientali (st.)
     E   la Compañía General de las Indias Orientales (hist.)
     SU   Ост-И́ндская компа́ния (ист.)

1078 GB   East Indies, the (hist.)
     F   les Indes orientales (hist.)
     D   Ostindien (Gesch.)
     I   le Indie Orientali (st.)
     E   las Indias Orientales (hist.)
     SU   Ост-И́ндия (ист.)

1079 GB   *East of Eden* (Steinbeck, 1952)
     F   *À l'est d'Éden*
     D   *Jenseits von Eden*
     I   *La Valle dell'Eden*
     E   *Al este del Edén*
     SU   «К восто́ку от ра́я» (Сте́йнбек)

1080 GB   *East Wind, West Wind* (Buck, 1930)
     F   *Vent d'est, vent d'ouest*
     D   *Ostwind-Westwind*
     I   *Vento d'est, vento di ponente*
     E   *Viento del Este, viento del Oeste*
     SU   «Восто́чный ве́тер, за́падный ве́тер» (Бак)

1081 GB *Easy Street* (Chaplin, 1917)
       F *Charlot ne s'en fait pas*
       D *Easy Street*
       I *Charlot poliziotto*
       E *Charlot en la calle de la Paz*
       SU «Тихая улица» (Чаплин)

1082 GB Ecclesiastes (Bib.)
       F l'Ecclésiaste (m.) (Bib.)
       D Prediger Salomonis (Bib.)
       I l'Ecclesiaste (Bib.)
       E El Eclesiastés (Bib.)
       SU «Екклезиаст» (библ.)

1083 GB Ecclesiasticus (Bib.)
       F l'Ecclésiastique (m.) (Bib.)
       D Die Weisheit des Jesus Sirach (Bib.)
       I l'Ecclesiastico (Bib.)
       E El Eclesiástico (Bib.)
       SU «Мудрость Иисуса сына Сирахова» (библ.)

1084 GB Echidna, the (myth.)
       F Échidna (myth.)
       D Echidna (myth.)
       I Echidna (mit.)
       E Equidna (mit.)
       SU Ехидна (миф.)

1085 GB Echo (myth.)
       F Écho (myth.)
       D Echo (myth.)
       I Eco (mit.)
       E Eco (mit.)
       SU Эхо (миф.)

1086 GB *Eclogues*, the [*Eclogae*] (Virgil, −37)
       F les *Églogues* (Virgile)
       D die *Eklogen* (Vergil)
       I le *Ecloghe* (Virgilio)
       E las *Églogas* (Virgilio)
       SU «Эклоги» (Вергилий)

1087 GB Ecuador
       F l'Équateur (m.)
       D Ecuador
       I l'Ecuador
       E el Ecuador
       SU Экуадор

1088 GB Eden (Bib.)
       F Éden (Bib.)
       D Eden (Bib.)
       I Eden (Bib.)
       E Edén (Bib.)
       SU Эдём (библ.)

1089 GB Edict of Nantes, the (1598)
       F l'édit de Nantes
       D das Edikt von Nantes
       I l'editto di Nantes
       E el edicto de Nantes
       SU Нантский эдикт

1090 GB Edinburgh (Scotland)
       F Édimbourg (Écosse)
       D Edinburgh (Schottland)
       I Edimburgo (Scozia)
       E Edimburgo (Escocia)
       SU Эдинбург (Шотландия)

1091 GB Edward (saint, king)
       F Édouard (saint, roi)
       D Eduard (Heiliger, König)
       I Edoardo (santo, rey)
       E Eduardo (santo, rey)
       SU Эдуард (св., прав.)

1092 GB Edward the Confessor (*1003*–1066)
       F Édouard le Confesseur
       D Eduard der Bekenner
       I Edoardo il Confessore
       E Eduardo el Confesor
       SU Эдуард Исповедник

       GB *Edwin Drood→Mystery of Edwin Drood*

1093 GB *Egmont* (Goethe, 1788)
       F *Egmont*
       D *Egmont*
       I *Egmont*
       E *Egmont*
       SU «Эгмонт» (Гёте)

1094 GB *Ego and the Id, The* (Freud, 1923)
       F *Le Moi et le soi*
       D *Das Ich und das Es*
       I *L'Io e l'Es*
       E *El yo y el ello*
       SU «Я и Оно» (Фрейд)

1095 GB *Egoist, The* (Meredith, 1879)
       F *L'Égoïste*
       D *Der Egoist*
       I *L'egoista*
       E *El egoísta*
       SU «Эгоист» (Мередит)

1096 GB Egypt
       F l'Égypte (f.)
       D Ägypten
       I l'Egitto
       E Egipto
       SU Египет

1097 GB Eiffel Tower, the (Paris)
      F   la tour Eiffel (Paris)
      D   der Eiffelturm (Paris)
      I   la Torre Eiffel (Parigi)
      E   la torre Eiffel (París)
      SU Эйфелова башня (Париж)

1098 GB *Eight and a Half* (Fellini, 1963)
      F   *Huit et demi*
      D   *Achtundeinhalb*
      I   *Otto e mezzo*
      E   *Ocho y media*
      SU «Восемь с половиной» (Феллини)

1099 GB *El* [*Him*] (Buñuel, 1953)
      F   *Él*
      D   *Er*
      I   *Él*
      E   *Él*
      SU «Он» (Бюнюэль)

1100 GB Elba (Italy)
      F   Elbe (Italie)
      D   Elba (Italien)
      I   Elba (Italia)
      E   Elba (Italia)
      SU Эльба (Италия)

1101 GB Elbe (River) the (Germany)
      F   l'Elbe (m.) (Allemagne)
      D   die Elbe (Deutschland)
      I   l'Elba (Germania)
      E   el Elba (Alemania)
      SU Эльба (Германия)

1102 GB Eldorado (myth.)
      F   Eldorado (myth.)
      D   Eldorado (myth.)
      I   Eldorado (mit.)
      E   El Dorado (mit.)
      SU Эльдорадо (миф.)

1103 GB Electra (myth., + Euripides, −413; Sophocles, −413)
      F   Électre (myth., + Euripide, Sophocle)
      D   Elektra (myth., + Euripides, Sophokles)
      I   Elettra (mit., + Euripide, Sofocle)
      E   Electra (mit., + Eurípides, Sófocles)
      SU Электра (миф., + Еврипид, Софокл)

1104 GB *Elegies* [*Elegiae*] (Propertius, −1)
      F   *Élégies* (Properce)
      D   *Elegien* (Propertius)
      I   *Elegie* (Properzio)
      E   *Elegías* (Propercio)
      SU «Элегии» (Проперций)

1105 GB *Elegy (Written) in a Country Churchyard* (Gray, 1751)
      F   *Élégie écrite dans un cimetière de campagne*
      D   *Elegie auf einem Dorfkirchhof*
      I   *Elegia scritta in un cimitero di campagna*
      E   *Elegía escrita en un cementerio de aldea*
      SU «Элегия, написанная на сельском кладбище» (Грей)

1106 GB *Elephant Boy* (Flaherty, 1937)
      F   *Sabu*
      D   *Elefanten-Boy*
      I   *La Danza degli elefanti*
      E   *Sabú*
      SU «Сабу» (Флаэрти)

1107 GB Eleusinian Mysteries, the (rel.)
      F   les mystères d'Eleusis (relig.)
      D   die Eleusinischen Mysterien (relig.)
      I   i misteri eleusini (relig.)
      E   los misterios de Eleusis (relig.)
      SU Элевсинские мистерии (рел.)

1108 GB Elijah (Bib.)
      F   Élie (Bib.)
      D   Elias (Bib.)
      I   Elia (Bib.)
      E   Elías (Bib.)
      SU Илия (библ.)

1109 GB Elisha (Bib.)
      F   Élisée (Bib.)
      D   Elisa (Bib.)
      I   Eliseo (Bib.)
      E   Eliseo (Bib.)
      SU Елисей (библ.)

1110 GB *Elixir of Love, The* (Donizetti, 1832)
      F   *L'Elixir d'amour*
      D   *Der Liebestrank*
      I   *L'elisir d'amore*
      E   *El elixir de amor*
      SU «Любовный напиток» (Доницетти)

1111 GB Elizabeth (saint, sovereign)
      F   Élisabeth (sainte, souveraine)
      D   Elisabeth (Heilige, Herr.)
      I   Elisabetta (santa, sovrana)
      E   Isabel (santa, sob.)
      SU Елизавета (св., прав.)

1112 GB El Salvador
      F   le Salvador
      D   El Salvador
      I   El Salvador
      E   El Salvador
      SU Сальвадор

1113 GB Elysium (myth.)
F l'Élysée (m.) (myth.)
D Elysium (myth.)
I Elisio (mit.)
E Elíseo (mit.)
SU Элизиум (миф.)

1114 GB *Embezzlers, The* (Katayev, 1926)
F *Les Gaspilleurs* (Kataiev)
D *Die Verschwender* (Katajew)
I *I truffatori* (Kataiev)
E *Desfalco en Moscú* (Katayev)
SU «Растратчики» (Катаев)

1115 GB *Emil and the Detectives* (Kästner, 1929)
F *Émile et les détectives*
D *Emil und die Detektive*
I *Emilio e i detectives*
E *Emilio y los policías*
SU «Эмиль и сыщики» (Кёстнер)

1116 GB Emilia-Romagna (Italy)
F l'Émilie-Romagne (f.) (Italie)
D Emilia Romagna (Italien)
I l'Emilia Romagna (Italia)
E Emilia (Italia)
SU Эмилия-Романья (Италия)

1117 GB *Emil, or a New System of Education* (Rousseau, 1762)
F *Émile ou De l'éducation*
D *Emile, oder Über die Erziehung*
I *Emilio o dell'educazione*
E *Emilio, o De la educación*
SU «Эмиль, или О воспитании» (Руссо)

1118 GB *Emma* (Austen, 1816)
F *Emma*
D *Emma*
I *Emma*
E *Emma*
SU «Эмма» (Остен)

1119 GB Emmanuel (Immanuel) (Bib.)
F Emmanuel (Bib.)
D Emanuel (Bib.)
I Emanuele (Bib.)
E Emmanuel (Bib.)
SU Еммануил (библ.)

1120 GB Empedocles (−V)
F Empédocle
D Empedokles
I Empedocle
E Empédocles
SU Эмпедокл

1121 GB *Emperor and Galilean* [*Kejser og Galilaeer*] (Ibsen, 1873)
F *Empereur et Galiléen*
D *Kaiser und Galiläer*
I *Cesare e Galileo*
E *Emperador y galileo*
SU «Кесарь и галилеянин» (Ибсен)

1122 GB *Emperor Jones, The* (O'Neill, 1920)
F *L'Empereur Jones*
D *Kaiser Jones*
I *L'imperatore Jones*
E *El emperador Jones*
SU «Император Джонс» (О'Нил)

1123 GB *Emperor's New Clothes, The* [*Kejserens nye klaeder*] (Andersen, 1835)
F *Les Nouveaux Vêtements de l'empereur*
D *Des Kaisers neue Kleider*
I *Il vestito nuovo dell'imperatore*
E *El traje nuevo del emperador*
SU «Новое платье короля» (Андерсен)

1124 GB *Empire Strikes Back, The* (Kershner, 1980)
F *L'empire contre-attaque*
D *Das Imperium schlägt zurück*
I *L'impero colpisce ancora*
E *El imperio contraataca*
SU «Империя контратакует» (Кёршнер)

1125 GB *Enamels and Cameos* (Gautier, 1852)
F *Émaux et Camées*
D *Emailmalereien und geschnittene Steine*
I *Smalti e cammei*
E *Esmaltes y camafeos*
SU «Эмали и камеи» (Готье)

1126 GB *Enchanted, The* (Giraudoux, 1933)
F *Intermezzo*
D *Intermezzo*
I *Intermezzo*
E *Intermezzo*
SU «Интермеццо» (Жироду)

1127 GB *Endgame* (Beckett, 1957)
F *Fin de partie*
D *Endspiel*
I *Fine di partita*
E *Fin de partida*
SU «Конец игры» (Беккет)

1128 GB *End of the Affair, The* (Greene, 1951)
F *La Fin d'une liaison*
D *Der Ausgangspunkt*
I *La fine dell'avventura*
E *El fin de la aventura*
SU «Конец дела» (Грин)

1129 GB Endymion (myth., + Keats, 1818)
    F Endymion (myth.)
    D Endymion (myth.)
    I Endimione (mit.)
    E Endimión (mit.)
    SU Эндимио́н (миф., + Китс)

1130 GB *Enemy of the People, An* [*En folkefiende*] (Ibsen, 1882)
    F *Un ennemi du peuple*
    D *Ein Volksfeind*
    I *Un nemico del popolo*
    E *Un enemigo del pueblo*
    SU «Враг наро́да» (Йбсен)

1131 GB *Enfants du Paradis, Les* [*Children of Paradise*] (Carné, 1944)
    F *Les Enfants du paradis*
    D *Kinder des Olymp*
    I *Les enfants du paradis*
    E *Les enfants du paradis*
    SU «Де́ти райка́» (Карне́)

1132 GB England
    F l'Angleterre (f.)
    D England
    I l'Inghilterra
    E Inglaterra
    SU А́нглия

1133 GB English Channel, the
    F la Manche
    D der Ärmenkanal
    I la Manica
    E el Canal de la Mancha
    SU Ла-Ма́нш

1134 GB English Civil War, the (1642–51)
    F la guerre civile anglaise
    D der englische Bürgerkrieg
    I la guerra civile inglese
    E la guerra civil inglesa
    SU Английская буржуа́зная револю́ция

1135 GB *English Humorists of the Eighteenth Century* (Thackeray, 1851)
    F *Les Humoristes anglais*
    D *Die englischen Humoristen*
    I *Gli umoristi inglesi del secolo XVIII*
    E *Los humoristas ingleses del siglo XVIII*
    SU «Англи́йские юмори́сты XVIII ве́ка» (Те́ккерей)

1136 GB Enlightenment, the (XVIII)
    F le siècle des lumières
    D die Aufklärung
    I l'illuminismo
    E la ilustración
    SU Просвеще́ние

1137 GB *Enneads*, the [*Nines*] (Plotinus, −III)
    F *Ennéades* (Plotin)
    D *Enneaden* (Plotinos)
    I *Enneadi* (Plotino)
    E *Enneadas* (Plotino)
    SU «Энне́ды» (Плоти́н)

1138 GB *Enoch Arden* (Tennyson, 1864)
    F *Enoch Arden*
    D *Enoch Arden*
    I *Enoch Arden*
    E *Enoch Arden*
    SU «Йнок А́рден» (Те́ннисон)

1139 GB Entente Cordiale, the (1904)
    F l'Entente cordiale
    D die Entente cordiale
    I l'Intesa cordiale
    E la Entente cordial
    SU Анта́нта

1140 GB *Entertainer, The* (Osborne, 1957)
    F *Comique*
    D *Der Entertainer*
    I *La persona divertente*
    E *El comediante*
    SU «Комедиа́нт» (О́сборн)

1141 GB Epaminondas (*410*–362)
    F Épaminondas
    D Epaminondas
    I Epaminonda
    E Epaminondas
    SU Эпамино́нд

1142 GB Ephesians, the Epistle of Paul to the (Bib.)
    F l'Épître de Saint Paul aux Éphésiens (Bib.)
    D der Epheserbrief (Bib.)
    I la lettera di Paolo agli Efesini (Bib.)
    E la Epístola de San Pablo a los efesios (Bib.)
    SU «Посла́ние к Ефе́сянам» (библ.)

1143 GB Ephesus (Bib.)
    F Éphèse (Bib.)
    D Ephesos (Bib.)
    I Efeso (Bib.)
    E Éfeso (Bib.)
    SU Эфе́с (библ.)

1144 GB Ephraim (Bib.)
    F Éphraïm (Bib.)
    D Ephraim (Bib.)
    I Efraim (Bib.)
    E Efraín (Bib.)
    SU Ефре́м (библ.)

1145 GB *Epicoene, or the Silent Woman*
(Jonson, 1609)
F *Épicène ou La Femme silencieuse*
D *Das stumme Mädchen*
I *La silenziosa*
E *Epicena o la mujer silenciosa*
SU «Эписи́н, и́ли Молчали́вая же́нщина»
(Джо́нсон)

1146 GB Epicurus (341–270)
F Épicure
D Epikur
I Epicuro
E Epicuro
SU Эпику́р

1147 GB Epimetheus (myth.)
F Épiméthée (myth.)
D Epimetheus (myth.)
I Epimeteo (mit.)
E Epimeteo (mit.)
SU Эпиметéй (миф.)

1148 GB Epiphany, the (rel.)
F l'Épiphanie (f.) (relig.)
D das Epiphaniusfest (relig.)
I l'Epifania (relig.)
E la Epifanía (relig.)
SU креще́ние (рел.)

GB Epistle of Paul to the . . . (Bib.)→
. . . , Epistle of Paul to the

1149 GB Equatorial Guinea
F la Guinée équatoriale
D Äquatorialguinea
I la Guinea Equatoriale
E Guinea Ecuatorial
SU Эквиториáльная Гвинéя

1150 GB Erasmus (*1466*–1536)
F Erasme
D Erasmus
I Erasmo
E Erasmo
SU Эрáзм Роттердáмский

1151 GB Erebus (myth.)
F Érèbe (myth.)
D Erebus (myth.)
I Erebo (mit.)
E Erebus (mit.)
SU Эрéб (миф.)

1152 GB *Erewhon* (Butler, 1872)
F *Erewhon*
D *Erewhon*
I *Erewhon*
E *Erewhon*
SU «Éгдин» (Бáтлер)

1153 GB *Erewhon Revisited* (Butler, 1901)
F *Nouveaux Voyages en Erewhon*
D *Das wiederbesuchte Erewhon*
I *Ritorno a Erewhon*
E *Regreso a Erewhon*
SU «Возвраще́ние в Éгдин» (Бáтлер)

1154 GB Eric the Red (X)
F Erik le Rouge
D Erich der Rote
I Erik il Rosso
E Erico el Rojo
SU Эйрик Рáуди

1155 GB Erik (king)
F Erik (roi)
D Erich (König)
I Erik (re)
E Erico (rey)
SU Эрик (прав.)

1156 GB Erinyes, the (myth.)
F les Érinyes (myth.)
D die Erinnyen (myth.)
I le Erinni (mit.)
E las Erinias (mit.)
SU Эри́нии (миф.)

1157 GB Eritrea (Ethiopia)
F l'Erythrée (f.) (Éthiopie)
D Eritrea (Äthiopien)
I l'Eritrea (Etiopia)
E Eritrea (Etiopia)
SU Эритрéя (Эфиóпия)

1158 GB *Ermine, The* (Anouilh, 1932)
F *L'Hermine*
D *Der Hermelin*
I *L'ermellino*
E *El armiño*
SU «Горностáй» (Анýй)

1159 GB *Ernani* (Verdi, 1844)
F *Ernani*
D *Ernani*
I *Ernani*
E *Ernani*
SU «Эрнáни» (Вéрди)

1160 GB *Eroica* Symphony, the (Beethoven, 1804)
F la symphonie *Héroïque*
D die *Eroica-Sinfonie*
I la sinfonia *Eroica*
E la sinfonía *Eroica*
SU «Герои́ческая» симфо́ния (Бетхо́вен)

1161 GB Eros (myth.)
F Éros (myth.)
D Eros (myth.)
I Eros (mit.)
E Eros (mit.)
SU Эро́т (миф.)

1162 GB Esau (Bib.)
F Ésaü (Bib.)
D Esau (Bib.)
I Esaù (Bib.)
E Esaú (Bib.)
SU Иса́в (библ.)

1163 GB Esdras (Bib.)
F Esdras (Bib.)
D Esdras (Bib.)
I Esdra (Bib.)
E Esdras (Bib.)
SU Э́здра (библ.)

1164 GB Eskimos, the
F les Esquimaux
D die Eskimos
I gli eschimesi
E los esquimales
SU эскимо́сы

1165 GB *Essay Concerning Human Understanding* (Locke, 1689)
F *Essai sur l'entendement humain*
D *Versuch über den menschlichen Verstand*
I *Saggio sull'intelletto umano*
E *Ensayo sobre el entendimiento humano*
SU «О́пыт о челове́ческом ра́зуме» (Локк)

1166 GB *Essay on Conic Sections, An* (Pascal, 1639)
F *Essai sur les coniques*
D *Abhandlung über die Kegelschnitte*
I *Saggio sulle coniche*
E *Ensayo sobre las secciones cónicas*
SU «Опыт тео́рии кони́ческих сече́ний» (Паска́ль)

1167 GB *Essay on Dramatic Poesy, An* (Dryden, 1668)
F *Essai sur la poésie dramatique*
D *Essay über dramatische Dichtung*
I *Saggio sulla poesia drammatica*
E *Ensayo sobre la poesía dramática*
SU «О́пыт о драмати́ческой поэ́зии» (Дра́йден)

1168 GB *Essay on Indifference Toward Religion* (Lamennais, 1817–23)
F *Essai sur l'indifférence en matière religieuse*
D *Über religiöse Gleichgültigkeit*
I *Saggio sull'indifferenza in materia di religione*
E *Ensayo sobre la indiferencia en materia de religión*
SU «О́пыт о безразли́чии к рели́гии» (Ламенне́)

1169 GB *Essay on Man, An* (Pope, 1734)
F *Essai sur l'homme*
D *Versuch über den Menschen*
I *Saggio sull'uomo*
E *Ensayo sobre el hombre*
SU «О́пыт о челове́ке» (Поп)

1170 GB *Essay on the Customs and the Spirit of Nations* (Voltaire, 1756–69)
F *Essai sur l'histoire générale et sur les moeurs et l'esprit des Nations*
D *Abhandlung über die allgemeine Geschichte und über Sitten und Geist der Völker*
I *Saggio sui costumi e sullo spirito delle nazioni*
E *Ensayo sobre las costumbres y el espíritu de los naciones*
SU «О́пыт о нра́вах и ду́хе наро́дов» (Вольте́р)

1171 GB *Essay on the Immediate Data of Consciousness, An* (Bergson, 1889)
F *Essai sur les données immédiates de la conscience*
D *Essay über die unmittelbaren Gaben des Bewußtseins*
I *Saggio sui dati immediati della coscienza*
E *Ensayo sobre los datos inmediatos de la conciencia*
SU «О́пыт о непосре́дственных да́нных созна́ния» (Бергсо́н)

1172   GB   *Essay on the Inequality of the Human*
            Races (Gobineau, 1853–5)
      F   *Essai sur l'inégalité des races humaines*
      D   *Essay über die Ungleichheit der*
            Menschenrassen
      I   *Saggio sulla ineguaglianza delle razze*
            umane
      E   *Ensayo sobre la desigualdad de las*
            razas humanas
      SU «О нера́венстве челове́ческих рас»
            (Гобино́)

1173   GB   *Essay on the Principle of Population,*
            An (Malthus, 1798)
      F   *Essai sur le principe de population*
      D   *Mensches Bevölkerungsgesetz*
      I   *Saggio sul principio della popolazione*
      E   *Ensayo sobre el principio de la*
            población
      SU «О́пыт о зако́не народонаселе́ния»
            (Ма́льтус)

1174   GB   *Essays* (Montaigne, 1580–8)
      F   les *Essais*
      D   die *Essais*
      I   *Saggi*
      E   los *Ensayos*
      SU «О́пыты» (Монте́нь)

1175   GB   Esther (Bib.; + Racine, 1689; Adams,
            1884)
      F   Esther (Bib.)
      D   Esther (Bib.)
      I   Ester (Bib.)
      E   Ester (Bib.)
      SU Эсфи́рь (библ., + Раси́н, А́дамс)

1176   GB   *Esther Waters* (Moore, 1894)
      F   *Esther Waters*
      D   *Esther Waters*
      I   *Esther Waters*
      E   *Esther Waters*
      SU «Э́стер Уо́терс» (Мур)

1177   GB   Estonia (USSR)
      F   l'Estonie (f.) (URSS)
      D   Estland (UdSSR)
      I   l'Estonia (URSS)
      E   Estonia (URSS)
      SU Эсто́ния (СССР)

1178   GB   Estremadura (Extremadura) (Spain)
      F   l'Estrémadure (f.) (Espagne)
      D   Estremadura (Spanien)
      I   l'Estremadura (Spagna)
      E   Extremadura (España)
      SU Эстремаду́ра (Испа́ния)

1179   GB   Eternal City, the (= Rome)
      F   la Ville éternelle (= Rome)
      D   die Ewige Stadt (= Rom)
      I   la Città Eterna (= Roma)
      E   la Ciudad Eterna (= Roma)
      SU «Ве́чный го́род» (= Рим)

1180   GB   *Eternal Husband, The* (Dostoievsky,
            1870)
      F   *Le Mari éternel* (Dostoïevski)
      D   *Der ewige Mann* (Dostojewskij)
      I   *Il marito eterno* (Dostoevskij)
      E   *El marido eterno* (Dostoievski)
      SU «Ве́чный муж» (Достое́вский)

1181   GB   *Ethics* (Spinoza, 1675)
      F   l'*Éthique*
      D   *Die Ethik*
      I   *L'Etica*
      E   *Ética*
      SU «Э́тика» (Спино́за)

1182   GB   Ethiopia
      F   l'Éthiopie
      D   Äthiopien
      I   l'Etiopia
      E   Etiopía
      SU Эфио́пия

1183   GB   Etna, Mount (Italy)
      F   Etna (Italie)
      D   Ätna (Italien)
      I   Etna (Italia)
      E   Etna (Italia)
      SU Э́тна (Ита́лия)

1184   GB   Etruscans, the (hist.)
      F   les Étrusques (hist.)
      D   die Etrusker (Gesch.)
      I   gli etruschi (st.)
      E   los etruscos (hist.)
      SU этру́ски (ист.)

1185   GB   *E.T. the Extra-Terrestrial* (Spielberg,
            1982)
      F   *E.T.*
      D   *E.T. Der Außerirdische*
      I   *E.T. L'extraterrestre*
      E   *E.T.*
      SU «Э.Т. – Внеземно́й» (Спи́лберг)

1186   GB   Euboea (Greece)
      F   l'Eubée (f.) (Grèce)
      D   Euböa (Griechenland)
      I   l'Eubea (Grecia)
      E   Eubea (Grecia)
      SU Эфбе́я (Гре́ция)

1187   GB   Euclid (−III)
       F   Euclide
       D   Euklides
       I   Euclide
       E   Euclides
       SU   Евклид

1188   GB   *Eugene Aram* (Bulwer-Lytton, 1832)
       F   *Eugène Aram*
       D   *Eugene Aram*
       I   *Eugene Aram*
       E   *Eugene Aram*
       SU   «Юджин Арам» (Булвер-Литтон)

1189   GB   *Eugene Onegin* (Pushkin, 1833;
            Tchaikovsky, 1879)
       F   *Eugène Onéguine* (Pouchkine,
            Tchaikovski)
       D   *Eugen Onegin* (Puschkin,
            Tschaikowskij)
       I   *Eugenio Onegin* (Puškin, Čajkovskij)
       E   *Eugenio Onieguin* (Puschkin,
            Tchaikovski)
       SU   «Евгений Онегин» (Пушкин,
            Чайковский)

1190   GB   *Eugénie Grandet* (Balzac, 1833)
       F   *Eugénie Grandet*
       D   *Eugénie Grandet*
       I   *Eugenia Grandet*
       E   *Eugenia Grandet*
       SU   «Евгения Гранде» (Бальзак)

1191   GB   Eugenius (pope)
       F   Eugène (pape)
       D   Eugen (Papst)
       I   Eugenio (papa)
       E   Eugenio (papa)
       SU   Евгений (папа римский)

1192   GB   Eumenes (king)
       F   Eumène (roi)
       D   Eumenes (König)
       I   Eumene (re)
       E   Eumenes (rey)
       SU   Евмен (царь)

1193   GB   Eumenides, the (myth., + Aeschylus,
            −458)
       F   les Euménides (myth., + Eschyle)
       D   die Eumeniden (myth., + Äschylus)
       I   le Eumenidi (mit., + Eschilo)
       E   las Euménides (mit., + Esquilo)
       SU   Евмениды (миф., + Эсхил)

1194   GB   *Eunuch, The* [*Eunuchus*] (Terence)
       F   *L'Eunuque* (Térence)
       D   *Der Eunuch* (Terentius)
       I   *Il eunuco* (Terenzio)
       E   *El eunuco* (Terencio)
       SU   «Евнух» (Теренций)

1195   GB   Euphrates (River), the (Asia)
       F   l'Euphrate (Asie)
       D   der Euphrat (Asien)
       I   l'Eufrate (Asia)
       E   el Éufrates (Asia)
       SU   Евфрат (Азия)

1196   GB   Euphrosyne (myth.)
       F   Euphrosyne (myth.)
       D   Euphrosyne (myth.)
       I   Eufrosine (mit.)
       E   Eufrosina (mit.)
       SU   Евфросина (миф.)

1197   GB   Eurasia
       F   l'Eurasie (f.)
       D   Eurasien
       I   l'Eurasia
       E   Eurasia
       SU   Евразия

1198   GB   Euripides (*480*–406)
       F   Euripide
       D   Euripides
       I   Euripide
       E   Eurípides
       SU   Еврипид

1199   GB   Europa (myth.)
       F   Europe (myth.)
       D   Europa (myth.)
       I   Europa (mit.)
       E   Europa (mit.)
       SU   Европа (миф.)

1200   GB   Europe
       F   l'Europe (f.)
       D   Europa
       I   l'Europa
       E   Europa
       SU   Европа

1201 GB European Atomic Energy Community, the (Euratom)
F la Communauté européenne de l'énergie atomique (Euratom)
D die Europäische Atomgemeinschaft (Euratom)
I la Comunità europea dell'energia atomica (Euratom)
E la Comunidad Europea de la Energía Atómica (Euratom)
SU Европейское сообщество по áтомной энéргии (Еврáтом)

1202 GB European Coal and Steel Community, the (ECSC)
F la Communauté européenne du charbon et de l'acier (CECA)
D die Europäische Gemeinschaft für Kohle und Stahl (EGKS)
I la Comunità europea del carbone e dell'acciaio (CECA)
E la Comunidad Europea del Carbón y del Acero (CECA)
SU Европейское объединéние ýгля и стáли (ЕОУС)

1203 GB European Council for Nuclear Research, the (CERN)
F le Conseil européen pour la recherche nucléaire (CERN)
D die Europäische Organization für Kernforschung (CERN)
I il Consiglio europeo per la ricerca nucleare (CERN)
E el Consejo Europeo por la Investigación Nuclear (CERN)
SU Европейская организáция я́дерных исслéдований (ЦЕРН)

1204 GB European Economic Community, the (EEC)
F la Communauté économique européenne (CEE)
D die Europäische Wirtschaftsgemeinschaft (EWG)
I la Comunità economica europea (CEE)
E la Comunidad Económica Europea (CEE)
SU Европейское экономи́ческое сообщество (ЕЭС)

1205 GB European Free Trade Association, the (EFTA)
F l'Association européenne de libre-échange (AELE)
D die Europäische Freihandelszone (EFTA)
I l'Associazione europea di libero scambio (EFTA)
E la Asociación europea del librecambio (EFTA)
SU Европéйская ассоциáция свобóдной торгóвли (ЕАСТ)

1206 GB Eurydice (myth.)
F Eurydice (myth.)
D Eurydike (myth.)
I Euridice (mit.)
E Eurídice (mit.)
SU Эвриди́ка (миф.)

1207 GB Eusebius (pope)
F Eusèbe (pape)
D Eusebius (Papst)
I Eusebio (papa)
E Eusebio (papa)
SU Евсéбий (пáпа ри́мский)

1208 GB Eustace (sovereign)
F Eustache (souverain)
D Eustachius (Herr.)
I Eustazio (sovrano)
E Eustaquio (sob.)
SU Евстáхий (прав.)

1209 GB *Evangeline* (Longfellow, 1847)
F *Évangéline*
D *Evangeline*
I *Evangelina*
E *Evangelina*
SU «Эванджели́на» (Лонгфéлло)

1210 GB Eve (Bib.)
F Ève (Bib.)
D Eva (Bib.)
I Eva (Bib.)
E Eva (Bib.)
SU Éва (библ.)

1211 GB *Evenings on a Farm near Dikanka* (Gogol, 1831–2)
F *Les Veillées à la ferme de Dikanka*
D *Abende auf dem Vorwerk bei Dikanka*
I *Veglie alla fattoria presso Dikan'ka*
E *Veladas en un caserío de Dikanka*
SU «Вечерá на хýторе близ Дикáньки» (Гóголь)

1212 GB   *Eve of St Agnes, The* (Keats, 1819)
  F   *La Veille de la Sainte-Agnès*
  D   *Sankt Agnes-Abend*
  I   *La vigilia di santa Agnese*
  E   *La víspera de Santa Inés*
  SU «Канýн святóй Агнéссы» (Китс)

1213 GB   Everest, Mount
  F   le mont Everest
  D   der Mount Everest
  I   l'Everest
  E   el monte Everest
  SU Эверéст

1214 GB   *Every Man In His Humour* (Jonson, 1598)
  F   *Chacun dans son caractère*
  D   *Jeder im Gleichgewicht*
  I   *Ognuno nel proprio umore*
  E   *Cada uno en su papel*
  SU «Всяк в своём нрáве» (Джóнсон)

1215 GB   *Execution of Emperor Maximilian of Mexico, The* (Manet, 1867)
  F   *L'Exécution de Maximilien*
  D   *Die Erschießung Maximilians von Mexiko*
  I   *La fucilazione dell'imperatore Massimiliano*
  E   *Fusilamiento del emperador Maximiliano*
  SU «Казнь импера́тора Максимилиа́на» (Мане́)

1216 GB   *Exile* (Saint-John Perse, 1942)
  F   *Exil*
  D   *Exil*
  I   *Esilio*
  E   *Exilio*
  SU «Изгна́ние» (Сен-Жон Перс)

1217 GB   Exodus (Bib.)
  F   l'Exode (m.) (Bib.)
  D   Exodus (Bib.)
  I   l'Esodo (Bib.)
  E   el Éxodo (Bib.)
  SU «Исхо́д» (библ.)

1218 GB   *Exorcist, The* (Friedkin, 1974)
  F   *L'Exorciste*
  D   *Der Exorzist*
  I   *L'esorcista*
  E   *El exorcista*
  SU «Заклина́тель» (Фри́дкин)

1219 GB   *Expedition of Humphry Clinker, The* (Smollett, 1771)
  F   *L'Expédition de Humphry Clinker*
  D   *Humphry Clinkers denkwürdige Reise*
  I   *La spedizione di Humphry Clinker*
  E   *La expedición de Humphry Clinker*
  SU «Путеше́ствие Ха́мфри Кли́нкера» (Смо́ллетт)

1220 GB   *Exterminating Angel, The* (Buñuel, 1962)
  F   *L'Ange exterminateur*
  D   *Der Würgengel*
  I   *L'angelo sterminatore*
  E   *El ángel exterminador*
  SU «А́нгел истребле́ния» (Бюнюэ́ль)

1221 GB   *Extraordinary Adventures of Julio Jurenito, The* (Ehrenburg, 1922)
  F   *Les Aventures extraordinaires de Julio Jurenito* (Ehrenbourg)
  D   *Die ungewöhnlichen Abenteuer des Julio Jurenito* (Ehrenburg)
  I   *Le straordinarie avventure di Julio Jurenito* (Erenburg)
  E   *Las aventuras de Julio Jurenito* (Ehrenburg)
  SU «Необыча́йные похожде́ния Ху́лио Хурени́то» (Эренбу́рг)

1222 GB   *Eyeless in Gaza* (Huxley, 1936)
  F   *La Paix des profondeurs*
  D   *Geblendet in Gaza*
  I   *La catena del passato*
  E   *Ciego en Gaza*
  SU «Слепо́й в Га́зе» (Ха́ксли)

  GB   Extremadura→Estremadura

1223 GB   Ezekiel (Bib.)
  F   Ézéchiel (Bib.)
  D   Hesekiel (Bib.)
  I   Ezechiele (Bib.)
  E   Ezequiel (Bib.)
  SU Иезеки́ль (библ.)

1224 GB   Ezra (Bib.)
  F   Ezra (Bib.)
  D   Ezra (Bib.)
  I   Ezra (Bib.)
  E   Ezra (Bib.)
  SU Éзра (библ.)

F

1225
GB	Fabius Cunctator (−II)
F	Fabius Cunctator
D	Fabius Cunctator
I	Fabio il Temporeggiatore
E	Fabio Cunctátor
SU	Фа́бий Макси́м (Кункта́тор)

1226
GB	*Fables*, the (La Fontaine, 1668–94)
F	les *Fables*
D	die *Fabeln*
I	le *Favole*
E	las *Fábulas*
SU	«Ба́сни» (Лафонте́н)

1227
GB	Fabricius (−III)
F	Fabricius
D	Fabricius
I	Fabrizio
E	Fabricio
SU	Фабри́ций

1228
GB	*Face in the Crowd, A* (Kazan, 1957)
F	*Un homme dans la foule*
D	*Ein Gesicht in der Menge*
I	*Un volto nella folla*
E	*Una cara en el gentío*
SU	«Лицо́ в толпе́» (Ка́зан)

1229
GB	*Faerie Queene, The* (Spenser, 1590–1690)
F	*La Reine des fées*
D	*Die Feenkönigin*
I	*La regina delle fate*
E	*La reina de las hadas*
SU	«Короле́ва фей» (Спе́нсер)

1230
GB	Faeroe Islands, the
F	les îles Féroé
D	die Färöer-Inseln
I	le isole Faer Øer
E	las islas Feroe
SU	Фаре́рские острова́

1231
GB	*Fahrenheit 451* (Truffaut, 1966)
F	*Fahrenheit 451*
D	*Fahrenheit 451*
I	*Fahrenheit 451*
E	*Fahrenheit 451*
SU	«Фаренге́йт 451» (Трюффо́)

1232
GB	*Fair Helen, The* (Offenbach, 1864)
F	*La Belle Hélène*
D	*Die schöne Helena*
I	*La belle Hélène*
E	*La bella Helena*
SU	«Прекра́сная Еле́на» (Оффенба́х)

1233
GB	*Fair Maid of Perth, The* (Scott, 1828)
F	*La Jolie Fille de Perth*
D	*Das schöne Mädchen von Perth*
I	*La bella fanciulla di Perth*
E	*La linda muchacha de Perth*
SU	«Пе́ртская краса́вица» (Скотт)

1234
GB	*Faithful Shepherd, The* (Guarini, 1580–90)
F	*Le Pasteur fidèle*
D	*Der getreue Hirte*
I	*Il pastor fido*
E	*El pastor fiel*
SU	«Ве́рный па́стух» (Гвари́ни)

1235
GB	Falkland Islands, the
F	les îles Falkland
D	die Falklandinseln
I	le isole Falkland
E	las islas Malvinas
SU	Фолкле́ндские острова́

1236
GB	*Fallen Idol, The* (Reed, 1948)
F	*Première désillusion*
D	*Kleines Herz in Not*
I	*Idolo infranto*
E	*El ídolo caído*
SU	«Па́вший и́дол» (Рид)

1237 GB *Fall of the House of Usher, The* (Poe, 1839)
F   *La Chute de la maison Usher*
D   *Der Untergang des Hauses Usher*
I   *La rovina della casa degli Usher*
E   *El fin de la casa Usher*
SU «Падéние дóма Эшер» (По)

1238 GB *False Confidences* (Marivaux, 1737)
F   *Les Fausses Confidences*
D   *Die falschen Vertraulichkeiten*
I   *Le false confidenze*
E   *Falsas confidencias*
SU «Лóжные призна́ния» (Мариво́)

1239 GB *Falstaff* (Verdi, 1893)
F   *Falstaff*
D   *Falstaff*
I   *Falstaff*
E   *Falstaff*
SU «Фáльстаф» (Вéрди)

1240 GB *Family Reunion, The* (Eliot, 1939)
F   *Réunion de famille*
D   *Der Familientag*
I   *La riunione di famiglia*
E   *La reunión de familia*
SU «Семéйная встрéча» (Э́лиот)

1241 GB *Famine* (O'Flaherty, 1934)
F   *Famine*
D   *Das schwarze Tal*
I   *Carestia*
E   *Hambre*
SU «Гóлод» (О'Фла́эрти)

1242 GB *Fanny* (Pagnol, 1931)
F   *Fanny*
D   *Fanny*
I   *Fanny*
E   *Fanny*
SU «Фанни́» (Панью́ль)

1243 GB *Fantasia* (Disney, 1940)
F   *Fantasia*
D   *Fantasia*
I   *Fantasia*
E   *Fantasía*
SU «Фанта́зия» (Ди́сней)

1244 GB *Fantastic Symphony*, the (Berlioz, 1830)
F   la *Symphonie fantastique*
D   die *Fantastische-Sinfonie*
I   la *Sinfonia fantastica*
E   la *Sinfonía fantástica*
SU «Фантасти́ческая симфóния» (Берлио́з)

1245 GB *Fantasy Pieces* (Hoffmann, 1814–15)
F   *Fantaisies dans la manière de Callot*
D   *Fantasiestücke in Callots Manier*
I   *Fantasie secondo Callot*
E   *Trozos de fantasía*
SU «Фанта́зии в ду́хе Калло́» (Гóфман)

1246 GB *Far East, the*
F   l'*Extrême-Orient*
D   der *Ferne Osten*
I   l'*Estremo Oriente*
E   el *Extremo Oriente*
SU Да́льний Востóк

1247 GB *Farewell to Arms, A* (Hemingway, 1929)
F   *L'Adieu aux armes*
D   *In einem anderen Land*
I   *Addio alle armi*
E   *El adiós a las armas*
SU «Проща́й, ору́жие!» (Хемингу́эй)

1248 GB *Far from the Madding Crowd* (Hardy, 1874)
F   *Loin de la foule hallucinante*
D   *Fern von der verwirrenden Menge*
I   *Via dalla pazza folla*
E   *Lejos de la muchedumbre enloquecedora*
SU «Вдали́ от обезуме́вшей толпы́» (Ха́рди)

1249 GB *Fasti* [*Calendar*] (Ovid)
F   les *Fastes* (m.) (Ovide)
D   die *Fasti* (Ovidius)
I   i *Fasti* (Ovidio)
E   los *Fastos* (Ovidio)
SU «Фа́сты» (Ови́дий)

1250 GB *Fates, the* (myth.)
F   les *Parques* (myth.)
D   die *Parzen* (myth.)
I   le *Parche* (mit.)
E   las *Parcas* (mit.)
SU па́рки (миф.)

1251 GB *Father, The* [*Fadren*] (Strindberg)
F   *Père*
D   *Der Vater*
I   *Il padre*
E   *Padre*
SU «Отéц» (Стри́ндберг)

GB Father Christmas→Santa Claus

1252　GB　*Father of the Family, The* (Diderot, 1758)
　　　F　*Le Père de famille*
　　　D　*Unterredung eines Vaters mit seinen Kindern*
　　　I　*Il padre di famiglia*
　　　E　*El padre de familia*
　　　SU　«Отец семейства» (Дидро́)

1253　GB　*Fathers and Sons* (Turgenev, 1862)
　　　F　*Pères et fils* (Tourgueniev)
　　　D　*Väter und Söhne* (Turgenjew)
　　　I　*Padri e figli* (Turgenev)
　　　E　*Padres e hijos* (Turgueniev)
　　　SU　«Отцы́ и де́ти» (Турге́нев)

1254　GB　Faunus (myth.)
　　　F　Faune (myth.)
　　　D　Faunus (myth.)
　　　I　Fauno (mit.)
　　　E　Fauno (mit.)
　　　SU　Фавн (миф.)

1255　GB　Faust (XVI; + Gounod, 1859)
　　　F　Faust
　　　D　Faust
　　　I　Faust
　　　E　Fausto
　　　SU　Фа́уст (+ Гуно́)

1256　GB　*Favourite, The* (Donizetti, 1840)
　　　F　*La Favorite*
　　　D　*Die Liebste*
　　　I　*La favorita*
　　　E　*La favorita*
　　　SU　«Фаворитка» (Доницетти)

1257　GB　*Feeling of Time, The* (Ungaretti, 1933)
　　　F　*Sentiment du temps*
　　　D　*Zeitgefühl*
　　　I　*Sentimento del tempo*
　　　E　*Sentimiento del tiempo*
　　　SU　«Чу́вство вре́мени» (Унгаре́тти)

1258　GB　Felix (pope)
　　　F　Félix (pape)
　　　D　Felix (Papst)
　　　I　Felice (papa)
　　　E　Félix (papa)
　　　SU　Фе́ликс (па́па ри́мский)

1259　GB　*Felix Holt* (Eliot, 1866)
　　　F　*Felix Holt*
　　　D　*Felix Holt*
　　　I　*Felix Holt*
　　　E　*Felix Holt*
　　　SU　«Фе́ликс Холт, радика́л» (Э́лиот)

1260　GB　Ferdinand (sovereign)
　　　F　Ferdinand (souverain)
　　　D　Ferdinand (Herr.)
　　　I　Ferdinando (sovrano)
　　　E　Fernando (sob.)
　　　SU　Фердина́нд (прав.)

1261　GB　*Fiery Angel, The* (Prokofiev, 1919–27)
　　　F　*L'Ange de feu*
　　　D　*Der Feuerengel*
　　　I　*L'angelo di fuoco*
　　　E　*El ángel de fuego*
　　　SU　«О́гненный а́нгел» (Проко́фьев)

1262　GB　Fiji
　　　F　les îles Fidji
　　　D　die Fidschi-Inseln
　　　I　le Figi
　　　E　Fidji
　　　SU　Фи́джи

1263　GB　*Financier, The* (Dreiser, 1912)
　　　F　*Le Financier*
　　　D　*Der Finanzmann*
　　　I　*Il finanziere*
　　　E　*El financiero*
　　　SU　«Финанси́ст» (Дра́йзер)

1264　GB　*Fin du jour, La* [*The End of the Day*] (Duvivier, 1939)
　　　F　*La Fin du jour*
　　　D　*Lebensabend*
　　　I　*Prigionieri del sogno*
　　　E　*Fin de jornada*
　　　SU　«Коне́ц дня» (Дювивье́)

1265　GB　*Fine Friend* (Maupassant, 1885)
　　　F　*Bel-Ami*
　　　D　*Bel-ami*
　　　I　*Bel-Ami*
　　　E　*Bel Ami*
　　　SU　«Ми́лый друг» (Мопасса́н)

1266　GB　*Fingal's Cave* (Mendelssohn, 1830)
　　　F　*La Grotte de Fingal* (Mendelssohn-Bartholdy)
　　　D　*Die Fingalshöhle* (Mendelssohn- Bartholdy)
　　　I　*La grotta di Fingal* (Mendelssohn-Bartholdy)
　　　E　*La gruta de Fingal* (Mendelssohn-Bartholdy)
　　　SU　«Финга́лова пеще́ра» (Мендельсо́н-Барто́льди)

1267 GB Finland
F la Finlande
D Finnland
I la Finlandia
E Finlandia
SU Финля́ндия

1268 GB Finland, the Gulf of
F le golfe de Finland
D der Finnische Meerbusen
I il golfo di Finlandia
E el golfo de Finlandia
SU Фи́нский зали́в

1269 GB *Finlandia* (Sibelius, 1899)
F *Finlandia*
D *Finlandia*
I *Finlandia*
E *Finlandia*
SU «Финля́ндия» (Сибе́лиус)

1270 GB *Finnegans Wake* (Joyce, 1939)
F *Finnegans Wake*
D *Finnegans Wake*
I *La veglia di Finnegan*
E *El despertar de Finnegan*
SU «Поми́нки по Фи́ннегану» (Джойс)

1271 GB *Firebird, The* (Stravinsky, 1910)
F *L'Oiseau de feu* (Stravinski)
D *Der Feuervogel* (Strawinski)
I *L'uccello di fuoco* (Stravinskij)
E *El pájaro de fuego* (Stravinski)
SU «Жар-пти́ца» (Страви́нский)

1272 GB *First Circle, The* (Solzhenitsyn, 1969)
F *Le Premier Cercle* (Soljenitsyne)
D *Der erste Kreis der Hölle* (Solschenizyn)
I *Il primo cerchio* (Solženicyn)
E *El primer círculo* (Soljenitsyn)
SU «В кру́ге пе́рвом» (Солжени́цын)

1273 GB *First Men in the Moon, The* (Wells, 1901)
F *Les Premiers Hommes dans la Lune*
D *Die ersten Menschen auf dem Mond*
I *I primi uomini sulla Luna*
E *Los primeros hombres en la Luna*
SU «Пе́рвые лю́ди на луне́» (Уэ́ллс)

1274 GB First World War, the (1914–18)
F la Première Guerre mondiale
D der erste Weltkrieg
I la prima guerra mondiale
E la primera guerra mundial
SU пе́рвая мирова́я война́

1275 GB *Fistful of Dollars, A* (Leone, 1964)
F *Pour une poignée de dollars*
D *Für eine Handvoll Dollar*
I *Per un pugno di dollari*
E *Por un puñado de dólares*
SU «Ра́ди приго́ршни до́лларов» (Лео́не)

1276 GB *Five Easy Pieces* (Rafelson, 1970)
F *Cinq Pièces faciles*
D *Fünf leichte Stücke*
I *Cinque pezzi facili*
E *Mi vida es mi vida*
SU «Пять лёгких музыка́льных пьес» (Ра́фельсон)

1277 GB *Five Weeks in a Balloon* (Verne, 1863)
F *Cinq Semaines en ballon*
D *Fünf Wochen im Ballon*
I *Cinque settimane in pallone*
E *Cinco semanas en globo*
SU «Пять неде́ль на возду́шном ша́ре» (Верн)

1278 GB Flanders (Belgium/France)
F la Flandre (Belge/France)
D Flandern (Belgien/Frankreich)
I le Fiandre (Belgio/Francia)
E Flandes (Bélgica/Francia)
SU Фла́ндрия (Бе́льгия/Фра́нция)

1279 GB Flavius (Roman name)
F Flavius (nom romain)
D Flavius (Römername)
I Flavio (nome romano)
E Flavio (nombre romano)
SU Фла́вий (древнери́мское и́мя)

1280 GB *Flies, The* (Sartre, 1942)
F *Les Mouches*
D *Die Fliegen*
I *Le mosche*
E *Las moscas*
SU «Му́хи» (Сартр)

1281 GB *Flight into Egypt, The* (art)
F *La Fuite en Égypte* (art)
D *Die Flucht nach Ägypten* (Kunst)
I *La fuga in Egitto* (arte)
E *La huida a Egipto* (arte)
SU «Бе́гство в Еги́пет» (иск.)

1282 GB *Flight to Arras* (Saint-Exupéry, 1942)
F *Pilote de guerre*
D *Flug nach Arras*
I *Pilota di guerra*
E *Piloto de guerra*
SU «Лётчик» (Сент-Экзюпери́)

1283 GB Flora (myth.)
F Flore (myth.)
D Flora (myth.)
I Flora (mit.)
E Flora (mit.)
SU Флóра (миф.)

1284 GB Florence (Italy)
F Florence (Italie)
D Florenz (Italien)
I Firenze (Italia)
E Florencia (Italia)
SU Флорéнция (Итáлия)

1285 GB Florida (USA)
F la Floride (USA)
D Florida (USA)
I Florida (USA)
E Florida (USA)
SU Флорúда (США)

1286 GB *Flowers of Evil, The* (Baudelaire, 1857)
F *Les Fleurs du mal*
D *Die Blumen der Bösen*
I *I fiori del male*
E *Las flores del mal*
SU «Цветы́ зла» (Бодлéр)

1287 GB Flushing (Netherlands)
F Flessingue (Pays-Bas)
D Vlissingen (Niederlande)
I Flessinga (Paesi Bassi)
E Flesinga (Holanda)
SU Флúссинген (Нидерлáнды)

1288 GB *Flying Dutchman, The* (Wagner, 1843)
F *Le Vaisseau fantôme*
D *Der fliegende Holländer*
I *L'Olandese volante*
E *El buque fantasma*
SU «Летýчий голлáндец» (Вáгнер)

1289 GB *Foma Gordeev* (Gorky, 1899)
F *Foma Gordeïev* (Gorki)
D *Foma Gordejew* (Gorkij)
I *Foma Gordeev* (Gor'kij)
E *Tomás Gordeief* (Gorki)
SU «Фомá Гордéев» (Гóрький)

1290 GB *Fontamara* (Silone, 1930)
F *Fontamara*
D *Fontamara*
I *Fontamara*
E *Fontamara*
SU «Фонтамáра» (Силóне)

1291 GB *Forbidden Paradise* (Lubitsch, 1924)
F *Paradis défendu*
D *Das verbotene Paradies*
I *La zarina*
E *La frivolidad de una dama*
SU «Запрéтный рай» (Лю́бич)

1292 GB *Force of Destiny, The* (Verdi, 1862)
F *La Force du destin*
D *Die Macht des Schicksals*
I *La forza del destino*
E *La fuerza del destino*
SU «Сúла судьбы́» (Вéрди)

1293 GB *Forefathers' Festival, The* [*Dziady*] (Mickiewicz, 1823–32)
F *Les Aïeux*
D *Ahnenfeier*
I *Gli avi*
E *Los antepasados*
SU «Дзя́ды» (Мицкéвич)

1294 GB Foreign Legion, the (France)
F la légion étrangère (France)
D die Fremdenlegion (Frankreich)
I la legione straniera (Francia)
E la legión extranjera (Francia)
SU инострáнный легиóн (Фрáнция)

1295 GB *Forge, The* (Le Nain, *1640*)
F *La Forge*
D *Die Schmiede*
I *La fucina*
E *La fragua*
SU «Кýзница» (Ленéн)

1296 GB *Forsyte Saga, The* (Galsworthy, 1922)
F *La Saga des Forsyte*
D *Die Forsyte Saga*
I *La saga dei Forsyte*
E *La saga de los Forsyte*
SU «Сáга о Фóрсайтах» (Гóлсуорси)

1297 GB Fortuna (Fortune) (myth.)
F Fortune (myth.)
D Fortuna (myth.)
I Fortuna (mit.)
E Fortuna (mit.)
SU Фортýна (миф.)

1298 GB *Fortunes of Nigel, The* (Scott, 1822)
F *La Fortune de Nigel*
D *Nigels Abenteuer*
I *Le avventure di Nigel*
E *La fortuna de Nigel*
SU «Приключéния Нáйджела» (Скотт)

1299   GB   *Forty-second Parallel, The* (Dos Passos, 1930)
      F   *Le 42ᵉ Parallèle*
      D   *Der 42. Breitengrad*
      I   *Il 42° parallelo*
      E   *Paralelo 42*
      SU   «42-я параллéль» (Дос Пáссос)

1300   GB   *For Whom the Bell Tolls* (Hemingway, 1940)
      F   *Pour qui sonne le glas*
      D   *Wem die Stunde schlägt*
      I   *Per chi suona la campana*
      E   *Por quién doblan las campanas*
      SU   «По ком звонúт кóлокол» (Хемингуэй)

      GB   Founding Fathers→Pilgrim Fathers

1301   GB   *Fountains of Rome, The* (Respighi, 1917)
      F   *Fontaines de Rome*
      D   *Die Fontänen in Rom*
      I   *Le fontane di Roma*
      E   *Las fuentes de Roma*
      SU   «Фонтáны Рúма» (Респúги)

1302   GB   *Four Feathers, The* (Mason, 1902)
      F   *Les Quatre Plumes blanches*
      D   *Vier Federn*
      I   *Le quattro piume*
      E   *Las cuatro plumas*
      SU   «Четы́ре перá» (Мéйсон)

1303   GB   Four Horsemen of the Apocalypse, the (Bib.) (+ Blasco Ibáñez, 1916; Ingram, 1921)
      F   les Quatre Cavaliers de l'Apocalypse (Bib.)
      D   die vier apokalyptischen Reiter (Bib.)
      I   i quattro cavalieri dall'Apocalisse (Bib.)
      E   los cuatro jinetes del Apocalipsis (Bib.)
      SU   «четы́ре всáдника Апокалúпсиса» (библ., + Блáско Ибáньес, Йнграм)

1304   GB   *Four Hundred Blows, The* (Truffaut, 1958)
      F   *Les Quatre Cents Coups*
      D   *Sie küßten und sie schlugen ihn*
      I   *I quattrocento colpi*
      E   *Los cuatrocientos golpes*
      SU   «Четы́реста удáров» (Трюффó)

1305   GB   *Four Quartets* (Eliot, 1936–42)
      F   *Les Quatre Quatuors*
      D   *Vier Quartette*
      I   *Quattro quartetti*
      E   *Cuatro cuartetos*
      SU   «Четы́ре квартéта» (Э́лиот)

1306   GB   *Four Seasons, The* (Vivaldi, *1725*)
      F   *Les Quatre Saisons*
      D   *Die Jahreszeiten*
      I   i *Concerti delle stagioni*
      E   *Las cuatro estaciones*
      SU   «Временá гóда» (Вивáльди)

      GB   Fra Angelico→Angelico, Fra

1307   GB   France
      F   la France
      D   Frankreich
      I   la Francia
      E   Francia
      SU   Фрáнция

1308   GB   Franche-Comté (France)
      F   la Franche-Comté (France)
      D   Franche-Comté (Frankreich)
      I   la Franca Contea (Francia)
      E   el Franco Condado (Francia)
      SU   Франш-Контé (Фрáнция)

1309   GB   *Franciada, The* (Ronsard, 1574)
      F   *La Franciade*
      D   *La Franciade*
      I   *La Franciade*
      E   *La Franciada*
      SU   «Франсиáда» (Ронсáр)

1310   GB   Francis (saint, sovereign)
      F   François (saint, souverain)
      D   Franz (Heiliger, Herr.)
      I   Francesco (santo, sovrano)
      E   Francisco (santo, sob.)
      SU   Францúск (св., прав.)

1311   GB   Francis Bacon (1561–1626)
      F   Francis Bacon
      D   Francis Bacon
      I   Francesco Bacone
      E   Francis Bacon
      SU   Фрэ́нсис Бэ́кон

1312   GB   Franciscans, the (rel.)
      F   les Franciscains (relig.)
      D   die Franziskaner (relig.)
      I   i francescani (relig.)
      E   los Franciscanos (relig.)
      SU   францискáнцы (рел.)

1313 GB Francis of Assisi (saint, 1181–1226)
  F François d'Assise (saint)
  D Franz von Assisi (Heiliger)
  I Francesco d'Assisi (santo)
  E Francisco de Asís (santo)
  SU Франци́ск Асси́зский (св.)

1314 GB Francis of Sales (saint, 1567–1622)
  F François de Sales (saint)
  D Franz von Sales (Heiliger)
  I Francesco di Sales (santo)
  E Francisco de Sales (santo)
  SU Франци́ск Са́льский (св.)

1315 GB Francis Xavier (1506–52)
  F François Xavier
  D Franz Xavier
  I Francesco Saverio
  E Francisco Javier
  SU Франци́ск Ксавье́

1316 GB Franconia (hist.)
  F la Franconie (hist.)
  D Franken (Gesch.)
  I la Franconia (st.)
  E Franconia (hist.)
  SU Франко́ния (ист.)

1317 GB Franco-Prussian War, the (1870–1)
  F la guerre franco-allemande
  D der Deutsch-Französische Krieg
  I la guerra franco-prussiana
  E la guerra franco-alemana
  SU Фра́нко-пру́сская война́

1318 GB Frankfurt am Main (Germany)
  F Francfort-sur-le-Main (Allemagne)
  D Frankfurt am Main (Deutschland)
  I Francoforte sul Meno (Germania)
  E Francfort del Meno (Alemania)
  SU Фра́нкфурт-на-Ма́йне (Герма́ния)

1319 GB Frankfurt an der Oder (Germany)
  F Francfort-sur-l'Oder (Alllemagne)
  D Frankfurt an der Oder (Deutschland)
  I Francoforte sull'Oder (Germania)
  E Francfort del Oder (Alemania)
  SU Фра́нкфурт-на-О́дере (Герма́ния)

1320 GB Franz Josef Land (USSR)
  F l'archipel François-Joseph (URSS)
  D Franz-Joseph-Land (UdSSR)
  I la Terra di Francesco Giuseppe (URSS)
  E la Tierra de Francisco José (URSS)
  SU Земля́ Фра́нца-Ио́сифа (СССР)

1321 GB Frederick (sovereign)
  F Frédéric (souverain)
  D Friedrich (Herr.)
  I Federico (sovrano)
  E Federico (sob.)
  SU Фре́дерик (прав.)

1322 GB Frederick the Great (1712–86)
  F Frédéric le Grand
  D Friedrich der Große
  I Federico il Grande
  E Federico el Grande
  SU Фре́дерик Вели́кий

1323 GB *Free Fall* (Golding, 1959)
  F *Chute libre*
  D *Freier Fall*
  I *Caduta libera*
  E *Caída libre*
  SU «Свобо́дное паде́ние» (Го́лдинг)

1324 GB Free French, the (1940)
  F la France Libre
  D das Freie Frankreich
  I la Francia libera
  E la Francia libre
  SU «Свобо́дная Фра́нция»

1325 GB *Freeshooter, The* (Weber, 1821)
  F *Le Freischütz*
  D *Der Freischütz*
  I *Il franco cacciatore*
  E *El freischütz*
  SU «Во́льный стрело́к» (Ве́бер)

1326 GB Freiburg (Germany)
  F Fribourg (Allemagne)
  D Freiburg (Deutschland)
  I Friburgo (Germania)
  E Friburgo (Alemania)
  SU Фре́йбург (Герма́ния)

1327 GB French Congo, the (hist.)
  F le Congo français (hist.)
  D Französisch-Kongo (Gesch.)
  I il Congo Francese (st.)
  E Congo Francés (hist.)
  SU Францу́зское Ко́нго (ист.)

1328 GB *French Connection, The* (Friedkin, 1971)
  F *La Loi de New-York*
  D *Brennpunkt Brooklyn*
  I *Il braccio violento della legge*
  E *Contra el imperio de la droga*
  SU «Францу́зская систе́ма свя́зи» (Фри́дкин)

1329 GB French Equatorial Africa (hist.)
       F   l'Afrique-Équatoriale française (AEF)
          (hist.)
       D   Französisch-Äquatorialafrika (Gesch.)
       I   l'Africa Equatoriale Francese (st.)
       E   África Ecuatorial Francesa (hist.)
      SU Францу́зская Экваториа́льная А́фрика
          (ист.)

1330 GB French Guiana
       F   la Guyana française
       D   Französisch-Guayana
       I   la Guayana Francese
       E   Guayana Francesa
      SU Францу́зская Гвиа́на

1331 GB *French Lieutenant's Woman, The*
          (Fowles, 1969; Reisz, 1981)
       F   *La Maîtresse du lieutenant français*
       D   *Die Geliebte des französichen*
          Leutnants
       I   *La donna del tenente francese*
       E   *La querida del teniente francés*
      SU «Же́нщина францу́зского лейтена́нта»
          (Фа́улс, Райс)

1332 GB French Revolution, the (1789–1815)
          (+ Carlyle, 1837)
       F   la Révolution française
       D   die Französische Revolution
       I   la rivoluzione francese
       E   la Revolución Francesa
      SU Вели́кая францу́зская револю́ция
          (+ Карле́йль)

1333 GB French Riviera, the (France)
       F   la Côte d'Azur (France)
       D   die französische Riviera (Frankreich)
       I   la Costa Azzurra (Francia)
       E   la Costa Azul (Francia)
      SU Лазу́рный бе́рег (Фра́нция)

1334 GB French West Africa (hist.)
       F   l'Afrique-Occidentale française (ADF)
          (hist.)
       D   Französisch-Westafrika (Gesch.)
       I   l'Africa Occidentale Francese (AOF)
          (st.)
       E   África Occidental Francesa (hist.)
      SU Францу́зская За́падная А́фрика (ист.)

1335 GB Fribourg (Switzerland)
       F   Fribourg (Suisse)
       D   Freiburg (Schweiz)
       I   Friburgo (Svizzera)
       E   Friburgo (Suiza)
      SU Фрубу́р (Швейца́рия)

1336 GB Friendly Islands, the (= Tonga)
       F   les îles des Amis
       D   die Freundschaftsinseln
       I   le isole degli Amici
       E   las islas de los Amigos
      SU острова́ Дру́жбы (= То́нга)

1337 GB *Friends for Life* (Rossi, 1955)
       F   *Amis pour la vie*
       D   *Freunde fürs Leben*
       I   *Amici per la pelle*
       E   *Inolvidable amistad*
      SU «Неразлу́чные друзья́» (Ро́сси)

1338 GB Frisian Islands, the
       F   les îles de la Frise
       D   die Friesischen Inseln
       I   le isole Frisone
       E   las islas Frisias
      SU Фри́зские острова́

1339 GB Friuli-Venezia Giulia (Italy)
       F   le Frioul-Vénétie Julienne (Italie)
       D   Friaul-Julisch-Venetien (Italien)
       I   il Friuli-Venezia Giulia (Italia)
       E   Friuli-Venecia Julia (Italia)
      SU Фриу́ли-Вене́ция-Джу́лия (Ита́лия)

1340 GB *Frogs, The* [*Batrachoi*] (Aristophanes,
          −405)
       F   *Les Grenouilles* (Aristophane)
       D   *Die Frösche* (Aristophanes)
       I   *Le rane* (Aristofane)
       E   *Las ranas* (Aristófanes)
      SU «Лягу́шки» (Аристофа́н)

1341 GB *From Here to Eternity* (Jones, 1951;
          Zinnemann, 1953)
       F   *Tant qu'il y aura des hommes*
       D   *Verdammt in alle Ewigkeit*
       I   *Da qui all'eternità*
       E   *De aquí a la eternidad*
      SU «Отны́не и во ве́ки веко́в» (Джонс,
          Зи́ннеманн)

1342 GB *From the Earth to the Moon* (Verne,
          1865)
       F   *De la Terre à la Lune*
       D   *Von der Erde zum Mond*
       I   *Dalla terra alla luna*
       E   *De la tierra a la luna*
      SU «С Земли́ на Луну́» (Верн)

1343   GB   *From the Life of a Ne'er-Do-Well*
                 (Eichendorff, 1826)
    F   *La Vie d'un propre à rien*
    D   *Aus dem Leben eines Taugenichts*
    I   *Storia di un fannullone*
    E   *Episodios de una vida tunante*
    SU «Из жи́зни одного́ безде́льника»
                 (Э́йхендорф)

1344   GB   *From the Morning Angelus to the*
                 Evening Angelus (Jammes, 1897)
    F   *De l'Angélus de l'aube à l'Angélus du*
                 soir
    D   *Vom Morgen- bis zum Abendläuten*
    I   *Dall'Angelus della mattina all'Angelus*
                 della sera
    E   *Del Toque del alba al Toque de la tarde*
    SU «От у́треннего бла́говеста до
                 вече́рнего» (Жамм)

1345   GB   Fronde, the (France, 1648–52)
    F   la Fronde (France)
    D   die Fronde (Frankreich)
    I   la Fronda (Francia)
    E   la Fronda (Francia)
    SU Фро́нда (Фра́нция)

1346   GB   *Frontenac Mystery, The* (Mauriac,
                 1933)
    F   *Le Mystère Frontenac*
    D   *Geheimnis Frontenac*
    I   *Il mistero Frontenac*
    E   *El misterio Frontenac*
    SU «Та́йна Фронтена́ка» (Мориа́к)

1347   GB   *Fruits of the Earth* (Gide, 1895)
    F   *Les Nourritures terrestres*
    D   *Uns nährt die Erde*
    I   *I nutrimenti terrestri*
    E   *Alimentos terrestres*
    SU «Я́ства земны́е» (Жид)

1348   GB   Furies, the (myth.)
    F   les Furies (myth.)
    D   die Furien (myth.)
    I   le Furie (mit.)
    E   las Furias (mit.)
    SU фу́рии (миф.)

1349   GB   *Fury* (Lang, 1936)
    F   *Furie*
    D   *Raserei*
    I   *Furia*
    E   *Furia*
    SU «Я́рость» (Ланг)

1350   GB   *Future of Science, The* (Renan, 1848)
    F   *L'Avenir de la science*
    D   *Die Zukunft der Wissenschaft*
    I   *L'avvenire della scienza*
    E   *El porvenir de la ciencia*
    SU «Бу́дущее нау́ки» (Рена́н)

G

1351	GB	Gabon	**1356**	GB	Galatea (myth.)
	F	le Gabon		F	Galatée (myth.)
	D	Gabun		D	Galatea (myth.)
	I	il Gabon		I	Galatea (mit.)
	E	Gabón		E	Galatea (mit.)
	SU	Габóн		SU	Галатéя (миф.)

1352 GB Gabriel (Bib.)
  F Gabriel (Bib.)
  D Gabriel (Bib.)
  I Gabriele (Bib.)
  E Gabriel (Bib.)
  SU Гаврии́л (библ.)

1353 GB Gaels, the (hist.)
  F les Gaëls (hist.)
  D die Gälen (Gesch.)
  I i gaeli (st.)
  E los gaeles (hist.)
  SU гэ́лы (ист.)

  GB Gaia (myth.)→Ge

1354 GB *Gaiety of Shipwrecks, The* (Ungaretti, 1919)
  F *La Joie des naufrages*
  D *Fröhlichkeit Schiffbrüchiger*
  I *Allegria di naufragi*
  E *Alegría de naufragios*
  SU «Весéлье кораблекрушéний» (Унгарéтти)

1355 GB Gaius (Roman name)
  F Gaius (nom romain)
  D Gajus (Römername)
  I Gaio (nome romano)
  E Gayo (nombre romano)
  SU Гай (древнери́мское и́мя)

1357 GB Galatia (hist.)
  F la Galatie (hist.)
  D Galatea (Gesch.)
  I la Galazia (st.)
  E Galacia (hist.)
  SU Галáтия (ист.)

1358 GB Galatians, the Epistle of Paul to the (Bib.)
  F l'Épître de Saint Paul aux Galates Bib.)
  D der Galaterbrief (Bib.)
  I la lettera di Paolo ai Galati (Bib.)
  E la Epístola de San Pablo a los gálatas (Bib.)
  SU «Послáние к Галáтам» (библ.)

1359 GB Galen (129–199)
  F Galien
  D Galenus
  I Galeno
  E Galeno
  SU Галéн

1360 GB Galicia (Spain)
  F la Galicie (Espagne)
  D Galizien (Spanien)
  I la Galizia (Spagna)
  E Galicia (España)
  SU Гали́ция (Испáния)

1361 GB Galilee (Bib.)
F la Galilée (Bib.)
D Galiläa (Bib.)
I la Galilea (Bib.)
E Galilea (Bib.)
SU Галилéя (библ.)

1362 GB Galilee, the Sea of (Bib.)
F le lac de Tibériade (Bib.)
D das Galiläische Meer (Bib.)
I il lago Tiberiade (Bib.)
E el lago de Tiberíades (Bib.)
SU Галилéйское мóре (библ.)

1363 GB Galileo (1564–1642)
F Galilée
D Galilei
I Galilei
E Galileo
SU Галилéо Галилéй

1364 GB *Gallic Wars [De Bello Gallico]*
(Caesar, 52–51)
F *Sur la guerre des Gaules* (César)
D *Der Gallische Krieg* (Cäsar)
I *La Guerra Gallica* (Cesare)
E *De la guerra de las Galias* (César)
SU «Запи́ски о гáлльской войнé» (Цéзарь)

1365 GB Gambia
F la Gambie
D Gambia
I il Gambia
E Gambia
SU Гáмбия

1366 GB *Gambler, The* (Dostoievsky, 1866)
F *Le Joueur* (Dostoïevski)
D *Der Spieler* (Dostojewskij)
I *Il giocatore* (Dostoevskij)
E *El jugador* (Dostoievski)
SU «Игрóк» (Достоéвский)

1367 GB *Game of Love and Chance, The*
(Marivaux, 1730)
F *Le Jeu de l'amour et du hasard*
D *Spiel von Liebe und Zufall*
I *Il gioco dell'amore e del caso*
E *Los juegos del amor y del azar*
SU «Игрá любви́ и слу́чая» (Маривó)

1368 GB Ganges (River), the (India)
F la Gange (Inde)
D der Ganges (Indien)
I il Gange (India)
E el Ganges (India)
SU Ганг (Ѝндия)

1369 GB Ganymede (myth.)
F Ganymède (myth.)
D Ganymed (myth.)
I Ganimede (mit.)
E Ganimedes (mit.)
SU Ганимéд (миф.)

1370 GB *Garden Party, The* (Mansfield, 1922)
F *La Garden Party*
D *Das Gartenfest*
I *La festa in giardino*
E *Garden Party*
SU «Прáздник в саду́» (Мэнсфильд)

1371 GB *Gargantua and Pantagruel* (Rabelais,
1532–64)
F *Gargantua et Pantagruel*
D *Gargantua und Pantagruel*
I *Gargantua e Pantagruel*
E *Gargantúa y Pantagrúel*
SU «Гаргантюá и Пантагрюэ́ль» (Раблé)

1372 GB Garonne (River), the (France)
F la Garonne (France)
D die Garonne (Frankreich)
I la Garonna (Francia)
E el Garona (Francia)
SU Гарóнна (Фрáнция)

GB Garter→Order of the Garter

1373 GB Gascony (France)
F la Gascogne (France)
D die Gaskogne (Frankreich)
I la Guascogna (Francia)
E Gascuña (Francia)
SU Гаскóнь (ж.) (Фрáнция)

1374 GB *Gates of Hell, The* (Rodin, 1880–1917)
F *La Porte de l'Enfer*
D *Das Höllentor*
I *La porta dell'Inferno*
E *La puerta del infierno*
SU «Вратá áда» (Родéн)

1375 GB Gaul (hist.)
F la Gaule (hist.)
D Gallien (Gesch.)
I la Gallia (st.)
E la Galia (hist.)
SU Гáллия (ист.)

1376 GB *Gay India* (Rameau, 1735)
F *Les Indes galantes*
D *Galantes Indien*
I *Les Indes galantes*
E *Les Indes galantes*
SU «Галáнтная Ѝндия» (Рамó)

1377 GB *Gay Parties* (Verlaine, 1869)
    F *Fêtes galantes*
    D *Schäferfeste*
    I *Feste galanti*
    E *Fiestas galantes*
    SU «Галáнтные прáзднества» (Верлéн)

1378 GB Gdansk (Poland)
    F Gdansk (Pologne)
    D Danzig (Polen)
    I Danzica (Polonia)
    E Gdansk (Polonia)
    SU Гдáньск (Пóльша)

1379 GB Ge (Gaia) (myth.)
    F Gaia (myth.)
    D Gäa (myth.)
    I Gea (mit.)
    E Gea (mit.)
    SU Гéя (миф.)

1380 GB Gemini (astron.)
    F les Gémeaux (astron.)
    D die Zwillinge (Astron.)
    I il Gemelli (astr.)
    E los Gemelos (astr.)
    SU Близнецы́ (астр.)

1381 GB General Agreement on Tariffs and Trade, the (GATT)
    F l'Accord général sur les tarifs et le commerce (GATT)
    D das Allgemeine Zoll- und Handelsabkommen (GATT)
    I l'Accordo generale sulle tariffe dogonali e il commercio (GATT)
    E el Acuerdo general sobre los aranceles y el comercio (GATT)
    SU Генерáльное соглашéние о тари́фах и торгóвле (ГАТТ)

1382 GB General Assembly, the (UNO)
    F l'Assemblée générale (ONU)
    D die Vollversammlung (UNO)
    I l'assemblea generale (ONU)
    E la Asamblea General (ONU)
    SU Генерáльная ассамблéя (ООН)

1383 GB *Generation, A [Pokolenie]* (Wajda, 1954)
    F *Une fille a parlé*
    D *Generation*
    I *Generazione*
    E *Generación*
    SU «Поколéние» (Вáйда)

1384 GB Genesis (Bib.)
    F la Genèse (Bib.)
    D Genesis (Bib.)
    I la Genesi (Bib.)
    E el Génesis (Bib.)
    SU «Бытиé» (библ.)

1385 GB Geneva (Switzerland)
    F Genève (f.) (Suisse)
    D Genf (Schweiz)
    I Ginevra (Svizzera)
    E Ginebra (Suiza)
    SU Женéва (Швейцáрия)

1386 GB Geneva, Lake (France/Switzerland)
    F le lac Léman (France/Suisse)
    D der Genfer See (Frankreich/Schweiz)
    I il lago di Ginevra (Francia/Svizzera)
    E el lago Leman (Francia/Suiza)
    SU Женéвское óзеро (Фрáнция/Швейцáрия)

1387 GB Genevieve (saint, *422–512*)
    F Geneviève (sainte)
    D Genoveva (Heilige)
    I Genoveffa (santa)
    E Genoveva (santa)
    SU Женевьéва (св.)

1388 GB Genghis Khan (*1162*–1227)
    F Gengis Khan
    D Dschingis Chan
    I Gengis Khan
    E Gengis Kan
    SU Чингисхáн

1389 GB *Genitrix* (Mauriac, 1923)
    F *Génitrix*
    D *Der Tod der jungen Frau*
    I *Genitrice*
    E *Genitrix*
    SU «Роди́тельница» (Мориáк)

1390 GB *Genius, The* (Dreiser, 1915)
    F *Le Génie*
    D *Das Genie*
    I *Il genio*
    E *El genio*
    SU «Гéний» (Дрáйзер)

1391 GB *Genius of Christianity, The* (Chateaubriand, 1802)
    F *Le Génie du christianisme*
    D *Der Geist des Christentums*
    I *Il genio del cristianesimo*
    E *El genio del cristianismo*
    SU «Гéний христиáнства» (Шатобриáн)

1392 GB Genoa (Italy)
    F Gênes (f.) (Italie)
    D Genua (Italien)
    I Genova (Italia)
    E Génova (Italia)
    SU Ге́нуя (Ита́лия)

1393 GB *Gentleman Dancing Master, The*
       (Wycherley, 1671)
    F *Le Gentleman maître de danse*
    D *Der ehrenwerte Tanzmeister*
    I *Il maestro di ballo gentiluomo*
    E *Caballero maestro de baile*
    SU «Джентльме́н – учи́тель та́нцев»
       (Уи́черли)

1394 GB *Gentleman's Agreement* (Kazan, 1947)
    F *Le Mur invisible*
    D *Tabu der Gerechten*
    I *Barriera invisibile*
    E *La barrera invisible*
    SU «Джентльме́нское соглаше́ние»
       (Ка́зан)

1395 GB *Gentlemen Prefer Blondes* (Hawks,
       1953)
    F *Les hommes préfèrent les blondes*
    D *Blondinen bevorzugt*
    I *Gli uomini preferiscono le bionde*
    E *Los caballeros las prefieren rubias*
    SU «Джентльме́ны предпочита́ют
       блонди́нок» (Хокс)

1396 GB George (saint, sovereign)
    F Georges (saint, roi de Grèce), George
       (roi d'Angleterre)
    D Georg (Heiliger, Herr.)
    I Giorgio (santo, sovrano)
    E Jorge (santo, sob.)
    SU Гео́ргий (св.), Гео́рг (коро́ль Гре́ции,
       А́нглии)

1397 GB Georgia (USA)
    F la Géorgie (USA)
    D Georgia (USA)
    I la Georgia (USA)
    E Georgia (USA)
    SU Джо́рджия (США)

1398 GB Georgia (USSR)
    F la Géorgie (URSS)
    D Georgien (UdSSR)
    I la Georgia (URSS)
    E Georgia (URSS)
    SU Гру́зия (СССР)

1399 GB *Georgics*, the [*Georgica*] (Virgil, −30)
    F les *Géorgiques* (Virgile)
    D die *Landleben* (Vergil)
    I le *Georgiche* (Virgilio)
    E las *Geórgicas* (Virgilio)
    SU «Гео́ргики» (Верги́лий)

1400 GB German Democratic Republic, the
       (GDR)
    F la République démocratique
       d'Allemagne (RDA)
    D die Deutsche Demokratische Republik
       (DDR)
    I la Repubblica Democratica Tedesca
       (RDT)
    E la República Democrática Alemana
       (RDA)
    SU Герма́нская Демократи́ческая
       Респу́блика (ГДР)

1401 GB German East Africa (hist.)
    F l'Afrique-Orientale allemande (hist.)
    D Deutsch-Ostafrika (Gesch.)
    I l'Africa Orientale Tedesca (st.)
    E África Oriental Alemana (hist.)
    SU Герма́нская Восто́чная А́фрика (ист.)

1402 GB German Federal Republic, the (GFR)
    F la République fédérale d'Allemagne
       (RFA)
    D die Bundesrepublik Deutschland (BR)
    I la Repubblica Federale Tedesca (RFT)
    E la República Federal de Alemania
       (RFA)
    SU Федерати́вная Респу́блика Герма́нии
       (ФРГ)

1403 GB *German Requiem, A* (Brahms, 1868)
    F le *Requiem allemand*
    D *Ein Deutsches Requiem*
    I il *Requiem tedesco*
    E el *Réquiem alemán*
    SU «Неме́цкий реквие́м» (Брамс)

1404 GB Germany
    F l'Allemagne (f.)
    D Deutschland
    I la Germania
    E Alemania
    SU Герма́ния

1405 GB *Germinal* (Zola, 1885)
    F *Germinal*
    D *Germinal*
    I *Germinale*
    E *Germinal*
    SU «Жермина́ль» (Золя́)

1406 GB Gethsemane (Bib.)
      F   Gethsémani (Bib.)
      D   Gethsemane (Bib.)
      I   Getsemani (Bib.)
      E   Getsemaní (Bib.)
      SU Гефсимания (библ.)

1407 GB Ghent (Gent) (Belgium)
      F   Gand (Belge)
      D   Gent (Belgien)
      I   Gand (Belgio)
      E   Gante (Bélgica)
      SU Гент (Бельгия)

1408 GB *Ghost Goes West, The* (Clair, 1936)
      F   *Fantôme à vendre*
      D   *Ein Gespenst auf Reisen*
      I   *Il fantasma galante*
      E   *El fantasma va al oeste*
      SU «Привидéние éдет на Зáпад» (Клер)

1409 GB *Ghosts* [*Gengangere*] (Ibsen, 1881)
      F   *Les Revenants*
      D   *Gespenster*
      I   *Gli spettri*
      E   *Espectros*
      SU «Привидéния» (Йбсен)

1410 GB Gibraltar
      F   Gibraltar
      D   Gibraltar
      I   Gibilterra
      E   Gibraltar
      SU Гибралтáр

1411 GB Gideon (Bib.)
      F   Gédéon (Bib.)
      D   Gideon (Bib.)
      I   Gedeone (Bib.)
      E   Gedeón (Bib.)
      SU Гедеóн (библ.)

1412 GB *Gil Blas* (Lesage, 1715–35)
      F   *Gil Blas de Santillane*
      D   *Gil Blas de Santillane*
      I   *Storia di Gil Blas di Santillana*
      E   *Gil Blas de Santillana*
      SU «Истóрия Жиль Блáза из
          Сантильáны» (Лесáж)

1413 GB *Girl from Arles, The* (Daudet/Bizet,
          1872)
      F   *L'Arlésienne*
      D   *Das Mädchen von Arles*
      I   *L'Arlesiana*
      E   *La Arlesiana*
      SU «Арлезиáнка» (Додé, Бизé)

      GB Girl Guides (Girl Scouts)→Guides

1414 GB *Girl of the Golden West, The* (Belasco,
          1905; Puccini, 1910)
      F   *La Fille de l'Ouest doré*
      D   *Das Mädchen aus dem goldenen
          Westen*
      I   *La fanciulla del West*
      E   *La muchacha del dorado Oeste*
      SU «Дéвушка с Зáпада» (Белáско,
          Пуччúни)

1415 GB *Girls of Slender Means, The* (Spark,
          1963)
      F   *Jeunes Filles de ressources exiguës*
      D   *Mädchen mit begrenzten Möglichkeiten*
      I   *Ragazze di mezzi scarsi*
      E   *Las señoritas de escasos medios*
      SU «Дéвушки со скýдными срéдствами»
          (Спарк)

1416 GB *Girl, 20* (Amis, 1971)
      F   *Fille, vingt ans*
      D   *Mädchen, 20*
      I   *Signorina, venti anni*
      E   *Señorita, veinti años*
      SU «Дéвушка, 20 лет» (Эмис)

1417 GB Gironde (Estuary), the (France)
      F   la Gironde (France)
      D   die Gironde (Frankreich)
      I   la Gironda (Francia)
      E   el Gironda (Francia)
      SU Жирóнда (Фрáнция)

1418 GB *Giselle* (Adam, 1841)
      F   *Giselle*
      D   *Giselle*
      I   *Giselle*
      E   *Giselle*
      SU «Жизéль» (Адáн)

1419 GB *Glass Menagerie, The* (Williams, 1944)
      F   *La Ménagerie de verre*
      D   *Glasmenagerie*
      I   *Lo zoo di vetro*
      E   *El zoo de cristal*
      SU «Стеклянный зверинец» (Уúльямс)

1420 GB *Gleaners, The* (Millet, 1857)
      F   *Les Glaneuses*
      D   *Die Ährenleserinnen*
      I   *Le spigolatrici*
      E   *Las espigadoras*
      SU «Сбóрщицы колóсьев» (Миллé)

1421 GB *Godfather, The* (Coppola, 1972)
F *Le Parrain*
D *Der Pate*
I *Il padrino*
E *El padrino*
SU «Крёстный отéц» (Кóппола)

1422 GB *Go Down, Moses* (Faulkner, 1942)
F *Descends, Moïse*
D *Das verworfene Erbe*
I *Scendi, Mosè*
E *Desciende, Moisés*
SU «Сойди, Моисéй» (Фóлкнер)

1423 GB *God's Little Acre* (Caldwell, 1933)
F *Le Petit Arpent du Bon Dieu*
D *Gottes kleiner Acker*
I *Piccolo campo*
E *El pequeño campo de Dios*
SU «Акр гóспода бóга» (Кóлдуэлл)

1424 GB *Gods Reborn, The* (Merezhkovsky, 1901)
F *Les Dieux ressuscités* (Merejkovski)
D *Die auferstandenen Götter* (Mereschkowskij)
I *La resurrezione degli dei* (Merežkovskij)
E *La resurrección de los dioses* (Merejkovski)
SU «Воскрéсшие бóги» (Мережкóвский)

1425 GB *Goetz von Berlichingen* (Goethe, 1773)
F *Götz von Berlichingen*
D *Götz von Berlichingen*
I *Götz von Berlichingen*
E *Goetz de Berlichingen*
SU «Гёц фон Бéрлихинген» (Гёте)

1426 GB Golan Heights, the (Syria)
F le plateau du Golan (Syrie)
D die Golanhöhen (Syrien)
I le alture del Golan (Siria)
E la meseta del Golán (Siria)
SU Голáнские высóты (Сúрия)

1427 GB *Goldberg Variations*, the (Bach, 1742)
F les variations *Goldberg*
D die *Goldberg-Variationen*
I i *Variazioni Goldberg*
E las variaciones *Goldberg*
SU «Гóльдбергские вариáции» (Бах)

1428 GB *Gold Bug, The* (Poe, 1843)
F *Le Scarabée d'or*
D *Der Goldkäfer*
I *Lo scarabeo d'oro*
E *El escarabajo de oro*
SU «Золотóй жук» (По)

1429 GB Gold Coast, the (hist.)
F la Côte-de-l'Or (hist.)
D die Goldküste (Gesch.)
I la Costa d'Oro (st.)
E la Costa de Oro (hist.)
SU Золотóй Бéрег (ист.)

1430 GB *Golden Age, The* (Buñuel, 1930)
F *L'Âge d'or*
D *Das goldene Zeitalter*
I *L'Âge d'or*
E *L'Âge d'or*
SU «Золотóй век» (Бюнюэль)

1431 GB Golden Age, the (myth., hist.)
F l'âge d'or (myth., hist.)
D das goldene Zeitalter (myth., Gesch.)
I l'età dell'oro (mit., st.)
E la edad de oro (mit., hist.)
SU Золотóй век (миф., ист.)

1432 GB *Golden Ass, The* (Apuleius, II)
F *L'Âne d'or* (Apulée)
D *Der goldene Esel* (Apuleius)
I *L'asino d'oro* (Apuleio)
E *El asno de oro* (Apuleyo)
SU «Золотóй осёл» (Апулéй)

1433 GB *Golden Bough, The* (Frazer, 1890–1915)
F *Le Rameau d'or*
D *Der goldene Zweig*
I *Il ramo d'oro*
E *La rama dorada*
SU «Золотáя ветвь» (Фрéйзер)

1434 GB *Golden Bowl, The* (James, 1904)
F *La Coupe d'or*
D *Die goldene Schale*
I *La coppa d'oro*
E *La copa de oro*
SU «Золотáя чáша» (Джеймс)

1435 GB *Golden Cockerel, The* (Rimsky-Korsakov, 1909)
F *Le Coq d'or* (Rimski-Korsakov)
D *Der goldene Hahn* (Rimskij-Korsakow)
I *Il gallo d'oro* (Rimskij-Korsakov)
E *El gallo de oro* (Rimsky-Korsakov)
SU «Золотóй петушóк» (Рúмский-Кóрсаков)

1436 GB Golden Fleece, the (myth.)
F la Toison d'or (myth.)
D das goldene Vlies (myth.)
I il vello d'oro (mit.)
E el Vellocino de oro (mit.)
SU золотóе рунó (миф.)

1437 GB Golden Gate, the (San Francisco)
F la Golden Gate
D die Golden Gate
I il Golden Gate
E la Golden Gate
SU Золотьíе Воро́та (Сан-Франци́ско)

1438 GB Golden Horde, the (hist.)
F la Horde d'or (hist.)
D die Goldene Horde (Gesch.)
I l'Orda d'oro (st.)
E la Horda de oro (hist.)
SU Золота́я о́рда (ист.)

1439 GB Golden Horn, the (Istanbul)
F la Corne d'or (Istanbul)
D das Goldene Horn (Istanbul)
I il Corno d'oro (Istanbul)
E el Cuerno de oro (Estambul)
SU Золото́й Рог (Стамбу́л)

1440 GB *Golden Legend*, the (XIII)
F la *Légende dorée*
D die *Legenda aurea*
I la *Legenda aurea*
E la *Leyenda áurea*
SU «Золота́я леге́нда»

1441 GB *Gold of the Rhine, The* (Wagner, 1869)
F *L'Or du Rhin*
D *Das Rheingold*
I *L'oro del Reno*
E *El oro del Rin*
SU «Зо́лото Ре́йна» (Ва́гнер)

1442 GB *Gold Rush, The* (Chaplin, 1924)
F *La Ruée vers l'or*
D *Der Goldrausch*
I *La febbre dell'oro*
E *La quimera del oro*
SU «Золота́я лихора́дка» (Ча́плин)

1443 GB Golgotha (Bib.)
F Golgotha (Bib.)
D Golgatha (Bib.)
I Golgota (Bib.)
E Gólgota (Bib.)
SU Голго́фа (библ.)

1444 GB Goliath (Bib.)
F Goliath (Bib.)
D Goliath (Bib.)
I Golia (Bib.)
E Goliat (Bib.)
SU Голиа́ф (библ.)

1445 GB *Gone with the Wind* (Mitchell, 1936)
F *Autant en emporte le vent*
D *Vom Winde verweht*
I *Via col vento*
E *Lo que el viento se llevó*
SU «Унесённые ве́тром» (Ми́тчелл)

1446 GB *Goodbye, Mr Chips* (Wood, 1939)
F *Au revoir, Mr Chips*
D *Auf Wiedersehen, Mr Chips*
I *Addio, Mr Chips*
E *Adiós, Mr Chips*
SU «Проща́йте, ми́стер Чипс» (Вуд)

1447 GB *Goodbye To All That* (Graves, 1929)
F *Adieu à tout cela*
D *Strich drunter!*
I *Addio a tutto questo*
E *Adiós a todo eso*
SU «Со всем э́тим поко́нчено» (Гре́йвс)

1448 GB *Goodbye to Berlin* (Isherwood, 1939)
F *Adieu, Berlin*
D *Leb' wohl, Berlin*
I *Addio a Berlino*
E *Adiós a Berlín*
SU «Проща́й, Берли́н» (Йшервуд)

1449 GB *Good Companions, The* (Priestley, 1929)
F *Les Bons Compagnons*
D *Die guten Gefährten*
I *I buoni compagni*
E *Los buenos compañeros*
SU «До́брые това́рищи» (При́стли)

1450 GB *Good Daughter, The* (Piccinni, 1760)
F *La Bonne Fille*
D *Die gute Tochter*
I *La buona figliola*
E *La buena hija*
SU «Чекки́на, или До́брая до́чка» (Пиччи́нни)

1451 GB *Good Earth, The* (Buck, 1931)
F, *La Terre chinoise*
D *Die gute Erde*
I *La buona terra*
E *La buena tierra*
SU «Земля́» (Бак)

1452 GB Good Friday (rel.)
F le Vendredi saint (relig.)
D der Karfreitag (relig.)
I il venerdì santo (relig.)
E Viernes Santo (relig.)
SU страстна́я пя́тница (рел.)

GB Good Hope, Cape of→Cape of Good
Hope

1453 GB *Good Soldier Schweik, The* [*Osudy
dobrého vojáka Švejka za světové
války*] (Hašek, 1920–3)
F *Les Aventures du brave soldat Švejk*
D *Die Abenteuer des braven Soldaten
Schwejk*
I *Le avventure del buon soldato Švejk*
E *Las aventuras del valeroso soldado
Schwejk*
SU «Похождéния брáвого солдáта
Швéйка» (Гáшек)

1454 GB *Good Woman of Setzuan, The* (Brecht,
1943)
F *La Bonne Âme de Setchouan*
D *Der gute Mensch von Sezuan*
I *L'anima buona di Sezuan*
E *La buena persona de Sezuan*
SU «Дóбрый человéк из Сезуáна» (Брехт)

1455 GB Gordian knot, the (myth.)
F Le noeud gordien (myth.)
D der Gordische Knoten (myth.)
I il nodo gordiano (mit.)
E el nudo gordiano (mit.)
SU Гóрдиев ýзел (миф.)

1456 GB *Gorgias* (Plato, IV)
F *Gorgias* (Platon)
D *Gorgias* (Platon)
I *Gorgia* (Platone)
E *Gorgias* (Platón)
SU «Гóргий» (Платóн)

1457 GB Gorgons, the (myth.)
F les Gorgones (myth.)
D die Gorgonen (myth.)
I le Gorgoni (mit.)
E las Gorgonas (mit.)
SU горгóны (миф.)

GB Gospel According to . . . (Bib.)→
. . . , Gospel According to

1458 GB Gospels, the (Bib.)
F les Évangiles (Bib.)
D die Evangelien (Bib.)
I i Vangeli (Bib.)
E los Evangelios (Bib.)
SU Евáнгелия (библ.)

1459 GB Goths, the (hist.)
F les Goths (hist.)
D die Goten (Gesch.)
I i goti (st.)
E los godos (hist.)
SU гóты (ист.)

1460 GB Gracchi, the (II)
F les Gracques
D die Gracchen
I i Gracchi
E los Gracos
SU Грáкхи

1461 GB Graces, the (myth.)
F les Grâces (myth.)
D die Grazien (myth.)
I le Grazie (mit.)
E las Gracias (mit.)
SU грáции (миф.)

1462 GB *Graduate, The* (Nichols, 1967)
F *Le Lauréat*
D *Die Reifeprüfung*
I *Il laureato*
E *El graduado*
SU «Аспирáнт» (Нúколс)

GB Grail→Holy Grail

1463 GB Grampian Mountains, the (Scotland)
F les monts Grampians (Écosse)
D die Grampians (Schottland)
I i monti Grampiani (Scozia)
E los montes Grampianos (Escocia)
SU Грампиáнские гóры (Шотлáндия)

1464 GB Granada (Spain)
F Grenade (Espagne)
D Granada (Spanien)
I Granada (Spagna)
E Granada (España)
SU Гранáда (Испáния)

1465 GB Grand Canal, the (Venice)
F le Grand Canal (Venise)
D der Canal Grande (Venedig)
I il Canal Grande (Venezia)
E el Gran Canal (Venecia)
SU Большóй канáл (Венéция)

1466 GB Grand Canyon, the (USA)
F le Grand Canyon (USA)
D der Gran Cañon (USA)
I il Grand Canyon (USA)
E el Cañon del Colorado (USA)
SU Большóй каньóн (США)

1467 GB *Grande Illusion, La* [*The Great
Illusion*] (Renoir, 1937)
F *La Grande Illusion*
D *Die Große Illusion*
I *La grande illusione*
E *La gran ilusión*
SU «Вели́кая иллю́зия» (Ренуа́р)

1468 GB *Grand Hotel* (Goulding, 1932)
F *Grand Hôtel*
D *Menschen im Hotel*
I *Grand Hotel*
E *Gran Hotel*
SU «Грандоте́ль» (Гу́лдинг)

1469 GB *Grand Jeu, Le* [*The Great Gamble*]
(Feyder, 1933)
F *Le Grand Jeu*
D *Das große Spiel*
I *La donna dai due volti*
E *El signo de la muerte*
SU «Больша́я игра́» (Фейде́р)

1470 GB *Grand Odalisque, The* (Ingres, 1814)
F *Grande Odalisque*
D *Odaliske*
I *Grande Odalisca*
E *La odalisca*
SU «Больша́я одали́ска» (Энгр)

1471 GB *Grapes of Wrath, The* (Steinbeck,
1939)
F *Les Raisins de la colère*
D *Die Früchte des Zorns*
I *Furore*
E *Las uvas de la ira*
SU «Гро́здья гне́ва» (Сте́йнбек)

1472 GB Gratian (359–383)
F Gratien
D Gratianus
I Graziano
E Graciano
SU Грациа́н

1473 GB *Graveyard by the Sea, The* (Valéry,
1920)
F *Le Cimetière marin*
D *Der Friedhof am Meer*
I *Il cimitero marino*
E *El cementerio marino*
SU «Морско́е кла́дбище» (Валери́)

GB Gray's *Elegy*→*Elegy Written in a
Country Churchyard*

1474 GB Great Australian Bight, the
F la Grande Baie Australienne
D der Australische Golf
I la Gran Baia Australiana
E la Gran Bahia Australiana
SU Большо́й Австрали́йский зали́в

1475 GB Great Barrier Reef, the (Australia)
F la Grànde Barrière Australienne
(Australie)
D das Große Barriereriff (Australien)
I la Grande Barriera Corallina
(Australia)
E la Gran Barrera de Arrecifes
(Australia)
SU Большо́й Барье́рный риф
(Австра́лия)

1476 GB Great Basin, The (USA)
F le Grand Bassin (USA)
D der Große Stromgebiet (USA)
I il Gran Bacino (USA)
E la Gran Cuenca (USA)
SU Большо́й Бассе́йн (США)

1477 GB Great Bear, the (Ursa Major) (astron.)
F la Grande Ourse (astron.)
D der Große Bär (Astron.)
I l'Orsa Maggiore (astr.)
E la Osa Mayor (astr.)
SU Больша́я Медве́дица (астр.)

1478 GB Great Bear Lake, the (Canada)
F le Grand Lac de l'Ours (Canada)
D der Große Bärensee (Kanada)
I il Gran Lago degli Orsi (Canada)
E el Gran Lago del Oso (Canadá)
SU Большо́е Медве́жье о́зеро
(Кана́да)

1479 GB Great Britain
F la Grande-Bretagne
D Großbritannien
I la Gran Bretagna
E la Gran Bretaña
SU Великобрита́ния

GB *Greatcoat, The*→*Overcoat, The*

1480 GB *Great Dictator, The* (Chaplin, 1940)
F *Le Dictateur*
D *Der große Diktator*
I *Il grande dittatore*
E *El gran dictador*
SU «Вели́кий дикта́тор» (Ча́плин)

1481 GB   Great Dividing Range, the (Australia)
F   la Cordillère Australienne (Australie)
D   die Ost-Kordilleren (Australien)
I   la Grande Catena Divisoria (Australia)
E   la Cordillera Australiana (Australia)
SU   Большо́й Водоразде́льный хребе́т (Австра́лия)

1482 GB   Greater Antilles, the (West Indies)
F   les Grandes Antilles (Antilles)
D   die Großen Antillen (Westindien)
I   le Grandi Antille (Antille)
E   las Antillas Mayores (Antillas)
SU   Больши́е Анти́льские острова́ (Вест-Йндия)

1483 GB   Greater London (England)
F   le Grand Londres (Angleterre)
D   Große London (England)
I   il Gran Londra (Inghilterra)
E   el Gran Londres (Inglaterra)
SU   Большо́й Ло́ндон (А́нглия)

1484 GB   *Greatest Show on Earth, The* (De Mille, 1952)
F   *Le Plus Grand Chapiteau du monde*
D   *Die größte Schau der Welt*
I   *Il più grande spettacolo del mondo*
E   *El mayor espectáculo del mundo*
SU   «Грандио́знейшее представле́ние на земле́» (Де Милль)

1485 GB   *Great Expectations* (Dickens, 1860–1)
F   *Les Grandes Espérances*
D   *Große Erwartungen*
I   *Grandi speranze*
E   *Grandes esperanzas*
SU   «Больши́е ожида́ния» (Ди́ккенс)

1486 GB   *Great Galeoto, The* (Echegaray, 1881)
F   *Le Grand Galeoto*
D   *Der Kuppler Galeotto*
I   *Il gran galeotto*
E   *El gran galeoto*
SU   «Вели́кий Галео́то» (Эчегара́й-и-Эйсаги́рре)

1487 GB   *Great Gatsby, The* (Fitzgerald, 1925)
F   *Gatsby, le Magnifique*
D   *Der große Gatsby*
I   *Il grande Gatsby*
E   *El gran Gatsby*
SU   «Вели́кий Гэ́тсби» (Фицдже́ральд)

1488 GB   Great Lakes, the (Canada/USA)
F   les Grands Lacs (Canada/USA)
D   die Großen Seen (Kanada/USA)
I   i Grandi Laghi (Canada/USA)
E   los Grandes Lagos (Canadá/USA)
SU   Вели́кие озёра (Кана́да/США)

1489 GB   *Great Manoeuvres* (Clair, 1955)
F   *Les Grandes Manoeuvres*
D   *Das große Manöver*
I   *Le grandi manovre*
E   *Las maniobras del amor*
SU   «Больши́е манёвры» (Клер)

1490 GB   Great Salt Lake, the (USA)
F   le Grand Lac Salé (USA)
D   der Große Salzsee (USA)
I   il Gran Lago Salato (USA)
E   el Gran Lago Salado (USA)
SU   Большо́е Солёное о́зеро (США)

1491 GB   Great Sandy Desert, the (Australia)
F   le Grand Désert de Sable (Australie)
D   die Große Sandwüste (Australien)
I   il Gran Deserto Sabbioso (Australia)
E   el Gran Desierto de Arena (Australia)
SU   Больша́я Песча́ная пусты́ня (Австра́лия)

1492 GB   Great Schism (Western Schism), the (rel., 1378–1417)
F   le Grand Schisme d'Occident (relig.)
D   das Abendländische Schisma (relig.)
I   il scisma d'occidente (relig.)
E   el Gran Cisma (relig.)
SU   «Вели́кий раско́л» (рел.)

1493 GB   Great Slave Lake, the (Canada)
F   le Grand Lac de l'Esclave (Canada)
D   der Große Sklavensee (Kanada)
I   il Gran Lago degli Schiavi (Canada)
E   el Gran Lago del Esclavo (Canadá)
SU   Большо́е Нево́льничье о́зеро (Кана́да)

1494 GB   *Great Testament, The* (Villon, 1461)
F   *Grand Testament*
D   *Das große Testament*
I   *Gran testamento*
E   *Gran testamento*
SU   «Большо́е завеща́ние» (Вийо́н)

1495 GB   *Great Train Robbery, The* (Porter, 1903)
F   *Great Train Robbery*
D   *Der große Eisenbahnraub*
I   *L'assalto al treno*
E   *Asalto y robo de un tren*
SU   «Вели́кое ограбле́ние по́езда» (По́рте

1496 GB Great Wall of China, the
F la Grande Muraille de Chine
D die Große Mauer von China
I la Grande Muraglia Cinese
E la Gran Muralla de China
SU Вели́кая кита́йская стена́

GB Great War→First World War

1497 GB Greco, El (1541–1614)
F Le Greco
D El Greco
I El Greco
E el Greco
SU Эль Гре́ко

1498 GB Greece
F le Grèce
D Griechenland
I la Grecia
E Grecia
SU Гре́ция

1499 GB *Greed* (Stroheim, 1923)
F *Les Rapaces*
D *Gier nach Geld*
I *Greed*
E *Avaricia*
SU «А́лчность» (Стро́хайм)

1500 GB *Greek Anthology*, the (−VII−+X)
F l'*Anthologie grecque*
D die griechische *Anthologie*
I l'*Antologia Palatina*
E la *Antología griega*
SU «Гре́ческая антоло́гия»

1501 GB *Green Henry* (Keller, 1854)
F *Henri le Vert*
D *Der Grüne Heinrich*
I *Enrico il verde*
E *Enrique el Verde*
SU «Зелёный Ге́нрих» (Ке́ллер)

1502 GB *Green Hills of Africa, The*
(Hemingway, 1935)
F *Les Vertes Collines d'Afrique*
D *Die grünen Hügel Afrikas*
I *Verdi colline d'Africa*
E *Las verdes colinas de África*
SU «Зелёные холмы́ А́фрики»
(Хемингуэ́й)

1503 GB Greenland
F le Groenland
D Grönland
I la Groenlandia
E Groenlandia
SU Гренла́ндия

1504 GB *Green Mirror, The* (Walpole, 1918)
F *Le Miroir vert*
D *Der grüne Spiegel*
I *Lo specchio verde*
E *El espejo verde*
SU «Зелёное зе́ркало» (Уо́лпол)

1505 GB Gregory (saint, pope)
F Grégoire (saint, pape)
D Gregor (Heiliger, Papst)
I Gregorio (santo, papa)
E Gregorio (santo, papa)
SU Григо́рий (св., па́па ри́мский)

1506 GB Gregory of Nyssa (*335–394*)
F Grégoire de Nysse
D Gregor von Nyssa
I Gregorio Nisseno
E Gregorio Niceno
SU Григо́рий Ни́сский

1507 GB Gregory of Tours (*538–594*)
F Grégoire de Tours
D Gregor von Tours
I Gregorio di Tours
E Gregorio de Tours
SU Григо́рий Ту́рский

1508 GB Gregory the Great (*540–604*)
F Grégoire le Grand
D Gregor der Große
I Gregorio Magno
E Gregorio Magno
SU Григо́рий Вели́кий

1509 GB Grenada (West Indies)
F le Grenade (Antilles)
D Grenada (Westindien)
I Grenada (Antille)
E Granada (Antillas)
SU Грена́да (Вест-И́ндия)

1510 GB Grenadines, the
F les Grenadines (f.)
D die Grenadinen
I le Grenadine
E las Granadinas
SU Гренади́ны (ж.)

1511 GB Grimms' *Fairy Tales* (1812–22)
F les *Contes d'enfants et du foyer* des
frères Grimm
D *Kinder- und Hausmärchen* der Brüder
Grimm
I le *Fiabe per bambini e famiglie* dei
fratelli Grimm
E los *Cuentos* dos hermanos Grimm
SU «Де́тские и семе́йные ска́зки» (бра́тья
Гримм)

1512 GB Groningen (Netherlands)
F   Groningue (Pays-Bas)
D   Groningen (Niederlande)
I   Groninga (Paesi Bassi)
E   Groninga (Holanda)
SU Грóнинген (Нидерлáнды)

1513 GB *Group, The* (Lumet, 1966)
F   *Le Groupe*
D   *Die Clique*
I   *Il gruppo e le sue passioni*
E   *El grupo*
SU «Грýппа» (Лю́мет)

1514 GB Guadeloupe
F   la Guadeloupe
D   Guadeloupe
I   Guadalupa
E   Guadalupe
SU Гваделýпа

1515 GB Guatemala
F   le Guatemala
D   Guatemala
I   il Guatemala
E   Guatemala
SU Гватемáла

1516 GB Guernsey (Channel Islands)
F   Guernesey (îles Anglo-Normandes)
D   Guernsey (Kanalinseln)
I   Guernsey (isole Normanne)
E   Guernesey (islas Anglonormandas)
SU Гéрнси (Нормáндские островá)

1517 GB *Guess Who's Coming to Dinner*
(Kramer, 1967)
F   *Devine qui vient dîner?*
D   *Rat mal, wer zum Essen kommt*
I   *Indovina chi viene a cena*
E   *Adivina quién viene esta noche*
SU «Угадáй, кто прихóдит к нам обéдать»
(Крéймер)

1518 GB Guides (Girl Guides) (Girl Scouts,
USA), the
F   les Guides (catholiques), les
Éclaireuses (neutres)
D   die Mädchenpfadfinder
I   le guide (cattoliche), le giovini
esploratrici (neutre)
E   las niñas exploradoras
SU гёрлгáйды

1519 GB *Guide to Geography* [*Geographike
hyphegesis*] (Ptolemy, II)
F   *Guide géographique* (Ptolémée)
D   *Geographische Anleitung* (Ptolemaios)
I   *Introduzione geografica* (Tolomeo)
E   *Geografía* (Ptolomeo)
SU «Руковóдство по геогрáфии»
(Птолемéй)

1520 GB Guinea
F   la Guinée
D   Guinea
I   la Guinea
E   Guinea
SU Гвинéя

1521 GB Guinea, the Gulf of
F   le golfe de Guinée
D   der Golf von Guinea
I   il golfo di Guinea
E   el golfo de Guinea
SU Гвинéйский залúв

1522 GB Guinea-Bissau
F   la Guinée-Bissau
D   Guinea-Bissau
I   la Guinea-Bissau
E   Guinea-Bissau
SU Гвинéя-Бисáу

1523 GB *Guinness Book of Records*, the
(McWhirter, 1955–)
F   le *Livre Guinness des records*
D   das *Guinness Buch der Rekorde*
I   il *Guinness dei primati*
E   el *Guinness libro de los récords*
SU «Кнúга рекóрдов Гúннесса»
(Макуúртер)

1524 GB *Gulag Archipelago, The* (Solzhenitzyn,
1974–78)
F   *L'Archipel du Goulag* (Soljenitsyne)
D   *Archipel Gulag* (Solschenizyn)
I   *Arcipelago Gulag* (Solženicyn)
E   *Archipiélago Gulag* (Soljenitsyn)
SU «Архипелáг ГУЛÁГ» (Солженúцын)

GB ´Gulf of . . . → . . . , Gulf of

1525 GB Guldinus (1577–1653)
F   Guldin
D   Guldin
I   Guldino
E   Guldino
SU Гýльдин

1526 GB Gulf Stream, the
     F le Gulf Stream
     D der Golfstrom
     I la corrente del Golfo
     E la corriente del Golfo
     SU Гольфстри́м

1527 GB *Gulliver's Travels* (Swift, 1721–5)
     F *Les Voyages de Gulliver*
     D *Gullivers Reisen*
     I *I viaggi di Gulliver*
     E *Los viajes de Gulliver*
     SU «Путеше́ствия Гулливе́ра» (Свифт)

1528 GB *Gun for Sale, A* (Greene, 1936)
     F *Tueur à gages*
     D *Das Attentat*
     I *Una pistola da vendere*
     E *Una pistola en venta*
     SU «Продаётся пистоле́т» (Грин)

1529 GB Gunpowder Plot, the (1605)
     F la Conspiration des poudres
     D die Pulververschwörung
     I la congiura delle polveri
     E la Conspiración de la Pólvora
     SU «Порохово́й за́говор»

1530 GB Gurkhas, the (Nepal)
     F les gurkhas (Nepal)
     D die Gurkhas (Nepal)
     I i gurkha (Nepal)
     E los gurkhas (Nepal)
     SU гу́ркхи (Непа́л)

1531 GB Gustav (king)
     F Gustave (roi)
     D Gustav (König)
     I Gustavo (re)
     E Gustavo (rey)
     SU Густа́в (прав.)

1532 GB *Gustav Vasa* (Strindberg, 1899)
     F *Gustàve Vasa*
     D *Gustav Vasa*
     I *Gustav Vasa*
     E *Gustavo Vasa*
     SU «Густа́в Ва́са» (Стри́ндберг)

1533 GB Guyana
     F la Guyana
     D Guayana
     I la Guyana
     E Guyana
     SU Гайа́на

1534 GB *Guy Mannering* (Scott, 1815)
     F *Guy Mannering*
     D *Guy Mannering*
     I *Guy Mannering*
     E *Guy Mannering*
     SU «Гай Мэ́ннеринг» (Скотт)

H

1535 GB Habakkuk (Bib.)
F Habacuc (Bib.)
D Habakuk (Bib.)
I Abacuc (Bib.)
E Habacuc (Bib.)
SU Авваку́м (библ.)

1536 GB Habsburgs (Hapsburgs), the (house)
F les Habsbourg (maison)
D die Habsburger (Herrschergeschlecht)
I gli Asburgo (casata)
E los Habsburgo (casa)
SU Га́бсбурги (дина́стия)

1537 GB Hades (myth.)
F Hadès (myth.)
D Hades (myth.)
I Ade (mit.)
E Hades (mit.)
SU Аи́д (миф.)

1538 GB Hadrian (76–138)
F Hadrien
D Hadrian
I Adriano
E Adriano
SU Адриа́н

1539 GB Hadrian's Wall (England)
F le mur d'Hadrien (Angleterre)
D der Hadrianswall (England)
I il vallo di Adriano (Inghilterra)
E la muralla de Adriano (Inglaterra)
SU Адриа́нов вал (А́нглия)

1540 GB Hagar (Bib.)
F Agar (Bib.)
D Hagar (Bib.)
I Agar (Bib.)
E Agar (Bib.)
SU Ага́рь (библ.)

1541 GB Haggai (Bib.)
F Aggée (Bib.)
D Haggai (Bib.)
I Aggeo (Bib.)
E Ageo (Bib.)
SU Агге́й (библ.)

1542 GB Hague, The (Netherlands)
F La Haye (Pays-Bas)
D Den Haag (Niederlande)
I L'Aia (Paesi Bassi)
E La Haya (Holanda)
SU Гаа́га (Нидерла́нды)

1543 GB Hainaut (Hainault) (Belgium)
F Hainaut (Belgique)
D Hennegau (Belgien)
I Hainaut (Belgio)
E Henao (Bélgica)
SU Эно́ (Бе́льгия)

1544 GB *Hairy Ape, The* (O'Neill, 1922)
F *Le Singe velu*
D *Der haarige Affe*
I *Lo scimmione*
E *El mono velludo*
SU «Косма́тая обезья́на» (О'Ни́л)

1545 GB Haiti
F Haïti
D Haïti
I Haiti
E Haití
SU Гаи́ти

GB Halicarnassus→Mausoleum of Halicarnassus

1546 GB Ham (Bib.)
F Cham (Bib.)
D Ham (Bib.)
I Cam (Bib.)
E Cam (Bib.)
SU Хам (библ.)

1547 GB Hamburg (Germany)
F Hambourg (Allemagne)
D Hamburg (Deutschland)
I Amburgo (Germania)
E Hamburgo (Alemania)
SU Гáмбург (Гермáния)

1548 GB *Hamburg Dramaturgy* (Lessing, 1767–8)
F *Dramaturgie de Hambourg*
D *Hamburgische Dramaturgie*
I *Drammaturgia amburghese*
E *Dramaturgia Hamburguesa*
SU «Гáмбургская драматургѝя» (Лéссинг)

1549 GB Hamilcar Barca (−III)
F Hamilcar Barca
D Hamilcar Barca
I Amilcare Barca
E Amílcar Barca
SU Гамилькáр Бáрка

1550 GB *Hamlet* (Shakespeare, 1601)
F *Hamlet*
D *Hamlet*
I *Amleto*
E *Hamlet*
SU «Гáмлет» (Шекспѝр)

1551 GB *Hamlet, The* (Faulkner, 1940)
F *Le Hameau*
D *Das Dorf*
I *Il borgo*
E *El villorrio*
SU «Деревýшка» (Фóлкнер)

1552 GB *Handful of Blackberries, A* (Silone, 1952)
F *Une poignée de mûres*
D *Eine Handvoll Brombeeren*
I *Una manciata di more*
E *Un puñado de moras*
SU «Горсть ежевѝки» (Силóне)

1553 GB *Handful of Dust, A* (Waugh, 1934)
F *Une poignée de poussière*
D *Eine Handvoll Staub*
I *Una manciata di polvere*
E *Un puñado de polvo*
SU «Пригóршня прáха» (Во)

1554 GB Hanging Gardens of Babylon, the
F les jardins suspendus de Sémiramis
D die hängenden Gärten der Semiramis
I i giardini pensili di Babele
E los jardines colgantes de Semíramis
SU висячие сады́ Семирамѝды

1555 GB *Hangman, The [Bödeln]* (Lagerkvist, 1933)
F *Le Bourreau*
D *Der Henker*
I *Il boia*
E *El verdugo*
SU «Палáч» (Лáгерквист)

1556 GB Hannah (Bib.)
F Anne (Bib.)
D Anna (Bib.)
I Anna (Bib.)
E Ana (Bib.)
SU Áнна (библ.)

1557 GB Hannibal (247–182)
F Hannibal
D Hannibal
I Annibale
E Aníbal
SU Ганнибáл

1558 GB Hanover (Germany)
F Hanovre (Allemagne)
D Hannover (Deutschland)
I Hannover (Germania)
E Hannover (Alemania)
SU Ганнóвер (Гермáния)

1559 GB Hanseatic League, the (hist.)
F la Ligue hanséatique (hist.)
D die Hanse (Gesch.)
I la lega anseatica (st.)
E la liga hanseática (hist.)
SU Ганзéйский сою́з (ист.)

1560 GB *Hänsel and Gretel* (Grimm, 1812; Humperdinck, 1893)
F *Hänsel et Gretel*
D *Hänsel und Gretel*
I *Hänsel e Gretel*
E *Hänsel y Gretel*
SU «Гéнзель и Грéтель» (Гримм, Хýмпердинк)

1561 GB *Happy Valley* (White, 1939)
F *Eden-Ville*
D *Glückstal*
I *La valle felice*
E *Valle feliz*
SU «Счастлѝвая долѝна» (Уáйт)

GB   Hapsburgs (house)→Habsburgs

1562   GB   *Hard Cash* (Reade, 1859)
  F   *Argent comptant*
  D   *Hartes Geld*
  I   *Contanti*
  E   *El dinero fatal*
  SU   «Звóнкая монéта» (Рид)

1563   GB   *Hard Times* (Dickens, 1854)
  F   *Les Temps difficiles*
  D   *Harte Zeiten*
  I   *Tempi difficili*
  E   *Tiempos difíciles*
  SU   «Тяжёлые временá» (Дúккенс)

1564   GB   Harlequin
  F   Arlequin
  D   Harlekin
  I   Arlecchino
  E   Arlequín
  SU   Арлекúн

1565   GB   *Harlot's Progress, A* (Hogarth, 1731)
  F   *La Carrière de la prostituée*
  D   *Der Weg einer Dirne*
  I   *Carriera di una prostituta*
  E   *La carrera de la prostituta*
  SU   «Карьéра проститýтки» (Хóгарт)

1566   GB   Harmonia (myth.)
  F   Harmonie (myth.)
  D   Harmonie (myth.)
  I   Armonia (mit.)
  E   Armonía (mit.)
  SU   Гармóния (миф.)

1567   GB   *Harmonies* (Lamartine, 1830)
  F   *Les Harmonies poétiques et religieuses*
  D   *Harmonien*
  I   *Armonie poetiche e religiose*
  E   *Armonías*
  SU   «Поэтúческие и религиóзные гармóнии» (Ламартúн)

1568   GB   *Harmony of the World, The* (Hindemith, 1957)
  F   *L'Harmonie du monde*
  D   *Die Harmonie der Welt*
  I   *L'armonia del mondo*
  E   *La armonía del mundo*
  SU   «Гармóния мúра» (Хúндемит)

1569   GB   Harold (king)
  F   Harold (roi)
  D   Harold (König)
  I   Aroldo (re)
  E   Haroldo (rey)
  SU   Гáрольд (прав.)

1570   GB   Harpies, the (myth.)
  F   les Harpyes (myth.)
  D   die Harpyien (myth.)
  I   le arpie (mit.)
  E   las Arpías (mit.)
  SU   гáрпии (миф.)

1571   GB   *Harvey* (Koster, 1950)
  F   *Harvey*
  D   *Mein Freund Harvey*
  I   *Harvey*
  E   *El invisible Harvey*
  SU   «Хáрви» (Кóстер)

1572   GB   *Háry János* (Kodály, 1926)
  F   *Háry János*
  D   *Háry János*
  I   *Háry János*
  E   *Háry János*
  SU   «Хáри Янош» (Кóдай)

1573   GB   *Hatter's Castle* (Cronin, 1931)
  F   *Le Chapelier et son château*
  D   *Der Hutmacher und sein Schloß*
  I   *Il castello del cappellaio*
  E   *El castillo del sombrero*
  SU   «Зáмок Брóуди» (Крóнин)

1574   GB   Havana (Cuba)
  F   la Havane (Cuba)
  D   Habana (Kuba)
  I   L'Avana (Cuba)
  E   la Habana (Cuba)
  SU   Гавáна (Кýба)

GB   Havre, Le→Le Havre

1575   GB   Hawaii
  F   les îles Hawaii
  D   die Hawaii-Inseln
  I   le Hawaii
  E   las islas Hawai
  SU   Гавáйи

1576   GB   *Haywain, The* (Constable, 1821)
  F   *La Charrette de foin*
  D   *Der Heuwagen*
  I   *Il carro di fieno*
  E   *La carreta de heno*
  SU   «Телéга для сéна» (Кóнстебл)

1577   GB   *Headless Horseman, The* (Reid, 1866)
  F   *Le Cavalier sans tête*
  D   *Vogelfrei im Urwald*
  I   *Il cavaliere senza testa*
  E   *El jinete sin cabeza*
  SU   «Всáдник без головы́» (Рид)

1578 GB *Heartbreak House* (Shaw, 1919)
  F *La Maison des coeurs brisés*
  D *Haus Herzenstod*
  I *Casa Cuorinfranto*
  E *La casa de la congoja*
  SU «Дом, где разбива́ются сердца́» (Шо́у)

1579 GB *Heart of Darkness* (Conrad, 1902)
  F *Au coeur des ténèbres*
  D *Herz der Finsternis*
  I *Cuore di tenebra*
  E *Corazón de las tinieblas*
  SU «Се́рдце тьмы» (Ко́нрад)

1580 GB *Heart of Midlothian* (Scott, 1818)
  F *La Prison d'Édimbourg*
  D *Das Herz von Midlothian*
  I *Il cuore del Midlothian*
  E *El corazón de Midlothian*
  SU «Эдинбу́ргская темни́ца» (Скотт)

1581 GB *Heart of the Matter, The* (Greene, 1948)
  F *Le Fond du problème*
  D *Das Herz aller Dinge*
  I *Il nocciolo della questione*
  E *Un sentido de realidad*
  SU «Суть де́ла» (Грин)

1582 GB Hebe (myth.)
  F Hébé (myth.)
  D Hebe (myth.)
  I Ebe (mit.)
  E Hebe (mit.)
  SU Ге́ба (миф.)

1583 GB Hebrews, the Epistle of Paul to the (Bib.)
  F l'Épître de Saint Paul aux Hébreux (Bib.)
  D der Hebräerbrief (Bib.)
  I la lettera di Paolo agli Ebrei (Bib.)
  E la Epístola de San Pablo a los hebreos
  SU «Посла́ние к Евре́ям» (библ.)

1584 GB Hebrides, the (Scotland)
  F les îles Hébrides (Écosse)
  D die Hebriden (Schottland)
  I le Ebridi (Scozia)
  E las Hébridas (Escocia)
  SU Гебри́дские острова́ (Шотла́ндия)

1585 GB Hebron (Bib.)
  F Hébron (Bib.)
  D Hebron (Bib.)
  I Ebron (Bib.)
  E Hebrón (Bib.)
  SU Хевро́н (библ.)

1586 GB Hecate (myth.)
  F Hécate (myth.)
  D Hekate (myth.)
  I Ecate (mit.)
  E Hécate (mit.)
  SU Гека́та (миф.)

1587 GB Hector (myth.)
  F Hector (myth.)
  D Hektor (myth.)
  I Ettore (mit.)
  E Héctor (mit.)
  SU Ге́ктор (миф.)

1588 GB Hecuba (myth., + Euripides, −425)
  F Hécube (myth., + Euripide)
  D Hekuba (myth., + Euripides)
  I Ecuba (mit., + Euripide)
  E Hécuba (mit., + Eurípides)
  SU Геку́ба (миф., + Еврипи́д)

1589 GB *Hedda Gabler* (Ibsen, 1890)
  F *Hedda Gabler*
  D *Hedda Gabler*
  I *Edda Gabler*
  E *Hedda Gabler*
  SU «Ге́дда Га́блер» (Й́бсен)

1590 GB *Heir, The* (Regnard, 1708)
  F *Le Légataire universel*
  D *Der Universalerbe*
  I *L'erede universale*
  E *El heredero universal*
  SU «Еди́нственный насле́дник» (Ренья́р)

1591 GB Helen (myth., + Euripides, −412)
  F Hélène (myth., + Euripide)
  D Helena (myth., + Euripides)
  I Elena (mit., + Euripide)
  E Helena (mit., + Eurípides)
  SU Еле́на (миф., + Еврипи́д)

1592 GB Heligoland
  F Helgoland
  D Helgoland
  I Helgoland
  E Helgoland
  SU Ге́льголанд

1593 GB Helios (myth.)
  F Hélios (myth.)
  D Helios (myth.)
  I Elio (mit.)
  E Helios (mit.)
  SU Ге́лиос (миф.)

1594 GB *Hellenica*, the (Xenophon, −IV)
  F   *Helléniques* (Xénophon)
  D   *Griechische Geschichten* (Xenophon)
  I   le *Elleniche* (Senofonte)
  E   *Helénicas* (Jenofonte)
  SU «Гре́ческая исто́рия» (Ксенофо́нт)

1595 GB Hellespont, the (hist.)
  F   le Hellespont (hist.)
  D   der Hellespont (Gesch.)
  I   l'Ellesponto (st.)
  E   el Helesponto (hist.)
  SU Геллеспо́нт (ист.)

1596 GB Helsinki (Finland)
  F   Helsinki (Finlande)
  D   Helsinki (Finnland)
  I   Helsinki (Finlandia)
  E   Helsinki (Finlandia)
  SU Хе́льсинки (Финля́ндия)

1597 GB *Henderson, the Rain King* (Bellow, 1959)
  F   *Le Faiseur de pluie*
  D   *Henderson der Regenkönig*
  I   *Il re della pioggia*
  E   *Henderson, el rey de la lluvia*
  SU «Хе́ндерсон – властели́н дождёй» (Бе́ллоу)

1598 GB *Henriada, the* [*History of Henry*] (Voltaire, 1723)
  F   la *Henriade*
  D   die *Henriade*
  I   la *Enriade*
  E   la *Henriada*
  SU «Генриа́да» (Вольте́р)

1599 GB Henry (sovereign)
  F   Henri (souverain)
  D   Heinrich (Herr.)
  I   Enrico (sovrano)
  E   Enrique (sob.)
  SU Ге́нрих (прав.)

1600 GB *Henry Esmond* (Thackeray, 1852)
  F   *Henri Esmond*
  D   *Henry Esmond*
  I   *Henry Esmond*
  E   *Enerico Esmond*
  SU «Исто́рия Ге́нри Э́смонда» (Те́ккерей)

1601 GB Henry the Lion (1130–95)
  F   Henri le Lion
  D   Heinrich der Löwe
  I   Enrico il Leone
  E   Enrique el León
  SU Ге́нрих Лев

1602 GB Henry the Navigator (1394–1460)
  F   Henri le Navigateur
  D   Heinrich der Seefahrer
  I   Enrico il Navigatore
  E   Enrique el Navegante
  SU Ге́нрих Морепла́ватель

1603 GB Hephaestus (myth.)
  F   Hephaïstos (myth.)
  D   Hephästos (myth.)
  I   Efesto (mit.)
  E   Hefestos (mit.)
  SU Гефе́ст (миф.)

1604 GB *Heptameron*, the (Margaret of Navarre, 1559)
  F   l'*Heptaméron* (Marguerite de Navarre)
  D   das *Heptameron* (Margarete von Navarra)
  I   l'*Eptamerone* (Margherita di Navarra)
  E   el *Heptamerón* (Margarita de Angulema)
  SU «Гептамеро́н» (Маргари́та Нава́ррская)

1605 GB Hera (myth.)
  F   Héra (myth.)
  D   Hera (myth.)
  I   Era (mit.)
  E   Hera (mit.)
  SU Ге́ра (миф.)

1606 GB Heracles (myth.)
  F   Héraclès (myth.)
  D   Herakles (myth.)
  I   Eracle (mit.)
  E   Heracles (mit.)
  SU Гера́кл (миф.)

1607 GB Heraclitus (−V)
  F   Héraclite
  D   Heraklit
  I   Eraclito
  E   Heráclito
  SU Геракли́т

1608 GB Hercules (myth.)
  F   Hercule (myth.)
  D   Herkules (myth.)
  I   Ercole (mit.)
  E   Hércules (mit.)
  SU Геркуле́с (миф.)

1609 GB *Hermann and Dorothea* (Goethe,
              1797)
          F   *Hermann et Dorothée*
          D   *Hermann und Dorothea*
          I   *Arminio e Dorotea*
          E   *Hermann y Dorotea*
          SU «Гéрман и Доротéя» (Гёте)

1610 GB Hermes (myth.)
          F   Hermès (myth.)
          D   Hermes (myth.)
          I   Ermes (mit.)
          E   Hermes (mit.)
          SU Гермéс (миф.)

1611 GB Hermione (myth.)
          F   Hermione (myth.)
          D   Hermine (myth.)
          I   Ermione (mit.)
          E   Hermiona (mit.)
          SU Гермиóна (миф.)

1612 GB Hermitage, the (Leningrad)
          F   l'Ermitage (Leningrad)
          D   die Eremitage (Leningrad)
          I   l'Ermitage (Leningrado)
          E   la Ermita (Leningrado)
          SU Эрмитáж (Ленингрáд)

1613 GB *Hernani* (Hugo, 1830)
          F   *Hernani*
          D   *Hernani*
          I   *Ernani*
          E   *Hernani*
          SU «Эрнáни» (Гюгó)

1614 GB Hero (myth.)
          F   Héro (myth.)
          D   Hero (myth.)
          I   Ero (mit.)
          E   Hero (mit.)
          SU Герó (миф.)

1615 GB Hero and Leander (myth., + Marlowe,
              1598)
          F   Héro et Léandre (myth.)
          D   Hero und Leander (myth.)
          I   Ero e Leandro (mit.)
          E   Hero y Leandro (mit.)
          SU Герó и Леáндр (миф., + Мáрло)

1616 GB Herod Agrippa (king)
          F   Hérode Agrippa (roi)
          D   Herodes Agrippa (König)
          I   Erode Agrippa (re)
          E   Herodes Agripa (rey)
          SU Ѝрод Агрѝппа (царь)

1617 GB Herod Antipas (king)
          F   Hérode Antipas (roi)
          D   Herodes Antipas (König)
          I   Erode Antipa (re)
          E   Herodes Antipas (rey)
          SU Ѝрод Антѝпа (царь)

1618 GB Herodias (Bib., + Massenet, 1881)
          F   Hérodiade (Bib.)
          D   Herodias (Bib.)
          I   Erodiade (Bib.)
          E   Herodías (Bib.)
          SU Иродиáда (библ., + Массне́)

1619 GB Herodotus (*484–430*)
          F   Hérodote
          D   Herodot
          I   Erodoto
          E   Herodoto
          SU Геродóт

1620 GB Herod the Great (73–4)
          F   Hérode le Grand
          D   Herodes der Große
          I   Erode il Grande
          E   Herodes el Grande
          SU Ѝрод Велѝкий

1621 GB *Hero of Our Time, A* (Lermontov,
              1840)
          F   *Un héros de notre temps* (Lermontov)
          D   *Ein Held unserer Zeit* (Lermontow)
          I   *Un eroe del nostro tempo* (Lermontov)
          E   *Un héroe de nuestro tiempo*
              (Lermontov)
          SU «Герóй нáшего врéмени»
              (Лéрмонтов)

1622 GB *Herzog* (Bellow, 1964)
          F   *Herzog*
          D   *Herzog*
          I   *Herzog*
          E   *Herzog*
          SU «Гéрцог» (Бéллоу)

1623 GB Hesiod (−IX)
          F   Hésiode
          D   Hesiodos
          I   Esiodo
          E   Hesíodo
          SU Гесиóд

1624 GB Hesperides, the (myth.)
          F   les Hespérides (myth.)
          D   die Hesperiden (myth.)
          I   le Esperidi (mit.)
          E   las Hespérides (mit.)
          SU Гесперѝды (миф.)

1625   GB   Hestia (myth.)
      F   Hestia (myth.)
      D   Hestia (myth.)
      I   Estia (mit.)
      E   Hestia (mit.)
      SU   Гéстия (миф.)

1626   GB   Hezekiah (Bib.)
      F   Ézéchias (Bib.)
      D   Hiskia (Bib.)
      I   Ezechia (Bib.)
      E   Ezequías (Bib.)
      SU   Езекúя (библ.)

      GB   *Hiawatha→Song of Hiawatha*

1627   GB   *High Noon* (Zinnemann, 1952)
      F   *Le train sifflera trois fois*
      D   *Zwölf Uhr mittags*
      I   *Mezzogiorno di fuoco*
      E   *Solo ante el peligro*
      SU   «Тóчно в пóлдень» (Зúннеманн)

1628   GB   *High Wind in Jamaica, A* (Hughes, 1929)
      F   *Grand Vent en Jamaïque*
      D   *Sturm über Jamaica*
      I   *Un ciclone nella Giamaica*
      E   *Un viento fuerte en Jamaica*
      SU   «Урагáн на Ямáйке» (Хьюз)

1629   GB   Hilary (saint, 429–449)
      F   Hilaire (saint)
      D   Hilarius (Heiliger)
      I   Ilario (santo)
      E   Hilario (santo)
      SU   Илларióн (св.)

1630   GB   *Hilda Lessways* (Bennett, 1911)
      F   *Hilda Lessways*
      D   *Hilda Lessways*
      I   *Hilda Lessways*
      E   *Hilda Lessways*
      SU   «Хúльда Лéссуэйс» (Бéннетт)

1631   GB   Himalayas, the
      F   l'Himalaya (m.)
      D   der Himalaja
      I   l'Himalaia
      E   el Himalaya
      SU   Гималáйские гóры

1632   GB   Hindustan
      F   l'Hindoustan (m.)
      D   Hindostan
      I   Indostan
      E   Indostán
      SU   Хиндустáн

1633   GB   Hippocrates (*460–377*)
      F   Hippocrate
      D   Hippokrates
      I   Ippocrate
      E   Hipócrates
      SU   Гиппокрáт

1634   GB   Hippolyta (myth.)
      F   Hippolyte (myth.)
      D   Hippolyta (myth.)
      I   Ippolita (mit.)
      E   Hipólita (mit.)
      SU   Ипполúта (миф.)

1635   GB   Hippolytus (myth., + Euripides, −428)
      F   Hippolyte (myth., + Euripide)
      D   Hippolytos (myth., + Euripides)
      I   Ippolito (mit., + Euripide)
      E   Hipólito (mit., + Eurípides)
      SU   Ипполúт (миф., + Еврипúд)

1636   GB   *Hippolytus and Aricia* (Rameau, 1733)
      F   *Hippolyte et Aricie*
      D   *Hippolytos und Aricia*
      I   *Ippolito e Aricia*
      E   *Hipólito y Aricia*
      SU   «Ипполúт и Арисúя» (Рамó)

1637   GB   *Hiroshima, mon amour* [*Hiroshima, My Love*] (Resnais, 1959)
      F   *Hiroshima, mon amour*
      D   *Hiroshima, mon amour*
      I   *Hiroshima, mon amour*
      E   *Hiroshima, mon amour*
      SU   «Хирóсúма, моя любóвь» (Ренé)

1638   GB   *Historia Naturalis* [*Natural History*] (Pliny the Elder, I)
      F   l'*Histoire naturelle* (Pline l'Ancien)
      D   die *Naturgeschichte* (Plinius der Ältere)
      I   la *Naturalis historia* (Plinio il Vecchio)
      E   la *Historia natural* (Plinio el Viejo)
      SU   «Естéственная истóрия» (Плúний Стáрший)

1639   GB   *Histories, the* [*Historiae*] (Polybius, −II)
      F   les *Histoires* (Polybe)
      D   die *Geschichten* (Polybios)
      I   le *Storie* (Polibio)
      E   *Historia general de Roma* (Polibio)
      SU   «Истóрия» (Полúбий)

1640 GB *History of Charles XII, The* (Voltaire, 1731)
F *L'Histoire de Charles XII*
D *Die Geschichte Karls XII von Schweden*
I *La storia di Carlo XII*
E *Historia de Carlos XII*
SU «История Ка́рла XII» (Вольте́р)

1641 GB *History of France, The* (Michelet, 1833–44)
F *Histoire de France*
D *Geschichte Frankreichs*
I *Storia di Francia*
E *Historia de Francia*
SU «Исто́рия Фра́нции» (Мишле́)

1642 GB *History of Italy, The* (Guicciardini, 1483–1540)
F *Histoire d'Italie* (Guichardin)
D *Geschichte Italiens* (Guicciardini)
I *Storia d'Italia* (Guicciardini)
E *Historia de Italia desde 1494 a 1532* (Guicciardini)
SU «Исто́рия Ита́лии» (Гвиччарди́ни)

1643 GB *History of New York* (Irving, 1809)
F *Histoire de New-York*
D *Geschichte New-Yorks*
I *Storia di New York*
E *Historia de Nueva York*
SU «Исто́рия Нью-Йо́рка» (Йрвинг)

1644 GB *History of Sir Charles Grandison, The* (Richardson, 1754)
F *L'Histoire de Sir Charles Grandison*
D *Die Geschichte von Sir Charles Grandison*
I *La storia di Sir Charles Grandison*
E *La historia de Sir Carlos Grandison*
SU «Исто́рия сэ́ра Ча́рльза Грандисо́на» (Ри́чардсон)

1645 GB *History of the Adventures of Joseph Andrews* (Fielding, 1742)
F *L'Histoire des aventures de Joseph Andrews*
D *Die Geschichte der Abenteuer Joseph Andrews*
I *La storia delle avventure di Joseph Andrews*
E *La historia de las aventuras de Joseph Andrews*
SU «Исто́рия приключе́ний Джо́зефа Э́ндруса» (Фи́лдинг)

1646 GB *History of the Conquest of Mexico, A* (Prescott, 1843)
F *La Conquête du Mexique*
D *Die Eroberung von Mexiko*
I *Storia della conquista del Messico*
E *Historia de la conquista de México*
SU «Исто́рия завоева́ния Ме́ксики» (Пре́скотт)

1647 GB *History of the Conquest of Peru, A* (Prescott, 1847)
F *La Conquête du Pérou*
D *Die Eroberung von Peru*
I *Storia della conquista del Perù*
E *Historia de la conquista del Perú*
SU «Исто́рия завоева́ния Перу́» (Пре́скотт)

1648 GB *History of the Consulate and the Empire, A* (Thiers, 1845–62)
F *Histoire du Consulat et de l'Empire*
D *Geschichte des Konsulats und des Empires*
I *Storia del consolato e dell'impero*
E *Historia del Consulado y del Imperio*
SU «Исто́рия ко́нсульства и импе́рии» (Тьер)

1649 GB *History of the French Revolution, A* (Thiers, 1823–7)
F *Histoire de la Révolution*
D *Geschichte der französischen Revolution*
I *Storia della rivoluzione francese*
E *Historia de la Revolución Francesa*
SU «Исто́рия Францу́зской револю́ции» (Тьер)

1650 GB *History of the Life and Voyages of Christopher Columbus* (Irving, 1828)
F *Histoire de la vie et des voyages de Christophe Colomb*
D *Leben und Reisen von Christopher Columbus*
I *Vita e viaggi di Cristoforo Colombo*
E *Vida y viajes de Cristóbal Colón*
SU «Исто́рия жи́зни и путеше́ствий Христофо́ра Колу́мба» (Йрвинг)

1651 GB *History of the Origins of Christianity, The* (Renan, 1863–83)
F *Histoire des origines du christianisme*
D *Geschichte der Anfänge des Christentums*
I *Storia delle origini del cristianesimo*
E *Historia de los orígenes del cristianismo*
SU «Исто́рия происхожде́ния христиа́нства» (Рена́н)

1652   GB   *History of the Peloponnesian War*
            [Syngraphe] (Thucydides, −IV)
       F   *Histoire de la guerre du Péloponnèse*
            (Thucydide)
       D   *Geschichte des Peloponnesischen*
            Krieges (Thukydides)
       I   *Guerra del Peloponneso* (Tucidide)
       E   *La historia de la guerra del Peloponeso*
            (Tucídides)
       SU   «Истóрия Пелопоннéсской войнь́»
            (Фукидúд)

1653   GB   *History of the Pugachov Rebellion*
            (Pushkin, 1834)
       F   *Histoire de la révolte de Pougatchev*
            (Pouchkine)
       D   *Geschichte des Pugatschowschen*
            Aufstandes (Puschkin)
       I   *Storia della rivolta di Pugačëv* (Puškin)
       E   *Historia de la rebelión de Pugachov*
            (Puschkin)
       SU   «Истóрия Пугачёва» (Пýшкин)

1654   GB   *History of the Reformation in*
            Germany, A (Ranke, 1839–47)
       F   *Histoire d'Allemagne au temps de la*
            Réforme
       D   *Deutsche Geschichte im Zeitalter der*
            Reformation
       I   *Storia della Germania nell'età della*
            riforma
       E   *Historia de Alemania en tiempos de la*
            reforma
       SU   «Немéцкая истóрия в эпóху
            Реформáции» (Рáнке)

1655   GB   Hittites, the (Bib.)
       F   les Hittites (Bib.)
       D   die Hethiter (Bib.)
       I   gli ittiti (Bib.)
       E   los hititas (Bib.)
       SU   хéтты (библ.)

1656   GB   Holland
       F   la Hollande
       D   Holland
       I   l'Olanda
       E   Holanda
       SU   Голлáндия

1657   GB   *Hollow Men, The* (Eliot, 1925)
       F   *Les Hommes creux*
       D   *Die hohlen Menschen*
       I   *Gli uomini vuoti*
       E   *Los hombres huecos*
       SU   «Пóлые лю́ди» (Э́лиот)

1658   GB   Holy Alliance, the (1815)
       F   la Sainte-Alliance
       D   die Heilige Allianz
       I   la santa alleanza
       E   la Santa Alianza
       SU   Свящéнный сою́з

1659   GB   Holy Bible, the
       F   la Sainte Bible
       D   die Heilige Bibel
       I   la Sacra Bibbia
       E   la Santa Biblia
       SU   Бúблия

1660   GB   Holy Family, the (art, + Marx, 1845)
       F   la Sainte Famille (art)
       D   die Heilige Familie (Kunst)
       I   la Sacra Famiglia (arte)
       E   la Familia Sagrada (arte)
       SU   святóе семéйство (иск., + Маркс)

       GB   Holy Ghost→Holy Spirit

1661   GB   Holy Grail, the (rel.)
       F   le Saint Graal (relig.)
       D   der Gral (relig.)
       I   il Graal (relig.)
       E   el Santo Grial (relig.)
       SU   Граáль (м.) (рел.)

1662   GB   Holy Innocents Day (rel.)
       F   les Saints Innocents (relig.)
       D   das Fest der Unschuldigen Kinder
            (relig.)
       I   i santi innocenti (relig.)
       E   el día de los Santos Inocentes (relig.)
       SU   День избиéния младéнцев (рел.)

1663   GB   Holy Land, the (= Israel)
       F   la Terre sainte (= Isräel)
       D   das Heilige Land (= Israel)
       I   la Terra Santa (= Israele)
       E   la Tierra Santa (= Israel)
       SU   святáя земля́ (= Изрáиль)

1664   GB   Holy League, the (1511)
       F   la Ligue Sainte
       D   die Heilige Liga
       I   la Lega Santa
       E   la Santa Liga
       SU   Свящéнная лúга

1665   GB   Holy Roman Empire, the (hist.)
       F   le Saint Empire Romain (hist.)
       D   das Heilige Römische Reich (Gesch.)
       I   il Sacro Romano Impero (st.)
       E   el Sacro Imperio Romano (hist.)
       SU   «Свящéнная Рúмская импéрия» (ист.)

1666 GB Holy Scriptures, the (Bib.)
F l'Écriture sainte (Bib.)
D die Heilige Schrift (Bib.)
I la Santa Scrittura (Bib.)
E la Sagrada Escritura (Bib.)
SU «свяще́нное писа́ние» (библ.)

1667 GB Holy Sepulchre, the (Jerusalem)
F le Saint-Sépulcre (Jérusalem)
D die Grabeskirche (Jerusalem)
I il Santo Sepulcro (Gerusalemme)
E el Santo Sepulcro (Jerusalén)
SU «Гроб госпо́день» (Иерусали́м)

1668 GB Holy Spirit (Holy Ghost), the (rel.)
F le Saint-Esprit (relig.)
D der Heilige Geist (relig.)
I lo Spirito Santo (relig.)
E el Espíritu Santo (relig.)
SU свято́й дух (рел.)

1669 GB Holy Week (rel.)
F la Semaine sainte (relig.)
D die Karwoche (relig.)
I la settimana santa (relig.)
E la Semana Santa (relig.)
SU страстна́я неде́ля (рел.)

1670 GB *Homecoming, The* (Pinter, 1965)
F *Le Retour*
D *Die Heimkehr*
I *Ritorno a casa*
E *Retorno al hogar*
SU «Возвраще́ние домо́й» (Пи́нтер)

1671 GB Homer (?–IX)
F Homère
D Homeros
I Omero
E Homero
SU Гоме́р

1672 GB Honduras
F le Honduras
D Honduras
I l'Honduras
E Honduras
SU Гондура́с

1673 GB Honorius (pope)
F Honorius (pape)
D Honorius (Papst)
I Onorio (papa)
E Honorio (papa)
SU Гоно́рий (па́па ри́мский)

1674 GB Hook of Holland, the (Netherlands)
F Hoek van Holland (Pays-Bas)
D Hoek van Holland (Niederlande)
I Hoek van Holland (Paesi Bassi)
E Hoek van Holland (Holanda)
SU Хук-ван-Хо́лланд (Нидерла́нды)

1675 GB Horace (65–8, + Corneille, 1640)
F Horace
D Horaz
I Orazio
E Horacio
SU Гора́ций (+ Корне́ль)

GB Horn, Cape→Cape Horn

1676 GB *Horse's Mouth, The* (Cary, 1944)
F *La Bouche du cheval*
D *Des Pudels Kern*
I *La bocca della verità*
E *La boca del caballo*
SU «Уста́ми худо́жника» (Кэ́ри)

1677 GB Hosea (Bib.)
F Osée (Bib.)
D Hosea (Bib.)
I Osea (Bib.)
E Oseas (Bib.)
SU Оси́я (библ.)

1678 GB *Hostage, The* (Claudel, 1909)
F *L'Otage*
D *Der Bürge*
I *L'ostaggio*
E *El rehén*
SU «Зало́жник» (Клоде́ль)

GB Hôtel des Invalides (Paris)→Invalides,
Hôtel des

1679 GB Hottentots, the (Africa)
F les Hottentots (Afrique)
D die Hottentotten (Afrika)
I gli ottentotti (Africa)
E los hotentotes (África)
SU готтенто́ты (А́фрика)

1680 GB *Hound of the Baskervilles, The* (Doyle,
1902)
F *Le Chien des Baskerville*
D *Der Hund von Baskervilles*
I *Il mastino dei Baskerville*
E *El sabueso de los Baskerville*
SU «Соба́ка Баскерви́лей» (Дойл)

1681   GB   Hours, the (myth.)
F   les Heures (myth.)
D   die Horen (myth.)
I   le Ore (mit.)
E   las Horas (mit.)
SU   Óры (миф.)

1682   GB   *House of Bernarda Alba* (Lorca, 1936)
F   *La Maison de Bernarda Alba*
D   *Bernarda Albas Haus*
I   *La casa di Bernarda Alba*
E   *La casa de Bernarda Alba*
SU   «Дом Бернáрды Áльбы» (Гарсúа Лóрка)

1683   GB   House of Commons, the (London)
F   la Chambre des communes (Londres)
D   das Unterhaus (London)
I   la camera dei comuni (Londra)
E   la Cámara de los Comunes (Londres)
SU   палáта óбщин (Лóндон)

1684   GB   House of Lords, the (London)
F   la Chambre des lords (Londres)
D   das Oberhaus (London)
I   la camera dei lords (Londra)
E   la Cámara de los Lores (Londres)
SU   палáта лóрдов (Лóндон)

1685   GB   House of Representatives, the (Washington)
F   la Chambre des représentants (Washington)
D   das Repräsentenhaus (Washington)
I   la camera dei deputati (Washington)
E   la Cámara de los Representantes (Washington)
SU   палáта представúтелей (Вашингтóн)

1686   GB   *House of the Dead* (Dostoievsky, 1861)
F   *Souvenirs de la maison des morts* (Dostoïevski)
D   *Aufzeichnungen aus einem Totenhaus* (Dostojewskij)
I   *Memorie da una casa di morti* (Dostoevskij)
E   *La casa de los muertos* (Dostoievski)
SU   «Запúски из мёртвого дóма» (Достоéвский)

1687   GB   *House of the Seven Gables, The* (Hawthorne, 1851)
F   *La Maison aux sept pignons*
D   *Das Haus der sieben Giebel*
I   *La casa delle sette torri*
E   *La casa de los siete altillos*
SU   «Дом о семú шпúлях» (Хóторн)

1688   GB   Houses of Parliament, the (London)
F   le palais de Westminster (Londres)
D   das Parlamentsgebäude (London)
I   il palazzo del Parlamento (Londra)
E   el Palacio de Westminster (Londres)
SU   здáние парлáмента (Лóндон)

1689   GB   *Howards End* (Forster, 1910)
F   *Howards End*
D   *Howards End*
I   *Casa Howard*
E   *La Mansión*
SU   «Хóуардс-Энд» (Фóрстер)

1690   GB   *How Green Was My Valley* (Llewellyn, 1939; Ford, 1941)
F   *Qu'elle était verte, ma vallée*
D   *So grün war mein Tal*
I   *Com'era verde la mia valle*
E   *Que verde era mi valle*
SU   «Как зеленá былá моя долúна» (Левéлин, Форд)

   GB   *Huckleberry Finn*→*Adventures of Huckleberry Finn*

1691   GB   *Hudibras* (Butler, 1663–78)
F   *Hudibras*
D   *Hudibras*
I   *Hudibras*
E   *Hudibras*
SU   «Гýдибрас» (Бáтлер)

1692   GB   Hugh (king)
F   Hugues (roi)
D   Hugo (König)
I   Ugo (re)
E   Hugo (rey)
SU   Гугó (прав.)

1693   GB   Huguenots, the (hist., + Meyerbeer, 1836)
F   les Huguenots (hist.)
D   die Hugenotten (Gesch.)
I   gli ugonotti (st.)
E   los Hugonotes (hist.)
SU   гугенóты (ист., + Мейербéр)

1694   GB   *Human, All Too Human* (Nietzsche, 1878)
F   *Humain, trop humain*
D   *Menschliches, Allzumenschliches*
I   *Umano, troppo umano*
E   *Humano, demasiado humano*
SU   «Человéческое, слúшком человéческое» (Нúцше)

1695 GB *Human Comedy, The* (Balzac, 1842–
        89)
     F *La Comédie humaine*
     D *Die menschliche Komödie*
     I *La commedia umana*
     E *La comedia humana*
     SU «Челове́ческая коме́дия» (Бальза́к)

1696 GB *Human Condition, The* (Malraux,
        1933)
     F *La Condition humaine*
     D *So lebt der Mensch*
     I *La condizione umana*
     E *La condición humana*
     SU «Усло́вия челове́ческого
        существова́ния» (Мальро́)

1697 GB *Humble Ones, The* (Coppée, 1872)
     F *Les Humbles*
     D *Die Niedrigen*
     I *Gli umili*
     E *Los humildes*
     SU «Смире́нные» (Коппе́)

     GB *Humphry Clinker*→*Expedition of
        Humphry Clinker*

1698 GB *Hunchback of Notre Dame, The*
        (Hugo, 1831)
     F *Notre-Dame de Paris*
     D *Der Glöckner von Notre-Dame*
     I *Notre-Dame de Paris*
     E *Nuestra Señora de París*
     SU «Собо́р Пари́жской богома́тери»
        (Гюго́)

1699 GB Hundred Days, the (1815)
     F les Cent-Jours
     D die Hundert Tage
     I i cento giorni
     E los Cien Días
     SU «Сто дней»

1700 GB Hundred Years' War, the (1337–1453)
     F la guerre de Cent Ans
     D der Hundertjährige Krieg
     I la guerra dei cent'anni
     E la guerra de los Cien Años
     SU столе́тняя война́

1701 GB *Hungarian Rhapsodies* (Liszt, 1860)
     F *Rapsodies hongroises*
     D *Ungarische Rhapsodien*
     I *Rapsodie ungheresi*
     E *Rapsodias húngaras*
     SU «Венге́рские рапсо́дии» (Лист)

1702 GB Hungary
     F la Hongrie
     D Ungarn
     I l'Ungheria
     E Hungría
     SU Ве́нгрия

1703 GB *Hunger* [*Sult*] (Hamsun, 1890)
     F *La Faim*
     D *Hunger*
     I *Fame*
     E *El hambre*
     SU «Го́лод» (Га́мсун)

1704 GB Huns, the (hist.)
     F les Huns (hist.)
     D die Hunnen (Gesch.)
     I gli unni (st.)
     E los hunos (hist.)
     SU гу́нны (ист.)

1705 GB *Hunting of the Snark, The* (Carroll,
        1876)
     F *La Chasse au snark*
     D *Der Jagd nach den Snark*
     I *La caccia allo Snark*
     E *La caza del snark*
     SU «Охо́та на Сна́рка» (Кэ́рролл)

1706 GB Hyacinth(us) (myth.)
     F Hyacinthos (myth.)
     D Hyakinthos (myth.)
     I Giacinto (mit.)
     E Jacinto (mit.)
     SU Гиаци́нт (миф.)

1707 GB Hyades, the (myth.)
     F les Hyades (myth.)
     D die Hyaden (myth.)
     I le Iade (mit.)
     E las Híades (mit.)
     SU Гиа́ды (миф.)

1708 GB Hydra (myth.)
     F l'Hydre (f.) (myth.)
     D die Hydra (myth.)
     I l'Idra (mit.)
     E la Hidra (mit.)
     SU Ги́дра (миф.)

1709 GB *Hymns* (Ronsard, 1555–6)
     F *Hymnes*
     D *Hymnen*
     I *Inni*
     E *Himnos*
     SU «Ги́мны» (Ронса́р)

1710 GB *Hymns to the Night* (Novalis, 1800)
    F *Hymnes à la nuit*
    D *Hymnen an die Nacht*
    I *Inni alla notte*
    E *Himnos de la noche*
    SU «Гимны к ночи» (Новалис)

1711 GB Hypatia (*370*–415, + Kingsley, 1853)
    F Hypatie
    D Hypathia
    I Ipazia
    E Hypatia
    SU Гупатия (+ Кингсли)

1712 GB Hyperboreans, the (myth.)
    F les Hyperboréens (myth.)
    D die Hyperboreer (myth.)
    I gli iperborei (mit.)
    E los hiperbóreos (mit.)
    SU гипербореи (миф.)

1713 GB Hyperion (myth., + Keats, 1820; Longfellow, 1839)
    F Hypérion (myth.)
    D Hyperion (myth.)
    I Iperione (mit.)
    E Hyperion (mit.)
    SU Гиперион (миф., + Китс, Лонгфелло)

I

1714 GB *I Am a Fugitive From a Chain Gang*
             (Le Roy, 1932)
        F   *Je suis un évadé*
        D   *Ich bin ein entflohener Kettensträfling*
        I   *Io sono un evaso*
        E   *Soy un fugitivo*
        SU «Я – бéглый кáторжник» (Ле Рой)

1715 GB Iberia (hist.)
        F   l'Ibérie (f.) (hist.)
        D   Iberia (Gesch.)
        I   l'Iberia (st.)
        E   Iberia (hist.)
        SU Ибéрия (ист.)

1716 GB Icarus (myth.)
        F   Icare (myth.)
        D   Ikarus (myth.)
        I   Icaro (mit.)
        E   Ícaro (mit.)
        SU Икáр (миф.)

1717 GB Ice Age, the (hist.)
        F   la période glaciaire (hist.)
        D   die Eiszeit (Gesch.)
        I   l'era glaciale (st.)
        E   el período glaciar (hist.)
        SU ледникóвый перńод (ист.)

1718 GB Iceland
        F   l'Islande (f.)
        D   Island
        I   l'Islanda
        E   Islandia
        SU Ислáндия

1719 GB *Iceland Fisherman, An* (Loti, 1866)
        F   *Pêcheur d'Islande*
        D   *Der Islandfischer*
        I   *Pescatore d'Islanda*
        E   *El pescador de Islandia*
        SU «Ислáндский рыбáк» (Лотń)

1720 GB *Iceman Cometh, The* (O'Neill, 1946)
        F   *La Venue de l'homme des glaces*
        D   *Der Eismann kommt*
        I   *Viene l'uomo del ghiaccio*
        E   *Viene el hombre de los hielos*
        SU «Разнóсчик льдá грядёт» (О'Нńл)

1721 GB *I, Claudius* (Graves, 1934)
        F   *Moi, Claude*
        D   *Ich, Claudius*
        I   *Io, Claudio*
        E   *Yo, Claudio*
        SU «Я, Клáвдий» (Грéйвс)

1722 GB *Ides of March, The* (Wilder, 1948)
        F   *Les Ides de mars*
        D   *Die Iden des März*
        I   *Le idi di marzo*
        E   *Los Idus de marzo*
        SU «Мáртовские ńды» (Уáйлдер)

1723 GB *Idiot, The* (Dostoievsky, 1868–9)
        F   *L'Idiot* (Dostoïevski)
        D   *Der Idiot* (Dostojewskij)
        I   *L'idiota* (Dostoevskij)
        E   *El idiota* (Dostoievski)
        SU «Идиóт» (Достоéвский)

1724 GB Idomencus (**myth.**, + Mozart, 1781)
        F   Idoménée (myth.)
        D   Idomeneo (myth.)
        I   Idomeneo (mit.)
        E   Idomeneo (mit.)
        SU Идоменéй (миф., + Мóцарт)

1725 GB *Idylls*, the [*Bukolika eidyllia*]
             (Theocritus, −III)
        F   *Idylles* (Théocrite)
        D   *Die Idyllen* (Theokritus)
        I   *Idilli* (Teocrito)
        E   los *Idilios* (Teócrito)
        SU «Идńллии» (Феокрńт)

1726 GB *Idylls of the King* (Tennyson, 1842–85)
F   *Les Idylles du roi*
D   *Die Königsidyllen*
I   *Idilli del re*
E   *Los idilios del rey*
SU «Короле́вские иди́ллии» (Те́ннисон)

1727 GB *If . . .* (Anderson, 1968)
F   *If*
D   *If . . .*
I   *Se . . .*
E   *Si . . .*
SU «Е́сли . . .» (А́ндерсон)

1728 GB *If It Die . . .* (Gide, 1926)
F   *Si le grain ne meurt*
D   *Stirb und werde*
I   *Se il grano non muore*
E   *Si la semilla no muere*
SU «Е́сли зерно́ не умрёт» (Жид)

1729 GB *If I were King* (Adam, 1852)
F   *Se j'étais roi*
D   *Wenn ich König wär'*
I   *Se fossi re*
E   *Si fuera rey*
SU «Е́сли б я был королём» (Ада́н)

1730 GB Ignatius of Loyola (saint, 1491–1556)
F   Ignace de Loyola (saint)
D   Ignatius von Loyola (Heiliger)
I   Ignazio di Loyola (santo)
E   Ignacio de Loyola (santo)
SU Игна́тий Лойо́ла (св.)

1731 GB *Iliad*, the (Homer, ?–VIII)
F   l'*Iliade* (f.) (Homère)
D   die *Ilias* (Homeros)
I   l'*Iliade* (Omero)
E   la *Ilíada* (Homero)
SU «Илиа́да» (Гоме́р)

1732 GB *I Like it Here* (Amis, 1958)
F   *Je l'aime ici*
D   *Hier hab' ich's gern*
I   *Mi piace qui*
E   *Me gustaría estar aquí*
SU «Мне нра́вится здесь» (Э́мис)

1733 GB *Illuminations* (Rimbaud, 1872–3)
F   *Illuminations*
D   *Illuminations*
I   *Illuminazioni*
E   *Las iluminaciones*
SU «Озаре́ния» (Рембо́)

1734 GB Illyria (hist.)
F   l'Illyrie (f.) (hist.)
D   Illyrien (Gesch.)
I   l'Illiria (st.)
E   Iliria (hist.)
SU Илли́рия (ист.)

1735 GB *Imaginary Invalid, The* (Molière, 1673)
F   *Le Malade imaginaire*
D   *Der eingebildete Kranke*
I   *Il malato immaginario*
E   *El enfermo imaginario*
SU «Мни́мый больно́й» (Молье́р)

1736 GB *Imitation of Christ* [*De imitatione Christi*] (Thomas à Kempis, *1418*)
F   *L'Imitation de Jésus-Christ* (Thomas a Kempis)
D   *Von der Nachfolge Christi* (Thomas a Kempis)
I   *Imitazione di Cristo* (Tommaso da Kempis)
E   *Imitación de Cristo* (Tomás de Kempis)
SU «О подража́нии Христу́» (Фома́ Кемпи́йский)

1737 GB *Imitation of Our Lady the Moon, The* (Laforgue, 1886)
F   *L'Imitation de Notre-Dame la Lune*
D   *Die Nachfolge der Notre-Dame-la-Lune*
I   *Imitazione di Nostra Signora la Luna*
E   *Imitación de Nuestra Señora la Luna*
SU «Подража́ние Луне́-богома́тери» (Лафо́рг)

1738 GB Immaculate Conception, the (rel.)
F   l'Immaculée Conception (relig.)
D   die Unbefleckte Empfängnis (relig.)
I   l'Immacolata Concezione (relig.)
E   la Inmaculada Concepción (relig.)
SU непоро́чное зача́тие (рел.)

1739 GB *Immoralist, The* (Gide, 1902)
F   *L'Immoraliste*
D   *Der Immoralist*
I   *L'immoralista*
E   *El inmoralista*
SU «Имморали́ст» (Жид)

1740 GB *Impertinents, The* (Moliere, 1661)
F   *Les Fâcheux*
D   *Die Lästigen*
I   *I seccatori*
E   *Los enfadosos*
SU «Доку́чные» (Молье́р)

1741 GB *Importance of Being Earnest, The*
(Wilde, 1895)
F *De l'importance d'être constant*
D *Bunbury*
I *L'importanza di chiamarsi Ernesto*
E *La importancia de llamarse Ernesto*
SU «Как важно быть серьёзным»
(Уайльд)

1742 GB *In Camera* (Sartre, 1944)
F *Huis clos*
D *Die Eingeschlossenen*
I *A porte chiuse*
E *Puerta cerrada*
SU «За запертой дверью» (Сартр)

1743 GB Incas, the (hist.)
F les Incas (hist.)
D die Inkas (Gesch.)
I gli incas (st.)
E los Incas (hist.)
SU инки (ист.)

1744 GB *In Chancery* (Galsworthy, 1920)
F *Aux aguets*
D *In Fesseln*
I *Alla sbarra*
E *En litigio*
SU «В петле» (Голсуорси)

1745 GB Independence, (American) War of
(American Revolution, USA), the
(1775–83)
F la guerre de l'Indépendance (USA)
D der Unabhängigkeitskrieg (USA)
I la guerra d'indipendenza (USA)
E la guerra de la Independencia (USA)
SU Война за независимость (США)

1746 GB Index Librorum Prohibitorum [Index
of Banned Books], the (1559–1966)
F l'Index
D der Index librorum prohibitorum
I l'indice dei libri proibiti
E el Índice de libros prohibidos
SU «Индекс запрещённых книг»

1747 GB India
F l'Inde (f.)
D Indien
I l'India
E la India
SU Индия

1748 GB *Indiana* (Sand, 1832)
F *Indiana*
D *Indiana*
I *Indiana*
E *Indiana*
SU «Индиана» (Санд)

1749 GB Indian Mutiny, the (1857–9)
F la Révolte des cipayes
D der Aufstand der Sepoys
I la rivolta dei sepoys
E la Sublevación de los cipayos
SU Индейское народное восстание

1750 GB Indian Ocean, the
F l'océan Indien
D der Indische Ozean
I l'oceano Indiano
E el océano Índico
SU Индийский океан

1751 GB *Indian Summer* (Stifter, 1857)
F *L'Été de la Saint-Martin*
D *Der Nachsommer*
I *L'estate di San Martino*
E *El veranillo de San Martín*
SU «Бабье лето» (Штифтер)

1752 GB Indochina (hist.)
F l'Indochine (f.) (hist.)
D Indochina (Gesch.)
I l'Indochina (st.)
E Indochina (hist.)
SU Индокитай (ист.)

1753 GB Indonesia
F l'Indonésie (f.)
D Indonesien
I l'Indonesia
E Indonesia
SU Индонезия

1754 GB *In Dubious Battle* (Steinbeck, 1936)
F *En un combat douteux*
D *Stürmische Ernte*
I *La battaglia*
E *La fuerza bruta*
SU «В схватке с сомнительным исходом»
(Стейнбек)

1755 GB Indus (River), the
F l'Indus (m.)
D der Indus
I l'Indo
E el Indo
SU Инд

1756 GB Industrial Revolution, the (hist.)
F la révolution industrielle (hist.)
D die industrielle Umwälzung (Gesch.)
I la rivoluzione industriale (st.)
E la revolución industrial (hist.)
SU промы́шленный переворо́т (ист.)

1757 GB *Infernal Machine, The* (Cocteau, 1934)
F *La Machine infernale*
D *Die Höllenmaschine*
I *La macchina infernale*
E *La máquina infernal*
SU «А́дская маши́на» (Кокто́)

1758 GB *Informer, The* (Ford + Steiner, 1935)
F *Le Mouchard*
D *Der Verräter*
I *Il traditore*
E *El delator*
SU «Осведоми́тель» (Форд/Сте́йнер)

1759 GB *Informer, The* (O'Flaherty, 1925)
F *Le Mouchard*
D *Die Nacht nach dem Verrat*
I *Il traditore*
E *El delator*
SU «Осведоми́тель» (О'Фла́эрти)

1760 GB *Inheritors, The* (Golding, 1955)
F *Les Hériteurs*
D *Die Erben*
I *Gli eredi*
E *Los herederos*
SU «Насле́дники» (Го́лдинг)

1761 GB *Inherit the Wind* (Kramer, 1960)
F *Procès de singe*
D *Wer den Wind sät*
I *. . . e l'uomo creò Satana*
E *Inherit the Wind*
SU «Пожнёшь бу́рю» (Кре́ймер)

1762 GB Inner Mongolia (China)
F la Mongolie-Intérieure (Chine)
D die Innere Mongolei (China)
I la Mongolia Interna (Cina)
E la Mongolia Interior (China)
SU Вну́тренняя Монго́лия (Кита́й)

1763 GB *Inner Voices* (Hugo, 1837)
F *Les Voix intérieures*
D *Innere Stimmen*
I *Le voci interiori*
E *Las voces interiores*
SU «Вну́тренние голоса́» (Гюго́)

1764 GB *Innocence of Father Brown, The* (Chesterton, 1911)
F *L'Innocence du Père Brown*
D *Der Hammer Gottes*
I *L'innocenza di Padre Brown*
E *El candor del Padre Brown*
SU «Неве́дение отца́ Бра́уна» (Че́стертон)

1765 GB Innocent (pope)
F Innocent (pape)
D Innozenz (Papst)
I Innocenzo (papa)
E Inocencio (papa)
SU Инноке́нтий (па́па ри́мский)

1766 GB *Innocent, The* (Voltaire, 1767)
F *L'Ingénu*
D *Der Unbefangene*
I *L'ingenuo*
E *El ingenuo*
SU «Простоду́шный» (Вольте́р)

1767 GB *Innocents Abroad, The* (Twain, 1869)
F *Les Innocents en voyage*
D *Die arglosen im Ausland*
I *Gli ingenui all'estero*
E *Los inocentes de viaje*
SU «Простаки́ за грани́цей» (Твен)

1768 GB *Inn of the Sixth Happiness, The* (Robson, 1958)
F *L'Auberge du Sixième Bonheur*
D *Die Herberge zur sechsten Glüchseligkeit*
I *La locanda della sesta felicità*
E *El albergue de la sexta felicidad*
SU «Гости́ница шесто́го сча́стья» (Ро́бсон)

1769 GB Inquisition, the (XIII–XIX)
F l'Inquisition
D die Inquisition
I l'inquisizione
E la Inquisición
SU инквизи́ция

1770 GB *Inspector Calls, An* (Priestley, 1947)
F *Un inspecteur vous demande*
D *Ein Inspektor kommt*
I *Un ispettore in casa Birling*
E *Ha llamado un inspector*
SU «Инспе́ктор пришёл» (При́стли)

1771 GB *Inspector General, The* (Gogol, 1836)
F *Le Revizor*
D *Der Revisor*
I *L'ispettore generale*
E *El inspector*
SU «Ревизо́р» (Го́голь)

1772 GB *Institutes of the Christian Religion*
(Calvin, 1536)
F *Institution de la religion chrétienne*
(Calvin)
D *Unterricht in der christlichen Religion*
(Calvin)
I *Istituzioni della religione cristiana*
(Calvino)
E *Institución de la Religión Cristiana*
(Calvino)
SU «Наставле́ние в христиа́нской ве́ре»
(Кальви́н)

1773 GB *Insulted and Injured, The*
(Dostoievsky, 1861)
F *Humiliés et offensés* (Dostoïevski)
D *Die Erniedrigten und Beleidigten*
(Dostojewskij)
I *Umiliati e offesi* (Dostoevskij)
E *Humillados y ofendidos* (Dostoievski)
SU «Уни́женные и оскорблённые»
(Достое́вский)

1774 GB *Interior Castle, The* (St Teresa of
Avila, 1588)
F *Le Château intérieur* (Thérèse de
Jésus)
D *Die Wohnungen, oder Innere Burg*
(Teresa de Jesus)
I *Libro delle dimore o castello interiore*
(Teresa de Avila)
E *Castillo Interior* (Santa Teresa de
Jesús)
SU «Вну́тренний за́мок» (Тере́за
Ави́льская)

1775 GB *Intermezzo* (Heine, 1823)
F *Intermezzo*
D *Intermezzo*
I *Intermezzo lirico*
E *Intermezzo*
SU «Интерме́ццо» (Ге́йне)

1776 GB International Court of Justice, the
(The Hague)
F la Cour internationale de justice (La
Haye)
D der Internationale Gerichtshof (Den
Haag)
I la Corte internazionale di giustizia
(L'Aia)
E la Corte Internacional de Justicia (La
Haya)
SU Междунаро́дный суд ООН (Гаа́га)

1777 GB International Monetary Fund (IMF),
the
F le Fonds monétaire international
(FMI)
D der Weltwährungsfonds (IMF)
I il Fonda monetario internazionale
(FMI)
E el Fondo Monetario Internacional
(FMI)
SU Междунаро́дный валю́тный фонд
(МВФ)

1778 GB Inter-Parliamentary Union (IPU), the
F l'Union interparlementaire (UIP)
D die Interparlamentarische Union
(IPU)
I l'Unione interparlamentare (UIP)
E la Unión interparlamentaria (UIP)
SU Межпарла́ментский сою́з (МС)

1779 GB *In the Heat of the Night* (Jewison, 1967)
F *Dans la chaleur de la nuit*
D *In der Hitze der Nacht*
I *La calda notte dell'ispettore Tibbs*
E *En el calor de la noche*
SU «В ночну́ю жару́» (Джу́исон)

1780 GB *In the Open Alley* (Ehrenburg, 1927)
F *Moscou ne croit pas aux larmes*
(Ehrenbourg)
D *Gasse am Moskau-Fluß* (Ehrenburg)
I *Nel vicolo Protočnyj* (Erenburg)
E *Una callejuela de Moscú* (Ehrenburg)
SU «В Прото́чном переу́лке» (Эренбу́рг)

1781 GB *In the Ravine* (Chekhov, 1900)
F *Dans le ravin* (Tchekhov)
D *In der Schlucht* (Tschechow)
I *Nel burrone* (Čechov)
E *En barranco* (Chejov)
SU «В овра́ге» (Че́хов)

1782 GB *In the South Seas* (Stevenson, 1896)
F *Dans les mers du Sud*
D *Südsee-Nachtgeschichten*
I *Nei mari del Sud*
E *De vuelta del mar*
SU «В ю́жных моря́х» (Сти́венсон)

1783 GB *In the Steppes of Central Asia* (Borodin, 1880)
F *Dans les steppes de l'Asie centrale* (Borodine)
D *In der Steppen von Mittel-Asien* (Borodin)
I *Nelle steppe dell'Asia centrale* (Borodin)
E *En las estepas del Asia Central* (Borodín)
SU «В Сре́дней А́зии» (Бороди́н)

1784 GB *In the World* (Gorky, 1915–16)
F *En gagnant mon pain* (Gorki)
D *Unter fremden Menschen* (Gor'kij)
I *Fra la gente* (Gor'kij)
E *Entre la gente* (Gorki)
SU «В лю́дях» (Го́рький)

1785 GB *Intimacy* (Sartre, 1939)
F *Le Mur*
D *Die Mauer*
I *Il muro*
E *El muro*
SU «Стена́» (Сартр)

1786 GB *Intolerance* (Griffith, 1916)
F *Intolérance*
D *Intoleranz*
I *Intolleranza*
E *Intolerancia*
SU «Нетерпи́мость» (Гри́ффит)

1787 GB *Intruder, The* (Maeterlinck, 1890)
F *L'Intruse*
D *Die Ungebetene*
I *L'intrusa*
E *La intrusa*
SU «Непро́шеная» (Ме́терли́нк)

1788 GB Invalides, the Hôtel des (Paris)
F l'hôtel des Invalides (Paris)
D der Invalidendom (Paris)
I l'Hôtel des Invalides (Parigi)
E el Hotel de los Invalidos (París)
SU Дом инвали́дов (Пари́ж)

GB Invincible Armada→Spanish Armada

1789 GB *Invisible Man, The* (Wells, 1897)
F *L'Homme invisible*
D *Der Unsichtbare*
I *L'uomo invisibile*
E *El hombre invisible*
SU «Челове́к-невиди́мка» (Уэ́ллс)

1790 GB *In Which We Serve* (Lean, 1942)
F *Ceux qui servent en mer*
D *Wofür wir dienen*
I *Il cacciatorpediniere Torrin*
E *Sangre, sudor y lágrimas*
SU «В кото́ром мы слу́жим» (Лин)

1791 GB Ion (myth., + Euripides, *418*)
F Ion (myth., + Euripide)
D Ion (myth., + Euripides)
I Ione (mit., + Euripide)
E Ion (mit. + Eurípides)
SU Ио́н (миф., + Еврипи́д)

1792 GB Ionian Islands, the (Greece)
F les îles Ioniennes (Grèce)
D die Ionischen Inseln (Griechenland)
I le isole Ionie (Grecia)
E las islas Jónicas (Grecia)
SU Иони́ческие острова́ (Гре́ция)

1793 GB Ionian Sea, the (Greece)
F la mer Ionienne (Grèce)
D das Ionische Meer (Griechenland)
I il mare Ionio (Grecia)
E el mar Jónico (Grecia)
SU Иони́ческое мо́ре (Гре́ция)

1794 GB Iphigeneia (myth.)
F Iphigénie (myth.)
D Iphigenie (myth.)
I Ifigenia (mit.)
E Ifigenia (mit.)
SU Ифиге́ния (миф.)

1795 GB *Iphigeneia in Aulis* (Euripides, 406; Gluck, 1774)
F *Iphigénie à Aulis* (Euripide, Gluck)
D *Iphigenie in Aulis* (Euripides, Gluck)
I *Ifigenia in Aulide* (Euripide, Gluck)
E *Ifigenia en Áulide* (Eurípides, Gluck)
SU «Ифиге́ния в Авли́де» (Еврипи́д, Глюк)

1796 GB *Iphigeneia in Tauris* (Euripides, −414;
          Gluck, 1779; Goethe, 1787)
      F   *Iphigénie en Tauride* (Euripide, Gluck,
          Goethe)
      D   *Iphigenie in Taurerland* (Euripides);
          Iphigenie in Tauris (Gluck, Goethe)
      I   *Ifigenia in Tauride* (Euripide, Gluck,
          Goethe)
      E   *Ifigenia en Táuride* (Eurípides, Gluck,
          Goethe)
      SU «Ифигéния в Таврúде» (Еврипúд,
          Глюк, Гёте)

1797 GB Iran
      F   l'Iran (m.)
      D   Iran
      I   l'Iran
      E   el Irán
      SU Ирáн

1798 GB Iraq
      F   l'Iraq (m.)
      D   Irak
      I   l'Iraq
      E   Irak
      SU Ирáк

1799 GB Ireland
      F   l'Irlande (f.)
      D   Irland
      I   l'Irlanda
      E   Irlanda
      SU Ирлáндия

1800 GB Iris (myth.)
      F   Iris (myth.)
      D   Iris (myth.)
      I   Iride (mit.)
      E   Iris (mit.)
      SU Ирúда (миф.)

1801 GB Irish Free State, the (hist.)
      F   l'État libre d'Irlande (hist.)
      D   der irische Freistaat (Gesch.)
      I   lo Stato Libero d'Irlanda (st.)
      E   el Estado libre de Irlanda (hist.)
      SU Ирлáндское своббдное госудáрство
          (ист.)

1802 GB Irish Sea, the
      F   la mer d'Irlande
      D   die Irische See
      I   il mare d'Irlanda
      E   el mar de Irlanda
      SU Ирлáндское мóре

1803 GB *Irma la Douce* [*Irma the Gentle*]
          (Wilder, 1963)
      F   *Irma la Douce*
      D   *Das Mädchen Irma la Douce*
      I   *Irma la dolce*
      E   *Irma, la dulce*
      SU «Крóткая Йрма» (Уáйлдер)

1804 GB Iron Age, the (hist.)
      F   l'âge de fer (hist.)
      D   die Eisenzeit (Gesch.)
      I   l'età del ferro (st.)
      E   el siglo de hierro (hist.)
      SU желéзный век (ист.)

1805 GB Iron Gate(s), the (Romania)
      F   les Portes de Fer (Roumanie)
      D   das Eiserne Tor (Rumänien)
      I   le Porte di Ferro (Romania)
      E   las Puertas de Hierro (Rumania)
      SU Желéзные Ворóта (Румы́ния)

1806 GB Isaac (Bib.)
      F   Isaac (Bib.)
      D   Isaak (Bib.)
      I   Isacco (Bib.)
      E   Isaac (Bib.)
      SU Исаáк (библ.)

1807 GB *Isabey and His Daughter* (Gérard,
          1795)
      F   *Isabey et sa fille*
      D   *Isabey und seine Tochter*
      I   *Isabey e sua figlia*
      E   *Isabey y su hija*
      SU «Изабé с дóчкой» (Жерáр)

1808 GB Isaiah (Bib.)
      F   Isaïe (Bib.)
      D   Jesaias (Bib.)
      I   Isaia (Bib.)
      E   Isaías (Bib.)
      SU Исáия (библ.)

1809 GB Isis (myth.)
      F   Isis (myth.)
      D   Isis (myth.)
      I   Isi (mit.)
      E   Isis (mit.)
      SU Исúда (миф.)

1810 GB Isocrates (436–338)
      F   Isocrate
      D   Isokrates
      I   Isocrate
      E   Isócrates
      SU Исокрáт

1811 GB Israel
    F Israël
    D Israel
    I Israele
    E Israel
    SU Изра́иль (м.)

1812 GB *Israel in Egypt* (Handel, 1739)
    F *Israël in Égypte* (Haendel)
    D *Israel in Ägypten* (Händel)
    I *Israele in Egitto* (Händel)
    E *Israel en Egipto* (Haendel)
    SU «Изра́иль в Еги́пте» (Ге́ндель)

1813 GB Istanbul (Turkey)
    F Istanbul (Turquie)
    D Istanbul (Türkei)
    I Istanbul (Turchia)
    E Estambul (Turquía)
    SU Стамбу́л (Ту́рция)

1814 GB *Italian, The* (Radcliffe, 1797)
    F *L'Italien*
    D *Der Italiener*
    I *L'italiano*
    E *El italiano*
    SU «Италья́нец» (Ра́дклиф)

1815 GB *Italian Girl in Algiers, The* (Rossini, 1812)
    F *L'Italienne à Alger*
    D *Die Italienerin in Algier*
    I *L'italiana in Algeri*
    E *La italiana en Argel*
    SU «Италья́нка в Алжи́ре» (Росси́ни)

1816 GB *Italian Straw Hat, An* (Labiche, 1851; Clair, 1928)
    F *Un chapeau de paille d'Italie*
    D *Der italienische Strohhut*
    I *Un cappello di paglia di Firenze*
    E *Un sombrero de paja de Italia*
    SU «Соло́менная шля́пка» (Лаби́ш, Клер)

1817 GB *Italian Symphony*, the (Mendelssohn, 1833)
    F la *Symphonie italienne* (Mendelssohn-Bartholdy)
    D die *Italienische Sinfonie* (Mendelssohn-Bartholdy)
    I la sinfonia *Italiana* (Mendelssohn-Bartholdy)
    E la *Sinfonía italiana* (Mendelssohn-Bartholdy)
    SU «Италья́нская» симфо́ния (Мендельсо́н-Барто́льди)

1818 GB Italy
    F l'Italie (f.)
    D Italien
    I l'Italia
    E Italia
    SU Ита́лия

1819 GB *It Can't Happen Here* (Lewis, 1935)
    F *Ça ne peut pas arriver ici*
    D *Das ist bei uns nicht möglich*
    I *Qui non può accadere*
    E *Aquí no puede suceder*
    SU «У нас э́то невозмо́жно» (Лью́ис)

1820 GB Ithaca (Greece)
    F Ithaque (f.) (Grèce)
    D Ithaka (Griechenland)
    I Itaca (Grecia)
    E Itaca (Grecia)
    SU Ита́ка (Гре́ция)

1821 GB *It Happened One Night* (Capra, 1934)
    F *New York-Miami*
    D *Es geschah in einer Nacht*
    I *Accadde una notte*
    E *Sucedió una noche*
    SU «Э́то случи́лось одна́жды но́чью» (Ка́пра)

1822 GB *It Is Never Too Late To Mend* (Reade, 1853)
    F *Jamais trop tard pour bien faire*
    D *Zur Besserung ist es nie zu spät*
    I *Non è mai troppo tardi per correggersi*
    E *Nunca es demasiado tarde para corregirse*
    SU «Испра́виться никогда́ не по́здно» (Рид)

1823 GB *It's A Mad Mad Mad Mad World* (Kramer, 1963)
    F *Un monde fou, fou, fou*
    D *Eine total, total verrückte Welt*
    I *Questo pazzo, pazzo, pazzo, pazzo mondo*
    E *El mundo está loco, loco, loco*
    SU «Безу́мный, безу́мный, безу́мный мир» (Кре́ймер)

1824 GB *It's My Life* (Godard, 1962)
    F *Vivre sa vie*
    D *Die Geschichte der Nana S.*
    I *Questa è la mia vita*
    E *Ésta es mi vida*
    SU «Жить свое́й жи́знью» (Года́р)

1825 GB *Ivanhoe* (Scott, 1819)
       F   *Ivanhoé*
       D   *Ivanhoe*
       I   *Ivanhoe*
       E   *Ivanhoe*
       SU «Айвéнго» (Скотт)

1826 GB Ivan the Great (1440–1505)
       F   Ivan le Grand
       D   Iwan der Großc
       I   Ivan il Grande
       E   Iván el Grande
       SU Ивáн Велúкий

1827 GB Ivan the Terrible (1530–84; + Eisenstein, 1944)
       F   Ivan le Terrible
       D   Iwan der Schreckliche
       I   Ivan il Terribile
       E   Iván el Terrible
       SU Ивáн Грóзный (+ Эйзенштéйн)

1828 GB Ivory Coast, the
       F   la Côte-d'Ivoire
       D   die Elfenbeinküste
       I   la Costa d'Avorio
       E   Costa de Marfil
       SU Бéрег Слонóвой Кóсти

J

1829	GB	Jacob (Bib.)
	F	Jacob (Bib.)
	D	Jakob (Bib.)
	I	Giacobbe (Bib.)
	E	Jacob (Bib.)
	SU	Иа́ков (библ.)

1830	GB	Jacobins, the (XVIII)
	F	les Jacobins
	D	die Jakobiner
	I	i giacobini
	E	los Jacobinos
	SU	якоби́нцы

1831	GB	Jacobites, the (XVII)
	F	les Jacobites
	D	die Jakobiten
	I	i giacobiti
	E	los Jacobitas
	SU	якоби́ты

1832	GB	*Jacob's Room* (Woolf, 1922)
	F	*La Chambre de Jacob*
	D	*Jacobs Zimmer*
	I	*La camera di Giacobbe*
	E	*El cuarto de Jacob*
	SU	«Ко́мната Дже́коба» (Вулф)

1833	GB	*Jacques the Fatalist* (Diderot, 1796)
	F	*Jacques le Fataliste*
	D	*Jakob und sein Herr*
	I	*Giacomo il fatalista*
	E	*Jacques el fatalista*
	SU	«Жак-фатали́ст и его́ хозя́ин» (Дидро́)

1834	GB	Jamaica
	F	la Jamaïque
	D	Jamaika
	I	la Giamaica
	E	Jamaica
	SU	Яма́йка

1835	GB	James (Bib., saint, sovereign)
	F	Jacques (Bib., saint, souverain)
	D	Jakobus (Bib., Heiliger, Herr.)
	I	Giacomo (Bib., santo, soverano)
	E	Jacobo (Bib., santo, sob.)
	SU	Иа́ков (библ., св., прав.)

1836	GB	*Jane Eyre* (Brontë, 1847)
	F	*Jane Eyre*
	D	*Jane Eyre*
	I	*Jane Eyre*
	E	*Jane Eyre*
	SU	«Джен Эйр» (Бро́нте)

1837	GB	Janus (myth.)
	F	Janus (myth.)
	D	Janus (myth.)
	I	Giano (mit.)
	E	Jano (mit.)
	SU	Я́нус (миф.)

1838	GB	Japan
	F	le Japon
	D	Japan
	I	il Giappone
	E	el Japón
	SU	Япо́ния

1839	GB	Japan, the Sea of
	F	la mer du Japon
	D	das Japanische Meer
	I	il mare del Giappone
	E	el mar del Japón
	SU	Япо́нское море

1840	GB	Japheth (Bib.)
	F	Japhet (Bib.)
	D	Japhet (Bib.)
	I	Jafet (Bib.)
	E	Jafet (Bib.)
	SU	Иафе́т (библ.)

1841	GB	Jason (myth.)
	F	Jason (myth.)
	D	Jason (myth.)
	I	Giasone (mit.)
	E	Jasón (mit.)
	SU	Ясо́н (миф.)

1842	GB	Java
	F	Java
	D	Java
	I	Giava
	E	Java
	SU	Я́ва

1843	GB	*Jaws* (Spielberg, 1975)
	F	*Les Dents de la mer*
	D	*Der weiße Hai*
	I	*Lo squalo*
	E	*Mandíbulas*
	SU	«Че́люсти» (Спи́лберг)

1844	GB	*Jazz Singer, The* (Crosland, 1927)
	F	*Le Chanteur de jazz*
	D	*Der Jazzsänger*
	I	*Il cantante di jazz*
	E	*El cantante de jazz*
	SU	«Певе́ц джа́за» (Кро́сленд)

1845	GB	*Jealous God, The* (Braine, 1964)
	F	*Le Dieu jaloux*
	D	*Der eifersüchtige Gott*
	I	*Il dio geloso*
	E	*El dios celoso*
	SU	«Ревни́вый бог» (Брейн)

1846	GB	*Jean-Christophe* (Rolland, 1904–12)
	F	*Jean-Christophe*
	D	*Johann Christof*
	I	*Gian Cristoforo*
	E	*Juan Cristóbal*
	SU	«Жан-Кристо́ф» (Ролла́н)

1847	GB	Jehovah (Bib.)
	F	Jéhovah (Bib.)
	D	Jehova (Bib.)
	I	Geova (Bib.)
	E	Jehová (Bib.)
	SU	Иего́ва (библ.)

1848	GB	Jehovah's Witnesses (rel.)
	F	les Témoins de Jéhovah (relig.)
	D	die Zeugen Jehovas (relig.)
	I	i testimoni di Geova (relig.)
	E	los Testigos de Jehová (relig.)
	SU	«Свиде́тели Иего́вы» (рел.)

1849	GB	Jehu (Bib.)
	F	Jéhu (Bib.)
	D	Jehu (Bib.)
	I	Ieu (Bib.)
	E	Jehú (Bib.)
	SU	Ииу́й (библ.)

1850	GB	*Jennie Gerhardt* (Dreiser, 1911)
	F	*Jennie Gerhardt*
	D	*Jennie Gerhardt*
	I	*Jennie Gerhardt*
	E	*Jennie Gerhardt*
	SU	«Дже́нни Ге́рхардт» (Дра́йзер)

1851	GB	*Jenůfa* (Janáček, 1904)
	F	*Jenufa* (Janáček)
	D	*Jenufa* (Janáček)
	I	*Jenufa* (Janáček)
	E	*Jenufa* (Janachek)
	SU	«Йе́нуфа» (Яна́чек)

1852	GB	Jephthah (Bib.)
	F	Jephté (Bib.)
	D	Jiftach (Bib.)
	I	Iefte (Bib.)
	E	Jefte (Bib.)
	SU	Иеффа́й (библ.)

1853	GB	Jeremiah (Bib.)
	F	Jérémie (Bib.)
	D	Jeremias (Bib.)
	I	Geremia (Bib.)
	E	Jeremías (Bib.)
	SU	Иеремия́ (библ.)

1854	GB.	Jericho (Bib.)
	F	Jéricho (Bib.)
	D	Jericho (Bib.)
	I	Gerico (Bib.)
	E	Jericó (Bib.)
	SU	Иерихо́н (библ.)

1855	GB	Jeroboam (Bib.)
	F	Jéroboam (Bib.)
	D	Jerobeam (Bib.)
	I	Geroboamo (Bib.)
	E	Jeroboán (Bib.)
	SU	Иеровоа́м (библ.)

1856	GB	Jerome (saint, *347–420*)
	F	Jérôme (saint)
	D	Hieronymus (Heiliger)
	I	Girolamo (santo)
	E	Jerónimo (santo)
	SU	Иерони́м (св.)

1857   GB   Jerusalem (Israel)
     F   Jérusalem (Israël)
     D   Jerusalem (Israel)
     I   Gerusalemme (Israele)
     E   Jerusalén (Israel)
     SU   Иерусалим (Израиль)

1858   GB   Jesuits, the (rel.)
     F   les jésuites (relig.)
     D   die Jesuiten (relig.)
     I   i gesuiti (relig.)
     E   los jesuitas (relig.)
     SU   иезуиты (рел.)

1859   GB   Jesus, the Society of (rel.)
     F   la Société de Jésus (relig.)
     D   die Gesellschaft Jesu (relig.)
     I   la Compagnia di Gesù (relig.)
     E   la Compañía de Jesús (relig.)
     SU   Общество Иисуса (рел.)

1860   GB   Jesus Christ (Bib.)
     F   Jésus-Christ (Bib.)
     D   Jesus (Bib.)
     I   Gesù Cristo (Bib.)
     E   Jesucristo (Bib.)
     SU   Иисус Христос (библ.)

1861   GB   *Jesus Christ Superstar* (Webber + Rice, 1969)
     F   *Jésus-Christ Superstar*
     D   *Jesus Christ Superstar*
     I   *Jesus Christ Superstar*
     E   *Jesus Christ Superstar*
     SU   «Иисус Христос – суперзвезда» (Уэббер/Райс)

1862   GB   *Jeux Interdits, Les* [*Forbidden Games*] (Clément, 1952)
     F   *Les Jeux interdits*
     D   *Verbotene Spiele*
     I   *Giochi proibiti*
     E   *Juegos prohibidos*
     SU   «Запрещённые игры» (Клеман)

1863   GB   *Jewels of the Madonna, The* (Wolf-Ferrari, 1911)
     F   *Les Joyaux de la Madone*
     D   *Der Schmuck der Madonna*
     I   *I gioielli della Madonna*
     E   *Las joyas de la Madona*
     SU   «Ожерелье Мадонны» (Вольф-Феррари)

1864   GB   *Jewess, The* (Halévy, 1835)
     F   *La Juive*
     D   *Die Judin*
     I   *L'ebrea*
     E   *La hebrea*
     SU   «Жидовка» (Галеви)

1865   GB   *Jewish State, The* (Herzl, 1896)
     F   *L'État juif*
     D   *Der Judenstaat*
     I   *Lo stato ebraico*
     E   *El Estado judío*
     SU   «Еврейское государство» (Герцль)

1866   GB   *Jew of Malta, The* (Marlowe, 1589)
     F   *Le Juif de Malte*
     D   *Der Jude von Malta*
     I   *L'ebreo di Malta*
     E   *El judío de Malta*
     SU   «Мальтийский еврей» (Марло)

1867   GB   Jews, the (rel.)
     F   les juifs (relig.)
     D   die Juden (relig.)
     I   gli ebrai (relig.)
     E   los judíos (relig.)
     SU   евреи (рел.)

1868   GB   Jezebel (Bib.)
     F   Jézabel (Bib.)
     D   Isebel (Bib.)
     I   Gezabele (Bib.)
     E   Jezabel (Bib.)
     SU   Иезавель (библ.)

1869   GB   Joachim (saint, I)
     F   Joachim (saint)
     D   Joachim (Heiliger)
     I   Gioacchino (santo)
     E   Joaquín (santo)
     SU   Иоахим (св.)

1870   GB   Joan (sovereign)
     F   Jeanne (souveraine)
     D   Johanna (Herr.)
     I   Giovanna (sovrana)
     E   Juana (sob.)
     SU   Иоанна (прав.)

1871   GB   Joan of Arc (*1412*–31)
     F   Jeanne d'Arc
     D   Jeanne d'Arc
     I   Giovanna d'Arco
     E   Juana de Arco
     SU   Жанна д'Арк

1872 GB *Joan of Arc at the Stake* (Honegger, 1938)
F *Jeanne d'Arc au Bûcher*
D *Johanna auf dem Scheiterhaufen*
I *Giovanna d'Arco al rogo*
E *Juana de Arco en la hoguera*
SU «Жа́нна д'Арк на костре́» (Онегге́р)

1873 GB Joan the Mad (1479–1555)
F Jeanne la Folle
D Johanna die Wahnsinnige
I Giovanna la Pazza
E Juana la Loca
SU Хуа́на Безу́мная

1874 GB Job (Bib.)
F Job (Bib.)
D Hiob (Bib.)
I Giobbe (Bib.)
E Job (Bib.)
SU Ио́в (библ.)

1875 GB Jocasta (myth.)
F Jocaste (myth.)
D Jokaste (myth.)
I Giocasta (mit.)
E Yocasta (mit.)
SU Иока́ста (миф.)

1876 GB *Jocelyn* (Lamartine, 1836)
F *Jocelyn*
D *Jocelyn*
I *Jocelyn*
E *Jocelyn*
SU «Жоселе́н» (Ламарти́н)

1877 GB Joel (Bib.)
F Joël (Bib.)
D Joël (Bib.)
I Gioele (Bib.)
E Joel (Bib.)
SU Иои́ль (библ.)

1878 GB Johannesburg (South Africa)
F Johannesburg (Afrique du Sud)
D Johannesburg (Südafrika)
I Johannesburg (Africa del Sud)
E Johannesburgo (África del Sur)
SU Иога́ннесбург (Ю́жная А́фрика)

1879 GB John (Bib., saint, sovereign)
F Jean (Bib., saint, souverain)
D Johann(es) (Bib., Heiliger, Herr.)
I Giovanni (Bib., santo, sovrano)
E Juan (Bib., santo, sob.)
SU Иоа́нн (библ., св., прав.)

1880 GB John, the Gospel According to [Saint] (Bib.)
F l'Évangile selon saint Jean (Bib.)
D das Johannes-Evangelium (Bib.)
I il Vangelo di Giovanni (Bib.)
E el Evangelio de San Juan (Bib.)
SU «Ева́нгелие от Иоа́нна» (библ.)

1881 GB *John Bull's Other Island* (Shaw, 1904)
F *L'Autre Île de John Bull*
D *John Bulls andere Insel*
I *L'altra isola di John Bull*
E *La otra isla de John Bull*
SU «Друго́й о́стров Джо́на Бу́лля» (Шо́у)

1882 GB John Chrysostom (saint, *345*–407)
F Jean Chrysostome (saint)
D Johannes Chrysostomus (Heiliger)
I Giovanni Crisostomo (santo)
E Juan Crisóstomo (santo)
SU Иоа́нн Златоу́ст (св.)

1883 GB John Lackland (1167–1216)
F Jean sans Terre
D Johann ohne Land
I Giovanni Senza Terra
E Juan Sin Tierra
SU Иоа́нн Безземе́льный

1884 GB John of Damascus (675–749)
F Jean Damascène
D Johannes Damascenus
I Giovanni Damasceno
E Juan Damasceno
SU Иоа́нн Дамаски́н

1885 GB John of Salisbury (*1115*–80)
F Jean de Salisbury
D Johann von Salisbury
I Giovanni di Salisbury
E Juan de Salisbury
SU Иоа́нн Солсбери́йский

1886 GB John of the Cross (saint, 1542–91)
F Jean de la Croix (saint)
D Johannes vom Kreuz (Heiliger)
I Giovanni della Croce (santo)
E Juan de la Cruz (santo)
SU Хуа́н де ла Крус (св.)

1887 GB John the Baptist (Bib., saint)
F Jean-Baptiste (Bib., saint)
D Johannes der Täufer (Bib., Heiliger)
I Giovanni Battista (Bib., santo)
E Juan Bautista (Bib., santo)
SU Иоа́нн Крести́тель (библ., св.)

1888 GB John the Fearless (1371–1419)
F Jean sans Peur
D Johannes der Furchtlose
I Giovanni Senza Paura
E Juan Sin Miedo
SU Иоа́нн Бесстра́шный

1889 GB Jonah (Bib.)
F Jonas (Bib.)
D Jonas (Bib.)
I Giona (Bib.)
E Jonás (Bib.)
SU Ио́на (библ.)

1890 GB Jonathan (Bib.)
F Jonathan (Bib.)
D Jonathan (Bib.)
I Gionata (Bib.)
E Jonatás (Bib.)
SU Ионафа́н (библ.)

1891 GB *Jonathan Wild the Great* (Fielding, 1743)
F *Vie de Jonathan Wild le Grand*
D *Mr. Jonathan Wild der Große*
I *Gionata Wild il grande*
E *Vida de Jonathan Wild*
SU «Исто́рия поко́йного Джо́натана Уа́йльда Вели́кого» (Фи́лдинг)

1892 GB Jordan
F la Jordanie
D Jordanien
I la Giordania
E Jordania
SU Иорда́ния

1893 GB Jordan (River), the
F le Jourdain
D der Jordan
I il Giordano
E el Jordán
SU Иорда́н

1894 GB Joseph (Bib., saint, sovereign)
F Joseph (Bib., saint, souverain)
D Joseph (Bib., Heiliger, Herr.)
I Giuseppe (Bib., santo, sovrano)
E José (Bib., santo, sob.)
SU Ио́сиф (библ., св., прав.)

1895 GB *Joseph and His Brothers* (Mann, 1933–43)
F *Joseph et ses frères*
D *Joseph und seine Brüder*
I *Giuseppe e i suoi fratelli*
E *José y sus hermanos*
SU «Ио́сиф и его́ бра́тья» (Манн)

GB *Joseph Andrews*→*History of the Adventures of Joseph Andrews*

1896 GB Josephine (1763–1815)
F Joséphine
D Josephine
I Giuseppina
E Josefina
SU Жозефи́на

1897 GB Joseph of Arimathea (Bib.)
F Joseph d'Arimathie (Bib.)
D Joseph von Arimathia (Bib.)
I Giuseppe d'Arimatea (Bib.)
E José de Arimatea (Bib.)
SU Ио́сиф из Аримафе́и (библ.)

1898 GB Josephus (*37–100*)
F Josèphe Flavius
D Josephus
I Giuseppe Flavio
E Josefo
SU Ио́сиф Фла́вий

1899 GB Joshua (Bib.)
F Josué (Bib.)
D Josua (Bib.)
I Giosuè (Bib.)
E Josué (Bib.)
SU Иису́с Нави́н (библ.)

1900 GB Josiah (Bib.)
F Josias (Bib.)
D Josias (Bib.)
I Giosia (Bib.)
E Josías (Bib.)
SU Иоси́я (библ.)

1901 GB *Jour de Fête* [*Holiday*] (Tati, 1949)
F *Jour de Fête*
D *Tatis Schützenfest*
I *Giorno di festa*
E *Jour de fête*
SU «Пра́здничный день» (Тати́)

1902 GB *Journal of the Plague Year, A* (Defoe, 1722)
F *Journal de l'année de la peste*
D *Tagebuch des Pestjahrs*
I *La peste di Londra*
E *Diario de la peste*
SU «Дневни́к чумы́» (Дефо́)

1903 GB *Journal to Stella* (Swift, 1710–13)
F *Journal à Stella*
D *Tagebuch für Stella*
I *Diario a Stella*
E *El Diario a Stella*
SU «Дневни́к для Сте́ллы» (Свифт)

1904 GB *Journey to the End of Night* (Céline, 1932)
    F *Voyage au bout de la nuit*
    D *Reise ans Ende der Nacht*
    I *Viaggio al termine della notte*
    E *Viaje al fin de la noche*
    SU «Путешéствие на край нóчи» (Селúн)

1905 GB *Journey to the Moon, A* (Verne, 1870)
    F *Autour de la lune*
    D *Die Reise zum Mond*
    I *Attorno alla luna*
    E *Un viaje a la luna*
    SU «Вокрýг Лунь́ı» (Верн)

1906 GB *Jour se lève, Le* [*The Day Dawns*] (Carné, 1939)
    F *Le jour se lève*
    D *Der Tag bricht an*
    I *Alba tragica*
    E *Amanecer*
    SU «День начинáется» (Карнé)

1907 GB Judaea (Bib.)
    F la Judée (Bib.)
    D Judäa (Bib.)
    I la Guidea (Bib.)
    E Judea (Bib.)
    SU Иудéя (библ.)

1908 GB Judah (Bib.)
    F Juda (Bib.)
    D Juda (Bib.)
    I Giuda (Bib.)
    E Judá (Bib.)
    SU Иýда (библ.)

1909 GB Judas (Bib.)
    F Judas (Bib.)
    D Judas (Bib.)
    I Giuda (Bib.)
    E Judas (Bib.)
    SU Иýда (библ.)

1910 GB Judas Iscariot (Bib.)
    F Judas Iscariote (Bib.)
    D Judas Ischariot (Bib.)
    I Giuda Iscariota (Bib.)
    E Judas Iscariote (Bib.)
    SU Иýда Искариóт (библ.)

1911 GB Judas Maccabeus (200–160; + Handel, 1745)
    F Judas Maccabée (+ Haendel)
    D Judas Makkabäus (+ Händel)
    I Giuda Maccabeo (+ Händel)
    E Judas Macabeo (+ Haendel)
    SU Иýда Маккавéй (+ Гéндель)

1912 GB Jude (Bib.)
    F Jude (Bib.)
    D Juda (Bib.)
    I Giuda (Bib.)
    E Judas (Bib.)
    SU Иýда (библ.)

1913 GB *Jude the Obscure* (Hardy, 1895)
    F *Jude l'Obscur*
    D *Juda der Unberühmte*
    I *Giuda l'oscuro*
    E *Judas el oscuro*
    SU «Джуд Незамéтный» (Хáрди)

1914 GB *Judgement, The* (Kafka, 1912)
    F *Le Verdict*
    D *Das Urteil*
    I *La condanna*
    E *La condena*
    SU «Прúговор» (Кáфка)

1915 GB Judges, the Book of (Bib.)
    F le Livre des Juges (Bib.)
    D das Buch der Richter (Bib.)
    I il libro dei Giudici (Bib.)
    E el Libro de los Jueces (Bib.)
    SU «Кнúга Судéй» (библ.)

1916 GB Judith (Bib.)
    F Judith (Bib.)
    D Judith (Bib.)
    I Giuditta (Bib.)
    E Judit (Bib.)
    SU Юдúфь (библ.)

    GB Jugoslavia→Yugoslavia

1917 GB *Jugurthine War, The* [*Bellum Iugurthinum*] (Sallust, 41–40)
    F *La Guerre de Jugurtha* (Salluste)
    D *Der Krieg gegen Jugurtha* (Sallustius)
    I *La guerra giugurtina* (Sallustio)
    E *La guerra de Yugurta* (Salustio)
    SU «Югýртинская войнá» (Саллю́стий)

1918 GB *Jules et Jim* [*Jules and Jim*] (Truffaut, 1961)
    F *Jules et Jim*
    D *Jules und Jim*
    I *Jules e Jim*
    E *Jules et Jim*
    SU «Жюль и Джим» (Трюффó)

1919 GB Julia (Roman name)
    F Julia (nom romain)
    D Julia (Römername)
    I Giulia (nome romano)
    E Julia (nombre romano)
    SU Ю́лия (древнерúмское úмя)

1920 GB   Julian the Apostate (*331*–363)
F   Julien l'Apostat
D   Julianus Apostata
I   Giuliano l'Apostata
E   Juliano el Apóstata
SU   Юлиа́н Отсту́пник

1921 GB   Julius (saint, pope)
F   Jules (saint, pape)
D   Julius (Heiliger, Papst)
I   Giulio (santo, papa)
E   Julio (santo, papa)
SU   Ю́лий (св., па́па ри́мский)

1922 GB   Julius Caesar (100–44, + Shakespeare, 1599)
F   Jules César
D   Julius Cäsar
I   Giulio Cesare
E   Julio César
SU   Ю́лий Це́зарь (+ Шекспи́р)

1923 GB   *Jungle, The* (Sinclair, 1906)
F   *La Jungle*
D   *Der Sumpf*
I   *La giungla*
E   *La jungla*
SU   «Джу́нгли» (Си́нклер)

1924 GB   *Jungle Book, The* (Kipling, 1894)
F   *Le Livre de la jungle*
D   *Das Dschungelbuch*
I   *Il libro della giungla*
E   *El libro de la selva*
SU   «Кни́га джу́нглей» (Ки́плинг)

1925 GB   Juno (myth.)
F   Junon (myth.)
D   Juno (myth.)
I   Giunone (mit.)
E   Juno (mit.)
SU   Юно́на (миф.)

1926 GB   *Juno and the Paycock* (O'Casey, 1924)
F   *Junon et le paon*
D   *Juno und der Pfau*
I   *Giunone e il pavone*
E   *Juno y el pavo real*
SU   «Юно́на и павли́н» (О`Ке́йси)

1927 GB   Jupiter (myth., astron.)
F   Jupiter (myth., astron.)
D   Jupiter (myth., Astron.)
I   Giove (mit., astr.)
E   Júpiter (mit., astr.)
SU   Юпи́тер (миф., астр.)

1928 GB   *Justice* (Galsworthy, 1910)
F   *Justice*
D   *Justiz*
I   *Giustizia*
E   *Justicia*
SU   «Справедли́вость» (Го́лсуорси)

1929 GB   Justin (saint, *100*–165)
F   Justin (saint)
D   Justin (Heiliger)
I   Giustino (santo)
E   Justino (santo)
SU   Юсти́н (св.)

1930 GB   Justinian (483–565)
F   Justinien
D   Justinian
I   Giustiniano
E   Justiniano
SU   Юстиниа́н

1931 GB   *Just So Stories* (Kipling, 1902)
F   *Les Histoires comme ça*
D   *Das kommt davon*
I   *Storie proprio così*
E   *Cuentos y no otra cosa*
SU   «Расска́зы про́сто так» (Ки́плинг)

1932 GB   Jutes, the (hist.)
F   les Jutes (hist.)
D   die Jüten (Gesch.)
I   gli juti (st.)
E   los jutos (hist.)
SU   ю́ты (ист.)

1933 GB   Jutland
F   le Jylland
D   Jütland
I   lo Jutland
E   Jutlandia
SU   Ютла́ндия

1934 GB   Jutland, the Battle of (1916)
F   la bataille (navale) du Jutland
D   die Skagerrakschlacht
I   la battaglia dello Jutland
E   la batalla (naval) de Jutlandia
SU   Ютла́ндское сраже́ние

1935 GB   Juvenal (*55*–127)
F   Juvénal
D   Juvenalis
I   Giovenale
E   Juvenal
SU   Ювена́л

K

1936 GB Kaliningrad (USRR)
    F Kaliningrad (URSS)
    D Königsberg (UdSSR)
    I Kaliningrad (URSS)
    E Kaliningrado (URSS)
    SU Калинингра́д (СССР)

1937 GB *Kangaroo* (Lawrence, 1923)
    F *Kangourou*
    D *Känguruh*
    I *Canguro*
    E *Canguro*
    SU «Кенгуру́» (Ло́ренс)

1938 GB *Kaputt* (Malaparte, 1944)
    F *Kaputt*
    D *Kaputt*
    I *Kaputt*
    E *Kaputt*
    SU «Капу́т» (Малапа́рте)

1939 GB Kashmir (India)
    F le Cachemire (Inde)
    D Kaschmir (Indien)
    I il Kashmir (India)
    E Cachemira (India)
    SU Кашми́р (И́ндия)

1940 GB Katowice (Poland)
    F Katowice (Pologne)
    D Kattowitz (Polen)
    I Katowice (Polonia)
    E Katovice (Polonia)
    SU Катови́це (По́льша)

1941 GB *Kenilworth* (Scott, 1821)
    F *Kenilworth*
    D *Kenilworth*
    I *Kenilworth*
    E *Kenilworth*
    SU «Ке́нилворт» (Скотт)

1942 GB Kenya
    F le Kenya
    D Kenia
    I il Kenia
    E Kenia
    SU Ке́ния

1943 GB *Keys of the Kingdom, The* (Cronin, 1942)
    F *Les Clefs du royaume*
    D *Der Schlüssel zum Königreich*
    I *Le chiavi del regno*
    E *Las llaves del reino*
    SU «Ключи́ от не́ба» (Кро́нин)

1944 GB *Khovanshchina* (Mussorgsky, 1886)
    F *Khovanchtchina* (Moussorgski)
    D *Chowantschina* (Mussorgskij)
    I *Chovanščina* (Musorgskij)
    E *Kovanchina* (Mussorgski)
    SU «Хова́нщина» (Му́соргский)

1945 GB Krushchev (1894–1971)
    F Khrouchchev
    D Chruschtshow
    I Chruščëv
    E Kruschef
    SU Хрущёв

1946 GB *Kid, The* (Chaplin, 1920)
    F *Le Gosse*
    D *Das Gör*
    I *Il monello*
    E *El niño*
    SU «Малы́ш» (Ча́плин)

1947 GB *Kidnapped* (Stevenson, 1886)
    F *Enlevé*
    D *Entführt*
    I *Il fanciullo rapito*
    E *El dinamitero secuestrado*
    SU «Похи́щенный» (Сти́венсон)

1948 GB Kiev (USSR)
    F Kiev (URSS)
    D Kiew (UdSSR)
    I Kijev (URSS)
    E Kiev (URSS)
    SU «Ки́ев (СССР)

1949 GB *Kim* (Kipling, 1901)
    F *Kim*
    D *Kim*
    I *Kim*
    E *Kim*
    SU «Ким» (Ки́плинг)

1950 GB *Kind Hearts and Coronets* (Hamer, 1949)
    F *Noblesse oblige*
    D *Adel Verpflichtet*
    I *Sangue blu*
    E *Ocho sentencias de muerte*
    SU «Си́няя кровь» (Хе́ймер)

1951 GB *Kind of Loving, A* (Barstow, 1960; Schlesinger, 1962)
    F *Un amour pas comme les autres*
    D *Nur ein Hauch Glückseligkeit*
    I *Una maniera d'amare*
    E *Esa clase de amor*
    SU «Любо́вь . . . любо́вь?» (Ба́рстоу, Шле́зингер)

1952 GB *Kindred by Choice* (Goethe, 1809)
    F *Les Affinités électives*
    D *Die Wahlverwandtschaften*
    I *Le affinità elettive*
    E *Las afinidades electivas*
    SU «Избира́тельное сро́дство» (Гёте)

1953 GB *King Coal* (Sinclair, 1917)
    F *Le Roi Charbon*
    D *König Kohle*
    I *Re carbone*
    E *El rey carbón*
    SU «Коро́ль У́голь» (Си́нклер)

1954 GB *King David* (Honegger, 1921)
    F *Le Roi David*
    D *König David*
    I *Il re Davide*
    E *El Rey David*
    SU «Царь Дави́д» (Онегге́р)

1955 GB *King John* (Shakespeare, 1596)
    F *Le Roi Jean*
    D *König Johannes*
    I *Re Giovanni*
    E *La vida y muerte del rey Juan*
    SU «Коро́ль Джон» (Шекспи́р)

1956 GB *King Lear* (Shakespeare, 1605)
    F *Le Roi Lear*
    D *König Lear*
    I *Re Lear*
    E *El rey Lear*
    SU «Коро́ль Лир» (Шекспи́р)

1957 GB *King of Ys, The* (Lalo, 1888)
    F *Le Roi d'Ys*
    D *Der König von Ys*
    I *Il re d'Ys*
    E *El rey de Ys*
    SU «Коро́ль го́рода Ис» (Лало́)

1958 GB Kings, the Book of (Bib.)
    F le Livre des Rois (Bib.)
    D das Buch der Könige (Bib.)
    I il Libro dei Re (Bib.)
    E el Libro de los Reyes (Bib.)
    SU «Кни́га Царств» (библ.)

1959 GB *Kings in Exile* (Daudet, 1879)
    F *Les Rois en exile*
    D *König im Exil*
    I *I re in esilio*
    E *Los reyes en el destierro*
    SU «Короли́ в изгна́нии» (Доде́)

1960 GB *King Solomon's Mines* (Haggard, 1885)
    F *Les Mines du roi Salomon*
    D *Die Goldgruben des Königs Salomonis*
    I *Le miniere del re Salamone*
    E *Las minas del rey Salomón*
    SU «Ко́пи царя́ Соломо́на» (Ха́ггард)

1961 GB *King Ubu* (Jarry, 1896)
    F *Ubu Roi*
    D *König Ubu*
    I *Ubu re*
    E *Ubu-Rey*
    SU «Юбю́-коро́ль» (Жарри́)

1962 GB *Kipps* (Wells, 1905)
    F *Kipps*
    D *Kipps*
    I *Kipps*
    E *Kipps*
    SU «Киппс» (Уэ́ллс)

1963 GB *Kiss, The* (Smetana, 1876; Rodin, 1886)
    F *Le Baiser*
    D *Der Kuß*
    I *Il bacio*
    E *El beso*
    SU «Поцелу́й» (Сме́тана, Роде́н)

1964 GB *Kiss Me, Kate* (Porter, 1948)
    F *Embrasse-moi, Kate!*
    D *Küß mich, Kätchen*
    I *Baciami, Kate!*
    E *¡Bésame, Kate!*
    SU «Целу́й меня́, Кэт» (По́ртер)

1965 GB *Knack . . . And How To Get It, The* (Lester, 1965)
    F *The Knack . . . et comment l'avoir*
    D *Der gewisse Kniff*
    I *Non tutti ce l'hanno*
    E *El knack . . . y cómo conseguirlo*
    SU «Сноро́вка – и как её приобрести́» (Ле́стер)

1966 GB *Knight of the Burning Pestle, The* (Beaumont + Fletcher, 1607)
    F *Le Chevalier au pilon ardent*
    D *Der Ritter mit der feurigen Mörserkeule*
    I *Il cavaliere dal pestello ardente*
    E *El caballero del mazo ardiente*
    SU «Ры́царь пламене́ющего пе́стика» (Бо́монт/Флё́тчер)

1967 GB *Knights, The [Hippeis]* (Aristophanes, −424)
    F *Les Chevaliers* (Aristophane)
    D *Die Ritter* (Aristophanes)
    I *I cavalieri* (Aristofane)
    E *Los caballeros* (Aristófanes)
    SU «Вса́дники» (Аристофа́н)

1968 GB *Knock, or the Triumph of Medicine* (Romains, 1923)
    F *Knock, ou le triomphe de la médecine*
    D *Dr. Knock*
    I *Knock, o il trionfo della medicina*
    E *Knock, o el triunfo de la medicina*
    SU «Кнок, или Торжество́ медици́ны» (Роме́н)

1969 GB Koblenz (Germany)
    F Coblence (Allemagne)
    D Koblenz (Deutschland)
    I Coblenza (Germania)
    E Coblenza (Alemania)
    SU Кобле́нц (Герма́ния)

1970 GB *Konrad Wallenrod* (Mickiewicz, 1828)
    F *Konrad Wallenrod*
    D *Konrad Wallenrod*
    I *Konrad Wallenrod*
    E *Konrad Wallenrod*
    SU «Ко́нрад Ва́лленрод» (Мицке́вич)

1971 GB *Kon-Tiki Expedition, The* (Heyerdahl, 1948)
    F *L'Expédition du Kon-Tiki*
    D *Kon-Tiki*
    I *Kon Tiki*
    E *La expedición de la Kon-Tiki*
    SU «Путеше́ствие на „Кон-Ти́ки"» (Хе́йердал)

1972 GB Koran, the (rel.)
    F le Coran (relig.)
    D der Koran (relig.)
    I il Corano (relig.)
    E el Corán (relig.)
    SU Кора́н (рел.)

1973 GB Korea
    F la Corée
    D Korea
    I la Corea
    E Corea
    SU Коре́я

1974 GB Krakow (Cracow) (Poland)
    F Cracovie (Pologne)
    D Krakau (Polen)
    I Cracovia (Polonia)
    E Cracovia (Polonia)
    SU Кра́ков (По́льша)

1975 GB *Krupp's Last Tape* (Beckett, 1958)
    F *La Dernière Bande*
    D *Das letzte Band*
    I *Finale di partita*
    E *La última cinta*
    SU «После́дняя ле́нта магнитофо́на» (Бе́ккет)

1976 GB Kremlin, the (Moscow)
    F le Kremlin (Moscou)
    D der Kreml (Moskau)
    I il Cremlino (Mosca)
    E el Kremlin (Moscú)
    SU Кремль (м.) (Москва́)

1977 GB *Kreutzer Sonata, the* (Beethoven, 1803; Tolstoy, 1890)
    F *La Sonate à Kreutzer* (Beethoven, Tolstoï)
    D der *Kreutzersonate* (Beethoven, Tolstoj)
    I *La Sonata a Kreutzer* (Beethoven, Tolstoj)
    E *La sonata a Kreutzer* (Beethoven, Tolstoi)
    SU «Кре́йцерова сона́та» (Бетхо́вен, Толсто́й)

1978   GB   *Kristin Lavransdatter* (Undset, 1920–2)
     F   *Kristin Lavransdatter*
     D   *Kristin Lavranstochter*
     I   *Kristin figlia di Lavran*
     E   *Cristina Lavransdatter*
     SU «Кри́стин, дочь Ла́вранса» (У́нсет)

1979   GB   Kuwait
     F   le Kuweït
     D   Kuwait
     I   il Kuwait
     E   Kuwait
     SU Куве́йт

L

1980   GB   Labour Party, the
        F   le Labour Party
        D   die Labour Party
        I   il Partito laburista
        E   el Partido Laborista
        SU   лейбори́стская па́ртия

1981   GB   Labrador (Canada)
        F   le Labrador (Canada)
        D   Labrador (Kanada)
        I   Labrador (Canada)
        E   Labrador (Canadá)
        SU   Лабрадо́р (Кана́да)

1982   GB   Laconia (Greece)
        F   la Laconie (Grèce)
        D   Lakonien (Griechenland)
        I   la Laconia (Grecia)
        E   Laconia (Grecia)
        SU   Лако́ния (Гре́ция)

1983   GB   *Lady and the Tramp* (Disney, 1956)
        F   *La Belle et le Clochard*
        D   *Susi und Strolch*
        I   *Lilli e il vagabondo*
        E   *La dame y el vagabundo*
        SU   «Ле́ди и бродя́га» (Ди́сней)

1984   GB   *Lady Chatterley's Lover* (Lawrence, 1928)
        F   *L'Amant de lady Chatterley*
        D   *Lady Chatterley*
        I   *L'amante di Lady Chatterley*
        E   *El amante de Lady Chatterley*
        SU   «Любо́вник ле́ди Ча́ттерли» (Ло́уренс)

1985   GB   *Ladykillers, The* (Mackendrick, 1955)
        F   *Tueurs de dames*
        D   *Ladykillers*
        I   *La signora omicida*
        E   *El quinteto de la muerte*
        SU   «Стару́шка-уби́йца» (Маке́ндрик)

1986   GB   *Lady of the Camelias, The* (Dumas, 1848)
        F   *La Dame aux camélias*
        D   *Die Kameliendame*
        I   *La signora dalle camelie*
        E   *La dama de las Camelias*
        SU   «Да́ма с каме́лиями» (Дюма́)

1987   GB   Lady of the Lake, the (myth., + Scott, 1810; Rossini, 1819)
        F   la Dame du lac (myth.)
        D   die Dame vom See (myth.)
        I   la signora del lago (mit.)
        E   la dama del lago (mit.)
        SU   Де́ва о́зера (миф., + Скотт, Росси́ни)

1988   GB   *Lady's Not for Burning, The* (Fry, 1949)
        F   *La dame ne brûlera pas*
        D   *Die dame ist nicht fürs Feuer*
        I   *La signora non è da bruciare*
        E   *La dama no está para quemar*
        SU   «Да́му не сожгу́т» (Фрай)

1989   GB   *Lady Vanishes, The* (Hitchcock, 1938)
        F   *Une femme disparaît*
        D   *Eine Dame verschwindet*
        I   *La signora sparisce*
        E   *Alarma en el expreso*
        SU   «Ле́ди исчеза́ет» (Хи́чкок)

1990   GB   *Lady Windermere's Fan* (Wilde, 1892)
        F   *L'Éventail de lady Windermere*
        D   *Lady Windermeres Fächer*
        I   *Il ventaglio di Lady Windermere*
        E   *El abanico de Lady Windermere*
        SU   «Ве́ер ле́ди Уи́ндермир» (Уа́йльд)

1991 GB *Lady with a Little Dog, The* (Chekhov, 1899)
F *La Dame au petit chien* (Tchekhov)
D *Die Dame mit dem Hündchen* (Tschechow)
I *La signora col cagnolino* (Čechov)
E *La señora del perillo* (Chejov)
SU «Да́ма с соба́чкой» (Че́хов)

1992 GB Laërtes (myth.)
F Laërte (myth.)
D Laertes (myth.)
I Laerte (mit.)
E Laertes (mit.)
SU Лаэ́рт (миф.)

GB Lake . . . → . . ., Lake

1993 GB Lake District, the (England)
F le district des lacs (Angleterre)
D das Seengebiet (England)
I la regione dei laghi (Inghilterra)
E el país de los lagos (Inglaterra)
SU Край озёр (А́нглия)

1994 GB *Lakme* (Delibes, 1883)
F *Lakmé*
D *Lakme*
I *Lakmé*
E *Lakmé*
SU «Лакме́» (Дели́б)

1995 GB *Lalla Rookh* (Moore, 1817)
F *Lalla Rookh*
D *Lalla Rookh*
I *Lalla Rookh*
E *Lalla Rookh*
SU «Ла́лла Рук» (Мур)

1996 GB La Mancha (Spain)
F la Manche (Espagne)
D La Mancha (Spanien)
I la Mancia (Spagna)
E la Mancha (España)
SU Ла-Ма́нча (Испа́ния)

1997 GB Lamentations (of Jeremiah), the (Bib.)
F les Lamentations (de Jérémie) (Bib.)
D die Klagelieder Jeremias (Bib.)
I le Lamentazioni (di Geremia) (Bib.)
E las Lamentaciones (de Jeremías) (Bib.)
SU «Плач Иереми́и» (библ.)

1998 GB Lamia (myth., + Keats, 1820)
F Lamia (myth.)
D Lamia (myth.)
I Lamia (mit.)
E Lamia (mit.)
SU Ла́мия (миф., + Китс)

1999 GB Lancelot (myth.)
F Lancelot (myth.)
D Lancelot (myth.)
I Lancelot (mit.)
E Lancelote (mit.)
SU Лансело́т (миф.)

2000 GB *Land of Heart's Desire, The* (Yeats, 1894)
F *Le Pays du désir du coeur*
D *Das Land der Sehnsucht*
I *Il paese del desiderio del cuore*
E *El país del deseo del corazón*
SU «Земля́ на́шего жела́ния» (Йитс)

2001 GB Languedoc (France)
F le Languedoc (France)
D Languedoc (Frankreich)
I la Linguadoca (Francia)
E Languedoc (Francia)
SU Лангедо́к (Фра́нция)

2002 GB *Laocöon, or On the Limits of Painting* (Lessing, 1766)
F *Laokoon, ou Des limites de la peinture*
D *Laokoon, oder Über die Grenzen der Malerei*
I *Laocoonte, o Dei limiti della pintura*
E *Laoconte, o de los límites de la pintura*
SU «Лаоко́он, и́ли О преде́лах жи́вописи» (Ле́ссинг)

2003 GB Laomedon (myth.)
F Laomédon (myth.)
D Laomedon (myth.)
I Laomedonte (mit.)
E Laomedonte (mit.)
SU Лаомедо́н (миф.)

2004 GB Lapiths, the (myth.)
F les Lapithes (myth.)
D die Lapithen (myth.)
I i lapiti (mit.)
E los lapitas (mit.)
SU ла́пифы (миф.)

2005 GB Lapland
F la Laponie
D Lappland
I la Lapponia
E Laponia
SU Лапла́ндия

2006 GB *Lark, The* (Anouilh, 1953)
F *L'Alouette*
D *Jeanne oder die Lerche*
I *L'allodola*
E *La alondra*
SU «Жа́воронок» (Ану́й)

2007 GB La Rochelle (France)
 F La Rochelle (France)
 D La Rochelle (Frankreich)
 I La Rochelle (Francia)
 E La Rochela (Francia)
 SU Ла-Рошéль (ж.) (Фрáнция)

2008 GB *Last Days of Pompeii, The*
  (Bulwer-Lytton, 1834)
 F *Les Derniers Jours de Pompéi*
 D *Die letzten Tage von Pompeji*
 I *Gli ultimi giorni di Pompei*
 E *Los últimos días de Pompeya*
 SU «Послéдние дни Помпéи»
  (Бýлвер-Лѝттон)

2009 GB Last Judgment, the (art)
 F le Jugement dernier (art)
 D das Jüngste Gericht (Kunst)
 I il Giudizio universale (arte)
 E El Juicio final (arte)
 SU «стрáшный суд» (иск.)

2010 GB *Last of the Mohicans, The* (Cooper,
  1826)
 F *Le Dernier des Mohicans*
 D *Der Letzte der Mohikaner*
 I *L'ultimo dei moicani*
 E *El último mohicano*
 SU «Послéдний из могикáн» (Кýпер)

2011 GB Last Supper, the (Bib., art)
 F la Cène (Bib., art)
 D das (heilige) Abendmahl (Bib., Kunst)
 I l'Ultima cena (Bib., arte)
 E La Cena (Bib., arte)
 SU «Тáйная вéчеря» (библ., иск.)

2012 GB *Last Tango in Paris* (Bertolucci, 1972)
 F *Dernier Tango à Paris*
 D *Der letzte Tango in Paris*
 I *Ultimo tango a Parigi*
 E *El último tango en París*
 SU «Послéднее тáнго в Парѝже»
  (Бертолýччи)

2013 GB *Last Tycoon, The* (Fitzgerald, 1941)
 F *Le Dernier Nabab*
 D *Der letzte Taikun*
 I *Gli ultimi fuochi*
 E *El último magnate*
 SU «Послéдний магнáт» (Фицджéральд)

2014 GB *Last Year at Marienbad* (Resnais,
  1961)
 F *L'Année dernière à Marienbad*
 D *Letztes Jahr in Marienbad*
 I *L'anno scorso a Marienbad*
 E *El año pasado en Marienbad*
 SU «В прóшлом годý в Марѝенбаде»
  (Ренé)

2015 GB *Late Mattia Pascal, The* (Pirandello,
  1904)
 F *Le feu Mattia Pascal*
 D *Die Wandlungen des Mattia Pascal*
 I *Il fu Mattia Pascal*
 E *El difunto Matías Pascal*
 SU «Покóйный Маттѝа Паскáль»
  (Пирандéлло)

2016 GB Latin America
 F l'Amérique latine
 D Lateinamerika
 I l'America latina
 E Latinoamérica
 SU Латѝнская Амéрика

2017 GB Latium (Italy)
 F le Latium (Italie)
 D Latium (Italien)
 I il Lazio (Italia)
 E Lacio (Italia)
 SU Лáцио (Итáлия)

2018 GB Latter-Day Saints, the (= Mormons)
  (rel.)
 F les Saints du dernier jour
  (= Mormons) (relig.)
 D die Heilige der letzten Tage
  (= Mormonen) (relig.)
 I i Santi dell'ultimo giorno (= mormoni)
  (relig.)
 E los Santos del último día
  (= Mormones) (relig.)
 SU «святы́е послéднего дня»
  (= мормóны) (рел.)

2019 GB Latvia (USSR)
 F la Lettonie (URSS)
 D Lettland (UdSSR)
 I la Lettonia (URSS)
 E Letonia (URSS)
 SU Лáтвия (СССР)

2020 GB *Laughing Cavalier* (Hals, 1624)
 F *Chevalier souriant*
 D *Lachender Kavalier*
 I *Cavaliere sorridente*
 E *Caballero risueño*
 SU «Улыбáющийся кавалéр» (Халс)

GB Laurence→Lawrence

2021 GB Lausanne (Switzerland)
F Lausanne (Suisse)
D Lausanne (Schweiz)
I Losanna (Svizzera)
E Lausana (Suiza)
SU Лоза́нна (Швейца́рия)

2022 GB Lawrence (saint, III)
F Laurent (saint)
D Laurentius (Heiliger)
I Lorenzo (santo)
E Lorenzo (santo)
SU Лавре́нтий (св.)

2023 GB *Lawrence of Arabia* (Lean, 1962)
F *Lawrence d'Arabie*
D *Lawrence von Arabien*
I *Lawrence d'Arabia*
E *Lawrence de Arabia*
SU «Ло́уренс Арави́йский» (Лин)

2024 GB *Laws* [*Laches*] (Plato, −IV)
F *Lois* (Platon)
D *Gesetze* (Platon)
I *Leggi* (Platone)
E *Leyes* (Platón)
SU «Зако́ны» (Плато́н)

2025 GB *Lay of the Last Minstrel, The* (Scott, 1805)
F *Le Lai du dernier ménestrel*
D *Des letzten Minnesängers Sang*
I *Il lamento dell'ultimo menestrello*
E *El lamento del último ministril*
SU «Песнь после́днего менестре́ля» (Скотт)

2026 GB Lazarus (Bib.)
F Lazare (Bib.)
D Lazarus (Bib.)
I Lazzaro (Bib.)
E Lázaro (Bib.)
SU Ла́зарь (библ.)

2027 GB League of Arab States, the
F la Ligue arabe
D die arabische Liga
I la Lega araba
E la Liga Árabe
SU Ли́га ара́бских госуда́рств

2028 GB League of Nations, the (hist.)
F la Société des Nations (SDN) (hist.)
D der Völkerbund (Gesch.)
I la Società delle nazioni (st.)
E la Sociedad de Naciones (hist.)
SU Ли́га на́ций (ист.)

2029 GB Leah (Bib.)
F Lia (Bib.)
D Lea (Bib.)
I Lia (Bib.)
E Lea (Bib.)
SU Ли́я (библ.)

2030 GB Leaning Tower of Pisa, the (Italy)
F la Tour penchée de Pise (Italie)
D der schiefe Glockenturm von Pisa (Italien)
I la Torre pendente di Pisa (Italia)
E la Torre inclinada de Pisa (Italia)
SU «Па́дающая ба́шня» в Пи́зе (Ита́лия)

2031 GB *Learned Ladies, The* (Molière, 1672)
F *Les Femmes savantes*
D *Die gelehrten Frauen*
I *Le donne saccenti*
E *Las mujeres sabias*
SU «Учёные же́нщины» (Молье́р)

2032 GB *Leaves of Autumn, The* (Hugo, 1831)
F *Feuilles d'automne*
D *Herbstblätter*
I *Foglie d'autunno*
E *Las hojas de otoño*
SU «Осе́нние ли́стья» (Гюго́)

2033 GB *Leaves of Grass* (Whitman, 1855)
F *Feuilles d'herbe*
D *Grashalme*
I *Foglie d'erba*
E *Hojas de hierba*
SU «Ли́стья травы́» (Уи́тмен)

2034 GB Lebanon
F le Liban
D Libanon
I il Libano
E el Líbano
SU Лива́н

2035 GB Leeward Islands, the
F les îles Sous-le-Vent
D die Leeward-Inseln
I le isole Sottovento
E las islas de Sotavento
SU Подве́тренные острова́

2036 GB *Legend of Gösta Berling, The* [*Gösta Berlings Saga*] (Lagerlöf, 1890−1)
F *La Saga de Gösta Berling*
D *Gösta Berling*
I *La saga di Gösta Berling*
E *La leyenda de Gösta Berling*
SU «Са́га о Йёсте Бе́рлинге» (Ла́герлёф)

2037 GB *Legend of Montrose, A* (Scott, 1819)
F   *La Légende de Montrose*
D   *Montrose*
I   *La leggenda di Montrose*
E   *La leyenda de Montrose*
SU «Леге́нда о Монтро́зе» (Скотт)

2038 GB *Legend of Orpheus, The* (Monteverdi, 1607)
F   *Orfeo*
D   *Orfeo*
I   *La favola d'Orfeo*
E   *Orfeo*
SU «Орфе́й» (Монтеве́рди)

2039 GB *Legend of the Ages, The* (Hugo, 1859–83)
F   *La Légende des siècles*
D   *Die Legende des Zeitalters*
I   *La leggenda dei secoli*
E   *La leyenda de los siglos*
SU «Леге́нда веко́в» (Гюго́)

GB Leghorn→Livorno

2040 GB Legion of Honour, the (France)
F   la Légion d'honneur (France)
D   die Ehrenlegion (Frankreich)
I   la legione d'onoro (Francia)
E   la Legión de Honor (Francia)
SU О́рден почётного легио́на (Фра́нция)

2041 GB Le Havre (France)
F   Le Havre (France)
D   Le Havre (Frankreich)
I   Le Havre (Francia)
E   El Havre (Francia)
SU Гавр (Фра́нция)

2042 GB Leiden (Netherlands)
F   Leyde (Pays-Bas)
D   Leiden (Niederlande)
I   Leida (Paesi Bassi)
E   Leyden (Holanda)
SU Ле́йден (Нидерла́нды)

2043 GB Leipzig (Germany)
F   Leipzig (Allemagne)
D   Leipzig (Deutschland)
I   Lipsia (Germania)
E   Leipzig (Alemania)
SU Ле́йпциг (Герма́ния)

2044 GB *Lelia* (Sand, 1833)
F   *Lélia*
D   *Lelia*
I   *Lelia*
E   *Lelia*
SU «Ле́лия» (Санд)

2045 GB Leningrad (USSR)
F   Leningrad (USSR)
D   Leningrad (UdSSR)
I   Leningrado (URSS)
E   Leningrado (URSS)
SU Ленингра́д (СССР)

2046 GB Lent (rel.)
F   le carême (relig.)
D   die Fasten (relig.)
I   la quaresima (relig.)
E   la cuaresma (relig.)
SU вели́кий пост (рел.)

2047 GB Leo (astron., saint, pope, emperor)
F   le Lion (astron.); Léon (saint, pape, empereur)
D   der Löwe (Astron.); Leo (Heiliger, Papst, Kaiser)
I   il Leone (astr.); Leone (santo, papa, imperatore)
E   León (astr., santo, papa, emperador)
SU Лев (астр., св., па́па ри́мский, импера́тор)

2048 GB Leonardo da Vinci (1452–1519)
F   Léonard de Vinci
D   Leonardo da Vinci
I   Leonardo da Vinci
E   Leonardo da Vinci
SU Леона́рдо да Ви́нчи

2049 GB *Leopard, The* (Lampedusa, 1956; Visconti, 1963)
F   *Le Léopard*
D   *Der Leopard*
I   *Il gattopardo*
E   *El gatopardo*
SU «Леопа́рд» (Тома́зи де Лампеду́са, Виско́нти)

2050 GB Leopold (emperor, sovereign)
F   Léopold (empereur, souverain)
D   Leopold (Kaiser, Herr.)
I   Leopoldo (imperatore, sovrano)
E   Leopoldo (emperador, sob.)
SU Леопо́льд (импера́тор, прав.)

2051 GB Lesotho
F   le Lesotho
D   Lesotho
I   il Lesotho
E   Lesotho
SU Лесо́то

2052　GB　Lesser Antilles, the (West Indies)
　　　F　les Petites Antilles (Antilles)
　　　D　die Kleinen Antillen (Westindien)
　　　I　le Piccole Antille (Antille)
　　　E　las Antillas Minores (Antillas)
　　　SU　Мáлые Антúльские островá
　　　　　(Вест-Úндия)

2053　GB　Lesser Slave Lake, the (Canada)
　　　F　le Petit Lac de l'Esclave (Canada)
　　　D　der Kleine Sklavesee (Kanada)
　　　I　il Piccolo Lago degli Schiavi (Canada)
　　　E　el Pequeño Lago del Esclavo (Canadá)
　　　SU　Мáлое Невóльничье óзеро (Канáда)

2054　GB　Lethe (myth.)
　　　F　Léthé (myth.)
　　　D　Lethe (myth.)
　　　I　Lete (mit.)
　　　E　Lete (mit.)
　　　SU　Лéта (миф.)

2055　GB　*Letter From an Unknown Woman*
　　　　　(Ophüls, 1948)
　　　F　*Lettre d'une inconnue*
　　　D　*Brief einer Unbekannken*
　　　I　*Lettera da una sconosciuta*
　　　E　*Carta de una desconocida*
　　　SU　«Письмó от незнакóмой жéнщины»
　　　　　(Офю́лс)

2056　GB　*Letters* [*Epistulae*] (Horace, −I)
　　　F　*Épîtres* (Horace)
　　　D　*Briefe* (Horaz)
　　　I　*Epistole* (Orazio)
　　　E　*Epístolas* (Horacio)
　　　SU　«Послáния» (Горáций)

2057　GB　*Letters from my Mill* (Daudet, 1869)
　　　F　*Lettres de mon moulin*
　　　D　*Briefe aus meiner Mühle*
　　　I　*Lettere dal mio mulino*
　　　E　*Cartas desde mi molino*
　　　SU　«Пúсьма с моéй мéльницы» (Додé)

2058　GB　*Letters from the Black Sea*, the
　　　　　[*Epistulae ex Ponto*] (Ovid, I)
　　　F　les *Pontiques* (Ovide)
　　　D　die *Briefe vom Schwarzen Meer*
　　　　　(Ovidius)
　　　I　le *Epistole dal Ponte* (Ovidio)
　　　E　las *Pónticas* (Ovidio)
　　　SU　«Понтúйские послáния» (Овúдий)

2059　GB　Levant, the
　　　F　le Levant
　　　D　die Levante
　　　I　il Levante
　　　E　el Levante
　　　SU　Левáнт

2060　GB　Levi (Bib.)
　　　F　Lévi (Bib.)
　　　D　Levi (Bib.)
　　　I　Levi (Bib.)
　　　E　Leví (Bib.)
　　　SU　Лéвий (библ.)

2061　GB　Leviathan (Bib., + Hobbes, 1651)
　　　F　Léviathan (Bib.)
　　　D　der Leviathan (Bib.)
　　　I　Leviatano (Bib.)
　　　E　Leviatán (Bib.)
　　　SU　левиафáн (библ., + Гоббс)

2062　GB　Levites, the (Bib.)
　　　F　les Lévites (Bib.)
　　　D　die Leviten (Bib.)
　　　I　i leviti (Bib.)
　　　E　los levitas (Bib.)
　　　SU　левúты (библ.)

2063　GB　Leviticus (Bib.)
　　　F　le Lévitique (Bib.)
　　　D　Leviticus (Bib.)
　　　I　il Levitico (Bib.)
　　　E　Levítico (Bib.)
　　　SU　«Левúт» (библ.)

2064　GB　Liberal Party, the
　　　F　le parti libéral
　　　D　die Liberalpartei
　　　I　il partito liberale
　　　E　el Partido Liberal
　　　SU　либерáльная пáртия

2065　GB　Liberia
　　　F　le Libéria
　　　D　Liberia
　　　I　la Liberia
　　　E　Liberia
　　　SU　Либéрия

　　　GB　Liberty, Statue of→Statue of Liberty

2066　GB　*Liberty Leading the People*
　　　　　(Delacroix, 1830)
　　　F　*La Liberté guidant le peuple*
　　　D　*Die Freiheit führt das Volk an*
　　　I　*La libertà che guida il popolo*
　　　E　*La libertad guiando el pueblo*
　　　SU　«Свобóда, ведýщая нарóд»
　　　　　(Делакруá)

2067　GB　Libra (astron.)
　　　F　la Balance (astron.)
　　　D　die Waage (Astron.)
　　　I　la Bilancia (astr.)
　　　E　Libra (astr.)
　　　SU　Весы́ (астр.)

2068 GB Libya
   F la Libye
   D Libyen
   I   la Libia
   E Libia
   SU Ли́вия

2069 GB Liège (Belgium)
   F Liège (Belge)
   D Lüttich (Belgien)
   I   Liegi (Belgio)
   E Lieja (Bélgica)
   SU Льеж (Бе́льгия)

2070 GB *Life, A* (Maupassant, 1883)
   F *Une vie*
   D *Ein Leben*
   I   *Una vita*
   E *Una vida*
   SU «Жизнь» (Мопасса́н)

2071 GB *Life and Adventures of Salavin, The* (Duhamel, 1920–32)
   F *Vie et aventures de Salavin*
   D *Salavins Leben und Abenteuer*
   I   *Vita e avventura di Salavin*
   E *Vida y aventuras de Salavin*
   SU «Жизнь и приключе́ния Салаве́на» (Дюаме́ль)

   GB *Life and Opinions of Tristram Shandy, Gentleman, The*→*Tristram Shandy*

2072 GB *Life at the Top* (Braine, 1962)
   F *La Vie au sommet*
   D *Ein Mann der Gesellschaft*
   I   *L'arrivato*
   E *Vida en la cumbre*
   SU «Жизнь наверху́» (Брейн)

2073 GB *Life for the Tsar, A* (Glinka, 1836)
   F *La Vie pour le tzar*
   D *Iwan Sussanin*
   I   *Una vita per lo zar*
   E *La vida por el Zar*
   SU «Ива́н Суса́нин» (Гли́нка)

2074 GB *Life is Not a Dream* (Quasimodo, 1949)
   F *La vie n'est pas un songe*
   D *Das Leben ist kein Traum*
   I   *La vita non è sogno*
   E *La vida no es sueño*
   SU «Жизнь не сон» (Квази́модо)

2075 GB *Life of Agricola [De vita Agricolae]* (Tacitus, 97)
   F *Vie d'Agricola* (Tacite)
   D *Leben des Agricola* (Tacitus)
   I   *Vita e costumi di Giulio Agricola* (Tacito)
   E *Vida de Agrícola* (Tácito)
   SU «Агри́кола» (Та́цит)

2076 GB *Life of Galileo, The* (Brecht, 1938–9)
   F *La vie de Galilée*
   D *Das Leben des Galilei*
   I   *La vita di Galileo*
   E *La vida de Galileo*
   SU «Жизнь Галиле́я» (Брехт)

2077 GB *Life of Henri Brulard, The* (Stendhal, 1835)
   F *La Vie d'Henri Brulard*
   D *Das Leben des Henri Brulard*
   I   *La vita di Henry Brulard*
   E *Vida de Henry Brulard*
   SU «Жизнь Анри́ Брюла́ра» (Стенда́ль)

2078 GB *Life of Jesus, A* (Renan, 1863)
   F *Vie de Jésus*
   D *Leben Jesu*
   I   *Vita di Gesù*
   E *Vida de Jesús*
   SU «Жизнь Иису́са» (Рена́н)

2079 GB *Life of Marian, The* (Marivaux, 1731–41)
   F *La Vie de Marianne*
   D *Das Leben Mariannes*
   I   *La vita di Marianna*
   E *La vida de Mariana*
   SU «Жизнь Мариа́нны» (Мариво́)

2080 GB *Life of St. Bruno* (Le Sueur, *1648*)
   F *Vie de saint Bruno*
   D *Das Leben des Heiligen Bruno*
   I   *Vita di S. Bruno*
   E *Vida de San Bruno*
   SU «Жизнь свято́го Бруно́» (Лесюэ́р)

2081 GB *Life of Samuel Johnson, The* (Boswell, 1791)
   F *Vie de Samuel Johnson*
   D *Das Leben von Samuel Johnson*
   I   *La vita di Samuel Johnson*
   E *La vida de Samuel Johnson*
   SU «Жизнь Сэ́мюэля Джо́нсона» (Бо́суэлл)

2082 GB *Life of the Bee, The* (Maeterlinck, 1901)
      F   *La Vie des abeilles*
      D   *Leben der Bienen*
      I   *La vita delle api*
      E   *Vida de las abejas*
      SU «Жизнь пчёл» (Métерли́нк)

2083 GB *Life of Washington, A* (Irving, 1855–9)
      F   *Vie de Washington*
      D   *Leben Washingtons*
      I   *Vita di Washington*
      E   *Vida de Washington*
      SU «Жизнеописа́ние Вашингто́на» (Йрвинг)

2084 GB *Life on the Mississippi* (Twain, 1883)
      F   *La Vie sur le Mississippi*
      D   *Leben auf dem Mississippi*
      I   *Vita sul Mississippi*
      E   *La vida sobre el Misisipí*
      SU «Жизнь на Миссиси́пи» (Твен)

2085 GB *Light in August* (Faulkner, 1932)
      F   *Lumière d'août*
      D   *Licht im August*
      I   *Luce d'agosto*
      E   *Luz de agosto*
      SU «Свет в а́вгусте» (Фо́лкнер)

2086 GB *Light that Failed, The* (Kipling, 1890)
      F   *La Lumière qui s'éteint*
      D   *Erloschenes Licht*
      I   *La luce che si spense*
      E   *La luz que se extingue*
      SU «Свет пога́с» (Ки́плинг)

2087 GB Liguria (Italy)
      F   la Ligurie (Italie)
      D   Ligurien (Italien)
      I   la Liguria (Italia)
      E   Liguria (Italia)
      SU Лигу́рия (Ита́лия)

2088 GB Lille (France)
      F   Lille (France)
      D   Lille (Frankreich)
      I   Lilla (Francia)
      E   Lila (Francia)
      SU Лилль (м.) (Фра́нция)

2089 GB *Lily of the Valley, The* (Balzac, 1835–6)
      F   *Le Lys dans la vallée*
      D   *Das Maiglöckchen*
      I   *Il mughetto*
      E   *La azucena del valle*
      SU «Ла́ндыш» (Бальза́к)

2090 GB Limbourg (Belgium)
      F   Limbourg (Belgique)
      D   Limburg (Belgien)
      I   Limburgo (Belgio)
      E   Limburgo (Bélgica)
      SU Ли́мбург (Бе́льгия)

2091 GB *Limelight* (Chaplin, 1952)
      F   *Les Feux de la rampe*
      D   *Rampenlicht*
      I   *Luci della ribalta*
      E   *Las candilejas*
      SU «Огни́ ра́мпы» (Ча́плин)

2092 GB Limousin (France)
      F   le Limousin (France)
      D   Limousin (Frankreich)
      I   il Limosino (Francia)
      E   Lemosín (Francia)
      SU Лимузе́н (Фра́нция)

2093 GB Linnaeus (1707–78)
      F   Linné
      D   von Linné
      I   Linneo
      E   Linneo
      SU Линне́й

2094 GB Lion Gate, the (Mycenae)
      F   la porte des Lionnes (Mycènes)
      D   das Löwentor (Mykene)
      I   la porta dei leoni (Micene)
      E   la Puerta de las Leonas (Micenas)
      SU Льви́ные воро́та (Мике́ны)

2095 GB Lions, the Gulf of (France)
      F   le golfe du Lion (France)
      D   der Golfe du Lion (Frankreich)
      I   il golfo del Leone (Francia)
      E   el Golfo de León (Francia)
      SU Лио́нский зали́в (Фра́нция)

2096 GB Lipari Islands (Aeolian Islands) (Italy)
      F   les îles Éoliennes (Italie)
      D   die Liparischen Inseln (Italien)
      I   le isole Eolie (Italia)
      E   las islas Lípari (Italia)
      SU Липа́рские острова́ (Ита́лия)

2097 GB Lisbon (Portugal)
      F   Lisbonne (f.) (Portugal)
      D   Lissabon (Portugal)
      I   Lisbona (Portogallo)
      E   Lisboa (Portugal)
      SU Лисабо́н (Португа́лия)

2098 GB Lithuania (USSR)
  F la Lituanie (URSS)
  D Litauen (UdSSR)
  I la Lituania (URSS)
  E Lituania (URSS)
  SU Ли́тва (СССР)

2099 GB *Litigants, The* (Racine, 1668)
  F *Les Plaideurs*
  D *Die Prozeßsüchtigen*
  I *I litiganti*
  E *Los litigantes*
  SU «Сутя́ги» (Раси́н)

2100 GB Little Bear, the (Ursa Minor) (astron.)
  F la Petite Ourse (astron.)
  D der Kleine Bär (Astron.)
  I l'Orsa Minore (astr.)
  E la Osa Menor (astr.)
  SU Ма́лая Медве́дица (астр.)

2101 GB *Little Dorrit* (Dickens, 1858)
  F *La Petite Dorrit*
  D *Klein-Dorrit*
  I *La piccola Dorrit*
  E *La pequeña Dorrit*
  SU «Кро́шка До́ррит» (Ди́ккенс)

2102 GB *Little Fadette* (Sand, 1849)
  F *La Petite Fadette*
  D *Die kleine Fadette*
  I *La piccola Fadette*
  E *La pequeña Fadette*
  SU «Ма́ленькая Фаде́тта» (Санд)

2103 GB *Little Foxes, The* (Hellman, 1939; Wyler, 1941)
  F *La Vipère*
  D *Die kleinen Füchse*
  I *I piccole volpi*
  E *La loba*
  SU «Лиси́чки» (Хе́лман, Уа́йлер)

2104 GB *Little Goose Man, The* (Wassermann, 1915)
  F *L'Homme aux oies*
  D *Das Gänsemännchen*
  I *L'ometto delle oche*
  E *El hombrecillo de los gansos*
  SU «Челове́к с гуся́ми» (Ва́ссерман)

2105 GB *Little Lord Fauntleroy* (Burnett, 1886)
  F *Le Petit Lord Fauntleroy*
  D *Der kleine Lord Fauntleroy*
  I *Il piccolo Lord Fauntleroy*
  E *El pequeño lord Fauntleroy*
  SU «Ма́ленький лорд Фа́унтлерой» (Бёрнетт)

2106 GB *Little Man, What Now?* (Fallada, 1932; Borzage, 1933)
  F *Et maintenant?*
  D *Kleiner Mann, was nun?*
  I *E adesso, pover'uomo?*
  E *¿Y ahora qué?*
  SU «Что же да́льше, ма́ленький челове́к?» (Фа́ллада, Бо́рзидж)

2107 GB *Little Match Girl, The* [*Den lille pige med svovlsrikkerne*] (Andersen, 1835)
  F *La Petite Fille aux allumettes*
  D *Das kleine Mädchen mit den Schwefelhölzchen*
  I *La piccola fiammiferaia*
  E *La muchacha de los fósforos*
  SU «Де́вочка со спи́чками» (А́ндерсен)

2108 GB *Little Mermaid, The* [*Den lille havfrue*] (Andersen, 1835)
  F *La Petite Sirène*
  D *Die kleine Seejungfrau*
  I *La sirenetta*
  E *La sirenita*
  SU «Руса́лочка» (А́ндерсен)

2109 GB *Little Prince, The* (Saint-Exupéry, 1943)
  F *Le Petit Prince*
  D *Der kleine Prinz*
  I *Il piccolo principe*
  E *El principito*
  SU «Ма́ленький принц» (Сент-Экзюпери́)

  GB *Little Red Riding-Hood*→*Red Riding Hood*

2110 GB *Little Women* (Alcott, 1868)
  F *Les Quatres Filles du Dr March*
  D *Die vier Schwestern*
  I *Piccole donne*
  E *Mujercitas*
  SU «Ма́ленькие же́нщины» (О́лкотт)

2111 GB *Lives of the Most Eminent Painters, Sculptors and Architects, The* (Vasari, 1550)
  F *Les Vies des plus excellents peintres, sculpteurs et architectes italiens*
  D *Lebensläufe der berühmtesten Maler, Bildhauer und Architekten*
  I *Le vite de'più eccellenti architetti, pittori e scultori italiani*
  E *Vidas de los más excelentes pintores, escultores y arquitectos*
  SU «Жизнеописа́ния наибо́лее знамени́тых живопи́сцев, вая́телей и зо́дчих» (Ваза́ри)

2112 GB *Lives of the Poets* (Johnson, 1779–80)
F *Vies des poètes anglais les plus célèbres*
D *Lebensbilder der englischen Dichter*
I *Vite dei poeti inglesi*
E *Vidas de los poetas ingleses*
SU «Жизнеописа́ния наибо́лее вы́дающихся англи́йских поэ́тов» (Джо́нсон)

2113 GB *Living Desert, The* (Disney, 1953)
F *Le Désert vivant*
D *Die Wüste lebt*
I *Il deserto che vive*
E *El desierto viviente*
SU «Жива́я пусты́ня» (Ди́сней)

2114 GB Livonia (hist.)
F la Livonie (hist.)
D Livland (Gesch.)
I la Livonia (st.)
E Livonia (hist.)
SU Ливо́ния (ист.)

2115 GB Livorno (Leghorn) (Italy)
F Livourne (Italie)
D Livorno (Italien)
I Livorno (Italia)
E Liorno (Italia)
SU Ливо́рно (Ита́лия)

2116 GB Livy (−59−+17)
F Tite-Live
D Livius
I Livio
E Tito Livio
SU Ли́вий

2117 GB *Liza of Lambeth* (Maugham, 1897)
F *Liza de Lambeth*
D *Liza von Lambeth*
I *Liza di Lambeth*
E *Liza de Lambeth*
SU «Ли́за из Ла́мбета» (Мо́эм)

2118 GB *Lohengrin* (Wagner, 1848)
F *Lohengrin*
D *Lohengrin*
I *Lohengrin*
E *Lohengrin*
SU «Лоэнгри́н» (Ва́гнер)

2119 GB Loire (River), the (France)
F la Loire (France)
D die Loire (Frankreich)
I la Loira (Francia)
E el Loira (Francia)
SU Луа́ра (Фра́нция)

2120 GB *Lolita* (Nabokov, 1958)
F *Lolita*
D *Lolita*
I *Lolita*
E *Lolita*
SU «Лоли́та» (Набо́ков)

2121 GB Lombards, the
F les Lombards
D die Lombarden
I i lombardi
E los lombardos
SU ломба́рды

2122 GB Lombardy (Italy)
F la Lombardie (Italie)
D die Lombardei (Italien)
I la Lombardia (Italia)
E Lombardía (Italia)
SU Ломба́рдия (Ита́лия)

2123 GB London (England)
F Londres (Angleterre)
D London (England)
I Londra (Inghilterra)
E Londres (Inglaterra)
SU Ло́ндон (А́нглия)

2124 GB *Loneliness of the Long Distance Runner, The* (Sillitoe, 1959)
F *La Solitude du coureur de fond*
D *Die Einsamkeit des Langstreckenläufers*
I *La solitudine del maratoneta*
E *La soledad del corredor de fondo*
SU «Одино́кий бегу́н» (Си́ллитоу)

2125 GB *Long Day's Journey into Night* (O'Neill, 1956)
F *Long Voyage dans la nuit*
D *Eine langen Tages Reise in die Nacht*
I *Lungo viaggio verso la notte*
E *El largo viaje de regreso*
SU «До́лгий день ухо́дит в по́лночь» (О'Ни́л)

2126 GB *Longest Day, The* (Annakin, 1962)
F *La Plus Longue Journée*
D *Der längste Tag*
I *Il giorno il più lungo*
E *El día más largo*
SU «Са́мый дли́нный день» (А́ннакин)

2127 GB *Longest Journey, The* (Forster, 1907)
F *Le Plus Long Voyage*
D *Die längste Reise*
I *Il cammino più lungo*
E *El más largo viaje*
SU «Сáмое длѝнное путешéствие» (Фóрстер)

2128 GB Longinus (III)
F Longin
D Longinos
I Longino
E Longino
SU Лонгѝн

2129 GB Long Parliament, the (1640–60)
F le Long Parlement
D das Lange Parlament
I il Parlamento lungo
E el Parlamento largo
SU Дóлгий парлáмент

2130 GB *Look Back in Anger* (Osborne, 1956)
F *La Paix du dimanche*
D *Blick zurück im Zorn*
I *Ricorda con rabbia*
E *Recordando con ira*
SU «Оглянѝсь во гнéве» (Óсборн)

2131 GB *Look Homeward, Angel* (Wolfe, 1929)
F *Mon ange, détourne ton regard vers la maison*
D *Schau heimwärts, Engel!*
I *Angelo, guarda il passato*
E *Mira hacia atrás, Ángel*
SU «Обернѝсь к дóму, áнгел» (Вулф)

2132 GB Lord Chancellor, the (England)
F le lord-chancelier (Angleterre)
D der Lordkanzler (England)
I il Lord cancelliere (Inghilterra)
E el lord canciller (Inglaterra)
SU лорд-кáнцлер (Áнглия)

2133 GB *Lord Jim* (Conrad, 1900)
F *Lord Jim*
D *Lord Jim*
I *Lord Jim*
E *Lord Jim*
SU «Лорд Джим» (Кóнрад)

2134 GB *Lord of the Flies* (Golding, 1954)
F *Le Seigneur des mouches*
D *Herr der Fliegen*
I *Il signore delle mosche*
E *El señor de las moscas*
SU «Повелѝтель мух» (Гóлдинг)

2135 GB *Lord of the Isles, The* (Scott, 1815)
F *Le Lord des îles*
D *Herr der Inseln*
I *Il lord delle isole*
E *El lord de las islas*
SU «Влады́ка островóв» (Скотт)

2136 GB *Lord of the Rings* (Tolkien, 1954–5)
F *Le Seigneur des anneaux*
D *Herr der Ringen*
I *Il signore degli anelli*
E *El señor de los anillos*
SU «Властелѝн колéц» (Тóлкин)

GB Lords, House of→House of Lords

2137 GB Lord's Prayer, the (rel.)
F le Pater (relig.)
D das Vaterunser (relig.)
I il Padre nostro (relig.)
E el Padre Nuestro (relig.)
SU «Óтче наш» (рел.)

2138 GB *Lorenzaccio* (Musset, 1834)
F *Lorenzaccio*
D *Lorenzaccio*
I *Lorenzaccio*
E *Lorenzaccio*
SU «Лоренцáччо» (Мюссé)

2139 GB Lorraine (France)
F la Lorraine (France)
D Lothringen (Frankreich)
I la Lorena (Francia)
E Lorena (Francia)
SU Лотарѝнгия (Фрáнция)

2140 GB *Lost Domain, The* (Alain-Fournier, 1913)
F *Le Grand Meaulnes*
D *Der große Kamerad*
I *Il grande amico Meaulnes*
E *El gran Meaulnes*
SU «Большóй Мольн» (Алéн-Фурньé)

2141 GB *Lost Horizon* (Capra, 1937)
F *Les Horizons perdus*
D *In Fesseln von Shangri-La*
I *Orizzonte perduto*
E *Horizontes perdidos*
SU «Потéрянные горизóнты» (Кáпра)

2142 GB *Lost Steps* (Breton, 1924)
F *Les Pas perdus*
D *Verlorene Schritten*
I *Passi perduti*
E *Los pasos perdidos*
SU «Потéрянные шагѝ» (Бретóн)

2143 GB *Lost Weekend, The* (Wilder, 1945)
     F *Le Poison*
     D *Das verlorene Wochenende*
     I *Giorni perduti*
     E *Días sin huella*
     SU «Потéрянные дни» (Уáйлдер)

2144 GB Lot (Bib.)
     F Loth (Bib.)
     D Lot (Bib.)
     I Lot (Bib.)
     E Lot (Bib.)
     SU Лот (библ.)

2145 GB Lothair (sovereign, + Disraeli, 1870)
     F Lothaire (souverain)
     D Lothar (Herr.)
     I Lotario (sovrano)
     E Lotario (sob.)
     SU Лóтарь (прав., + Дизраéли)

2146 GB *Lotte in Weimar* (Mann, 1939)
     F *Lotte à Weimar*
     D *Lotte in Weimar*
     I *Carlotta a Weimar*
     E *Carlota en Weimar*
     SU «Лóтта в Вéймаре» (Манн)

2147 GB Lotus-Eaters, the (myth.)
     F les Lotophages (myth.)
     D die Lotosesser (myth.)
     I i Lotofagi (mit.)
     E los Lotofagos (mit.)
     SU лотофáги (миф.)

2148 GB Louis (king)
     F Louis (roi)
     D Ludwig (König)
     I Luigi (re)
     E Luis (rey)
     SU Людóвик (прав.)

2149 GB Louis-Philippe (1773–1850)
     F Louis-Philippe
     D Louis Philippe
     I Luigi Filippo
     E Luis Felipe
     SU Луй Филипп

2150 GB Louvain (Belgium)
     F Louvain (Belge)
     D Löwen (Belgien)
     I Lovanio (Belgio)
     E Lovaina (Bélgica)
     SU Лёвен (Бéльгия)

2151 GB Louvre, the (Paris)
     F le Louvre (Paris)
     D der Louvre (Paris)
     I il Louvre (Parigi)
     E el Louvre (París)
     SU Лувр (Парúж)

2152 GB *Love and Mr Lewisham* (Wells, 1900)
     F *L'Amour et M. Lewisham*
     D *Liebe und Herr Lewisham*
     I *L'amore e il signor Lewisham*
     E *El amor y Mr. Lewisham*
     SU «Любóвь и мúстер Лю́ишем» (Уэ́ллс)

2153 GB *Loved One, The* (Waugh, 1948;
              Richardson, 1965)
     F *Ce cher disparu*
     D *Tod in Hollywood*
     I *Il caro estinto*
     E *El querido difunto*
     SU «Незабвéнная» (Во, Рúчардсон)

2154 GB *Love for Love* (Congreve, 1895)
     F *Amour pour amour*
     D *Liebe für Liebe*
     I *Amore per amore*
     E *Amor por amor*
     SU «Любóвь за любóвь» (Кóнгрив)

2155 GB *Love for Three Oranges, The*
           (Prokofiev, 1921)
     F *L'Amour des trois oranges* (Prokofiev)
     D *Die Liebe zu den drei Orangen*
        (Prokofiev)
     I *L'amore delle tre melarance*
        (Prokof'ev)
     E *El amor por las tres naranjas*
        (Prokofiev)
     SU «Любóвь к трём апельсúнам»
        (Прокóвьев)

2156 GB *Love of Danae, The* (Strauss, 1952)
     F *L'Amour de Danaé*
     D *Die Liebe der Danae*
     I *L'amore di Danae*
     E *El amor de Dánae*
     SU «Любóвь Данáи» (Штрáус)

2157 GB *Love Punished* (Anouilh, 1950)
     F *L'amour puni*
     D *Die bestrafte Liebe*
     I *L'amore castigato*
     E *El amor castigado*
     SU «Накáзанная любóвь» (Анýй)

2158 GB *Lover, The* (Pinter, 1963)
F *L'Amant*
D *Der Liebhaber*
I *Il amante*
E *El amante*
SU «Любóвник» (Пи́нтер)

2159 GB *Loves [Amores]* (Ovid, −I)
F *Amours* (Ovide)
D *Liebeselegien* (Ovidius)
I *Amori* (Ovidio)
E *Amores* (Ovidio)
SU «Любóвные эле́гии» (Ови́дий)

2160 GB *Love's Labour's Lost* (Shakespeare, 1594)
F *Peines d'amour perdues*
D *Verlorene Liebesmüh*
I *Pene d'amore perdute*
E *Trabajo de amor perdito*
SU «Беспло́дные уси́лия любви́» (Шекспи́р)

2161 GB *Love Story* (Hiller, 1970)
F *Love Story*
D *Love Story*
I *Love Story*
E *Love Story*
SU «Любóвная исто́рия» (Хи́ллер)

2162 GB Low Countries, the (hist.)
F les Pays-Bas (hist.)
D die Niederlande (Gesch.)
I i Paesi Bassi (st.)
E los Países Bajos (hist.)
SU Нидерла́нды (ист.)

2163 GB *Lower Depths, The* (Gorky, 1902)
F *Les Bas-Fonds* (Gorki)
D *Nachtasyl* (Gorkij)
I *Bassifondi* (Gor'kij)
E *Los bajos fondos* (Gorki)
SU «На дне» (Гóрький)

2164 GB *Lower Depths* (Renoir, 1936)
F *Les Bas-Fonds*
D *Nachtasyl*
I *Verso la vita*
E *Los bajos fondos*
SU «На дне» (Ренуа́р)

2165 GB *Loyalties* (Galsworthy, 1922)
F *Loyautés*
D *Treue*
I *Lealtà*
E *Lealtad*
SU «Ве́рность» (Гóлсуорси)

2166 GB Loyalty Islands, the
F les îles Loyauté
D die Loyalty-Inseln
I le isole Lealtà
E las islas de la Lealtad
SU острова́ Луайоте́

2167 GB Lübeck (Germany)
F Lübeck (Allemagne)
D Lübeck (Deutschland)
I Lubecca (Germania)
E Lübeck (Alemania)
SU Лю́бек (Герма́ния)

2168 GB Lublin (Poland)
F Lublin (Pologne)
D Lublin (Polen)
I Lublino (Polonia)
E Lublín (Polonia)
SU Лю́блин (Пóльша)

2169 GB Lucan (39–65)
F Lucain
D Lukan
I Lucano
E Lucano
SU Лука́н

GB Lucerne→Luzern

2170 GB Lucerne, Lake (Switzerland)
F le lac des Quatre-Cantons (Suisse)
D der Vierwaldstättersee (Schweiz)
I il lago di Lucerna (Svizzera)
E el lago de los Cuatro Cantones (Suiza)
SU Фирвальдште́тское óзеро (Швейца́рия)

2171 GB *Lucia di Lammermoor* (Donizetti, 1835)
F *Lucie de Lammermoor*
D *Lucia von Lammermoor*
I *Lucia di Lammermoor*
E *Lucía de Lammermoor*
SU «Лучи́я ди Ла́ммермур» (Донице́тти)

2172 GB Lucian (120–180)
F Lucien
D Lukianos
I Luciano
E Luciano
SU Лукиа́н

2173 GB Lucifer (myth., Bib.)
F Lucifer (myth., Bib.)
D Luzifer (myth., Bib.)
I Lucifero (mit., Bib.)
E Lucifer (mit., Bib.)
SU Люцифе́р (миф., библ.)

2174 GB Lucius (Roman name)
F Lucius (nom romain)
D Lucius (Römername)
I Lucio (nome romano)
E Lucio (nombre romano)
SU Лу́ций (древнери́мское и́мя)

2175 GB *Luck of Barry Lyndon, The*
(Thackeray, 1844)
F *Barry Lyndon*
D *Das Glück von Barry Lyndon*
I *Barry Lyndon*
E *Barry Lyndon*
SU «Уда́ча Ба́рри Ли́ндона» (Те́ккерей)

2176 GB *Luck of Roaring Camp, The* (Harte,
1868)
F *La chance entre au camp*
D *Das Glück von Roaring Camp*
I *La fortuna di Roaring Camp*
E *La buena suerte de Roaring Camp*
SU «Сча́стье реву́щего ста́на» (Гарт)

2177 GB *Lucky Jim* (Amis, 1954)
F *Jim la Chance*
D *Glück für Jim*
I *Jim il fortunato*
E *Jim y la suerte*
SU «Счастли́вчик Джим» (Э́мис)

2178 GB Lucretia (−IV)
F Lucrèce
D Lukrezia
I Lucrezia
E Lucrecia
SU Лукре́ция

2179 GB *Lucretia Borgia* (Hugo, 1833)
F *Lucrèce Borgia*
D *Lucrezia Borgia*
I *Lucrèce Borgia*
E *Lucrecia Borgia*
SU «Лукре́ция Бо́рджа» (Гюго́)

2180 GB Lucretius (−I)
F Lucrèce
D Lukrez
I Lucrezio
E Lucrecio
SU Лукре́ций

2181 GB Ludwig (sovereign)
F Louis (souverain)
D Ludwig (Herr.)
I Ludovico (sovrano)
E Luis (sob.)
SU Лю́двиг (прав.)

2182 GB Lugano, Lake (Italy/Switzerland)
F le lac de Lugano (Italie/Suisse)
D der Luganer See (Italien/Schweiz)
I il lago di Lugano (Italia/Svizzera)
E el lago de Lugano (Italia/Suiza)
SU о́зеро Луга́но (Ита́лия/Швейца́рия)

2183 GB Luke (saint, Bib.)
F Luc (saint, Bib.)
D Lukas (Heiliger, Bib.)
I Luca (santo, Bib.)
E Lucas (santo, Bib.)
SU Лука́ (св., библ.)

2184 GB Luke, the Gospel According to [Saint]
(Bib.)
F l'Évangile selon saint Luc (Bib.)
D das Lukas-Evangelium (Bib.)
I il Vangelo di Luca (Bib.)
E el Evangelio de San Lucas (Bib.)
SU «Ева́нгелие от Луки́» (библ.)

2185 GB *Luncheon on the Grass* (Manet, 1863)
F *Le Déjeuner sur l'herbe*
D *Frühstück im Freien*
I *Colazione sull'erba*
E *Colación en el campo*
SU «За́втрак на траве́» (Мане́)

2186 GB Lusatia (hist.)
F la Lusace (hist.)
D die Lausitz (Gesch.)
I la Lusazia (st.)
E Lusacia (hist.)
SU Лу́жица (ист.)

2187 GB Lusitania (hist.)
F la Lusitanie (hist.)
D Lusitanien (Gesch.)
I la Lusitania (st.)
E Lusitania (hist.)
SU Лузита́ния (ист.)

2188 GB Lutetia (hist.)
F Lutèce (hist.)
D Lutetia (Gesch.)
I Lutetia (st.)
E Lutecia (hist.)
SU Люте́ция (ист.)

2189 GB Luther (1483–1546; + Osborne, 1961)
F Luther
D Luther
I Lutero
E Lutero
SU Лю́тер (+ О́сборн)

2190	GB	Luxembourg
	F	le Luxembourg
	D	Luxembourg
	I	il Lussemburgo
	E	Luxemburgo
	SU	Люксембу́рг

2191 GB Luzern (Lucerne) (Switzerland)
F Lucerne (Suisse)
D Luzern (Schweiz)
I Lucerna (Svizzera)
E Lucerna (Suiza)
SU Люце́рн (Швейца́рия)

2192 GB Lycia (hist.)
F la Lycie (hist.)
D Lykien (Gesch.)
I la Licia (st.)
E Licia (hist.)
SU Ли́кия (ист.)

2193 GB *Lycidas* (Milton, 1637)
F *Lycidas*
D *Lycidas*
I *Lycidas*
E *Lycidas*
SU «Лю́сидас» (Ми́льтон)

2194 GB Lycurgus (myth.)
F Lycurgue (myth.)
D Licurgo (myth.)
I Licurgo (mit.)
E Licurgo (mit.)
SU Лику́рг (миф.)

2195 GB Lydia (hist.)
F la Lydie (hist.)
D Lydien (Gesch.)
I la Lidia (st.)
E Lidia (hist.)
SU Ли́дия (ист.)

2196 GB Lyon(s) (France)
F Lyon (France)
D Lyon (Frankreich)
I Lione (Francia)
E Lyon (Francia)
SU Лио́н (Фра́нция)

2197 GB Lysander (−IV)
F Lysandre
D Lysander
I Lisandro
E Lisandro
SU Лиса́ндр

2198 GB Lysimachus (*355–281*)
F Lysimaque
D Lysimachos
I Lisimaco
E Lisímacho
SU Лисима́х

2199 GB Lysippus (IV)
F Lysippe
D Lysippos
I Lisippo
E Lisipo
SU Лиси́пп

2200 GB *Lysistrata* (Aristophanes, −411)
F *Lysistrata* (Aristophane)
D *Lysistrata* (Aristophanes)
I *Lisistrata* (Aristofane)
E *Lisístrata* (Aristófanes)
SU «Лиси́страта» (Аристофа́н)

M

2201 GB Macau
  F le Macao
  D Macau
  I Macao
  E Macao
  SU Макáо

2202 GB *Macbeth* (Shakespeare, 1605)
  F *Macbeth*
  D *Macbeth*
  I *Macbeth*
  E *Macbeth*
  SU «Макбéт» (Шекспúр)

2203 GB Maccabees, the (rel.)
  F les Maccabées (relig.)
  D die Makkabäer (relig.)
  I i Maccabei (relig.)
  E los Macabeos (relig.)
  SU Маккавéи (рел.)

  GB Maccabeus, Judas→Judas Maccabeus

2204 GB Macedonia (Europe)
  F la Macédoine (Europe)
  D Mazedonien (Europa)
  I la Macedonia (Europa)
  E Macedonia (Europa)
  SU Македóния (Еврóпа)

2205 GB Machiavelli (1469–1527)
  F Machiavel
  D Machiavelli
  I Machiavelli
  E Maquiavelo
  SU Макиавéлли

2206 GB Madagascar
  F le Madagascar
  D Madagaskar
  I il Madagascar
  E Madagascar
  SU Мадагаскáр

2207 GB *Madame Angot's Daughter* (Lecocq, 1872)
  F *La Fille de Madame Angot*
  D *Die Tochter der Madame Angot*
  I *La figlia di Mme Angot*
  E *La hija de Madame Angot*
  SU «Дочь мадáм Ангó» (Лекóк)

2208 GB *Madame Bovary* (Flaubert, 1857)
  F *Madame Bovary*
  D *Madame Bovary*
  I *Madame Bovary*
  E *Madame Bovary*
  SU «Госпожá Бовари́» (Флобéр)

2209 GB *Madame Butterfly* (Puccini, 1904)
  F *Madame Butterfly*
  D *Madame Butterfly*
  I *Madama Butterfly*
  E *Madame Butterfly*
  SU «Чúо-Чúо-сáн» (Пуччúни)

2210 GB *Madame Chrysanthemum* (Loti, 1887)
  F *Madame Chrysanthème*
  D *Madame Chrysanthème*
  I *La signora dei crisantemi*
  E *Madame Crisantemo*
  SU «Госпожá Хризантéма» (Лотú)

2211 GB Madeira
  F Madère
  D Madeira
  I Madera
  E Madera
  SU Мадéйра

2212 GB Madonna, the (rel., art)
  F la madone (relig., art)
  D die Madonna (Maria) (relig., Kunst)
  I la Madonna (relig., arte)
  E la Madona (relig., arte)
  SU Мадóнна (рел., иск.)

2213 GB *Madonna of the Magnificat* (Botticelli, 1482–3)
F *Madone du Magnificat*
D *Madonna del Magnificat*
I *Madonna del Magnificat*
E *Madona del Magnificat*
SU «Мадо́нна дель Маньифика́т» (Боттиче́лли)

2214 GB *Madwoman of Chaillot, The* (Giraudoux, 1946)
F *La Folle de Chaillot*
D *Die Irre von Chaillot*
I *La pazza di Chaillot*
E *La loca de Chaillot*
SU «Беснова́тая из Шайо́» (Жироду́)

2215 GB Maecenas (*70–8*)
F Mécène
D Mäcenas
I Mecenate
E Mecenas
SU Мецена́т

2216 GB Maenads, the (myth.)
F les Ménades (myth.)
D die Mänaden (myth.)
I le menadi (mit.)
E las ménades (mit.)
SU мена́ды (миф.)

2217 GB Magellan (*1480–1521*)
F Magellan
D Magellan
I Magellano
E Magallanes
SU Магелла́н

2218 GB Magellan, the Strait of
F le détroit de Magellan
D die Magellan-Straße
I lo stretto di Magellano
E el estrecho de Magallanes
SU Магелла́нов проли́в

2219 GB *Maggie: A Girl of the Streets* (Crane, 1893)
F *Maggie, fille des rues*
D *Maggie, ein Straßenmädchen*
I *Maggie, ragazza di strada*
E *Maggie, una chica de la calle*
SU «Мэ́гги, де́вушка с у́лицы» (Крейн)

2220 GB Maggiore, Lake (Italy)
F le lac Majeur (Italie)
D der Lago Maggiore (Italien)
I il lago Maggiore (Italia)
E el lago Mayor (Italia)
SU о́зеро Ла́го-Маджо́ре (Ита́лия)

2221 GB Magi, the (rel.)
F les Rois mages (relig.)
D die Magier (relig.)
I i magi (relig.)
E los Reyes Magos (relig.)
SU волхвы́ (рел.)

2222 GB *Magic Flute, The* (Mozart, 1791)
F *La Flûte enchantée*
D *Die Zauberflöte*
I *Il flauto magico*
E *La flauta encantada*
SU «Волше́бная фле́йта» (Мо́царт)

2223 GB *Magic Mountain, The* (Mann, 1924)
F *La Montagne magique*
D *Der Zauberberg*
I *La montagna incantata*
E *La montaña mágica*
SU «Волше́бная гора́» (Манн)

2224 GB Magna Carta (Magna Charta), the (1215)
F la Grande Charte
D die Magna Charta (Libertatum)
I la Magna charta (libertatum)
E la Carta Magna
SU Вели́кая ха́ртия во́льностей

2225 GB Magnesia (Greece)
F la Magnésie (Grèce)
D Magnesia (Griechenland)
I la Magnesia (Grecia)
E Magnesia (Grecia)
SU Магне́сия (Гре́ция)

2226 GB *Magnificent Ambersons, The* (Welles, 1942)
F *La Splendeur des Amberson*
D *Der Glanz des Hauses Amberson*
I *L'orgoglio degli Amberson*
E *El cuarto mandamiento*
SU «Великоле́пные Э́мберсоны» (Уэ́ллс)

2227 GB *Magnificent Obsession* (Stahl, 1935)
F *Le Secret magnifique*
D *Die wunderbare Macht*
I *Al di là delle tenebre*
E *Obsesión*
SU «Великоле́пная иде́я» (Стал)

2228 GB *Magnificent Seven, The* (Sturges, 1961)
F *Les Sept Mercenaires*
D *Die glorreichen Sieben*
I *I magnifici sette*
E *Los siete magníficos*
SU «Великоле́пная семёрка» (Стёрджес)

GB   *Mahagonny→Rise and Fall of the*
     Town Mahagonny

GB   Mahomet→Muhammad

2229 GB   Maia (myth.)
      F   Maia (myth.)
      D   Maia (myth.)
      I   Maia (mit.)
      E   Maia (mit.)
      SU   Ма́йя (миф.)

2230 GB   *Maid of Orleans, The* (Schiller, 1801;
           Tchaikovsky, 1879)
      F   *La Pucelle d'Orléans* (Schiller,
           Tchaikovski)
      D   *Die Jungfrau von Orléans* (Schiller,
           Tschaikowskij)
      I   *La pulcella di Orléans* (Schiller,
           Čajkovskij)
      E   *La doncella de Orleáns* (Schiller,
           Tchaikovski)
      SU   «Орлеа́нская де́ва» (Ши́ллер,
           Чайко́вский)

2231 GB   *Maids, The* (Genêt, 1948)
      F   *Les Bonnes*
      D   *Die Zofen*
      I   *Le cameriere*
      E   *Las criadas*
      SU   «Го́рничные» (Жене́)

2232 GB   *Maid's Tragedy, The* (Beaumont +
           Fletcher, 1611)
      F   *La Tragédie de la jeune fille*
      D   *Eine Mädchentragödie*
      I   *La tragedia della fanciulla*
      E   *La tragedia de una joven*
      SU   «Траге́дия де́вушки» (Бо́монт/
           Фле́тчер)

2233 GB   *Main Street* (Lewis, 1920)
      F   *Main Street*
      D   *Hauptstraße*
      I   *Strada maestra*
      E   *Calle mayor*
      SU   «Гла́вная у́лица» (Лью́ис)

2234 GB   Mainz (Germany)
      F   Mayence (Allemagne)
      D   Mainz (Deutschland)
      I   Magonza (Germania)
      E   Maguncia (Alemania)
      SU   Майнц (Герма́ния)

2235 GB   *Major Barbara* (Shaw, 1905)
      F   *Commandant Barbara*
      D   *Major Barbara*
      I   *Il maggiore Barbara*
      E   *El comandante Bárbara*
      SU   «Майо́р Ба́рбара» (Шо́у)

2236 GB   Majorca
      F   Majorque
      D   Mallorca
      I   Maiorca
      E   Mallorca
      SU   Малью́рка

2237 GB   *Makropoulos Secret, The* [*Věc*
           Makropulos] (Čapek, 1925)
      F   *L'Affaire Makropoulos*
      D   *Die Sache Makropoulos*
      I   *L'affare Makropoulos*
      E   *El asunto Makropoulos*
      SU   «Сре́дство Макро́пулоса» (Ча́пек)

2238 GB   Malacca, the Strait of
      F   le détroit de Malacca
      D   die Malakka-Straße
      I   lo stretto di Malacca
      E   el estrecho de Malaca
      SU   Мала́ккский проли́в

2239 GB   Malachi (Bib.)
      F   Malachie (Bib.)
      D   Maleachi (Bib.)
      I   Malachia (Bib.)
      E   Malaquías (Bib.)
      SU   Мала́хий (библ.)

2240 GB   *Malatesta* (Montherlant, 1948)
      F   *Malatesta*
      D   *Malatesta*
      I   *Malatesta*
      E   *Malatesta*
      SU   «Малате́ста» (Монтерла́н)

2241 GB   *Malavoglias, The* (Verga, 1881)
      F   *La Malavoglia*
      D   *I Malavoglia*
      I   *I Malavoglia*
      E   *I Malavoglia*
      SU   «Семья́ Малаво́лья» (Ве́рга)

2242 GB   Malawi
      F   le Malawi
      D   Malawi
      I   il Malawi
      E   Malawi
      SU   Мала́ви

2243 GB   Malaya
      F   la Malaisie
      D   Malaia
      I   la Malaysia Occidentale
      E   Malaya
      SU   Мала́йя

2244 GB Malay Peninsula, the
F la presqu'île Malaise
D die Malaiische Halbinsel
I la penisola di Malacca
E la Península Malaya
SU полуо́стров Мала́кка

2245 GB Malaysia
F la Malaysia
D Malaysia
I la Malaysia
E Malaysia
SU Мала́йзия

2246 GB Maldive Islands, the
F les îles Maldives
D die Malediven
I le Maldive
E las Maldivas
SU Мальди́вские острова́

2247 GB Mali
F le Mali
D Mali
I il Mali
E el Malí
SU Мали́

2248 GB *Malone Dies* (Beckett, 1951)
F *Malone meurt*
D *Malone stirbt*
I *Malone muore*
E *Malone muere*
SU «Мало́н умира́ет» (Бе́ккет)

2249 GB Malta
F Malte (f.)
D Malta
I Malta
E Malta
SU Ма́льта

2250 GB Mamelukes, the (hist.)
F les mamelouks (hist.)
D die Mameluken (Gesch.)
I i mamelucchi (st.)
E los mamelucos (hist.)
SU мамлю́ки (ист.)

2251 GB *Man and a Woman, A* (Lelouch, 1966)
F *Un homme et une femme*
D *Ein Mann und eine Frau*
I *Un uomo, una donna*
E *Un hombre y una mujer*
SU «Оди́н мужчи́на, одна́ же́нщина» (Лелу́ш)

2252 GB *Man and Superman* (Shaw, 1905)
F *Homme et surhomme*
D *Mensch und Übermensch*
I *Uomo e superuomo*
E *Hombre y superhombre*
SU «Челове́к и сверхчелове́к» (Шо́у)

2253 GB Manasseh (Manasses) (Bib.)
F Manassé (Bib.)
D Manasse (Bib.)
I Manasse (Bib.)
E Manasés (Bib.)
SU Мана́ссия (библ.)

2254 GB Manchuria (China)
F la Mandchourie (Chine)
D die Mandschurei (China)
I la Manciuria (Cina)
E Manchuria (China)
SU Маньчжу́рия (Кита́й)

2255 GB *Mandarins, The* (Beauvoir, 1954)
F *Les Mandarins*
D *Die Mandarine von Paris*
I *I mandarini*
E *Los mandarinos*
SU «Мандари́ны» (Бовуа́р)

2256 GB *Mandragola, La* [*The Mandrake*] (Machiavelli, 1504)
F *La Mandragore* (Machiavel)
D *Mandragola* (Machiavelli)
I *La Mandragola* (Machiavelli)
E *La Mandrágora* (Maquiavelo)
SU «Мандраго́ра» (Макиаве́лли)

2257 GB *Man – Finished, A* (Papini, 1912)
F *Un homme fini*
D *Ein fertiger Mensch*
I *Un uomo finito*
E *Un hombre acabado*
SU «Ко́нченый челове́к» (Папи́ни)

2258 GB *Man For All Seasons, A* (Bolt, 1960; Zinnemann, 1966)
F *Un homme pour toutes les saisons*
D *Ein Mann zu jeder Jahreszeit*
I *Un uomo per tutte le stagioni*
E *Un hombre para la eternidad*
SU «Челове́к на все времена́» (Болт, Зи́ннеманн)

2259 GB Manfred (1232–66; + Byron, 1817; Tchaikovsky, 1885)
F Manfred (+ Byron, Tchaikovski)
D Manfred (+ Byron, Tschaikowskij)
I Manfredi (+ Byron, Čajkovskij)
E Manfredo (+ Byron, Tchaikovski)
SU Ма́нфред (+ Ба́йрон, Чайко́вский)

2260 GB Man Friday (*Robinson Crusoe*)
F Vendredi
D Freitag
I Venerdì
E Viernes
SU Пя́тница («Робинзо́н Кру́зо»)

2261 GB *Manhattan Transfer* (Dos Passos, 1925)
F *Manhattan Transfer*
D *Manhattan Transfer*
I *Nuova York*
E *Manhattan Transfer*
SU «Манхе́ттен» (Дос Па́ссос)

2262 GB Manilla (Philippines)
F Manille (Philippines)
D Manila (Philippinen)
I Manila (Filippine)
E Manila (Filipinas)
SU Мани́ла (Филиппи́ны)

2263 GB *Man of Aran* (Flaherty, 1934)
F *L'Homme d'Aran*
D *Die Männer von Aran*
I *L'uomo di Aran*
E *El hombre de Aran*
SU «Челове́к из А́рана» (Фла́эрти)

2264 GB *Man of Property, The* (Galsworthy, 1906)
F *Le Propriétaire*
D *Der reiche Mann*
I *Il possidente*
E *El propietario*
SU «Со́бственник» (Го́лсуорси)

2265 GB *Manon* (Massenet, 1884)
F *Manon*
D *Manon*
I *Manon*
E *Manon*
SU «Мано́н» (Массне́)

2266 GB *Manon Lescaut* (Prévost, 1728–31; Puccini, 1893)
F *Manon Lescaut*
D *Manon Lescaut*
I *Manon Lescaut*
E *Manon Lescaut*
SU «Мано́н Леско́» (Прево́, Пуччи́ни)

2267 GB *Mansfield Park* (Austen, 1814)
F *Le Parc de Mansfield*
D *Mansfield Park*
I *Mansfield Park*
E *El parque de Mansfield*
SU «Ме́нсфилд парк» (О́стин)

2268 GB *Man's Hope* (Malraux, 1937)
F *L'Espoir*
D *Die Hoffnung*
I *La speranza*
E *La esperanza*
SU «Наде́жда» (Мальро́)

2269 GB Mantua (Italy)
F Mantoue (Italie)
D Mantua (Italien)
I Mantova (Italia)
E Mantua (Italia)
SU Ма́нтуя (Ита́лия)

2270 GB *Man Who Knew Coolidge, The* (Lewis, 1928)
F *L'Homme qui connaissait Coolidge*
D *Der Mann, der den Präsidenten kannte*
I *L'uomo che conobbe Coolidge*
E *El hombre que conocía Coolidge*
SU «Челове́к, кото́рый знал Ку́лиджа» (Лью́ис)

2271 GB *Man Who Knew Too Much, The* (Hitchcock, 1934)
F *L'Homme qui en savait trop*
D *Der Mann, der zuviel wußte*
I *L'uomo che sapeva troppo*
E *El hombre que sabía demasiado*
SU «Челове́к, кото́рый сли́шком мно́го знал» (Хи́чкок)

2272 GB *Man Who Shot Liberty Valance, The* (Ford, 1962)
F *L'Homme qui tua Liberty Valance*
D *Der Mann, der Liberty Valance erschoß*
I *L'uomo che uccise Liberty Valance*
E *El hombre que mató a Liberty Valance*
SU «Челове́к, уби́вший Ли́берти Вэ́ланса» (Форд)

2273 GB *Man Who Was Thursday, The* (Chesterton, 1908)
F *Le Nommé Jeudi*
D *Der Mann, der Donnerstag war*
I *L'uomo che fu Giovedì*
E *El hombre que fue jueves*
SU «Челове́к, кото́рый был Четверго́м» (Че́стертон)

2274 GB *Marat/Sade* (Weiss, 1965)
F *Marat-Sade*
D *Die Ermordung Jean-Paul Marats*
I *L'assassinio di Jean Paul Marat*
E *Marat Sade*
SU «Мара́т-Сад» (Вайс)

2275	GB	*Marble Faun, The* (Hawthorne, 1860)
	F	*Faune de marbre*
	D	*Der Marmorfaun*
	I	*Il fauno di marmo*
	E	*Fauno de mármol*
	SU	«Мра́морный фавн» (Хо́торн)

2276	GB	Marcellus (saint, pope)
	F	Marcel (saint, pape)
	D	Marcellus (Heiliger, Papst)
	I	Marcello (santo, papa)
	E	Marcelo (santo, papa)
	SU	Марце́лл (св., па́па ри́мский)

2277	GB	Marches, the (Italy)
	F	les Marches (f.) (Italie)
	D	die Marken (Italien)
	I	le Marche (Italia)
	E	las Marcas (Italia)
	SU	Ма́рке (Ита́лия)

2278	GB	Marcian (396–457)
	F	Marcien
	D	Marcian
	I	Marciano
	E	Marciano
	SU	Марциа́н

2279	GB	Marcus (Roman name)
	F	Marc (nom romain)
	D	Marcus (Römername)
	I	Marco (nome romano)
	E	Marco (nombre romano)
	SU	Марк (древнери́мское имя)

2280	GB	Marcus Aurelius (121–180)
	F	Marc Aurèle
	D	Marcus Aurelius
	I	Marco Aurelio
	E	Marco Aurelio
	SU	Марк Авре́лий

2281	GB	Margaret (saint, *255–275*)
	F	Marguerite (sainte)
	D	Margarete (Heilige)
	I	Margherita (santa)
	E	Margarita (santa)
	SU	Маргари́та (св.)

2282	GB	Margaret of Anjou (1430–82)
	F	Marguerite d'Anjou
	D	Margarete von Anjou
	I	Margherita d'Angiò
	E	Margarita de Anjou
	SU	Маргари́та Анжу́йская

2283	GB	Margaret of Navarre (Margaret of Angoulême) (1492–1549)
	F	Marguerite d'Angoulême
	D	Margarete von Navarra
	I	Margherita d'Angoulême
	E	Margarita de Angulema
	SU	Маргари́та Нава́ррская

2284	GB	*Maria Chapdelaine* (Hémon, 1916)
	F	*Maria Chapdelaine*
	D	*Maria Chapdelaine*
	I	*Marie Chapdelaine*
	E	*Marie Chapdelaine*
	SU	«Мари́я Шапдле́н» (Эмо́н)

2285	GB	Mariana Islands, the
	F	les îles Mariannes
	D	die Marianen
	I	le Marianne
	E	las islas Marianas
	SU	Мариа́нские острова́

2286	GB	*Marian's Whims* (Musset, 1833)
	F	*Les Caprices de Marianne*
	D	*Die launische Marianne*
	I	*I capricci di Marianna*
	E	*Los caprichos de Mariana*
	SU	«Капри́з Мариа́нны» (Мюссе́)

2287	GB	*Maria Stuart* (Schiller, 1800)
	F	*Marie Stuart*
	D	*Maria Stuart*
	I	*Maria Stuarda*
	E	*María Estuardo*
	SU	«Мари́я Стю́арт» (Ши́ллер)

2288	GB	Maria Theresa (1717–80)
	F	Marie-Thérèse
	D	Maria Theresia
	I	Maria Teresa
	E	María Teresa
	SU	Мари́я Тере́зия

2289	GB	Marie-Antoinette (1755–93)
	F	Marie-Antoinette
	D	Maria Antonietta
	I	Maria Antonietta
	E	María Antonieta
	SU	Мари́я Антуане́тта

2290	GB	Marie Byrd Land (Antarctica)
	F	le terre Marie-Byrd (Antarctique)
	D	Marie-Byrd-Land (Antarktika)
	I	la terra di Byrd (Antartide)
	E	la tierra de María Byrd (Antártida)
	SU	Земля́ Мэ́ри Бэрд (Антаркти́да)

2291 GB Maria de Médicis (1573–1642)
　　F Marie de Médicis
　　D Maria von Medici
　　I Maria de' Medici
　　E María de Médicis
　　SU Мари́я Ме́дичи

2292 GB Marie-Louise (1791–1847)
　　F Marie-Louise
　　D Marie-Louise
　　I Maria Luisa
　　E María Luisa
　　SU Мари́я Луи́за

2293 GB Marie-Thérèse (1638–83)
　　F Marie-Thérèse
　　D Maria Theresia
　　I Maria Teresa
　　E María Teresa
　　SU Мари́я Тере́зия

2294 GB *Mario and the Magician* (Mann, 1930)
　　F *Mario et le magicien*
　　D *Mario und der Zauberer*
　　I *Mario e il mago*
　　E *Mario y el encantador*
　　SU «Мари́о и волше́бник» (Манн)

2295 GB *Marion de Lorme* (Hugo, 1829)
　　F *Marion Delorme*
　　D *Marion Delorme*
　　I *Marione Delorme*
　　E *Marión Delorme*
　　SU «Марио́н Дело́рм» (Гюго́)

2296 GB *Marius* (Pagnol, 1929)
　　F *Marius*
　　D *Marius*
　　I *Marius*
　　E *Marius*
　　SU «Мариу́с» (Панью́ль)

2297 GB Mark (saint, Bib.)
　　F Marc (saint, Bib.)
　　D Markus (Heiliger, Bib.)
　　I Marco (santo, Bib.)
　　E Marcos (santo, Bib.)
　　SU Марк (св., библ.)

2298 GB Mark, the Gospel According to [Saint] (Bib.)
　　F l'Évangile selon saint Marc (Bib.)
　　D das Markus-Evangelium (Bib.)
　　I il Vangelo di Marco (Bib.)
　　E el Evangelio de San Marcos (Bib.)
　　SU «Ева́нгелие от Ма́рка» (библ.)

2299 GB Mark Antony (83–30)
　　F Marc Antoine
　　D Marcus Antonius
　　I Marco Antonio
　　E Marco Antonio
　　SU Марк Анто́ний

2300 GB Marmara, the Sea of (Turkey)
　　F la mer de Marmara (Turquie)
　　D das Marmarameer (Türkei)
　　I il mare di Marmara (Turchia)
　　E el mar de Mármara (Turquía)
　　SU Мра́морное мо́ре (Ту́рция)

2301 GB *Marmion* (Scott, 1808)
　　F *Marmion*
　　D *Marmion*
　　I *Marmion*
　　E *Marmion*
　　SU «Ма́рмион» (Скотт)

2302 GB Marne (River), the (France)
　　F la Marne (France)
　　D die Marne (Frankreich)
　　I la Marna (Francia)
　　E el Marne (Francia)
　　SU Ма́рна (Фра́нция)

2303 GB *Marriage, The* (Mussorgsky, 1868)
　　F *Le Mariage* (Moussorgski)
　　D *Die Heirat* (Mussorgskij)
　　I *Il matrimonio* (Musorgskij)
　　E *El matrimonio* (Mussorgski)
　　SU «Жени́тьба» (Му́соргский)

2304 GB *Marriage à la Mode* (Hogarth, 1743–5)
　　F *Mariage à la mode*
　　D *Hochzeit nach der Mode*
　　I *Matrimonio alla moda*
　　E *Matrimonio a la moda*
　　SU «Мо́дный брак» (Хо́гарт)

2305 GB *Marriage at Cana, The* (Veronese, 1562–3)
　　F *Les Noces de Cana* (Véronèse)
　　D *Die Hochzeit zu Kana* (Veronese)
　　I *Le nozze di Cana* (Veronese)
　　E *Las bodas de Cana* (Veronés)
　　SU «Брак в Ка́не» (Вероне́зе)

2306 GB *Marriage of Figaro, The* (Beaumarchais, 1784; Mozart, 1786)
　　F *Le Mariage de Figaro*
　　D *Die Hochzeit des Figaro*
　　I *Le nozze di Figaro*
　　E *Las bodas de Fígaro*
　　SU «Сва́дьба Фи́гаро» (Бомарше́, Мо́царт)

2307 GB *Marriage of Giovanni Arnolfini and*
         Giovanna Cenami, The (Van Eyck,
         1434)
     F   *Les Époux Arnolfini*
     D   *Giovanni Arnolfini mit seiner Gattin*
     I   *Ritratto dei coniugi Arnolfini*
     E   *Arnolfini y su esposa*
     SU «Портрёт супру́гов Арнольфи́ни» (Ван
         Эйк)

2308 GB *Marriage of Heaven and Hell, The*
         (Blake, 1790)
     F   *Le Mariage du Ciel et de l'Enfer*
     D   *Die Heirat des Himmels und der Hölle*
     I   *Il matrimonio del cielo e dell'inferno*
     E   *Las bodas del cielo y del infierno*
     SU «Брак нёба и а́да» (Блейк)

2309 GB *Marriage of Loti, The* (Loti, 1880)
     F   *Le Mariage de Loti*
     D   *Die Hochzeit des Loti*
     I   *Il matrimonio di Loti*
     E   *El matrimonio de Loti*
     SU «Брак Лоти́» (Лоти́)

2310 GB Mars (myth., astron.)
     F   Mars (myth., astron.)
     D   Mars (myth., Astron.)
     I   Marte (mit., astr.)
     E   Marte (mit., astr.)
     SU Марс (миф., астр.)

2311 GB Marseillaise, the (Rouget de Lisle,
         1792)
     F   la Marseillaise
     D   die Marseillaise
     I   la Marsigliese
     E   la Marsellesa
     SU «Марсельё́за» (Руже́ де Лиль)

2312 GB Marseille(s) (France)
     F   Marseille (France)
     D   Marseille (Frankreich)
     I   Marsiglia (Francia)
     E   Marsella (Francia)
     SU Марсе́ль (м.) (Фра́нция)

2313 GB *Marshal's Wife of Ancre, The* (Vigny,
         1831)
     F   *La Maréchale d'Ancre*
     D   *Die Frau des Marshalls Ancre*
     I   *La marescialla d'Ancre*
     E   *La mariscala de Ancre*
     SU «Жена́ ма́ршала д'А́нкра» (Виньи́)

2314 GB Martha (Bib.)
     F   Marthe (Bib.)
     D   Martha (Bib.)
     I   Marta (Bib.)
     E   Marta (Bib.)
     SU Ма́рфа (библ.)

2315 GB Martial (*38–103*)
     F   Martial
     D   Martialis
     I   Marziale
     E   Marcial
     SU Марциа́л

2316 GB Martin (saint, *316–397*)
     F   Martin (saint)
     D   Martin (Heiliger)
     I   Martino (santo)
     E   Martín (santo)
     SU Марти́н (св.)

2317 GB *Martin Chuzzlewit* (Dickens, 1843–4)
     F   *Martin Chuzzlewit*
     D   *Martin Chuzzlewit*
     I   *Martin Chuzzlewit*
     E   *Martín Chuzzlewit*
     SU «Ма́ртин Чёзлвит» (Ди́ккенс)

2318 GB *Martin Eden* (London, 1909)
     F   *Martin Eden*
     D   *Martin Eden*
     I   *Martin Eden*
     E   *Martín Eden*
     SU «Ма́ртин Йден» (Ло́ндон)

2319 GB Martinique (West Indies)
     F   Martinique (Antilles)
     D   Martinique (Westindien)
     I   Martinica (Antille)
     E   Martinica (Antillas)
     SU Мартини́ка (Вест-Йндия)

2320 GB Mary (Bib., saint, sovereign)
     F   Marie (Bib., sainte, souveraine)
     D   Maria (Bib., Heilige, Herr.)
     I   Maria (Bib., santa, sovrana)
     E   María (Bib., santa, sob.)
     SU Мари́я (библ., св., прав.)

2321 GB *Mary Barton* (Gaskell, 1848)
     F   *Mary Barton*
     D   *Mary Barton*
     I   *Maria Barton*
     E   *Mary Barton*
     SU «Мёри Ба́ртон» (Га́скелл)

2322 GB Mary Magdalene (Bib.)
    F Marie-Madeleine (Bib.)
    D Maria Magdalena (Bib.)
    I Maria di Magdala (Bib.)
    E María Magdalena (Bib.)
    SU Мари́я Магдали́на (библ.)

2323 GB Mary, Queen of Scots (1542–87)
    F Marie Stuart
    D Maria Stuart
    I Maria Stuarda
    E María Estuardo
    SU Мари́я Стю́арт

2324 GB Mary Tudor (1496–1533)
    F Marie Tudor
    D Maria Tudor
    I Maria Tudor
    E María Tudor
    SU Мари́я Тю́дор

2325 GB *Masked Ball, A* (Verdi, 1859)
    F *Un bal masqué*
    D *Ein Maskenball*
    I *Un ballo in maschera*
    E *Un baile de máscaras*
    SU «Бал-маскара́д» (Ве́рди)

2326 GB Massacre of the Innocents, the (Bib., art)
    F le massacre des innocents (Bib., art)
    D der Bethlehemitische Kindermord (Bib., Kunst)
    I la strage degli innocenti (Bib., arte)
    E la degollación de los Inocentes (Bib., arte)
    SU избие́ние младе́нцев (библ., иск.)

2327 GB Massif Central, the (France)
    F le Massif central (France)
    D das Zentralmassiv (Frankreich)
    I el Massiccio Centrale (Francia)
    E el Macizo Central (Francia)
    SU Центра́льный масси́в (Фра́нция)

2328 GB *Master Builder, The [Bygmester Solness]* (Ibsen, 1893)
    F *Solness le Constructuer*
    D *Baumeister Solneß*
    I *Il costruttore Solness*
    E *El constructor Solness*
    SU «Строи́тель Со́льнес» (Йбсен)

2329 GB *Master of Ballantrae, The* (Stevenson, 1889)
    F *Le Maître de Ballantrae*
    D *Die feindlichen Brüder*
    I *Il signore di Ballantrae*
    E *El señor de Balantry*
    SU «Владе́лец Баллантре́» (Сти́венсон)

2330 GB *Master of the World* (Verne, 1904)
    F *Maître du monde*
    D *Herr über die Welt*
    I *Padrone del mondo*
    E *Dueño del mundo*
    SU «Властели́н ми́ра» (Верн)

2331 GB *Master Olaf [Mäster Olof]* (Strindberg, 1874)
    F *Maître Olof*
    D *Meister Olaf*
    I *Maestro Olaf*
    E *Maestro Olaf*
    SU «Ме́стер У́луф» (Стри́ндберг)

2332 GB *Master Peter's Puppet Show* (Falla, 1923)
    F *Le Retable de maître Pierre*
    D *Meister Peters Schauspiel*
    I *Il teatrino di mastro Pietro*
    E *El retablo de Maese Pedro*
    SU «Балага́нчик маэ́стро Пе́дро» (Фа́лья)

2333 GB *Mastersingers of Nuremberg, The* (Wagner, 1868)
    F *Les Maîtres chanteurs de Nuremberg*
    D *Die Meistersinger von Nürnberg*
    I *I maestri cantori di Norimberga*
    E *Los maestros cantores de Nuremberg*
    SU «Нюрнбе́ргские мейстерзи́нгеры» (Ва́гнер)

2334 GB *Master Thaddeus [Pan Tadeusz]* (Mickiewicz, 1934)
    F *Monsieur Thadée*
    D *Herr Thaddäus*
    I *Il signor Taddeo*
    E *Pan Tadeusz*
    SU «Пан Таде́уш» (Мицке́вич)

2335 GB *Mathematical Collection, The [Hē mathēmatikē syntaxis]* (Ptolemy, II)
    F *Composition mathématique* (Ptolémée)
    D *Systematisches Handbuch der Astronomie* (Ptolemaios)
    I *Composizione matematica* (Tolomeo)
    E *Composición matemática* (Ptolomeo)
    SU «Вели́кое математи́ческое построе́ние астроно́мии» (Птолеме́й)

2336 GB *Mathis the Painter* (Hindemith, 1934)
F *Mathis le peintre*
D *Mathis der Maler*
I *Mathis il pittore*
E *Matías, el pintor*
SU «Худо́жник Ма́тис» (Хи́ндемит)

2337 GB *Matriona's House* (Solzhenitsyn, 1963)
F *La Maison de Matriona* (Soljenitsyne)
D *Matrjonas Hof* (Solschenizyn)
I *La casa di Matrjona* (Solženicyn)
E *La casa de Matriona* (Soljenitsyn)
SU «Матрёнин двор» (Солжени́цын)

2338 GB Matterhorn, the (Switzerland)
F le mont Cervin (Suisse)
D das Matterhorn (Schweiz)
I il monte Cervino (Svizzera)
E el Monte Cervino (Suiza)
SU Ма́ттерхорн (Швейца́рия)

2339 GB *Matter of Life and Death, A* (Powell, 1946)
F *Question de vie ou de mort*
D *Irrtum im Jenseits*
I *Scala al paradiso*
E *A vida o muerte*
SU «Вопро́с жи́зни и сме́рти» (Па́уэлл)

2340 GB Matthew (saint, Bib.)
F Matthieu (saint, Bib.)
D Matthäus (Heiliger, Bib.)
I Matteo (santo, Bib.)
E Mateo (santo, Bib.)
SU Матфе́й (св., библ.)

2341 GB Matthew, the Gospel According to [Saint] (Bib.)
F l'Évangile selon saint Matthieu (Bib.)
D das Matthäus-Evangelium (Bib.)
I il Vangelo di Matteo (Bib.)
E el Evangelio de San Mateo (Bib.)
SU «Ева́нгелие от Матфе́я» (библ.)

2342 GB Matthias (saint, Bib.)
F Mathias (saint, Bib.)
D Matthias (Heiliger, Bib.)
I Mattias (santo, Bib.)
E Matías (santo, Bib.)
SU Матфе́й (св., библ.)

2343 GB Maundy Thursday (rel.)
F le jeudi saint (relig.)
D der Gründonnerstag (relig.)
I il giovedì santo (relig.)
E el Jueves Santo (relig.)
SU вели́кий четве́рг (рел.)

2344 GB Mauretania (hist.)
F la Mauritanie (hist.)
D Mauretanien (Gesch.)
I la Mauretania (st.)
E Mauritania (hist.)
SU Маврета́ния (ист.)

2345 GB Mauritania
F la Mauritanie
D Mauretanien
I la Mauritania
E Mauritania
SU Маврита́ния

2346 GB Mauritius
F l'île Maurice
D Mauritius
I Maurizio
E Mauricio
SU Маври́кий

2347 GB *Maurizius Case, The* (Wassermann, 1928)
F *L'Affaire Maurizius*
D *Der Fall Maurizius*
I *Il caso Maurizius*
E *El caso Maurizius*
SU «Де́ло Маури́циуса» (Ва́ссерман)

2348 GB Mausoleum of Halicarnassus, the
F le Mausolée d'Halicarnasse
D das Mausoleum zu Halikarnaß
I il mausoleo ad Alicarnasso
E el mausoleo de Halicarnaso
SU Галикарна́сский мавзоле́й

2349 GB Mausolus (−IV)
F Mausole
D Mausolus
I Mausolo
E Mausolo
SU Мавсо́л

2350 GB Maximilian (sovereign)
F Maximilien (souverain)
D Maximilian (Herr.)
I Massimiliano (sovrano)
E Maximiliano (sob.)
SU Максимилиа́н (прав.)

2351 GB *Maxims*, the (La Rochefoucauld, 1665)
F les *Maximes*
D die *Maximen*
I le *Massime*
E las *Máximas*
SU «Макси́мы» (Ларошфуко́)

2352 GB   May Day
    F   le premier mai
    D   der erste Mai
    I   il primo maggio
    E   el primero de mayo
    SU   Пе́рвое ма́я

2353 GB   *Mayor of Casterbridge, The* (Hardy, 1886)
    F   *Le Maire de Casterbridge*
    D   *Der Bürgermeister von Casterbridge*
    I   *Il sindaco di Casterbridge*
    E   *El alcalde de Casterbridge*
    SU   «Мэр Кэ́стербриджа» (Ха́рди)

2354 GB   *Measure for Measure* (Shakespeare, 1604)
    F   *Mesure pour Mesure*
    D   *Maß für Maß*
    I   *Misura per misura*
    E   *Medida por medida*
    SU   «Ме́ра за ме́ру» (Шекспи́р)

2355 GB   Mecca (Saudi Arabia)
    F   la Mecque (Arabie Saoudite)
    D   Mekka (Saudi-Arabien)
    I   la Mecca (Arabia Saudiana)
    E   la Meca (Arabia Saudita)
    SU   Ме́кка (Са́удовская Ара́вия)

2356 GB   Mechelen (Mechlin) (Belgium)
    F   Malines (Belge)
    D   Mecheln (Belgien)
    I   Malines (Belgio)
    E   Malinas (Bélgica)
    SU   Ме́хелен (Бе́льгия)

2357 GB   Mecklenburg (Germany)
    F   le Mecklembourg (Allemagne)
    D   Mecklenburg (Deutschland)
    I   il Meclemburgo (Germania)
    E   Mecklemburgo (Alemania)
    SU   Ме́кленбург (Герма́ния)

2358 GB   Medea (myth.,+ Euripides, −V; Corneille, 1635)
    F   Médée (myth., + Euripide, Corneille)
    D   Medea (myth., + Euripides, Corneille)
    I   Medea (mit., + Euripide, Corneille)
    E   Medea (mit., + Eurípide, Corneille)
    SU   Меде́я (миф., + Еврипи́д, Корне́ль)

2359 GB   Medes, the (hist.)
    F   les Mèdes (hist.)
    D   die Medien (Gesch.)
    I   i medi (st.)
    E   los medos (hist.)
    SU   мидя́не (ист.)

2360 GB   Medina (Saudi Arabia)
    F   Médine (Arabie Saoudite)
    D   Medina (Saudi-Arabien)
    I   Medina (Arabia Saudiana)
    E   Medina (Arabia Saudita)
    SU   Меди́на (Са́удовская Ара́вия)

2361 GB   *Meditations*, the (Marcus Aurelius, II)
    F   les *Méditations* (Marc Aurèle)
    D   *Selbstbetrachtungen* (Marcus Aurelius)
    I   *Colloqui con se stesso* (Marco Aurelio)
    E   los *Pensamientos* (Marco Aurelio)
    SU   «Наедине́ с собо́й» (Марк Авре́лий)

2362 GB   Mediterranean Sea, the
    F   la mer Méditerranée
    D   das Mittelmeer
    I   il mare Mediterraneo
    E   el mar Mediterráneo
    SU   Средизе́мное мо́ре

2363 GB   *Medium, The* (Menotti, 1946)
    F   *Le Médium*
    D   *Das Medium*
    I   *La medium*
    E   *El médium*
    SU   «Ме́диум» (Мено́тти)

2364 GB   Medusa (myth.)
    F   Méduse (myth.)
    D   Medusa (myth.)
    I   Medusa (mit.)
    E   Medusa (mit.)
    SU   Меду́за (миф.)

2365 GB   Megaera (myth.)
    F   Mégère (myth.)
    D   Megäre (myth.)
    I   Megera (mit.)
    E   Megera (mit.)
    SU   Меге́ра (миф.)

2366 GB   Megara (Greece)
    F   la Mégare (Grèce)
    D   Megara (Griechenland)
    I   la Megara (Grecia)
    E   Megara (Grecia)
    SU   Ме́гара (Гре́ция)

2367 GB   Melanchthon (1497–1560)
    F   Melanchthon
    D   Melanchthon
    I   Melantone
    E   Melanchton
    SU   Мела́нхтон

2368   GB   Melanesia
　　　 F   la Mélanésie
　　　 D   Melanesien
　　　 I   la Melanesia
　　　 E   Melanesia
　　　 SU   Меланéзия

2369   GB   Melchizedek (Bib.)
　　　 F   Melchisédech (Bib.)
　　　 D   Melchisedek (Bib.)
　　　 I   Melchisedec (Bib.)
　　　 E   Melchisedec (Bib.)
　　　 SU   Мелхиседéк (библ.)

2370   GB   Meleager (myth.)
　　　 F   Méléagre (myth.)
　　　 D   Meleagros (myth.)
　　　 I   Meleagro (mit.)
　　　 E   Meleagro (mit.)
　　　 SU   Мелеáгр (миф.)

2371   GB   Melpomene (myth.)
　　　 F   Melpomène (myth.)
　　　 D   Melpomene (myth.)
　　　 I   Melpomene (mit.)
　　　 E   Melpómene (mit.)
　　　 SU   Мельпомéна (миф.)

2372   GB   Memnon (myth.)
　　　 F   Memnon (myth.)
　　　 D   Memnon (myth.)
　　　 I   Memnone (mit.)
　　　 E   Memnón (mit.)
　　　 SU   Мéмнон (миф.)

2373   GB   *Memoirs of a Dutiful Daughter*
　　　　　　(Beauvoir, 1958)
　　　 F   *Mémoires d'une jeune fille rangée*
　　　 D   *Memoiren einer Tochter aus gutem*
　　　　　　Hause
　　　 I   *Memorie d'una ragazza perbene*
　　　 E   *Memorias de una joven formal*
　　　 SU   «Мемуáры хорошó воспúтанной
　　　　　　дéвушки» (Бовуáр)

2374   GB   *Memorabilia of Socrates, The*
　　　　　　[Apomnemoneumata] (Xenophon,
　　　　　　−IV)
　　　 F   *Apologie de Socrate* (Xénophon)
　　　 D   *Erinnerungen an Sokrates* (Xenophon)
　　　 I   *Apologia di Socrate* (Senofonte)
　　　 E   *Apología de Sócrates* (Jenofonte)
　　　 SU   «Апологúя Сокрáта» (Ксенофóнт)

2375   GB   *Memories from Beyond the Grave*
　　　　　　(Chateaubriand, 1848–50)
　　　 F   *Mémoires d'outre-tombe*
　　　 D   *Denkwürdigkeiten von jenseits des*
　　　　　　Grabes
　　　 I   *Memorie d'oltre-tomba*
　　　 E   *Memorias de ultratumba*
　　　 SU   «Замогúльные запúски» (Шатобриáн)

2376   GB   Memphis (Egypt)
　　　 F   Memphis (Égypte)
　　　 D   Memphis (Ägypten)
　　　 I   Menfi (Egitto)
　　　 E   Menfis (Egipto)
　　　 SU   Мéмфис (Егúпет)

2377   GB   Menander (342–292)
　　　 F   Ménandre
　　　 D   Menander
　　　 I   Menandro
　　　 E   Menandro
　　　 SU   Менáндр

2378   GB   Menelaus (myth.)
　　　 F   Ménélas (myth.)
　　　 D   Menelaos (myth.)
　　　 I   Menelas (mit.)
　　　 E   Menelao (mit.)
　　　 SU   Менелáй (миф.)

2379   GB   *Meninas, Las* [*The Maids of Honour*]
　　　　　　(Velázquez, *1656*)
　　　 F   *Les Menines*
　　　 D   *Las Meninas*
　　　 I   *Las Meninas*
　　　 E   *Las Meninas*
　　　 SU   «Менúны» (Велáскес)

2380   GB   *Men of Good Will* (Romains, 1932–46)
　　　 F   *Les Hommes de bonne volonté*
　　　 D   *Die guten Willens sind*
　　　 I   *Gli uomini di buona volontà*
　　　 E   *Los hombres de buena voluntad*
　　　 SU   «Лю́ди дóброй вóли» (Ромéн)

　　　 GB   Menorca→Minorca

2381   GB   Mensheviks, the (hist.)
　　　 F   les mencheviks (hist.)
　　　 D   die Menschewiken (Gesch.)
　　　 I   i menscevichi (st.)
　　　 E   los mencheviques (hist.)
　　　 SU   меньшевикú (ист.)

2382   GB   Mentor (myth.)
     F   Mentor (myth.)
     D   Mentor (myth.)
     I   Mentore (mit.)
     E   Mentor (mit.)
     SU   Ме́нтор (миф.)

2383   GB   *Men Without Women* (Hemingway,
           1927)
     F   *Hommes sans femmes*
     D   *Männer ohne Frauen*
     I   *Uomini senza donne*
     E   *Hombres sin mujeres*
     SU   «Мужчи́ны без же́нщин» (Хемингуэ́й)

2384   GB   Mephistopheles (myth.)
     F   Méphistophélès (myth.)
     D   Mephistopheles (myth.)
     I   Mefistofele (mit.)
     E   Mefistófeles (mit.)
     SU   Мефисто́фель (миф.)

2385   GB   *Mer, La* [*The Sea*] (Debussy)
     F   *La Mer*
     D   *La Mer*
     I   *La mer*
     E   *El mar*
     SU   «Мо́ре» (Дебюсси́)

2386   GB   *Merchant of Venice, The* (Shakespeare,
           1596)
     F   *Le Marchand de Venise*
     D   *Der Kaufmann von Venedig*
     I   *Il mercante di Venezia*
     E   *El mercader de Venecia*
     SU   «Венециа́нский купе́ц» (Шекспи́р)

2387   GB   Mercury (myth., astron.)
     F   Mercure (myth., astron.)
     D   Merkurius (myth., Astron.)
     I   Mercurio (mit., astr.)
     E   Mercurio (mit., astr.)
     SU   Мерку́рий (миф., астр.)

2388   GB   Merlin (myth., + Emerson, 1874)
     F   Merlin (myth.)
     D   Merlin (myth.)
     I   Merlino (mit.)
     E   Merlín (mit.)
     SU   Ме́рлин (миф., + Э́мерсон)

2389   GB   *Merry-Go-Round* (Schnitzler, 1897;
           Ophüls, 1950)
     F   *La Ronde*
     D   *Der Reigen*
     I   *Girotondo*
     E   *La ronda*
     SU   «Хорово́д» (Шни́цлер, Офю́лс)

2390   GB   *Merry Widow, The* (Lehar, 1905)
     F   *La Veuve joyeuse*
     D   *Die lustige Witwe*
     I   *La vedova allegra*
     E   *La viuda alegre*
     SU   «Весёлая вдова́» (Лега́р)

2391   GB   *Merry Wives of Windsor, The*
           (Shakespeare, 1601; Nicolai, 1849)
     F   *Les Joyeuses Commères de Windsor*
     D   *Die lustigen Weiber von Windsor*
     I   *Le allegre comari di Windsor*
     E   *Las alegres comadres de Windsor*
     SU   «Виндзо́рские прока́зницы»
           (Шекспи́р, Никола́и)

2392   GB   Mesopotamia (Asia)
     F   la Mésopotamie (Asie)
     D   Mesopotamien (Asia)
     I   la Mesopotamia (Asia)
     E   Mesopotamia (Asia)
     SU   Месопота́мия (А́зия)

2393   GB   Mesenia (Greece)
     F   la Messénie (Grèce)
     D   Messenien (Griechenland)
     I   la Messenia (Grecia)
     E   Mesenia (Grecia)
     SU   Мессе́ния (Гре́ция)

2394   GB   *Messiah*, the (Handel, 1741)
     F   *Le Messie* (Haendel)
     D   der *Messias* (Händel)
     I   il *Messia* (Händel)
     E   *El Mesías* (Haendel)
     SU   «Мессия» (Ге́ндель)

2395   GB   Messina (Sicily)
     F   Messine (Sicile)
     D   Messina (Sizilien)
     I   Messina (Sicilia)
     E   Messina (Sicilia)
     SU   Месси́на (Сици́лия)

2396   GB   *Metamorphoses*, the (Ovid, −I)
     F   les *Métamorphoses* (Ovide)
     D   die *Metamorphosen* (Ovidius)
     I   le *Metamorfosi* (Ovidio)
     E   las *Metamorfosis* (Ovidio)
     SU   «Метаморфо́зы» (Ови́дий)

2397   GB   *Metamorphosis, The* (Kafka, 1915)
     F   *La Métamorphose*
     D   *Die Verwandlung*
     I   *La metamorfosi*
     E   *La metamorfosis*
     SU   «Превраще́ние» (Ка́фка)

2398 GB Methodists, the (rel.)
 F les méthodistes (relig.)
 D die Methodisten (relig.)
 I i metodisti (relig.)
 E los metodistas (relig.)
 SU методи́сты (рел.)

2399 GB Methuselah (Bib.)
 F Mathusalem (Bib.)
 D Mathusalem (Bib.)
 I Matusalem (Bib.)
 E Matusalén (Bib.)
 SU Мафусаи́л (библ.)

2400 GB Meuse (River), the (France)
 F la Meuse (France)
 D die Maas (Frankreich)
 I la Mosa (Francia)
 E el Mosa (Francia)
 SU Мааc (Фра́нция)

2401 GB Mexico
 F le Mexique
 D Mexiko
 I il Messico
 E México
 SU Ме́ксика

2402 GB Mexico, the Gulf of
 F le Golfe du Mexique
 D der Golf von Mexiko
 I il golfo del Messico
 E el golfo de México
 SU Мексика́нский зали́в

2403 GB Mexico City (Mexico)
 F Mexico (Mexique)
 D Mexiko (Mexiko)
 I Città di Messico (Messico)
 E México (México)
 SU Ме́хико (Ме́ксика)

2404 GB Micah (Bib.)
 F Michée (Bib.)
 D Micha (Bib.)
 I Michea (Bib.)
 E Miqueas (Bib.)
 SU Михе́й (библ.)

2405 GB Michael (saint, sovereign)
 F Michel (saint, souverain)
 D Michael (Heiliger, Herr.)
 I Michele (santo, sovrano)
 E Miguel (santo, sob.)
 SU Михаи́л (св., прав.)

2406 GB *Michael Strogoff* (Verne, 1876)
 F *Michel Strogoff*
 D *Michel Strogoff*
 I *Michel Strogoff*
 E *Miguel Strogoff*
 SU «Михаи́л Стро́гов» (Верн)

2407 GB Michelangelo (1475–1564)
 F Michel-Ange
 D Michelangelo
 I Michelangelo Buonarroti
 E Miguel Ángel Buonarroti
 SU Микела́нджело

2408 GB Mickey Mouse (Disney, 1932)
 F Mickey la Souris
 D Mickey-Maus
 I Topolino
 E el Ratón Mickey
 SU Мышо́нок Ми́кки

2409 GB *Micromegas* (Voltaire, 1752)
 F *Micromégas*
 D *Micromegas*
 I *Micromega*
 E *Micromegas*
 SU «Микроме́гас» (Вольте́р)

2410 GB Micronesia
 F la Micronésie
 D Mikronesien
 I la Micronesia
 E Micronesia
 SU Микроне́зия

2411 GB Midas (myth.)
 F Midas (myth.)
 D Midas (myth.)
 I Mida (mit.)
 E Midas (mit.)
 SU Мида́с (миф.)

2412 GB *Middle Age of Mrs Eliot, The* (Wilson, 1958)
 F *Quarante Ans de Mrs Eliot*
 D *Meg Eliot*
 I *Una signora di mezza età*
 E *La madurez de la señora Eliot*
 SU «Же́нщина сре́дних лет» (Уи́лсон)

2413 GB Middle Ages, the (hist.)
 F le moyen âge (hist.)
 D das Mittelalter (Gesch.)
 I il medioevo (st.)
 E la Edad Media (hist.)
 SU сре́дние века́ (ист.)

2414 GB Middle East, the
F le Moyen-Orient
D Vorderasien
I il Levante
E el Oriente Medio
SU Сре́дний Восто́к

2415 GB *Middlemarch* (Eliot, 1872)
F *Middlemarch*
D *Middlemarch*
I *Middlemarch*
E *Middlemarch*
SU «Ми́ддлмарч» (Э́лиот)

2416 GB *Midnight Cowboy* (Schlesinger, 1969)
F *Macadam Cowboy*
D *Asphalt Cowboy*
I *Un uomo da marciapiede*
E *Midnight Cowboy*
SU «Ковбо́й с у́лицы» (Шле́зингер)

2417 GB *Midsummer Night's Dream, A*
(Shakespeare, 1596; Mendelssohn,
1843)
F *Le Songe d'une nuit d'été*
(Shakespeare, Mendelssohn-
Bartholdy)
D *Ein Sommernachtstraum*
(Shakespeare, Mendelssohn-
Bartholdy)
I *Sogno di una notte di mezza estate*
(Shakespeare, Mendelssohn-
Bartholdy)
E *El sueño de una noche de verano*
(Shakespeare, Mendelssohn-
Bartholdy)
SU «Сон в ле́тнюю ночь» (Шекспи́р,
Мендельсо́н-Барто́льди)

2418 GB Midway Islands, the
F les îles Midway
D die Midway-Inseln
I le isole Midway
E las islas Midway
SU острова́ Ми́дуэй

2419 GB *Mignon* (Thomas, 1866)
F *Mignon*
D *Mignon*
I *Mignon*
E *Mignon*
SU «Минье́н» (Тома́)

2420 GB Milan (Italy)
F Milan (Italie)
D Mailand (Italien)
I Milano (Italia)
E Milán (Italia)
SU Мила́н (Ита́лия)

2421 GB Miletus (Turkey)
F Milet (Turquie)
D Milet (Türkei)
I Mileto (Turchia)
E Mileto (Turquía)
SU Миле́т (Ту́рция)

2422 GB *Military Necessity, The* (Vigny, 1835)
F *Servitude et grandeur militaires*
D *Des Soldatenstandes Knechtschaft und
Größe*
I *Servitù e grandezza militari*
E *Servidumbre y grandeza militar*
SU «Нево́ля и вели́чие солда́та» (Виньи́)

2423 GB Milky Way, the (astron.)
F la Voie lactée (astron.)
D die Milchstraße (Astron.)
I la Via Lattea (astr.)
E la Vía láctea (astr.)
SU Мле́чный путь (астр.)

2424 GB *Million, Le* [*The Million*] (Clair, 1930)
F *Le Million*
D *Die Million*
I *Il milione*
E *El millón*
SU «Миллио́н» (Клер)

2425 GB *Mill on the Floss, The* (Eliot, 1860)
F *Le Moulin sur la Floss*
D *Die Mühle am Floß*
I *Il mulino sulla Floss*
E *El molino del Floss*
SU «Ме́льница на Фло́ссе» (Э́лиот)

2426 GB Minerva (myth.)
F Minerve (myth.)
D Minerva (myth.)
I Minerva (mit.)
E Minerva (mit.)
SU Мине́рва (миф.)

2427 GB Minorca (Spain)
F Minorque (Espagne)
D Menorca (Spanien)
I Minorca (Spagna)
E Menorca (España)
SU Мено́рка (Испа́ния)

2428 GB Minos (myth.)
F Minos (myth.)
D Minos (myth.)
I Minosse (mit.)
E Minos (mit.)
SU Ми́нос (миф.)

2429   GB   Minotaur, the (myth.)
       F   le Minotaure (myth.)
       D   der Minotaurus (myth.)
       I   il Minotauro (mit.)
       E   el Minotauro (mit.)
       SU   Минотáвр (миф.)

2430   GB   *Minstrelsy of the Scottish Border*
            (Scott, 1802–3)
       F   *Chansons de la frontière écossaise*
       D   *Spielmannsdichtung des schottischen*
            Grenzlandes
       I   *Canti giullareschi della frontiera*
            scozzese
       E   *Juglaría de la frontiera escocesa*
       SU   «Пéсни шотлáндской грани́цы»
            (Скотт)

2431   GB   *Miracle of the Rose, The* (Genêt,
            1945–6)
       F   *Le Miracle de la rose*
       D   *Wunder der Rose*
       I   *Il miracolo della rosa*
       E   *El milagro de la rosa*
       SU   «Чу́до ро́зы» (Жене́)

2432   GB   *Mireille* (Gounod, 1864)
       F   *Mireille*
       D   *Mireille*
       I   *Mirella*
       E   *Mireille*
       SU   «Мире́йль» (Гуно́)

2433   GB   *Mirgorod* (Gogol, 1835)
       F   *Mirgorod*
       D   *Mirgorod*
       I   *Mirgorod*
       E   *Mirgorod*
       SU   «Ми́ргород» (Го́голь)

2434   GB   *Misanthrope, Le* [*The Misanthropist*]
            (Molière, 1666)
       F   *Le Misanthrope*
       D   *Der Menschenfeind*
       I   *Il misantropo*
       E   *El misántropo*
       SU   «Мизантро́п» (Молье́р)

2435   GB   *Miser, The* (Molière, 1668)
       F   *L'Avare*
       D   *Der Geizige*
       I   *L'avaro*
       E   *El avaro*
       SU   «Скупо́й» (Молье́р)

2436   GB   *Misérables, Les* [*The Wretched Ones*]
            (Hugo, 1862)
       F   *Les Misérables*
       D   *Die Elenden*
       I   *I miserabili*
       E   *Los miserables*
       SU   «Отвéрженные» (Гюго́)

2437   GB   *Miss Fifi* (Maupassant, 1882)
       F   *Mademoiselle Fifi*
       D   *Fräulein Fifi*
       I   *Mademoiselle Fifi*
       E   *La señorita Fifí*
       SU   «Мадемуазéль Фифи́» (Мопассáн)

2438   GB   Mississippi (River), the (USA)
       F   le Mississippi (USA)
       D   der Mississippi (USA)
       I   il Mississippi (USA)
       E   el Misisipí (USA)
       SU   Миссиси́пи (США)

2439   GB   *Miss Julie* [*Fröken Julie*] (Strindberg,
            1889)
       F   *Mademoiselle Julie*
       D   *Fräulein Julie*
       I   *La signorina Giulia*
       E   *La señorita Julia*
       SU   «Фрёкен Ю́лия» (Стри́ндберг)

2440   GB   Missouri (River), the (USA)
       F   le Missouri (USA)
       D   der Missouri (USA)
       I   il Missouri (USA)
       E   el Misuri (USA)
       SU   Миссу́ри (США)

2441   GB   *Mr Blandings Builds His Dream House*
            (Potter, 1948)
       F   *Un million de clefs en mains*
       D   *Nur meiner Frau zuliebe*
       I   *La casa dei nostri sogni*
       E   *Los Blandings ya tienen casa*
       SU   «Ми́стер Бла́ндингс стро́ит дом свои́х
            грёз» (По́ттер)

2442   GB   *Mr Deeds Goes to Town* (Capra, 1936)
       F   *L'Extravagant Mr Deeds*
       D   *Mr Deeds geht in die Stadt*
       I   *È arrivata la felicità*
       E   *El deseo de vivir*
       SU   «Ми́стер Дидс переезжáет в го́род»
            (Кáпра)

2443 GB Mr Midshipman Easy (Marryat, 1836)
     F   Mr le Midshipman Easy
     D   Seekadett Jack Freimut
     I   Il guardiamarina Easy
     E   El guardia marina Easy
     SU «Мичман Изи» (Марриет)

2444 GB Mr Norris Changes Trains (Isherwood,
         1935)
     F   Mr Norris change de train
     D   Mr Norris steigt um
     I   Il signor Norris se ne va
     E   Mr Norris cambia de trenes
     SU «Мистер Норрис делает пересадку»
         (Ишервуд)

2445 GB Mrs Dalloway (Woolf, 1925)
     F   Mrs Dalloway
     D   Eine Frau von 50 Jahren
     I   La signora Dalloway
     E   Mrs. Dalloway
     SU «Миссис Дэллоуэй» (Вулф)

2446 GB Mrs Warren's Profession (Shaw, 1898)
     F   La Profession de Mme Warren
     D   Frau Warrens Gewerbe
     I   La professione della signora Warren
     E   La profesión de la señora Warren
     SU «Профéссия госпожи Уóррен» (Шóу)

2447 GB Mithra(s) (myth.)
     F   Mithra (myth.)
     D   Mithras (myth.)
     I   Mitra (mit.)
     E   Mitra (mit.)
     SU Митра (миф.)

2448 GB Mithridates (king, + Racine, 1673)
     F   Mithridate (roi)
     D   Mithridates (König)
     I   Mitridate (re)
     E   Mitrídates (rey)
     SU Митридáт (царь, + Расин)

2449 GB Mnemosyne (myth.)
     F   Mnémosyne (myth.)
     D   Mnemosyne (myth.)
     I   Mnemosine (mit.)
     E   Mnemosina (mit.)
     SU Мнемосина (миф.)

2450 GB Moby Dick, or the White Whale
         (Melville, 1851)
     F   Moby Dick ou la Baleine blanche
     D   Moby Dick oder der Wal
     I   Moby Dick o La balena bianca
     E   Moby Dick o la ballena blanca
     SU «Мóби Дик, или Бéлый кит»
         (Мéлвилл)

2451 GB Modern Love (Meredith, 1862)
     F   L'Amour moderne
     D   Moderne Liebe
     I   Amore moderno
     E   Amor moderno
     SU «Совремéнная любóвь» (Мéредит)

2452 GB Modern Painters (Ruskin, 1843)
     F   Peintres modernes
     D   Moderne Maler
     I   Pittori moderni
     E   Pintores modernos
     SU «Совремéнные живопúсцы» (Рéскин)

2453 GB Modern Times (Chaplin, 1936)
     F   Les Temps modernes
     D   Moderne Zeiten
     I   Tempi moderni
     E   Tiempos modernos
     SU «Нóвые временá» (Чáплин)

2454 GB Modern Utopia, A (Wells, 1905)
     F   Une utopie moderne
     D   Jenseits des Sirius
     I   Un'utopia moderna
     E   Una utopía moderna
     SU «Совремéнная утóпия» (Уэллс)

     GB Mohammed→Muhammad

2455 GB Moldavia (USSR)
     F   la Moldavie (URSS)
     D   Moldau (UdSSR)
     I   la Moldavia (URSS)
     E   Moldavia (URSS)
     SU Молдáвия (СССР)

2456 GB Moll Flanders (Defoe, 1721)
     F   Moll Flanders
     D   Moll Flanders
     I   Moll Flanders
     E   Moll Flanders
     SU «Молль Флéндерс» (Дефó)

2457 GB Molloy (Beckett, 1951)
     F   Molloy
     D   Molloy
     I   Molloy
     E   Molloy
     SU «Моллóй» (Бéккет)

2458 GB Moluccas, the (Indonesia)
     F   les îles Moluques (Indonésie)
     D   die Molukken (Indonesien)
     I   le Molucche (Indonesia)
     E   las Molucas (Indonesia)
     SU Молýккские островá (Индонéзия)

2459 GB Monaco
    F le Monaco
    D Monaco
    I il Monaco
    E Mónaco
    SU Мóнако

2460 GB *Monadology, The* (Leibniz, 1714)
    F *La Monadologie*
    D die *Monadologie*
    I la *Monadologia*
    E la *Monadología*
    SU «Монадолóгия» (Лéйбниц)

2461 GB *Mona Lisa*, the (Leonardo da Vinci, 1503)
    F la *Joconde* (Léonard de Vinci)
    D die *Mona Lisa* (Leonardo da Vinci)
    I la *Gioconda* (Leonardo da Vinci)
    E la *Gioconda* (Leonardo de Vinci)
    SU «Джокóнда» (Леонáрдо да Вúнчи)

2562 GB *Monday Chats* (Sainte-Beuve, 1851–62)
    F *Causeries du lundi*
    D *Montagsplaudereien*
    I *Conversazioni del lunedì*
    E *Charlas del lunes*
    SU «Бесéды по понедéльникам» (Сент-Бёв)

2463 GB *Monday Tales, The* (Daudet, 1873)
    F *Contes du lundi*
    D *Montagsgeschichten*
    I *Racconti del lunedì*
    E *Cuentos del lunes*
    SU «Расскáзы по понедéльникам» (Додé)

2464 GB Mongolia
    F la Mongolie
    D die Mongolei
    I la Mongolia
    E Mongolia
    SU Монгóлия

2465 GB Mongolian People's Republic, the
    F la République populaire de Mongolie
    D die Mongolische Volksrepublik
    I la Repubblica Popolare di Mongolia
    E la República Popular de Mongolia
    SU Монгóльская Нарóдная Респýблика

2466 GB Mongols, the (hist.)
    F les mongols (hist.)
    D die Mongolen (Gesch.)
    I i mongoli (st.)
    E los mongoles (hist.)
    SU монгóлы (ист.)

2467 GB *Monk, The* (Lewis, 1796)
    F *Le Moine*
    D *Der Gottsucher*
    I *Il monaco*
    E *Ambrosio o el Monje*
    SU «Монáх» (Льюúис)

2468 GB *Monna Vanna* (Maeterlinck, 1902)
    F *Monna Vanna*
    D *Monna Vanna*
    I *Monna Vanna*
    E *Monna Vanna*
    SU «Мóнна Вáнна» (Мéтерлинк)

2469 GB *Monsieur Hulot's Holiday* (Tati, 1952)
    F *Les Vacances de M. Hulot*
    D *Die Ferien des Herrn Ülol*
    I *Le vacanze del signor Hulot*
    E *Las vacaciones de Monsieur Hulot*
    SU «Óтпуск мосьé Юлó» (Татú)

2470 GB *Monsieur Perrichon's Journey* (Labiche, 1860)
    F *Le Voyage de Monsieur Perrichon*
    D *Die Reise des Herrn Perrichon*
    I *Il viaggio del signor Perrichon*
    E *El viaje de Sr. Perrichón*
    SU «Путешéствие господúна Перришóна» (Лабúш)

2471 GB Mont Blanc (France)
    F le mont Blanc (France)
    D Montblanc (Frankreich)
    I il monte Bianco (Francia)
    E el Monte Blanco (Francia)
    SU Монблáн (Фрáнция)

2472 GB Montenegro (Yugoslavia)
    F le Monténégro (Yougoslavie)
    D Montenegro (Jugoslawien)
    I il Montenegro (Iugoslavia)
    E Montenegro (Yugoslavia)
    SU Черногóрия (Югослáвия)

2473 GB *Month in the Country, A* (Turgenev, 1850)
    F *Un mois à la campagne* (Tourgueniev)
    D *Ein Monat auf dem Lande* (Turgenjew)
    I *Un mese alla campagna* (Turgenev)
    E *Un mes en la campaña* (Turgueniev)
    SU «Мéсяц в дерéвне» (Тургéнев)

2474 GB Montreal (Canada)
    F Montréal (Canada)
    D Montreal (Kanada)
    I Montreal (Canada)
    E Montreal (Canadá)
    SU Монреáль (м.) (Канáда)

2475 GB *Moon and Sixpence, The* (Maugham, 1919)
F *L'Envoûté*
D *Silbermond und Kupfermünze*
I *La luna e sei soldi*
E *La luna y seis peniques*
SU «Луна́ и грош» (Мо́эм)

2476 GB *Moonlight Sonata*, the (Beethoven, 1801)
F la sonate *Clair de lune*
D die *Mondscheinsonate*
I la sonata *Chiaro di luna*
E la sonata *Claro de luna*
SU «Лу́нная» сона́та (Бетхо́вен)

2477 GB *Moonstone, The* (Collins, 1868)
F *La Pierre de lune*
D *Der Mondstein*
I *La pietra di luna*
E *La piedra lunar*
SU «Лу́нный ка́мень» (Ко́ллинз)

2478 GB Moors, the (hist.)
F les Maures (hist.)
D die Mauren (Gesch.)
I i mauri (st.)
E los moros (hist.)
SU ма́вры (ист.)

2479 GB *Moral Letters to Lucilius [Epistulae morales ad Lucilium]* (Seneca, 63–5)
F *Lettres à Lucilius* (Sénèque)
D *Briefe an Lucilius über Ethik* (Seneca)
I *Epistulae morales ad Lucilium* (Seneca)
E *Cartas a Lucilio* (Séneca)
SU «Пи́сьма к Люци́лию» (Сене́ка)

2480 GB Moravia (Czechoslavakia)
F la Moravie (Tchécoslovaquie)
D Mähren (Tschechoslowakei)
I la Moravia (Cecoslovacchia)
E Moravia (Checoslovaquia)
SU Мора́вия (Чехослова́кия)

2481 GB *Morgan: A Suitable Case for Treatment* (Reisz, 1966)
F *Morgan fou à lier*
D *Protest*
I *Morgan, matto da legare*
E *Morgan, un caso clínico*
SU «Мо́рган спя́тивший» (Райс)

2482 GB Mormons, the (rel.)
F les mormons (relig.)
D die Mormonen (relig.)
I i mormoni (relig.)
E los mormones (relig.)
SU мормо́ны (рел.)

2483 GB Morocco
F le Maroc
D Marokko
I il Marocco
E Marruecos
SU Маро́кко

2484 GB Morpheus (myth.)
F Morphée (myth.)
D Morpheus (myth.)
I Morfeo (mit.)
E Morfeo (mit.)
SU Морфе́й (миф.)

2485 GB *Morte d'Arthur, Le* ["The Death of Arthur"] (Malory, *1469*)
F *La Mort d'Arthur*
D *Der Tod Arthurs*
I *La morte di Artù*
E *La muerte de Arturo*
SU «Смерть Арту́ра» (Мэ́лори)

2486 GB Moscow (USSR)
F Moscou (URSS)
D Moskau (UdSSR)
I Mosca (URSS)
E Moscú (URSS)
SU Москва́ (СССР)

2487 GB Moselle (River), the (France/Germany)
F la Moselle (France/Allemagne)
D die Mosel (Frankreich/Deutschland)
I la Mosella (Francia/Germania)
E el Mosela (Francia/Alemania)
SU Мозе́ль (м.) (Фра́нция/Герма́ния)

2488 GB Moses (Bib.)
F Moïse (Bib.)
D Moses (Bib.)
I Mosè (Bib.)
E Moisés (Bib.)
SU Моисе́й (библ.)

2489 GB Mosquito Coast, the (Nicaragua)
F la côte des Mosquitos Nicaragua)
D die Moskitoküste (Nicaragua)
I la Costa dei Mosquito (Nicaragua)
E la Costa de los Mosquitos (Nicaragua)
SU Моски́товый бе́рег (Никара́гуа)

2490 GB *Mother, The* (Gorky, 1907)
    F *La Mère* (Gorki)
    D *Die Mutter* (Gorkij)
    I *La madre* (Gor`kij)
    E *La madre* (Gorki)
    SU «Мать» (Го́рький)

2491 GB *Mother Courage and Her Children* (Brecht, 1939)
    F *Mère Courage et ses enfants*
    D *Mutter Courage und ihre Kinder*
    I *Madre Courage e i suoi figli*
    E *Madre Coraje y sus hijos*
    SU «Мама́ша Кура́ж и её де́ти» (Брехт)

2492 GB *Mother Goose Tales* (Perrault, 1697)
    F *Contes de ma mère l'Oye*
    D *Märchen meiner Mutter, der Gans*
    I *Racconti di mia madre l'Oca*
    E *Cuentos de mi madre la oca*
    SU «Ска́зки мое́й ма́тушки Гусы́ни» (Перро́)

2493 GB *Mother-in-Law, The* [*Hecyra*] (Terence, −165, −160)
    F *La Belle-Mère* (Térence)
    D *Die Schwiegermutter* (Terentius)
    I *La suocera* (Terenzio)
    E *La suegra* (Terencio)
    SU «Свекро́вь» (Теренций)

    GB Mount . . . → . . . , Mount

2494 GB *Mourning Becomes Electra* (O'Neill, 1931)
    F *Le deuil sied à Électre*
    D *Trauer muß Elektra tragen*
    I *Il lutto si addice ad Elettra*
    E *A Electra le sienta bien el luto*
    SU «Тра́ур – у́часть Эле́ктры» (О'Ни́л)

2495 GB *Mousetrap, The* (Christie, 1952)
    F *La Souricière*
    D *Die Mausefalle*
    I *Trappola per topi*
    E *La ratonera*
    SU «Мышело́вка» (Кри́сти)

2496 GB Mozambique
    F le Mozambique
    D Mosambik
    I il Mozambico
    E Mozambique
    SU Мозамби́к

2497 GB *Mozart on His Trip to Prague* (Mörike, 1856)
    F *Voyage de Mozart à Prague*
    D *Mozart auf der Reise nach Prag*
    I *Mozart in viaggio per Praga*
    E *Viaje de Mozart a Praga*
    SU «Мо́царт на пути́ в Пра́гу» (Мёрике)

2498 GB *Much Ado About Nothing* (Shakespeare, 1598)
    F *Beaucoup de bruit pour rien*
    D *Viel Lärm um nichts*
    I *Molto rumore per nulla*
    E *Mucho ruido para nada*
    SU «Мно́го шу́ма из ничего́» (Шекспи́р)

2499 GB Muhammad (Mahomet, Mohammed) (*570–632*)
    F Muhammad
    D Mohammed
    I Maometto
    E Mahoma
    SU Муха́ммед

2500 GB Mulhouse (France)
    F Mulhouse (France)
    D Mülhausen (Frankreich)
    I Mulhouse (Francia)
    E Mulhouse (Francia)
    SU Мюлу́з (Фра́нция)

2501 GB Munich (Germany)
    F Munich (Allemagne)
    D München (Deutschland)
    I Monaco (Germania)
    E Munich (Alemania)
    SU Мю́нхен (Герма́ния)

2502 GB *Murder Considered as One of the Fine Arts* (De Quincey, 1827, 1839)
    F *De l'assassinat considéré comme un des beaux-arts*
    D *Der Mord als eine schöne Kunst betrachtet*
    I *L'assassinio come una delle belle arti*
    E *El asesinato considerado como una de las bellas artes*
    SU «Уби́йство, рассма́триваемое как одно́ из изя́щных иску́сств» (Де Куи́нси)

2503 GB *Murder in the Cathedral* (Eliot, 1935)
    F *Meurtre dans la cathédrale*
    D *Mord im Dom*
    I *Assassinio nella cattedrale*
    E *Asesinato en la catedral*
    SU «Уби́йство в собо́ре» (Э́лиот)

2504 GB *Murder of Roger Ackroyd, The*
(Christie, 1926)
F *Le Meurtre de Roger Ackroyd*
D *Der Mord an Roger Ackroyd*
I *Dalle nove alle dieci*
E *El asesinato de Roger Ackroyd*
SU «Убийство Роджера Экройда»
(Кристи)

2505 GB *Murder on the Orient Express*
(Christie, 1934; Lumet, 1973)
F *Le Meurtre de l'Orient-Express*
D *Der blaue Express*
I *Assassinio sull'Orient Express*
E *El crimen del Oriente-Express*
SU «Восточный экспресс» (Кристи,
Люмет)

2506 GB *Murders in the Rue Morgue, The* (Poe,
1841)
F *Double Assassinat dans la rue Morgue*
D *Der Doppelmord in der Rue Morgue*
I *Il delitto della Rue Morgue*
E *Doble asesinato en la calle Morgue*
SU «Убийство на улице Морг» (По)

2507 GB Muses, the (myth.)
F les Muses (myth.)
D die Musen (myth.)
I le Muse (mit.)
E las musas (mit.)
SU музы (миф.)

2508 GB *Musical Offering, The* (Bach, 1747)
F *L'Offrande musicale*
D *Das musikalische Opfer*
I *L'offerta musicale*
E *La ofrenda musical*
SU «Музыкальное приношение» (Бах)

2509 GB *Music for the Royal Fireworks*
(Handel, 1749)
F *Musique pour les feux d'artifice*
(Haendel)
D *Feuerwerkmusik* (Händel)
I *Musica per i fuochi d'artificio* (Händel)
E *Música para los fuegos artificiales*
(Haendel)
SU «Музыка к фейерверку» (Гендель)

2510 GB *Mutiny on the Bounty* (Nordhoff +
Hall, 1932)
F *Les révoltés du Bounty*
D *Meuterei auf der "Bounty"*
I *La tragedia del Bounty*
E *Rebelión a bordo*
SU «Мятеж на ,,Баунти''» (Нордхоф/
Холл)

2511 GB Mycenae (Greece)
F Mycènes (Grèce)
D Mykene (Griechenland)
I Micene (Grecia)
E Micenas (Grecia)
SU Микены (ж.) (Греция)

2512 GB *My Fair Lady* (Lerner, 1956)
F *Pygmalion*
D *My Fair Lady*
I *My Fair Lady*
E *Mi bella dama*
SU «Моя прекрасная леди» (Лернер)

2513 GB *My Friend from Limousin* (Giraudoux,
1922)
F *Siegfried et le Limousin*
D *Siegfried*
I *Il romanzo di Siegfried*
E *Sigfrido y el Limosino*
SU «Зигфрид и Лимузен» (Жироду)

2514 GB *My Name is Aram* (Saroyan, 1940)
F *Quand même un Américain*
D *Ich heiße Aram*
I *Il mio nome è Aran*
E *Mi nombre es Aram*
SU «Меня зовут Арам» (Сароян)

2515 GB Myrmidons, the (myth.)
F les Myrmidons (myth.)
D die Myrmidonen (myth.)
I i mirmidoni (mit.)
E los mirmidones (mit.)
SU мирмидонцы (миф.)

2516 GB *My Sister Life* (Pasternak, 1922)
F *Ma soeur la vie*
D *Meine Schwester, das Leben*
I *Sorella mia la vita*
E *Mi hermana, la vida*
SU «Сестра моя – жизнь» (Пастернак)

2517 GB *Mysteries of Udolpho, The* (Radcliffe,
1794)
F *Les Mystères d'Udolphe*
D *Udolphos Geheimnisse*
I *I misteri di Udolfo*
E *Los misterios de Udolfo*
SU «Удольфские тайны» (Радклиф)

2518 GB *Mysterious Island, The* (Verne, 1875)
F *L'Île mystérieuse*
D *Die geheimnisvolle Insel*
I *L'isola misteriosa*
E *La isla misteriosa*
SU «Таинственный остров» (Верн)

2519 GB *Mystery of Edwin Drood, The*
                (Dickens, 1870)
         F   *Le Mystère d'Edwin Drood*
         D   *Das Geheimnis des Edwin Drood*
         I   *Il mistero di Edwin Drood*
         E   *El misterio de Edwin Drood*
         SU «Тайна Эдвина Друда» (Диккенс)

2520 GB *Mystery of the Charity of Joan of Arc,*
                The (Péguy, 1910)
         F   *Le Mystère de la charité de Jeanne*
                d'Arc
         D   *Das Mysterium der Erbarmung*
         I   *Il mistero della carità di Giovanna*
                d'Arco
         E   *Misterio de la caridad de Juana de Arco*
         SU «Мистéрия о Жáнне д'Арк» (Пегú)

2521 GB *Mysticism and Logic* (Russell, 1957)
         F   *Mysticisme et logique*
         D   *Mystizismus und Logik*
         I   *Misticismo e logica*
         E   *Misticismo y lógica*
         SU «Мистицúзм и лóгика» (Рáссел)

2522 GB *Myth of Sisyphus, The* (Camus, 1942)
         F   *Le Mythe de Sisyphe*
         D   *Der Mythos von Sisyphos*
         I   *Il mito di Sisifo*
         E   *El mito de Sísifo*
         SU «Миф о Сизúфе» (Камю́)

2523 GB *My Universities* (Gorky, 1923)
         F   *Mes universités* (Gorki)
         D   *Meine Universitäten* (Gor'kij)
         I   *Le mie università* (Gor'kij)
         E   *Mis universidades* (Gorki)
         SU «Мои́ университéты» (Гóрький)

N

2524	GB	*Naked and the Dead, The* (Mailer, 1948)
	F	*Les Nus et les morts*
	D	*Die Nackten und die Toten*
	I	*Il nudo e il morto*
	E	*Los desnudos y los muertos*
	SU	«Нагúе и мёртвые» (Мéйлер)

2525	GB	*Naked City* (Dassin, 1948)
	F	*La Cité sans voiles*
	D	*Die nackte Stadt*
	I	*La città nuda*
	E	*La ciudad desnuda*
	SU	«Гóлый гóрод» (Дассéн)

2526	GB	*Naked Year, The* (Pilnyak, 1921)
	F	*L'Année nue* (Pilniak)
	D	*Das nackte Jahr* (Pil'njak)
	I	*L'anno nudo* (Pil'njak)
	E	*El año desnudo* (Pilniak)
	SU	«Гóлый год» (Пильня́к)

2527	GB	Namibia
	F	la Namibie
	D	Namibia
	I	la Namibia
	E	Namibia
	SU	Намúбия

2528	GB	*Namouna* (Lalo, 1882)
	F	*Namouna*
	D	*Namouna*
	I	*Namouna*
	E	*Namouna*
	SU	«Намýна» (Лалó)

2529	GB	*Nana* (Zola, 1880
	F	*Nana*
	D	*Nana*
	I	*Nanà*
	E	*Nana*
	SU	«Нанá» (Золя́)

2530	GB	*Nanook of the North* (Flaherty, 1922)
	F	*Nanouk l'Esquimau*
	D	*Nanuk, der Eskimo*
	I	*Nanuk l'eschimiese*
	E	*Nanuk, El Esquimal*
	SU	«Нанýк с Сéвера» (Флáэрти)

2531	GB	Naples (Italy)
	F	Naples (Italie)
	D	Neapel (Italien)
	I	Napoli (Italia)
	E	Nápoles (Italia)
	SU	Неáполь (м.) (Итáлия)

2532	GB	Napoleon (1769–1821)
	F	Napoléon
	D	Napoleon
	I	Napoleone
	E	Napoleón
	SU	Наполеóн

2533	GB	*Napoleon Crowning the Empress Josephine* (David, 1805–8)
	F	*Le Sacre de Napoléon*
	D	*Napoleons Krönungsfeier*
	I	*Consacrazione di Napoleone*
	E	*Coronación de Napoleón y Josefina*
	SU	«Коронáция Наполеóна» (Давúд)

2534	GB	Napoleonic Wars, the (1805–15)
	F	les guerres contre Napoléon
	D	der Kampf gegen Napoleon
	I	le guerre contro Napoleone
	E	las guerras contra Napoleón
	SU	наполеóновские вóйны

2535 GB   *Napoleon of Notting Hill, The*
            (Chesterton, 1904)
      F   *Le Napoléon de Notting Hill*
      D   *Der Held von Notting Hill*
      I   *Il Napoleone di Notting Hill*
      E   *El Napoleón de Notting Hill*
      SU   «Наполеóн из Нóттинг-хѝлла»
            (Чéстертон)

2536 GB   Narbonne (France)
      F   Narbonne (France)
      D   Narbonne (Frankreich)
      I   Narbona (Francia)
      E   Narbona (Francia)
      SU   Нарбóнн (Фрáнция)

2537 GB   Narcissus (myth.)
      F   Narcisse (myth.)
      D   Narziß (myth.)
      I   Narciso (mit.)
      E   Narciso (mit.)
      SU   Нарцѝсс (миф.)

2538 GB   *Narcissus and Goldmund* (Hesse,
            1930)
      F   *Narcisse et Goldmund*
      D   *Narziß und Goldmund*
      I   *Narciso e Boccadoro*
      E   *Narciso y Goldmundo*
      SU   «Нарцѝсс и Гóлдмунд» (Хéссе)

2539 GB   Nathan (Bib.)
      F   Nathan (Bib.)
      D   Nathan (Bib.)
      I   Nathan (Bib.)
      E   Natán (Bib.)
      SU   Нафáн (библ.)

2540 GB   National Assembly, the (France, hist.)
      F   l'Assemblée nationale (France, hist.)
      D   die National-Versammlung
            (Frankreich, Gesch.)
      I   l'assemblea nazionale (Francia, st.)
      E   la Asamblea Nacional (Francia, hist.)
      SU   Национáльная ассамблéя (Фрáнция,
            ист.)

2541 GB   Nativity, the (rel., art)
      F   la Nativité (relig., art)
      D   die Geburt Christi (relig., Kunst)
      I   la Natività (relig., arte)
      E   la Natividad (relig., arte)
      SU   рождествó Христá (рел., иск.)

2542 GB   *Natural History* (Lacépède, 1830)
      F   *Histoire naturelle*
      D   *Naturgeschichte*
      I   *Storia naturale*
      E   *Historia natural*
      SU   «Естéственная истóрия» (Ласепéд)

2543 GB   *Natural Son, The* (Diderot, 1757)
      F   *Le Fils naturel*
      D   *Der außereheliche Sohn*
      I   *Il figlio naturale*
      E   *El hijo natural*
      SU   «Побóчный сын» (Дидрó)

2544 GB   *Nausea* (Sartre, 1938)
      F   *La Nausée*
      D   *Der Ekel*
      I   *La nausea*
      E   *La náusea*
      SU   «Тошнотá» (Сартр)

2545 GB   Nausicaä (myth.)
      F   Nausicaa (myth.)
      D   Nausikaa (myth.)
      I   Nausicaa (mit.)
      E   Nausicaa (mit.)
      SU   Навсикáя (миф.)

2546 GB   Navarre (Navarra) (Spain)
      F   la Navarre (Espagne)
      D   Navarra (Spanien)
      I   la Navarra (Spagna)
      E   Navarra (España)
      SU   Навáрра (Испáния)

2547 GB   Nazareth (Bib.)
      F   Nazareth (Bib.)
      D   Nazareth (Bib.)
      I   Nazareth (Bib.)
      E   Nazaret (Bib.)
      SU   Назарéт (библ.)

2548 GB   Nazis, the (hist.)
      F   les nazis (hist.)
      D   die Nationalsozialisten (Gesch.)
      I   i nazisti (st.)
      E   los nazis (hist.)
      SU   нацѝсты (ист.)

2549 GB   Near East, the
      F   le Proche-Orient
      D   der Nahe Osten
      I   il Levante
      E   el Próximo Oriente
      SU   Блѝжний Востóк

2550 GB Nebuchadnezzar (Nebuchadrezzar)
(Bib.)
F Nabuchodonosor (Bib.)
D Nebukadnezar (Bib.)
I Nabucodonosor (Bib.)
E Nabucodonosor (Bib.)
SU Навуходоно́сор (библ.)

2551 GB Nehemiah (Bib.)
F Néhémie (Bib.)
D Nehemia (Bib.)
I Neemia (Bib.)
E Nehemias (Bib.)
SU Нееми́я (библ.)

2552 GB Nemesis (myth.)
F Némésis (myth.)
D Nemesis (myth.)
I Nemesi (mit.)
E Némesis (mit.)
SU Немеси́да (миф.)

2553 GB Neoptolemus (myth.)
F Néoptolème (myth.)
D Neoptolemos (myth.)
I Neottolomeo (mit.)
E Neoptolemo (mit.)
SU Неоптоле́м (миф.)

2554 GB Nepal
F le Népal
D Nepal
I il Nepal
E Nepal
SU Непа́л

2555 GB Neptune (myth., astron.)
F Neptune (myth., astron.)
D Neptun (myth., Astron.)
I Nettuno (mit., astr.)
E Neptuno (mit., astr.)
SU Непту́н (миф., астр.)

2556 GB Nereus (myth.)
F Nérée (myth.)
D Nereus (myth.)
I Nereo (mit.)
E Nereo (mit.)
SU Нере́й (миф.)

2557 GB Nero (37–68)
F Néron
D Nero
I Nerone
E Nerón
SU Неро́н

2558 GB *Nest of Gentlefolk, A* (Turgenev, 1859)
F *Un nid de gentilshommes*
(Tourgueniev)
D *Das Adelsnest* (Turgenjew)
I *Un nido di nobili* (Turgenev)
E *Nido de hidalgos* (Turgueniev)
SU «Дворя́нское гнездо́» (Турге́нев)

2559 GB Nestor (myth.)
F Nestor (myth.)
D Nestor (myth.)
I Nestore (mit.)
E Néstor (mit.)
SU Не́стор (миф.)

2560 GB Netherlands, the
F les Pays-Bas
D die Niederlande
I i Paesi Bassi
E Holanda
SU Нидерла́нды (м.)

2561 GB Neuchâtel (Switzerland)
F Neuchâtel (Suisse)
D Neuenburg (Schweiz)
I Neuchâtel (Svizzera)
E Neuchâtel (Suiza)
SU Невшате́ль (м.) (Швейца́рия)

2562 GB *Never on Sunday* (Dassin, 1960)
F *Jamais le dimanche*
D *Sonntags . . . nie!*
I *Mai di domenica*
E *Nunca en Domingo*
SU «Никогда́ по воскресе́ньям» (Дассе́н)

2563 GB *New Arabian Nights, The* (Stevenson,
1882)
F *Nouvelles Mille et Une Nuits*
D *Neue Arabische Nächte*
I *Le nuove notti arabe*
E *Las nuevas noches árabes*
SU «Но́вые ара́бские но́чи» (Сти́венсон)

2564 GB *New Art of Writing Plays, The* (Lope
de Vega, 1609)
F *Le Nouvel Art de faire les comédies*
D *Die Neue Kunst, Comedias zu
schreiben*
I *La nuova arte di far commedie*
E *El arte nuevo de hacer comedias*
SU «Но́вое иску́сство сочиня́ть коме́дии»
(Ве́га Ка́рпьо)

2565 GB New Britain (Papua New Guinea)
F   la Nouvelle-Bretagne (Papouasie-
Nouvelle-Guinée)
D   Neubritannien (Papua-Neuguinea)
I   la Nuova Britannia (Papua-Nuova
Guinea)
E   Nueva Bretaña (Papuasia-Nueva
Guinea)
SU Но́вая Брита́ния (Па́пуа-Но́вая
Гвине́я)

2566 GB New Brunswick (Canada)
F   le Nouveau-Brunswick (Canada)
D   Neubraunschweig (Kanada)
I   il New Brunswick (Canada)
E   Nuevo Brunswick (Canadá)
SU Нью-Бра́нсуик (Кана́да)

2567 GB New Caledonia
F   la Nouvelle-Calédonie
D   Neukaledonien
I   la Nuova Caledonia
E   Nueva Caledonia
SU Но́вая Каледо́ния

2568 GB New Castile (Spain)
F   la Nouvelle-Castille (Espagne)
D   Neu-Kastilien (Spanien)
I   la Castiglia Nuova (Spagna)
E   Castilla la Nueva (España)
SU Но́вая Касти́лия (Испа́ния)

2569 GB *Newcomes, The* (Thackeray, 1855)
F   *Newcomes*
D   *Familie Newcome*
I   *I Newcome*
E   *Los Newcomes*
SU «Нью́комы» (Те́ккерей)

2570 GB New Economic Policy, the (NEP)
(USSR, 1921–9)
F   la Nouvelle politique économique (NEP)
(URSS)
D   die Neue Ökonomische Politik (NEP)
(UdSSR)
I   la Nuova politica economica (NEP)
(URSS)
E   la nueva política económica (Nep)
(URSS)
SU Но́вая экономи́ческая поли́тика
(НЭП) (СССР)

2571 GB New England (USA)
F   la Nouvelle-Angleterre (USA)
D   Neuengland (USA)
I   la Nuova Inghilterra (USA)
E   la Nueva Inglaterra (USA)
SU Но́вая А́нглия (США)

2572 GB *New Essays Concerning Human
Understanding* (Leibniz, 1704)
F   *Nouveaux Essais sur l'entendement
humain*
D   *Neue Abhandlungen über den
menschlichen Verstand*
I   *Nuovi saggi sull'intelletto umano*
E   *Nuevo tratado sobre el entendimiento
humano*
SU «Но́вые о́пыты о челове́ческом
ра́зуме» (Ле́йбниц)

2573 GB Newfoundland (Canada)
F   Terre-Neuve (Canada)
D   Neufundland (Kanada)
I   Terranova (Canada)
E   Terranova (Canadá)
SU Ньюфаундле́нд (Кана́да)

2574 GB New Guinea (Papua New Guinea)
F   la Nouvelle-Guinée (Papouasie-
Nouvelle-Guinée)
D   Neuguinea (Papua-Neuguinea)
I   la Nuova Guinea (Papua-Nuova
Guinea)
E   Nueva Guinea (Papuasia-Nueva
Guinea)
SU Но́вая Гвине́я (Па́пуа-Но́вая Гвине́я)

2575 GB New Hampshire (USA)
F   le New Hampshire (USA)
D   New Hampshire (USA)
I   il New Hampshire (USA)
E   New Hampshire (USA)
SU Нью-Хэ́мпшир (США)

2576 GB New Hebrides, the
F   les Nouvelles-Hébrides
D   die Neuen Hebriden
I   le Nuove Ebridi
E   las Nuevas Hébridas
SU Но́вые Гебри́ды (ж.)

2577 GB New Ireland (Papua New Guinea)
      F   la Nouvelle-Irlande (Papouasie-
          Nouvelle-Guinée)
      D   Neuirland (Papua-Neuguinea)
      I   la Nuova Irlanda (Papua-Nuova-
          Guinea)
      E   Nueva Irlanda (Papuasia-Nueva
          Guinea)
      SU Но́вая Ирла́ндия (Па́пуа-Но́вая
          Гвине́я)

2578 GB New Jersey (USA)
      F   le New Jersey (USA)
      D   New Jersey (USA)
      I   il New Jersey (USA)
      E   Nueva Jersey (USA)
      SU Нью-Дже́рси (США)

2579 GB *New Kingdom, The* (George, 1928)
      F   *Le Nouveau Règne*
      D   *Das neue Reich*
      I   *Il nuovo regno*
      E   *Nuevo imperio*
      SU «Но́вое ца́рство» (Гео́рге)

2580 GB *New Kingdom, The* [*Det nya riket*]
          (Strindberg, 1882)
      F   *Le Royaume nouveau*
      D   *Das neue Reich*
      I   *Il nuovo regno*
      E   *El nuevo reino*
      SU «Но́вое ца́рство» (Стри́ндберг)

2581 GB *New Louise, The* (Rousseau, 1761)
      F   *La Nouvelle Héloïse*
      D   *Die neue Heloise*
      I   *La nuova Eloisa*
      E   *Julia o la Nueva Eloísa*
      SU «Ю́лия, и́ли Но́вая Элои́за» (Руссо́)

2582 GB *New Men, The* (Snow, 1954)
      F   *Nouveaux Hommes*
      D   *Die neuen Männer*
      I   *I nuovi uomini*
      E   *Nuevos hombres*
      SU «Но́вые лю́ди» (Сно́у)

2583 GB New Mexico (USA)
      F   le Nouveau-Mexique (USA)
      D   New Mexico (USA)
      I   il Nuovo Messico (USA)
      E   Nuevo México (USA)
      SU Нью-Ме́ксико (США)

2584 GB New Orleans (USA)
      F   La Nouvelle-Orléans (USA)
      D   New Orleans (USA)
      I   New Orleans (USA)
      E   Nueva Orleáns (USA)
      SU Но́вый Орлеа́н (США)

2585 GB New Siberian Islands, the (USSR)
      F   la Nouvelle-Sibérie (URSS)
      D   die Neusibirischen Inseln (UdSSR)
      I   la Nuova Siberia (URSS)
      E   Nueva Siberia (URSS)
      SU Новосиби́рские острова́ (СССР)

2586 GB New South Wales (Australia)
      F   la Nouvelle-Galles du Sud (Australie)
      D   Neusüdwales (Australien)
      I   il Nuovo Galles del Sud (Australia)
      E   Nueva Gales del Sur (Australia)
      SU Но́вый Ю́жный Уэ́льс (Австра́лия)

2587 GB New Testament, the (Bib.)
      F   le Nouveau Testament (Bib.)
      D   das Neue Testament (Bib.)
      I   il Nuovo Testamento (Bib.)
      E   el Nuevo Testamento (Bib.)
      SU Но́вый заве́т (библ.)

2588 GB *New Way to Pay Old Debts, A*
          (Massinger, *1625*)
      F   *Une nouvelle façon de payer de vieilles
          dettes*
      D   *Neues Rezept, alte Schulden zu zahlen*
      I   *Un nuovo modo di pagare vecchi debiti*
      E   *Una nueva manera de pagar viejas
          deudas*
      SU «Но́вый спо́соб плати́ть ста́рые долги́»
          (Ме́ссинджер)

2589 GB *New World Symphony*, the (Dvořák)
      F   la *Symphonie du Nouveau Monde*
      D   die Sinfonie *Aus der Neuen Welt*
      I   la sinfonia *Dal Nuovo Mondo*
      E   la *Sinfonía del Nuevo Mundo*
      SU симфо́ния «Но́вый свет» (Дво́ржак)

2590 GB New Year, the
      F   le Nouvel an
      D   das Neue Jahr
      I   il capodanno
      E   el Año Nuevo
      SU Но́вый год

2591 GB New Year's Day
      F   le jour de l'an
      D   der Neujahrstag
      I   il capodanno
      E   el día de Año Nuevo
      SU день Но́вого го́да

2592 GB New York (USA)
      F   New-York (USA)
      D   New-York (USA)
      I   New York (USA)
      E   Nueva York (USA)
      SU Нью-Йо́рк (США)

2593 GB New Zealand
    F   la Nouvelle-Zélande
    D Neuseeland
    I   la Nuova Zelanda
    E Nueva Zelanda
    SU Нóвая Зелáндия

2594 GB Niagara Falls, the (Canada/USA)
    F   les chutes du Niagara (Canada/USA)
    D die Niagarafälle (Kanada/USA)
    I   le cascate del Niagara (Canada/USA)
    E la catarata del Niágara (Canadá/USA)
    SU Ниагáрский водопáд (Канáда/США)

2595 GB Nicaea (hist.)
    F   Nicée (hist.)
    D Nicäa (Gesch.)
    I   Nicea (st.)
    E Nicea (hist.)
    SU Никéя (ист.)

2596 GB Nicaragua
    F   le Nicaragua
    D Nicaragua
    I   il Nicaragua
    E Nicaragua
    SU Никарáгуа

2597 GB Nicc (France)
    F   Nice (France)
    D Nizza (Frankreich)
    I   Nizza (Francia)
    E Niza (Francia)
    SU Нúцца (Фрáнция)

2598 GB Nicholas (saint, pope, sovereign)
    F   Nicolas (saint, pape, souverain)
    D Nikolaus (Heiliger, Papst, Herr.)
    I   Nicola (santo, papa, sovrano)
    E Nicolás (santo, papa, sob.)
    SU Николáй (св., пáпа рúмский, прав.)

2599 GB *Nicholas Nickleby* (Dickens, 1838–9)
    F   *Nicolas Nickleby*
    D *Nicholas Nickleby*
    I   *Nicholas Nickleby*
    E *Nicolás Nickleby*
    SU «Нúколас Нúкльби» (Дúккенс)

2600 GB Nicodemus (Bib.)
    F   Nicodème (Bib.)
    D Nikodemus (Bib.)
    I   Nicodemo (Bib.)
    E Nicodemo (Bib.)
    SU Никодúм (библ.)

2601 GB *Nicomède* (Corneille, 1651)
    F   *Nicomède*
    D *Nicomède*
    I   *Nicomede*
    E *Nicomedes*
    SU «Никомéд» (Корнéль)

2602 GB Niger
    F   le Niger
    D Niger
    I   il Niger
    E Níger
    SU Нúгер

2603 GB Nigeria
    F   le Nigeria
    D Nigerien
    I   la Nigeria
    E Nigeria
    SU Нигéрия

2604 GB *Nigger of the "Narcissus", The*
      (Conrad, 1897)
    F   *Le Nègre du "Narcisse"*
    D *Der Nigger von der "Narzissus"*
    I   *Il negro del "Narciso"*
    E *El negro del "Narciso"*
    SU «Негр с ,,Нарцúсса"» (Кóнрад)

2605 GB *Night and Day* (Woolf, 1919)
    F   *La Nuit et le Jour*
    D *Nacht und Tag*
    I   *Notte e giorno*
    E *Noche y día*
    SU «Ночь и день» (Вулф)

2606 GB *Night Flight* (Saint-Exupéry, 1931)
    F   *Vol de nuit*
    D *Nachtflug*
    I   *Volo di notte*
    E *Vuelo de noche*
    SU «Ночнóй полёт» (Сент-Экзюперú)

2607 GB *Nightingale, The* [*Nattergalen*]
      (Andersen, 1835)
    F   *Le Rossignol*
    D *Die Nachtigall*
    I   *L'usignolo*
    E *El ruiseñor*
    SU «Соловéй» (Áндерсен)

2608 GB *Nightmare Abbey* (Peacock, 1818)
    F   *L'Abbaye de Cauchemar*
    D *Schreckensabtei*
    I   *L'abbazia degli incubi*
    E *La mansión de las pesadillas*
    SU «Аббáтство кошмáров» (Пúкок)

2609 GB *Night of the Demon, The* (Tourneur, 1957)
    F *Rendez-vous avec la peur*
    D *Die Nacht des Teufels*
    I *La notte del demonio*
    E *Noche del diablo*
    SU «Ночь дья́вола» (Турнёр)

2610 GB *Night of the Iguana, The* (Williams, 1961)
    F *La Nuit de l'iguane*
    D *Die Nacht des Leguan*
    I *La notte dell'iguana*
    E *La noche de la iguana*
    SU «Ночь игуа́ны» (Уи́льямс)

2611 GB *Night on the Bald Mountain, A* (Mussorgski, 1867)
    F *Une nuit sur le mont Chauve* (Moussorgski)
    D *Eine Nacht auf dem Kahlenberge* (Mussorgskij)
    I *Una notte sul Monte Calvo* (Musòrgskij)
    E *Una noche en el Monte Pelado* (Mussorgski)
    SU «Ночь на Лы́сой горе́» (Му́соргский)

2612 GB *Nights, The* (Musset, 1835–37)
    F *Les Nuits*
    D *Die Nächte*
    I *Le notti*
    E *Las noches*
    SU «Но́чи» (Мюссе́)

2613 GB *Night Thoughts* (Young, 1742–6)
    F *Pensées nocturnes*
    D *Nachtgedanken*
    I *Pensieri notturni*
    E *Pensamientos nocturnos*
    SU «Ночны́е размышле́ния» (Юнг)

2614 GB *Night Watch, The* (Rembrandt, 1642)
    F *Ronde de nuit*
    D *Nachtwache*
    I *Ronda di notte*
    E *Ronda nocturna*
    SU «Ночно́й дозо́р» (Ре́мбрандт)

2615 GB Nijmegen (Netherlands)
    F Nimègue (Pays-Bas)
    D Nimwegen (Niederlande)
    I Nimega (Paesi Bassi)
    E Nimega (Holanda)
    SU Не́ймеген (Нидерла́нды)

2616 GB Nike (myth.)
    F Niké (myth.)
    D Nike (myth.)
    I Nike (mit.)
    E Niké (mit.)
    SU Ни́ка (миф.)

2617 GB Nile (River), the
    F le Nil
    D der Nil
    I il Nilo
    E el Nilo
    SU Нил

2618 GB *Nineteen Eighty-Four* (Orwell, 1949)
    F *Mil neuf cent quatre-vingt-quatre*
    D *Neunzehnhundertvierundachtzig*
    I *Mille novecento ottantaquattro*
    E *Mil nuevecientos ochenta y cuatro*
    SU «1984-й год» (О́руэлл)

2619 GB *Nineteen-Nineteen* (Dos Passos, 1932)
    F *1919*
    D *Auf Trümmern*
    I *1919*
    E *1919*
    SU «1919» (Дос Па́ссос)

2620 GB *Ninety-Three* (Hugo, 1874)
    F *Quatre-vingt-treize*
    D *Dreiundneunzig*
    I *Il novantatrè*
    E *El noventa y tres*
    SU «Девяно́сто тре́тий год» (Гюго́)

2621 GB Nineveh (Bib.)
    F Ninive (Bib.)
    D Ninive (Bib.)
    I Ninive (Bib.)
    E Nínive (Bib.)
    SU Ниневи́я (библ.)

2622 GB *Ninotchka* (Lubitsch, 1939)
    F *Ninotchka*
    D *Ninotschka*
    I *Ninotchka*
    E *Ninotchka*
    SU «Ни́ночка» (Лю́бич)

2623 GB Niobe (myth.)
    F Niobé (myth.)
    D Niobe (myth.)
    I Niobe (mit.)
    E Níobe (mit.)
    SU Нио́ба (миф.)

2624 GB Noah (Bib.)
F Noé (Bib.)
D Noah (Bib.)
I Noè (Bib.)
E Noé (Bib.)
SU Ной (библ.)

2625 GB Noah's ark (Bib.)
F l'arche de Noé (Bib.)
D die Arche Noah (Bib.)
I l'arca di Noè (Bib.)
E la arca de Noé (Bib.)
SU Нóев ковчéг (библ.)

2626 GB Nobel prize, the
F le prix Nobel
D der Nobelpreis
I il premio Nobel
E el premio Nóbel
SU Нóбелевская прéмия

2627 GB Norman Conquest, the (1066)
F la conquête normande d'Angleterre
D die normannische Eroberung
I la conquista normanna
E la conquista normanda de Inglaterra
SU Нормáндское завоевáние Áнглии

2628 GB Normandy (France)
F la Normandie (France)
D die Normandie (Frankreich)
I la Normandia (Francia)
E Normandía (Francia)
SU Нормáндия (Фрáнция)

2629 GB Normans, the (hist.)
F les Normands (hist.)
D die Normannen (Gesch.)
I i normanni (st.)
E los normandos (hist.)
SU нормáнны (ист.)

2930 GB North Africa
F l'Afrique du Nord
D Nordafrika
I l'Africa settentrionale
E África del Norte
SU Сéверная Áфрика

2631 GB *North Against South* (Verne, 1887)
F *Nord contre Sud*
D *Nord gegen Süden*
I *Nord contro sud*
E *Norte contra sur*
SU «Сéвер прóтив Ю́га» (Верн)

2632 GB North America
F l'Amérique du Nord
D Nordamerika
I l'America settentrionale
E América del Norte
SU Сéверная Амéрика

2633 GB *Northanger Abbey* (Austen, 1817)
F *L'Abbaye de Northanger*
D *Northanger Abbey*
I *L'abbazia di Northanger*
E *La abadía de Northanger*
SU «Нортéнгерское аббáтство» (Óстин)

2634 GB North Atlantic Treaty Organization, the (NATO)
F l'Organisation du traité de l'Atlantique Nord (OTAN)
D der Nordatlantikpakt (NATO)
I l'Organizzazione del patto del Nord Atlantico (NATO)
E la Organización del Tratado del Atlántico Norte (OTAN)
SU Организáция Североатлантú́ческого договóра (НÁТО)

2635 GB *North by Northwest* (Hitchcock, 1959)
F *La Mort aux trousses*
D *Der unsichtbare Dritte*
I *Intrigo internazionale*
E *Con la muerte en los talones*
SU «Смерть слéдует по пятáм» (Хú́чкок)

2636 GB North Carolina (USA)
F la Caroline du Nord (USA)
D Nordkarolina (USA)
I la Carolina del Nord (USA)
E Carolina del Norte (USA)
SU Сéверная Каролú́на (США)

2637 GB North Dakota (USA)
F le Dakota du Nord (USA)
D Norddakota (USA)
I la Dakota del Nord (USA)
E Dakota del Norte (USA)
SU Сéверная Дакóта (США)

2638 GB Northern Ireland
F l'Irlande du Nord
D Nordirland
I l'Irlanda del Nord
E Irlanda del Norte
SU Сéверная Ирлáндия

2639 GB Northern Sporades, the (Greece)
     F les Sporades du Nord (Grèce)
     D die nördlichen Sporaden
        (Griechenland)
     I le Sporadi settentrionali (Grecia)
     E las Espóradas Septentrionales (Grecia)
    SU Céверные Споpáды (Гpéция)

2640 GB Northern Territory (Australia)
     F le Territoire du Nord (Australie)
     D Nordterritorium (Australien)
     I il Territorio del Nord (Australia)
     E Australia del Norte (Australia)
    SU Céверная Территóрия (Австрáлия)

2641 GB North Island (New Zealand)
     F l'île du Nord (Nouvelle-Zélande)
     D die Nordinsel (Neuseeland)
     I l'isola del Nord (Nuova Zelanda)
     E la isla del Norte (Nueva Zelanda)
    SU Céверный óстров (Нóвая Зелáндия)

2642 GB North Pole, the
     F le pôle Nord
     D der Nordpol
     I il polo Nord
     E el Polo Norte
    SU Céверный пóлюс

2643 GB North Sea, the
     F la mer du Nord
     D die Nordsee
     I il mare del Nord
     E el mar del Norte
    SU Céверное мóре

2644 GB North Vietnam (hist.)
     F le Viêt-Nam du Nord (hist.)
     D Nordvietnam (Gesch.)
     I il Vietnam del Nord (st.)
     E Vietnam del Norte (hist.)
    SU Céверный Вьетнáм (ист.)

2645 GB Northwest Passage, the (hist.)
     F le passage du Nord-ouest (hist.)
     D die nordwestliche Durchfahrt (Gesch.)
     I il passaggio di nord-ovest (st.)
     E el paso del noroeste (hist.)
    SU Céверо-зáпадный прохóд (ист.)

2646 GB Northwest Territories, the (Canada)
     F les Territoires du Nord-ouest (Canada)
     D die Nordwestterritorien (Kanada)
     I i Territori del Nord-Ovest (Canada)
     E el Territorio del Noroeste (Canadá)
    SU Céверо-Зáпадные территóрии
       (Канáда)

2647 GB Norway
     F la Norvège
     D Norwegen
     I la Norvegia
     E Noruega
    SU Норвéгия

2648 GB *Nose, The* (Gogol, 1835)
     F *Le Nez*
     D *Die Nase*
     I *Il naso*
     E *La nariz*
    SU «Нос» (Гóголь)

2649 GB *Notebook of Malte Laurids Brigge, The*
       (Rilke, 1904–10)
     F *Les Cahiers de Malte Laurids Brigge*
     D *Die Aufzeichnungen des Malte Laurids*
       Brigge
     I *I quaderni di Malte Laurids Brigge*
     E *Los cuadernos de Malte Laurids Brigge*
    SU «Замéтки Мáльте Лáуридса Брúгге»
       (Рúльке)

     GB *Notes from the House of the Dead→*
       House of the Dead

2650 GB Notre-Dame (Cathedral) (Paris)
     F Notre-Dame (de Paris) (Paris)
     D die Kathedrale Notre-Dame (Paris)
     I la cattedrale Notre-Dame (Parigi)
     E Nuestra Señora de París (París)
    SU собóр Парúжской богомáтери
       (Парúж)

2651 GB Nova Scotia (Canada)
     F la Nouvelle-Écosse (Canada)
     D Neuschottland (Kanada)
     I la Nuova Scozia (Canada)
     E la Nueva Escocia (Canadá)
    SU Нóвая Шотлáндия (Канáда)

2652 GB Novaya Zemlya (USSR)
     F la Nouvelle-Zemble (URSS)
     D Nowaja Semlja (UdSSR)
     I la Nuova Zemlja (URSS)
     E Nueva Zembla (URSS)
    SU Нóвая Земля́ (СССР)

2653 GB *Novum Organum* ["The New
       Instrument"] (Bacon, 1620)
     F le *Novum organum* (Bacon)
     D *Das neue Organon* (Bacon)
     I il *Novum Organum* (Bacone)
     E *Novum Organum* (Bacon)
    SU «Нóвый органóн» (Бэкон)

2654 GB   Nubia (Sudan/Egypt)
      F   la Nubie (Soudan/Égypte)
      D   Nubien (Sudan/Ägypten)
      I   la Nubia (Sudan/Egitto)
      E   Nubia (Sudán/Egipto)
      SU   Нубия (Судáн/Егѝпет)

2655 GB   Numbers (Bib.)
      F   les Nombres (Bib.)
      D   Numeri (Bib.)
      I   il libro dei Numeri (Bib.)
      E   el Libro de los Números (Bib.)
      SU   «Кнѝга чѝсел» (библ.)

2656 GB   Nuremberg Trial, the (1945–6)
      F   le procès de Nuremberg
      D   die Nürnberger Prozesse
      I   il processo di Norimberga
      E   el proceso de Nuremberg
      SU   Нюрнбéргский процéсс

2657 GB   Nürnberg (Nuremberg) (Germany)
      F   Nuremberg (Allemagne)
      D   Nürnberg (Deutschland)
      I   Norimberga (Germania)
      E   Nuremberg (Alemania)
      SU   Нюрнберг (Гермáния)

2658 GB   *Nutcracker, The* (Tchaikovsky, 1892)
      F   la *Casse-Noisette* (Tchaikovski)
      D   der *Nußknacker* (Tschaikowskij)
      I   il *Schiaccianoci* (Čajkovskij)
      E   el *Cascanueces* (Tchaikovski)
      SU   «Щелкýнчик» (Чайкóвский)

2659 GB   Nyasaland (hist.) (= Malawi)
      F   le Nyassaland (hist.)
      D   Njassaland (Gesch.)
      I   il Nyasaland (st.)
      E   Nyassalandia (hist.)
      SU   Ньясаленд (ист.) (= Малáви)

O

2660 GB *Oath of the Horatii*, the (David, 1784)
F *Serment des Horaces*
D *Lehnseid der Horazen*
I *Giuramento degli Orazi*
E *Juramento de los Horacios*
SU «Кля́тва Гора́циев» (Дави́д)

2661 GB Obadiah (Bib.)
F Abdias (Bib.)
D Obadja (Bib.)
I Abdia (Bib.)
E Abdías (Bib.)
SU А́вдий (библ.)

2662 GB Oberon (myth., + Weber, 1826)
F Obéron (myth.)
D Oberon (myth.)
I Oberon (mit.)
E Oberón (mit.)
SU Оберо́н (миф., + Ве́бер)

2663 GB *Oblomov* (Goncharov, 1858)
F *Oblomov* (Gontcharov)
D *Oblomow* (Gontscharow)
I *Oblomov* (Gončarov)
E *Oblomov* (Gontcharov)
SU «Обло́мов» (Гончаро́в)

2664 GB *Occupe-Toi d'Amélie* [*Look After Amelia!*] (Autant-Lara, 1949)
F *Occupe-toi d'Amélie!*
D *Pflege Amelia!*
I *Occupati di Amelia!*
E *¡Te ocupa de Amelia!*
SU «Займи́сь Аме́лией» (Ота́н-Лара́)

2665 GB Oceania
F l'Océanie (f.)
D Ozeanien
I l'Oceania
E Oceanía
SU Океа́ния

2666 GB Octavian (−63−+14)
F Octave
D Octavianus
I Ottaviano
E Octavio
SU Октавиа́н

2667 GB October Revolution, the (Russia, 1917)
F la révolution d'Octobre (Russie)
D die Oktoberrevolution (Rußland)
I la rivoluzione d'Ottobre (Russia)
E la Revolución de Octubre (Rusia)
SU Октя́брьская револю́ция (Росси́я)

2668 GB *Odd Man Out* (Reed, 1947)
F *Huit Heures de sursis*
D *Ausgestoßen*
I *Fuggiasco*
E *Larga es la noche*
SU «Вы́бывший из игры́» (Рид)

2669 GB *Ode on a Grecian Urn* (Keats, 1819)
F *Ode sur une urne grecque*
D *Ode über eine griechische Urne*
I *Ode sopra un'urna greca*
E *Oda a una urna griega*
SU «О́да гре́ческой ва́зе» (Китс)

2670 GB *Ode on Melancholy* (Keats, 1820)
F *Ode sur la Mélancolie*
D *Ode an die Melancholie*
I *Alla melanconia*
E *Oda a la melancolía*
SU «О́да меланхо́лии» (Китс)

2671 GB Oder (River), the (Europe)
F l'Oder (Europe)
D die Oder (Europa)
I l'Oder (Europa)
E el Oder (Europa)
SU О́дра (Евро́па)

2672 GB *Odes* [*Carmina*] (Horace, −I)
    F *Odes* (Horace)
    D *Oden* (Horaz)
    I *Odi* (Orazio)
    E *Odas* (Horacio)
    SU «Óды» (Горáций)

2673 GB *Odes of Pindar*, the [*Épinikia*] (Pindar, −V)
    F les *Épinicies* (Pindare)
    D die *Siegeslieder* (Pindaros)
    I gli *Odi* (Pindaro)
    E *Epinicios* (Píndaro)
    SU «Óды» (Пиндáр)

2674 GB *Odessa Tales* (Babel, 1931)
    F *Contes d'Odessa*
    D *Geschichten aus Odessa*
    I *Racconti di Odessa*
    E *Cuentos de Odesa*
    SU «Одéсские расскáзы» (Бáбель)

2675 GB *Ode to a Nightingale* (Keats, 1819)
    F *Ode à un rossignol*
    D *Ode an eine Nachtigall*
    I *Ode a un usignolo*
    E *Oda del ruiseñor*
    SU «Óда к соловью́» (Китс)

    GB *Ode to a Skylark*→*To a Skylark*

2676 GB *Ode to Autumn* (Keats, 1820)
    F *Ode à l'automne*
    D *An den Herbst*
    I *All'autunno*
    E *Al otoño*
    SU «К óсени» (Китс)

2677 GB *Ode to the West Wind* (Shelley, 1820)
    F l'*Ode au vent d'ouest*
    D *Ode an den Westwind*
    I l'*Ode al vento dell'ovest*
    E *Oda al viento del Oeste*
    SU «Óда к зáпадному вéтру» (Шéлли)

2678 GB Odysseus (myth.)
    F Ulysse (myth.)
    D Odysseus (myth.)
    I Odisseo (mit.)
    E Odiseo (mit.)
    SU Одиссéй (миф.)

2679 GB *Odyssey*, the (Homer, ?−VII)
    F l'*Odyssée* (f.) (Homère)
    D die *Odyssee* (Homeros)
    I l'*Odissea* (Omero)
    E la *Odisea* (Homero)
    SU «Одиссéя» (Гомéр)

2680 GB Oedipus (myth.)
    F Oedipe (myth.)
    D Ödipus (myth.)
    I Edipo (mit.)
    E Edipo (mit.)
    SU Эдúп (миф.)

2681 GB *Oedipus at Colonus* [*Oidipous epi Kolono*] (Sophocles, −401)
    F *Oedipe à Colone* (Sophocle)
    D *Ödipus auf Colonus* (Sophokles)
    I *Edipo a Colono* (Sofocle)
    E *Edipo en Colona* (Sófocles)
    SU «Эдúп в Колóне» (Софóкл)

2682 GB *Oedipus the King* [*Oidipous Tyrannos*] [*Oedipus Rex*] (Sophocles, −V)
    F *Oedipe roi* (Sophocle)
    D *König Ödipus* (Sophokles)
    I *Edipo re* (Sofocle)
    E *Edipo rey* (Sófocles)
    SU «Эдúп-царь» (Софóкл)

2683 GB *Officers and Gentleman* (Waugh, 1955)
    F *Officiers et Gentlemen*
    D *Offiziere und Herren*
    I *Ufficiali e signori*
    E *Oficiales y caballeros*
    SU «Офицéры и джентльмéны» (Во)

2684 GB *Of Human Bondage* (Maugham, 1915)
    F *Servitude humaine*
    D *Der Menschen Hörigkeit*
    I *Schiavo d'amore*
    E *Servidumbre humana*
    SU «Брéмя страстéй человéческих» (Мóэм)

2685 GB *Of Mice and Men* (Steinbeck, 1937; Milestone, 1939)
    F *Des souris et des hommes*
    D *Von Mäusen und Menschen*
    I *Uomini e topi*
    E *Hombres y ratones*
    SU «О мышáх и лю́дях» (Стéйнбек, Мáйлстон)

2686 GB *Oil!* (Sinclair, 1927)
    F *Le Pétrole*
    D *Petroleum*
    I *Petrolio*
    E *Petróleo*
    SU «Нефть» (Сúнклер)

2687 GB Oise (River), the (France)
　　　F l'Oise (f.) (France)
　　　D die Oise (Frankreich)
　　　I l'Oise (Francia)
　　　E el Oise (Francia)
　　　SU Уа́за (Фра́нция)

2688 GB *Oh! What a Lovely War*
　　　　　(Attenborough, 1969)
　　　F *Ah, Dieu, que la guerre est jolie*
　　　D *Ach, was für ein wunderschöner Krieg*
　　　I *Oh che bella guerra*
　　　E *¡Oh! qué bella guerra*
　　　SU «Ах, кака́я чуде́сная война́!»
　　　　　(А́ттенборо)

2689 GB *Old Castile* (Spain)
　　　F la Vieille-Castille (Espagne)
　　　D Alt-Kastilien (Spanien)
　　　I la Castiglia Vecchia (Spagna)
　　　E Castilla la Vieja (España)
　　　SU Ста́рая Касти́лия (Испа́ния)

2690 GB *Old Curiosity Shop, The* (Dickens,
　　　　　1841)
　　　F *Le Magasin d'antiquités*
　　　D *Der Antiquitätenladen*
　　　I *La bottega dell'antiquario*
　　　E *La tienda de antigüedades*
　　　SU «Ла́вка дре́вностей» (Ди́ккенс)

2691 GB *Old Goriot* (Balzac, 1834)
　　　F *Le Père Goriot*
　　　D *Der alte Goriot*
　　　I *Papa Goriot*
　　　E *Papá Goriot*
　　　SU «Оте́ц Горио́» (Бальза́к)

2692 GB *Old Man and the Sea, The*
　　　　　(Hemingway, 1952)
　　　F *Le Vieil Homme et la mer*
　　　D *Der alte Mann und das Meer*
　　　I *Il vecchio e il mare*
　　　E *El viejo y el mar*
　　　SU «Стари́к и мо́ре» (Хемингуэ́й)

2693 GB Old Man of the Mountain, the (hist.)
　　　F le Vieux de la montagne (hist.)
　　　D der Alte des Gebirges (Gesch.)
　　　I il Vecchio della montagna (st.)
　　　E el Viejo de la montaña (hist.)
　　　SU «стари́к с гор» (ист.)

2694 GB *Old Men at the Zoo, The* (Wilson,
　　　　　1961)
　　　F *La Girafe et les vieillards*
　　　D *Die alten Männer im Zoo*
　　　I *Vecchi allo zoo*
　　　E *Viejos en el zoo*
　　　SU «Старики́ в зоопа́рке» (Уи́лсон)

2695 GB *Old Mortality* (Scott, 1816)
　　　F *Les Puritains d'Écosse*
　　　D *Altes Sterben*
　　　I *I puritani*
　　　E *Los puritanos de Escocia*
　　　SU «Пурита́не» (Скотт)

2696 GB Old Testament, the (Bib.)
　　　F l'Ancien Testament (Bib.)
　　　D das Alte Testament (Bib.)
　　　I l'Antico Testamento (Bib.)
　　　E el Antiguo Testamento (Bib.)
　　　SU Ве́тхий заве́т (библ.)

2697 GB *Old Wives' Tale, The* (Bennett, 1908)
　　　F *Histoire de vieilles femmes*
　　　D *Konstanze und Sophie*
　　　I *Racconto delle vecchie*
　　　E *Porqué matan las mujeres*
　　　SU «По́весть о ста́рых же́нщинах»
　　　　　(Бе́ннетт)

2698 GB *Oliver Twist* (Dickens, 1838)
　　　F *Olivier Twist*
　　　D *Oliver Twist*
　　　I *Le avventure di Oliver Twist*
　　　E *Oliver Twist*
　　　SU «О́ливер Твист» (Ди́ккенс)

2699 GB *O Lucky Man!* (Anderson, 1972)
　　　F *Le Meilleur des mondes possibles*
　　　D *Der Erfolgreiche*
　　　I *O Lucky Man!*
　　　E *¡Oh!, hombre afortunado*
　　　SU «О, счастли́вец» (А́ндерсон)

2700 GB *Olvidados, Los* [*The Forgotten Ones*]
　　　　　(Buñuel, 1950)
　　　F *Pitié pour eux*
　　　D *Die Vergessenen*
　　　I *I figli della violenza*
　　　E *Los olvidados*
　　　SU «Забы́тые» (Бюнюэ́ль)

2701 GB Olympia (Greece)
　　　F Olympie (Grèce)
　　　D Olympia (Griechenland)
　　　I Olimpia (Grecia)
　　　E Olimpia (Grecia)
　　　SU Оли́мпия (Гре́ция)

2702 GB Olympic Games, the
F les Jeux olympiques
D die Olympischen Spiele
I i giochi olimpici
E los Juegos Olímpicos
SU Олимпи́йские и́гры

2703 GB Olympus, Mount (Greece)
F le mont Olympe (Grèce)
I der Olymp (Griechenland)
I l'Olimpo (Grecia)
E Olimpo (Grecia)
SU Оли́мп (Гре́ция)

2704 GB Oman
F l'Oman
D Oman
I il Oman
E Omán
SU Ома́н

2705 GB *Omoo* (Melville, 1847)
F *Omoo*
D *Omoo*
I *Omoo*
E *Omoo*
SU «Ому́» (Ме́лвилл)

2706 GB *Ondine* (Giraudoux, 1939)
F *Ondine*
D *Ondine*
I *Ondine*
E *Ondina*
SU «Онди́на» (Жироду́)

2707 GB *One Day in the Life of Ivan Denisovich* (Solzhenitsyn, 1962)
F *Une journée d'Ivan Denisovitch* (Soljenitsyne)
D *Ein Tag im Leben des Iwan Denissowitsch* (Solschenizyn)
I *Una giornata di Ivan Denissovič* (Solženicyn)
E *Un día en la vida de Iván Denisovich* (Soljenitsyn)
SU «Оди́н день Ива́на Дени́совича» (Солжени́цын)

2708 GB *One Flew Over the Cuckoo's Nest* (Forman, 1975)
F *Vol au-dessus du nid de coucous*
D *Einer flog über das Kuckucksnest*
I *Qualcuno volò sul nido del cuculo*
E *Vuelo sobre el nido de cuclillos*
SU «Кто-то перелете́л куку́шечье гнездо́» (Фо́рман)

2709 GB *On Germany* (Staël, 1810–13)
F *De l'Allemagne*
D *Über Deutschland*
I *La Germania*
E *De Alemania*
SU «О Герма́нии» (Сталь)

2710 GB *On Oratory* [*De Oratore*] (Cicero, −I)
F *De l'éloquence* (Cicéron)
D *Vom Redner* (Cicero)
I *Dell'oratore* (Cicerone)
E *De la oratoria* (Cicerón)
SU «Об ора́торском иску́сстве» (Цицеро́н)

2711 GB *On Religion* (Schleiermacher, 1799)
F *Discours sur la religion*
D *Über die Religion*
I *Discorsi sulla religione*
E *Discurso sobre la religión*
SU «Ре́чи о рели́гии» (Шле́йермахер)

2712 GB Ontario (Canada)
F Ontario (Canada)
D Ontario (Kanada)
I Ontario (Canada)
E Ontario (Canadá)
SU Онта́рио (Кана́да)

2713 GB *On the Beach* (Kramer, 1959)
F *Le Dernier Rivage*
D *Das letzte Ufer*
I *L'ultima riva*
E *La hora final*
SU «На после́днем берегу́» (Кре́ймер)

2714 GB *On the Education of Girls* (Fénelon, 1687)
F *Traité de l'éducation des filles*
D *Über Mädchenerziehung*
I *Trattato sull'educazione delle fanciulle*
E *La educación de las niñas*
SU «О воспита́нии де́вочек» (Фенело́н)

2715 GB *On the Eve* (Turgenev, 1860)
F *À la veille* (Tourgueniev)
D *Am Vorabend* (Turgenjew)
I *Alla vigilia* (Turgenev)
E *En vísperas* (Tourgueniev)
SU «Накану́не» (Турге́нев)

2716 GB *On the History of Religion and*
Philosophy in Germany (Heine, 1834)
F   *La Religion et la Philsophie en*
Allemagne
D   *Zur Geschichte der Religion und*
Philosophie in Deutschland
I   *Storia della religione e della filosofia in*
Germania
E   *Contribución a la historia de la religión*
y de la filosofía en Alemania
SU «К истóрии релúгии и философии в
Гермáнии» (Гéйне)

2717 GB *On the Marble Cliffs* (Jünger, 1939)
F   *Sur les falaises de marbre*
D   *Auf den Marmorklippen*
I   *Sugli scogli di marmo*
E   *Arrecifes de mármol*
SU «На мрáморных утёсах» (Юнгер)

2718 GB *On the Nature of the Gods [De Natura*
Deorum] (Cicero, −I)
F   *De la nature des dieux* (Cicéron)
D   *Vom Wesen der Götter* (Cicero)
I   *Della natura degli dei* (Cicerone)
E   *De la naturaleza de los dioses* (Cicerón)
SU «О прирóде богóв» (Цицерóн)

2719 GB *On the Nature of Things [De Rerum*
natura] (Lucretius, −I)
F   *De rerum natura* (Lucrèce)
D   *Das Wesen des Weltalls* (Lucretius)
I   *De rerum natura* (Lucrezio)
E   *De la naturaleza de las cosas* (Lucrecio)
SU «О прирóде вещéй» (Лукрéций)

2720 GB *On the Road* (Kerouac, 1957)
F   *Sur la route*
D   *Unterwegs*
I   *Sulla strada*
E   *En la carretera*
SU «На дорóге» (Керуáк)

2721 GB *On the Soul [Peri psyches] [De Anima]*
(Aristotle, −IV)
F   *De l'âme* (Aristote)
D   *Über die Seele* (Aristoteles)
I   *Sull'anima* (Aristotele)
E   *El tratado del alma* (Aristóteles)
SU «О душé» (Аристóтель)

2722 GB *On the Training of an Orator [Institutio*
oratoria] (Quintilian, I)
F   *L'Institution oratoire* (Quintilien)
D   *Redner-Lehrgang* (Quintilianus)
I   *L'educazione del oratore* (Quintiliano)
E   *La educación del orador* (Quintiliano)
SU «Об образовáнии орáтора»
(Квинтилиáн)

2723 GB *On the Truth of the Catholic Faith*
[Summa contra Gentiles] (Thomas
Aquinas, 1258−64)
F   *Summa contra Gentiles* (Thomas
d'Aquin)
D   *Summe wider die Heiden* (Thomas von
Aquilo)
I   *Summa contra gentiles* (Tommaso
d'Aquino)
E   *Summa contra gentiles* (Tomás de
Aquino)
SU «Сýмма прóтив язы́чников» (Фомá
Аквúнский)

2724 GB *On the Waterfront* (Kazan, 1954)
F   *Sur les quais*
D   *Die Faust im Nacken*
I   *Fronte del porto*
E   *La ley del silencio*
SU «Закóн молчáния» (Кáзан)

2725 GB Opatija (Yugoslavia)
F   Opatija (Yougoslavie)
D   Opatija (Jugoslawien)
I   Abbazia (Iugoslavia)
E   Opatija (Yugoslavia)
SU Опáтия (Югослáвия)

2726 GB Oporto (Portugal)
F   Porto (Portugal)
D   Porto (Portugal)
I   Oporto (Portogallo)
E   Oporto (Portugal)
SU Пóрту (Португáлия)

2727 GB *Opportunities, The* (Montale, 1939)
F   *Les Occasions*
D   *Die Gelegenheiten*
I   *Le occasioni*
E   *Las ocasiones*
SU «Случáйности» (Монтáле)

2728 GB Orange Free State, the (South Africa)
F   l'État libre d'Orange (Afrique du Sud)
D   die Oranje-Freistaat (Südafrika)
I   lo Stato Libero dell'Orange (Africa del
Sud)
E   el Estado Libre de Orange (África del
Sur)
SU Орáнжевая провúнция (Южная
Áфрика)

2729 GB Orange River, the (South Africa)
F   l'Orange (m.) (Afrique du Sud)
D   der Oranje (Südafrika)
I   l'Orange (Africa del Sud)
E   el río Orange (África del Sur)
SU Орáнжевая рекá (Южная Áфрика)

2730 GB *Orators' Dialogues* [*Dialogus de*
          oratoribus] (Tacitus, 102)
      F   *Dialogue des orateurs* (Tacite)
      D   *Dialog über die Redner* (Tacitus)
      I   *Dialogo sull'oratoria* (Tacito)
      E   *Diálogos de los oradores* (Tácito)
      SU «Диало́г об ора́торах» (Та́цит)

2731 GB *Ordeal of Richard Feverel, The*
          (Meredith, 1859)
      F   *L'Épreuve de Richard Feverel*
      D   *Richard Feverels Prüfung*
      I   *La prova di Richard Feverel*
      E   *La prueba sacra de Ricardo Feverel*
      SU «Испыта́ния Ри́чарда Фе́вереля»
          (Ме́редит)

2732 GB Order of the Garter, the
      F   l'ordre de la Jarretière
      D   der Hosenbandorden
      I   l'ordine della Giarrettiera
      E   la orden de la Jarretera
      SU о́рден Повя́зки

2733 GB *Oresteia*, the (Aeschylus, −458)
      F   l'*Orestie* (Eschyle)
      D   *Orestie* (Aischylos)
      I   l'*Orestea* (Eschilo)
      E   la *Orestíada* (Esquilo)
      SU «Оресте́я» (Эсхи́л)

2734 GB Orestes (myth., + Euripides, −408;
          Voltaire, 1750)
      F   Oreste (myth., + Euripide, Voltaire)
      D   Orestes (myth., + Euripides, Voltaire)
      I   Oreste (mit., + Euripide, Voltaire)
      E   Orestes (mit., + Eurípides, Voltaire)
      SU Оре́ст (миф., + Еврипи́д, Вольте́р)

2735 GB Organisation for Economic
          Co-operation and Development
          (OECD), the
      F   l'Organisation de coopération et de
          développement économique (OCDE)
      D   die Organisation für wirtschaftlichen
          Zusammenarbeit und Entwicklung
          (OECD)
      I   l'Organizzazione per la cooperazione e
          lo sviluppo economici (OCSE)
      E   la Organización de cooperación y
          desarrollo económico (OCDE)
      SU Организа́ция экономи́ческого
          сотру́дничества и разви́тия (ОЭСР)

2736 GB Organisation of African Unity (OAU),
          the
      F   l'Organisation de l'unité africaine
          (OUA)
      D   die Organisation für Afrikanische
          Einheit (OAE)
      I   l'Organizzazione per l'unità africana
          (OUA)
      E   la Organización por la unidad africana
          (OUA)
      SU Организа́ция африка́нского еди́нства
          (OAE)

2737 GB Organisation of American States
          (OAS), the
      F   l'Organisation des États américains
          (OEA)
      D   die Organisation Amerikanischer
          Staaten (OAS)
      I   l'Organizzazione degli Stati americani
          (OSA)
      E   la Organización de los Estados
          Americanos (OEA)
      SU Организа́ция америка́нских госуда́рств
          (ОА́Г)

2738 GB Organisation of the Petroleum
          Exporting Countries, the (OPEC)
      F   l'Organisation des pays exportateurs
          de pétrole (OPEP)
      D   der Zusammenschluß
          erdölexportierenden Länder (OPEC)
      I   l'Organizzazione dei paesi esportatori
          di petrolio (OPEC)
      E   la Organización de los países
          exportadores de petrólio (OPEP)
      SU Организа́ция стран – экспортёров
          не́фти (ОПЕ́К)

2739 GB *Organon*, the [*The Instrument*]
          (Aristotle, −IV)
      F   *Organon* (Aristote)
      D   *Organon* (Aristoteles)
      I   *Organon* (Aristotele)
      E   *Organon* (Aristóteles)
      SU «Органо́н» (Аристо́тель)

2740 GB Origen (*185–254*)
      F   Origène
      D   Origenes
      I   Origene
      E   Orígenes
      SU Ориге́н

2741 GB *Origin of Ideas, The* (Rosmini-Serbati, 1830)
F *Nouvel Essai sur l'origine des idées*
D *Der Ursprung der Ideen*
I *Nuovo saggio sull'origine delle idee*
E *Nuevo ensayo sobre el origen de las ideas*
SU «Нóвый óпыт о происхождéнии идéй» (Розмúни-Сербáти)

2742 GB *Origin of Species* (Darwin, 1859)
F *De l'origine des espèces*
D *Abstammung der Menschen*
I *Sull'origine delle specie*
E *Del origen de las especies*
SU «Происхождéние вúдов» (Дáрвин)

2743 GB Orion (myth., astron.)
F Orion (myth., astron.)
D Orion (myth., Astron.)
I Orione (mit., astr.)
E Orión (mit., astr.)
SU Орióн (миф., астр.)

2744 GB Orkney Islands, the (Scotland)
F les Orcades (f.) (Écosse)
D die Orkneyinseln (Schottland)
I le Orcadi (Scozia)
E las Orcadas (Escocia)
SU Оркнéйские островá (Шотлáндия)

2745 GB *Orlando Furioso [Roland Mad]* (Ariosto, 1516)
F *Roland furieux* (Arioste)
D *Der rasende Roland* (Ariosto)
I *Orlando furioso* (Ariosto)
E *Orlando furioso* (Ariosto)
SU «Нeúстовый Рóланд» (Ариóсто)

2746 GB Orléans (France)
F Orléans (France)
D Orléans (Frankreich)
I Orléans (Francia)
E Orleáns (Francia)
SU Орлеáн (Фрáнция)

2747 GB Orpheus (myth., + Gluck, 1774)
F Orphée (myth.)
D Orpheus (myth.)
I Orfeo (mit.)
E Orfeo (mit.)
SU Орфéй (миф., + Глюк)

2748 GB Orpheus and Eurydice (myth., + Gluck, 1762)
F Orphée et Eurydice (myth.)
D Orpheus und Eurydike (myth.)
I Orfeo ed Euridice (mit.)
E Orfeo y Eurídice (mit.)
SU Орфéй и Эвридúка (миф., + Глюк)

2749 GB *Orpheus in the Underworld* (Offenbach, 1858)
F *Orphée aux enfers*
D *Orpheus in der Unterwelt*
I *Orphée aux enfers*
E *Orfeo en los infiernos*
SU «Орфéй в адý» (Оффенбáх)

2750 GB Osiris (myth.)
F Osiris (myth.)
D Osiris (myth.)
I Osiri (mit.)
E Osiris (mit.)
SU Осúрис (миф.)

2751 GB Ostend (Belgium)
F Ostende (Belgique)
D Ostende (Belgien)
I Ostenda (Belgio)
E Ostende (Bélgica)
SU Остéнде (Бéльгия)

2752 GB Oslo (Norway)
F Oslo (Norvège)
D Oslo (Norwegen)
I Oslo (Norvegia)
E Oslo (Noruega)
SU Óсло (Норвéгия)

2753 GB *Othello* (Shakespeare, 1604; Rossini, 1816; Verdi, 1887)
F *Othello*
D *Othello*
I *Otello*
E *Otelo*
SU «Отéлло» (Шекспúр, Россúни, Вéрди)

2754 GB *Our Lady of the Flowers* (Genêt, 1949)
F *Notre-Dame-des-Fleurs*
D *Notre-Dame-des-Fleurs*
I *Nostra Signora dei Fiori*
E *Nuestra Señora de las Flores*
SU «Нотр-дам-де-флёр» (Женé)

2755 GB *Our Man in Havana* (Greene, 1958)
F *Notre agent à la Havane*
D *Unser Mann in Havanna*
I *Il nostro agente all'Avana*
E *Nuestro hombre en La Habana*
SU «Наш человéк в Гавáне» (Грин)

2756 GB *Our Mutual Friend* (Dickens, 1864–5)
  F *Notre ami commun*
  D *Unser gemeinsamer Freund*
  I *Il nostro comune amico*
  E *Nuestro común amigo*
  SU «Наш о́бщий друг» (Ди́ккенс)

2757 GB *Our Town* (Wilder, 1938)
  F *Notre petite ville*
  D *Unsere kleine Stadt*
  I *Piccola città*
  E *Nuestra ciudâd*
  SU «Наш городо́к» (Уа́йлдер)

2758 GB *Outcast of the Islands, An* (Conrad, 1896)
  F *Banni des îles*
  D *Der Verdammte der Inseln*
  I *Un reietto delle isole*
  E *Desterrado de las islas*
  SU «И́згнанный с острово́в» (Ко́нрад)

2759 GB Outer Mongolia (hist.)
  F la Mongolie-Extérieure (hist.)
  D die Äußere Mongolei (Gesch.)
  I la Mongolia Esterna (st.)
  E Mongolia Exterior (hist.)
  SU Вне́шняя Монго́лия (ист.)

2760 GB *Outline of History, The* (Wells, 1920)
  F *L'Esquisse de l'histoire universelle*
  D *Grundlinien der Weltgeschichte*
  I *Excursus di storia*
  E *Las grandes líneas de la historia*
  SU «О́черк исто́рии» (Уэ́ллс)

2761 GB *Outsider, The* (Camus, 1942; Wilson, 1956)
  F *L'Étranger*
  D *Der Fremde*
  I *Lo straniero*
  E *El extranjero*
  SU «Посторо́нний» (Камю́, Уи́лсон)

2762 GB *Overcoat, The* (Gogol, 1842)
  F *Le Manteau*
  D *Der Mantel*
  I *Il cappotto*
  E *El capote*
  SU «Шине́ль» (Го́голь)

2763 GB Ovid (−43–+17)
  F Ovide
  D Ovidius
  I Ovidio
  E Ovidio
  SU Ови́дий

2764 GB *Ox-Bow Incident, The* (Wellman, 1943)
  F *L'Étrange Incident*
  D *Ritt zum Ox-Bow*
  I *Alba fatale*
  E *Alba fatal*
  SU «Стра́нный слу́чай» (Уэ́ллман)

2765 GB Oxus (River), the (hist.)
  F l'Oxus (hist.)
  D der Oxus (Gesch.)
  I l'Oxus (st.)
  E el Oxo (hist.)
  SU Окс (ист.)

P

2766 GB Pacific Ocean, the
F l'océan Pacifique
D der Stille Ozean
I l'oceano Pacifico
E el océano Pacífico
SU Тихий океан

2767 GB *Pacific 231* (Honegger, 1923)
F *Pacific 231*
D *Pacific 231*
I *Pacific 231*
E *Pacific 231*
SU «Пасифик 231» (Онеггер)

2768 GB Padua (Italy)
F Padoue (Italie)
D Padua (Italien)
I Padova (Italia)
E Padua (Italia)
SU Падуя (Италия)

2769 GB *Pagliacchi, I* [*The Clowns*]
(Leoncavallo, 1892)
F *Paillasse*
D *Bajazzo*
I *I pagliacchi*
E *I pagliacci*
SU «Паяцы» (Леонкавалло)

2770 GB *Painted Veil, The* (Maugham, 1925)
F *Le Voile peint*
D *Der bunte Schleier*
I *Il velo dipinto*
E *El velo pintado*
SU «Пёстрая вуаль» (Моэм)

2771 GB *Pajama Game, The* (Donen, 1957)
F *Pique-nique en pyjama*
D *Picknick im Pyjama*
I *Il gioco del pigiama*
E *El juego del pijama*
SU «Пикник в пижаме» (Донен)

2772 GB Pakistan
F le Pakistan
D Pakistan
I il Pakistan
E el Paquistán
SU Пакистан

2773 GB Palatine Hill, the (Rome)
F le mont Palatin (Rome)
D der Palatin (Rom)
I il Palatino (Roma)
E el monte Palatino (Roma)
SU Палатин (Рим)

2774 GB Palermo (Italy)
F Palerme (Italie)
D Palermo (Italien)
I Palermo (Italia)
E Palermo (Italia)
SU Палермо (Италия)

2775 GB Palestine (Bib.)
F la Palestine (Bib.)
D Palästina (Bib.)
I la Palestina (Bib.)
E Palestina (Bib.)
SU Палестина (библ.)

2776 GB Palestine Liberation Organisation
(PLO), the
F l'Organisation de la libération de la
Palestine (OLP)
D die Palästinische
Befreiungsorganisation (PLO)
I l'Organizzazione per la liberazione
della Palestina (OLP)
E la Organización por la liberación de
Palestina (OLP)
SU Организация освобождения
Палестины (ООП)

2777 GB Palladium, the (myth.)
F le palladium (myth.)
D das Palladium (myth.)
I il Palladio (mit.)
E el Paladio (mit.)
SU палла́диум (миф.)

2778 GB Pallas (= Athena)
F Pallas (= Athène)
D Pallas (= Athene)
I Pallade (= Atena)
E Palas (= Atenea)
SU Палла́да (= Афи́на)

2779 GB Palm Sunday (rel.)
F le dimanche des Rameaux (relig.)
D der Palmsonntag (relig.)
I la Domenica delle Palme (relig.)
E el Domingo de Ramos (relig.)
SU ве́рбное воскресе́нье (рел.)

2780 GB *Pamela, or Virtue Rewarded*
(Richardson, 1740)
F *Paméla ou la Vertu récompensée*
D *Pamela oder Belohnte Tugend*
I *Pamela o la virtù ricompensata*
E *Pamela o la virtud recompensada*
SU «Паме́ла, и́ли Вознаграждённая
добро́детель» (Ри́чардсон)

2781 GB Pamphylia (Bib.)
F la Pamphylie (Bib.)
D Pamphylien (Bib.)
I la Panfilia (Bib.)
E Panfilia (Bib.)
SU Памфи́лия (библ.)

2782 GB Pamplona (Spain)
F Pampelune (Espagne)
D Pamplona (Spanien)
I Pamplona (Spagna)
E Pamplona (España)
SU Пампло́на (Испа́ния)

2783 GB Pan (myth.; + Hamsun, 1894)
F Pan (myth.)
D Pan (myth.)
I Pan (mit.)
E Pan (mit.)
SU Пан (миф., + Га́мсун)

2784 GB Panama
F le Panama
D Panama
I il Panamá
E Panamá
SU Пана́ма

2785 GB Panama Canal, the
F le canal de Panama
D der Panamakanal
I il canale di Panamá
E el canal de Panamá
SU Пана́мский кана́л

2786 GB Panama Canal Zone, the
F la zone du canal de Panama
D die Panamakanalzone
I la Zona del canale di Panamá
E la Zona del Canal de Panamá
SU Зо́на Пана́мского кана́ла

2787 GB Pandora (myth.)
F Pandore (myth.)
D Pandora (myth.)
I Pandora (mit.)
E Pandora (mit.)
SU Пандо́ра (миф.)

2788 GB *Pandora's Box* (Wedekind, 1901)
F *La Boîte de Pandore*
D *Die Büchse der Pandora*
I *Il vaso di Pandora*
E *La caja de Pandora*
SU «Я́щик Пандо́ры» (Ве́декинд)

2789 GB Pantaloon
F Pantalon
D der Hanswurst
I Pantalone
E Pantalón
SU Пантало́не

2790 GB Pantheon, the (Rome)
F le Panthéon (Rome)
D das Pantheon (Rom)
I il Pantheon (Roma)
E el Panteón (Roma)
SU Пантео́н (Рим)

2791 GB Papal States, the (hist.)
F les États pontificaux (hist.)
D der Kirchenstaat (Gesch.)
I lo Stato Pontificio (st.)
E los Estados Pontificios (hist.)
SU Па́пская о́бласть (ист.)

2792 GB *Paper Moon* (Bogdanovich, 1973)
F *Barbe à papa*
D *Paper Moon*
I *Luna di carta*
E *El papel de la luna*
SU «Бума́жная луна́» (Богда́нович)

2793 GB Papua-New Guinea
F la Papouasie-Nouvelle-Guinée
D Papua-Neuguinea
I la Papua-Nuova Guinea
E Papuasia-Nueva Guinea
SU Пáпуа-Нóвая Гвинéя

2794 GB *Paradise Lost* (Milton, 1667)
F *Le Paradis perdu*
D *Das verlorene Paradies*
I *Paradiso perduto*
E *El Paraíso perdido*
SU «Потéрянный рай» (Мúльтон)

2795 GB *Paradise Regained* (Milton, 1671)
F *Le Paradis reconquis*
D *Das wiedergewonnene Paradies*
I *Paradiso riguadagnato*
E *Paraíso reconquistado*
SU «Возвращённый рай» (Мúльтон)

2796 GB Paraguay
F le Paraguay
D Paraguay
I il Paraguay
E el Paraguay
SU Парагвáй

2797 GB *Parallel Lives* [*Bioi paralleloi*]
(Plutarch, II)
F *Vies parallèles* (Plutarque)
D *Parallelbiographien* (Plutarchos)
I *Vite parallele* (Plutarco)
E *Las vidas paralelas* (Plutarco)
SU «Параллéльные жизнеописáния»
(Плутáрх)

2798 GB *Parents Terribles, Les* [*The Terrible Parents*] (Cocteau, 1948)
F *Les Parents terribles*
D *Die schrecklichen Eltern*
I *I parenti terribili*
E *Los padres terribles*
SU «Трýдные родúтели» (Коктó)

2799 GB Paris (myth.)
F Pâris (myth.)
D Paris (myth.)
I Paride (mit.)
E Paris (mit.)
SU Парúс (миф.)

2800 GB Paris (France)
F Paris (France)
D Paris (Frankreich)
I Parigi (Francia)
E París (Francia)
SU Парúж (Фрáнция)

2801 GB *Paris Qui Dort* [*Paris Asleep*] (Clair, 1924)
F *Paris qui dort*
D *Das schlafende Paris*
I *Paris qui dort*
E *Paris qui dort*
SU «Парúж уснýл» (Клер)

2802 GB *Parsifal* (Wagner, 1882)
F *Parsifal*
D *Parsifal*
I *Parsifal*
E *Parsifal*
SU «Пáрсифаль» (Вáгнер)

2803 GB Parma (Italy)
F Parme (Italie)
D Parma (Italien)
I Parma (Italia)
E Parma (Italia)
SU Пáрма (Итáлия)

2804 GB Parnassus (Greece)
F le mont Parnasse (Grèce)
D Parnaß (Griechenland)
I il monte Parnaso (Grecia)
E Parnaso (Grecia)
SU Парнáс (Грéция)

2805 GB Parsees, the (hist.)
F les Parsis (hist.)
D die Parsen (Gesch.)
I i parsi (st.)
E los parsis (hist.)
SU пáрсы (ист.)

2806 GB Parthenon, the (Athens)
F le Parthénon (Athènes)
D der Parthenon (Athen)
I il Partenone (Atene)
E el Partenón (Atenas)
SU Парфенóн (Афúны)

2807 GB Parthians, the (hist.)
F les Parthes (hist.)
D die Parther (Gesch.)
I i parti (st.)
E los partos (hist.)
SU парфяне (ист.)

2808 GB *Parties in St. Petersburg* (Maistre, 1821)
F *Les Soirées de Saint-Pétersbourg*
D *Petersburger Abende*
I *Le serate di Pietroburgo*
E *Las veladas de San Petersburgo*
SU «Петербýргские вечерá» (Местр)

2809 GB Pasiphaë (myth.)
F Pasiphaé (myth.)
D Pasiphaë (myth.)
I Pasifae (mit.)
E Pasífae (mit.)
SU Пасифая (миф.)

2810 GB *Pasquier Chronicles, The* (Duhamel, 1933–44)
F *Chronique des Pasquier*
D *Chronik der Familie Pasquier*
I *Cronache dei Pasquier*
E *La crónica de los Pasquier*
SU «Хрóника семьй Паскьé» (Дюамéль)

2811 GB *Passage to India, A* (Forster, 1924)
F *Route des Indes*
D *Auf der Suche nach Indien*
I *Passaggio in India*
E *Ruta de las Indias*
SU «Поéздка в Ѝндию» (Фóрстер)

2812 GB *Passing of the Third Floor Back, The* (Jerome, 1908)
F *Le Locataire du troisième étage*
D *Der Fremde*
I *Il passaggero del terzo piano*
E *El inquilino del tercero*
SU «Жилéц с четвёртого этажá» (Джерóм)

2813 GB *Passion of Joan of Arc, The* (Dreyer, 1928)
F *La Passion de Jeanne d'Arc*
D *Johanna von Orleans*
I *La passione di Giovanna d'Arco*
E *La Pasión de Juana de Arco*
SU «Стрáсти Жáнны д'Арк» (Дрéйер)

2814 GB Passion Sunday (rel.)
F le dimanche de la Passion (relig.)
D der Sonntag Judika (relig.)
I la Domenica di Passione (relig.)
E el Domingo de Pasión (relig.)
SU страстнóе воскресéнье (рел.)

2815 GB Passover, the (rel.)
F la Pâque (relig.)
D Passah (relig.)
I la Pasqua (relig.)
E la pascua (relig.)
SU пáсха (рел.)

2816 GB *Pastoral Symphony*, the (Beethoven, 1808)
F la symphonie *Pastorale*
D die *Sinfonie Pastorale*
I la *Sinfonia Pastorale*
E la *Sinfonía pastoral*
SU «Пасторáльная» симфóния (Бетхóвен)

2817 GB *Pastoral Symphony, The* (Gide, 1919)
F *La Symphonie pastorale*
D *Pastoral-Symphonie*
I *La sinfonia pastorale*
E *Sinfonía pastoral*
SU «Пасторáльная симфóния» (Жид)

2818 GB Patagonia
F la Patagonie
D Patagonien
I la Patagonia
E Patagonia
SU Патагóния

2819 GB *Pathetic* (*Pathétique*) *Symphony*, the (Tchaikovsky, 1893)
F la *Symphonie Pathétique* (Tchaikovski)
D die *Sinfonie Pathétique* (Tschaikowski)
I la *Sinfonia Patetica* (Čajkowskij)
E la sinfonía *Patética* (Tchaikovski)
SU «Патетѝческая» симфóния (Чайкóвский)

2820 GB *Pathétique Sonata*, the (Beethoven, 1798)
F la sonate *Pathétique*
D die *Sonate Pathétique*
I la *Sonata Patetica*
E la sonata *Patética*
SU «Патетѝчсская» сонáта (Бетхóвен)

2821 GB *Pathfinder, The* (Cooper, 1840)
F *Le Trappeur*
D *Der Pfadfinder*
I *La guida*
E *El piloto*
SU «Следопы̆т, ѝли Óзеро-мóре» (Кýпер)

2822 GB *Paths of Glory* (Kubrick, 1957)
F *Les Sentiers de la gloire*
D *Wege zum Ruhm*
I *Orizzonti di gloria*
E *Paths of glory*
SU «Путѝ слáвы» (Кýбрик)

2823 GB Patrick (saint, V)
     F Patrick (saint)
     D Patrick (Heiliger)
     I Patrizio (santo)
     E Patricio (santo)
     SU Па́трик (св.)

2824 GB Paul (saint, pope, sovereign)
     F Paul (saint, pape, souverain)
     D Paulus (Heiliger, Papst, Herr.)
     I Paolo (santo, papa, sovrano)
     E Paulo (santo, papa, sob.)
     SU Па́вел (св., па́па ри́мский, прав.)

2825 GB *Peace, The* [*Eirene*] (Aristophanes, −421)
     F *La Paix* (Aristophane)
     D *Der Frieden* (Aristophanes)
     I *La pace* (Aristofane)
     E *La paz* (Aristófanes)
     SU «Мир» (Аристофа́н)

2826 GB *Pearl Fishers, The* (Bizet, 1863)
     F *Les Pêcheurs de perles*
     D *Die Perlenfischer*
     I *I pescatori di perle*
     E *Los pescadores de perlas*
     SU «Иска́тели же́мчуга» (Бизе́)

2827 GB *Peasant of Paris, The* (Aragon, 1926)
     F *Le Paysan de Paris*
     D *Pariser Landleben*
     I *Il contadino di Parigi*
     E *El campesino de París*
     SU «Пари́жский мужи́к» (Араго́н)

2828 GB *Peasants* (Chekhov, 1897)
     F *Les Paysans* (Tchekhov)
     D *Die Bauern* (Tschechow)
     I *I contadini* (Čechov)
     E *Los campesinos* (Chejov)
     SU «Мужики́» (Че́хов)

2829 GB *Peasants, The* [*Chłopi*] (Reymont, 1924)
     F *Les Paysans*
     D *Die polnischen Bauern*
     I *I contadini*
     E *Los campesinos*
     SU «Мужики́» (Ре́ймонт)

2830 GB Peasants' Revolt, the (1381, 1524–5)
     F La Guerre des paysans
     D der Bauernkrieg
     I la guerra dei contadini
     E la guerra dos campesinos
     SU крестья́нское восста́ние

2831 GB *Peer Gynt* (Ibsen, 1867; Grieg, 1876)
     F *Peer Gynt*
     D *Peer Gynt*
     I *Peer Gynt*
     E *Peer Gynt*
     SU «Пер Гюнт» (И́бсен, Григ)

2832 GB Pegasus (myth.)
     F Pégase (myth.)
     D Pegasus (myth.)
     I Pegaso (mit.)
     E Pegaso (mit.)
     SU Пега́с (миф.)

2833 GB Peking (China)
     F Pékin (Chine)
     D Peking (China)
     I Pechino (Cina)
     E Pekín (China)
     SU Пеки́н (Кита́й)

2834 GB Peleus (myth.)
     F Pélée (myth.)
     D Peleus (myth.)
     I Peleo (mit.)
     E Peleo (mit.)
     SU Пеле́й (миф.)

2835 GB *Pelham* (Bulwer-Lytton, 1828)
     F *Pelham*
     D *Pelham*
     I *Pelham*
     E *Pelham*
     SU «Пе́лэм» (Бу́лвер-Ли́ттон)

2836 GB *Pelleas and Melisande* (Maeterlinck, 1892; Debussy, 1902)
     F *Pelléas et Mélisande*
     D *Pelléas et Mélisande*
     I *Pelléas et Mélisande*
     E *Pelléas et Mélisande*
     SU «Пелеа́с и Мелиса́нда» (Ме́терли́нк, Дебюсси́)

2837 GB Peloponnese, the (Greece)
     F le Péloponnèse (Grèce)
     D der Peloponnes (Griechenland)
     I il Peloponneso (Grecia)
     E el Peloponeso (Grecia)
     SU Пелопонне́с (Гре́ция)

2838 GB Peloponnesian Wars, the (431–404)
     F la guerre du Péloponnèse
     D der Peloponnesische Krieg
     I la guerra del Peloponneso
     E la guerra del Peloponeso
     SU Пелопонне́сская война́

2839 GB Pelops (myth.)
F Pélops (myth.)
D Pelops (myth.)
I Pelope (mit.)
E Pélope (mit.)
SU Пелóпс (миф.)

2840 GB *Pendennis* (Thackeray, 1849–50)
F *Pendennis*
D *Pendennis*
I *La storia di Pendennis*
E *La historia de Pendennis*
SU «Пендéннис» (Тéккерей)

2841 GB Penelope (myth.)
F Pénélope (myth.)
D Penelope (myth.)
I Penelope (mit.)
E Penélope (mit.)
SU Пенелóпа (миф.)

2842 GB *Penguin Island* (France, 1908)
F *L'Île des pingouins*
D *Die Insel der Pinguine*
I *L'isola dei pinguini*
E *La isla de los pinguinos*
SU «Óстров пингвúнов» (Франс)

2843 GB Peninsular War, the (1808–14)
F la guerre d'Espagne
D der Krieg in Spanien
I la guerra della Spagna
E la guerra de Independencia
SU войнá в Испáнии

2844 GB Pennines, the (England)
F les Pennines (Angleterre)
D das Penninische Gebirge (England)
I i monti Pennini (Inghilterra)
E los montes Peninos (Inglaterra)
SU Пеннúнские гóры (Áнглия)

2845 GB Pennsylvania (USA)
F la Pennsylvanie (USA)
D Pennsylvanien (USA)
I la Pennsylvania (USA)
E Pensilvania (USA)
SU Пенсильвáния (США)

2846 GB *Penseroso, Il* ["The Contemplative One"] (Milton, 1631)
F *Penseroso*
D *Der Nachdenkliche*
I *Il penseroso*
E *El pensador*
SU «Задýмчивый» (Мúльтон)

2847 GB Pentateuch, the (Bib.)
F la Pentateuque (Bib.)
D der Pentateuch (Bib.)
I il Pentateuco (Bib.)
E el Pentateuco (Bib.)
SU «пятикнúжие» (библ.)

2848 GB Pentecost (rel.)
F la Pentecôte (relig.)
D Pfingsten (relig.)
I la Pentecoste (relig.)
E la Pentecostés (relig.)
SU пятидесятница (рел.)

2849 GB Penthesilea (myth., + Kleist, 1808)
F Penthésilée (myth.)
D Penthesilea (myth.)
I Pentesilea (mit.)
E Pentesilea (mit.)
SU Пентесúлея (миф., + Клейст)

2850 GB *Percival* (Chrétien de Troyes, 1175)
F *Perceval*
D *Perceval*
I *Perceval*
E *Perceval*
SU «Персевáль, úли Пóвесть о Граáле» (Кретьéн де Труá)

GB *Peregrine Pickle→Adventures of Peregrine Pickle*

2851 GB *Pergamum (Pergamon)* (Greece)
F Pergame (Grèce)
D Pergamon (Griechenland)
I Pergamo (Grecia)
E Pérgamo (Grecia)
SU Пергáм (Грéция)

2852 GB Pericles (*495–429*, + Shakespeare, 1608)
F Périclès
D Perikles
I Pericle
E Pericles
SU Перúкл (+ Шекспúр)

2853 GB Perpignan (France)
F Perpignan (France)
D Perpignan (Frankreich)
I Perpignano (Francia)
E Perpiñán (Francia)
SU Перпиньян (Фрáнция)

2854
GB Persephone (myth.)
F Perséphone (myth.)
D Persephone (myth.)
I Persefone (mit.)
E Perséfone (mit.)
SU Персефо́на (миф.)

2855
GB Persepolis (Iran)
F Persépolis (Iran)
D Persepolis (Iran)
I Persepoli (Iran)
E Persépolis (Irán)
SU Персе́поль (м.) (Ира́н)

2856
GB Perseus (myth.)
F Persée (myth.)
D Perseus (myth.)
I Perseo (mit.)
E Perseo (mit.)
SU Персе́й (миф.)

2857
GB Persia (hist.)
F la Perse (hist.)
D Persien (Gesch.)
I la Persia (st.)
E Persia (hist.)
SU Пе́рсия (ист.)

2858
GB Persian Gulf, the
F le golfe Persique
D der Persische Golf
I il golfo Persico
E el golfo Pérsico
SU Перси́дский зали́в

2859
GB *Persian Letters* (Montesquieu, 1721)
F *Lettres persanes*
D *Persische Briefe*
I *Lettere persiane*
E *Cartas persas*
SU «Перси́дские пи́сьма» (Монтескьё)

2860
GB *Persians, The* [*Persai*] (Aeschylus, −472)
F *Les Perses* (Eschyle)
D *Die Perser* (Aischylos)
I *I persiani* (Eschilo)
E *Los Persas* (Esquilo)
SU «Пе́рсы» (Эсхи́л)

2861
GB Persian Wars, the (500−449)
F les guerres Médiques
D die Persekriege
I le guerre persiane
E las guerras Médicas
SU гре́ко-перси́дские во́йны

2862
GB *Persuasion* (Austen, 1817)
F *Persuasion*
D *Überredung*
I *Persuasione*
E *Persuasión*
SU «Убежде́ние» (О́стин)

2863
GB Peru
F le Pérou
D Peru
I il Perù
E el Perú
SU Перу́

2864
GB Perugia (Italy)
F Pérouse (Italie)
D Perugia (Italien)
I Perugia (Italia)
E Perusa (Italia)
SU Перу́джа (Ита́лия)

2865
GB Peter (saint, sovereign)
F Pierre (saint, souverain)
D Peter (Heiliger, Herr.)
I Pietro (santo, sovrano)
E Pedro (santo, sob.)
SU Пётр (св., прав.)

2866
GB *Peter and the Wolf* (Prokofiev, 1940)
F *Pierre et le Loup* (Prokofiev)
D *Peter und der Wolf* (Prokofjew)
I *Pierino e il lupo* (Prokof'ev)
E *Pedrito y el lobo* (Prokofiev)
SU «Пе́тя и волк» (Проко́фьев)

2867
GB *Peter Camenzind* (Hesse, 1904)
F *Peter Camenzind*
D *Peter Camenzind*
I *Peter Camenzind*
E *Peter Camenzind*
SU «Пе́тер Ка́менцинд» (Хе́ссе)

2868
GB *Peter Pan* (Barrie, 1904)
F *Peter Pan*
D *Peter Pan*
I *Peter Pan*
E *Peter Pan*
SU «Пи́тер Пан» (Ба́рри)

2869 GB *Peter Schlemihl's Remarkable Story, or*
              The Man Who Lost His Shadow
              (Chamisso, 1814)
       F   *La Merveilleuse Histoire de Peter*
              Schlemihl, ou L'Homme qui a perdu
              son ombre
       D   *Peter Schlemihls Wundersame*
              Geschichte, oder der Mann, der seinen
              Schatten verloren hat
       I   *La meraviglia storia di Peter Schlemihl,*
              o L'uomo che perdè la sua ombra
       E   *Historia de Pedro Schlemihl o El*
              hombre que perdió su sombra
       SU «Необычáйная истóрия Пéтера
              Шлéмиля, и́ли Человéк, котóрый
              потеря́л свою́ тень» (Шами́ссо)

2870 GB *Peter Simple* (Marryat, 1834)
       F   *Peter Simple*
       D   *Peter Simple*
       I   *Pietro il Semplice*
       E   *Pedro el Simple*
       SU «Пи́тер Симпл» (Мáрриет)

2871 GB Peter the Great (1672–1725)
       F   Pierre le Grand
       D   Peter der Große
       I   Pietro il Grande
       E   Pedro el Grande
       SU Пётр Вели́кий

2872 GB Peter the Hermit (1050–1115)
       F   Pierre l'Ermite
       D   Peter der Einsiedler
       I   Pietro l'Eremita
       E   Pedro el Ermitaño
       SU Пётр Пусты́нник

2873 GB Petition of Right, the (1628)
       F   la Pétition des droits
       D   die Bitte um Rechte
       I   la Petizione dei diritti
       E   la Petición dos derechos
       SU Пети́ция о прáве

2874 GB Petrarch (1304–74)
       F   Pétrarque
       D   Petrarca
       I   Petrarca
       E   Petrarca
       SU Петрáрка

2875 GB Petronius (Arbiter) (I)
       F   Pétrone (Arbiter)
       D   Petronius (Arbiter)
       I   Petronio (Arbitro)
       E   Petronio (Arbitro)
       SU Петрóний (Арби́тр)

2876 GB *Petrushka* (Stravinsky, 1911)
       F   *Petrouchka* (Stravinski)
       D   *Petruschka* (Strawinski)
       I   *Petrouchka* (Stravinskij)
       E   *Petruchka* (Stravinski)
       SU «Петру́шка» (Страви́нский)

2877 GB Phaedra (myth., + Racine 1677)
       F   Phèdre (myth.)
       D   Phädra (myth.)
       I   Fedra (mit.)
       E   Fedra (mit.)
       SU Фéдра (миф., + Раси́н)

2878 GB *Phaedrus* (Plato, −VI)
       F   *Phèdre* (Platon)
       D   *Phädrus* (Platon)
       I   *Fedro* (Platone)
       E   *Fedro* (Platón)
       SU «Федр» (Платóн)

2879 GB Phaethon (myth.)
       F   Phaéton (myth.)
       D   Phaethon (myth.)
       I   Fetonte (mit.)
       E   Faetón (mit.)
       SU Фаэтóн (миф.)

2880 GB Pharisees, the (Bib.)
       F   les pharisiens (Bib.)
       D   die Pharisäer (Bib.)
       I   i farisei (Bib.)
       E   los fariseos (Bib.)
       SU фарисéи (библ.)

2881 GB Pharos of Alexandria, the
       F   le Phare d'Alexandrie
       D   der Leuchtturm auf Pharos
       I   il faro di Alessandria
       E   el faro de Alejandría
       SU маáк в Алексáндрии

2882 GB *Phenomenology of Mind, The* (Hegel,
              1807)
       F   *Phénoménologie de l'esprit*
       D   *Die Phänomenologie des Geistes*
       I   *Fenomenologia dello spirito*
       E   *Fenomenología del espíritu*
       SU «Феноменолóгия дýха» (Гéгель)

2883 GB Philadelphia (Bib., USA)
       F   Philadelphie (Bib., USA)
       D   Philadelphia (Bib., USA)
       I   Filadelfia (Bib., USA)
       E   Filadelfia (Bib., USA)
       SU Филадéльфия (библ., США)

2884 GB Philemon (Bib., myth)
     F   Philémon (Bib., myth)
     D   Philemon (Bib., myth)
     I   Filemone (Bib., mit.)
     E   Filemón (Bib., mit.)
     SU Филемо́н (библ., миф.)

2885 GB Philemon and Baucis (myth.)
     F   Philémon et Baucis (myth.)
     D   Philemon und Baucis (myth.)
     I   Filemone e Bauci (mit.)
     E   Filemón y Baucis (mit.)
     SU Филемо́н и Бавки́да (миф.)

2886 GB Philip (saint, pope, sovereign)
     F   Philippe (saint, pape, souverain)
     D   Philipp (Heiliger, Papst, Herr.)
     I   Filippo (santo, papa, sovrano)
     E   Felipe (santo, papa, sob.)
     SU Фили́пп (св., па́па ри́мский, прав.)

2887 GB Philippi (Greece)
     F   Philippes (Grèce)
     D   Philippi (Griechenland)
     I   Filippi (Grecia)
     E   Filipos (Grecia)
     SU Фили́ппы (Гре́ция)

2888 GB Philippians, the Epistle of Paul to the
         (Bib.)
     F   l'Épître de Saint Paul aux Philippiens
         (Bib.)
     D   der Philipperbrief (Bib.)
     I   la Lettera di Paolo ai Filippesi (Bib.)
     E   la Epístola de San Pablo a los filipinos
         (Bib.)
     SU «Посла́ние к Филиппи́йцам» (библ.)

2889 GB *Philippics*, the [*Kata Philippou*]
         (Demosthenes, 351–341)
     F   les *Philippiques* (Démosthène)
     D   *Gegen Philipp* (Demosthenes)
     I   le *Filippiche* (Demostene)
     E   las *Filípicas* (Demóstenes)
     SU «Фили́ппики» (Демосфе́н)

2890 GB Philippines, the
     F   les Philippines (f.)
     D   die Philippinen
     I   le Filippine
     E   las Filipinas
     SU Филиппи́ны (ж.)

2891 GB Philip the Fair (1288–1314)
     F   Philippe le Bel
     D   Philipp der Schöne
     I   Filippo il Bello
     E   Felipe el Hermoso
     SU Фили́пп Краси́вый

2892 GB Philistines, the (Bib.)
     F   les Philistins (Bib.)
     D   die Philister (Bib.)
     I   i filistei (Bib.)
     E   los filisteos (Bib.)
     SU филисти́мляне (библ.)

2893 GB Philoctetes (myth., + Sophocles,
         −408)
     F   Philoctète (myth., + Sophocle)
     D   Philoktetes (myth., + Sophokles)
     I   Filottete (mit., + Sofocle)
     E   Filoctetes (mit., + Sófocles)
     SU Филокте́т (миф., + Софо́кл)

2894 GB Philomela (myth.)
     F   Philomèle (myth.)
     D   Philomela (myth.)
     I   Filomela (mit.)
     E   Filomela (mit.)
     SU Филоме́ла (миф.)

2895 GB Philo of Alexandria (I)
     F   Philon d'Alexandrie
     D   Philon von Alexandrien
     I   Filone di Alessandria
     E   Filón de Alejandría
     SU Фило́н Александри́йский

2896 GB *Philsophical Essays Concerning
         Human Understanding* (Hume, 1748)
     F   les *Essais sur l'entendement humain*
     D   *Über den menschlichen Verstand*
     I   *Ricerca sull'intelletto umano*
     E   *Ensayo sobre el entendimiento humano*
     SU «Тракта́т о челове́ческой приро́де»
         (Юм)

2897 GB *Philosophical Letters* (Voltaire, 1734)
     F   *Lettres philosphiques*
     D   *Philosophische Briefe*
     I   *Lettere filosofiche*
     E   *Cartas filosóficas*
     SU «Филосо́фские пи́сьма» (Вольте́р)

2898 GB *Philosophy of Right, The* (Hegel, 1820
         −1)
     F   *Philosophie du droit*
     D   *Grundlinien der Philosophie des Rechts*
     I   *Lineamenti di filosofia del diritto*
     E   *Filosofía del derecho*
     SU «Филосо́фия пра́ва» (Ге́гель)

2899 GB *Philosophy of the History of Mankind,*
A (Herder, 1784–91)

F *Idées sur la philosophie de l'histoire de*
l'humanité

D *Ideen zur Philosophie der Geschichte*
der Menschheit

I *Idee sulla filosofia della storia*
dell'umanità

E *Filosofía de la historia de la humanidad*

SU «Идéи к филосóфии истóрии
человéчества» (Гéрдер)

2900 GB *Phineas Finn* (Trollope, 1869)

F *Phineas Finn*

D *Phineas Finn*

I *Phineas Finn*

E *Phineas Finn*

SU «Фи́ниас Финн» (Трóллоп)

2901 GB Phoebe (myth.)

F Phébé (myth.)

D Phöbe (myth.)

I Feba (mit.)

E Feba (mit.)

SU Фéба (миф.)

2902 GB Phoebus (myth.)

F Phébus (myth.)

D Phöbus (myth.)

I Febo (mit.)

E Febo (mit.)

SU Феб (миф.)

2903 GB Phoenicia (hist.)

F la Phénicie (hist.)

D Phönizien (Gesch.)

I la Fenicia (st.)

E Fenicia (hist.)

SU Финики́я (ист.)

2904 GB *Phoenician Women, The* [*Phoinissae*]
(Euripides, −410)

F *Les Phéniciennes* (Euripide)

D *Die Phönizierinnen* (Euripides)

I *Le fenicie* (Euripide)

E *Las fenicias* (Eurípides)

SU «Финики́йки» (Еврипи́д)

2905 GB *Phormio* (Terence, −161)

F *Phormion* (Térence)

D *Phormio* (Terentius)

I *Phormio* (Terenzio)

E *Formio* (Terencio)

SU «Формиóн» (Терéнций)

2906 GB Phrygia (Bib.)

F la Phrygie (Bib.)

D Phrygien (Bib.)

I la Frigia (Bib.)

E Frigia (Bib.)

SU Фри́гия (библ.)

2907 GB *Physician of His Own Honour, The*
(Calderón de la Barca, 1635)

F *Le Médecin de son honneur*

D *Der Arzt seiner Ehre*

I *Medico del proprio onore*

E *El médico de su honra*

SU «Врач своéй чéсти» (Кальдерóн де ла
Бáрка)

2908 GB *Physicists, The* (Dürrenmatt, 1962)

F *Les Physiciens*

D *Die Physiker*

I *I fisici*

E *Los físicos*

SU «Фи́зики» (Дю́рренматт)

2909 GB Piacenza (Italy)

F Plaisance (Italie)

D Piacenza (Italien)

I Piacenza (Italia)

E Piacenza (Italia)

SU Пьячéнца (Итáлия)

2910 GB Picardy (France)

F la Picardie (France)

D die Picardie (Frankreich)

I la Piccardia (Francia)

E la Picardía (Francia)

SU Пикарди́я (Фрáнция)

2911 GB *Pickwick Papers, The* (Dickens, 1836–
7)

F *Les Aventures de M. Pickwick*

D *Die Pickwickier*

I *Il circolo Pickwick*

E *Los papeles póstumos del Club*
Pickwick

SU «Посмéртные запи́ски Пи́квикского
клу́ба» (Ди́ккенс)

2912 GB Picts, the (hist.)

F les Pictes (hist.)

D die Pikten (Gesch.)

I i pitti (st.)

E los pictos (hist.)

SU пи́кты (ист.)

2913 GB *Picture of Dorian Gray, The* (Wilde, 1891)
F *Le Portrait de Dorian Gray*
D *Das Bildnis des Dorian Gray*
I *Il ritratto di Dorian Gray*
E *El retrato de Dorian Gray*
SU «Портре́т До́риана Гре́я» (Уа́йльд)

2914 GB *Pictures from an Exhibition* (Mussorgsky, 1874)
F *Tableaux d'une exposition* (Moussorgski)
D *Gemälde aus einer Ausstellung* (Mussorgski)
I *Quadri di una esposizione* (Musorgskij)
E *Cuadros de una exposición* (Mussorgski)
SU «Карти́нки с вы́ставки» (Му́соргский)

2915 GB *Pictures of Travel* (Heine, 1826–31)
F *Tableaux de voyage*
D *Reisebilder*
I *Impressioni di viaggio*
E *Cuadros de viajes*
SU «Путевы́е карти́ны» (Ге́йне)

2916 GB Piedmont (Italy)
F le Piémont (Italie)
D Piemont (Italien)
I il Piemonte (Italia)
E el Piamonte (Italia)
SU Пьемо́нт (Ита́лия)

2917 GB Pierre Abelard (1079–1142)
F Pierre Abélard
D Peter Abelard
I Pietro Abelardo
E Pedro Abelardo
SU Пьер Абеля́р

2918 GB Pierrot
F Pierrot
D Pierrot
I Pedrolino
E Pierrot
SU Пьеро́

2919 GB *Piers Plowman* (Langland, 1362–1387)
F *La Vision de Piers le Laboureur*
D *Peter der Pflüger*
I *Pietro l'aratore*
E *Pedro el arador*
SU «Виде́ние о Петре́ Па́харе» (Ле́нгленд)

2920 GB *Pietà* [*The Deposition*] (Michelangelo, 1550–6)
F *Pietà* (Michel-Ange)
D *Pietà* (Michelangelo)
I *Pietà* (Michelangelo)
E *La Piedad* (Miguel Ángel)
SU «Пьета́» (Микела́нджело)

GB Pilate, Pontius→Pontius Pilate

2921 GB Pilgrim Fathers, the (XVII)
F les Pèlerins
D die Pilgerväter
I i padri pellegrini
E los padres peregrinos
SU «Отцы́-пилигри́мы»

2922 GB *Pilgrim Kamanita, The* [*Pilgrimen Kamanita*] (Gjellerup, 1906)
F *Le Pèlerin Kamanita*
D *Pilger Kamanita*
I *Il pellegrino Camanita*
E *El peregrino Camanita*
SU «Пилигри́м Камани́та» (Гье́ллеруп)

2923 GB *Pilgrim's Progress* (Bunyan, 1678, 1684)
F *Le Voyage du pèlerin*
D *Des Pilgers Wanderschaft*
I *Il viaggio del pellegrino*
E *Viaje del peregrino*
SU «Путеше́ствие пилигри́ма» (Бе́ньян)

2924 GB *Pillars of Society* [*Samfundets støtter*] (Ibsen, 1877)
F *Les Soutiens de la société*
D *Stützen der Gesellschaft*
I *Le colonne della società*
E *Los puntales de la sociedad*
SU «Столпы́ о́бщества» (Йбсен)

2925 GB Pindar (*518–438*)
F Pindare
D Pindar
I Pindaro
E Píndaro
SU Пинда́р

2926 GB *Pines of Rome, The* (Respighi, 1924)
F *Pins de Rome*
D *Die Pinien in Rom*
I *I pini di Roma*
E *Los pinos de Roma*
SU «Пи́нии Ри́ма» (Респи́ги)

GB *Pinocchio*→*Adventures of Pinocchio*

2927 GB *Pioneers, The* (Cooper, 1823)
    F *Les Pionniers*
    D *Die Pioniere*
    I *I pionieri*
    E *Los colonizadores*
    SU «Пионе́ры» (Ку́пер)

2928 GB *Pippa Passes* (Browning, 1841)
    F *Pippa passe*
    D *Pippa geht vorüber*
    I *Pippa passa*
    E *Pippa pasa*
    SU «Пи́ппа прохо́дит» (Бра́унинг)

2929 GB Piraeus (Greece)
    F Le Pirée (Grèce)
    D Piräus (Griechenland)
    I Il Pireo (Grecia)
    E El Pireo (Grecia)
    SU Пире́й (Гре́ция)

2930 GB Pirithous (myth.)
    F Pirithoos (myth.)
    D Pirithoos (myth.)
    I Piritoo (mit.)
    E Piritoo (mit.)
    SU Пирифо́й (миф.)

2931 GB Pisa (Italy)
    F Pise (Italie)
    D Pisa (Italien)
    I Pisa (Italia)
    E Pisa (Italia)
    SU Пи́за (Ита́лия)

2932 GB Pisces (astron.)
    F les Poissons (astron.)
    D die Fische (Astron.)
    I i Pesci (astr.)
    E Piscis (astr.)
    SU Ры́бы (астр.)

2933 GB Pisistratus (*612*–527)
    F Pisistrate
    D Pisistratus
    I Pisistrato
    E Pisístrato
    SU Писистра́т

2934 GB Pius (saint, pope)
    F Pie (saint, pape)
    D Pius (Heiliger, Papst)
    I Pio (santo, papa)
    E Pío (santo, papa)
    SU Пий (св., па́па ри́мский)

2935 GB *Place in the Sun, A* (Stevens, 1951)
    F *Une place au soleil*
    D *Ein Platz in der Sonne*
    I *Un posto al sole*
    E *Un lugar en el sol*
    SU «Ме́сто на со́лнце» (Сти́венс)

2936 GB *Plague, The* (Camus, 1947)
    F *La Peste*
    D *Die Pest*
    I *La peste*
    E *La peste*
    SU «Чума́» (Камю́)

2937 GB *Plain Dealer, The* (Wycherley, 1676)
    F *L'Homme de bonne foi*
    D *Der offen Handelnde*
    I *Il dabben uomo*
    E *El hombre sin doblez*
    SU «Прямоду́шный» (Уи́черли)

2938 GB *Plain Tales from the Hills* (Kipling, 1887)
    F *Simples Contes des collines*
    D *Schlichte Geschichten aus Indien*
    I *Racconti dalle colline*
    E *Sencillos cuentos de las colinas*
    SU «Просты́е расска́зы с гор» (Ки́плинг)

2939 GB Plate, the River (Argentina/Uruguay)
    F le Río de la Plata (Argentine/Uruguay)
    D der Platafluß (Argentinien/Uruguay)
    I il Río de la Plata (Argentina/Uruguay)
    E el Río de la Plata (Argentina/Uruguay)
    SU Ла-Пла́та (Аргенти́на/Уругва́й)

2940 GB Plato (*428–348*)
    F Platon
    D Platon
    I Platone
    E Platón
    SU Плато́н

2941 GB Plautus (*254*–184)
    F Plaute
    D Plautus
    I Plauto
    E Plauto
    SU Плавт

2942 GB *Playboy of the Western World, The* (Synge, 1907)
    F *Le Baladin du monde occidental*
    D *Ein wahrer Held*
    I *Il furfantello dell'Ovest*
    E *El danzarín del mundo occidental*
    SU «Удало́й молоде́ц – го́рдость За́пада» (Синг)

2943 GB Pleiades, the (myth., astron.)
      F   les Pléiades (myth., astron.)
      D   die Plejaden (myth., Astron.)
      I   le Pleiadi (mit., astr.)
      E   las Pléyades (mit., astr.)
      SU Плея́ды (миф., астр.)

2944 GB Pliny the Elder (23–79)
      F   Pline l'Ancien
      D   Plinius der Ältere
      I   Plinio il Vecchio
      E   Plinio el Viejo
      SU Пли́ний Ста́рший

2945 GB Pliny the Younger (*61–113*)
      F   Pline le Jeune
      D   Plinius der Jüngere
      I   Plinio il Giovane
      E   Plinio el Joven
      SU Пли́ний Мла́дший

2946 GB Plotinus (205–270)
      F   Plotin
      D   Plotin
      I   Plotino
      E   Plotino
      SU Плоти́н

2947 GB Plough, the (astron.)
      F   le Chariot (astron.)
      D   der Wagen (Astron.)
      I   il Carro (astr.)
      E   el Carro (astr.)
      SU Больша́я Медве́дица (астр.)

2948 GB *Plumed Serpent, The* (Lawrence, 1926)
      F   *Le Serpent à plumes*
      D   *Die gefiedete Schlange*
      I   *Il serpente piumato*
      E   *La serpiente emplumada*
      SU «Перна́тый змий» (Ло́ренс)

2949 GB Plutarch (*46–119*)
      F   Plutarque
      D   Plutarch
      I   Plutarco
      E   Plutarco
      SU Плута́рх

2950 GB Pluto (myth., astron.)
      F   Pluton (myth., astron.)
      D   Pluto (myth., Astron.)
      I   Plutone (mit., astr.)
      E   Plutón (mit., astr.)
      SU Плуто́н (миф., астр.)

2951 GB *Pnin* (Nabokov, 1957)
      F   *Pnin*
      D   *Pnin*
      I   *Pnin*
      E   *Pnin*
      SU «Пнин» (Набо́ков)

2952 GB *Poems Ancient and Modern* (Vigny, 1826)
      F   *Poèmes antiques et modernes*
      D   *Gedichte alten und neuen*
      I   *Poemi antichi e moderni*
      E   *Poemas antiguos y modernos*
      SU «Поэ́мы стари́нные и совреме́нные» (Виньи́)

2953 GB *Poems and Ballads* (Swinburne, 1866, 1878)
      F   *Poésies et Ballades*
      D   *Gedichte und Balladen*
      I   *Poesie e Ballate*
      E   *Poemas y baladas*
      SU «Стихи́ и балла́ды» (Су́йнберн)

2954 GB *Poems, Chiefly in the Scottish Dialect* (Burns, 1786)
      F   *Poèmes, la plupart en langage écossais*
      D   *Gedichte, hauptsächlich in schottischer Mundart*
      I   *Poesie, sopratutto in dialetto scozzese*
      E   *Cantos populares de Escocia*
      SU «Стихотворе́ния, напи́санные преиму́щественно на шотла́ндском диале́кте» (Бёрнс)

2955 GB *Poems in Prose* (Turgenev, 1878)
      F   *Poèmes en Prose* (Tourgueniev)
      D   *Gedichte in Prosa* (Turgenjew)
      I   *Poemi in prosa* (Turgenev)
      E   *Poemas en prosa* (Turgueniev)
      SU «Стихотворе́ния в про́зе» (Турге́нев)

2956 GB *Poems of Ossian*, the (Macpherson, 1765)
      F   *Poèmes d'Ossian*
      D   *Volksdichtungen von Ossian*
      I   *Canti d'Ossian*
      E   *Cantos de Osián*
      SU «Сочине́ния Оссиа́на» (Макфе́рсон)

2957 GB *Poet and Peasant* overture, the (Suppé, 1846)
      F   l'ouverture *Poète et Paysan*
      D   die Ouvertüre *Dichter und Bauer*
      I   l'ouverture *Poeta e contadino*
      E   la obertura *Poeta y aldeano*
      SU увертю́ра «Поэ́т и крестья́нин» (Зу́ппе)

GB   *Poetic Art, The→Art of Poetry*

2958   GB   *Poetics, The* (Aristotle, 335–322)
  F   *Poétique* (Aristote)
  D   *Poetik* (Aristoteles)
  I   *Poetica* (Aristotele)
  E   *Poética* (Aristóteles)
  SU   «Поэ́тика» (Аристо́тель)

2959   GB   *Poetry and Truth* (Goethe, 1811–4)
  F   *Poésie et vérité*
  D   *Dichtung und Wahrheit*
  I   *Poesia e verità*
  E   *Poesía y verdad*
  SU   «Поэ́зия и пра́вда» (Гёте)

2960   GB   *Poet's Love* (Schumann, 1840)
  F   *Les Amours du poète*
  D   *Dichterliebe*
  I   *Amore di poeta*
  E   *Amor de poeta*
  SU   «Любо́вь поэ́та» (Шу́ман)

2961   GB   *Poil de Carotte* [*Carrots*] (Duvivier, 1932)
  F   *Poil de Carotte*
  D   *Rotschopf*
  I   *Pelo di carota*
  E   *Pelirrojo*
  SU   «Ры́жик» (Дювивье́)

2962   GB   *Point Counter Point* (Huxley, 1928)
  F   *Contrepoint*
  D   *Kontrapunkt des Lebens*
  I   *Punto contro punto*
  E   *Contrapunto*
  SU   «Контрапу́нкт» (Ха́ксли)

2963   GB   Poland
  F   la Pologne
  D   Polen
  I   la Polonia
  E   Polonia
  SU   По́льша

2964   GB   Pole Star, the
  F   l'étoile polaire
  D   der Polarstern
  I   la stella polare
  E   la estrella polar
  SU   Поля́рная звезда́

2965   GB   Polybius (*200–118*)
  F   Polybe
  D   Polybios
  I   Polibio
  E   Polibio
  SU   Поли́бий

2966   GB   Polycarp (saint, II)
  F   Polycarpe (saint)
  D   Polykarp (Heiliger)
  I   Policarpo (santo)
  E   Policarpo (santo)
  SU   Полика́рп (св.)

2967   GB   Polydorus (myth.)
  F   Polydore (myth.)
  D   Polydoros (myth.)
  I   Polidoro (mit.)
  E   Polidoro (mit.)
  SU   Полидо́р (миф.)

2968   GB   *Polyeucte* (Corneille, 1641)
  F   *Polyeucte*
  D   *Polyeukt*
  I   *Poliuto*
  E   *Polyeucto*
  SU   «Полие́вкт» (Корне́ль)

2969   GB   Polynesia
  F   la Polynésie
  D   Polynesien
  I   la Polinesia
  E   Polinesia
  SU   Полине́зия

2970   GB   Polyphemus (myth.)
  F   Polyphème (myth.)
  D   Polyphemos (myth.)
  I   Polifemo (mit.)
  E   Polifemo (mit.)
  SU   Полифе́м (миф.)

2971   GB   Pomerania (hist.)
  F   la Poméranie (hist.)
  D   Pommern (Gesch.)
  I   la Pomerania (st.)
  E   Pomerania (hist.)
  SU   Помо́рье (ист.)

2972   GB   Pompeii (Italy)
  F   Pompéi (Italie)
  D   Pompeji (Italien)
  I   Pompei (Italia)
  E   Pompeya (Italia)
  SU   Помпе́и (Ита́лия)

2973   GB   Pompey (106–48)
  F   Pompée
  D   Pompejus
  I   Pompeo
  E   Pompeyo
  SU   Помпе́й

2974 GB Pontius Pilate (Bib., I)
F Ponce Pilate (Bib.)
D Pontius Pilatus (Bib.)
I Ponzio Pilato (Bib.)
E Poncio Pilato (Bib.)
SU Понтий Пилат (библ.)

2975 GB *Poor Bitos* (Anouilh, 1956)
F *Pauvre Bitos*
D *Der arme Bitos*
I *Povero Bitos*
E *Pobre Bitós*
SU «Бедняга Битóс» (Ануй)

2976 GB *Poor Folk* (Dostoievsky, 1846)
F *Les Pauvres Gens* (Dostoïevski)
D *Arme Leute* (Dostojewskij)
I *Povera gente* (Dostoevskij)
E *Pobres gentes* (Dostoievski)
SU «Бедные люди» (Достоевский)

2977 GB *Pope, The* (Maistre, 1819)
F *Du Pape*
D *Vom Papst*
I *Del Papa*
E *El Papa*
SU «О папе» (Местр)

2978 GB Poppaea (−I)
F Poppée
D Poppea
I Poppea
E Popea
SU Поппея

2979 GB Po (River), the (Italy)
F le Pô (Italie)
D der Po (Italien)
I il Po (Italia)
E el Po (Italia)
SU По (Италия)

2980 GB *Porgy and Bess* (Gershwin, 1935)
F *Porgy and Bess*
D *Porgy and Bess*
I *Porgy and Bess*
E *Porgy and Bess*
SU «Порги и Бесс» (Гершвин)

2981 GB Porphyry (233–*301*)
F Porphyre
D Porphyrios
I Porfirio
E Porfirio
SU Порфирий

2982 GB Port au Prince (Haiti)
F Port-au-Prince (Haïti)
D Port-au-Prince (Haiti)
I Port-au-Prince (Haiti)
E Puerto Príncipe (Haití)
SU Порт-о-Пренс (Гаити)

2983 GB *Portrait in a Mirror* (Morgan, 1944)
F *Portrait dans un miroir*
D *Das Bildnis*
I *Ritratto allo specchio*
E *Relato en un espejo*
SU «Портрет в зеркале» (Морган)

2984 GB *Portrait of a Lady, The* (James, 1881)
F *Un portrait de femme*
D *Das Bildnis einer Dame*
I *Ritratto di signora*
E *Retrato de una dama*
SU «Женский портрет» (Джеймс)

2985 GB *Portrait of Jennie* (Dieterle, 1948)
F *Le Portrait de Jennie*
D *Jenny*
I *Il ritratto di Jennie*
E *Jennie*
SU «Портрет Дженни» (Дитерле)

2986 GB *Portrait of the Artist as a Young Dog* (Thomas, 1940)
F *Portrait de l'artiste en jeune chien*
D *Porträt des Künstlers als junger Dachs*
I *Ritratto dell'artista da cucciolo*
E *Retrato del artista de calavera*
SU «Портрет художника – молодого пса» (Томас)

2987 GB *Portrait of the Artist as a Young Man, A* (Joyce, 1916)
F *Dédalus, portrait de l'artiste par lui-même*
D *Jugendbildnis des Dichters*
I *Ritratto dell'artista giovane*
E *Retrato del artista adolescente*
SU «Портрет художника в юности» (Джойс)

2988 GB *Port-Royal* (Montherlant, 1954)
F *Port-Royal*
D *Port-Royal*
I *Port-Royal*
E *Port-Royal*
SU «Пор-Рояль» (Монтерлан)

2989   GB   Port Said (Egypt)
     F   Port-Saïd (Égypte)
     D   Port Said (Ägypten)
     I   Porto Said (Egitto)
     E   Port Said (Egipto)
     SU   Порт-Сайд (Егúпет)

2990   GB   Portugal
     F   le Portugal
     D   Portugal
     I   il Portogallo
     E   Portugal
     SU   Португáлия

2991   GB   Portuguese East Africa (hist.)
     F   l'Afrique-Orientale Portugaise (hist.)
     D   Portugiesisch-Ost-Afrika (Gesch.)
     I   l'Africa Orientale Portoghese (st.)
     E   África oriental Portuguesa (hist.)
     SU   Португáльская Востóчная Áфрика
         (ист.)

2992   GB   Portuguese Guinea (hist.)
     F   la Guinée-Portugaise (hist.)
     D   Portugiesisch-Guinea (Gesch.)
     I   la Guinea Portoghese (st.)
     E   Guinea Portuguesa (hist.)
     SU   Португáльская Гвинéя (ист.)

2993   GB   Poseidon (myth.)
     F   Poséidon (myth.)
     D   Poseidon (myth.)
     I   Poseidone (mit.)
     E   Poseidón (mit.)
     SU   Посейдóн (миф.)

2994   GB   *Poseidon Adventure, The* (Neame,
        1972)
     F   *L'Aventure du Poséidon*
     D   *Die Höllenfahrt der Poseidon*
     I   *L'avventura del Poseidone*
     E   *La aventura del Poseidón*
     SU   «Приключéние с „Посейдóном"» (Ним)

2995   GB   *Possessed, The* (Dostoievsky, 1871–2)
     F   *Les Possédés* (Dostoïevski)
     D   *Die Dämonen* (Dostojewskij)
     I   *I demoni* (Dostoevskij)
     E   *Los endemoniados* (Dostoievski)
     SU   «Бéсы» (Достоéвский)

2996   GB   *Postilion of Longjumeau, The* (Adam,
        1836)
     F   *Le Postillon de Longjumeau*
     D   *Der Postillion von Lonjumeau*
     I   *Il postiglione di Longjumeau*
     E   *El postillón de Longjumeau*
     SU   «Почтальóн из Лонжюмó» (Адáн)

2997   GB   Potsdam Conference, the (1945)
     F   la conférence de Potsdam
     D   das Potsdamer Abkommen
     I   la conferenza di Potsdam
     E   la conferencia de Potsdam
     SU   Потсдáмская конферéнция

2998   GB   *Power and the Glory, The* (Greene,
        1940)
     F   *La Puissance et la Gloire*
     D   *Die Kraft und die Herrlichkeit*
     I   *Il potere e la gloria*
     E   *El poder y la gloria*
     SU   «Власть и слáва» (Грин)

2999   GB   *Power of Darkness, The* (Tolstoy,
        1888)
     F   *La Puissance des ténèbres* (Tolstoï)
     D   *Macht der Finsternis* (Tolstoj)
     I   *La potenza delle tenebre* (Tolstoy)
     E   *El poder de las tinieblas* (Tolstoi)
     SU   «Власть тьмы» (Толстóй)

3000   GB   Poznan (Poland)
     F   Poznan (Pologne)
     D   Posen (Polen)
     I   Poznan (Polonia)
     E   Poznan (Polonia)
     SU   Пóзнань (ж.) (Пóльша)

3001   GB   Prague (Czechoslovakia)
     F   Prague (Tchécoslovaquie)
     D   Prag (Tscechoslovakei)
     I   Praga (Cecoslovacchia)
     E   Praga (Checoslovaquia)
     SU   Прáга (Чехословáкия)

3002   GB   *Prairie, The* (Cooper, 1827)
     F   *La Prairie*
     D   *Die Prärie*
     I   *La prateria*
     E   *La pampa*
     SU   «Прéрия» (Кýпер)

3003   GB   *Praise of Folly, The* [*Encomium
        moriae, seu laus stultitiae*] (Erasmus,
        1509)
     F   *Éloge de la folie* (Erasme)
     D   *Lob der Torheit* (Erasmus)
     I   *Elogio della pazzia* (Erasmo)
     E   *Elogio de la locura* (Erasmo)
     SU   «Похвáла Глупости» (Эрáзм
        Роттердáмский)

3004 GB Praxiteles (−IV)
    F Praxitèle
    D Praxiteles
    I Prassitele
    E Praxiteles
    SU Пракси́тель

3005 GB *Prelude to "The Afternoon of a Faun"*
    (Debussy, 1894)
    F *Prélude à "l'Après-midi d'un faune"*
    D *Präludium an "L'Après-midi d'un faune"*
    I *Prélude à l'après-midi d'un faune*
    E *Preludio a la siesta de un fauno*
    SU «Прелю́дия к послеполу́дню фа́вна» (Дебюсси́)

3006 GB Premonstratensians, the (rel.)
    F les Prémontrés (relig.)
    D die Prämonstratensen (relig.)
    I i premostratensi (relig.)
    E los premonstratenses (relig.)
    SU премонстра́нты (рел.)

3007 GB Presbyterians, the (rel.)
    F les presbytériens (relig.)
    D die Presbyterianen (relig.)
    I i presbiteri (relig.)
    E los presbitarianos (relig.)
    SU пресвитериа́нцы (рел.)

3008 GB *Pretenders, The* [*Kongsemnerne*]
    (Ibsen, 1863)
    F *Les Prétendants à la couronne*
    D *Kronprätendenten*
    I *I pretendenti al trono*
    E *Los pretendientes de la corona*
    SU «Борьба́ за пре́стол» (И́бсен)

3009 GB Priam (myth.)
    F Priam (myth.)
    D Priamus (myth.)
    I Priamo (mit.)
    E Príamo (mit.)
    SU Приа́м (миф.)

3010 GB Priapus (myth.)
    F Priape (myth.)
    D Priapus (myth.)
    I Priapo (mit.)
    E Príapo (mit.)
    SU Приа́п (миф.)

3011 GB *Pride and Prejudice* (Austen, 1813)
    F *Orgueil et préjugé*
    D *Stolz und Vorurteil*
    I *Orgoglio e pregiudizio*
    E *Orgullo y prejuicio*
    SU «Го́рдость и предупрежде́ние» (О́стин)

3012 GB *Prime of Miss Jean Brodie, The* (Spark, 1961)
    F *Le Bel Âge de Miss Brodie*
    D *Die Lehrerin*
    I *Gli anni in fiore della signorina Brodie*
    E *La flor de la señorita Brodie*
    SU «Расцве́т мисс Джин Бро́ди» (Спарк)

3013 GB *Prince, The* (Machiavelli, *1513*)
    F *Le Prince* (Machiavel)
    D *Der Fürst* (Machiavelli)
    I *Il Principe* (Machiavelli)
    E *El Príncipe* (Maquiavelo)
    SU «Князь» (Макиаве́лли)

3014 GB *Prince and the Pauper, The* (Twain, 1881)
    F *Le Prince et le mendiant*
    D *Prinz und Betteljunge*
    I *Il principe e il povero*
    E *El príncipe y el pobre*
    SU «Принц и ни́щий» (Твен)

3015 GB Prince Edward Island (Canada)
    F l'île de Prince-Édouard (Canada)
    D Prinz-Eduard-Insel (Kanada)
    I l'isola Principe Edoardo (Canada)
    E la isla del Príncipe Eduardo (Canadá)
    SU о́стров При́нца Э́дуарда (Кана́да)

3016 GB *Prince Igor* (Borodin, 1889)
    F *Prince Igor* (Borodine)
    D *Fürst Igor* (Borodin)
    I *Il principe Igor* (Borodin)
    E *El príncipe Igor* (Borodín)
    SU «Князь И́горь» (Бороди́н)

3017 GB *Prince Otto* (Stevenson, 1885)
    F *Le Prince Otto*
    D *Fürst Otto*
    I *Il principe Otto*
    E *El príncipe Otón*
    SU «Принц О́тто» (Сти́венсон)

3018 GB *Princess and The Pea, The* [*Prinsessen på aerten*] (Andersen, 1835)
    F *La Princesse et le Petit Pois*
    D *Die Prinzessin auf der Erbse*
    I *Principessa sopra un pisello*
    E *La Princesa y el guisante*
    SU «Принце́сса на горо́шине» (А́ндерсен)

3019 GB *Princess of Clèves, The* (La Fayette, 1678)
    F *La Princesse de Clèves*
    D *Die Prinzessin von Clèves*
    I *La principessa di Clèves*
    E *La princesa de Clèves*
    SU «Принце́сса Кле́вская» (Лафайе́т)

3020 GB *Principia Mathematica* ["The Principles
of Mathematics"] (Russell, 1910–13)
F *Principia Mathematica*
D *Die Grundsätze der Mathematik*
I *Principia Mathematica*
E *Principia mathematica*
SU «Principia Mathematica» (Рáссел)

3021 GB *Principia Philosophiae* [*Principles of
Philosophy*] (Descartes, 1644)
F *Principes de la philosophie* (Descartes)
D *Grundlagen der Philosophie*
(Descartes)
I *Principi della filosofia* (Cartesio)
E *Principios de la filosofía* (Descartes)
SU «Начáла филосóфии» (Декáрт)

3022 GB *Principles of a New Science Regarding
the General Nature of Nations, The*
(Vico, 1725)
F *Principes d'une science nouvelle relative
à la nature commune des nations*
D *Grundzüge einer neuen Wissenschaft
über die gemeinschaftliche Natur der
Völker*
I *Principi di una scienza nuova d'intorno
alla comune natura delle nazioni*
E *Principios de una ciencia nueva acerca
de la naturaleza común de los naciones*
SU «Основáния нóвой наýки об óбщей
прирóде нáций» (Викó)

3023 GB *Principles of Human Knowledge*
(Berkeley, 1710)
F *Traité sur les principes de la
connaissance*
D *Die Prinzipien des menschlichen
Wissens*
I *Trattato sui principi della conoscenza
umana*
E *Tratado sobre los principios del
conocimiento humano*
SU «Трактáт о начáлах человéческого
знáния» (Бéркли)

3024 GB *Principles of Political Economy, The*
(Mill, 1822)
F *Les Principes d'économie politique*
D *Die Grundsätze der politischen ·
Ökonomie*
I *Principi di economia politica*
E *Principios de economía política*
SU «Элемéнты политической экономии»
(Милль)

3025 GB *Prisoner, The* (Dallapiccola, 1950)
F *Le Prisonnier*
D *Der Gefangene*
I *Il prigioniero*
E *El prisionero*
SU «Заключённый» (Даллапи́ккола)

3026 GB *Prisoner of Chillon, The* (Byron, 1816)
F *Le Prisonnier de Chillon*
D *Der Gefangene von Chillon*
I *Il prigioniero di Chillon*
E *El prisionero de Chillon*
SU «Шильóнский ýзник» (Бáйрон)

3027 GB *Prisoner of the Caucasus, The*
(Pushkin, 1822)
F *Le Prisonnier du Caucase* (Pouchkine)
D *Der Gefangene im Kaukasus*
(Puschkin)
I *Il prigioniero del Caucaso* (Puškin)
E *El prisionero del Cáucaso* (Puschkin)
SU «Кавкáзский плéнник» (Пýшкин)

3028 GB *Prisoner of Zenda, The* (Hope, 1894)
F *Le Prisonnier de Zenda*
D *Der Gefangene von Zenda*
I *Il prigioniero di Zenda*
E *El prisionero de Zenda*
SU «Зéндский ýзник» (Хóуп)

3029 GB *Private Life of Henry VIII, The*
(Korda, 1932)
F *La Vie privée d'Henri VIII*
D *Das Privatleben Heinrichs VIII*
I *Le sei mogli di Enrico VIII*
E *La vida privada de Enrique VIII*
SU «Чáстная жизнь Гéнриха VIII»
(Кóрда)

3030 GB Privy Council, the (London)
F le Conseil privé (Londres)
D der Geheime Rat (London)
I il Consiglio privato (Londra)
E el Consejo privado (Londres)
SU «Тáйный совéт» (Лóндон)

3031 GB Proclus (*410–485*)
F Proclus
D Proklos
I Proclo
E Proclo
SU Прокл

3032 GB Procrustes (myth.)
F Procruste (myth.)
D Prokrustes (myth.)
I Procuste (mit.)
E Procusto (mit.)
SU Прокрýст (миф.)

3033 GB Prodigal Son, the (Bib., art)
      F   l'enfant prodigue (Bib., art)
      D   der verlorene Sohn (Bib., Kunst)
      I   il figlio prodigo (Bib., arte)
      E   el hijo pródigo (Bib., arte)
      SU блу́дный сын (библ., иск.)

3034 GB *Prodigious Adventures of Tartarin of*
          Tarascon, The (Daudet, 1872)
      F   *Les Aventures prodigieuses de Tartarin*
          de Tarascon
      D   *Die wunderbaren Abenteuer des*
          Tartarin de Tarascon
      I   *Tartarino di Tarascona*
      E   *Tartarín de Tarascón*
      SU «Необыча́йные приключе́ния
          Тартаре́на из Тараско́на» (Доде́)

3035 GB *Professor Unrat* (Mann, 1905)
      F   *Professeur Unrat*
      D   *Professor Unrat*
      I   *Il professore Unrat*
      E   *El profesor Unrat*
      SU «Учи́тель гнус» (Манн)

3036 GB Prohibition, the (USA, 1919–33)
      F   la Prohibition (USA)
      D   die Prohibition (USA)
      I   il proibizionismo (USA)
      E   la prohibición (USA)
      SU запреще́ние прода́жи спиртны́х
          напи́тков (США)

3037 GB Prometheus (myth.)
      F   Prométhée (myth.)
      D   Prometheus (myth.)
      I   Prometeo (mit.)
      E   Prometeo (mit.)
      SU Промете́й (миф.)

3038 GB *Prometheus Bound* [*Prometheus*
          desmotes] (Aeschylus, –467)
      F   *Prométhée enchaîné* (Eschyle)
      D   *Der gefesselte Prometheus* (Aischylos)
      I   *Prometeo incatenato* (Eschilo)
      E   *Prometeo encadenado* (Esquilo)
      SU «Прико́ванный Промете́й» (Эсхи́л)

3039 GB *Prometheus Unbound* (Shelley, 1820)
      F   *Prométhée délivré*
      D   *Der entfesselte Prometheus*
      I   *Prometeo liberato*
      E   *Prometeo liberado*
      SU «Освобождённый Промете́й» (Шёлли)

3040 GB Promised Land, the (Bib.)
      F   la Terre promise (Bib.)
      D   das gelobte Land (Bib.)
      I   la terra promessa (Bib.)
      E   la tierra de promisión (Bib.)
      SU земля́ обетова́нная (библ.)

3041 GB Propertius (−I)
      F   Properce
      D   Properz
      I   Properzio
      E   Propercio
      SU Проперций

3042 GB *Prophet, The* (Meyerbeer, 1849)
      F   *Le Prophète*
      D   *Der Prophet*
      I   *Il profeta*
      E   *El profeta*
      SU «Проро́к» (Мейербе́р)

3043 GB Proserpine (myth.)
      F   Proserpine (myth.)
      D   Proserpina (myth.)
      I   Proserpina (mit.)
      E   Proserpina (mit.)
      SU Прозерпи́на (миф.)

3044 GB *Protagoras* (Plato, −IV)
      F   *Protagoras* (Platon)
      D   *Protagoras* (Platon)
      I   *Protagora* (Platone)
      E   *Protágoras* (Platón)
      SU «Протаго́р» (Плато́н)

3045 GB Protestants, the (rel., hist.)
      F   les protestants (relig., hist.)
      D   die Protestanten (relig., Gesch.)
      I   i protestanti (relig., st.)
      E   los protestantes (relig., hist.)
      SU протеста́нты (рел., ист.)

3046 GB Proteus (myth.)
      F   Protée (myth.)
      D   Proteus (myth.)
      I   Proteo (mit.)
      E   Proteo (mit.)
      SU Проте́й (миф.)

3047 GB Provence (France)
      F   la Provence (France)
      D   die Provence (Frankreich)
      I   la Provenza (Francia)
      E   Provenza (Francia)
      SU Прова́нс (Фра́нция)

3048 GB Proverbs (Bib.)
F les Proverbes (Bib.)
D die Sprüche Salomonis (Bib.)
I i Proverbi (Bib.)
E el Libro de los Proverbios (Bib.)
SU «Кни́га при́тчей Соломо́новых» (библ.)

3049 GB *Provincial Letters* (Pascal, 1656–7)
F *Les Provinciales*
D *Briefe an einen Provinzialen*
I *Le provinciali*
E *Las cartas provinciales*
SU «Пи́сьма к провинциа́лу» (Паска́ль)

3050 GB Prussia (hist.)
F la Prusse (hist.)
D Preußen (Gesch.)
I la Prussia (st.)
E Prusia (hist.)
SU Пру́ссия (ист.)

3051 GB Psalms, the (Bib.)
F les Psaumes (Bib.)
D die Psalmen (Bib.)
I i Salmi (Bib.)
E los Salmos (Bib.)
SU Псалты́рь (ж.) (библ.)

3052 GB *Psalmus Hungaricus* [*Hungarian Psalm*] (Kodály, 1923)
F *Psalmus Hungaricus*
D *Psalmus hungaricus*
I *Psalmus hungaricus*
E *Psalmus hungaricus*
SU «Венге́рский псало́м» (Ко́дай)

3053 GB Psyche (myth.)
F Psyché (myth.)
D Psyche (myth.)
I Psiche (mit.)
E Psique (mit.)
SU Психе́я (миф.)

3054 GB *Psycho* (Hitchcock, 1960)
F *Psychose*
D *Psycho*
I *Psycho*
E *Psicosis*
SU «Пси́хо» (Хи́чкок)

3055 GB *Psychology of Art, The* (Malraux, 1948 –50)
F *La Psychologie de l'art*
D *Psychologie der Kunst*
I *Psicologia dell'arte*
E *La psicología del arte*
SU «Психоло́гия иску́сства» (Мальро́)

3056 GB Ptolemy (king)
F Ptolémée (roi)
D Ptolemäus (König)
I Tolomeo (re)
E Ptolomeo (rey)
SU Птолеме́й (царь)

3057 GB Publius (Roman name)
F Publius (nom romain)
D Publius (Römername)
I Publio (nome romano)
E Publio (nombre romano)
SU Пу́блий (древнери́мское и́мя)

3058 GB *Pudd'nhead Wilson* (Twain, 1894)
F *Pudd'nhead Wilson*
D *Dummkopf Wilson*
I *Wilson lo svitato*
E *Cabezahueca Wilson*
SU «Простофи́ля Ви́льсон» (Твен)

3059 GB Puerto Rico
F Porto Rico
D Puerto Rico
I Portorico
E Puerto Rico
SU Пуэ́рто-Ри́ко

3060 GB Punch
F Polochinelle
D Kasper
I Pulcinella
E Polichinela
SU Петру́шка

3061 GB Punic Wars, the (III–II)
F les guerres puniques
D die punischen Kriege
I le guerre puniche
E las guerras púnicas
SU пуни́ческие во́йны

3062 GB *Punishments* (Hugo, 1853)
F *Les Châtiments*
D *Züchtigungen*
I *Castighi*
E *Los castigos*
SU «Возме́здие» (Гюго́)

3063 GB *Punishment without Revenge* (Lope de Vega, 1635)
F *Le Châtiment sans vengeance*
D *Strafe ohne Rache*
I *Il castigo senza vendetta*
E *El castigo sin venganza*
SU «Наказа́ние не мще́ние» (Ве́га Ка́рпьо)

3064 GB Puritans, the (rel., hist.)
F les puritains (relig., hist.)
D die Puritaner (relig., Gesch.)
I i puritani (relig., st.)
E los puritanos (relig., hist.)
SU пуритáне (рел., ист.)

3065 GB *Puritans of Scotland, The* (Bellini, 1835)
F *Les Puritains*
D *Die Puritaner*
I *I puritani*
E *Los puritanos*
SU «Пуритáне» (Беллúни)

3066 GB Pushkin (1799–1837)
F Pouchkine
D Puschkin
I Puškin
E Puschkin
SU Пýшкин

3067 GB *Puss in Boots* (Perrault, 1697)
F *Le Chat botté*
D *Der gestiefelte Kater*
I *Il gatto con gli stivali*
E *El gato con botas*
SU «Кот в сапогáх» (Перрó)

3068 GB Pygmalion (myth.; + Shaw, 1913)
F Pygmalion (myth.)
D Pygmalion (myth.)
I Pigmalione (mit.)
E Pigmalión (mit.)
SU Пигмалиóн (миф., + Шóу)

3069 GB Pyramids of Egypt, the
F les Pyramides d'Égypte
D die Pyramiden von Ägypten
I i Piramidi d'Egitto
E las Pirámides de Egipto
SU египетские пирамúды

3070 GB Pyrenees, the (France/Spain)
F les Pyrénées (f.) (France/Espagne)
D die Pyrenäen (Frankreich/Spanien)
I i Pirenei (Francia/Spagna)
E los Pirineos (Francia/España)
SU Пиренéи (м.) (Фрáнция/Испáния)

3071 GB Pyrrha (myth.)
F Pyrrha (myth.)
D Pyrrha (myth.)
I Pirra (mit.)
E Pirra (mit.)
SU Пúрра (миф.)

3072 GB Pyrrhus (myth.)
F Pyrrhos (myth.)
D Pyrrhus (myth.)
I Pirro (mit.)
E Pirro (mit.)
SU Пирр (миф.)

3073 GB Pythagoras (−II)
F Pythagore
D Pythagoras
I Pitagora
E Pitágoras
SU Пифагóр

3074 GB Pythian Games, the (hist.)
F les Jeux Pythiques (hist.)
D die Pythischen Spiele (Gesch.)
I i giochi pitici (st.)
E los Juegos Píticos (hist.)
SU пифийские úгры (ист.)

3075 GB Python (myth.)
F Python (myth.)
D Python (myth.)
I Pitone (mit.)
E Pitón (mit.)
SU пифóн (миф.)

Q

3076	GB	Qatar
	F	le Qatar
	D	Qatar
	I	il Qatar
	E	Katar
	SU	Ка́тар

3077	GB	*Quai des Brumes* [*Port of Mists*] (Carné, 1938)
	F	*Quai des brumes*
	D	*Hafen im Nebel*
	I	*Il porto delle nebbie*
	E	*Puerto de las brumas*
	SU	«На́бережная тума́нов» (Карне́)

3078	GB	Quakers, the (rel.)
	F	les Quakers (relig.)
	D	die Quäker (relig.)
	I	i quaccheri (relig.)
	E	los cuáqueros (relig.)
	SU	квáкеры (рел.)

3079	GB	Quebec (Canada)
	F	Québec (Canada)
	D	Quebec (Kanada)
	I	Quebec (Canada)
	E	Quebec (Canadá)
	SU	Квебе́к (Канáда)

3080	GB	*Queen After Death* (Montherlant, 1942)
	F	*La Reine morte*
	D	*Die tote Königin*
	I	*La regina morta*
	E	*La reina muerta*
	SU	«Мёртвая короле́ва» (Монтерлáн)

3081	GB	Queen Elizabeth Islands, the (Canada)
	F	les îles de la Reine-Élisabeth (Canada)
	D	die Königen-Elisabeth-Inseln (Kanada)
	I	le isole Regina Elisabetta (Canada)
	E	las islas de la Reina Isabel (Canadá)
	SU	островá Короле́вы Елизаве́ты (Канáда)

3082	GB	*Queen Mab* (Shelley, 1812–3)
	F	*La Reine Mab*
	D	*Feenkönigin*
	I	*La regina Mab*
	E	*La Reina Mab*
	SU	«Короле́ва Маб» (Шéлли)

3083	GB	Queen Maud Land (Antarctica)
	F	la terre de la Reine-Maud (Antarctique)
	D	Königin-Maud-Land (Antarktika)
	I	la terra Regina Maud (Antartide)
	E	la tierra de la Reina Maud (Antártida)
	SU	Земля́ Короле́вы Мод (Антаркти́да)

3084	GB	*Queen of Spades, The* (Pushkin, 1833; Tchaikovsky, 1890)
	F	*La Dame de Pique* (Pouchkine, Tchaikovski)
	D	*Pique Dame* (Puschkin, Tschaikowskij)
	I	*La dama di picche* (Puškin, Čajkovskij)
	E	*La dama de los tres naipes* (Puschkin, Tchaikovski)
	SU	«Пи́ковая дáма» (Пýшкин, Чайкóвский)

3085 GB Queensland (Australia)
F le Queensland (Australie)
D Queensland (Australien)
I il Queensland (Australia)
E Queensland (Australia)
SU Квинсленд (Австра́лия)

3086 GB *Quentin Durward* (Scott, 1823)
F *Quentin Durward*
D *Quentin Durward*
I *Quentin Durward*
E *Quentin Durward*
SU «Кве́нтин До́рвард» (Скотт)

3087 GB *Quiet American, The* (Greene, 1956)
F *Un Américain bien tranquille*
D *Der stille Amerikaner*
I *Il tranquillo americano*
E *Un americano impasible*
SU «Ти́хий америка́нец» (Грин)

3088 GB Quintilian (35–96)
F Quintilien
D Quintilianus
I Quintiliano
E Quintiliano
SU Квинтилиа́н

3089 GB Quintus (Roman name)
F Quinte (nom romain)
D Quintus (Römername)
I Quinto (nome romano)
E Quinto (nombre romano)
SU Квинт (древнери́мское и́мя)

3090 GB Quirinal Hill, the (Rome)
F le mont Quirinal (Rome)
D der Quirinalis (Rom)
I il Quirinale (Roma)
E il monte Quirinal (Roma)
SU Квирина́л (Рим)

3091 GB *Quo Vadis?* ["Where are You Going?"] (Sienkiewicz, 1895; Le Roy, 1951)
F *Quo vadis?*
D *Quo vadis?*
I *Quo vadis?*
E *Quo vadis?*
SU «Ка́мо гряде́ши?» (Сенке́вич, Ле Рой)

GB Qur'an→Koran

R

3092   GB   Rachel (Bib.)
      F   Rachel (Bib.)
      D   Rahel (Bib.)
      I   Rachele (Bib.)
      E   Raquel (Bib.)
      SU   Рахи́ль (библ.)

3093   GB   *Raft of the Medusa, The* (Géricault, 1818–19)
      F   *Le Radeau de la "Méduse"*
      D   *Das Floß der Medusa*
      I   *La zattera della Medusa*
      E   *La balsa de la Medusa*
      SU   «Плот Меду́зы» (Жерико́)

3094   GB   Ragusa (Italy)
      F   Raguse (Italie)
      D   Ragusa (Italien)
      I   Ragusa (Italia)
      E   Ragusa (Italia)
      SU   Рагу́за (Ита́лия)

3095   GB   *Raiders of the Lost Ark* (Spielberg, 1981)
      F   *Les Aventuriers de l'arche perdue*
      D   *Jäger des verlorenen Schatzes*
      I   *I predatori dell'arca perduta*
      E   *En busca de la arca perdida*
      SU   «В по́исках поте́рянного ковче́га» (Спи́лберг)

3096   GB   *Rainbow, The* (Lawrence, 1915)
      F   *L'Arc-en-ciel*
      D   *Der Regenbogen*
      I   *L'arcobaleno*
      E   *El arco iris*
      SU   «Ра́дуга» (Ло́ренс)

3097   GB   *Rain, Steam and Speed* (Turner, 1844)
      F   *Pluie, vapeur et vitesse*
      D   *Regen, Dampf und Geschwindigkeit*
      I   *Pioggia, vapore e velocità*
      E   *Lluvia, vapor y velocidad*
      SU   «Дождь, пар и ско́рость» (Тёрнер)

3098   GB   *Rake's Progress, The* (Hogarth, 1735; Stravinsky, 1951)
      F   *La Carrière du roué* (Hogarth, Stravinski)
      D   *Der Weg des Wüstlings* (Hogarth, Strawinski)
      I   *La carriera di un libertino* (Hogarth, Stravinskij)
      E   *La carrera de un libertino* (Hogarth, Stravinski)
      SU   «Карье́ра мо́та» (Хо́гарт, Страви́нский)

3099   GB   *Ralph Roister Doister* (Udall, 1553)
      F   *Ralph Roister Doister*
      D   *Ralph Prahlhans*
      I   *Ralph Roister Doister*
      E   *Ralph Roister Doister*
      SU   «Ральф Ро́йстер До́йстер» (Ю́далл)

3100   GB   Rameses (Bib.)
      F   Ramesès (Bib.)
      D   Ramses (Bib.)
      I   Ramesse (Bib.)
      E   Ramsés (Bib.)
      SU   Рамсе́с (библ.)

3101   GB   Rangoon (Burma)
      F   Rangoon (Birmanie)
      D   Rangun (Birma)
      I   Rangoon (Birmania)
      E   Rangún (Birmania)
      SU   Рангу́н (Би́рма)

3102 GB *Rape of Lucrece, The* (Shakespeare, 1594)
    F *Le Viol de Lucrèce*
    D *Lucretia*
    I *Lucrezia violata*
    E *Lucrecia violada*
    SU «Лукре́ция» (Шекспи́р)

3103 GB *Rape of the Lock, The* (Pope, 1712, 1714)
    F *La Boucle de cheveux enlevée*
    D *Der Lockenraub*
    I *Il riccio rapito*
    E *El rizo robado*
    SU «Похище́ние ло́кона» (Поп)

3104 GB *Rape of the Sabines, The* (art)
    F *L'Enlèvement des Sabines* (art)
    D *Der Raub der Sabinerinnen* (Kunst)
    I *Il ratto delle sabine* (arte)
    E *El rapto de las sabinas* (arte)
    SU «Похище́ние сабиня́нок» (иск.)

3105 GB Raphael (1483–1520)
    F Raphaël
    D Raffael
    I Raffaello
    E Rafael
    SU Рафаэ́ль Са́нти

3106 GB *Raven, The* (Poe, 1845)
    F *Le Corbeau*
    D *Der Rabe*
    I *Il corvo*
    E *El cuervo*
    SU «Во́рон» (По)

3107 GB Ravenna (Italy)
    F Ravenne (Italie)
    D Ravenna (Italien)
    I Ravenna (Italia)
    E Ravena (Italia)
    SU Раве́нна (Ита́лия)

3108 GB *Razor's Edge, The* (Maugham, 1944)
    F *Le Fil du rasoir*
    D *Auf Messers Schneide*
    I *Sul filo del rasoio*
    E *El filo de la navaja*
    SU «Острие́ бри́твы» (Мо́эм)

3109 GB *Rear Window* (Hitchcock, 1954)
    F *Fenêtre sur cour*
    D *Das Fenster zum Hof*
    I *La finestra sul cortile*
    E *La ventana indiscreta*
    SU «Окно́ с ви́дом на двор» (Хи́чкок)

3110 GB Rebecca (Bib.)
    F Rébecca (Bib.)
    D Rebekka (Bib.)
    I Rebecca (Bib.)
    E Rebeca (Bib.)
    SU Реве́кка (библ.)

3111 GB *Rebel, The* (Camus, 1951)
    F *L'Homme révolté*
    D *Der Mensch in der Revolte*
    I *L'uomo in rivolta*
    E *El hombre se rebela*
    SU «Взбунтова́вшийся челове́к» (Камю́)

3112 GB *Rebel Without a Cause* (Ray, 1955)
    F *La Fureur de vivre*
    D *. . . denn sie wissen nicht, was sie tun*
    I *Gioventù bruciata*
    E *Rebelde sin causa*
    SU «Бунта́рь без причи́ны» (Рей)

3113 GB *Red and the Black, The* (Stendhal, 1830)
    F *Le Rouge et le Noir*
    D *Rot und Schwarz*
    I *Il rosso e il nero*
    E *Rojo y negro*
    SU «Кра́сное и чёрное» (Стенда́ль)

3114 GB *Red Badge of Courage, The* (Crane, 1895)
    F *La Conquête du courage*
    D *Das rote Siegel*
    I *Il segno rosso del coraggio*
    E *La roja insignia del valor*
    SU «А́лый знак до́блести» (Крейн)

3115 GB *Redburn* (Melville, 1849)
    F *Redburn*
    D *Redburn*
    I *Redburn*
    E *Redburn*
    SU «Ре́дберн» (Ме́лвилл)

3116 GB Red Cross, the
    F la Croix-Rouge
    D das Rote Kreuz
    I la Croce rossa
    E la Cruz roja
    SU Кра́сный Крест

3117 GB *Redgauntlet* (Scott, 1824)
    F *Redgauntlet*
    D *Redgauntlet*
    I *Redgauntlet*
    E *Redgauntlet*
    SU «Редго́нтлет» (Скотт)

3118 GB *Red Riding-Hood (Little Red*
              Riding-Hood) (Perrault, 1697)
        F *Le Petit Chaperon rouge*
        D *Rotkäppchen*
        I *Cappuccetto rosso*
        E *Caperucita Roja*
        SU «Кра́сная ша́почка» (Перро́)

3119 GB Red River, the (Vietnam)
        F le fleuve Rouge (Viêt-Nam)
        D der Rote Fluß (Vietnam)
        I il fiume Rosso (Vietnam)
        E el Río Rojo (Vietnam)
        SU Кра́сная река́ (Вьетна́м)

3120 GB *Red Room, The [Röda rummet]*
              (Strindberg, 1879)
        F *La Chambre rouge*
        D *Das rote Zimmer*
        I *La camera rossa*
        E *El cuarto rojo*
        SU «Кра́сная ко́мната» (Стри́ндберг)

3121 GB *Red Roses for Me* (O'Casey, 1943)
        F *Roses rouges pour moi*
        D *Rote Rosen für mich*
        I *Rose rosse per me*
        E *Rosas rojas para mí*
        SU «Кра́сные ро́зы для меня́» (О'Ке́йси)

3122 GB Red Sea, the
        F la mer Rouge
        D das Rote Meer
        I il mare Rosso
        E el mar Rojo
        SU Кра́сное мо́ре

3123 GB Red Square (Moscow)
        F la place Rouge (Moscou)
        D der Rote Platz (Moskau)
        I la piazza Rossa (Mosca)
        E la plaza Roja (Moscú)
        SU Кра́сная пло́щадь (Москва́)

3124 GB *Reflections on the Causes of the*
              Grandeur and Declension of the
              Romans (Montesquieu, 1734)
        F *Considérations sur les causes de la*
              grandeur des Romains et de leur
              décadence
        D *Betrachtungen über Größe und Verfall*
              der Römer
        I *Considerazioni sulle cause della*
              grandezza dei romani e della loro
              decadenza
        E *Consideraciones sobre las causas de la*
              grandeza de los romanos y de su
              decadencia
        SU «Размышле́ния о причи́нах вели́чия и
              паде́ния ри́млян» (Монтескье́)

3125 GB *Reflections on Violence* (Sorel, 1908)
        F *Réflexions sur la violence*
        D *Über die Gewalt*
        I *Riflessioni sulla violenza*
        E *Reflexiones sobre la violencia*
        SU «Размышле́ния о наси́лии» (Соре́ль)

3126 GB Reformation, the (XVI)
        F la Réforme
        D die Reformation
        I la riforma
        E la Reforma
        SU реформа́ция

3127 GB Regensburg (Ratisbon) (Germany)
        F Ratisbonne (Allemagne)
        D Regensburg (Deutschland)
        I Ratisbona (Germania)
        E Ratisbona (Alemania)
        SU Ре́генсбург (Герма́ния)

3128 GB Regiomontanus (1436–76)
        F Regiomontanus
        D Regiomontanus
        I Regiomontano
        E Regiomontano
        SU Региомонта́н

3129 GB *Règle du Jeu, La [The Rules of the*
              Game] (Renoir, 1939)
        F *La Règle du jeu*
        D *Die Spielregel*
        I *La règle du jeu*
        E *La règle du jeu*
        SU «Пра́вила игры́» (Ренуа́р)

3130 GB Rehoboam (Bib.)
        F Roboam (Bib.)
        D Rehabeam (Bib.)
        I Roboamo (Bib.)
        E Roboam (Bib.)
        SU Робоа́м (библ.)

3131 GB Reign of Terror, the (France, 1793–4)
    F la Terreur
    D der Terror
    I il terrore
    E el Terror
    SU террóр (Фрáнция)

3132 GB Reims (Rheims) (France)
    F Reims (France)
    D Reims (Frankreich)
    I Reims (Francia)
    E Reims (Francia)
    SU Реймс (Фрáнция)

3133 GB Reindeer Lake (Canada)
    F le lac Caribou (Canada)
    D der Rentiersee (Kanada)
    I il lago delle Renne (Canada)
    E el lago del Reno (Canadá)
    SU Олéнье óзеро (Канáда)

    GB Religious Wars→Wars of Religion

3134 GB *Remembrance of Things Past* (Proust, 1913–27)
    F *À la recherche du temps perdu*
    D *Auf der Suche nach der verlorenen Zeit*
    I *Alla ricerca del tempo perduto*
    E *En busca del tiempo perdido*
    SU «В пóисках утрáченного врéмени» (Пруст)

    GB Remus→Romulus and Remus

3135 GB Renaissance, the (XIV–XVI)
    F la Renaissance
    D die Renaissance
    I il rinascimento
    E el Renacimiento
    SU Ренессáнс

    GB Representatives, House of→House of Representatives

3136 GB *Republic, The [Politeia]* (Plato, –IV)
    F *La République* (Platon)
    D *Der Staat* (Platon)
    I *La Repubblica* (Platone)
    E *La República* (Platón)
    SU «Госудáрство» (Платóн)

3137 GB Republican Party, the
    F le parti républicain
    D die Republikanische Partei
    I il Partito repubblicano
    E el Partido republicano
    SU республикáнская пáртия

3138 GB Republic of South Africa, the
    F la République sud-africaine
    D die Republik Südafrika
    I la Repubblica Sudafricana
    E la República Sudafricana
    SU Ю́жно-Африкáнская Респýблика

3139 GB *Repulsion* (Polanski, 1965)
    F *Répulsion*
    D *Ekel*
    I *Repulsione*
    E *Repulsión*
    SU «Отвращéние» (Полáнский)

3140 GB *Requiem* (Mozart, 1791)
    F *Requiem*
    D *Requiem*
    I *Requiem*
    E *Réquiem*
    SU «Рéквием» (Мóцарт)

3141 GB *Requiem for a Nun* (Faulkner, 1951)
    F *Requiem pour une nonne*
    D *Requiem für eine Nonne*
    I *Requiem per una monaca*
    E *Réquiem por una mujer*
    SU «Рéквием по монáхине» (Фóлкнер)

3142 GB *Residence on Earth* (Neruda, 1933–5)
    F *Résidence sur la terre*
    D *Aufenthalt auf Erden*
    I *Residenza in terra*
    E *Residencia en la tierra*
    SU «Местожи́тельство – земля́» (Нерýда)

3143 GB Resistance, the (France, 1940–5)
    F la Résistance (France)
    D die Résistance (Frankreich)
    I la resistenza (Francia)
    E la Resistencia (Francia)
    SU Сопротивлéние (Фрáнция)

3144 GB *Resistible Rise of Arturo Ui, The* (Brecht, 1941)
    F *La Résistible Ascension d'Arturo Ui*
    D *Der aufhaltsame Aufstieg des Arturo Ui*
    I *La resistibile ascesa di Arturo Ui*
    E *La resistible ascensión de Arturo Ui*
    SU «Карьéра Артýро У́и» (Брехт)

3145 GB *Respectable Prostitute, The* (Sartre, 1946)
    F *La Putain respectueuse*
    D *Die ehrbare Dirne*
    I *La squaldrina timorata*
    E *La respetuosa*
    SU «Прили́чная проститýтка» (Сартр)

3146   GB   Restoration, the (1660; 1814–30)
    F   la Restauration
    D   die Restauration
    I   la restaurazione
    E   la Restauración
    SU   реставра́ция

3147   GB   Resurrection, the (rel., + Tolstoy, 1899)
    F   la Résurrection (relig., + Tolstoï)
    D   die Auferstehung (relig., + Tolstoj)
    I   la Resurrezione (relig., + Tolstoj)
    E   la Resurrección (relig., + Tolstoi)
    SU   воскресе́ние (рел., + Толсто́й)

3148   GB   *Return of the Native, The* (Hardy, 1878)
    F   *Retour au pays natal*
    D   *Der Heimgekehrte*
    I   *Il ritorno al paese*
    E   *El retorno al país natal*
    SU   «Возвраще́ние на ро́дину» (Ха́рди)

3149   GB   *Return of Ulysses to his Country, The* (Monteverdi, 1641)
    F   *Le Retour d'Ulysse*
    D   *Il Ritorno d'Ulisse*
    I   *Il ritorno d'Ulisse in patria*
    E   *El retorno de Ulises*
    SU   «Возвраще́ние Ули́сса» (Монтеве́рди)

3150   GB   Revelation (of St. John the Divine), the (Bib.)
    F   l'Apocalypse (f.) (de Saint Jean, le Théologien) (Bib.)
    D   die Offenbarung des Johannes (Bib.)
    I   l'Apocalisse (Bib.)
    E   el Apocalipsis (Bib.)
    SU   «Открове́ние (Иоа́нна Богосло́ва)» (библ.)

3151   GB   *Revenger's Tragedy, The* (Tourneur, 1607)
    F   *La Tragédie du vengeur*
    D   *Des Rächers Tragödie*
    I   *Tragedia del vendicatore*
    E   *La tragedia del vengador*
    SU   «Траге́дия мсти́теля» (Те́рнер)

3152   GB   *Reveries of a Solitary Walker, The* (Rousseau, 1777–8)
    F   *Les Rêveries du promeneur solitaire*
    D   *Träumereien eines einsamen Spaziergängers*
    I   *Le fantasticherie del passeggiatore solitario*
    E   *Reflexiones de un paseante solitario*
    SU   «Прогу́лки одино́кого мечта́теля» (Руссо́)

3153   GB   *Revolt of the Angels, The* (France, 1914)
    F   *La Révolte des Anges*
    D   *Aufruhr der Engel*
    I   *La rivolta degli angeli*
    E   *La caída de los ángeles*
    SU   «Восста́ние а́нгелов» (Франс)

3154   GB   *Revolt of the Masses* (Ortega y Gasset, 1929)
    F   *La Révolte des masses*
    D   *Der Aufstand der Massen*
    I   *La ribellione delle masse*
    E   *La rebelión de las masas*
    SU   «Восста́ние масс» (Орте́га-и-Гасе́т)

3155   GB   Rheinland-Pfalz (Rhineland-Palatinate) (Germany)
    F   la Rhénanie-Palatinat (Allemagne)
    D   Rheinland-Pfalz (Deutschland)
    I   la Renania-Palatinato (Germania)
    E   Renania-Palatinado (Alemania)
    SU   Ре́йнланд-Пфальц (Герма́ния)

3156   GB   Rhineland, the (Germany)
    F   la Rhénanie (Allemagne)
    D   das Rheinland (Deutschland)
    I   la Renania (Germania)
    E   la Renania (Alemania)
    SU   Ре́йнланд (Герма́ния)

    GB   Rhineland-Palatinate→Rheinland-Pfalz

3157   GB   Rhine (River), the (Europe)
    F   le Rhin (Europe)
    D   der Rhein (Europa)
    I   il Reno (Europa)
    E   el Rin (Europa)
    SU   Рейн (Евро́па)

3158   GB   *Rhinoceros* (Ionesco, 1958)
    F   *Le Rhinocéros*
    D   *Die Nashörner*
    I   *Il rinoceronte*
    E   *El rinoceronte*
    SU   «Носоро́г» (Ионе́ско)

3159   GB   Rhodes (Greece)
    F   Rhodes (Grèce)
    D   Rhodos (Griechenland)
    I   Rodi (Grecia)
    E   Rodas (Grecia)
    SU   Ро́дос (Гре́ция)

3160 GB Rhodesia (hist.)
F la Rhodésie (hist.)
D Rhodesien (Gesch.)
I la Rhodesia (st.)
E Rodesia (hist.)
SU Родéзия (ист.)

3161 GB Rhône (River), the (France)
F le Rhône (France)
D die Rhône (Frankreich)
I il Rodano (Francia)
E el Ródano (Francia)
SU Рóна (Фрáнция)

3162 GB Richard (saint, king)
F Richard (saint, roi)
D Richard (Heiliger, König)
I Riccardo (santo, re)
E Ricardo (santo, rey)
SU Рúчард (св., корóль)

3163 GB Richard Coeur-de-Lion (Richard the
Lion-Heart) (1157–99)
F Richard Coeur de Lion
D Richard Löwenherz
I Riccardo Cuor di Leone
E Ricardo Corazón de León
SU Рúчард Львúное Сéрдце

3164 GB *Riders to the Sea* (Synge, 1904)
F *À cheval vers la mer*
D *Reiter ans Meer*
I *Cavalcata a mare*
E *Jinetes hacia el mar*
SU «Скáчущие к мóрю» (Синг)

3165 GB *Ridiculous Blue-Stockings, The*
(Molière, 1659)
F *Les Précieuses Ridicules*
D *Die lächerlichen Preziösen*
I *Le preziose ridicole*
E *Las preciosas ridículas*
SU «Смешнúе жемáнницы» (Мольéр)

3166 GB *Rienzi* (Bulwer-Lytton, 1835; Wagner,
1840)
F *Rienzi*
D *Rienzi*
I *Rienzi*
E *Rienzi*
SU «Риéнци» (Бýлвер-Лúттон, Вáгнер)

3167 GB *Rififi [Free Fight]* (Dassin, 1955)
F *Du rififi ches les hommes*
D *Rififi*
I *Rififi*
E *Rififi*
SU «Рифифú» (Дассéн)

3168 GB *Rifle Rangers, The* (Reid, 1850)
F *Les Francs-Tireurs forestiers*
D *Das weiße Roß der Steppe*
I *I tiratori di fucile*
E *Los tiradores de rifle*
SU «Вóльные стрелкú» (Рид)

GB Rights, Bill of→Bill of Rights

3169 GB *Rights of Man, The* (Paine, 1791–2)
F *Les Droits de l'homme*
D *Die Menschenrechte*
I *I diritti dell'uomo*
E *Los derechos del hombre*
SU «Правá человéка» (Пейн)

3170 GB *Rigoletto* (Verdi, 1851)
F *Rigoletto*
D *Rigoletto*
I *Rigoletto*
E *Rigoletto*
SU «Риголéтто» (Вéрди)

3171 GB Rijeka (Yugoslavia)
F Rijeka (Yougoslavie)
D Rijeka (Jugoslawien)
I Fiume (Iugoslavia)
E Rijeka (Yugoslavia)
SU Риéка (Югослáвия)

3172 GB *Rime of the Ancient Mariner, The*
(Coleridge, 1798)
F *La Complainte du vieux marinier*
D *Der alte Matrose*
I *La Ballata del vecchio marinaio*
E *La Balada del viejo marinero*
SU «Поэ́ма о стáром морякé» (Кóлридж)

3173 GB *Ring and the Book, The* (Browning,
1869)
F *L'Anneau et le livre*
D *Der Ring und das Buch*
I *L'anello e il libro*
E *El anillo y el libro*
SU «Кольцó и кнúга» (Брáунинг)

3174 GB *Ring of the Nibelung, The* (Wagner,
1854–74)
F *L'Anneau du Nibelung*
D *Der Ring des Nibelungen*
I *L'anello del Nibelungo*
E *El anillo de los Nibelungos*
SU «Кольцó нибелýнга» (Вáгнер)

3175 GB *Rip van Winkle* (Irving, 1819)
  F *Rip van Winkle*
  D *Rip van Winkle*
  I *Rip van Winkle*
  E *Rip van Winkle*
  SU «Рип ван Ви́нкель» (И́рвинг)

3176 GB *Rise and Fall of the Town Mahagonny, The* (Brecht + Weill, 1927)
  F *La Grandeur et décadence de la ville de Mahagonny*
  D *Der Aufstieg und Fall der Stadt Mahagonny*
  I *L'ascesa e caduta della città di Mahagonny*
  E *El apogeo y caída de la ciudad Mahagonny*
  SU «Возвыше́ние и паде́ние го́рода Маха́гонни» (Брехт/Вейль)

3177 GB Risorgimento, the ["Resurgence"] (1831)
  F le Risorgimento
  D das Risorgimento
  I il Risorgimento
  E el Risorgimento
  SU Рисорджиме́нто

3178 GB *Rite of Spring, The* (Stravinsky, 1913)
  F *Le Sacre du printemps* (Stravinski)
  D *Le Sacre du Printemps* (Strawinski)
  I *La sagra della primavera* (Stravinskij)
  E *La consagración de la primavera* (Stravinski)
  SU «Весна́ свяще́нная» (Страви́нский)

3179 GB *Rivals, The* (Sheridan, 1775)
  F *Les Rivaux*
  D *Die Nebenbuhler*
  I *I rivali*
  E *Los rivales*
  SU «Сопе́рники» (Ше́ридан)

  GB River . . . → . . . (River)

  GB Riviera→French Riviera

3180 GB Riyadh (Saudi Arabia)
  F Riyad (Arabie Saoudite)
  D Riad (Saudi-Arabien)
  I Riyadh (Arabia Saudita)
  E Er Riad (Arabia Saudita)
  SU Эр-Рия́д (Са́удовская Ара́вия)

3181 GB *Roads to Freedom, The* (Sartre, 1945–9)
  F *Les Chemins de la liberté*
  D *Die Wege der Freiheit*
  I *Le vie della libertà*
  E *Los caminos de la libertad*
  SU «Доро́ги свобо́ды» (Сартр)

3182 GB *Road to Wigan Pier, The* (Orwell, 1937)
  F *La Route qui mène au quai Wigan*
  D *Die Straße nach Wigan Pier*
  I *La strada per Wigan Pier*
  E *El camino de Wigan Pier*
  SU «Доро́га на Уи́ган-Пир» (О́руэлл)

3183 GB *Robbers, The* (Schiller, 1782; Verdi, 1847)
  F *Les Brigands*
  D *Die Räuber*
  I *I masnadieri*
  E *Los bandidos*
  SU «Разбо́йники» (Ши́ллер, Ве́рди)

3184 GB Robert (king)
  F Robert (roi)
  D Robert (König)
  I Roberto (re)
  E Roberto (rey)
  SU Ро́берт (коро́ль)

3185 GB Robert the Bruce (1274–1329)
  F Robert Bruce
  D Robert Bruce
  I Roberto Bruce
  E Roberto Bruce
  SU Ро́берт Брус

3186 GB Robert the Devil (XI, + Meyerbeer, 1831)
  F Robert le Diable
  D Robert der Teufel
  I Roberto il diavolo
  E Roberto el Diablo
  SU Ро́берт-Дья́вол (+ Мейербе́р)

3187 GB Robin Hood (?myth.)
  F Robin des Bois (?myth.)
  D Robin Hood (?myth.)
  I Robin Hood (?mit.)
  E Robín de los Bosques (¿mit.?)
  SU Ро́бин Гуд (?миф.)

3188 GB *Robinson Crusoe* (Defoe, 1719)
  F *Robinson Crusoé*
  D *Robinson Crusoe*
  I *Robinson Crusoe*
  E *Robinson Crusoe*
  SU «Робинзо́н Кру́зо» (Дефо́)

3189 GB *Rob Roy* (Scott, 1817)
F *Rob Roy*
D *Rob Roy*
I *Rob Roy*
E *Rob Roy*
SU «Роб Рой» (Скотт)

3190 GB *Rocco and His Brothers* (Visconti, 1960)
F *Rocco et ses frères*
D *Rocco und seine Brüder*
I *Rocco e i suoi fratelli*
E *Rocco y sus hermanos*
SU «Рókко и егó брáтья» (Вискóнти)

GB Rockies→Rocky Mountains

3191 GB Rocky Mountains, the (Canada/USA)
F les montagnes Rocheuses (Canada/USA)
D das Felsengebirge (Kanada/USA)
I le Montagne Rocciose (Canada/USA)
E las Montañas Rocosas (Canadá/USA)
SU Скалúстые гóры (Канáда/США)

GB *Roderick Random*→*Adventures of Roderick Random*

3192 GB Roger Bacon (1214–*1293*)
F Roger Bacon
D Roger Bacon
I Ruggero Bacone
E Roger Bacon
SU Рóджер Бэ́кон

3193 GB *Roland in Love* (Boiardo, 1487)
F *Roland amoureux* (Boiardo)
D *Verliebter Roland* (Boiardo)
I *Orlando innamorato* (Boiardo)
E *Orlando enamorado* (Boyardo)
SU «Влюблённый Рóланд» (Боя́рдо)

3194 GB *Roman Actor, The* (Massinger, 1629)
F *L'Acteur romain*
D *Der römische Schauspieler*
I *L'attore romano*
E *El actor romano*
SU «Рúмский актёр» (Мéссинджер)

3195 GB *Romance of the Forest* (Radcliffe, 1791)
F *Le Roman de la forêt*
D *Adeline oder Das Abenteuer im Walde*
I *Il romanzo della selva*
E *Adelina*
SU «Ромáн в лесý» (Рáдклиф)

3196 GB *Romance of the Rose*, the (XIII)
F le *Roman de la Rose*
D der *Rosenroman*
I il *Roman de la Rose*
E el *Roman de la rose*
SU «Ромáн о рóзе»

3197 GB *Romances Without Words* (Verlaine, 1874)
F *Romances sans paroles*
D *Romanzen ohne Worte*
I *Romanze senza parole*
E *Romanzas sin palabras*
SU «Ромáнсы без слов» (Верлéн)

3198 GB *Roman Elegies* (Goethe, 1790)
F *Les Élégies romaines*
D *Römische Elegien*
I *Elegie Romane*
E *Elegías romanas*
SU «Рúмские элéгии» (Гёте)

GB Roman Empire→Holy Roman Empire

3199 GB Romania
F la Roumanie
D Rumänien
I la Romania
E Rumania
SU Румы́ния

3200 GB Romans, the Epistle of Paul to the (Bib.)
F l'Épître de Saint Paul aux Romains (Bib.)
D der Römerbrief (Bib.)
I la lettera di Paolo ai Romani (Bib.)
E la Epístola de San Pablo a los romanos (Bib.)
SU «Послáние к Рúмлянам» (библ.)

3201 GB *Roman Spring of Mrs Stone, The* (Williams, 1950)
F *Le Printemps romain de Mme Stone*
D *Mrs Stone und ihr römischer Frühling*
I *La primavera romana della signora Stone*
E *La primavera romana de la señora Stone*
SU «Рúмская веснá госпожú Стóун» (Уúльямс)

3202 GB *Romantic School, The* (Heine, 1836)
F *De l'école romantique*
D *Die Romantische Schule*
I *Scuola Romantica*
E *La escuela romántica*
SU «Романтúческая шкóла» (Гéйне)

3203 GB Romanus (pope, emperor)
F Romain (pape, empereur)
D Romanus (Papst, Kaiser)
I Romano (papa, imperatore)
E Romano (papa, emperador)
SU Рома́н (па́па ри́мский, импера́тор)

3204 GB Rome (Italy)
F Rome (Italie)
D Rom (Italien)
I Roma (Italia)
E Roma (Italia)
SU Рим (Ита́лия)

3205 GB *Romeo and Juliet* (Shakespeare, 1594; Berlioz, 1839)
F *Roméo et Juliette*
D *Romeo und Julia*
I *Giulietta e Romeo*
E *Romeo y Julieta*
SU «Роме́о и Джулье́тта» (Шекспи́р, Берлио́з)

3206 GB *Romola* (Eliot, 1863)
F *Romola*
D *Romola*
I *Romola*
E *Romola*
SU «Ро́мола» (Э́лиот)

3207 GB Romulus and Remus (myth.)
F Romulus et Remus (myth.)
D Romulus und Remus (myth.)
I Romolo e Remo (mit.)
E Rómulo y Remo (mit.)
SU Ро́мул и Рем (миф.)

3208 GB *Room, The* (Pinter, 1957)
F· *La Chambre*
D *Das Zimmer*
I *La stanza*
E *La habitación*
SU «Ко́мната» (Пи́нтер)

3209 GB *Room at the Top* (Braine, 1957)
F *Une pièce en haut*
D *Und nähme doch Schaden an seiner Seele*
I *La stanza di sopra*
E *Un lugar en la cumbre*
SU «Путь наве́рх» (Брейн)

3210 GB *Room at the Top* (Clayton, 1959)
F *Les Chemins de la haute ville*
D *Der Weg nach oben*
I *La stanza di sopra*
E *Un lugar en la cumbre*
SU «Путь наве́рх» (Кле́йтон)

3211 GB *Room of One's Own, A* (Woolf, 1929)
F *Une chambre à soi*
D *Ein eigenes Zimmer*
I *Una stanza propria*
E *Una habitación propia*
SU «Своя́ ко́мната» (Вулф)

3212 GB *Room with a View, A* (Forster, 1905)
F *Une chambre d'où l'on voit*
D *Ein Zimmer mit Aussicht*
I *Camera con vista*
E *Habitación con vistas*
SU «Ко́мната с ви́дом» (Фо́рстер)

3213 GB *Rope* (Hitchcock, 1948)
F *La Corde*
D *Cocktail für eine Leiche*
I *Nodo alla gola*
E *La cuerda*
SU «Верёвка» (Хи́чкок)

3214 GB *Rosamunde Overture*, the (Schubert, 1823)
F l'ouverture *Rosamunde*
D Musik zu *Rosamunde*
I l'ouverture *Rosamunda*
E la obertura *Rosamunda*
SU увертю́ра к «Розаму́нде» (Шу́берт)

3215 GB *Rose and the Ring, The* (Thackeray, 1855)
F *La Rose et l'anneau*
D *Die Rose und der Ring*
I *La rosa e l'anello*
E *La rosa y el anillo*
SU «Ро́за и кольцо́» (Те́ккерей)

3216 GB *Rose Garden, The* [*Golestan*] (Saadi, 1258)
F *La Roserie*
D *Der Rosengarten*
I *Il Roseto*
E *El jardín de las rosas*
SU «Гулиста́н» (Саади́)

3217 GB *Rosemary's Baby* (Polanski, 1968)
F *Rosemary's Baby*
D *Rosemaries Baby*
I *Rosemary's baby*
E *La semilla del diablo*
SU «Дитя́ дья́вола» (Пола́нский)

GB Roses, Wars of the→Wars of the Roses

3218   GB   *Rose Tattoo* (Williams, 1951)
     F   *La Rose tatouée*
     D   *Die tätowierte Rose*
     I   *La rosa tatuata*
     E   *La rosa tatuada*
     SU   «Татуи́рованная ро́за» (Уи́льямс)

3219   GB   Rosetta Stone, the (Egypt)
     F   la pierre de Rosette (Égypte)
     D   der Stein von Rosetta (Ägypten)
     I   la stele di Rosetta (Egitto)
     E   la piedra de Roseta (Egipto)
     SU   Розе́ттский ка́мень (Еги́пет)

3220   GB   Rosicrucians, the (rel.)
     F   les Rose-Croix (relig.)
     D   die Rosenkreuzer (relig.)
     I   i rosacroci (relig.)
     E   los Rosacruces (relig.)
     SU   розенкре́йцеры (рел.)

3221   GB   *Rosmersholm* (Ibsen, 1886)
     F   *Rosmersholm*
     D   *Rosmersholm*
     I   *Villa Rosmer*
     E   *Rosmersholm*
     SU   «Ро́смерсхольм» (И́бсен)

3222   GB   Rouen (France)
     F   Rouen (France)
     D   Rouen (Frankreich)
     I   Rouen (Francia)
     E   Ruán (Francia)
     SU   Руа́н (Фра́нция)

3223   GB   *Rouen Cathedral* (Monet, 1892–1904)
     F   *La Cathédrale de Rouen*
     D   *Die Kathedrale von Rouen*
     I   *Cattedrale di Rouen*
     E   *Catedral de Ruán*
     SU   «Руа́нский собо́р» (Моне́)

3224   GB   *Rougon-Macquart Family, The* (Zola, 1871–93)
     F   *Les Rougon-Macquart*
     D   *Die Rougon-Macquart*
     I   *I Rougon-Macquart*
     E   *Los Rougon-Macquart*
     SU   «Руго́н-Макка́ры» (Золя́)

3225   GB   Round Table, the (myth.)
     F   la Table ronde (myth.)
     D   die Tafelrunde (myth.)
     I   la Tavola rotonda (mit.)
     E   la Tabla Redonda (mit.)
     SU   Кру́глый стол (миф.)

3226   GB   Roussillon (France)
     F   Roussillon (France)
     D   Roussillon (Frankreich)
     I   Rossiglione (Francia)
     E   Rosellón (Francia)
     SU   Руссильо́н (Фра́нция)

3227   GB   *Royal Highness* (Mann, 1909)
     F   *Altesse royale*
     D   *Königliche Hoheit*
     I   *Altezza reale*
     E   *Alteza real*
     SU   «Короле́вское высо́чество» (Манн)

3228   GB   *Royal Way, The* (Malraux, 1930)
     F   *La Voie royale*
     D   *Der Königsweg*
     I   *La via reale*
     E   *La vía real*
     SU   «Короле́вская доро́га» (Мальро́)

3229   GB   *Rubáiyát, the* (Omar Khayyám, XI)
     F   les *Quatrains* (Umar Khayyam)
     D   der *Rubaiyyat* (Omar Chayyam)
     I   il *Rubaiyyat* (Omar Khayyam)
     E   el *Rubaiyat* (Omar Khayyam)
     SU   «Руба́и» (Ома́р Хайя́м)

3230   GB   *Rudin* (Turgenev, 1856)
     F   *Roudine* (Tourgueniev)
     D   *Rudin* (Turgenjew)
     I   *Rudin* (Turgenev)
     E   *Rudin* (Turgueniev)
     SU   «Ру́дин» (Турге́нев)

3231   GB   Rudolf (sovereign)
     F   Rodolphe (souvrain)
     D   Rudolf (Herr.)
     I   Rodolfo (sovrano)
     E   Rodolfo (sob.)
     SU   Рудо́льф (прав.)

     GB   Rumania→Romania

3232   GB   *R.U.R.* (Čapek, 1920)
     F   *R.U.R.*
     D   *R.U.R.*
     I   *R.U.R.*
     E   *R.U.R.*
     SU   «R.U.R.» (Ча́пек)

3233   GB   *Rusalka* (Dargomyzhsky, 1856; Dvořák, 1901)
     F   *Roussalka*
     D   *Russalka*
     I   *Rusalka*
     E   *Rusalka*
     SU   «Руса́лка» (Даргомы́жский, Дво́ржак)

3234 GB Russia
F la Russie
D Rußland
I la Russia
E Rusia
SU Россия

3235 GB *Russian Easter Festival*
(Rimsky-Korsakov, 1888)
F *La Grande Pâque russe*
(Rimski-Korsakov)
D *Die großen russischen Ostern*
(Rimskij-Korsakow)
I *La grande Pasqua russa*
(Rimskij-Korsakov)
E *La gran Pascua rusa*
(Rimsky-Korsakov)
SU «Светлый праздник» (Римский-
Корсаков)

3236 GB Russian Soviet Federated Socialist
Republic (RSFSR), the (USSR)
F la République socialiste fédérative
soviétique russe (RSFSR) (URSS)
D die Russische Sozialistische Föderative
Sowjetrepublik (RSFSR) (UdSSR)
I la Repubblica Socialista Federativa
Sovietica Russa (RSFSR) (URSS)
E la República Socialista Federativa
Soviética Rusa (RSFSR) (URSS)
SU Российская Советская Федеративная
Социалистическая Республика (РСФСР)
(СССР)

3237 GB *Russlan and Ludmilla* (Pushkin, 1820;
Glinka, 1842)
F *Rouslan et Lioudmila* (Pouchkine,
Glinka)
D *Russlan i Ljudmila* (Puschkin, Glinka)
I *Ruslan e Ludmilla* (Puškin, Glinka)
E *Ruslan y Ludmila* (Puschkin, Glinka)
SU «Руслан и Людмила» (Пушкин, Глинка)

3238 GB Russo-Japanese War, the (1904–5)
F la guerre russo-japonaise
D der Russisch-Japonische Krieg
I la guerra russo-giapponese
E la guerra ruso-japonesa
SU Русско-японская война

3239 GB *Rustic Chivalry* (Verga, 1883)
F *Cavalleria rusticana*
D *Sizilianische Bauernehre*
I *Cavalleria rusticana*
E *Caballería rusticana*
SU «Сельская честь» (Вёрга)

3240 GB Ruth (Bib.)
F Ruth (Bib.)
D Ruth (Bib.)
I Ruth (Bib.)
E Ruth (Bib.)
SU Руфь (библ.)

3241 GB *Ruy Blas* (Hugo, 1838)
F *Ruy Blas*
D *Ruy Blas*
I *Ruy Blas*
E *Ruy Blas*
SU «Рюй Блаз» (Гюго)

3242 GB Rwanda
F le Ruanda
D Rwanda
I il Ruanda
E Ruanda
SU Руанда

3243 GB *Ryan's Daughter* (Lean, 1971)
F *La Fille de Ryan*
D *Ryans Tochter*
I *La figlia di Ryan*
E *La hija de Ryan*
SU «Дочь Райана» (Лин)

S

3244 GB Saar (River), the (France/Germany)
    F la Sarre (France/Allemagne)
    D die Saar (Frankreich/Deutschland)
    I il Saar (Francia/Germania)
    E el Sarre (Francia/Alemania)
    SU Саáр (Фрáнция/Гермáния)

3245 GB Saarbrücken (Germany)
    F Sarrebruck (Allemagne)
    D Saarbrücken (Deutschland)
    I Saarbrücken (Germania)
    E Sarrebruck (Alemania)
    SU Саарбрю́ккен (Гермáния)

3246 GB Saarland, the (Germany)
    F la Sarre (Allemagne)
    D Saarland (Deutschland)
    I il Saarland (Germania)
    E el Sarre (Alemania)
    SU Саáр (Гермáния)

3247 GB *Sabine Women, The* (David, 1799)
    F *Les Sabines*
    D *Die Sabinerinnen*
    I *Le sabine*
    E *Las sabinas*
    SU «Сабúнянки» (Давúд)

3248 GB *Sacred and Profane Love* (Titian, 1512–15)
    F *Amour sacrée et profane* (Titien)
    D *Himmlische und irdische Liebe* (Tizien)
    I *Amor sacro e profano* (Tiziano)
    E *Amor sacro y profano* (Tiziano)
    SU «Любóвь земнáя и небéсная» (Тициáн)

3249 GB Sagittarius (astron.)
    F le Sagittaire (astron.)
    D der Schütze (Astron.)
    I il Sagittario (astr.)
    E el Sagitario (astr.)
    SU Стрелéц (астр.)

3250 GB St Bartholomew's Day Massacre, the (France, 1572)
    F la Saint-Barthélemy (France)
    D die Bartholomäusnacht (Frankreich)
    I la notte di San Bartolomeo (Francia)
    E la noche de San Bartolomé (Francia)
    SU Варфоломéевская ночь (Фрáнция)

3251 GB St Basil's Cathedral (Moscow)
    F l'église Basile-le-Bienheureux (Moscou)
    D die Basiliuskirche (Moskau)
    I la chiesa di San Basilio (Mosca)
    E la iglesia de San Basilio (Moscú)
    SU храм Васúлия Блажéнного (Москвá)

3252 GB St George's Channel
    F le canal Saint George
    D der Sankt-Georgskanal
    I il canale di San Giorgio
    E el canal de San Jorge
    SU пролúв Святóго Геóрга

3253 GB St Gotthard Pass, the (Switzerland)
    F le col du Saint-Gothard (Suisse)
    D der Sankt-Gotthard-Paß (Schweiz)
    I il passo del San Gottardo (Svizzera)
    E el puerto de San Gotardo (Suiza)
    SU перевáл Сен-Готáрд (Швейцáрия)

3254 GB St Helena
    F Saint-Hélène
    D Sankt Helena
    I Sant'Elena
    E Santa Elena
    SU óстров Святóй Елéны

3255   GB   *Saint Joan* (Shaw, 1923)
       F   *Sainte Jeanne*
       D   *Die heilige Johanna*
       I   *Santa Giovanna*
       E   *Santa Juana*
       SU   «Святáя Иоáнна» (Шóу)

3256   GB   St Lawrence, the Gulf of (Canada)
       F   le golfe du Saint-Laurent (Canada)
       D   der Sankt-Lorenz-Golf (Kanada)
       I   il golfo del San Lorenzo (Canada)
       E   el golfo del San Lorenzo (Canadá)
       SU   залúв Святóго Лаврéнтия (Канáда)

3257   GB   St Lawrence (River), the (Canada)
       F   le Saint-Laurent (Canada)
       D   der Sankt-Lorenz-Strom (Kanada)
       I   il San Lorenzo (Canada)
       E   el San Lorenzo (Canadá)
       SU   рекá Святóго Лаврéнтия (Канáда)

3258   GB   St Lucia (West Indies)
       F   Sainte Lucie (Antilles)
       D   Santa Lucia (Westindien)
       I   Santa Lucia (Antille)
       E   Santa Lucía (Antillas)
       SU   Сент-Люсúя (Вест-Úндия)

3259   GB   St Mark's Square (Venice)
       F   la place Saint-Marc (Venise)
       D   der Markusplatz (Venedig)
       I   la piazza San Marco (Venezia)
       E   la plaza de San Marcos (Venecia)
       SU   Пья́цца Сан-Мáрко (Венéция)

3260   GB   *St Matthew Passion* (Bach, 1729)
       F   la *Passion selon Saint Matthieu*
       D   die *Matthäuspassion*
       I   la *Passione secondo Matteo*
       E   la *Pasión según San Mateo*
       SU   «Стрáсти по Матфéю» (Бах)

3261   GB   St Paul's Cathedral (London)
       F   la cathédrale Saint-Paul (Londres)
       D   die Sankt-Pauls-Kirche (London)
       I   la cattedrale di San Paolo (Londra)
       E   la catedral de San Pablo (Londres)
       SU   собóр святóго Пáвла (Лóндон)

3262   GB   St Peter's Basilica (Rome)
       F   le basilique Saint-Pierre (Rome)
       D   die Peterskirche (Rom)
       I   la basilica di San Petro (Roma)
       E   la basílica de San Pedro (Roma)
       SU   собóр святóго Петрá (Рим)

3263   GB   St Petersburg (hist.)
       F   Saint-Pétersbourg (hist.)
       D   Sankt-Petersburg (Gesch.)
       I   Pietroburgo (st.)
       E   San Petersburgo (hist.)
       SU   Санкт-Петербýрг (ист.)

3264   GB   St Vincent (West Indies)
       F   Saint-Vincent (Antilles)
       D   Saint-Vincent (Westindien)
       I   San Vicenzo (Antille)
       E   San Vicente (Antillas)
       SU   Сент-Вúнсент (Вест-Úндия)

3265   GB   *Salammbô* (Flaubert, 1862)
       F   *Salammbô*
       D   *Salammbô*
       I   *Salammbô*
       E   *Salambó*
       SU   «Саламбó» (Флобéр)

3266   GB   Salic Law, the (V)
       F   la loi salique
       D   das salische Gesetz
       I   la legge salica
       E   la ley Sálica
       SU   Салúческая прáвда

3267   GB   *Salisbury Cathedral* (Constable, 1831)
       F   la *Cathédrale de Salisbury*
       D   *Salisbury Cathedral*
       I   *La cattedrale di Salisbury*
       E   *La catedral de Salisbury*
       SU   «Собóр в Сóлсбери» (Кóнстебл)

3268   GB   Sallust (86–34)
       F   Salluste
       D   Sallustius
       I   Sallustio
       E   Salustio
       SU   Саллю́стий

3269   GB   Salome (Bib., + Wilde, 1896; Strauss, 1905)
       F   Salomé (Bib.)
       D   Salome (Bib.)
       I   Salomé (Bib.)
       E   Salomé (Bib.)
       SU   Саломéя (библ., + Уáйльд, Штрáус)

3270   GB   Salonika (Greece)
       F   Salonique (Grèce)
       D   Saloniki (Griechenland)
       I   Salonicco (Grecia)
       E   Salónica (Grecia)
       SU   Салóники (м.) (Грéция)

3271 GB Saluzzo (Italy)
F Saluces (Italie)
D Saluzzo (Italien)
I Saluzzo (Italia)
E Saluces (Italia)
SU Салу́ццо (Ита́лия)

3272 GB Salvation Army, the (rel.)
F l'Armée du salut (relig.)
D die Heilsarmee (relig.)
I il Esercito della Salvezza (relig.)
E el Ejército de Salvación (relig.)
SU А́рмия спасе́ния (рел.)

3273 GB Salzburg (Austria)
F Salzbourg (Autriche)
D Salzburg (Österreich)
I Salisburgo (Austria)
E Salzburgo (Austria)
SU За́льцбург (А́встрия)

3274 GB Samaria (Bib.)
F la Samarie (Bib.)
D Samaria (Bib.)
I la Samaria (Bib.)
E Samaria (Bib.)
SU Сама́рия (библ.)

3275 GB Samaritans, the (Bib.)
F les Samaritains (Bib.)
D die Samariten (Bib.)
I i samaritani (Bib.)
E los samaritanos (Bib.)
SU самаритя́не (библ.)

3276 GB Samothrace (Greece)
F Samothrace (Grèce)
D Samothrake (Griechenland)
I Samotracia (Grecia)
E Samotracia (Grecia)
SU Самотра́ки (Гре́ция)

3277 GB *Samson et Dalila* [*Samson and Delilah*]
(Saint-Saëns, 1877)
F *Samson et Dalila*
D *Samson und Dalila*
I *Sansone e Dalila*
E *Sansón y Dalila*
SU «Самсо́н и Дали́ла» (Сен-Са́нс)

3278 GB *Samson Agonistes* ["Samson the
Struggler"] (Milton, 1671)
F *Samson Agonistes*
D *Samson Agonistes*
I *Sansone Agonista*
E *Sansón Agonista*
SU «Самсо́н-боре́ц» (Ми́льтон)

3279 GB Samuel (Bib.)
F Samuel (Bib.)
D Samuel (Bib.)
I Samuele (Bib.)
E Samuel (Bib.)
SU Самуи́л (библ.)

3280 GB *Sanctuary* (Faulkner, 1931)
F *Sanctuaire*
D *Die Freistatt*
I *Santuario*
E *Santuario*
SU «Святи́лище» (Фо́лкнер)

3281 GB *Sang d'un Poète, Le* [*The Blood of a
Poet*] (Cocteau, 1930)
F *Le Sang d'un Poète*
D *Das Blut eines Dichters*
I *Le sang d'un poète*
E *Le sang d'un poète*
SU «Кровь поэ́та» (Кокто́)

3282 GB San Marino
F le Saint-Marin
D San Marino
I il San Marino
E San Marino
SU Сан-Мари́но

3283 GB Santa Claus (Father Christmas)
F Père Noël
D der Weihnachtsmann
I Babbo Natale
E Papá Noel
SU дед-моро́з

3284 GB Santiago de Compostela (Spain)
F Saint-Jacques-de-Compostelle
(Espagne)
D Santiago de Compostela (Spanien)
I Santiago de Compostela (Spagna)
E Santiago de Compostela (España)
SU Сантья́го-де-Компосте́ла (Испа́ния)

3285 GB Saône (River), the (France)
F la Saône (France)
D die Saône (Frankreich)
I la Saona (Francia)
E el Saona (Francia)
SU Со́на (Фра́нция)

3286 GB Sappho (−VI)
F Sappho
D Sappho
I Saffo
E Safo
SU Сапфо́

3287 GB Saracens, the (hist.)
F les Sarrasins (hist.)
D die Sarazene (hist.)
I i saraceni (hist.)
E los sarracenos (hist.)
SU сараци́ны (ист.)

3288 GB Saragossa (Spain)
F Saragosse (Espagne)
D Saragossa (Spanien)
I Saragozza (Spagna)
E Zaragoza (España)
SU Сараго́са (Испа́ния)

3289 GB Sarah (Bib.)
F Sara (Bib.)
D Sara (Bib.)
I Sara (Bib.)
E Sara (Bib.)
SU Ца́рра (библ.)

3290 GB Sardinia (Italy)
F la Sardaigne (Italie)
D Sardinien (Italien)
I la Sardegna (Italia)
E Cerdeña (Italia)
SU Сарди́ния (Ита́лия)

3291 GB Sargasso Sea, the
F la mer des Sargasses
D das Sargasso-Meer
I il mare dei Sargassi
E el mar de los Sargazos
SU Сарга́ссово мо́ре

3292 GB Sark (Channel Islands)
F Sercq (îles Anglo-Normandes)
D Sark (Kanalinseln)
I Sark (isole Normanne)
E Sark (islas Anglonormandas)
SU Сарк (Норма́ндские острова́)

3293 GB *Sartor Resartus* ["The Tailor Re-tailored"] (Carlyle, 1836)
F *Sartor Resartus*
D *Der geflickte Flickschneider*
I *Sartor Resartus*
E *Sartor Resartus*
SU «Са́ртор Реза́ртус» (Ка́рлейль)

3294 GB Satan (rel.)
F Satan (relig.)
D Satan (relig.)
I Satana (relig.)
E Satanás (relig.)
SU сатана́ (рел.)

3295 GB *Satin Slipper, The* (Claudel, 1928–9)
F *Le Soulier de satin*
D *Der seidene Schuh*
I *Lo scarpino di raso*
E *El zapato de raso*
SU «Атла́сный башмачо́к» (Клоде́ль)

3296 GB *Satires*, the [*Satirae*] (Horace, −I; Juvenal, V)
F les *Satires* (Horace, Juvenal)
D die *Satiren* (Horaz, Juvenalis)
I le *Satire* (Orazio, Giovenale)
E las *Sátiras* (Horacio, Juvenal)
SU «Сати́ры» (Гора́ций, Ювена́л)

3297 GB *Saturday Night and Sunday Morning* (Sillitoe, 1958; Reisz, 1960)
F *Samedi soir et dimanche matin*
D *Samstagnacht und Sonntagmorgen*
I *Sabato notte e domenica mattina*
E *Sábado por la noche y domingo por la mañana*
SU «Суббо́тний ве́чер, воскре́сное у́тро» (Си́ллитоу, Райс)

3298 GB *Saturday Night Fever* (Badham, 1977)
F *La Fièvre du samedi soir*
D *Nur Samstag Nacht*
I *La febbre del sabato sera*
E *La fiebre del sábado en la noche*
SU «Лихора́дка в суббо́ту ве́чером» (Ба́дем)

3299 GB Saturn (myth., astron.)
F Saturne (myth., astron.)
D Saturnus (myth); Saturn (Astron.)
I Saturno (mit., astr.)
E Saturno (mit., astr.)
SU Сату́рн (миф., астр.)

3300 GB *Saturnine Poems* (Verlaine, 1866)
F *Poèmes saturniens*
D *Saturnische Gedichte*
I *Poemi saturnini*
E *Poemas saturnianos*
SU «Сату́рновские стихотворе́ния» (Верле́н)

3301 GB *Satyricon*, the (Petronius, I)
F le *Satiricon* (Pétrone)
D der *Satiricon* (Petronius)
I il *Satyricon* (Petronio)
E el *Satiricón* (Petronio)
SU «Сатирико́н» (Петро́ний)

3302 GB Saudi Arabia
      F   l'Arabie Saoudite
      D   Saudi-Arabien
      I   l'Arabia Saudita
      E   Arabia Saudita
      SU Сáудовская Арáвия

3303 GB Saul (Bib.)
      F   Saül (Bib.)
      D   Saul (Bib.)
      I   Saul (Bib.)
      E   Saúl (Bib.)
      SU Саýл (библ.)

3304 GB Savoy (France)
      F   la Savoie (France)
      D   Savoyen (Frankreich)
      I   la Savoia (Francia)
      E   Saboya (Francia)
      SU Савóйя (Фрáнция)

3305 GB Saxons, the (hist.)
      F   les Saxons (hist.)
      D   die Sachsen (Gesch.)
      I   i sassoni (hist.)
      E   los sajones (hist.)
      SU сáксы (ист.)

3306 GB Saxony (Germany)
      F   la Saxe (Allemagne)
      D   Sachsen (Deutschland)
      I   la Sassonia (Germania)
      E   Sajonia (Alemania)
      SU Саксóния (Гермáния)

3307 GB Scaevola (?myth.)
      F   Scaevola (?myth.)
      D   Scävola (?myth.)
      I   Scevola (?mit.)
      E   Escévola (¿mit.?)
      SU Сцéвола (?миф.)

3308 GB *Scalp-Hunters, The* (Reid, 1851)
      F   *Les Chasseurs de chevelures*
      D   *Die Skalpjäger*
      I   *Gli scotennatori*
      E   *Los cazadores de cabelleras*
      SU «Охóтники за скáльпами» (Рид)

3309 GB Scandinavia
      F   la Scandinavie
      D   Skandinavien
      I   la Scandinavia
      E   Escandinavia
      SU Скандинáвия

3310 GB Scaramouche
      F   Scaramouche
      D   Scaramouche
      I   Scaramuccia
      E   Escaramuza
      SU Скарамýш

3311 GB *Scarlet Letter, The* (Hawthorne, 1850)
      F   *La Lettre écarlate*
      D   *Der scharlachrote Buchstabe*
      I   *La lettera scarlatta*
      E   *La letra escarlata*
      SU «Áлая бýква» (Хóторн)

3312 GB *Scarlet Pimpernel, The* (Orczy, 1905)
      F   *La Primule écarlate*
      D   *Die scharlachrote Blume*
      I   *La primula rossa*
      E   *Pimpinela escarlata*
      SU «Áлая прúмула» (Óртси)

3313 GB *Scatterbrain, The* (Molière, 1655)
      F   *L'Étourdi*
      D   *Der Unbesonnene*
      I   *Lo stordito*
      E   *El aturdido*
      SU «Шáлый» (Мольéр)

3314 GB *Scenes from Bohemian Life* (Murger, 1848)
      F   *Scènes de la vie de bohème*
      D   *Szenen aus dem Leben der Bohème*
      I   *Scene della vita di Bohème*
      E   *Escenas de la vida bohemia*
      SU «Сцéны из жúзни богéмы» (Мюржé)

3315 GB *Scenes of Childhood* (Schumann, 1838)
      F   *Scènes d'enfants*
      D   *Kinderszenen*
      I   *Scene infantili*
      E   *Escenas infantiles*
      SU «Дéтские сцéны» (Шýман)

3316 GB *Scenes of Clerical Life* (Eliot, 1858)
      F   *Scènes de la vie du clergé*
      D   *Szenen aus dem Leben der Geistlichen*
      I   *Scene di vita clericale*
      E   *Escenas de la vida clerical*
      SU «Сцéны из клерикáльной жúзни» (Éлиот)

3317 GB Schaffhausen (Switzerland)
      F   Schaffhouse (Suisse)
      D   Schaffhausen (Schweiz)
      I   Sciaffusa (Svizzera)
      E   Schaffhausen (Suiza)
      SU Шафхáузен (Швейцáрия)

3318 GB Scheherazade (*Thousand and One Nights*) (+ Rimsky-Korsakov, 1888)
F Schéhérazade (*Mille et une nuits*) (+ Rimski-Korsakov)
D Scheherezade (*Tausendundeine Nacht*) (+ Rimskij-Korsakow)
I Scheherazade (*Mille e una notte*) (+ Rimskij-Korsakov)
E Scherezade (*Mil y una noches*) (+ Rimsky-Korsakov)
SU Шехераза́да («Ты́сяча и одна́ ночь») (+ Ри́мский-Ко́рсаков)

3319 GB Scheldt (River), the (France/Belgium/Netherlands)
F l'Escaut (France/Belgique/Pays-Bas)
D die Schelde (Frankreich/Belgien/Niederlande)
I la Schelda (Francia/Belgio/Paesi Bassi)
E el Escalda (Francia/Bélgica/Holanda)
SU Ше́льда (Фра́нция/Бе́льгия/Нидерла́нды)

3320 GB *School for Husbands, The* (Molière, 1661)
F *L'École des maris*
D *Die Schule der Männer*
I *La scuola dei mariti*
E *La escuela de los maridos*
SU «Шко́ла мужей» (Молье́р)

3321 GB *School for Indifference, The* (Giraudoux, 1911)
F *L'École des indifférents*
D *Die Schule des Hochmuts*
I *La scuola degli indifferenti*
E *La escuela de los indiferentes*
SU «Шко́ла равноду́шных» (Жироду́)

3322 GB *School for Scandal, The* (Sheridan, 1777)
F *L'École de la médisance*
D *Die Lästerschule*
I *La scuola della maldicenza*
E *La escuela de la maledicencia*
SU «Шко́ла злосло́вия» (Ше́ридан)

3323 GB *School for Wives, The* (Molière, 1662; Gide, 1929–36)
F *L'École des femmes*
D *Die Schule der Frauen*
I *La scuola delle mogli*
E *La escuela de las mujeres*
SU «Шко́ла жён» (Молье́р, Жид)

3324 GB *Schweik in the Second World War* [*Osudy dobrého vojáka Švejka za světové války*] (Hašek, 1943)
F *Chweik dans la seconde guerre mondiale*
D *Schweyk im zweiten Weltkrieg*
I *Schweyk nella seconda guerra mondiale*
E *Schweyk en la segunda guerra mundial*
SU «Похожде́ния бра́вого солда́та Швейка́ во время́ второ́й мирово́й войны́» (Га́шек)

3325 GB Scipio (185–129)
F Scipion
D Scipio
I Scipione
E Escipión
SU Сципио́н

3326 GB Scorpio (astron.)
F le Scorpion (astron.)
D der Skorpion (Astron.)
I il Scorpione (astr.)
E el Escorpión (astr.)
SU Скорпио́н (астр.)

3327 GB Scotland
F l'Écosse (f.)
D Schottland
I la Scozia
E Escocia
SU Шотла́ндия

3328 GB *Scottish Symphony*, the (Mendelssohn, 1842)
F la *Symphonie écossaise* (Mendelssohn-Bartholdy)
D die *Schottische Symphonie* (Mendelssohn-Bartholdy)
I la sinfonia *Scozzese* (Mendelssohn-Bartholdy)
E la sinfonía *Escocesa* (Mendelssohn-Bartholdy)
SU «Шотла́ндская» симфо́ния (Мендельсо́н-Барто́льди)

3329 GB Scouts (Boy Scouts, USA), the
F les Scouts (catholiques), les Éclaireurs (neutres)
D die Pfadfinder
I gli scouts (cattolici), i giovani esploratori (neutri)
E los niños exploradores
SU бойска́уты

3330 GB Scylla and Charybdis (myth.)
F Scylla et Charybde (myth.)
D Skylla und Charybdis (myth.)
I Scilla e Cariddi (mit.)
E Escila y Caribdis (mit.)
SU Сци́лла и Хари́бда (миф.)

3331 GB Scythians, the (hist.)
F les Scythes (hist.)
D die Skythen (Gesch.)
I i sciti (st.)
E los escitas (hist.)
SU скифы (ист.)

3332 GB *Seagull, The* (Chekhov, 1896)
F *La Mouette* (Tchekov)
D *Die Möwe* (Tschechow)
I *Il gabbiano* (Čechov)
E *La gaviota* (Chejov)
SU «Ча́йка» (Че́хов)

3333 GB *Seamarks* (Saint-John Perse, 1957)
F *Amers*
D *Seemarken*
I *Amari*
E *Los faros*
SU «Ориенти́ры» (Сен-Жон Перс)

GB Sea of . . . → . . . , Sea of

3334 GB *Seashell and the Clergyman, The* (Dulac, 1928)
F *La Coquille et le clergyman*
D *Die Muschel und der Pfarrer*
I *La coquille et le clergyman*
E *La concha y el clérigo*
SU «Ра́ковина и свяще́нник» (Дюла́к)

3335 GB *Season in Hell, A* (Rimbaud, 1873)
F *Une saison en enfer*
D *Ein Sommer in der Hölle*
I *Una stagione all'inferno*
E *Una temporada en el infierno*
SU «Сквозь ад» (Рембо́)

3336 GB *Seasons, The* (Thomson, 1726–30; Haydn, 1801)
F *Les Saisons*
D *Die Jahreszeiten*
I *Le stagioni*
E *Las estaciones*
SU «Времена́ го́да» (То́мсон, Гайдн)

3337 GB *Sea Wolf, The* (London, 1904)
F *Le Loup des mers*
D *Der Seewolf*
I *Il lupo di mare*
E *El lobo de mar*
SU «Морско́й волк» (Ло́ндон)

3338 GB Sebastian (saint)
F Sébastien (saint)
D Sebastian (Heiliger)
I Sebastiano (santo)
E Sebastián (santo)
SU Севастья́н (св.)

3339 GB *Second Mrs Tanqueray, The* (Pinero, 1893)
F *La Deuxième madame Tanqueray*
D *Die zweite Frau Tanqueray*
I *La seconda signora Tanqueray*
E *La segunda señora Tanqueray*
SU «Втора́я ми́ссис Те́нкерей» (Пине́ро)

3340 GB *Second Sex, The* (Beauvoir, 1949)
F *Le Deuxième Sexe*
D *Das andere Geschlecht*
I *Il secondo sesso*
E *El segundo sexo*
SU «Второ́й пол» (Бовуа́р)

3341 GB Second World War, the (1939–45)
F la Seconde Guerre mondiale
D der zweite Weltkrieg
I la seconda guerra mondiale
E la segunda guerra mundial
SU втора́я мирова́я война́

3342 GB *Secret Agent* (Conrad, 1907)
F *L'Agent secret*
D *Der Geheimagent*
I *L'agente segreto*
E *El agente secreto*
SU «Та́йный аге́нт» (Ко́нрад)

3343 GB *Secret Marriage, The* (Cimarosa, 1792)
F *Le Mariage secret*
D *Die heimliche Ehe*
I *Il matrimonio segreto*
E *El matrimonio secreto*
SU «Та́йный брак» (Чимаро́за)

3344 GB Security Council, the (UNO)
F le Conseil de sécurité (ONU)
D der Sicherheitsrat (UNO)
I il consiglio di sicurezza (ONU)
E el Consejo de Seguridad (ONU)
SU Сове́т безопа́сности (ООН)

3345 GB *Seed Beneath the Snow, The* (Silone, 1940)
F *Grain sous la neige*
D *Der Samen unter dem Schnee*
I *Il seme sotto la neve*
E *La semilla bajo la nieve*
SU «Се́мя под сне́гом» (Сило́не)

3346 GB Segovia (Spain)
F Ségovie (Espagne)
D Segovia (Spanien)
I Segovia (Spagna)
E Segovia (España)
SU Сего́вия (Испа́ния)

3347 GB Seine (River), the (France)
F la Seine (France)
D die Seine (Frankreich)
I la Senna (Francia)
E el Sena (Francia)
SU Се́на (Фра́нция)

3348 GB *Sejanus* (Jonson, 1603)
F *Sejanus*
D *Sejanus*
I *Sejanus*
E *Sejanus*
SU «Паде́ние Сея́на» (Джо́нсон)

3349 GB Selene (myth.)
F Séléné (myth.)
D Selene (myth.)
I Selene (mit.)
E Selene (mit.)
SU Селе́на (миф.)

3350 GB *Self-Tormentor, The*
[Heautontimoroumenos] (Terence,
−163)
F *Le Bourreau de lui-même* (Térence)
D *Der Selbstquäler* (Terentius)
I *Il punitore de se stesso* (Terenzio)
E *El hombre que se castiga a sí mismo*
(Terencio)
SU «Самоистяза́тель» (Тере́нций)

3351 GB Semiramis (myth.)
F Sémiramis (myth.)
D Semiramis (myth.)
I Semiramide (mit.)
E Semíramis (mit.)
SU Семирами́да (миф.)

3352 GB Seneca (−55−+39)
F Sénèque
D Seneca
I Seneca
E Séneca
SU Сене́ка

3353 GB Senegal
F le Sénégal
D Senegal
I il Senegal
E el Senegal
SU Сенега́л

3354 GB Sennacherib (Bib.)
F Sennachérib (Bib.)
D Sanherib (Bib.)
I Sennacherib (Bib.)
E Senaquerib (Bib.)
SU Сеннахири́м (библ.)

3355 GB *Sense and Sensibility* (Austen, 1811)
F *Raison et sensibilité*
D *Empfindung und Empfindlichkeit*
I *Senno e sensibilità*
E *Buen sentido y sensibilidad*
SU «Здра́вый смысл и чувстви́тельность»
(О́стин)

3356 GB *Sentimental Education* (Flaubert, 1869)
F *L'Éducation sentimentale*
D *Erziehung des Gefühls*
I *Educazione sentimentale*
E *La educación sentimental*
SU «Воспита́ние чувств» (Флобе́р)

3357 GB *Sentimental Journey Through France
and Italy, A* (Sterne, 1768)
F *Voyage sentimental en France et en
Italie*
D *Empfindsame Reise durch Frankreich
und Italien*
I *Viaggio sentimentale attraverso la
Francia e l'Italia*
E *Viaje sentimental a Francia e Italia*
SU «Сентимента́льное путеше́ствие по
Фра́нции и Ита́лии» (Стерн)

3358 GB *Separate Tables* (Rattigan, 1954)
F *Tables séparées*
D *An Einzeltischen*
I *Tavole separate*
E *Mesas separadas*
SU «Отде́льные столы́» (Ра́ттиган)

3359 GB Septuagint, the (Bib.)
F la version des Septante (Bib.)
D die Septuaginta (Bib.)
I la Settanta (Bib.)
E la versión de los Setenta (Bib.)
SU Септуаги́нта (библ.)

3360 GB Serbia (Yugoslavia)
F la Serbie (Yougoslavie)
D Serbien (Jugoslawien)
I la Serbia (Iugoslavia)
E Serbia (Yugoslavia)
SU Се́рбия (Югосла́вия)

3361 GB Sergius (saint, pope)
F   Serge (saint, pape)
D   Sergius (Heiliger, Papst)
I   Sergio (santo, papa)
E   Sergio (santo, papa)
SU Сéргий (св., пáпа рúмский)

3362 GB Sermon on the Mount, the (Bib.)
F   le Sermon sur la montagne (Bib.)
D   die Bergpredigt (Bib.)
I   il discorso della montagna (Bib.)
E   el Sermón de la Montaña (Bib.)
SU Нагóрная прóповедь (библ.)

3363 GB *Servant of Two Masters, A* (Goldoni, 1746)
F   *Le Serviteur de deux maîtres*
D   *Der Diener zweier Herren*
I   *Il servitore di due padroni*
E   *El criado de dos amos*
SU «Слугá двух госпóд» (Гольдóни)

3364 GB Servius (Roman name)
F   Servius (nom romain)
D   Servius (Römername)
I   Servio (nome romano)
E   Servio (nombre romano)
SU Сéрвий (древнерúмское úмя)

3365 GB *Sesame and Lilies* (Ruskin, 1865)
F   *Sésame et les Lys*
D   *Sesam und Lilien*
I   *Sesamo e gigli*
E   *Sésamo y lirios*
SU «Сезáм и лúлии» (Рéскин)

3366 GB Seth (Bib.)
F   Seth (Bib.)
D   Seth (Bib.)
I   Set (Bib.)
E   Set (Bib.)
SU Сиф (библ.)

3367 GB *Sevastopol Sketches* (Tolstoy, 1855)
F   *Récits de Sébastopol* (Tolstoï)
D   *Sewastopolj* (Tolstoj)
I   *Racconti di Sebastopoli* (Tolstoj)
E   *Cuentos de Sebastopol* (Tolstoi)
SU «Севастóпольские расскáзы» (Толстóй)

3368 GB Seven Against Thebes, the (myth., + Aeschylus, −467)
F   les Sept contre Thèbes (myth., + Eschyle)
D   Die Sieben gegen Theben (myth., + Aischylos)
I   I sette a Tebe (mit., + Eschilo)
E   Los siete contra Tebas (mit., + Esquilo)
SU Сéмеро прóтив Фив (миф., + Эсхúл)

3369 GB *Seven Brides for Seven Brothers* (Donen, 1954)
F   *Les Sept Femmes de Barberousse*
D   *Eine Braut für sieben Brüder*
I   *Sette spose per sette fratelli*
E   *Siete novias para siete hermanos*
SU «Семь невéст для семú брáтьев» (Дóнен)

3370 GB *Seven Days in May* (Frankenheimer, 1964)
F   *Sept Jours en mai*
D   *Sieben Tage im Mai*
I   *Sette giorni a maggio*
E   *Siete días de mayo*
SU «Семь дней в мáе» (Фрáнкенхаймер)

3371 GB *Seven Lamps of Architecture, The* (Ruskin, 1849)
F   *Les Sept Lampes de l'architecture*
D   *Die sieben Leuchter der Baukunst*
I   *Le sette lampade dell'architettura*
E   *Las siete lámparas de la arquitectura*
SU «Семь свéточей архитектýры» (Рéскин)

3372 GB *Seven Pillars of Wisdom, The* (Lawrence, 1926)
F   *Les Sept Piliers de la sagesse*
D   *Die sieben Säulen der Weisheit*
I   *I sette pilastri della saggezza*
E   *Los siete pilares de la Sabiduría*
SU «Семь столбóв мýдрости» (Лóуренс)

3373 GB *Seven Samurai* [*Shichi-nin no samurai*] (Kurosawa, 1954)
F   *Les Sept Samouraïs*
D   *Die sieben Samurai*
I   *I sette samurai*
E   *Los siete valientes*
SU «Семь самурáев» (Куросáва)

3374 GB Seventh-day Adventists, the (rel.)
F les Adventistes du septième jour (relig.)
D die Adventisten des Siebenten Tags (relig.)
I gli avventisti del settimo giorno (relig.)
E los adventistas del séptimo día (relig.)
SU адвентисты седьмóго дня (рел.)

3375 GB *Seventh Ring, The* (George, 1907)
F *Le Septième Anneau*
D *Der siebente Ring*
I *Il settimo anello*
E *Séptimo anillo*
SU «Седьмóе кольцó» (Геóрге)

3376 GB *Seventh Seal, The* [*Det sjunde inseglet*] (Bergman, 1957)
F *Le Septième Sceau*
D *Das siebente Siegel*
I *Il settimo sigillo*
E *El séptimo sello*
SU «Седьмáя печáть» (Бéргман)

3377 GB Seven Wonders of the World, the
F les Sept Merveilles du monde
D die Sieben Weltwunder
I le sette meraviglie del mondo
E las Siete Maravillas del Mundo
SU семь чудéс свéта

3378 GB Seven Years' War, the (1756–63)
F la guerre de Sept Ans
D der Siebenjährige Krieg
I la guerra dei sette anni
E la guerra de los Siete Años
SU Семилéтняя войнá

3379 GB *Severed Head, A* (Murdoch, 1961)
F *Une tête coupée*
D *Maskenspiel*
I *Una testa tagliata*
E *Cabeza cercenada*
SU «Отрýбленная головá» (Мёрдок)

3380 GB Severnaya Zemlya (USSR)
F Severnaïa Zemlia (URSS)
D Nordland (UdSSR)
I Severnaja Zemlja (URSS)
E Severnaia Zemlia (URSS)
SU Сéверная Земля́ (СССР)

3381 GB Severus (saint, emperor)
F Séverin (saint, empereur)
D Severus (Heiliger, Kaiser)
I Severo (santo, imperatore)
E Severo (santo, emperador)
SU Севéр (св., императóр)

3382 GB Seville (Spain)
F Séville (Espagne)
D Sevilla (Spanien)
I Siviglia (Spagna)
E Sevilla (España)
SU Севи́лья (Испáния)

3383 GB Sextus (Roman name)
F Sextus (nom romain)
D Sextus (Römername)
I Sesto (nome romano)
E Sesto (nombre romano)
SU Секст (древнери́мское и́мя)

3384 GB Seychelles, the
F les Seychelles
D die Seschellen
I le Seicelle
E las Seychelles
SU Сейшéльские островá

3385 GB Shalmaneser (king)
F Salmanasar (roi)
D Salmanassar (König)
I Salmanassar (re)
E Salmanasar (rey)
SU Салманасáр (царь)

3386 GB Shanghai (China)
F Chang-hai (Chine)
D Schanghai (China)
I Sciangai (Cina)
E Shanghai (China)
SU Шанхáй (Китáй)

3387 GB *Shanghai Express* (Sternberg, 1932)
F *Shanghai Express*
D *Schanghai Express*
I *Shanghai Express*
E *El expreso de Shanghai*
SU «Экспрéсс на Шанхáй» (Стéрнберг)

3388 GB *She Came to Stay* (Beauvoir, 1943)
F *L'Invitée*
D *Sie kam und blieb*
I *L'invitata*
E *La invitada*
SU «Гóстья» (Бовуáр)

3389 GB Shem (Bib.)
F Sem (Bib.)
D Sem (Bib.)
I Sem (Bib.)
E Sem (Bib.)
SU Сим (библ.)

3390 GB *Shepherd's Calendar, The* (Spenser, 1579)
    F *Le Calendrier du berger*
    D *Der Schäferkalender*
    I *Il calendario del pastore*
    E *El calendario del pastor*
    SU «Календáрь пáстуха» (Спéнсер)

3391 GB *Shepherd's Pipe, The* (Marino, 1620)
    F *Le Chalumeau*
    D *Die Schäferpfeife*
    I *La sampogna*
    E *La zampoña*
    SU «Волы́нка» (Марúно)

3392 GB Sherpas, the (Nepal)
    F les Sherpas (Népal)
    D die Sherpas (Nepal)
    I gli sherpa (Nepal)
    E los sherpas (Nepal)
    SU шéрпы (Непáл)

3393 GB *She Stoops to Conquer* (Goldsmith, 1773)
    F *Les Fautes d'une nuit*
    D *Sie läßt sich herab, um zu siegen*
    I *Ella si umilia per conquistare*
    E *Ella se humilla para vencer*
    SU «Ночь ошúбок, úли Унижéние пáче гóрдости» (Гóлсуорси)

3394 GB Shetland Islands, the (Scotland)
    F les îles Shetland (Écosse)
    D die Shetlandinseln (Schottland)
    I le isole Shetland (Scozia)
    E las islas Shetland (Escocia)
    SU Шетлéндские островá (Шотлáндия)

3395 GB *Shining, The* (Kubrick, 1980)
    F *Shining*
    D *Shining*
    I *Shining*
    E *El resplandor*
    SU «Сияние» (Кýбрик)

3396 GB *Ship of Fools, The* (Brant, 1494)
    F *Le Nef des fous*
    D *Das Narrenschiff*
    I *La nave dei pazzi*
    E *La nave de los locos*
    SU «Корáбль дуракóв» (Брант)

3397 GB *Shirley* (Brontë, 1849)
    F *Shirley*
    D *Shirley*
    I *Shirley*
    E *Shirley*
    SU «Шéрли» (Брóнте)

3398 GB *Shoot the Pianist* (Truffaut, 1960)
    F *Tirez sur le pianiste*
    D *Schießen Sie auf den Pianisten*
    I *Tirate sul pianista*
    E *Tirez le pianiste*
    SU «Стреля́йте в пианúста» (Трюффó)

3399 GB *Shropshire Lad, A* (Housman, 1896)
    F *Un gars du Shropshire*
    D *Ein Junge aus Shropshire*
    I *Un ragazzo dello Shropshire*
    E *Un muchacho del Shropshire*
    SU «Шропшúрский пáрень» (Хáусмен)

3400 GB Shrove Tuesday (rel.)
    F le mardi gras (relig.)
    D die Fastnacht (relig.)
    I il martedì grasso (relig.)
    E el martes de carnaval (relig.)
    SU втóрник на мáсленой недéле (рел.)

3401 GB Siam (hist.)
    F le Siam (hist.)
    D Siam (Gesch.)
    I il Siam (st.)
    E Siam (hist.)
    SU Сиáм (ист.)

3402 GB Siberia (USSR)
    F la Sibérie (URSS)
    D Sibirien (UdSSR)
    I la Sibiria (URSS)
    E Siberia (URSS)
    SU Сибúрь (ж.) (СССР)

3403 GB Sicilian Vespers, the (1282; + Verdi, 1855)
    F les Vêpres siciliennes
    D Die Sizilianische Vesper
    I I vespri siciliani
    E las Vísperas Sicilianas
    SU Сицилúйская вечéрня (+ Вéрди)

3404 GB Sicily (Italy)
    F la Sicile (Italie)
    D Sizilien (Italien)
    I la Sicilia (Italia)
    E Sicilia (Italia)
    SU Сицúлия (Итáлия)

3405 GB Sidon (Bib.)
    F Sidon (Bib.)
    D Sidon (Bib.)
    I Sidone (Bib.)
    E Sidón (Bib.)
    SU Сидóн (библ.)

3406 GB Siegfried (myth., + Wagner, 1876)
    F Siegfried (myth.)
    D Siegfried (myth.)
    I Sigfrido (mit.)
    E Sigfrido (mit.)
    SU Зи́гфрид (миф., + Ва́гнер)

3407 GB Siena (Italy)
    F Sienne (Italie)
    D Siena (Italien)
    I Siena (Italia)
    E Siena (Italia)
    SU Сиéна (Итáлия)

3408 GB Sierra Leone
    F la Sierra Leone
    D Sierra Leone
    I la Sierra Leone
    E Sierra Leone
    SU Сьéрра Леóне

    GB Sighs, Bridge of→Bridge of Sighs

3409 GB Sigismund (sovereign)
    F Sigismond (souverain)
    D Sigismund (Herr.)
    I Sigismondo (sovrano)
    E Sigismondo (sob.)
    SU Сугизму́нд (прав.)

3410 GB Sikhs, the (rel.)
    F les sikhs (relig.)
    D die Sikhs (relig.)
    I i sikh (relig.)
    E los sijs (relig.)
    SU си́кхи (рел.)

3411 GB *Silas Marner* (Eliot, 1861)
    F *Silas Marner*
    D *Silas Marner*
    I *Silas Marner*
    E *Silas Marner*
    SU «Cáйлес Мáрнер» (Э́лиот)

3412 GB *Silence of Colonel Bramble, The*
      (Maurois, 1918)
    F *Les Silences du colonel Bramble*
    D *Die Schweigen des Obersten Bramble*
    I *I silenzi del colonnello Bramble*
    E *Los silencios del coronel Bramble*
    SU «Молчáние полкóвника Брéмбля»
      (Моруá)

3413 GB *Silent Don, The (And Quiet Flows the*
      Don) (Sholokhov, 1928–40)
    F *Le Don paisible* (Cholokhov)
    D *Der stille Don* (Scholochow)
    I *Il placido Don* (Šolochov)
    E *El Don apacible* (Cholojov)
    SU «Ти́хий Дон» (Шóлохов)

3414 GB Silenus (myth.)
    F Silène (myth.)
    D Silen (myth.)
    I Sileno (mit.)
    E Sileno (mit.)
    SU Силéн (миф.)

3415 GB Silesia (Europe)
    F la Silésie (Europe)
    D Schlesien (Europa)
    I la Slesia (Europa)
    E Silesia (Europa)
    SU Силéзия (Еврóпа)

3416 GB *Silken Ladder, The* (Rossini, 1812)
    F *L'Échelle de soie*
    D *Die Seidenleiter*
    I *La scala di seta*
    E *La escala de seda*
    SU «Шёлковая лéстница» (Росси́ни)

3417 GB Silvanus (myth.)
    F Silvain (myth.)
    D Silvanus (myth.)
    I Silvano (mit.)
    E Silvano (mit.)
    SU Сильвáн (миф.)

3418 GB Simeon (Bib.)
    F Siméon (Bib.)
    D Simeon (Bib.)
    I Simeone (Bib.)
    E Simeón (Bib.)
    SU Симеóн (библ.)

3419 GB Simeon Stylites (saint, *390*–459)
    F Siméon Stylite (saint)
    D Simeon der Säulenheilige (Heiliger)
    I Simeone Stilito (santo)
    E Simeón Estilita (santo)
    SU Симеóн Стóлпник (св.)

3420 GB Simon (Bib.)
    F Simon (Bib.)
    D Simon (Bib.)
    I Simone (Bib.)
    E Simón (Bib.)
    SU Симóн (библ.)

3421 GB *Simon Boccanegra* (Verdi, 1857)
F *Simone Boccanegra*
D *Simone Boccanegra*
I *Simon Boccanegra*
E *Simon Boccanegra*
SU «Симо́н Бокканéгра» (Вéрди)

3422 GB *Simplicissimus* (Grimmelshausen, 1668)
F *La Vie de l'aventurier Simplicius Simplicissimus*
D *Der Abentheuerliche Simplizissimus Teutsch*
I *L'avventuroso Simplicissimus*
E *Simplicissimus*
SU «Симплици́ссимус» (Гри́ммельсхаузен)

3423 GB Simplon Pass, the (Switzerland)
F le tunnel du Simplon (Suisse)
D der Simplontunnel (Schweiz)
I il passo del Sempione (Svizzera)
E il paso del Simplón (Suiza)
SU перева́л Симпло́н (Швейца́рия)

3424 GB Sinai, Mount (Bib.)
F le mont Sinaï (Bib.)
D der Berg Sinai (Bib.)
I il monte Sinai (Bib.)
E el monte Sinaí (Bib.)
SU гора́ Сина́й (библ.)

3425 GB Sinai Peninsula, the (Egypt)
F la péninsule du Sinaï (Égypte)
D die Sinaihalbinsel (Ägypten)
I la penisola del Sinai (Egitto)
E la península del Sinaí (Egipto)
SU Сина́йский полуо́стров (Еги́пет)

3426 GB Sinbad (Sindbad) the Sailor (*Thousand and one Nights*)
F Sinbad le marin (*Mille et une Nuits*)
D Sindbad der Seefahrer (*Tausendundeine Nacht*)
I Sindibad il marinaio (*Mille e una notte*)
E Simbad el Marino (*Mil y una noches*)
SU Синдба́д-моря́к («Ты́сяча и одна́ ночь»)

3427 GB Singapore
F Singapour
D Singapur
I Singapore
E Singapur
SU Сингапу́р

3428 GB *Singin' in the Rain* (Kelly/Donen, 1952)
F *Chantons sous la pluie*
D *Du sollst mein Glücksstern sein*
I *Cantando sotto la pioggia*
E *Cantando bajo la lluvia*
SU «Пéсня под дождём» (Кéлли/До́нен)

GB *Sir Charles Grandison*→*History of Sir Charles Grandison*

3429 GB Sirens, the (myth.)
F les sirènes (myth.)
D die Sirenen (myth.)
I le Sirene (mit.)
E las sirenas (mit.)
SU сирéны (миф.)

3430 GB *Sir Gawain and the Green Knight* (1370)
F *Gauvain et le chevalier vert*
D *Gawain und der grüne Ritter*
I *Sir Galvano e il Cavaliere Verde*
E *Sir Galvano y el caballero verde*
SU «Сэр Га́вейн и Зелёный ры́царь»

3431 GB Sirius (astron.)
F Sirius (astron.)
D Sirius (Astron.)
I Sirio (astr.)
E Sirio (astr.)
SU Си́риус (астр.)

3432 GB *Sister Carrie* (Dreiser, 1900)
F *Soeur Carrie*
D *Schwester Carrie*
I *Nostra sorella Carrie*
E *Hermana Carrie*
SU «Сестра́ Кéрри» (Дра́йзер)

3433 GB Sistine Chapel, the (Vatican)
F la chapelle Sixtine (Vatican)
D die Sixtinische Kapelle (Vatican)
I la Cappella Sistina (Vaticano)
E la capilla Sixtina (Vaticano)
SU Сиксти́нская капéлла (Ватика́н)

3434 GB *Sistine Madonna*, the (Raphael, 1513)
F la *Madone sixtine* (Raphaël)
D die *Sixtinische Madonna* (Raffael)
I la *Madonna Sistina* (Raffaele)
E la *Madona sixtina* (Rafael)
SU «Сиксти́нская мадо́нна» (Рафаэ́ль Са́нти)

3435 GB Sisyphus (myth.)
      F   Sisyphe (myth.)
      D   Sisyphus (myth.)
      I   Sisifo (mit.)
      E   Sísifo (mit.)
      SU Сизиф (миф.)

3436 GB Siva (Shiva) (rel.)
      F   Çiva (relig.)
      D   Schiwa (relig.)
      I   Shiva (relig.)
      E   Siva (relig.)
      SU Шива (рел.)

3437 GB *Six Characters in Search of an Author*
          (Pirandello, 1921)
      F   *Six Personnages en quête d'auteur*
      D   *Sechs Personen suchen einen Autor*
      I   *Sei personaggi in cerca d'autore*
      E   *Seis personajes en busca de autor*
      SU «Шесть персонажей в поисках автора»
          (Пиранделло)

3438 GB *Six Moral Tales* (Laforgue, 1887)
      F   *Moralités légendaires*
      D   *Sagenhafte Sinnenspiele*
      I   *Moralità leggendarie*
      E   *Moralidades legendarias*
      SU «Легендарные рассказы с моралью»
          (Лафорг)

3439 GB Sixtus (saint, pope)
      F   Sixte (saint, pape)
      D   Sixtus (Heiliger, Papst)
      I   Sisto (santo, papa)
      E   Sixto (santo, papa)
      SU Сикст (св., папа римский)

3440 GB *Skin, The* (Malaparte, 1949)
      F   *La Peau*
      D   *Die Haut*
      I   *La pelle*
      E   *La piel*
      SU «Кожа» (Малапарте)

3441 GB Slave Coast, the (hist.)
      F   la côte des Esclaves (hist.)
      D   die Sklavenküste (Gesch.)
      I   la Costa degli Schiavi (st.)
      E   la Costa de los Esclavos (hist.)
      SU Невольничий берег (ист.)

3442 GB Slave River, the (Canada)
      F   la rivière de l'Esclave (Canada)
      D   der Sklavenfluß (Kanada)
      I   il fiume degli Schiavi (Canada)
      E   el río del Esclavo (Canadá)
      SU река Невольничья (Канада)

3443 GB Slavs, the (hist.)
      F   les Slaves (hist.)
      D   die Slawen (Gesch.)
      I   i slavi (st.)
      E   los eslavos (hist.)
      SU славяне (ист.)

3444 GB *Sleeping Beauty, The* (Perrault, 1697;
          Tchaikovsky, 1890)
      F   *La Belle au bois dormant* (Perrault,
          Tchaikovski)
      D   *Das Dornröschen* (Perrault,
          Tschaikowskij)
      I   *La bella addormentata nel bosco*
          (Perrault, Čaikovskij)
      E   *La bella durmiente del bosque*
          (Perrault, Tchaikovski)
      SU «Спящая красавица» (Перро,
          Чайковский)

3445 GB *Sleep of Prisoners, A* (Fry, 1951)
      F   *Le Songe du prisonnier*
      D   *Ein Schlaf Gefangener*
      I   *Sonno di prigionieri*
      E   *Sueño de prisioneros*
      SU «Сон узников» (Фрай)

3446 GB *Sleepwalker, The* (Bellini, 1831)
      F   *La Somnambule*
      D   *Die Nachtwandlerin*
      I   *La sonnambula*
      E   *La somnámbula*
      SU «Сомнамбула» (Беллини)

3447 GB Slovakia (Czechoslovakia)
      F   la Slovaquie (Tchécoslovaquie)
      D   die Slowakei (Tschechoslowakei)
      I   la Slovacchia (Cecoslovacchia)
      E   Eslovaquia (Checoslovaquia)
      SU Словакия (Чехословакия)

3448 GB Slovenia (Yugoslavia)
      F   la Slovénie (Yougoslavie)
      D   Slowenien (Jugoslawien)
      I   la Slovenia (Iugoslavia)
      E   Eslovenia (Yugoslavia)
      SU Словения (Югославия)

3449 GB *Small Testament, The* (Villon, 1456)
      F   *Petit Testament*
      D   *Das kleine Testament*
      I   *Piccolo testamento*
      E   *Pequeño Testamento*
      SU «Малое завещание» (Вийон)

3450 GB *Smiles of a Summer Night*
             [*Sommarnattens Leende*] (Bergman,
             1955)
         F   *Sourires d'une nuit d'été*
         D   *Das Lächeln einer Sommernacht*
         I   *Sorrisi di una notte d'estate*
         E   *Sonrisas de una noche de verano*
         SU «Улы́бки ле́тней но́чи» (Бе́ргман)

3451 GB *Smoke* (Turgenev, 1867)
         F   *Fumée* (Tourgueniev)
         D   *Rauch* (Turgenjew)
         I   *Fumo* (Turgenev)
         E   *El humo* (Turgueniev)
         SU «Дым» (Турге́нев)

3452 GB Smyrna (Bib.)
         F   Smyrne (Bib.)
         D   Smyrna (Bib.)
         I   Smirne (Bib.)
         E   Esmirna (Bib.)
         SU Сми́рна (библ.)

3453 GB *Snow Country* [*Yukiguni*] (Kawabata,
             1937)
         F   *Pays de neige*
         D   *Schneeland*
         I   *Il paese delle nevi*
         E   *País de la Nieve*
         SU «Сне́жная страна́» (Кавава́та)

3454 GB *Snow Maiden, The* (Rimsky-Korsakov,
             1882)
         F   *Fleur de neige*
         D   *Schneeflöckchen*
         I   *La fanciulla di neve*
         E   *La doncella de nieve*
         SU «Снегу́рочка» (Ри́мский-Ко́рсаков)

3455 GB *Snow Queen, The* [*Snedronningen*]
             (Andersen, 1844)
         F   *La Reine des neiges*
         D   *Die Schneekönigin*
         I   *Regina della neve*
         E   *La Reina de las nieves*
         SU «Сне́жная короле́ва» (А́ндерсен)

3456 GB *Snow White and the Seven Dwarfs*
             (Grimm, 1815; Disney, 1937)
         F   *Blanche-Neige et les sept nains*
         D   *Schneewittchen und die sieben Zwerge*
         I   *Biancaneve e i setti nani*
         E   *Blancanieves y los siete enanitos*
         SU «Белосне́жка и семь гно́мов»
             (Гримм, Ди́сней)

3457 GB *Social Contract, The* (Rousseau, 1762)
         F   *Le Contrat social*
         D   *Vom Gesellschaftsvertrag*
         I   *Il contratto sociale*
         E   *El contrato social*
         SU «Об обще́ственном догово́ре»
             (Руссо́)

3458 GB Social Democratic Party, the
         F   le parti social-démocrate
         D   die Sozialdemokratische Partei
         I   il partito socialdemocratico
         E   el Partido Socialdemocrático
         SU Социа́л-демократи́ческая па́ртия

3459 GB Socialist Party, the
         F   le parti socialiste
         D   die Sozialistische Partei
         I   il partito socialista
         E   el Partido Socialista
         SU Социалисти́ческая па́ртия

3460 GB Society Islands, the
         F   les îles de la Société
         D   die Gesellschaftsinseln
         I   le isole della Società
         E   las islas de la Sociedad
         SU острова́ О́бщества

3461 GB Socrates (*470–399*)
         F   Socrate
         D   Sokrates
         I   Socrate
         E   Sócrates
         SU Сокра́т

3462 GB Sodom and Gomorrah (Bib.)
         F   Sodome et Gomorrhe (Bib.)
         D   Sodom und Gomorrha (Bib.)
         I   Sodoma e Gomorra (Bib.)
         E   Sodoma y Gomorra (Bib.)
         SU Содо́м и Гомо́рра (библ.)

3463 GB Sofia (Bulgaria)
         F   Sofia (Bulgarie)
         D   Sofia (Bulgarien)
         I   Sofia (Bulgaria)
         E   Sofía (Bulgaria)
         SU Софи́я (Болга́рия)

3464 GB *Soldiers Three* (Kipling, 1888–9)
         F   *Trois Troupiers*
         D   *Soldaten-Geschichten*
         I   *Tre soldati*
         E   *Tres soldados*
         SU «Три солда́та» (Ки́плинг)

3465 GB Solomon (Bib.)
F Salomon (Bib.)
D Salomo (Bib.)
I Salomone (Bib.)
E Salomón (Bib.)
SU Соломóн (библ.)

3466 GB Solomon Islands, the
F les îles Salomon
D die Salomoninseln
I le isole Salomone
E las islas Salomón
SU Соломóновы островá

3467 GB Solon (*630–560*)
F Solon
D Solon
I Solone
E Solón
SU Солóн

3468 GB Somalia
F la Somalie
D Somalia
I la Somalia
E Somalia
SU Сомалú

3469 GB *Some Like It Hot* (Wilder, 1959)
F *Certains l'aiment chaud*
D *Manche mögen's heiß*
I *A qualcuno piace caldo*
E *Con faldas y a lo loco*
SU «Нéкоторым нрáвится, когдá жáрко»
(Уáйлдер)

3470 GB Somme (River), the (France)
F la Somme (France)
D die Somme (Frankreich)
I la Somme (Francia)
E el Somme (Francia)
SU Сóмма (Фрáнция)

3471 GB *Songbook*, the (Petrarch, 1360)
F *Rimes* (Pétrarque)
D *Gedichte* (Petrarca)
I il *Canzoniere* (Petrarca)
E *Cancionero* (Petrarca)
SU «Кнúга пéсен» (Петрáрка)

3472 GB *Song of Bernadette, The* (Werfel; 1941)
F *Le Chant de Bernadette*
D *Das Lied von Bernadette*
I *Bernadette*
E *La canción de Bernadette*
SU «Пéсня Бернадéтты» (Вéрфель)

3473 GB *Song of Hiawatha, The* (Longfellow,
1855)
F *Hiawatha*
D *Hiawatha*
I *Il canto di Hiawatha*
E *La canción de Hiawatha*
SU «Песнь о Гайавáте» (Лонгфéлло)

3474 GB *Song of Roland*, the (1170)
F la *Chanson de Roland*
D das *Rolandslied*
I la *Canzone di Orlando*
E la *Canción de Rolando*
SU «Песнь о Рóланде»

3475 GB Song of Solomon, the (Bib.)
F le Cantique de Salomon (Bib.)
D das hohe Lied Salomonis (Bib.)
I il Cantico dei Cantici (Bib.)
E El Cantor de los Cantores (Bib.)
SU «Песнь пéсней» (библ.)

3476 GB Song of Songs, the (Bib.)
F le Cantique des Cantiques (Bib.)
D das hohe Lied Salomonis (Bib.)
I il Cantico dei Cantici (Bib.)
E El Cantor de los Cantores (Bib.)
SU «Песнь пéсней» (библ.)

3477 GB *Song of the Earth, The* (Mahler, 1908)
F *Le Chant de la terre*
D *Das Lied von der Erde*
I *Il canto della terra*
E *La canción de la tierra*
SU «Песнь о землé» (Мáлер)

3478 GB *Song of the Nibelungs*, the (XIII)
F la *Chanson des Nibelungen*
D das *Nibelungenlied*
I il *Cantare dei Nibelunghi*
E la *Canción de los Nibelungos*
SU «Пéснь о Нибелýнгах»

3479 GB *Songs of a Wayfarer* (Mahler, 1883–5)
F *Chants d'un compagnon errant*
D *Lieder eines fahrenden Gesellen*
I *Canti di un giovanetto errante*
E *Canciones de un mozalbete viajante*
SU «Пéсни стрáнствующего подмастéрья»
(Мáлер)

3480 GB *Songs of Bilitis, The* (Louÿs, 1894)
F *Les Chansons de Bilitis*
D *Lieder der Bilitis*
I *Le canzoni di Bilitide*
E *Las canciones de Bilitis*
SU «Пéсни Билитúс» (Луúс)

3481 GB *Songs of Dusk, The* (Hugo, 1835)
   F   *Les Chants du crépuscule*
   D   *Dämmerungslieder*
   I   *Canti del crepuscolo*
   E   *Los cantos del crepúsculo*
   SU «Пéсни сýмерек» (Гюгó)

3482 GB *Songs of Experience* (Blake, 1794)
   F   *Les Chants d'expérience*
   D   *Lieder der Erfahrung*
   I   *Canti dell'esperienza*
   E   *Cantos de experiencia*
   SU «Пéсни óпыта» (Блейк)

3483 GB *Songs of Innocence* (Blake, 1789)
   F   *Les Chants d'innocence*
   D   *Lieder der Unschuld*
   I   *Canti dell'innocenza*
   E   *Cantos de inocencia*
   SU «Пéсни невúнности» (Блейк)

3484 GB *Songs Without Words* (Mendelssohn, 1829–45)
   F   *Romances sans paroles* (Mendelssohn-Bartholdy)
   D   *Lieder ohne Worte* (Mendelssohn-Bartholdy)
   I   *Lieder senza parole* (Mendelssohn-Bartholdy)
   E   *Romanzas sin palabras* (Mendelssohn-Bartholdy)
   SU «Пéсни без слов» (Мендельсóн-Бартóльди)

3485 GB *Sonnets to Orpheus* (Rilke, 1923)
   F   *Sonnets à Orphée*
   D   *Sonetten an Orpheus*
   I   *Sonetti a Orfeo*
   E   *Sonetos a Orfeo*
   SU «Сонéты к Орфéю» (Рúльке)

3486 GB *Son of a Servant, The* [*Tjänstekvinnans son*] (Strindberg, 1886)
   F   *Le Fils de la servante*
   D   *Der Sohn einer Magd*
   I   *Il figlio della serva*
   E   *El hijo de la criada*
   SU «Сын служáнки» (Стрúндберг)

3487 GB *Sons and Lovers* (Lawrence, 1913)
   F   *Fils et amants*
   D   *Söhne und Liebhaber*
   I   *Figli e amanti*
   E   *Hijos y amantes*
   SU «Сыновья́ и любóвники» (Лóренс)

3488 GB Sophists, the (−V)
   F   les sophistes
   D   die Sophisten
   I   i sofisti
   E   los sofistas
   SU софúсты

3489 GB Sophocles (*496–406*)
   F   Sophocle
   D   Sophokles
   I   Sofocle
   E   Sófocles
   SU Софóкл

3490 GB Sorbonne, the (Paris)
   F   la Sorbonne (Paris)
   D   die Sorbonne (Paris)
   I   la Sorbona (Parigi)
   E   la Sorbona (París)
   SU Сорбóнна (Парúж)

3491 GB *Sorochinsky Fair* (Mussorgsky, 1913)
   F   *La Foire de Sorotchinsti* (Moussorgski)
   D   *Der Jahrmarkt von Sorotschintzi* (Mussorgskij)
   I   *La fiera di Sorotčinsky* (Musorgskij)
   E   *La feria de Sorotchintsi* (Mussorgski)
   SU «Сорочúнская я́рмарка» (Мýсоргский)

3492 GB *Sorrows, the* [*Tristia*] (Ovid, I)
   F   les *Tristes* (Ovide)
   D   die *Trauerlieder* (Ovidius)
   I   le *Tristezze* (Ovidio)
   E   *Tristes* (Ovidio)
   SU «Скóрбные элéгии» (Овúдий)

3493 GB *Sorrows of Young Werther, The* (Goethe, 1774)
   F   *Les Souffrances du jeune Werther*
   D   *Die Leiden des jungen Werthers*
   I   *I dolori del giovane Werther*
   E   *Las desventuras del joven Werther*
   SU «Страдáния ю́ного Вéртера» (Гёте)

3494 GB Sosigenes (−I)
   F   Sosigène
   D   Sosigenes
   I   Sosigene
   E   Sosígenes
   SU Сосигéн

3495 GB *Sound and the Fury, The* (Faulkner, 1929)
   F   *Le Bruit et la fureur*
   D   *Schall und Wahn*
   I   *L'urlo e il furore*
   E   *El ruido y la furia*
   SU «Шум и я́рость» (Фóлкнер)

3496 GB *Sound of Music, The* (Wise, 1965)
F *La Mélodie du bonheur*
D *Meine Lieder – Meine Träume*
I *Tutti insieme appassionatamente*
E *Sonrisas y lágrimas*
SU «Улы́бки сквозь слёзы» (Уайз)

GB *Sous les Toits de Paris→ Under the Roofs of Paris*

3497 GB South Africa
F l'Afrique du Sud
D Südafrika
I l'Africa del Sud
E África del Sur
SU Ю́жная А́фрика

3498 GB South America
F l'Amérique du Sud
D Südamerika
I l'America meridionale
E América del Sur
SU Ю́жная Аме́рика

3499 GB South Australia (Australia)
F l'Australie-Méridionale (Australie)
D Südaustralien (Australien)
I l'Australia Meridionale (Australia)
E Australia Meridional (Australia)
SU Ю́жная Австра́лия (Австра́лия)

3500 GB South Carolina (USA)
F la Caroline du Sud (USA)
D Südcarolina (USA)
I la Carolina del Sud (USA)
E Carolina del Sur (USA)
SU Ю́жная Кароли́на (США)

3501 GB South China Sea, the
F la mer de Chine méridionale
D das Südchinesische Meer
I il mare Cinese Meridionale
E el mar de la China Meridional
SU Южно-Кита́йское мо́ре

3502 GB South Dakota (USA)
F le Dakota du Sud (USA)
D Süddakota (USA)
I la Dakota del Sud (USA)
E Dakota del Sur (USA)
SU Ю́жная Дако́та (США)

3503 GB Southeast Asia
F l'Asie du Sud-Est
D Südostasien
I l'Asia Sudorientale
E Asia sudoriental
SU Ю́го-Восто́чная А́зия

3504 GB South-East Asia Treaty Organisation, the (SEATO)
F l'Organisation du traité de l'Asie du Sud-Est (OTASE)
D der Südostasiatische Sicherheitsvertrag (SEATO)
I l'Organizzazione del trattato dell'Asia sudorientale (SEATO)
E la Organización del tratado de la Asia Sudeste (SEATO)
SU Организа́ция догово́ра Ю́го-Восто́чной А́зии (СЕА́ТО)

3505 GB Southern Cross, the (astron.)
F la Croix du Sud (astron.)
D das Kreuz des Südens (Astron.)
I la Croce del Sud (astr.)
E la Cruz del Sur (astr.)
SU Ю́жный крест (астр.)

3506 GB *Southern Mail* (Saint-Exupéry, 1927)
F *Courrier sud*
D *Südkurier*
I *Corriere Sud*
E *Correo del Sur*
SU «Ю́жный почто́вый» (Сент-Экзюпери́)

3507 GB South Georgia
F la Géorgie du Sud
D Süd-Georgien
I la Georgia del Sud
E Georgia del Sur
SU Ю́жная Гео́ргия

3508 GB South Island (New Zealand)
F l'île du Sud (Nouvelle-Zélande)
D die Südinsel (Neuseeland)
I l'isola del Sud (Nuova Zelanda)
E la isla del Sur (Nueva Zelanda)
SU Ю́жный о́стров (Но́вая Зела́ндия)

3509 GB South Korea
F la Corée du Sud
D Südkorea
I la Corea del Sud
E Corea del Sur
SU Ю́жная Коре́я

3510 GB South Pole, the
F le pôle Sud
D der Südpol
I il polo Sud
E el Polo Sur
SU Ю́жный по́люс

3511 GB South Sandwich Islands, the
    F   les îles Sandwich du Sud
    D   die Süd-Sandwichinseln
    I   le isole Sandwich Australi
    E   las islas Sandwich del Sur
    SU Южные Сáндвичевы островá

3512 GB South Vietnam (hist.)
    F   le Viêt-Nam du Sud (hist.)
    D   Südvietnam (Gesch.)
    I   il Vietnam del Sud (st.)
    E   Vietnam del Sur (hist.)
    SU Южный Вьетнáм (ист.)

3513 GB South West Africa
    F   le Sud-Ouest africain
    D   Südwestafrika
    I   l'Africa del Sud-Ovest
    E   África del Sudoeste
    SU Юго-Зáпадная Áфрика

3514 GB South Yemen
    F   le Yémen du Sud
    D   Südjemen
    I   lo Yemen del Sud
    E   Yemen del Sur
    SU Южный Йéмен

3515 GB Soviet Union, the
    F   l'Union Soviétique
    D   die Sowjetunion
    I   l'Unione Sovietica
    E   la Unión Soviética
    SU Совéтский Сою́з

3516 GB Spain
    F   l'Espagne (f.)
    D   Spanien
    I   la Spagna
    E   España
    SU Испáния

3517 GB Spanish Armada (Invincible Armada),
       the (1588)
    F   l'Invincible Armada
    D   die spanische Armada
    I   l'Invencible Armada
    E   la Armada Invencible
    SU «Непобедúмая армáда»

3518 GB Spanish Civil War, the (1936–9)
    F   la guerre civile d'Espagne
    D   der Spanische Bürgerkrieg
    I   la guerra civile in Spagna
    E   la guerra civil española
    SU граждáнская войнá в Испáния

3519 GB *Spanish Hour, The* (Ravel, 1911)
    F   *L'Heure espagnole*
    D   die *Heure espagnole*
    I   *L'Heure espagnole*
    E   *La hora española*
    SU «Испáнский час» (Равéль)

3520 GB Spanish Inquisition, the (hist.)
    F   l'Inquisition espagnole (hist.)
    D   die Spanische Inquisition (Gesch.)
    I   l'inquisizione spagnola (st.)
    E   la inquisición española (hist.)
    SU инквизúция в Испáнии (ист.)

3521 GB *Spanish Rhapsody* (Ravel, 1907)
    F   *Rhapsodie espagnole*
    D   *Spanische Rhapsodie*
    I   *Rapsodia spagnola*
    E   *Rapsodia española*
    SU «Испáнская рапсóдия» (Равéль)

3522 GB Spanish Sahara, the (hist.)
    F   le Sahara espagnol (hist.)
    D   Spanisch-Sahara (Gesch.)
    I   il Sahara Spagnolo (st.)
    E   el Sáhara Español (hist.)
    SU Испáнская Сахáра (ист.)

3523 GB Spanish Succession, the War of the
       (1701–14)
    F   la guerre de la Succession d'Espagne
    D   der Spanische Erbfolgekrieg
    I   la guerra di successione spagnola
    E   la guerra de Sucesión de España
    SU войнá за испáнское наслéдство

3524 GB *Spanish Symphony* (Lalo, 1873)
    F   *Symphonie espagnole*
    D   *Spanische Symphonie*
    I   *Sinfonia spagnola*
    E   *Sinfonía Española*
    SU «Испáнская симфóния» (Лалó)

3525 GB *Spanish Testament* (Koestler, 1938)
    F   *Le Testament espagnol*
    D   *Ein spanisches Testament*
    I   *Dialogo con la morte*
    E   *Testamento español*
    SU «Испáнское свидéтельство» (Кёстлер)

3526 GB Sparta (Greece)
    F   Sparte (Grèce)
    D   Sparta (Griechenland)
    I   Sparta (Grecia)
    E   Esparta (Grecia)
    SU Спáрта (Грéция)

3527 GB Spartacus (−I)
F Spartacus
D Spartacus
I Spartaco
E Espartaco
SU Спартáк

3528 GB Spartans, the (hist.)
F les Spartiates (hist.)
D die Spartaner (Gesch.)
I i spartiati (st.)
E los espartas (hist.)
SU спартáнцы (ист.)

3529 GB *Spectacles* (Prévert, 1951)
F *Spectacles*
D *Schauspiel*
I *Spettacolo*
E *Espectáculos*
SU «Зрéлище» (Превéр)

3530 GB Speyer (Spires) (Germany)
F Spire (Allemagne)
D Speyer (Deutschland)
I Spira (Germania)
E Espira (Alemania)
SU Шпéйер (Гермáния)

3531 GB Sphinx, the (myth.)
F le sphinx (myth.)
D die Sphinx (myth.)
I la Sfinge (mit.)
E la Esfinge (mit.)
SU сфинкс (миф.)

3532 GB *Spirit of Laws, The* (Montesquieu, 1748)
F *L'Esprit des lois*
D *Der Geist der Gesetze*
I *Lo spirito delle leggi*
E *El espíritu de las leyes*
SU «О дýхе закóнов» (Монтескьё)

3533 GB Split (Yugoslavia)
F Split (Yougoslavie)
D Split (Jugoslawien)
I Spalato (Iugoslavia)
E Split (Yugoslavia)
SU Сплит (Югослáвия)

3534 GB *Spring* (Botticelli, 1477)
F *Printemps*
D *Frühling*
I *Primavera*
E *Primavera*
SU «Веснá» (Боттичéлли)

3535 GB *Spring's Awakening* (Wedekind, 1891)
F *L'Éveil du printemps*
D *Frühlings Erwachen*
I *Risveglio di primavera*
E *Despertar de la primavera*
SU «Пробуждéние весны́» (Вéдекинд)

3536 GB *Sportsman's Notebook* [*Sportman's Sketches*], *A* (Turgenev, 1852)
F *Récits d'un chasseur* (Tourgueniev)
D *Aufzeichnungen eines Jägers* (Turgenjew)
I *Memorie di un cacciatore* (Turgenev)
E *Recuerdos de un cazador* (Turgueniev)
SU «Запи́ски охóтника» (Тургéнев)

3537 GB *Spy, The* (Cooper, 1821)
F *L'Espion*
D *Der Spion*
I *La spia*
E *El Espía*
SU «Шпиóн» (Кýпер)

3538 GB *Spy Who Came in From the Cold, The* (Le Carré, 1963; Ritt, 1965)
F *L'Espion qui venait du froid*
D *Der Spion, der aus der Kälte kam*
I *La spia che venne dal freddo*
E *El espía que surgió del frio*
SU «Шпиóн, пришéдший с хóлода» (Ле Каррé, Ритт)

3539 GB *Squaring the Circle* (Katayev, 1928)
F *La Quadrature du cercle* (Kataiev)
D *Die Quadratur des Kreises* (Katajew)
I *La quadratura del circolo* (Kataiev)
E *La cuadratura del círculo* (Kataiev)
SU «Квадратýра крýга» (Катáев)

3540 GB Sri Lanka
F Sri Lanka
D Sri Lanka
I Sri Lanka
E Sri Lanka
SU Шри-Лáнка

3541 GB *Stabat Mater* (Rossini, 1832−41)
F *Stabat Mater*
D *Stabat Mater*
I *Stabat Mater*
E *Stábat Máter*
SU «Стáбат мáтер» (Росси́ни)

GB Stamboul→Istanbul

3542 GB   *Star!* (Wise, 1968)
    F   *Star*
    D   *Star!*
    I   *Un giorno . . . di prima mattina*
    E   *La estrella*
    SU   «Звезда́» (Уа́йз)

3543 GB   Star Chamber, the (hist., London)
    F   la Chambre étoilée (hist., Londres)
    D   die Sternkammer (Gesch., London)
    I   la camera stellata (st., Londra)
    E   la Cámara Estrellada (hist., Londres)
    SU   Звёздная пала́та (ист., Ло́ндон)

3544 GB   *Star Is Born, A* (Wellman, 1937)
    F   *Une étoile est née*
    D   *Ein neuer Stern am Himmel*
    I   *È nata una stella*
    E   *Ha nacido una estrella*
    SU   «Родила́сь звезда́» (Уэ́ллман)

    GB   Stars and Stripes→Star-Spangled
        Banner

3545 GB   *Stars Look Down, The* (Cronin, 1935)
    F   *Sous le regard des étoiles*
    D   *Die Sterne blicken herab*
    I   *E le stelle stanno a guardare*
    E   *Las estrellas miran hacia abajo*
    SU   «Звёзды смо́трят вниз» (Кро́нин)

3546 GB   Star-Spangled Banner, the
    F   la bannière étoilée
    D   das Sternenbanner
    I   la bandiera stellata
    E   la bandera estrellada
    SU   Звёздное зна́мя

3547 GB   *Star Wars* (Lucas, 1977)
    F   *La guerre des étoiles*
    D   *Krieg der Sterne*
    I   *Guerre stellari*
    E   *Guerras de estrella*
    SU   «Звёздные во́йны» (Лу́кас)

3548 GB   *State of Siege* (Camus, 1948)
    F   *L'État de siège*
    D   *Belagerungszustand*
    I   *Stato d'assedio*
    E   *El estado de sitio*
    SU   «Оса́дное положе́ние» (Камю́)

3549 GB   States of the Church, the (hist.)
    F   les États de l'Église (hist.)
    D   der Kirchenstaat (Gesch.)
    I   lo Stato della Chiesa (st.)
    E   los Estados de la Iglesia (hist.)
    SU   па́пское госуда́рство (ист.)

3550 GB   Statue of Liberty, the (New York)
    F   la statue de la Liberté (New-York)
    D   die Freiheitsstatue (New-York)
    I   la statua della Libertà (New York)
    E   la estatua de la Libertad (Nueva York)
    SU   ста́туя Свобо́ды (Нью-Йо́рк)

3551 GB   *Stello* (Vigny, 1832)
    F   *Stello*
    D   *Stello*
    I   *Stello*
    E   *Stello*
    SU   «Сте́лло» (Виньи́)

3552 GB   Stephen (saint, pope, king)
    F   Étienne (saint, pape, roi)
    D   Stephan (Heiliger, Papst, König)
    I   Stefano (santo, papa, re)
    E   Esteban (santo, papa, rey)
    SU   Стефа́н (св., па́па ри́мский, коро́ль)

3553 GB   *Sting, The* (Hill, 1973)
    F   *Attaque*
    D   *Der Stachel*
    I   *La stangata*
    E   *El aguijón*
    SU   «Уку́с» (Хилл)

3554 GB   Stockholm (Sweden)
    F   Stockholm (Suède)
    D   Stockholm (Schweden)
    I   Stoccolma (Svezia)
    E   Estocolmo (Suecia)
    SU   Стокго́льм (Шве́ция)

3555 GB   *Stolen Kisses* (Truffaut, 1968)
    F   *Baisers volés*
    D   *Geraubte Küsse*
    I   *Baci rubati*
    E   *Besos robados*
    SU   «Укра́денные поцелу́и» (Трюффо́)

3556 GB   *Stones of Venice, The* (Ruskin, 1851–3)
    F   *Les Pierres de Venise*
    D   *Die Steine von Venedig*
    I   *Le pietre di Venezia*
    E   *Las piedras de Venecia*
    SU   «Ка́мни Вене́ции» (Ре́скин)

3557 GB   *Stories for a Year* (Pirandello, 1922–
        36)
    F   *Nouvelles pour un an*
    D   *Novellen für ein Jahr*
    I   *Novelle per un anno*
    E   *Novelas para un año*
    SU   «Нове́ллы на год» (Пиранде́лло)

3558 GB *Storm, The* (Ostrovsky)
    F *L'Orage* (Ostrovski)
    D *Das Gewitter* (Ostrowskij)
    I *L'uragano* (Ostrovskij)
    E *La tempestad* (Ostrovsky)
    SU «Гроза́» (Остро́вский)

3559 GB *Story of Christ, The* (Papini, 1921)
    F *L'Histoire du Christ*
    D *Die Lebensgeschichte Christi*
    I *Storia di Cristo*
    E *Vida de Cristo*
    SU «Жизнь Христа́» (Папи́ни)

3560 GB *Story of San Michele, The* (Munthe, 1929)
    F *Le Livre de San Michele*
    D *Das Buch von San Michele*
    I *La storia di San Michele*
    E *La historia de San Michele*
    SU «Кни́га о Сан-Мике́ле» (Мю́нте)

3561 GB Strabo (−64−+23)
    F Strabon
    D Strabon
    I Strabone
    E Estrabón
    SU Страбо́н

3562 GB *Strait is the Gate* (Gide, 1909)
    F *La Porte étroite*
    D *Die enge Pforte*
    I *La porta stretta*
    E *La puerta estrecha*
    SU «Те́сные врата́» (Жид)

    GB Strait(s) of . . . → . . . , Strait(s) of

3563 GB *Strange Case of Dr Jekyll and Mr Hyde, The* (Stevenson, 1886)
    F *Docteur Jekyll et M. Hyde*
    D *Dr Jekyll und Mr. Hyde*
    I *Lo strano caso del dottor Jekyll e del signor Hyde*
    E *El extraño caso del Dr. Jekyll y de Mr. Hyde*
    SU «Стра́нная исто́рия до́ктора Дже́келя и ми́стера Ха́йда» (Сти́венсон)

3564 GB *Strange Interlude* (O'Neill, 1928)
    F *L'Étrange Intermède*
    D *Seltsames Zwischenspiel*
    I *Strano interludio*
    E *Extraño interludio*
    SU «Стра́нная интерлю́дия» (О'Ни́л)

3565 GB *Stranger, The* (Kotzebue, 1789)
    F *Misanthropie et Repentir*
    D *Menschenhasse und Reue*
    I *Odio e pentimento*
    E *Misantropía y arrepentimiento*
    SU «Не́нависть к лю́дям и раска́яние» (Коцебу́)

3566 GB *Strangers and Brothers* (Snow, 1940)
    F *Étrangers et frères*
    D *Fremde und Brüder*
    I *Stranieri e fratelli*
    E *Extranjeros y hermanos*
    SU «Чужи́е и бра́тья» (Сно́у)

3567 GB Strasbourg (France)
    F Strasbourg (France)
    D Straßbourg (Frankreich)
    I Strasburgo (Francia)
    E Estrasburgo (Francia)
    SU Страсбу́р (Фра́нция)

3568 GB *Straw Dogs* (Peckinpah, 1971)
    F *Chiens de paille*
    D *Wer Gewalt sät*
    I *Cane di paglia*
    E *Perros de paja*
    SU «Соло́менные соба́ки» (Пе́кинпа)

3569 GB *Streetcar Named Desire, A* (Williams, 1947)
    F *Un tramway nommé Désir*
    D *Endstation Sehnsucht*
    I *Un tram chiamato desiderio*
    E *Un tranvía llamado deseo*
    SU «Трамва́й ,,Жела́ние''» (Уи́льямс)

3570 GB *Strife* (Galsworthy, 1909)
    F *Lutte*
    D *Kampf*
    I *Lotta*
    E *Disensión*
    SU «Борьба́» (Го́лсуорси)

3571 GB *Strong as Death* (Maupassant, 1889)
    F *Fort comme la mort*
    D *Stark wie der Tod*
    I *Forte come la morte*
    E *Fuerte como la muerte*
    SU «Сильна́ как смерть» (Мопасса́н)

3572 GB *Struggle Until Dawn* (Betti, 1945)
    F *Lutte à l'aube*
    D *Kampf bis zum Morgengrauen*
    I *Lotta fino all'alba*
    E *Lucha hasta el alba*
    SU «Борьба́ до рассве́та» (Бе́тти)

3573 GB *Student Prince, The* (Lubitsch, 1927)
    F *Vieil Heidelberg*
    D *Alt-Heidelberg*
    I *Il principe studente*
    E *El príncipe estudiante*
    SU «Принц-студе́нт» (Лю́бич)

3574 GB *Study in Scarlet, A* (Doyle, 1887)
    F *La Tache écarlate*
    D *Studien in Scharlachrot*
    I *Uno studio in rosso*
    E *Estudio en escarlata*
    SU «Этю́д в кра́сном» (Дойл)

3575 GB Stuttgart (Germany)
    F Stuttgart (Allemagne)
    D Stuttgart (Deutschland)
    I Stoccarda (Germania)
    E Stuttgart (Alemania)
    SU Штутгарт (Герма́ния)

3576 GB Styx, the (myth.)
    F le Styx (myth.)
    D der Styx (myth.)
    I lo Stige (mit.)
    E el Estigia (mit.)
    SU Стикс (миф.)

3577 GB Sudan, the
    F le Soudan
    D Sudan
    I il Sudan
    E Sudán
    SU Суда́н

3578 GB Sudetenland (hist.)
    F la région des Sudètes (hist.)
    D Sudetenland (Gesch.)
    I la regione dei sudeti (st.)
    E la región de los sudetes (hist.)
    SU Суде́тская о́бласть (ист.)

3579 GB Suetonius (*69–122*)
    F Suétone
    D Suetonius
    I Svetonio
    E Suetonio
    SU Свето́ний

3580 GB Suez, the Gulf of
    F le golfe de Suez
    D der Golf von Suez
    I il golfo di Suez
    E el golfo de Suez
    SU Су́эцкий зали́в

3581 GB Suez Canal, the
    F le canal de Suez
    D der Suezkanal
    I il canale di Suez
    E el canal de Suez
    SU Су́эцкий кана́л

3582 GB Sumerians, the (hist.)
    F les Sumériens (hist.)
    D die Sumerer (Gesch.)
    I i sumeri (st.)
    E los sumerios (hist.)
    SU шуме́ры (ист.)

3583 GB *Summa Theologiae* [*Summary of*
      Theology] (Thomas Aquinas, 1265–73)
    F *Summa Theologiae* (Thomas d'Aquin)
    D *Summe der Theologie* (Thomas von
      Aquilo)
    I *Summa theologiae* (Tommaso
      d'Aquino)
    E *Summa Theologiae* (Tomás de
      Aquino)
    SU «Су́мма теоло́гии» (Фома́ Акви́нский)

3584 GB *Sun Also Rises, The* (Hemingway,
      1926)
    F *Le soleil se lève aussi*
    D *Fiesta*
    I *Il sole sorge ancora*
    E *Fiesta*
    SU «И восхо́дит со́лнце» (Хемингуэ́й)

3585 GB *Sunday, Bloody Sunday* (Schlesinger,
      1971)
    F *Un dimanche comme les autres*
    D *Sunday, Bloody Sunday*
    I *Domenica, maledetta domenica*
    E *Domingo, maldito domingo*
    SU «Воскресе́нье, прокля́тое
      воскресе́нье» (Шле́зингер)

3586 GB *Sunken Bell, The* (Hauptmann, 1896;
      Respighi, 1927)
    F *La Cloche engloutie*
    D *Die versunkene Glocke*
    I *La campana sommersa*
    E *La campana sumergida*
    SU «Потону́вший ко́локол» (Га́уптман,
      Респи́ги)

3587 GB Sun King, the (= Louis XIV)
    F le Roi-Soleil (= Louis XIV)
    D der Sonnenkönig (= Ludwig XIV)
    I il Re Sole (= Luigi XIV)
    E el Rey Sol (= Luis XIV)
    SU «коро́ль-со́лнце» (= Людо́вик XIV)

3588 GB *Sunset Boulevard* (Wilder, 1950)
F *Boulevard du crépuscule*
D *Boulevard der Dämmerung*
I *Viale del tramonto*
E *El crepúsculo de los dioses*
SU «Бульва́р Со́лнечных зака́тов» (Уа́йлдер)

3589 GB Superior, Lake (Canada/USA)
F le lac Supérior (Canada/USA)
D der Obere See (Kanada/USA)
I il lago Superiore (Canada/USA)
E el lago Superior (Canadá/USA)
SU о́зеро Ве́рхнее (Кана́да/США)

3590 GB *Suppliant Women, The [Hiketides]* (Aeschylus, −490; Euripides, −421)
F *Les Suppliantes* (Eschyle, Euripide)
D *Die Schutzflehenden* (Aischylos, Euripides)
I *Le supplici* (Eschilo, Euripide)
E *Las suplicantes* (Esquilo, Eurípides)
SU «Проси́тельницы» (Эсхи́л, Еврипи́д)

3591 GB *Supposes, The* (Gascoigne, 1566)
F *Les Supposes*
D *Die Vermutungen*
I *Supposes*
E *Supposes*
SU «Подменённые» (Га́скойн)

3592 GB Surinam
F le Surinam
D Surinam
I il Suriname
E Surinam
SU Сурина́м

3593 GB *Surprise of Love, The* (Marivaux, 1722)
F *La Surprise de l'amour*
D *Der Überfall der Liebe*
I *La sorpresa dell'amore*
E *La sorpresa del amor*
SU «Сюрпри́з любви́» (Мариво́)

3594 GB *Susanna's Secret* (Wolf-Ferrari, 1909)
F *Le Secret de Suzanne*
D *Susannes Geheimnis*
I *Il segreto di Susanna*
E *El secreto de Susanna*
SU «Та́йна Суса́нны» (Вольф-Ферра́ри)

3595 GB *Suspicion* (Hitchcock, 1941)
F *Soupçons*
D *Verdacht*
I *Sospetto*
E *Sospecha*
SU «Подозре́ние» (Хи́чкок)

3596 GB Swabia (Germany)
F la Souabe (Allemagne)
D Schwaben (Deutschland)
I la Svevia (Germania)
E Suabia (Alemania)
SU Шва́бия (Герма́ния)

3597 GB *Swan Lake* (Tchaikovsky, 1876)
F *Le Lac des cygnes* (Tchaïkovski)
D *Schwanensee* (Tschaikowskij)
I *Il lago dei cigni* (Čaikovski)
E *El lago de los cisnes* (Tchaikovski)
SU «Лебеди́ное о́зеро» (Чайко́вский)

3598 GB *Swann's Way* (Proust, 1913)
F *Du côté de chez Swann*
D *Der Weg zu Swann*
I *La strada di Swann*
E *Por el camino de Swann*
SU «По направле́нию к Сва́ну» (Пруст)

3599 GB Swaziland
F le Swaziland
D Swasiland
I lo Swaziland
E Suazilandia
SU Свазиле́нд

3600 GB Sweden
F la Suède
D Schweden
I la Svezia
E Suecia
SU Шве́ция

3601 GB *Swing, The* (Fragonard, 1766)
F *Les Hasards heureux de l'escarpolette*
D *Die Schaukel*
I *Gli allegri rischi dell'altalena*
E *El columpio*
SU «Каче́ли» (Фрагона́р)

3602 GB Swiss Confederation, the
F la Confédération suisse
D die Schweizerische Eidgenossenschaft
I la Confederazione Elvetica
E la Confederación Suiza
SU Швейца́рская Конфедера́ция

3603 GB *Swiss Family Robinson, The* (Wyss, 1813)
F *Robinson suisse*
D *Der Schweizerische Robinson*
I *Robinson svizzero*
E *El Robinson suizo*
SU «Швейца́рский Робинзо́н» (Висс)

3604 GB Switzerland
F la Suisse
D die Schweiz
I la Svizzera
E Suiza
SU Швейца́рия

3605 GB Sylvester (saint, pope)
F Sylvestre (saint, pape)
D Silvester (Heiliger, Papst)
I Silvestro (santo, papa)
E Silvestre (santo, papa)
SU Сильве́стр (св., па́па ри́мский)

3606 GB *Symphonic Studies* (Schumann, 1834)
F *Études symphoniques*
D *Sinfonische Etüden*
I *Studi sinfonici*
E *Estudios sinfónicos*
SU «Симфони́ческие этю́ды» (Шу́ман)

3607 GB *Symphonic Variations* (Franck, 1885)
F les *Variations symphoniques*
D *Sinfonische Variationen*
I *Variazioni sinfoniche*
E *Variaciones sinfónicas*
SU «Симфони́ческие вариа́ции» (Франк)

3608 GB *Symposium* (Plato, IV)
F *Le Banquet* (Platon)
D *Das Gastmahl* (Platon)
I *Il simposio* (Platone)
E *El banquete* (Platón)
SU «Пир» (Плато́н)

3609 GB Syracuse (Italy)
F Syracuse (Italie)
D Syrakus (Italien)
I Siracusa (Italia)
E Siracusa (Italia)
SU Сираку́зы (ж.) (Ита́лия)

3610 GB Syria
F la Syrie
D Syrien
I la Siria
E Siria
SU Си́рия

3611 GB *System of Logic, A* (Mill, 1843)
F *Logique inductive et déductive*
D *Ein System der induktiven und deduktiven Logik*
I *Sistema di logica deduttiva e induttiva*
E *Lógica deductiva e inductiva*
SU «Систе́ма ло́гики» (Милль)

3612 GB *System of Nature, The* (Holbach, 1770)
F *Système de la nature*
D *System der Natur*
I *Sistema della natura*
E *Sistema de la naturaleza*
SU «Систе́ма приро́ды» (Го́льбах)

3613 GB Szczecin (Poland)
F Szczecin (Pologne)
D Stettin (Polen)
I Stettino (Polonia)
E Szczecin (Polonia)
SU Ще́цин (По́льша)

T

3614 GB Table Mountain, the (Cape Town)
F   la montagne de la Table (Le Cap)
D   der Tafelberg (Kapstadt)
I   la montagna della Tavola (Città del Capo)
E   la montaña de la Tabla (El Cabo)
SU Столóвая горá (Кейптáун)

3615 GB *Table Talk* (Hazlitt, 1821–2)
F   *Propos de table*
D   *Tischplauderei*
I   *Conversazione attorno alla tavola*
E   *Charla de sobremesa*
SU «Застóльная бесéда» (Хэ́злитт)

3616 GB Tacitus (*56–120*)
F   Tacite
D   Tacitus
I   Tacito
E   Tácito
SU Тáцит

3617 GB Tadzhikistan (USSR)
F   le Tadjikistan (URSS)
D   Tadschikistan (UdSSR)
I   il Tadžikistan (URSS)
E   Tadjikistán (URSS)
SU Таджикистáн (СССР)

3618 GB Tagus (River), the (Portugal/Spain)
F   le Tage (Portugal/Espagne)
D   der Tajo (Portugal/Spanien)
I   il Tago (Portogallo/Spagna)
E   el Tajo (Portugal/España)
SU Тáхо (Португáлия/Испáния)

3619 GB Tahiti
F   Tahiti (m.)
D   Tahiti
I   Tahiti
E   Tahiti
SU Таи́ти

3620 GB Taiwan
F   Taiwan
D   Taiwan
I   Taiwan
E   Taiwan
SU Тайвáнь (м.)

3621 GB Taj Mahal, the (Agra)
F   le Tadj Mahall (Agra)
D   das Tadsch Mahal (Agra)
I   il Taj-Mahal (Agra)
E   el Tadj-Mahall (Agra)
SU Тадж-Махáл (А́гра)

3622 GB *Tale of an Algerian Trooper, The* (Loti, 1881)
F   *Le Roman d'un spahi*
D   *Der Spahi*
I   *Il romanzo di un spahi*
E   *La novela de un espahí*
SU «Ромáн одногó спаги́» (Лоти́)

3623 GB *Tale of a Tub, A* (Swift, 1704)
F   *Le Conte du tonneau*
D   *Ein Märchen von der Tonne*
I   *La favola della botte*
E   *El cuento del tonel*
SU «Скáзка о бóчке» (Свифт)

3624 GB *Tale of the Love and Death of Cornet Christopher Rilke, The* (Rilke, 1899)
F   *Chant de l'amour et de la mort du cornette Christophe Rilke*
D   *Weise von Liebe und Tod des Cornets Christoph Rilke*
I   *Canto di amore e di morte dell'alfiere Christoph Rilke*
E   *Canción de amor y muerte del alférez Cristóbal Rilke*
SU «Песнь о любви́ и смéрти корнéта Христофóра Ри́льке» (Ри́льке)

3625 GB *Tale of Two Cities, A* (Dickens, 1859)
  F *Un Conte de Deux Villes*
  D *Die Geschichte zweier Städte*
  I *Le due città*
  E *Historia de dos ciudades*
  SU «Пóвесть о двух городáх» (Дѝккенс)

3626 GB *Tales from Shakespeare* (Lamb, 1808)
  F *Contes tirés de Shakespeare*
  D *Shakespeare-Erzählungen*
  I *Racconti tratti da Shakespeare*
  E *Cuentos inspirados en Shakespeare*
  SU «Расскáзы из Шекспѝра» (Лэм)

3627 GB *Tales from the Vienna Woods* (Strauss, 1868)
  F *Contes des bois de Vienne*
  D *Geschichten aus dem Wienerwald*
  I *Storielle del bosco viennese*
  E *Cuentos de los bosques de Viena*
  SU «Скáзки Вéнского лéса» (Штрáус)

3628 GB *Tales of a Wayside Inn* (Longfellow, 1863)
  F *Contes d'un auberge au bord de la route*
  D *Geschichten aus einem Gasthof an der Straße*
  I *Racconti di un'osteria lungo la strada*
  E *Cuentos de una posada a pie del camino*
  SU «Расскáзы придорóжной гостѝницы» (Лонгфéлло)

3629 GB *Tales of Belkin, The* (Pushkin, 1830)
  F *Les Récits de Bielkine* (Pouchkine)
  D *Belkins Erzählungen* (Puschkin)
  I *Racconti di Belkin* (Puškin)
  E *Los relatos de Belkin* (Puschkin)
  SU «Пóвести Бéлкина» (Пýшкин)

3630 GB *Tales of Hoffmann, The* (Offenbach, 1881)
  F *Les Contes d'Hoffmann*
  D *Hoffmanns Erzählungen*
  I *I racconti di Hoffmann*
  E *Cuentos de Hoffmann*
  SU «Скáзки Гóфмана» (Оффенбáх)

3631 GB *Tales of Spain and Italy* (Musset, 1830)
  F *Contes d'Espagne et d'Italie*
  D *Erzählungen aus Spanien und Italien*
  I *Racconti di Spagna e d'Italia*
  E *Cuentos de España y de Italia*
  SU «Испáнские и итальянские пóвести» (Мюссé)

3632 GB *Tales of the Grotesque and Arabesque* (Poe, 1834)
  F *Contes de la Grotesque et Arabesque*
  D *Unheimliche Geschichten*
  I *Racconti arabeschi*
  E *Narraciones extraordinarias*
  SU «Гротéски и арабéски» (По)

3633 GB *Tales of the Serapion Brothers* (Hoffmann, 1819–20)
  F *Contes des frères Serapion*
  D *Die Serapionsbrüder*
  I *I fratelli di San Serapione*
  E *Cuentos de los hermanos Serapión*
  SU «Серапиóновы брáтья» (Гóфман)

3634 GB *Talisman, The* (Scott, 1825)
  F *Le Talisman*
  D *Der Talisman*
  I *Il talismano*
  E *El talismán*
  SU «Талисмáн» (Скотт)

3635 GB Talmud, the (rel.)
  F le Talmud (relig.)
  D der Talmud (relig.)
  I il Talmud (relig.)
  E el Talmud (relig.)
  SU «Талмýд» (рел.)

3636 GB Tamburlaine the Great (1336–1405; + Marlowe, 1587)
  F Tamerlan le Grand
  D Tamerland der Große
  I Tamerlano il Grande
  E Tamerlán el Grande
  SU Тимýр Велѝкий (+ Мáрло)

3637 GB *Taming of the Shrew, The* (Shakespeare, 1593)
  F *La Mégère apprivoisée*
  D *Der Widerspenstigen Zähmung*
  I *La bisbetica domata*
  E *La fierecilla domada*
  SU «Укрощéние строптѝвой» (Шекспѝр)

3638 GB Tancred (king, + Rossini, 1813)
  F Tancrède (roi)
  D Tankred (König)
  I Tancredi (re)
  E Tancredo (rey)
  SU Танкрéд (царь, + Россѝни)

3639 GB Tanganyika (hist.)
  F le Tanganyika (hist.)
  D Tanganjika (Gesch.)
  I la Tanganica (st.)
  E Tanganica (hist.)
  SU Танганьѝка (ист.)

3640	GB	Tangier(s) (Morocco)
	F	Tanger (Maroc)
	D	Tanger (Marokko)
	I	Tangeri (Morocco)
	E	Tánger (Marruecos)
	SU	Танжéр (Марóкко)

3641	GB	Tannhäuser (XIII; + Wagner, 1845)
	F	Tannhäuser
	D	Tannhäuser
	I	Tannhäuser
	E	Tannhäuser
	SU	Тангéйзер (+ Вáгнер)

3642	GB	Tantalus (myth.)
	F	Tantale (myth.)
	D	Tantalus (myth.)
	I	Tantalo (mit.)
	E	Tántalo (mit.)
	SU	Тантáл (миф.)

3643	GB	Tanzania
	F	la Tanzanie
	D	Tansania
	I	la Tanzania
	E	Tanzania
	SU	Танзáния

3644	GB	Taranto (Italy)
	F	Tarente (Italie)
	D	Tarent (Italien)
	I	Taranto (Italia)
	E	Tarento (Italia)
	SU	Тарáнто (Итáлия)

3645	GB	*Taras Bulba* (Gogol, 1835)
	F	*Tarass Boulba*
	D	*Taras Bulba*
	I	*Taras Bul'ba*
	E	*Taras Bulba*
	SU	«Тарáс Бýльба» (Гóголь)

3646	GB	Tarquin (king)
	F	Tarquin (roi)
	D	Tarquinius (König)
	I	Tarquinio (re)
	E	Tarquino (rey)
	SU	Таркви́ний (царь)

3647	GB	Tarragona (Spain)
	F	Tarragone (Espagne)
	D	Tarragona (Spanien)
	I	Tarragona (Spagna)
	E	Tarragona (España)
	SU	Таррагóна (Испáния)

3648	GB	Tarsus (Bib.)
	F	Tarse (Bib.)
	D	Tarsus (Bib.)
	I	Tarso (Bib.)
	E	Tarso (Bib.)
	SU	Тарс (библ.)

	GB	*Tartarin of Tarascon→Prodigious Adventures of Tartarin of Tarascon*

3649	GB	Tartars (Tatars), the (hist.)
	F	les Tatars (hist.)
	D	die Tataren (Gesch.)
	I	i tatari (st.)
	E	los tátaros (hist.)
	SU	татáры (ист.)

3650	GB	Tartarus (myth.)
	F	Tartare (myth.)
	D	Tartarus (myth.)
	I	Tartaro (mit.)
	E	Tártaro (mit.)
	SU	Тáртар (миф.)

3651	GB	*Tartuffe* (Molière, 1664)
	F	*Tartuffe*
	D	*Tartuffe*
	I	*Tartufo*
	E	*Tartufo*
	SU	«Тартю́ф» (Мольéр)

3652	GB	*Tarzan* (Burroughs, 1912)
	F	*Tarzan*
	D	*Tarzan*
	I	*Tarzan*
	E	*Tarzán*
	SU	«Тарзáн» (Бéрроуз)

3653	GB	Tasmania (Australia)
	F	la Tasmanie (Australie)
	D	Tasmanien (Australien)
	I	la Tasmania (Australia)
	E	Tasmania (Australia)
	SU	Тасмáния (Австрáлия)

3654	GB	Tasso (1544–95)
	F	le Tasse
	D	Tasso
	I	Tasso
	E	Tasso
	SU	Тáссо

3655	GB	*Taste of Honey, A* (Delaney, 1958)
	F	*Un goût de miel*
	D	*Bitterer Honig*
	I	*Sapore di miele*
	E	*Sabor a miel*
	SU	«Вкус мёда» (Дилэ́ни)

GB   Tatars→Tartars

3656 GB   Taurus (astron.)
 F   le Taureau (astron.)
 D   der Stier (Astron.)
 I   il Toro (astr.)
 E   el Tauro (astr.)
 SU   Телец (астр.)

3657 GB   *Taxi Driver* (Scorsese, 1976)
 F   *Taxi Driver*
 D   *Taxi-Driver*
 I   *Taxi Driver*
 E   *Taxi Driver*
 SU   «Таксист» (Скорсéсе)

3658 GB   Tchaikovsky (1840–93)
 F   Tchaikovski
 D   Tschaikowskij
 I   Čaikovskij
 E   Tchaikovski
 SU   Чайкóвский

3659 GB   Tehran (Teheran) (Iran)
 F   Téhéran (Iran)
 D   Teheran (Iran)
 I   Teheran (Iran)
 E   Teherán (Irán)
 SU   Тегерáн (Ирáн)

3660 GB   Telemachus (myth., + Fénelon, 1699)
 F   Télémaque (myth.)
 D   Telemach (myth.)
 I   Telemaco (mit.)
 E   Telémaco (mit.)
 SU   Телемáх (+ Фенелóн)

GB   Tell, William→William Tell

3661 GB   *Tellier House, The* (Maupassant, 1881)
 F   *La Maison Tellier*
 D   *Das Haus Tellier*
 I   *La casa Tellier*
 E   *La casa Tellier*
 SU   «Заведéние Тельé» (Мопассáн)

3662 GB   *Tell-Tale Heart, The* (Poe, 1843)
 F   *Le Coeur révélateur*
 D   *Das verräterische Herz*
 I   *Il cuore rivelatore*
 E   *El corazón delator*
 SU   «Предáтельское сéрдце» (По)

3663 GB   *Tempest, The* (Shakespeare, 1611)
 F   *La Tempête*
 D   *Der Sturm*
 I   *La tempesta*
 E   *La tempestad*
 SU   «Бýря» (Шекспúр)

3664 GB   Templars, the (rel.)
 F   les Templiers (relig.)
 D   die Tempelherren (relig.)
 I   i templari (relig.)
 E   los templarios (relig.)
 SU   тамплиéры (рел.)

3665 GB   *Temptation of Saint Anthony, The* (Flaubert, 1874)
 F   *La Tentation de saint Antoine*
 D   *Die Versuchung des Heiligen Antonius*
 I   *Tentazione di sant'Antonio*
 E   *La tentación de San Antonio*
 SU   «Искушéние святóго Антóния» (Флобéр)

3666 GB   *Tenant of Wildfell Hall, The* (Brontë, 1848)
 F   *Le Locataire de Wildfell Hall*
 D   *Der Pächter von Wildfell Hall*
 I   *L'affittuaria di Wildfell Hall*
 E   *La dama de Wildfell Hall*
 SU   «Арендáтор Вáйлдфелл-Гóлла» (Брóнте)

3667 GB   Ten Commandments, the (Bib.)
 F   les dix commandements (Bib.)
 D   die zehn Gebote (Bib.)
 I   i dieci precetti (Bib.)
 E   los diez mandamientos (Bib.)
 SU   дéсять зáповедей (библ.)

3668 GB   *Ten Days That Shook the World* (Reed, 1919)
 F   *Dix Jours qui ebranlèrent le monde*
 D   *Zehn Tage, die die Welt erschütterten*
 I   *Dieci giorni che sconvolsero il mondo*
 E   *Diez días que conmovieron al mundo*
 SU   «Дéсять дней, котóрые потряслú мир» (Рид)

3669 GB   *Tender Husband, The* (Steele + Addison, 1705)
 F   *Le Tendre Époux*
 D   *Der zärtliche Ehemann*
 I   *Il marito affettuoso*
 E   *El marido afectuoso*
 SU   «Нéжный муж» (Стил/Áддисон)

3670 GB   *Tender is the Night* (Fitzgerald, 1934)
 F   *Tendre est la nuit*
 D   *Zärtlich ist die Nacht*
 I   *Tenera è la notte*
 E   *Tierna es la noche*
 SU   «Ночь нежнá» (Фицджéральд)

3671	GB	Terence (*186–159*)
	F	Térence
	D	Terenz
	I	Terenzio
	E	Terencio
	SU	Терéнций

3672	GB	Teresa of Avila (saint, 1515–82)
	F	Thérèse d'Avila (sainte)
	D	Theresia von Avila (Heilige)
	I	Teresa d'Avila (santa)
	E	Teresa de Jesús (santa)
	SU	Терéза Авѝльская (св.)

3673	GB	Terpsichore (myth.)
	F	Terpsichore (myth.)
	D	Terpsichore (myth.)
	I	Tersicore (mit.)
	E	Terpsícore (mit.)
	SU	Терпсихóра (миф.)

3674	GB	*Terrible Children, The* (Cocteau, 1929)
	F	*Les Enfants terribles*
	D	*Die schrecklichen Kinder*
	I	*I ragazzi terribili*
	E	*Los niños terribles*
	SU	«Трýдные дéти» (Коктó)

	GB	*Terrible Parents, The*→*Parents Terribles, Les*
	GB	Terror, the Reign of→Reign of Terror

3675	GB	Tertullian (*155–220*)
	F	Tertullien
	D	Tertullian
	I	Tertulliano
	E	Tertuliano
	SU	Тертуллиáн

3676	GB	*Tess of the D'Urbervilles* (Hardy, 1891)
	F	*Tess d'Urberville*
	D	*Tess von D'Urbervilles*
	I	*Tess dei D'Urbervilles*
	E	*Teresa la de Urberville*
	SU	«Тэсс из рóда д'Эрбервѝлей» (Хáрди)

3677	GB	Tethys (myth.)
	F	Téthys (myth.)
	D	Tethys (myth.)
	I	Teti (mit.)
	E	Tetis (mit)
	SU	Тефѝда (миф.)

3678	GB	Teutons, the (hist.)
	F	les Teutons (hist.)
	D	die Teutonen (Gesch.)
	I	i teutoni (st.)
	E	los teutones (hist.)
	SU	тевтóны (ист.)

3679	GB	Texas (USA)
	F	le Texas (USA)
	D	Texas (USA)
	I	il Texas (USA)
	E	Texas (USA)
	SU	Техáс (США)

3680	GB	Thailand
	F	le Thaïlande
	D	Thailand
	I	la Thailandia
	E	Tailandia
	SU	Таилáнд

3681	GB	*Thaïs* (Massenet, 1894)
	F	*Thaïs*
	D	*Thaïs*
	I	*Thaïs*
	E	*Thais*
	SU	«Таис» (Массné)

3682	GB	Thales (*624–546*)
	F	Thalès
	D	Thales
	I	Talete
	E	Tales
	SU	Фалéс

3683	GB	Thalia (myth.)
	F	Thalie (myth.)
	D	Thalia (myth.)
	I	Talia (mit.)
	E	Talía (mit.)
	SU	Тáлия (миф.)

3684	GB	Thames (River), the (England)
	F	la Tamise (Angleterre)
	D	die Themse (England)
	I	il Tamigi (Inghilterra)
	E	el Támesis (Inglaterra)
	SU	Тéмза (Áнглия)

3685	GB	*That Uncertain Feeling* (Amis, 1955)
	F	*Ce sentiment incertain*
	D	*Jenes ungewisse Gefühl*
	I	*Quel sentimento incerto*
	E	*Una extraña sensación*
	SU	«Это неопределённое чýвство» (Эмис)

3686 GB   *Thaw, The* (Ehrenburg, 1954–6)
    F   *Le Dégel* (Ehrenbourg)
    D   *Tauwetter* (Ehrenburg)
    I   *Il disgelo* (Erenburg)
    E   *El deshielo* (Ehrenburg)
    SU   «Óттепель» (Эренбу́рг)

3687 GB   *Theatre of Clara Gazul, The* (Mérimée, 1825)
    F   *Théâtre de Clara Gazul*
    D   *Theater von Clara Gazul*
    I   *Teatro di Clara Gazul*
    E   *Teatro de Clara Gazul*
    SU   «Теа́тр Кла́ры Гасу́ль» (Мериме́)

3688 GB   Thebes (Greece, Egypt)
    F   Thèbes (Grèce, Égypte)
    D   Theben (Griechenland, Ägypten)
    I   Tebe (Grecia, Egitto)
    E   Tebas (Grecia, Egipto)
    SU   Фи́вы (ж.) (Гре́ция, Еги́пет)

3689 GB   Themis (myth.)
    F   Thémis (myth.)
    D   Themis (myth.)
    I   Temi (mit.)
    E   Temis (mit.)
    SU   Феми́да (миф.)

3690 GB   Themistocles (*524–460*)
    F   Thémistocle
    D   Themistokles
    I   Temistocle
    E   Temístocles
    SU   Фемисто́кл

3691 GB   *Theodicy* (Leibniz, 1710)
    F   *Essais de Théodicée*
    D   *Theodizee*
    I   *Saggi di teodicea*
    E   *Teodicea*
    SU   «Теодице́я» (Ле́йбниц)

3692 GB   Theodore (saint, pope)
    F   Théodore (saint, pape)
    D   Theodor (Heiliger, Papst)
    I   Teodoro (santo, papa)
    E   Teodoro (santo, papa)
    SU   Теодо́р (св., па́па ри́мский)

3693 GB   Theodosius (emperor)
    F   Théodose (empereur)
    D   Theodosius (Kaiser)
    I   Teodosio (imperatore)
    E   Teodosio (emperador)
    SU   Феодо́сий (импера́тор)

3694 GB   *Theogony*, the (Hesiod, −*800*)
    F   la *Théogonie* (Hésiode)
    D   die *Theogonie* (Hesiodos)
    I   la *Teogonia* (Esiodo)
    E   la *Teogonía* (Hesíodo)
    SU   «Теого́ния» (Гесио́д)

3695 GB   Theophilus (emperor)
    F   Théophile (empereur)
    D   Theophil (Kaiser)
    I   Teofilo (imperatore)
    E   Teófilo (emperador)
    SU   Феофи́л (импера́тор)

3696 GB   *Thérèse Desqueyroux* (Mauriac, 1927)
    F   *Thérèse Desqueyroux*
    D   *Theresa Desqueyroux*
    I   *Thérèse Desqueyroux*
    E   *Teresa Desqueyroux*
    SU   «Тере́за Дескейру́» (Мориа́к)

3697 GB   *Thérèse Raquin* (Zola, 1867)
    F   *Thérèse Raquin*
    D   *Thérèse Raquin*
    I   *Teresa Raquin*
    E   *Teresa Raquin*
    SU   «Тере́за Раке́н » (Золя́)

3698 GB   Thermopylae (Greece)
    F   les Thermopyles (Grèce)
    D   die Thermopylen (Griechenland)
    I   le Termopili (Grecia)
    E   las Termópilas (Grecia)
    SU   Фермопи́лы (ж.) (Гре́ция)

3699 GB   Theseus (myth.)
    F   Thésée (myth.)
    D   Theseus (myth.)
    I   Teseo (mit.)
    E   Teseo (mit.)
    SU   Тезе́й (миф.)

3700 GB   Thessalonians, the Epistle of Paul to the (Bib.)
    F   l'Épître de Saint Paul aux Thessaloniciens (Bib.)
    D   die Thessalonicherbriefe (Bib.)
    I   le lettere di Paolo ai Tessalonicesi (Bib.)
    E   la Epístola de San Pablo a los tesalios (Bib.)
    SU   «Посла́ние к Фессалоники́йцам» (библ.)

3701 GB Thessalonica (Greece)
F Thessalonique (Grèce)
D Thessalonike (Griechenland)
I Tessalonica (Grecia)
E Tesalónica (Grecia)
SU Фессалóники (Грéция)

3702 GB Thessaly (Greece)
F la Thessalie (Grèce)
D Thessalien (Griechenland)
I la Tessaglia (Grecia)
E Tesalia (Grecia)
SU Фессáлия (Грéция)

3703 GB Thetis (myth.)
F Thétis (myth.)
D Thetis (myth.)
I Teti (mit.)
E Tetis (mit.)
SU Фетúда (миф.)

3704 GB *They Shoot Horses, Don't They?*
(Pollack, 1969)
F *On achève bien les chevaux*
D *Nur Pferden gibt man den*
Gnadenschuß
I *Non si uccidono così anche i cavalli?*
E *¿No se matan así también los caballos?*
SU «Лошадéй ведь тóже убивáют, не
прáвда ли?» (Пóллак)

3705 GB *Thibaults, The* (Martin du Gard, 1922–
40)
F *Les Thibault*
D *Les Thibault*
I *I Thibault*
E *Los Thibault*
SU «Семья́ Тибó» (Мартéн дю Гар)

3706 GB *Thief of Baghdad, The* (Powell, 1940)
F *Le Voleur de Bagdad*
D *Der Dieb von Bagdad*
I *Il ladro di Bagdad*
E *El ladrón de Bagdad*
SU «Багдáдский вор» (Пáуэлл)

3707 GB *Thieving Magpie, The* (Rossini, 1817)
F *La Pie voleuse*
D *Die diebische Elster*
I *La gazza ladra*
E *La urraca ladrona*
SU «Сорóка-ворóвка» (Россúни)

3708 GB *Things to Come* (Menzies, 1936)
F *Les Temps futurs*
D *Die Zukunft*
I *La vita futura*
E *La vida futura*
SU «Бýдущее врéмя» (Мéнзис)

3709 GB *Thinker, The* (Rodin, 1880)
F *Le Penseur*
D *Der Denker*
I *Il pensatore*
E *El pensador*
SU «Мыслúтель» (Родéн)

3710 GB *Third Man, The* (Reed, 1949)
F *Le Troisième Homme*
D *Der dritte Mann*
I *Il terzo uomo*
E *El tercero hombre*
SU «Трéтий человéк» (Рид)

3711 GB *Thirteen Pipes, The* (Ehrenburg, 1923)
F *Treize Pipes* (Ehrenbourg)
D *Dreizehn Pfeifen* (Ehrenburg)
I *Tredici tubi* (Erenburg)
E *Trece pipas* (Ehrenburg)
SU «Тринáдцать трýбок» (Эренбýрг)

3712 GB *Thirty-Nine Steps, The* (Buchan, 1915;
Hitchcock, 1935)
F *Les Trente-neuf Marches*
D *Die dreiunddreißig Stufen*
I *Il club dei trentanove*
E *Treinta y nueve escalones*
SU «Трúдцать дéвять ступéней» (Бáкен,
Хúчкок)

3713 GB Thirty Years' War, the (1618–48)
F la guerre de Trente Ans
D der Dreißigjährige Krieg
I la guerra dei trent'anni
E la guerra de los Treinta Años
SU Тридцатилéтняя войнá

3714 GB *This Side of Paradise* (Fitzgerald, 1920)
F *De ce côté-ci du Paradis*
D *Diesseits des Paradieses*
I *Di qua dal Paradiso*
E *A este lado del Paraíso*
SU «По эту стóрону рáя» (Фицджéральд)

3715 GB *This Sporting Life* (Anderson, 1963)
F *Le Prix d'un homme*
D *Lockender Lorbeer*
I *Io sono un campione*
E *El ingenuo salvaje*
SU «Эта спортúвная жизнь» (Áндерсон)

3716 GB Thomas (saint)
F Thomas (saint)
D Thomas (Heiliger)
I Tommaso (santo)
E Tomás (santo)
SU Фомá (св.)

3717 GB Thomas Aquinas (saint; 1224–1284)
      F   Thomas d'Aquin (saint)
      D   Thomas von Aquin (Heiliger)
      I   Tommaso d'Aquino (santo)
      E   Tomás de Aquino (santo)
      SU Фома́ Акви́нский (св.)

3718 GB Thor (myth.)
      F   Thor (myth.)
      D   Thor (myth.)
      I   Thor (mit.)
      E   Tor (mit.)
      SU Тор (миф.)

3719 GB *Those Cursed Tuscans* (Malaparte, 1957)
      F   *Maudits Toscans*
      D   *Verdammte Toskaner*
      I   *Maledetti toscani*
      E   *Esos malditos toscanos*
      SU «Уж э́ти прокля́тые тоска́нцы» (Малапа́рте)

3720 GB *Those Magnificent Men in Their Flying Machines* (Annakin, 1965)
      F   *Ces merveilleux fous volants dans leurs drôles de machines*
      D   *Die tollkühnen Männer in ihren fliegenden Kisten*
      I   *Quei temerari sulle macchine volanti*
      E   *Aquellos chalados en sus locos cacharros*
      SU «Уж э́ти молодцы́ на свои́х лета́тельных аппара́тах» (А́ннакин)

3721 GB *Thoughts* (Pascal, 1670)
      F   *Pensées*
      D   *Gedanken*
      I   *Pensieri*
      E   *Pensamientos*
      SU «Мы́сли» (Паска́ль)

3722 GB *Thousand and One Nights* (*Arabian Nights*), the [*Alf laylah wa laylah*]
      F   les *Mille et Une Nuits*
      D   die *Tausendundeine Nacht*
      I   le *Mille e una notte*
      E   las *Mil y una noches*
      SU «Ты́сяча и одна́ ночь»

3723 GB *Thousand Cranes, A* [*Sembazuru*] (Kawabata, 1959)
      F   *Nuée d'oiseaux blancs*
      D   *Tausend Kraniche*
      I   *Mille gru*
      E   *Mil grullas*
      SU «Ты́сячекры́лый жура́вль» (Кавábáта)

3724 GB Thrace (Greece)
      F   la Thrace (Grèce)
      D   Thrazien (Griechenland)
      I   la Tracia (Grecia)
      E   Tracia (Grecia)
      SU Фра́кия (Гре́ция)

3725 GB *Three Coins in the Fountain* (Negulesco, 1954)
      F   *La Fontaine des amours*
      D   *Drei Münzen im Brunnen*
      I   *Tre soldi nella fontana*
      E   *Creemos en el amor*
      SU «Три моне́тки в фонта́не» (Негуле́ско)

3726 GB *Three Contributions to the Theory of Sex* (Freud, 1905)
      F   *Trois Essais sur la théorie de la sexualité*
      D   *Drei Abhandlungen zur Sexualtheorie*
      I   *Tre saggi sulla teoria della sessualità*
      E   *Tres ensayos sobre la teoría sexual*
      SU «Три статьи́ о тео́рии полово́го влече́ния» (Фрейд)

3727 GB *Three-Cornered Hat, The* (Falla, 1919)
      F   *Le Tricorne*
      D   *Der Dreispitz*
      I   *Il cappello a tre punte*
      E   *El sombrero de tres picos*
      SU «Треуго́лка» (Фа́лья)

3728 GB *Three Men in a Boat* (Jerome, 1889)
      F   *Trois Hommes dans un bateau*
      D   *Drei Mann in einem Boot*
      I   *Tre uomini in barca*
      E   *Tres hombres en un bote*
      SU «Тро́е в ло́дке» (Джеро́м)

3729 GB *Three Musketeers, The* (Dumas, 1844)
      F   *Les Trois Mousquetaires*
      D   *Die drei Musketiere*
      I   *I tre moschettieri*
      E   *Los tres mosqueteros*
      SU «Три мушкетёра» (Дюма́)

3730 GB *Threepenny Opera, The* (Brecht, 1928)
      F   *L'Opéra de quat' sous*
      D   *Die Dreigroschenoper*
      I   *L'opera da tre soldi*
      E   *La ópera de cuatro peniques*
      SU «Трёхгрошо́вая о́пера» (Брехт)

3731 GB *Three Philosophers, The* (Giorgione, 1510)
      F   *Les Trois Philosophes*
      D   *Die drei Philosophen*
      I   *Tre filosofi*
      E   *Los tres filósofos*
      SU «Три филосо́фа» (Джорджо́не)

3732 GB *Three Sisters, The* (Chekhov, 1901)
F *Les Trois Soeurs* (Tchekhov)
D *Drei Schwestern* (Tschechow)
I *Le tre sorelle* (Čechov)
E *Las tres hermanas* (Chejov)
SU «Три сестры́» (Че́хов)

3733 GB *Three Soldiers* (Dos Passos, 1921)
F *Trois Soldats*
D *Drei Soldaten*
I *Tre soldati*
E *Tres soldados*
SU «Три солда́та» (Дос Па́ссос)

3734 GB Three Wise Men, the (Bib.)
F les Rois mages (Bib.)
D die drei Weisen (Bib.)
I i Re Magi (Bib.)
E los Reyes Magos (Bib.)
SU три волхва́ (библ.)

3735 GB *Through the Looking Glass* (Carroll, 1872)
F *Alice à travers le miroir*
D *Alice im Spiegelreich*
I *Attraverso lo specchio*
E *A través del espejo*
SU «В Зазерка́лье» (Кэ́рролл)

3736 GB Thucydides (−V)
F Thucydide
D Thukydides
I Tucidide
E Tucídides
SU Фукиди́д

3737 GB Thuringia (Germany)
F la Thuringe (Allemagne)
D Thüringen (Deutschland)
I la Turingia (Germania)
E Turingia (Alemania)
SU Тюри́нгия (Герма́ния)

3738 GB *Thus Spoke Zarathustra* (Nietzsche, 1883–4)
F *Ainsi parlait Zarathustra*
D *Also sprach Zarathustra*
I *Così parlò Zarathustra*
E *Así hablaba Zaratustra*
SU «Так говори́л Зарату́стра» (Ни́цше)

3739 GB Tiberias, Lake (Bib.)
F le lac de Tibériade (Bib.)
D der Tiberiassee (Bib.)
I il lago Tiberiade (Bib.)
E el lago de Tiberíades (Bib.)
SU Тивериа́дское о́зеро (библ.)

3740 GB Tiberius (emperor)
F Tibère (empereur)
D Tiberius (Kaiser)
I Tiberio (imperatore)
E Tiberio (emperador)
SU Тибе́рий (импера́тор)

3741 GB Tiber (River), the (Italy)
F le Tibre (Italie)
D der Tiber (Italien)
I il Tevere (Italia)
E el Tíber (Italia)
SU Тибр (Ита́лия)

3742 GB Tibet
F le Tibet
D Tibet
I il Tibet
E el Tíbet
SU Тибе́т

3743 GB Tierra del Fuego
F la Terre de Feu
D Feuerland
I la Terra del Fuoco
E Tierra del Fuego
SU О́гненная Земля́

3744 GB Tigris (River), the
F le Tigre
D der Tigris
I il Tigri
E el Tigris
SU Тигр

3745 GB *Till Eulenspiegel* (Strauss, 1894)
F *Till Eulenspiegel*
D *Till Eulenspiegel*
I *Till Eulenspiegel*
E *Till Eulenspiegel*
SU «Тиль Уленшпи́гель» (Штра́ус)

3746 GB Timbuktu (Tombouctou, Timbuctoo) (Mali)
F Tombouctou (Mali)
D Timbuktu (Mali)
I Tombouctou (Mali)
E Tombuctú (Malí)
SU Томбукту́ (Мали́)

3747 GB *Time and the Conways* (Priestley, 1937)
F *Le Temps et les Conway*
D *Zeit und die Conways*
I *Il tempo e la famiglia Conway*
E *El tiempo y los Conways*
SU «Вре́мя и семья́ Ко́нвей» (При́стли)

3748 GB   *Time Machine, The* (Wells, 1895)
    F   *La Machine à explorer le temps*
    D   *Die Zeitmaschine*
    I   *La macchina del tempo*
    E   *La máquina del tiempo*
    SU   «Маши́на вре́мени» (Уэ́ллс)

3749 GB   *Time of Hope* (Snow, 1949)
    F   *Temps d'espoir*
    D   *Zeit der Hoffnung*
    I   *Tempo di speranza*
    E   *Tiempo de esperanza*
    SU   «Пора́ наде́жд» (Сно́у)

3750 GB   Time of Troubles, the (Russia, 1598–1613)
    F   le Temps des troubles (Russie)
    D   die Zeit der Wirren (Rußland)
    I   il tempo turbato (Russia)
    E   el tiempo turbulento (Rusia)
    SU   Сму́тное вре́мя (Росси́я)

3751 GB   *Timon of Athens* (Shakespeare, 1607)
    F   *Timon d'Athènes*
    D   *Timon von Athen*
    I   *Timone di Atene*
    E   *Timón de Atenas*
    SU   «Тимо́н Афи́нский» (Шекспи́р)

3752 GB   Timothy (Bib.)
    F   Timothée (Bib.)
    D   Timotheus (Bib.)
    I   Timoteo (Bib.)
    E   Timoteo (Bib.)
    SU   Тимофе́й (библ.)

3753 GB   *Tin Drum, The* (Grass, 1959)
    F   *Le Tambour*
    D   *Die Blechtrommel*
    I   *Il tamburo di latta*
    E   *El tambor de hojalata*
    SU   «Жестяно́й бараба́н» (Грасс)

3754 GB   Tintoretto (*1518*–1594)
    F   le Tintoret
    D   Tintoretto
    I   il Tintoretto
    E   el Tintoreto
    SU   Тинторе́тто

3755 GB   Tiresias (myth.)
    F   Tirésias (myth.)
    D   Teiresias (myth.)
    I   Tiresia (mit.)
    E   Tiresias (mit.)
    SU   Тире́сий (миф.)

3756 GB   Tirol (Tyrol), the (Austria)
    F   le Tyrol (Autriche)
    D   Tirol (Österreich)
    I   il Tirolo (Austria)
    E   el Tirol (Austria)
    SU   Тиро́ль (м.) (А́встрия)

3757 GB   *'Tis Pity She's a Whore* (Ford, 1633)
    F   *Dommage qu'elle soit une putain*
    D   *Schade, daß sie eine Dirne ist*
    I   *Peccato che sia una sgualdrina*
    E   *Lástima que sea impura*
    SU   «Нельзя́ её развра́тницей назва́ть» (Форд)

3758 GB   Titans, the (myth.)
    F   les Titans (myth.)
    D   die Titanen (myth.)
    I   i Titani (mit.)
    E   los titanes (mit.)
    SU   тита́ны (миф.)

3759 GB   Titian (*1488*–1576)
    F   Titien
    D   Tizian
    I   Tiziano
    E   Tiziano
    SU   Тициа́н

3760 GB   Titus (Bib.)
    F   Tite (Bib.)
    D   Titus (Bib.)
    I   Tito (Bib.)
    E   Tito (Bib.)
    SU   Тит (библ.)

3761 GB   *Titus Andronicus* (Shakespeare, 1594)
    F   *Titus Andronicus*
    D   *Titus Andronicus*
    I   *Tito Andronico*
    E   *Tito Andrónico*
    SU   «Тит Андро́ник» (Шекспи́р)

3762 GB   *To a Skylark* (Shelley, 1820)
    F   *À une alouette*
    D   *An eine Lerche*
    I   *A un'allodola*
    E   *La alondra*
    SU   «Ла́сточке» (Ше́лли)

3763 GB   *Tobacco Road* (Caldwell, 1932)
    F   *La Route au tabac*
    D   *Die Tabakstraße*
    I   *La via del tabacco*
    E   *El camino del tabaco*
    SU   «Таба́чная доро́га» (Ко́лдуэлл)

3764 GB Tobias (Bib.)
F Tobie (Bib.)
D Tobias (Bib.)
I Tobia (Bib.)
E Tobías (Bib.)
SU Tóвия (библ.)

3765 GB Tobit (Bib.)
F Tobie (Bib.)
D Tobias (Bib.)
I Tobia (Bib.)
E Tobías (Bib.)
SU Tóвит (библ.)

3766 GB *To Damascus* [*Till Damascus*]
(Strindberg, 1898, 1904)
F *Chemin de Damas*
D *Nach Damaskus*
I *Verso Damasco*
E *A Damasco*
SU «Путь в Дамáск» (Стрúндберг)

3767 GB *To Have and To Have Not*
(Hemingway, 1937)
F *Avoir et ne pas avoir*
D *Haben und Nichthaben*
I *Avere e non avere*
E *Tener y no tener*
SU «Имéть и не имéть» (Хемингуэ́й)

3768 GB *Toilers of the Sea* (Hugo, 1866)
F *Les Travailleurs de la mer*
D *Die Arbeiter des Meeres*
I *I lavoratori del mare*
E *Los trabajadores del mar*
SU «Трýженики мóря» (Гюгó)

3769 GB *To Joy* (Schiller, 1786)
F *À la joie*
D *An die Freude*
I *Alla gioia*
E *A la alegría*
SU «К рáдости» (Шúллер)

3770 GB Tokyo (Japan)
F Tokyo (Japon)
D Tokio (Japan)
I Tokyo (Giappone)
E Tokio (Japón)
SU Tóкио (Япóния)

3771 GB *To Let* (Galsworthy, 1921)
F *À louer*
D *Zu vermieten*
I *Affittasi*
E *Se alquila*
SU «Сдаётся в наём» (Гóлсуорси)

3772 GB *Tomcat Murr* (Hoffmann, 1820–2)
F *Le Chat Murr*
D *Lebensansichten des Katers Murr*
I *La filosofia della vita del gatto Murr*
E *Opiniones del gato Murr*
SU «Житéйские воззрéния котá Мýрра»
(Гóфман)

GB *Tom Sawyer*→*Adventures of Tom
Sawyer*

3773 GB *Tom Thumb* (Perrault, 1697)
F *Le Petit Poucet*
D *Der Däumling*
I *Pollicino*
E *Pulgarcito*
SU «Мáльчик с пáльчик» (Перрó)

3774 GB *Tonight We Improvise* (Pirandello,
1930)
F *Ce soir, on improvise*
D *Heute abend wir improvisieren*
I *Questa sera si recita a soggetto*
E *Esta noche se improvisa*
SU «Сегóдня мы импровизúруем»
(Пирандéлло)

3775 GB *Tonio Kröger* (Mann, 1903)
F *Tonio Kröger*
D *Tonio Kröger*
I *Tonio Kröger*
E *Tonio Kröger*
SU «Тóнио Крéгер» (Манн)

3776 GB *Topaze* (Pagnol, 1928)
F *Topaze*
D *Das große ABC*
I *Topaze*
E *Topaze*
SU «Топáз» (Паньóль)

3777 GB Torah, the (Bib.)
F la Torah (Bib.)
D die Thora (Bib.)
I la Tora (Bib.)
E la Tora (Bib.)
SU «Тóра» (библ.)

3778 GB *Tortilla Flat* (Steinbeck, 1935)
F *Tortilla Flat*
D *Die wunderlichen Schelme von Tortilla
Flat*
I *Pian della Tortilla*
E *Tortilla Flat*
SU «Квартáл Тортúлья Флэт» (Стéйнбек)

3779   GB   *Tosca* (Puccini, 1900)
     F   *Tosca*
     D   *Tosca*
     I   *Tosca*
     E   *Tosca*
     SU   «Тóска» (Пуччи́ни)

3780   GB   *To the Lighthouse* (Woolf, 1927)
     F   *La Promenade au phare*
     D   *Die Fahrt zum Leuchtturm*
     I   *Gita al faro*
     E   *Paseo del fare*
     SU   «К маякý» (Вулф)

3781   GB   *Touch of Class, A* (Frank, 1972)
     F   *Une touche de classe*
     D   *Ein Druck der Klasse*
     I   *Un tocco di classe*
     E   *Un toque de clase*
     SU   «Печáть клáсса» (Франк)

3782   GB   Toulon (France)
     F   Toulon (France)
     D   Toulon (Frankreich)
     I   Tolone (Francia)
     E   Tolón (Francia)
     SU   Тулóн (Фрáнция)

3783   GB   Toulouse (France)
     F   Toulouse (France)
     D   Toulouse (Frankreich)
     I   Tolosa (Francia)
     E   Tolosa (Francia)
     SU   Тулýза (Фрáнция)

3784   GB   Touraine (France)
     F   la Touraine (France)
     D   die Touraine (Frankreich)
     I   la Turenna (Francia)
     E   Turena (Francia)
     SU   Турéн (Фрáнция)

3785   GB   *To Us the Freedom* (Clair, 1932)
     F   *À nous la liberté*
     D   *Es lebe die Freiheit*
     I   *A me la libertà*
     E   *¡Viva la libertad!*
     SU   «Свобóду нам!» (Клер)

3786   GB   *Towering Inferno, The* (Guillermin, 1974)
     F   *La Tour infernale*
     D   *Flammendes Inferno*
     I   *La torre infernale*
     E   *El infierno violento*
     SU   «Пылáющая бáшня» (Ги́ллермин)

     GB   Tower of Babel→Babel, Tower of

3787   GB   Tower of London, the (London)
     F   la Tour de Londres (Londres)
     D   die Tower (London)
     I   la Torre di Londra (Londra)
     E   la torre de Londres (Londres)
     SU   Тáуэр (Лóндон)

3788   GB   Trabzon (Trebizond) (Turkey)
     F   Trébizonde (Turquie)
     D   Trapezunt (Türkei)
     I   Trebisonda (Turchia)
     E   Trebisonda (Turquía)
     SU   Трабзóн (Тýрция)

3789   GB   *Trachinian Women, The* [*Trachiniai*] (Sophocles, −V)
     F   *Les Trachiniennes* (Sophocle)
     D   *Die Frauen von Trachis* (Sophokles)
     I   *Le Trachinie* (Sofocle)
     E   *Las Traquinias* (Sófocles)
     SU   «Трахи́нянки» (Софóкл)

3790   GB   *Tractatus theologico-politicus* ["A Theological and Political Treatise"] (Spinoza, 1670)
     F   *Traité théologico-politique*
     D   *Theologisch-politischer Traktat*
     I   *Tractatus theologico-politicus*
     E   *Tractatus theologico-politicus*
     SU   «Богослóвско-полити́ческий трактáт» (Спинóза)

3791   GB   *Traffic* (Tati, 1970)
     F   *Trafic*
     D   *Trafic*
     I   *Monsieur Hulot nel caos del traffico*
     E   *Trafic*
     SU   «Движéние» (Тати́)

3792   GB   *Tragical History of Doctor Faustus, The* (Marlowe, 1592)
     F   *La Tragique Histoire du docteur Faust*
     D   *Die tragische Geschichte von Doktor Faustus*
     I   *La tragica storia del dottor Faust*
     E   *La trágica historia del doctor Fausto*
     SU   «Траги́ческая истóрия дóктора Фáуста» (Мáрло)

3793   GB   Trajan (53–117)
     F   Trajan
     D   Trajanus
     I   Traiano
     E   Trajano
     SU   Трая́н

3794 GB Trajan's Column (Rome)
F la colonne de Trajan (Rome)
D die Trajanssäule (Rom)
I la colonna Traiana (Roma)
E la columna Trajana (Roma)
SU колóнна Трая́на (Рим)

3795 GB *Tramp, The* (Chaplin, 1915)
F *Charlot vagabond*
D *Der Tramp*
I *Il vagabondo*
E *El vagabundo*
SU «Бродя́га» (Ча́плин)

3796 GB Transcaucasia (USSR)
F la Transcaucasie (URSS)
D Transkaukasien (UdSSR)
I la Transcaucasia (URSS)
E Transcaucasia (URSS)
SU Закавка́зье (СССР)

3797 GB Transfiguration, the (rel.)
F la Transfiguration (relig.)
D die Verklärung (relig.)
I la Trasfigurazione (relig.)
E la Transfiguración (relig.)
SU преображе́ние (рел.)

3798 GB Transjordan (hist.)
F la Transjordanie (hist.)
D Transjordanien (Gesch.)
I la Transgiordania (st.)
E Transjordania (hist.)
SU Трансиорда́ния (ист.)

3799 GB Trans-Siberian Railway, the (USSR)
F le Transsibérien (URSS)
D die Sibirische Eisenbahn (UdSSR)
I la transiberiana (URSS)
E el Transiberiano (URSS)
SU Транссиби́рская магистра́ль (СССР)

3800 GB Transylvania (Romania, hist.)
F la Transylvanie (Roumanie, hist.)
D Siebenbürgen (Rumänien, Gesch.)
I la Transilvania (Romania, st.)
E Transilvania (Rumania, hist.)
SU Трансильва́ния (Румы́ния, ист.)

3801 GB *Traveller Without Luggage* (Anouilh, 1937)
F *Le Voyageur sans bagages*
D *Der Reisende ohne Gepäck*
I *Il viaggiatore senza bagaglio*
E *Viajero sin equipaje*
SU «Путеше́ственник без багажа́» (Ануй)

3802 GB *Travel Sketches* (Heine, 1826–31)
F *Tableaux de voyage*
D *Reisebilder*
I *Impressioni di viaggio*
E *Cuadros de viajes*
SU «Путевы́е карти́ны» (Ге́йне)

3803 GB *Travels with a Donkey* (Stevenson, 1879)
F *Voyage avec un âne*
D *Reisen mit einem Esel*
I *Viaggio a dorso d'asino*
E *Viajes con una burra*
SU «Путеше́ствие с осло́м» (Сти́венсон)

3804 GB *Traviata, La* [*The Lost One*] (Verdi, 1853)
F *La Traviata*
D *La Traviata*
I *La Traviata*
E *La Traviata*
SU «Травиа́та» (Ве́рди)

3805 GB *Treasure Island* (Stevenson, 1881–2)
F *L'Île au trésor*
D *Die Schatzinsel*
I *L'isola del tesoro*
E *La isla del tesoro*
SU «О́стров сокро́вищ» (Сти́венсон)

3806 GB *Treasure of the Humble, The* (Maeterlinck, 1896)
F *Le Trésor des humbles*
D *Der Schatz der Armen*
I *Il tesoro degli umili*
E *El tesoro de los humildes*
SU «Сокро́вище смире́нных» (Ме́терли́нк)

3807 GB *Treasure of the Sierra Madre, The* (Huston, 1948)
F *Le Trésor de la Sierra Madre*
D *Der Schatz der Sierra Madre*
I *Il tesoro della Sierra Madre*
E *El tesoro de la Sierra Madre*
SU «Сокро́вище с Сье́рра-Ма́дре» (Хью́стон)

3808 GB *Treatise on Painting* (Leonardo da Vinci, 1498–1518)
F *Traité de la peinture* (Léonard de Vinci)
D *Traktat von der Malerei* (Leonardo da Vinci)
I *Trattato di pittura* (Leonardo da Vinci)
E *Tratado de la pintura* (Leonardo de Vinci)
SU «Тракта́т о жи́вописи» (Леона́рдо да Ви́нчи)

3809 GB *Treatise on the Five Orders of Architecture, A* (Vignola, 1562)
F *Règle des cinq ordres de l'architecture* (Vignole)
D *Traktat von den fünf Säulenordnungen* (Vignola)
I *Regola delli cinque ordini di architettura* (Vignola)
E *Tratado de los cinco órdenes en la arquitectura* (Vignola)
SU «Пра́вило пяти́ о́рдеров архитекту́ры» (Виньо́ла)

3810 GB *Treatise on the Passions* (Descartes, 1649)
F *Traité des passions de l'âme* (Descartes)
D *Die Leidenschaften der Seele* (Descartes)
I *Trattato sulle passioni dell'anima* (Cartesio)
E *Tratado de las pasiones* (Descartes)
SU «Тракта́т о страстя́х» (Дека́рт)

3811 GB Trent, the Council of (1545–63)
F le concile de Trente
D das Tridentiner Konzil
I il concilio di Trento
E el Concilio de Trento
SU Триде́нтский собо́р

3812 GB Trentino-Alto Adige (Italy)
F le Trentin-Haut-Adige (Italie)
D Trentino-Südtirol (Italien)
I il Trentino-Alto Adige (Italia)
E Trentino-Alto Adigio (Italia)
SU Тренти́но-А́льто-Ади́дже (Ита́лия)

3813 GB Trento (Trent) (Italy)
F Trente (Italie)
D Trient (Italien)
I Trento (Italia)
E Trento (Italia)
SU Тре́нто (Ита́лия)

3814 GB *Trial, The* (Kafka, 1924–5)
F *Le Procès*
D *Der Prozeß*
I *Il processo*
E *El proceso*
SU «Проце́сс» (Ка́фка)

3815 GB *Trickeries of Scapin, The* (Molière, 1671)
F *Les Fourberies de Scapin*
D *Scappinos Gaunereien*
I *Le furberie di Scapino*
E *Las astucias de Scapin*
SU «Проде́лки Скапе́на» (Молье́р)

3816 GB Trier (Germany)
F Trèves (Allemagne)
D Trier (Deutschland)
I Treviri (Germania)
E Tréveris (Alemania)
SU Трир (Герма́ния)

3817 GB Trieste (Italy)
F Trieste (Italie)
D Triest (Italien)
I Trieste (Italia)
E Trieste (Italia)
SU Трие́ст (Ита́лия)

3818 GB Trinidad (West Indies)
F Trinité (Antilles)
D Trinidad (Westindien)
I Trinidad (Antille)
E Trinidad (Antillas)
SU Тринида́д (Вест-И́ндия)

3819 GB Trinitarians, the (rel.)
F les trinitaires (relig.)
D die Trinitarier (relig.)
I i Trinitari (relig.)
E los Trinitarios (relig.)
SU тринита́рии (рел.)

3820 GB Trinity, the (rel.)
F la Trinité (relig.)
D die Dreieinigkeit (relig.)
I la Trinità (relig.)
E la Trinidad (relig.)
SU тро́ица (рел.)

3821 GB Triple Alliance, the (1668, 1717)
F la Triple-Alliance
D der Dreibund
I la Triplice alleanza
E la Triple Alianza
SU Тро́йственный сою́з

3822 GB Tripolitania (Libya)
F la Tripolitaine (Libye)
D Tripolitanien (Libyen)
I Tripolitania (Libia)
E Tripolitania (Libia)
SU Триполита́ния (Ли́вия)

3823 GB *Tristana* (Buñuel, 1970)
F *Tristana*
D *Tristana*
I *Tristana*
E *Tristana*
SU «Триста́на» (Бюнюэ́ль)

3824 GB *Tristan and Isolde* (Wagner, 1865)
F *Tristan et Isolde*
D *Tristan und Isolde*
I *Tristan e Isolta*
E *Tristán e Isolda*
SU «Тристáн и Изóльда» (Вáгнер)

3825 GB *Tristram Shandy* (Sterne, 1760–9)
F *Vie et opinions de Tristram Shandy*
D *Tristram Shandys Leben und Meinungen*
I *Vita e opinioni di Tristram Shandy*
E *Tristán Shandy*
SU «Жизнь и мнéния Трúстрама Шéнди, джентльмéна» (Стерн)

3826 GB Triton (myth.)
F Triton (myth.)
D Triton (myth.)
I Tritone (mit.)
E Tritón (mit.)
SU Тритóн (миф.)

3827 GB *Triumph of Aphrodite, The* (Orff, 1953)
F *Le Triomphe d'Aphrodite*
D *Der Triumph der Aphrodite*
I *Il trionfo di Afrodite*
E *El triunfo de Afrodita*
SU «Триýмф Афродúты» (Орф)

3828 GB *Triumph of Love, The* (Lully, 1681)
F *Le Triomphe de l'amour*
D *Der Triumph der Liebe*
I *Il trionfo del amore*
E *El triunfo del amor*
SU «Торжествó любвú» (Люллú)

3829 GB *Triumphs, the* (Petrarch, 1354)
F les *Triomphes* (Pétrarque)
D die *Triumphe* (Petrarca)
I i *Trionfi* (Petrarca)
E los *Triunfos* (Petrarca)
SU «Триýмфы» (Петрáрка)

3830 GB *Troilus and Cressida* (Shakespeare, 1601)
F *Troïlus et Cressida*
D *Troilos und Cressida*
I *Troilo e Cressida*
E *Troilo y Crésida*
SU «Трóил и Крéссида» (Шекспúр)

3831 GB Trojan Horse, the (myth.)
F le cheval de Troie (myth.)
D das Trojanische Pferd (myth.)
I il cavallo di Troja (mit.)
E el caballo de Troya (mit.)
SU Троя́нский конь (миф.)

3832 GB *Trojans, The* (Berlioz, 1855–9)
F *Les Troyens*
D *Die Trojaner*
I *I troiani*
E *Los Troyanos*
SU «Троя́нцы» (Берлиóз)

3833 GB Trojan War, the (−XII)
F la guerre de Troie
D der Trojanische Krieg
I la guerra di Troia
E la guerra de Troya
SU Троя́нская войнá

3834 GB *Trojan War Will Not Take Place, The* (Giraudoux, 1935)
F *La guerre de Troie n'aura pas lieu*
D *Kein Krieg in Troja*
I *La guerra di Troia non si farà*
E *La guerra de Troya no tendrá lugar*
SU «Троя́нской войны́ не бýдет» (Жиродý)

3835 GB *Trojan Women, The* [*Troades*] (Euripides, −415)
F *Les Troyennes* (Euripide)
D *Die Troerinnen* (Euripides)
I *Le troiane* (Euripide)
E *Las troyanas* (Eurípides)
SU «Троя́нки» (Еврипúд)

3836 GB Tropic of Cancer, the
F le tropique du Cancer
D der Wendekreis des Krebses
I il tropico del Cancro
E el trópico de Cáncer
SU трóпик Рáка

3837 GB Tropic of Capricorn, the
F le tropique du Capricorne
D der Wendekreis des Steinbocks
I il tropico del Capricorno
E el trópico de Capricornio
SU трóпик Козерóга

3838 GB *Troubadour, The* (Verdi, 1852)
F *Le Trouvère*
D *Der Troubadour*
I *Il trovatore*
E *El trovador*
SU «Трубадýр» (Вéрди)

3839 GB *Trout Quintet, the* (Schubert, 1819)
F la quintette *La Truite*
D das *Forellenquintett*
I il quintetto *La trota*
E el quinteto *La trucha*
SU квинтéт «Форéль» (Шýберт)

GB   *Trovatore, Il*→ *Troubadour, The*

3840   GB   Troy (Greece)
       F   Troie (Grèce)
       D   Troja (Griechenland)
       I   Troia (Grecia)
       E   Troya (Grecia)
       SU   Трóя (Грéция)

3841   GB   Truce of God, the (X–XII)
       F   la Trêve de Dieu
       D   der Gottesfriede
       I   la tregua di Dio
       E   la Tregua de Dios
       SU   «Бóжий мир»

3842   GB   Trucial States, the (hist.)
       F   les États de la Trêve (hist.)
       D   die Vertragsstaaten (Gesch.)
       I   gli stati della Tregua (st.)
       E   los Trucial States (hist.)
       SU   Договóрный Омáн (ист.)

3843   GB   Tunis (Tunisia)
       F   Tunis (Tunisie)
       D   Tunis (Tunesien)
       I   Tunisi (Tunisia)
       E   Túnez (Túnez)
       SU   Тунúс (Тунúс)

3844   GB   Tunisia
       F   la Tunisie
       D   Tunesien
       I   la Tunisia
       E   Túnez
       SU   Тунúс

3845   GB   *Turcaret* (Lesage, 1709)
       F   *Turcaret*
       D   *Turcaret*
       I   *Turcaret*
       E   *Turcaret*
       SU   «Тюркарé» (Лесáж)

3846   GB   Turin (Italy)
       F   Turin (Italie)
       D   Turin (Italien)
       I   Torino (Italia)
       E   Turín (Italia)
       SU   Турúн (Итáлия)

3847   GB   Turkey
       F   la Turquie
       D   die Türkei
       I   la Turchia
       E   Turquía
       SU   Тýрция

3848   GB   *Turn of the Screw, The* (James, 1898;
             Britten, 1954)
       F   *Le Tour d'écrou*
       D   *Die Umdrehung der Schraube*
       I   *Il giro di vite*
       E   *La vuelta de tuerca*
       SU   «Поворóт винтá» (Джеймс, Брúттен)

3849   GB   Tuscany (Italy)
       F   la Toscane (Italie)
       D   Toskana (Italien)
       I   la Toscana (Italia)
       E   Toscana (Italia)
       SU   Тоскáна (Итáлия)

3850   GB   Tutankhamun (Tutankhamen)
             (–XIV)
       F   Tout Ankh Amon
       D   Tut-anch-amon
       I   Tutankhamon
       E   Tutankamón
       SU   Тутанхамóн

3851   GB   *Twelfth Night* (Shakespeare, 1601)
       F   *La Nuit des rois*
       D   *Was ihr wollt*
       I   *La dodicesima notte*
       E   *La duodécima noche*
       SU   «Двенáдцатая ночь» (Шекспúр)

3852   GB   *Twelve, The* (Blok, 1918)
       F   *Les Douze*
       D   *Die Zwölf*
       I   *I dodici*
       E   *Los doce*
       SU   «Двенáдцать» (Блок)

3853   GB   *Twenty Thousand Leagues Under the
             Sea* (Verne, 1869)
       F   *Vingt Mille Lieues sous les mers*
       D   *Zwanzig tausend Meilen unter dem
             Meer*
       I   *Ventimila leghe sotto i mari*
       E   *Veinte mil leguas de viaje submarino*
       SU   «Двáдцать тысяч льё под водóй»
             (Верн)

3854   GB   *Twenty Years After* (Dumas, 1845)
       F   *Vingt Ans après*
       D   *Zwanzig Jahre nachher*
       I   *Vent'anni dopo*
       E   *Veinte años después*
       SU   «Двáдцать лет спустя» (Дюмá)

3855 GB *Twice-Told Tales, The* (Hawthorne, 1837, 1842)
F *Contes racontés deux fois*
D *Zweimal erzählt*
I *Racconti narrati due volte*
E *Cuentos contados dos veces*
SU «Дважды рассказанные истории» (Хоторн)

3856 GB *Twilight of the Gods, The* (Wagner, 1876)
F *Le Crépuscule des dieux*
D *Götterdämmerung*
I *Il crepuscolo degli dei*
E *El crepúsculo de los dioses*
SU «Гибель богов» (Вагнер)

3857 GB *Two Cultures, The* (Snow, 1967)
F *Les Deux Cultures*
D *Die zwei Kulturen*
I *Le due culture*
E *Las dos culturas*
SU «Две культуры» (Сноу)

3858 GB *Two Days, The* (Cherubini, 1800)
F *Les Deux Journées*
D *Der Wasserträger*
I *Le due giornate*
E *Los dos días*
SU «Два дня» (Керубини)

3859 GB *Two Gentlemen of Verona, The* (Shakespeare, 1594)
F *Les Deux Gentilshommes de Vérone*
D *Die beiden Veroneser*
I *I due gentiluomini di Verona*
E *Los dos hidalgos de Verona*
SU «Два веронца» (Шекспир)

3860 GB *2001: A Space Odyssey* (Kubrick, 1968)
F *2001: l'Odyssée de l'espace*
D *2001: Odyssee im Weltraum*
I *2001: Odissea nello spazio*
E *2001: una Odisea del espacio*
SU «2001 год: Космическая Одиссея» (Кубрик)

3861 GB *Two Years Before the Mast* (Dana, 1840)
F *Une voix du gaillard d'avant*
D *Zwei Jahre vor'm Mast*
I *Marinaio per due anni*
E *Dos años al pie del mástil*
SU «Два года простым матросом» (Дана)

3862 GB Typhon (myth.)
F Typhon (myth.)
D Typhon (myth.)
I Tifone (mit.)
E Tifón (mit.)
SU Тифон (миф.)

3863 GB *Typhoon* (Conrad, 1903)
F *Typhon*
D *Taifun*
I *Tifone*
E *Tifón*
SU «Тайфун» (Конрад)

3864 GB Tyre (Bib.)
F Tyr (Bib.)
D Tyros (Bib.)
I Tiro (Bib.)
E Tiro (Bib.)
SU Тир (библ.)

GB Tyrol→Tirol

3865 GB Tyrrhenian Sea, the
F la mer Tyrrhénienne
D das Tyrrhenische Meer
I il mare Tirreno
E el mar Tirreno
SU Тирренское море

U

3866	GB	Uffizi Gallery, the (Florence)
	F	les Offices (Florence)
	D	die Uffizien (Florenz)
	I	gli Uffizi (Firenza)
	E	los Oficios (Florencia)
	SU	галере́я Уффи́ци (Флоре́нция)

3867	GB	Uganda
	F	l'Ouganda (m.)
	D	Uganda
	I	l'Uganda
	E	Uganda
	SU	Уга́нда

3868	GB	*Ugly Duckling, The [Den grimme aelling]* (Andersen, 1843)
	F	*Le Vilain Petit Canard*
	D	*Das häßliche Entlein*
	I	*Il brutto anatroccolo*
	E	*El patito feo*
	SU	«Га́дкий утёнок» (А́ндерсен)

3869	GB	Ukraine, the (USSR)
	F	l'Ukraine (f.) (URSS)
	D	die Ukraine (UdSSR)
	I	l'Ucraina (URSS)
	E	Ucrania (URSS)
	SU	Украи́на (СССР)

3870	GB	Ulysses (myth., + Joyce, 1922)
	F	Ulysse (myth.)
	D	Ulysses (myth.)
	I	Ulisse (mit.)
	E	Ulises (mit.)
	SU	Ули́сс (миф., + Джойс)

3871	GB	*Umberto D* (De Sica, 1952)
	F	*Umberto D*
	D	*Umberto D*
	I	*Umberto D*
	E	*Umberto D*
	SU	«Умбе́рто Д.» (Де Си́ка)

3872	GB	*Umbrellas of Cherbourg, The* (Demy, 1964)
	F	*Les Parapluies de Cherbourg*
	D	*Die Regenschirme von Cherbourg*
	I	*I parapioggia di Cherbourg*
	E	*Los paraguas de Cherburgo*
	SU	«Шербу́рские зо́нтики» (Деми́)

3873	GB	Umbria (Italy)
	F	l'Ombrie (f.) (Italie)
	D	Umbrien (Italien)
	I	l'Umbria (Italia)
	E	Umbría (Italia)
	SU	У́мбрия (Ита́лия)

3874	GB	*Uncle Tom's Cabin* (Beecher Stowe, 1852)
	F	*La Case de l'oncle Tom*
	D	*Onkel Toms Hütte*
	I	*La capanna dello zio Tom*
	E	*La cabaña del tío Tom*
	SU	«Хи́жина дя́ди То́ма» (Би́чер-Сто́у)

3875	GB	*Uncle Vanya* (Chekhov, 1899)
	F	*Oncle Vania* (Tchekhov)
	D	*Onkel Wanya* (Tschechow)
	I	*Zio Vanja* (Čechov)
	E	*El tío Vania* (Chejov)
	SU	«Дя́дя Ва́ня» (Че́хов)

3876	GB	*Under Milk Wood* (Thomas, 1953)
	F	*Au bois lacté*
	D	*Unter dem Milchwald*
	I	*Sotto il bosco di latte*
	E	*Bajo el bosque lácteo*
	SU	«Под моло́чным ле́сом» (То́мас)

3877 GB *Under the Greenwood Tree* (Hardy, 1872)
F *Sous la verte feuillée*
D *Die Liebe der Fancy Day*
I *Sotto l'albero del verde bosco*
E *Bajo el árbol del verde bosque*
SU «Под дéревом зелёным» (Хáрди)

3878 GB *Under the Net* (Murdoch, 1954)
F *Dans le filet*
D *Unter dem Netz*
I *Nella rete*
E *Bajo la red*
SU «Под сéтью» (Мёрдок)

3879 GB *Under the Roofs of Paris* (Clair, 1930)
F *Sous les toits de Paris*
D *Unter den Dächern von Paris*
I *Sotto i tetti di Parigi*
E *Bajo los techos de París*
SU «Под крышами Парижа» (Клер)

3880 GB *Under the Sun of Satan* (Bernanos, 1926)
F *Sous le soleil de Satan*
D *Die Sonne Satans*
I *Sotto il sole di Satana*
E *Bajo el sol de Satán*
SU «Под сóлнцем сатаны» (Бернанóс)

3881 GB *Under Western Eyes* (Conrad, 1911)
F *Sous les yeux d'Occident*
D *Mit den Augen des Westens*
I *Sotto gli occhi dell'Occidente*
E *Bajo los ojos del Occidente*
SU «Глазáми зáпада» (Кóнрад)

3882 GB *Unfinished Symphony*, the (Schubert, 1822)
F la *Symphonie inachevée*
D die *Unvollendete Sinfonie*
I la sinfonia *Incompiuta*
E la sinfonía *Incompleta*
SU «Неокóнченная» симфóния (Шýберт)

3883 GB Union of Soviet Socialist Republics (USSR), the
F l'Union des républiques socialistes soviétiques (URSS)
D die Union der Sozialistischen Sowjetrepubliken (UdSSR)
I l'Unione delle Repubbliche Socialiste Sovietiche (URSS)
E la Unión de Repúblicas Socialistas Soviéticas (URSS)
SU Сою́з Совéтских Социалисти́ческих Респýблик (СССР)

3884 GB Unitarians, the (rel.)
F les unitariens (relig.)
D die Unitarier (relig.)
I gli unitariani (relig.)
E los unitarios (relig.)
SU унитáрии (рел.)

3885 GB United Arab Emirates (UAE), the
F les Émirats arabes unis (EAU)
D die Vereinigten Arabischen Emirate (VAE)
I gli Emirati Arabi Uniti (EAU)
E los Emiratos Árabes Unidos (EAU)
SU Объединённые Арáбские Эмирáты (ОАЭ)

3886 GB United Arab Republic (UAR), the
F la République arabe unie (RAU)
D die Vereinigte Arabische Republik (VAR)
I la Repubblica Araba Unita
E la República Árabe Unida (RAU)
SU Объединённая Арáбская Респýблика (ОАР)

3887 GB United Kingdom of Great Britain and Northern Ireland, the
F le Royaume-Uni de Grande-Bretagne et Irlande du Nord
D das Vereinigte Königreich von Großbritannien und Nordirland
I il Regno Unito di Gran Bretagna e Irlanda del Nord
E el Reino Unido de Gran Bretaña e Irlanda del Norte
SU Соединённое Королéвство Великобритáнии и Сéверной Ирлáндии

3888 GB United Nations Conference on Trade and Development, the (UNCTAD)
F la Conférence des Nations unies pour le commerce et le développement (CNUCED)
D die Konferenz für Handel und Entwicklung und Welthandelsrat (UNCTAD)
I la Conferenza delle Nazioni unite sul commercio e lo sviluppo (UNCTAD)
E la Conferencia de las Naciones Unidas para el comercio y el desarrollo (CNUCED)
SU Конферéнция ОÓН по торгóвле и развńтию (ЮНКТÁД)

3889 GB United Nations Industrial
Development Organisation, the
(UNIDO)
F l'Organisation des Nations unies pour
le développement industriel
(ONUDI)
D die Organisation für industrielle
Entwicklung (UNIDO)
I l'Organizzazione delle Nazioni unite
per lo sviluppo industriale (UNIDO)
E la Organización de las Naciones
Unidas para el desarrollo industrial
(UNIDO)
SU Организáция ОÓН по
промы́шленному развúтию
(ЮНИДÓ)

3890 GB United Nations Organisation, the
(UNO)
F l'Organisation des Nations unies
(ONU)
D die Organisation der Vereinten
Nationen (UNO)
I l'Organizzazione delle Nazioni unite
(ONU)
E la Organización de las Naciones
Unidas (ONU)
SU Организáция Объединённых Нáций
(ОÓН)

3891 GB United Nations Children's Fund, the
(UNICEF)
F le Fonds des Nations Unies pour
l'enfance (UNICEF)
D der Internationale Kinderhilfsfonds
der Vereinten Nationen (UNICEF)
I il fondo internazionale delle Nazioni
unite per l'infanzia (UNICEF)
E el Fondo de las Naciones Unidas para
la Infancia (UNICEF)
SU Дéтский фонд ОÓН (ЮНИСÉФ)

3892 GB United Nations Educational, Scientific
and Cultural Organisation, the
(UNESCO)
F l'Organisation des Nations unies pour
l'éducation, la science, et la culture
(UNESCO)
D die Organisation der UNO für
Erziehung, Wissenschaft und Kultur
(UNESCO)
I l'Organizzazione delle Nazioni unite
per l'educazione, la scienza e la cultura
(UNESCO)
E la Organización de las Naciones
Unidas para la Educación, la Ciencia y
la Cultura (UNESCO)
SU Организáция Объединённых Нáций по
вопрóсам образовáния, наýки и
культýры (ЮНÉСКО)

3893 GB United States of America (USA), the
F les États-Unis d'Amérique (USA)
D die Vereinigten Staaten von Amerika
(USA)
I gli Stati Uniti d'America (USA)
E los Estados Unidos de América (USA)
SU Соединённые Штáты Амéрики (США)

3894 GB Upper Egypt
F la haute Égypte
D Oberägypten
I l'Alto Egitto
E Alto Egipto
SU Вéрхний Егúпет

3895 GB Upper Volta (hist.)
F la Haute-Volta (hist.)
D Obervolta (Gesch.)
I l'Alto Volta (st.)
E Alto Volta (hist.)
SU Вéрхняя Вóльта (ист.)

3896 GB Urals, the (USSR)
F les monts Oural (URSS)
D der Ural (UdSSR)
I gli Urali (URSS)
E los Urales (URSS)
SU Урáл (СССР)

3897 GB Uranus (myth., astron.)
F Ouranos (myth.), Uranus (astron.)
D Uranos (myth.), Uranus (Astron.)
I Urano (mit., astr.)
E Urano (mit., astr.)
SU Урáн (миф., астр.)

3898 GB Urban (pope)
    F Urbain (pape)
    D Urban (Papst)
    I Urbano (papa)
    E Urbano (papa)
    SU Урба́н (па́па ри́мский)

3899 GB Ursa Major (Great Bear) (astron.)
    F la Grande Ourse (astron.)
    D der Große Bär (Astron.)
    I l'Orsa Maggiore (astr.)
    E la Osa Mayor (astr.)
    SU Больша́я Медве́дица (астр.)

3900 GB Ursa Minor (Little Bear) (astron.)
    F la Petite Ourse (astron.)
    D der Kleine Bär (Astron.)
    I l'Orsa Minore (astr.)
    E la Osa Menor (astr.)
    SU Ма́лая Медве́дица (астр.)

3901 GB Uruguay
    F l'Uruguay (m.)
    D Uruguay
    I l'Uruguay
    E el Uruguay
    SU Уругва́й

3902 GB *Utopia* (More, 1516)
    F *Utopie* (More)
    D *Utopia* (More)
    I *Utopia* (Moro)
    E *Utopía* (Moro)
    SU «Уто́пия» (Мор)

V

3903 GB Valencia (Spain)
F Valence (Espagne)
D Valencia (Spanien)
I la Valencia (Spagna)
E Valencia (España)
SU Валéнсия (Испáния)

3904 GB Valentinian (emperor)
F Valentinien (empereur)
D Valentinianus (Kaiser)
I Valentiniano (imperatore)
E Valentiniano (emperador)
SU Валентиниáн (императóр)

3905 GB Valerian (195–260)
F Valérien
D Valerianus
I Valeriano
E Valeriano
SU Валериáн

3906 GB Valerius (Roman name)
F Valerius (nom romain)
D Valerius (Römername)
I Valerio (nome romano)
E Valerio (nombre romano)
SU Валéрий (древнерúмское úмя)

3907 GB Valetta (Valletta) (Malta)
F La Valette (Malte)
D Valletta (Malta)
I La Valletta (Malta)
E La Valetta (Malta)
SU Валлéтта (Мáльта)

3908 GB Valhalla (myth.)
F Walhalla (myth.)
D die Walhall (myth.)
I il Walhalla (mit.)
E Walhalla (mit.)
SU валгáлла (миф.)

3909 GB *Valkyrie, The* (Wagner, 1870)
F *La Valkyrie*
D *Die Walküre*
I *La Valchiria*
E *La Walkiria*
SU «Валькúрия» (Вáгнер)

3910 GB Valkyries, the (myth.)
F les Valkyries (myth.)
D die Walküren (myth.)
I le Valchirie (mit.)
E las Walkirias (mit.)
SU валькúрии (миф.)

3911 GB *Valley of the Dolls* (Robson, 1967)
F *La Vallée des poupées*
D *Das Tal der Puppen*
I *La valle delle bambole*
E *El valle de las muñecas*
SU «Долúна кýкол» (Рóбсон)

3912 GB *Valse Triste [Sad Waltz]* (Sibelius, 1903)
F *Valse triste*
D *Trauriger Walzer*
I *Valzer triste*
E *Vals triste*
SU «Грýстный вальс» (Сибéлиус)

3913 GB Vandals, the (hist.)
F les Vandales (hist.)
D die Wandalen (Gesch.)
I i vandali (st.)
E los vándalos (hist.)
SU вандáлы (ист.)

3914 GB *Vanity Fair* (Thackeray, 1848)
F *La Foire aux vanités*
D *Jahrmarkt der Eitelkeit*
I *La fiera della vanità*
E *La feria de las vanidades*
SU «Ярмарка тщеслáвия» (Тéккерей)

3915　GB　Vatican, the (Rome)
　　　　F　le Vatican (Rome)
　　　　D　der Vatikan (Rom)
　　　　I　il Vaticano (Roma)
　　　　E　el Vaticano (Roma)
　　　　SU　Ватикáн (Рим)

3916　GB　*Vatican Cellars, The* (Gide, 1914)
　　　　F　*Les Caves du Vatican*
　　　　D　*Die Verliese des Vaticans*
　　　　I　*I sotterranei del Vaticano*
　　　　E　*Las cuevas del Vaticano*
　　　　SU　«Подземéлья Ватикáна» (Жид)

3917　GB　Vatican Council, the (1869–70, 1962–5)
　　　　F　le concile du Vatican
　　　　D　das Vatikanische Konzil
　　　　I　il concilio Vaticano
　　　　E　el Concilio Vaticano
　　　　SU　Ватикáнский собóр

3918　GB　Vendée, the (France)
　　　　F　la Vendée (France)
　　　　D　die Vendée (Frankreich)
　　　　I　la Vendea (Francia)
　　　　E　Vendea (Francia)
　　　　SU　Вандéя (Фрáнция)

3919　GB　Venerable Bede, the (673–735)
　　　　F　Bède le Vénérable
　　　　D　Beda Venerabilis
　　　　I　Beda il Venerabile
　　　　E　Beda el Venerable
　　　　SU　Бéда Достопочтéнный

3920　GB　Veneto (Italy)
　　　　F　le Vénétie (Italie)
　　　　D　Venezien (Italien)
　　　　I　il Veneto (Italia)
　　　　E　Venecia (Italia)
　　　　SU　Венéция (Итáлия)

3921　GB　Venezuela
　　　　F　le Venezuela
　　　　D　Venezuela
　　　　I　il Venezuela
　　　　E　Venezuela
　　　　SU　Венесуэ́ла

3922　GB　Venice (Italy)
　　　　F　Venise (Italie)
　　　　D　Venedig (Italien)
　　　　I　Venezia (Italia)
　　　　E　Venecia (Italia)
　　　　SU　Венéция (Итáлия)

3923　GB　*Venice Preserv'd* (Otway, 1682)
　　　　F　*Venise sauvée*
　　　　D　*Das gerettete Venedig*
　　　　I　*Venezia salvata*
　　　　D　*Venecia salvada*
　　　　SU　«Спасённая Венéция» (Óтуэй)

3924　GB　Venus (myth., astron.)
　　　　F　Vénus (myth., astron.)
　　　　D　Venus (myth., Astron.)
　　　　I　Venere (mit., astr.)
　　　　E　Venus (mit., astr.)
　　　　SU　Венéра (миф., астр.)

3925　GB　*Venus and Adonis* (Shakespeare, 1593)
　　　　F　*Vénus et Adonis*
　　　　D　*Venus und Adonis*
　　　　I　*Venere e Adone*
　　　　E　*Venus y Adonis*
　　　　SU　«Венéра и Адонúс» (Шекспúр)

3926　GB　*Venus de Milo*, the (Paris)
　　　　F　la *Vénus de Milo* (Paris)
　　　　D　die *Venus von Milo* (Paris)
　　　　I　l'*Afrodite di Milo* (Parigi)
　　　　E　la *Venus de Milo* (París)
　　　　SU　«Афродúта Милóсская» (Парúж)

　　　　GB　Vergil→Virgil

3927　GB　Verona (Italy)
　　　　F　Vérone (Italie)
　　　　D　Verona (Italien)
　　　　I　Verona (Italia)
　　　　E　Verona (Italia)
　　　　SU　Верóна (Итáлия)

3928　GB　Versailles (France)
　　　　F　Versailles (France)
　　　　D　Versailles (Frankreich)
　　　　I　Versailles (Francia)
　　　　E　Versalles (Francia)
　　　　SU　Версáль (м.) (Фрáнция)

3929　GB　*Vertigo* (Hitchcock, 1958)
　　　　F　*Sueurs froides*
　　　　D　*Aus dem Reich der Toten*
　　　　I　*La donna che visse due volte*
　　　　E　*De entre los muertos*
　　　　SU　«Головокружéние» (Хúчкок)

3930　GB　Vespasian (9–79)
　　　　F　Vespasien
　　　　D　Vespasianus
　　　　I　Vespasiano
　　　　E　Vespasiano
　　　　SU　Веспасиáн

3931 GB *Vested Interests* (Benavente, 1907)
F *Les Affaires sont les affaires*
D *Der tugendhafte Glücksritter*
I *Gli interessi creati*
E *Los intereses creados*
SU «Игра́ интере́сов»
(Бенаве́нте-и-Марти́нес)

3932 GB Vesuvius, Mount (Italy)
F le mont Vésuve (Italie)
D Vesuv (Italien)
I il Vesuvio (Italia)
E el Vesubio (Italia)
SU Везу́вий (Ита́лия)

3933 GB *Vicar of Wakefield, The* (Goldsmith, 1766)
F *Le Vicaire de Wakefield*
D *Der Landpfarrer von Wakefield*
I *Il vicario di Wakefield*
E *El vicario de Wakefield*
SU «Векфи́льдский свяще́нник»
(Го́лдсмит)

3934 GB Victor (saint, pope)
F Victor (saint, pape)
D Viktor (Heiliger, Papst)
I Vittore (santo, papa)
E Víctor (santo, papa)
SU Ви́ктор (св., па́па ри́мский)

3935 GB Victoria (1819–1901)
F Victoria
D Viktoria
I Vittoria
E Victoria
SU Викто́рия

3936 GB *Victory* (Conrad, 1915)
F *Une victoire*
D *Sieg*
I *Vittoria*
E *Victoria*
SU «Побе́да» (Ко́нрад)

3937 GB Vienna (Austria)
F Vienne (Autriche)
D Wien (Österreich)
I Vienna (Austria)
E Viena (Austria)
SU Ве́на (А́встрия)

3938 GB Vietnam
F le Viêt-Nam
D Vietnam
I il Vietnam
E Vietnam
SU Вьетна́м

3939 GB *View from the Bridge, A* (Miller, 1955)
F *Vu du pont*
D *Ein Blick von der Brücke*
I *Uno sguardo dal ponte*
E *Panorama desde el puente*
SU «Вид с моста́» (Ми́ллер)

3940 GB Vikings, the (hist.)
F les Vikings (hist.)
D die Wikinger (Gesch.)
I i vichingi (st.)
E los vikingos (hist.)
SU вики́нги (ист.)

3941 GB *Village Doctor, The* (Balzac, 1833)
F *Le Médecin de campagne*
D *Der Landarzt*
I *Il medico di campagna*
E *El médico de aldea*
SU «Се́льский врач» (Бальза́к)

3942 GB Vilnius (USSR)
F Vilnious (URSS)
D Wilna (UdSSR)
I Vilna (URSS)
E Vilna (URSS)
SU Ви́льнюс (СССР)

3943 GB *Vipers' Tangle* (Mauriac, 1932)
F *Le Noeud de vipères*
D *Natterngezücht*
I *Nodo di vipere*
E *Nudo de víboras*
SU «Клубо́к змей» (Мориа́к)

3944 GB Virgil (Vergil) (70–19)
F Virgile
D Vergil
I Virgilio
E Virgilio
SU Верги́лий

3945 GB Virginia (USA)
F la Virginie (USA)
D Virginia (USA)
I la Virginia (USA)
E Virginia (USA)
SU Вирги́ния (США)

3946 GB *Virginians, The* (Thackeray, 1857–9)
F *Virginiens*
D *Die Virginier*
I *I virginiani*
E *Los virginianos*
SU «Вирги́нцы» (Те́ккерей)

3947 GB *Virginibus Puerisque* ["For Girls and Boys"] (Stevenson, 1881)
F   *Virginibus Puerisque*
D   *Für Mädchen und Knaben*
I   *Virginibus Puerisque*
E   *Virginibus Puerisque*
SU «Для ма́льчиков и де́вочек» (Сти́венсон)

3948 GB Virgin Islands, the (West Indies)
F   les îles Vierges (Antilles)
D   die Jungferninseln (Westindien)
I   le isole Vergini (Antille)
E   las islas Vírgenes (Antillas)
SU Вирги́нские острова́ (Вест-И́ндия)

3949 GB *Virgin Soil* (Turgenev, 1877)
F   *Terres vierges* (Tourgueniev)
D   *Neuland* (Turgenjew)
I   *Terra vergine* (Turgenev)
E   *Tierras vírgenes* (Turgueniev)
SU «Новь» (Турге́нев)

3950 GB *Virgin Soil Upturned* (Sholokhov, 1932, 1960)
F   *Terres défrichées* (Cholokhov)
D   *Neuland unterm Pflug* (Scholochow)
I   *I dissodatori* (Šolochov)
E   *Tierras roturadas* (Cholojov)
SU «По́днятая целина́» (Шо́лохов)

3951 GB Virgo (astron.)
F   la Vierge (astron.)
D   die Jungfrau (Astron.)
I   la Vergine (astr.)
E   Virgo (astr.)
SU Де́ва (астр.)

3952 GB *Viridiana* (Buñuel, 1961)
F   *Viridiana*
D   *Viridiana*
I   *Viridiana*
E   *Viridiana*
SU «Виридиа́на» (Бюнюэ́ль)

3953 GB *Viscount of Bragelonne, The* (Dumas, 1848–50)
F   *Le Vicomte de Bragelonne*
D   *Der Graf von Bragelonne*
I   *Il visconte di Bragelone*
E   *El vizconde de Bragelone*
SU «Вико́нт де Бражело́н» (Дюма́)

3954 GB Vistula (River), the (Poland)
F   la Vistule (Pologne)
D   die Weichsel (Polen)
I   la Vistola (Polonia)
E   el Vístula (Polonia)
SU Ви́сла (По́льша)

3955 GB Vladimir (saint, prince)
F   Vladimir (saint, prince)
D   Wladimir (Heiliger, Prinz)
I   Vladimiro (santo, principe)
E   Vladimiro (santo, príncipe)
SU Влади́мир (св., князь)

3956 GB *Voices of Silence, The* (Malraux, 1951)
F   *Les Voix du silence*
D   *Stimmen der Stille*
I   *Le voci del silenzio*
E   *Las voces del silencio*
SU «Голоса́ молча́ния» (Мальро́)

3957 GB *Voices of the Night* (Longfellow, 1839)
F   *Voix de la nuit*
D   *Stimmen der Nacht*
I   *Voci della notte*
E   *Voces de la noche*
SU «Ночны́е голоса́» (Лонгфе́лло)

3958 GB *Volpone, or The Fox* (Jonson, 1606)
F   *Volpone ou le Renard*
D   *Volpone oder der Fuchs*
I   *Volpone*
E   *Volpone o El zorro*
SU «Вольпо́не, и́ли Лиса́» (Джо́нсон)

3959 GB *Voluptuousness* (Sainte-Beuve, 1834)
F   *Volupté*
D   *Lust*
I   *Voluttà*
E   *Voluptuosidad*
SU «Сладостра́стие» (Сент-Бёв)

3960 GB Vosges (Mountains), the (France)
F   les Vosges (f.) (France)
D   die Vogesen (Frankreich)
I   i Vosgi (Francia)
E   los Vosgos (Francia)
SU Воге́зы (м.) (Фра́нция)

3961 GB *Voyage to the Centre of the Earth* (Verne, 1864)
F   *Voyage au centre de la Terre*
D   *Die Reise zum Mittelpunkt der Erde*
I   *Viaggio al centro della terra*
E   *Viaje al centro de la Tierra*
SU «Путеше́ствие к це́нтру Земли́» (Верн)

3962 GB Vulcan (myth.)
F   Vulcain (myth.)
D   Vulkan (myth.)
I   Vulcano (mit.)
E   Vulcano (mit.)
SU Вулка́н (миф.)

3963 GB Vulgate, the (Bib.)
F   la Vulgate (Bib.)
D   die Vulgata (Bib.)
I   la Volgata (Bib.)
E   la Vulgata (Bib.)
SU Вульга́та (библ.)

W

3964 GB *Wages of Fear, The* (Clouzot, 1953)
 F *Le Salaire de la peur*
 D *Lohn der Angst*
 I *Vite vendute*
 E *El salario del miedo*
 SU «Возмéздие за страх» (Клузó)

3965 GB *Wag of Seville, The* (Tirso de Molina, 1630)
 F *Le Trompeur de Séville*
 D *Der Verführer von Sevilla*
 I *Il beffatore di Siviglia*
 E *El burlador de Sevilla*
 SU «Севи́льский озóрник» (Ти́рсо де Моли́на)

3966 GB Wailing Wall, the (Jerusalem)
 F le Mur des Lamentations (Jérusalem)
 D die Klagemauer (Jerusalem)
 I il Muro del pianto (Gerusalemme)
 E el Muro de las Lamentaciones (Jerusalén)
 SU Стенá плáча (Иерусали́м)

3967 GB *Waiting for Godot* (Beckett, 1952)
 F *En attendant Godot*
 D *Warten auf Godot*
 I *Aspettando Godot*
 E *Esperando a Godot*
 SU «В ожидáнии Годó» (Бéккет)

3968 GB *Waiting for Lefty* (Odets, 1935)
 F *En attendant Lefty*
 D *Das Warten auf Lefty*
 I *Aspettando Lefty*
 E *Esperando a Lefty*
 SU «В ожидáнии Лéфти» (Одéтс)

3969 GB Walachia (Wallachia) (Romania)
 F la Valachie (Roumanie)
 D die Walachei (Rumänien)
 I la Valacchia (Romania)
 E Valaquia (Rumania)
 SU Валáхия (Румы́ния)

3970 GB *Walden, or Life in the Woods* (Thoreau, 1854)
 F *Walden ou La Vie dans les bois*
 D *Walden oder Leben in den Wäldern*
 I *Walden o la vita nei boschi*
 E *Walden o la vida en los bosques*
 SU «Уóлден, и́ли Жизнь в лесý» (Тóро)

3971 GB Wales
 F le pays de Galles
 D Wales
 I il Galles
 E el País de Gales
 SU Уэ́льс

3972 GB *Wallenstein* (Schiller, 1799)
 F *Wallenstein*
 D *Wallenstein*
 I *Wallenstein*
 E *Wallenstein*
 SU «Смерть Валленштéйна» (Ши́ллер)

3973 GB Walloons, the (Belgium)
 F les Wallons (Belgique)
 D die Wallonen (Belgien)
 I i valloni (Belgio)
 E los valones (Bélgica)
 SU валлóны (Бéльгия)

3974 GB Wandering Jew, the (rel., + Suë, 1844–5)
 F le Juif errant (relig.)
 D der ewige Jude (relig.)
 I l'ebreo errante (relig.)
 E el judío errante (relig.)
 SU Вéчный жид (рел., + Сю)

3975 GB   *War and Peace* (Tolstoy, 1865–9)
      F   *Guerre et Paix* (Tolstoï)
      D   *Krieg und Frieden* (Tolstoj)
      I   *Guerra e pace* (Tolstoj)
      E   *Guerra y Paz* (Tolstoi)
      SU   «Война́ и мир» (Толсто́й)

3976 GB   *Ward No. 6* (Chekhov, 1892)
      F   *La Chambre numéro 6* (Tchekhov)
      D   *Das Zimmer No. 6* (Tschechow)
      I   *La corsia n. 6* (Čechov)
      E   *La sala número 6* (Chejov)
      SU   «Пала́та № 6» (Че́хов)

      GB   War of Independence→Independence,
           War of

3977 GB   *War of the Worlds, The* (Wells, 1898)
      F   *Le Guerre des mondes*
      D   *Der Krieg der Welten*
      I   *La guerra dei mondi*
      E   *La guerra de los mundos*
      SU   «Война́ миро́в» (Уэ́ллс)

3978 GB   Warsaw (Poland)
      F   Varsovie (Pologne)
      D   Warschau (Polen)
      I   Varsavia (Polonia)
      E   Varsovia (Polonia)
      SU   Варша́ва (По́льша)

3979 GB   Warsaw Pact, the (1955)
      F   le pacte de Varsovie
      D   der Warschaupakt
      I   il patto di Varsavia
      E   el pacto de Varsovia
      SU   Варша́вский догово́р

3980 GB   Wars of Religion, the (1562–98)
      F   les guerres de Religion
      D   die Hugenottenkriege
      I   le guerre di religione
      E   las guerras de Religión
      SU   религио́зные во́йны

3981 GB   Wars of the Roses, the (1455–85)
      F   la guerre des Deux-Roses
      D   die Rosenkriege
      I   la guerra delle due rose
      E   la guerra de las Dos Rosas
      SU   во́йны А́лой и Бе́лой ро́зы

3982 GB   *Wasps, The [Sphekes]* (Aristophanes,
           −422)
      F   *Les Guêpes* (Aristophane)
      D   *Die Wespen* (Aristophanes)
      I   *Le vespe* (Aristofane)
      E   *Las avispas* (Aristófanes)
      SU   «О́сы» (Аристофа́н)

3983 GB   *Waste Land, The* (Eliot, 1922)
      F   *La Terre Gaste*
      D   *Das wüste Land*
      I   *La terra desolata*
      E   *La tierra desolada*
      SU   «Беспло́дная земля́» (Э́лиот)

3984 GB   *Waters and land* (Quasimodo, 1930)
      F   *Eaux et Terres*
      D   *Wasser und Erde*
      I   *Acque e terre*
      E   *Aguas y tierras*
      SU   «Вода́ и земля́» (Квази́модо)

3985 GB   *Waverley* (Scott, 1814)
      F   *Waverley*
      D   *Waverley*
      I   *Waverley*
      E   *Waverley*
      SU   «Уэ́верли» (Скотт)

3986 GB   *Waves, The* (Woolf, 1931)
      F   *Les Vagues*
      D   *Die Wellen*
      I   *Le onde*
      E   *Las olas*
      SU   «Во́лны» (Вулф)

3987 GB   *Way of All Flesh, The* (Butler, 1903)
      F   *Ainsi va toute chair*
      D   *Der Weg allen Fleisches*
      I   *Così muore la carne*
      E   *Así muere la carne*
      SU   «Путь вся́кой пло́ти» (Ба́тлер)

3988 GB   *Way of the World, The* (Congreve,
           1700)
      F   *Ainsi va le monde*
      D   *Der Lauf der Welt*
      I   *Così va il mondo*
      E   *El camino de la vida*
      SU   «Пути́ све́тской жи́зни» (Ко́нгрив)

3989 GB   *We* (Zamyatin, 1924)
      F   *Nous autres* (Zamiatine)
      D   *Wir* (Samjatin)
      I   *Noi* (Zamjatin)
      E   *Nosotros* (Zamjatin)
      SU   «Мы» (Замя́тин)

3990 GB   *Wealth of Nations, The* (Smith, 1776)
      F   *La Richesse des nations*
      D   *Der Nationalreichtum*
      I   *La ricchezza delle nazioni*
      E   *La riqueza de las naciones*
      SU   «Бога́тство наро́дов» (Смит)

3991 GB *Weavers, The* (Hauptmann, 1892)
F *Les Tisserands*
D *Die Weber*
I *I tessitori*
E *Los tejedores*
SU «Ткачи» (Гáуптман)

3992 GB *Week on the Concord and Merrimack Rivers, A* (Thoreau, 1849)
F *Une semaine sur les fleuves Concord et Merrimack*
D *Eine Woche an den Flüssen Concord und Merrimack*
I *Una settimana sui fiumi Concord e Merrimack*
E *Una semana en los ríos Concordia y Merrimack*
SU «Недéля на рéках Кóнкорд и Мéрримак» (Тóро)

3993 GB *Well of the Saints, The* (Synge, 1905)
F *La Fontaine aux saints*
D *Der heilige Brunnen*
I *La fonte dei santi*
E *El manantial de los santos*
SU «Истóчник святы́х» (Синг)

3994 GB *Well-Tempered Clavier, The* (Bach, 1722, 1744)
F *Le Clavecin bien tempéré*
D *Das wohltemperierte Klavier*
I *Il clavicembalo ben temperato*
E *El clave bien temperado*
SU «Хорошó темперúрованный клавúр» (Бах)

3995 GB Wenceslas (saint, 907–989)
F Venceslas (saint)
D Wenzel (Heiliger)
I Venceslao (santo
E Wenceslao (santo)
SU Вацлáв (св.)

3996 GB West Africa
F l'Afrique occidentale
D Westafrika
I l'Africa occidentale
E el África occidental
SU Зáпадная Áфрика

3997 GB West Berlin (Germany)
F Berlin-Ouest (Allemagne)
D West-Berlin (Deutschland)
I Berlino Ovest (Germania)
E Berlín Oeste (Alemania)
SU Зáпадный Берлúн (Гермáния)

3998 GB Western Australia (Australia)
F l'Australia-Occidentale (Australie)
D West-Australien (Australien)
I l'Australia Occidentale (Australia)
E Australia Occidental (Australia)
SU Зáпадная Австрáлия (Австрáлия)

3999 GB Western European Union (WEU), the
F l'Union de l'Europe Occidentale (UEO)
D die Westeuropäische Union (WEU)
I l'Unione europea occidentale (UEO)
E la Unión de Europa occidental (UEO)
SU Западноевропéйский сою́з (ЗЕС)

4000 GB Western Samoa
F les Samoa occidentales
D West-Samoa
I le Samoa Occidentali
E Samoa Occidental
SU Зáпадное Самóа

GB Western Schism (rel.)→Great Schism

4001 GB West Falkland (Falkland Islands)
F Falkland occidentale (îles Falkland)
D Westfalkland (Falklandinseln)
I Falkland Occidentale (isole Falkland)
E Gran Malvina (Malvinas)
SU Зáпадный Фóлкденд (Фолкдéндские островá)

4002 GB West Indies, the
F les Antilles (f.)
D Westindien
I le Antille
E las Antillas
SU Вест-Úндия

4003 GB Westminster Abbey (London)
F l'abbaye de Westminster (Londres)
D die Westminster-Abtei (London)
I l'abbazia di Westminster (Londra)
E la abadía de Westminster (Londres)
SU Вестминстерское аббáтство (Лóндон)

4004 GB Westphalia (Germany)
F la Westphalie (Allemagne)
D Westfalen (Deutschland)
I la Vestfalia (Germania)
E Westfalia (Alemania)
SU Вестфáлия (Гермáния)

4005 GB *West Side Story* (Bernstein, 1957)
F *West Side Story*
D *West Side Story*
I *West Side Story*
E *West Side Story*
SU «Вестсáйдская истóрия» (Бéрнстайн)

4006 GB West Virginia (USA)
     F la Virginie-Occidentale (USA)
     D West Virginia (USA)
     I la Virginia Occidentale (USA)
     E Virginia Occidental (USA)
     SU За́падная Виргѝния (США)

4007 GB *Westward Ho!* (Kingsley, 1855)
     F *Vers l'Ouest*
     D *Nach Westen!*
     I *Verso Ovest*
     E *Hacia el Oeste*
     SU «К за́паду!» (Ки́нгсли)

4008 GB *What is Art?* (Tolstoy, 1897–8)
     F *Qu'est-ce que l'art?* (Tolstoï)
     D *Was ist Kunst?* (Tolstoj)
     I *Che cos'è l'arte?* (Tolstoj)
     E *¿Qué es el arte?* (Tolstoi)
     SU «Что тако́е иску́сство?» (Толсто́й)

4009 GB *When We Dead Awaken [Naar vi døde vaagner]* (Ibsen, 1899)
     F *Quand nous nous réveillerons d'entre les morts*
     D *Wenn wir Toten erwachen*
     I *Quando noi morti ci destiamo*
     E *Cuando despertemos de entre los muertos*
     SU «Когда́ мы, мёртвые, воскресѝм» (Йбсен)

4010 GB *Where Angels Fear to Tread* (Forster, 1905)
     F *Où les anges ont peur d'avancer*
     D *Engel und Narren*
     I *Monteriano*
     E *Donde los ángeles no se aventuran*
     SU «Куда́ боя́тся ступѝть а́нгелы» (Фо́рстер)

4011 GB *Whim, A* (Musset, 1837)
     F *Un caprice*
     D *Eine Laune*
     I *Un capriccio*
     E *Un capricho*
     SU «Капрѝз» (Мюссе́)

4012 GB *White Chief, The* (Reid, 1859)
     F *Le Chef blanc*
     D *Der weiße Häuptling*
     I *Il capo bianco*
     E *El jefe blanco*
     SU «Бе́лый вождь» (Рид)

4013 GB *White Devil, The* (Webster, 1612)
     F *Le Démon blanc*
     D *Der weiße Teufel*
     I *Il diavolo bianco*
     E *El diablo blanco*
     SU «Бе́лый дья́вол» (Уэ́бстер)

4014 GB *White Fang* (London, 1905)
     F *Croc-Blanc*
     D *Wolfsblut*
     I *Zanna bianca*
     E *Colmillo blanco*
     SU «Бе́лый клык» (Ло́ндон)

4015 GB *White Girl, The* (Whistler, 1863)
     F *La Jeune Fille en blanc*
     D *Mädchen in weiß*
     I *Ragazza in bianco*
     E *Joven vestida de blanco*
     SU «Де́вушка в бе́лом» (Уѝстлер)

4016 GB *White Heat* (Walsh, 1949)
     F *L'enfer est à lui*
     D *Sprung in den Tod*
     I *La furia umana*
     E *Al rojo vivo*
     SU «Раскалённый добела́» (Уо́лш)

4017 GB White House, the (Washington)
     F la Maison Blanche
     D das Weiße Haus
     I la Casa Bianca
     E la Casa Blanca
     SU Бе́лый дом (Вашингто́н)

4018 GB *White Jacket* (Melville, 1850)
     F *La Blouse blanche*
     D *Weißjacke*
     I *Giachetta bianca*
     E *La chaqueta blanca*
     SU «Бе́лая ку́ртка» (Ме́лвилл)

4019 GB *White Lady, The* (Boïeldieu, 1825)
     F *La Dame blanche*
     D *Die weiße Dame*
     I *La dama bianca*
     E *La dama blanca*
     SU «Бе́лая да́ма» (Буальдьё)

4020 GB *White Nights* (Dostoievsky, 1848)
     F *Nuits blanches* (Dostoïevski)
     D *Weiße Nächte* (Dostojewskij)
     I *Le notti bianche* (Dostoevskij)
     E *Noches blancas* (Dostoievski)
     SU «Бе́лые но́чи» (Достое́вский)

4021	GB	White Nile (River), the
	F	le Nil Blanc
	D	der Weiße Nil
	I	il Nilo Bianco
	E	el Nilo Blanco
	SU	Бе́лый Нил

4022	GB	*White Peacock, The* (Lawrence, 1911)
	F	*Le Paon blanc*
	D	*Der weiße Pfau*
	I	*Il pavone bianco*
	E	*El pavón blanco*
	SU	«Бе́лый павли́н» (Ло́ренс)

4023	GB	White Russia (hist.)
	F	la Russie blanche (hist.)
	D	Weißrußland (Gesch.)
	I	la Russia Bianca (st.)
	E	Rusia Blanca (hist.)
	SU	Белору́ссия (СССР)

4024	GB	White Sea, the (USSR)
	F	la mer Blanche (URSS)
	D	das Weiße Meer (UdSSR)
	I	il mare Bianco (URSS)
	E	el mar Blanco (URSS)
	SU	Бе́лое мо́ре (СССР)

4025	GB	Whit Sunday (rel.)
	F	le dimanche de la Pentecôte (relig.)
	D	der Pfingstsonntag (relig.)
	I	la domenica di Pentecoste (relig.)
	E	el domingo de Pentecostés (relig.)
	SU	тро́ицын день (рел.)

4026	GB	*Who's Afraid of Virginia Woolf?* (Albee, 1962)
	F	*Qui a peur de Virginia Woolf?*
	D	*Wer hat Angst vor Virginia Woolf?*
	I	*Chi a paura di Virginia Woolf?*
	E	*¿Quién teme a Virginia Woolf?*
	SU	«Кто бои́тся Вирджи́нии Вулф?» (О́лби)

4027	GB	*Widowers' Houses* (Shaw, 1892)
	F	*L'argent n'a pas d'odeur*
	D	*Die Häuser der Herrn Sartorius*
	I	*Le case del vedovo*
	E	*Casas de viudos*
	SU	«Дома́ вдовца́» (Шо́у)

4028	GB	*Wild Ass's Skin, The* (Balzac, 1831)
	F	*La Peau de chagrin*
	D	*Das Chagrinleder*
	I	*La pelle di zigrino*
	E	*La piel de zapa*
	SU	«Шагре́невая ко́жа» (Бальза́к)

4029	GB	*Wild Duck, The* [*Vildanden*] (Ibsen, 1884)
	F	*Le Canard sauvage*
	D	*Die Wildente*
	I	*L'anitra selvatica*
	E	*El pato salvaje*
	SU	«Ди́кая у́тка» (Йбсен)

4030	GB	*Wild Strawberries* [*Smultronstället*] (Bergman, 1957)
	F	*Les Fraises sauvages*
	D	*Wilde Erdbeeren*
	I	*Il posto delle fragole*
	E	*Fresas salvajes*
	SU	«Земляни́чная поля́на» (Бе́ргман)

4031	GB	*Wilhelm Meister's Apprenticeship* (Goethe, 1795–6)
	F	*Les Années d'apprentissage de Wilhelm Meister*
	D	*Wilhelm Meisters Lehrjahre*
	I	*Anni di apprendistato di Wilhelm Meister*
	E	*Los años de aprendizaje de Guillermo Meister*
	SU	«Го́ды уче́ния Вильге́льма Ме́йстера» (Гёте)

4032	GB	William (emperor, sovereign)
	F	Guillaume (empereur, souverain)
	D	Wilhelm (Kaiser, Herr.)
	I	Gugliemo (imperatore, sovrano)
	E	Guillermo (emperador, sob.)
	SU	Вильге́льм (импера́тор, прав.)

4033	GB	William of Orange (1650–1702)
	F	Guillaume d'Orange
	D	Wilhelm von Oranien
	I	Gugliemo di Orange-Nassau
	E	Guillermo III de Nassau
	SU	Вильге́льм Ора́нский

4034	GB	William Rufus (*1056*–1100)
	F	Guillaume le Roux
	D	Wilhelm der Rote
	I	Gugliemo il Rosso
	E	Guillermo el Rojo
	SU	Вильге́льм Ры́жий

4035	GB	William Tell (XIV; + Schiller, 1804; Rossini, 1829)
	F	Guillaume Tell
	D	Wilhelm Tell
	I	Gugliemo Tell
	E	Guillermo Tell
	SU	Вильге́льм Телль (+ Ши́ллер, Росси́ни)

4036 GB William the Conqueror (*1028*–1087)
    F   Guillaume le Conquérant
    D   Wilhelm der Eroberer
    I   Guglielmo il Conquistadore
    E   Guillermo el Conquistador
    SU Вильгѐльм Завоевáтель

4037 GB William the Silent (1553–84)
    F   Guillaume le Taciturne
    D   Wilhelm der Schweigsame
    I   Guglielmo il Taciturno
    E   Guillermo el Taciturno
    SU Вильгѐльм Молчалѝвый

4038 GB *Wind Among the Reeds, The* (Yeats, 1899)
    F   *Le Vent dans les roseaux*
    D   *Der Wind im Rohr*
    I   *Il vento fra le canne*
    E   *El viento en los rosales*
    SU «Вѐтер в камышáх» (Йитс)

4039 GB *Wind, Sand and Stars* (Saint-Exupéry, 1939)
    F   *Terre des hommes*
    D   *Wind, Sand und Sterne*
    I   *Terra degli uomini*
    E   *Tierra de los hombres*
    SU «Планѐта людѐй» (Сент-Экзюперѝ)

4040 GB Windward Islands, the
    F   les îles du Vent
    D   die Inseln unter dem Winde
    I   le isole Sopravento
    E   las islas de Barlovento
    SU Навѐтренные островá

4041 GB *Winged Victory of Samothrace*, the (Paris)
    F   la *Victoire de Samothrace* (Paris)
    D   die *Nike von Samothrake* (Paris)
    I   la *Nike di Samotracia* (Parigi)
    E   la *Victoria de Samotracia* (París)
    SU «Нѝке Самофракѝйская» (Парѝж)

4042 GB *Wings of the Dove, The* (James, 1902)
    F   *Les Ailes de la colombe*
    D   *Die Flügel der Taube*
    I   *Le ali della colomba*
    E   *Las alas de la paloma*
    SU «Крѝлья гóлуби» (Джеймс)

4043 GB *Winter Journey* (Schubert, 1827)
    F   *Voyage d'hiver*
    D   *Winterreise*
    I   *Viaggio d'inverno*
    E   *Viaje de invierno*
    SU «Зѝмний путь» (Шýберт)

4044 GB *Winter of Our Discontent, The* (Steinbeck, 1961)
    F   *L'Hiver de notre mécontentement*
    D   *Geld bringt Geld*
    I   *L'inverno del nostro scontento*
    E   *El invierno de nuestro descontento*
    SU «Зимá тревóги нáшей» (Стѐйнбек)

4045 GB Winter Palace, the (Leningrad)
    F   la palais d'Hiver (Leningrad)
    D   der Winterpalais (Leningrad)
    I   il Palazzo d'Inverno (Leningrado)
    E   el palacio de Invierno (Leningrado)
    SU Зѝмний дворѐц (Ленинград)

4046 GB *Winter's Tale, The* (Shakespeare, 1610)
    F   *Le Conte d'hiver*
    D   *Das Wintermärchen*
    I   *Il racconto d'inverno*
    E   *El cuento de invierno*
    SU «Зѝмняя скáзка» (Шекспѝр)

4047 GB *Wisdom* (Verlaine, 1881)
    F   *Sagesse*
    D   *Weisheit*
    I   *Saggezza*
    E   *Cordura*
    SU «Мýдрость» (Верлѐн)

4048 GB *Wisdom of Women, The* (Tirso de Molina, 1621)
    F   *La Prudence de la femme*
    D   *Die Klugheit der Frauen*
    I   *La prudenza della donna*
    E   *La prudencia en la mujer*
    SU «Мýдрость жѐнщины» (Тѝрсо де Молѝна)

4049 GB *Within a Budding Grove* (Proust, 1919)
    F   *À l'ombre des jeunes filles en fleurs*
    D   *Im Schatten der jungen Mädchen*
    I   *All'ombra delle fanciulle in fiore*
    E   *A la sombra de las muchachas en flor*
    SU «Под сѐнью дѐвушек в цветý» (Пруст)

4050 GB *Witness for the Prosecution* (Christie, 1954)
    F   *Témoin à charge*
    D   *Zeugin der Anklage*
    I   *Teste a carico*
    E   *Testigo de cargo*
    SU «Свидѐтель обвинѐния» (Крѝсти)

4051 GB *Wizard of Oz, The* (Fleming, 1939)
    F   *Le Magicien d'Oz*
    D   *Der Magier von Oz*
    I   *Il mago di Oz*
    E   *El mago de Oz*
    SU «Колдýн из Óза» (Флѐминг)

4052 GB *Woe From Wit* (Griboyedov, 1822–4)
 F *Le Malheur d'avoir trop d'esprit* (Griboïedov)
 D *Verstand schafft Leiden* (Gribojedow)
 I *Che disgrazia l'ingegno!* (Griboedov)
 E *La razón daña* (Griboiedov)
 SU «Го́ре от ума́» (Грибое́дов)

4053 GB *Wolf of the Steppes, The* (Hesse, 1927)
 F *Le Loup des steppes*
 D *Der Steppenwolf*
 I *Il lupo della steppa*
 E *El lobo de las estepas*
 SU «Степно́й волк» (Хе́ссе)

4054 GB *Woman in White, The* (Collins, 1860)
 F *La Dame en blanc*
 D *Die Frau in weiß*
 I *La donna in bianco*
 E *La mujer de blanco*
 SU «Же́нщина в бе́лом» (Ко́ллинз)

4055 GB *Woman of No Importance, A* (Wilde, 1893)
 F *Une femme sans importance*
 D *Eine Frau ohne Bedeutung*
 I *Una donna senza importanza*
 E *Una mujer sin importancia*
 SU «Же́нщина, не сто́ящая внима́ния» (Уа́йльд)

4056 GB *Woman of Paris, A* (Chaplin, 1923)
 F *L'Opinion publique*
 D *Die Nächte einer schönen Frau*
 I *Una donna a Parigi*
 E *Una mujer de París*
 SU «Парижа́нка» (Ча́плин)

4057 GB *Woman of Rome, The* (Moravia, 1947)
 F *La Belle Romaine*
 D *Die Römerin*
 I *La romana*
 E *La romana*
 SU «Ри́млянка» (Мора́виа)

4058 GB *Woman Without a Shadow, The* (Strauss, 1919)
 F *La Femme sans ombre*
 D *Die Frau ohne Schatten*
 I *La donna senz'ombra*
 E *La mujer sin sombra*
 SU «Же́нщина без те́ни» (Штра́ус)

4059 GB *Women Beware Women* (Middleton, 1621)
 F *Que les femmes se défient des femmes*
 D *So mögen Frauen sich vor Frauen vorsehen*
 I *Donne diffidate delle donne*
 E *Guárdense las mujeres de las mujeres*
 SU «Же́нщины, остерега́йтесь же́нщин!» (Ми́длтон)

4060 GB *Women in Love* (Lawrence, 1920)
 F *Femmes amoureuses*
 D *Liebende Frauen*
 I *Donne innamorate*
 E *Mujeres enamoradas*
 SU «Влюблённые же́нщины» (Ло́ренс)

4061 GB *Women in Parliament* [*Ekklesiazousai*] (Aristophanes, –391)
 F *L'Assemblée des femmes* (Aristophane)
 D *Die Volksversammlung der Frauen* (Aristophanes)
 I *Le donne a parlamento* (Aristofano)
 E *La asamblea de las mujeres* (Aristófanes)
 SU «Же́нщины в наро́дном собра́нии» (Аристофа́н)

 GB *Women of Trachis, The*→*Trachinian Women, The*

4062 GB *Wonderful Adventures of Nils, The* [*Nils Holgerssons Underbara Resa genom Sverige*] (Lagerlöf, 1906–7)
 F *Les Merveilleux Voyages de Nils Holgersson*
 D *Nils Holgerssons wunderbare Reise durch Schweden*
 I *Il viaggio meraviglioso di Nils Holgersson attraverso la Svezia*
 E *El viaje maravilloso de Nils Holgersson*
 SU «Чуде́сное путеше́ствие Ни́льса Хо́льгерссона по Шве́ции» (Ла́герлёф)

4063 GB *Wonder-Working Magician, The* (Calderon de la Barca, 1637)
 F *Le Magicien prodigieux*
 D *Der wundertätige Magus*
 I *Il mago dei prodigi*
 E *El mágico prodigioso*
 SU «Чу́дный чароде́й» (Кальдеро́н де ла Ба́рка)

4064 GB *Woodlanders, The* (Hardy, 1887)
     F *Les Forestiers*
     D *Die Wäldler*
     I *Gli abitatori del bosco*
     E *Los habitantes del bosque*
     SU «В краю лесóв» (Хáрди)

4065 GB *Words* (Prévert, 1946)
     F *Paroles*
     D *Worte eines Gläubigen*
     I *Parole*
     E *Palabras*
     SU «Словá» (Превéр)

4066 GB *Words of a Believer* (Lamennais, 1834)
     F *Paroles d'un croyant*
     D *Worte eines Gläubigen*
     I *Parole d'un credente*
     E *Palabras de un creyente*
     SU «Словá вéрующего» (Ламеннé)

4067 GB *Working Class Goes to Heaven, The* (Petri, 1971)
     F *La classe ouvrière va au Paradis*
     D *Die Arbeiterklasse geht ins Paradies*
     I *La classe operaia va in Paradiso*
     E *La clase obrera va a Paraíso*
     SU «Рабóчий класс идёт в рай» (Пéтри)

4068 GB *Works and Days* [*Erga kai hemerai*] (Hesiod, −VII)
     F *Les Travaux et les jours* (Hésiode)
     D *Werke und Tage* (Hesiodos)
     I *Le opere e i giorni* (Esiodo)
     E *Los trabajos y los días* (Hesíodo)
     SU «Трудьí и дни» (Гесиóд)

4069 GB *World as Will and Idea, The* (Schopenhauer, 1819)
     F *Le Monde comme volonté et comme représentation*
     D *Die Welt als Wille und Vorstellung*
     I *Il mondo come volontà e rappresentazione*
     E *El mundo como voluntad y representación*
     SU «Мир как вóля и представлéние» (Шопенгáуэр)

4070 GB World Council of Churches (WCC), the
     F le Conseil oecuménique des Églises (COE)
     D der Weltkirchenrat
     I il Consiglio mondiale delle chiese (CMC)
     E el Concilio ecuménico de las Iglesias (CEI)
     SU Всемúрный совéт церквéй (ВСЦ)

4071 GB World Council of Peace (WCP), the
     F le Conseil Mondial de la Paix (CMP)
     D der Weltfriedenrat
     I il Consiglio mondiale della pace (CMP)
     E el Consejo mondial de la paz (CMP)
     SU Всемúрный Совéт Мúра (ВСМ)

4072 GB World Health Organisation (WHO), the
     F l'Organisation mondiale de la Santé (OMS)
     D die Weltgesundheitsorganisation (WHO)
     I l'Organizzazione mondiale della Sanità (OMS)
     E la Organización Mundial de la Salud (OMS)
     SU Всемúрная организáция здравоохранéния (ВОЗ)

4073 GB *Would-be Gentleman, The* (Molière, 1670)
     F *Le Bourgeois gentilhomme*
     D *Der Bürger als Edelmann*
     I *Il borghese gentiluomo*
     E *El burgués gentilhombre*
     SU «Мещанúн во дворя́нстве» (Мольéр)

4074 GB Wroclaw (Poland)
     F Wroclaw (Pologne)
     D Breslau (Polen)
     I Breslavia (Polonia)
     E Wroclaw (Polonia)
     SU Врóцлав (Пóльша)

4075 GB *Wrong Set, The* (Wilson, 1949)
     F *La Fausse Partie*
     D *Die falsche Serie*
     I *La parte sbagliata*
     E *La clase falsa*
     SU «Не тот набóр» (Уúлсон)

4076 GB *Wuthering Heights* (Brontë, 1847)
     F *Les Hauts de Hurlevent*
     D *Sturmhöhe*
     I *Cime tempestose*
     E *Cumbres borrascosas*
     SU «Грозовóй перевáл» (Брóнте)

X

4077   GB   Xanthippe (−V)
       F   Xanthippe
       D   Xanthippe
       I   Santippa
       E   Jantipa
       SU   Ксантиппа

       GB   Xavier, Francis→Francis Xavier

4078   GB   Xenophon (431–350)
       F   Xénophon
       D   Xenophon
       I   Senofonte
       E   Jenofonte
       SU   Ксенофо́нт

4079   GB   Xerxes (519–465)
       F   Xerxès
       D   Xerxes
       I   Serse
       E   Jerjes
       SU   Ксеркс

Y

4080
GB	Yakutia (USSR)
F	l'Iakoutie (f.) (URSS)
D	Jakutien (UdSSR)
I	la Jacuzia (URSS)
E	Yakutia (URSS)
SU	Якýтия (СССР)

4081
GB	*Year of the Soul, The* (George, 1897)
F	*L'Année de l'âme*
D	*Das Jahr der Seele*
I	*L'anno dell'anima*
E	*Año del alma*
SU	«Год душú» (Геóрге)

4082
GB	*Years, The* (Woolf, 1937)
F	*Les Années*
D	*Die Jahre*
I	*Gli anni*
E	*Los años*
SU	«Гóды» (Вулф)

4083
GB	*Yellow Christ, The* (Gauguin, 1889)
F	*Le Christ jaune*
D	*Der gelbe Christus*
I	*Il Cristo giallo*
E	*El Cristo amarillo*
SU	«Жёлтый Христóс» (Гогéн)

4084
GB	Yellow Sea, the
F	la mer Jaune
D	das Gelbe Meer
I	il mare Giallo
E	el mar Amarillo
SU	Жёлтое мóре

4085
GB	Yemen
F	le Yémen
D	Jemen
I	lo Yemen
E	el Yemen
SU	Йéмен

4086
GB	*You and I* (Géraldy, 1913)
F	*Toi et moi*
D	*Du und ich*
I	*Tu ed io*
E	*Tú y yo*
SU	«Ты и я» (Жеральдú)

4087
GB	*You Can't Take It With You* (Capra, 1938)
F	*Vous ne l'emporterez pas avec vous*
D	*Lebenskünstler*
I	*L'eterna illusione*
E	*Vive como quieras*
SU	«Вам э́того с собóй никогдá не унестú» (Кáпра)

4088
GB	*You Can't Trifle With Love* (Musset, 1834)
F	*On ne badine pas avec l'amour*
D	*Man scherzt nicht mit der Liebe*
I	*Con l'amore non si scherza*
E	*No hay burlas con el amor*
SU	«С любóвью не шýтят» (Мюссé)

4089
GB	*You Never Can Tell* (Shaw, 1897)
F	*On ne peut jamais dire*
D	*Mann kann nie wissen*
I	*Non si sa mai*
E	*No se puede decir nunca*
SU	«Поживём – увúдим!» (Шóу)

4090
GB	*Young Eagle, The* (Rostand, 1900)
F	*L'Aiglon*
D	*Der junge Aar*
I	*L'Aiglon*
E	*El Aguilucho*
SU	«Орлёнок» (Ростáн)

4091   GB   *Youngest of the Fates, The* (Valéry, 1917)
    F   *La Jeune Parque*
    D   *Die junge Parze*
    I   *La giovane parca*
    E   *La joven parca*
    SU   «Юная па́рка» (Валери́)

4092   GB   *Young Girls, The* (Montherlant, 1936–9)
    F   *Les Jeunes Filles*
    D   *Die jungen Mädchen*
    I   *Le fanciulle*
    E   *Las adolescentes*
    SU   «Де́вушки» (Монтерла́н)

4093   GB   *Young Guard, The* (Fadeyev, 1945)
    F   *La Jeune Garde* (Fadeïev)
    D   *Die junge Garde* (Fadejew)
    I   *La giovane guardia* (Fadeev)
    E   *La joven guardia* (Fadeiev)
    SU   «Молода́я гва́рдия» (Фаде́ев)

4094   GB   *Youth* (Conrad, 1902)
    F   *Jeunesse*
    D   *Jugend*
    I   *Gioventù*
    E   *Juventud*
    SU   «Ю́ность» (Ко́нрад)

4095   GB   Yugoslavia
    F   la Yougoslavie
    D   Jugosławien
    I   la Iugoslavia
    E   Yugoslavia
    SU   Югосла́вия

Z

4096 GB Zaïre
        F   le Zaïre
        D Zaire
        I   lo Zaire
        E Zaire
        SU Зайр

4097 GB Zambia
        F   la Zambie
        D Sambia
        I   lo Zambia
        E Zambia
        SU Зáмбия

4098 GB Zanzibar (Tanzania)
        F   Zanzibar (Tanzania)
        D Sansibar (Tansania)
        I   Zanzibar (Tanzania)
        E Zanzíbar (Tanzania)
        SU Занзибáр (Танзáния)

4099 GB *Zazie dans le Métro* [*Zazie on the Underground*] (Malle, 1960)
        F   *Zazie dans le Métro*
        D *Zazie*
        I   *Zazie nel metrò*
        E *Zazie en el metro*
        SU «Зазú в метрó» (Малль)

4100 GB Zechariah (Zachariah) (Bib.)
        F   Zacharie (Bib.)
        D Sacharja (Bib.)
        I   Zaccaria (Bib.)
        E Zacarías (Bib.)
        SU Захáрия (библ.)

4101 GB *Zéro de Conduite* [*Nought for Behaviour*] (Vigo, 1933)
        F   *Zéro de conduite*
        D *Betragen ungenügend*
        I   *Zero in condotta*
        E *Cero en conducta*
        SU «Ноль за поведéние» (Вигó)

4102 GB Zeus (myth.)
        F   Zeus (myth.)
        D Zeus (myth.)
        I   Zeus (mit.)
        E Zeus (mit.)
        SU Зевс (миф.)

4103 GB Zimbabwe
        F   le Zimbabwe
        D Simbabwe
        I   lo Zimbabwe
        E Zimbabwe
        SU Зимбáбве

4104 GB *Zorba the Greek* [*Víos kai politía tou Aléxi Zormpá*] (Kazantzakis, 1946)
        F   *Alexis Zorba*
        D *Alexis Zorbas*
        I   *Zorba il greco*
        E *Hechos y gestas de Alexis Zorba*
        SU «Жизнь и делá Алéксиса Зорбáса» (Казандзáкис)

4105 GB Zoroaster (−VI)
        F   Zoroastre
        D Zoroaster
        I   Zoroastro
        E Zoroastro
        SU Зороáстр

4106 GB Zululand (South Africa)
    F le Zoulouland (Afrique du Sud)
    D Zululand (Südafrika)
    I lo Zululand (Africa del Sud)
    E Zululandia (África del Sur)
    SU Зу́луленд (Ю́жная А́фрика)

4107 GB Zürich (Switzerland)
    F Zurich (Suisse)
    D Zürich (Schweiz)
    I Zurigo (Svizzera)
    E Zurich (Suiza)
    SU Цю́рих (Швейца́рия)

4108 GB Zweibrücken (Germany)
    F Deux-Ponts (Allemagne)
    D Zweibrücken (Deutschland)
    I Due Ponti (Germania)
    E Dos Puentes (Alemania)
    SU Цвейбрю́ккен (Герма́ния)

CROSS-INDEXES

The following cross-indexes will enable the user of the dictionary to find the equivalent name or title in any language by means of referring to the main body of the book.

To discover the English equivalent, the reader simply has to find the name he requires in the respective non-English language (French, German, Italian, Spanish or Russian), where it will be listed alphabetically. The number following the name will be that of the main entry, where the English equivalent will be found.

By means of the same number, the reader can also cross-refer from one language to any other, since all languages are grouped together under the English in the main section of the book.

The names and titles are given in the cross-indexes in their basic form, since all additional information, provision of definite articles and so on is supplied in the main entries.

When looking up an italicised title in the lists, it should be remembered that any initial article, definite or indefinite, should be ignored for alphabetical purposes, thus following the system used in most standard lists of literary and other titles.

Identical or very similar titles are distinguished by author (as the two French titles *L'Admirable Crichton*), and identical names are also distinguished for ease of reference.

In the very few cases where two reference numbers are given (as for French *Grande Ourse*), this means that there are two equally valid English equivalents.

FRANÇAIS

DEUTSCH

ITALIANO

Giobbe 1874
Giocasta 1875
Giocatore, Il 1366
giochi olimpici 2702
giochi pitici 3074
Giochi proibiti 1862
Gioco dell'amore e del caso, Il 1367
Gioco del pigiama, Il 2771
Gioconda 2461
Gioele 1877
Gioielli della Madonna, I 1863
Giona 1889
Gionata 1890
Gionata Wild il grande 1891
Giordania 1892
Giordano 1893
Giorgio 1396
Giornata di Ivan Denissovič, Una 2707
Giorni perduti 2143
Giorno della locusta, Il 930
Giorno di festa 1901
Giorno . . . di prima mattina, Un 3542
Giorno il più lungo, Il 2126
Giorno maledetto 331
Giosia 1900
Giosuè 1899
Giovane guardia, La 4093
Giovane Holden, Il 667
Giovane parca, La 4091
"giovani arrabbiati" 182
Giovani uccidono, I 481
Giovanna 1870
Giovanna d'Arco 1871
Giovanna d'Arco al rogo 1872
Giovanna la Pazza 1873
Giovanni 1879
Giovanni, vangelo di 1880
Giovanni Battista 1887
Giovanni Cristostomo 1882
Giovanni Damasceno 1884
Giovanni della Croce 1886
Giovanni di Salisbury 1885
Giovanni Senza Paura 1888
Giovanni Senza Terra 1883
Giove 1927
giovedì santo 2343
Giovenale 1935
Gioventù 4094
Gioventù bruciata 3112
giovini esploratrici 1518
Giro del mondo in ottanta giorni, Il 263
Giro di vite, Il 3848
Girolamo 1856
Gironda 1417
Girotondo 2389
Giselle 1418
Gita al faro 3780
Giuda (personaggio biblico, figlio di Giacobbe) 1908
Giuda (personaggio biblico, apostolo, santo) 1909
Giuda (personaggio biblico, autore della 'Lettera di Giuda') 1912
Giuda Iscariota 1910
Giuda l'oscuro 1913

Guida Maccabeo 1911
Giudea 1907
Giudici, libro dei 1915
Giuditta 1916
Giulia 1919
Giuliano l'Apostata 1920
Giuliano l'Apostata, o la morte degli dei 943
Giulietta e Romeo 3205
Giulio 1921
Giulio Cesare 1922
Giungla, La 1923
Giungla d'asfalto 282
Giunone 1925
Giunone e il pavone 1926
Giuramento degli Orazi 2660
Giuseppe 1894
Giuseppe d'Arimatea 1897
Giuseppe e i suoi fratelli 1895
Giuseppe Flavio 1898
Giuseppina 1896
Giustiniano 1930
Giustino 1929
Giustizia 1928
Gladiatori, I 565
Golan, alture del 1426
Golden Gate 1437
Golfo, corrente del 1526
Golgota 1443
Golia 1444
Gorgia 1456
Gorgoni 1457
goti 1459
Götz von Berlichingen 1425
Graal 1661
Gracchi 1460
Grampiani, monti 1463
Granada 1464
Gran Bacino 1476
Gran Baia Australiana 1474
Gran Bretagna 1479
Grand Canyon 1466
Grande amico Meaulnes, Il 2140
Grande Barriera Corallina 1475
Grande caldo, Il 443
Grande Catena Divisoria 1481
Grand Ciro, Il 266
Grande dittatore, Il 1480
Grande Gatsby, Il 1487
Grande illusione, La 1467
Grande Muraglia Cinese 1496
Grande Odalisca 1470
Grande Pasqua russa, La 3235
Gran Deserto Sabbioso 1491
Grande sonno, Il 445
Grand Hotel 1468
Grandi Antille 1482
Grandi cimiteri sotto la luna, I 994
Grandi Laghi 1488
Grandi manovre, Le 1489
Grandi speranze 1485
Gran Galeotto, Il 1486
Gran Lago degli Orsi 1478
Gran Lago degli Schiavi 1493
Gran Lago Salato 1490
Gran Londra 1483

ESPAÑOL

РУССКИЙ

APPENDIX
Common first names and their equivalents

ENGLISH	FRANÇAIS	DEUTSCH	ITALIANO	ESPAÑOL	РУССКИЙ
Adam	Adam	Adam	Adamo	Adán	Áдам
Adrian	Adrien	Adrian	Adriano	Adriano	Адриáн
Albert	Albert	Albert	Alberto	Alberto	Альбéрт
Alexander	Alexandre	Alexander	Alessandro	Alejandro	Алексáндр
Alfred	Alfred	Alfred	Alfredo	Alfredo	Альфрéд
Alice	Alice	Alice	Alicia	Alicia	Алúса
Alan	Alain	Alain	Alano	Alano	Алáн
Andrew	André	Andreas	Andrea	Andrés	Андрéй
Ann(e)	Anne	Anna	Anna	Ana	Áнна
Anthony	Antoine	Anton	Antonio	Antonio	Антóний
Arthur	Arthur	Artur	Arturo	Arturo	Артýр
Barbara	Barbe	Barbara	Barbara	Bárbara	Варвáра
Basil	Basile	Basilius	Basilio	Basilio	Васúлий
Benjamin	Benjamin	Benjamin	Beniamino	Benjamín	Вениамúн
Bernard	Bernard	Bernhard	Bernardo	Bernardo	Бернáрд
Caroline	Caroline	Karoline	Carolina	Carolina	Каролúна
Catherine	Catherine	Katharine	Caterina	Catalina	Екатерúна
Christopher	Christophe	Christoph	Cristoforo	Cristóbal	Христофóр
Daniel	Daniel	Daniel	Danielle	Daniel	Даниúл
David	David	David	David	David	Давúд
Dorothy	Dorothée	Dorothea	Dorotea	Dorotea	Дорофéя
Edmund	Edmond	Edmund	Edmondo	Edmundo	Эдмýнд
Edward	Édouard	Eduard	Edoardo	Eduardo	Эдуáрд
Elizabeth	Élisabeth	Elisabeth	Elisabetta	Isabel	Елизавéта
Ernest	Ernest	Ernst	Ernesto	Ernesto	Эрнéст
Frances	Françoise	Franziska	Francesca	Francisca	Францúска
Francis	François	Franz	Francesco	Francisco	Францúск
Frederick	Frédéric	Friedrich	Federico	Federico	Фредерúк
George	Georges	Georg	Giorgio	Jorge	Геóргий
Gregory	Grégoire	Gregor	Gregorio	Gregorio	Григóрий
Harold	Harold	Harald	Araldo	Araldo	Гáрольд
Helen	Hélène	Helena	Elena	Helena	Елéна
Henry	Henri	Heinrich	Enrico	Enrique	Гéнрих
Hugh	Hugues	Hugo	Ugo	Hugo	Хью
James	Jacques	Jakob	Giacobbe	Diego	Яков
Jeremy	Jérémie	Jeremias	Geremia	Jeremías	Еремéй
Jane/Joan	Jeanne	Johanna	Giovanna	Juana	Иоáнна
John	Jean	Johann	Giovanni	Juan	Ивáн
Joseph	Joseph	Joseph	Giuseppe	José	Иóсиф

ENGLISH	FRANÇAIS	DEUTSCH	ITALIANO	ESPAÑOL	РУССКИЙ
Laurence	Laurent	Lorenz	Lorenzo	Lorenzo	Лавре́нтий
Louis/Lewis	Louis	Ludwig	Luigi	Luis	Луи́
Lucy	Lucie	Lucia	Lucia	Lucía	Лю́си́я
Luke	Luc	Lukas	Luca	Lucas	Лука́
Mark	Marc	Markus	Marco	Marcos	Марк
Margaret	Marguerite	Margareta	Margherita	Margarita	Маргари́та
Martha	Marthe	Martha	Marta	Marta	Ма́рфа
Martin	Martin	Martin	Martino	Martín	Марти́н
Mary	Marie	Maria	Maria	María	Мари́я
Matthew	Mathieu	Matthäus	Matteo	Mateo	Матве́й
Michael	Michel	Michael	Michele	Miguel	Михаи́л
Nicholas	Nicolas	Nikolaus	Nicola	Nicolás	Никола́й
Oliver	Olivier	Oliver	Oliverio	Oliverio	О́ливер
Patrick	Patrice	Patrizius	Patrizio	Patricio	Патри́кий
Paul	Paul	Paul	Paolo	Pablo	Па́вел
Peter	Pierre	Peter	Pietro	Pedro	Пётр
Philip	Philippe	Philipp	Filippo	Felipe	Фили́пп
Rachel	Rachel	Rachel	Rachele	Raquel	Рахи́ль
Reginald	Regnault	Reinhold	Rinaldo	Reinaldos	Реджина́льд
Richard	Richard	Richard	Riccardo	Ricardo	Ри́чард
Robert	Robert	Robert	Roberto	Roberto	Ро́берт
Roderick	Rodrigue	Roderich	Rodrigo	Rodrigo	Рю́рик
Roland	Roland	Roland	Orlando	Rolando	Ро́ланд
Samuel	Samuel	Samuel	Samuele	Samuel	Самуи́л
Sarah	Sara	Sarah	Sara	Sara	Са́рра
Simon	Simon	Simon	Simone	Simón	Си́мон
Stephen	Étienne	Stefan	Stefano	Esteban	Степа́н
Susan	Suzanne	Susanna	Susanna	Susana	Суса́нна
Theresa	Thérèse	Theresia	Teresa	Teresa	Тере́за
Theodore	Théodore	Theodor	Teodoro	Teodoro	Фёдор
Thomas	Thomas	Thomas	Tomasso	Tomás	Фома́
Timothy	Timothée	Timotheus	Timoteo	Timoteo	Тимофе́й
Victor	Victor	Viktor	Vittorio	Victor	Ви́ктор
Vincent	Vincent	Vinzent	Vincentio	Vicente	Винсе́нт
Walter	Gauthier	Walter	Gualtiero	Gualterio	Ва́льтер
William	Guillaume	Wilhelm	Guiglielmo	Guillermo	Вильге́льм

BIBLIOGRAPHY

The select bibliography that follows represents only the hard core of what was actually consulted in the course of work on the dictionary and the search for names and titles in the different languages. Apart from the works listed, which are in the main encyclopedias and specialised reference books and dictionaries, a number of yearbooks, gazetteers, directories, catalogues and other publications were used, such as (for the literary titles) the regularly published *Les Livres disponibles* listing all French books currently in print at any given time, and the equivalent Spanish *Libros en venta* and *Libros Españoles*.

Many of the encyclopedias consulted were large, multivolume works, and could be suitably 'milked' for a large number of entries. One objective in consulting different encyclopedias, however, was as much to cross-check the form and spelling of names and titles as to add to the general content.

The bibliography is arranged in two parts. The first lists the encyclopedias and other works used, as mentioned, and the second lists the bilingual (English–foreign language) dictionaries that were regularly referred to. Even these, however, were also backed up with other, smaller dictionaries.

The absence of any significant title that occurs to the reader, therefore, does not necessarily mean that such a title was not consulted.

I have taken the liberty of translating the Russian titles since this language may not be so readily accessible to users of the dictionary.

I Encyclopedias and specialised reference works

ENGLISH

Aurousseau, M., *The Rendering of Geographical Names*, Hutchinson, London, 1957.
Benét, William Rose, *The Reader's Encyclopedia*, Adam & Charles Black, London, 1965.
Drabble, Margaret (ed.), *The Oxford Companion to English Literature*, 5th ed., OUP, Oxford, 1985.
Encyclopaedia Britannica, Encyclopaedia Britannica, Chicago, London, etc., 1976.
Evans, Ivor H., *Brewer's Dictionary of Phrase and Fable*, Cassell, London, 1981.
Girling, D. A. (ed.), *Everyman's Encyclopedia*, Dent, London, 1978.
Halliwell, Leslie, *Halliwell's Film Guide*, Granada Publishing, St Albans, 1985.
Hammond, N. G. L. and Scullard, H. H. (eds), *The Oxford Classical Dictionary*, Clarendon Press, Oxford, 1970.
Hart, James D. *The Oxford Companion to American Literature*, OUP, Oxford, 1983.
Hartnoll, Phyllis (ed.), *The Oxford Companion to the Theatre*, OUP, Oxford, 1983.
Harvey, Sir Paul, *The Oxford Companion to English Literature*, 4th ed. revised by Dorothy Eagle, Clarendon Press, Oxford, 1973.
Harvey, Sir Paul and Heseltine, J. E., *The Oxford Companion to French Literature*, Clarendon Press, Oxford, 1959.
Payton, Geoffrey (comp.), *Payton's Proper Names*, Warne, London, 1969.
Scholes, Percy A., *The Oxford Companion to Music*, 10th ed. edited by John Owen Ward, OUP, Oxford, 1978.
Webster's Biographical Dictionary, G. & C. Merriam, Springfield, Mass., USA, 1976.
Webster's New Geographical Dictionary, G. & C. Merriam, Springfield, Mass., USA, 1980.

FRANÇAIS

Encyclopédie alphabétique Larousse-Omnis, Librairie Larousse, Paris, 1977.
Encyclopédie internationale Focus, Bordas, Paris, 1962.
Grand Larousse encyclopédique, Librairie Larousse, Paris, 1960.
Grimal, Pierre, *Dictionnaire de la mythologie grecque et romaine*, Presses Universitaires de France, Paris, 1979.
Nouveau Larousse Classique, Librairie Larousse, Paris, 1957
Robert, Paul (dir.), *Le petit Robert 2: Dictionnaire universel des noms propres*, SNL-Le Robert, Paris, 1980.

DEUTSCH

Brockhaus Enzyklopädie, F. A. Brockhaus, Wiesbaden, 1966.
Der Grosse Brockhaus, F. A. Brockhaus, Wiesbaden, 1977.
Kleines literarisches Lexikon, Erster Band: Autoren I (Von den Anfängen bis zum 19. Jahrhundert), Francke Verlag, Bern, 1969.
Kleines literarisches Lexikon, Zweiter Band: Autoren II (20. Jahrhundert), Francke Verlag, Bern, 1972–3.
Knaurs Lexikon, Droemer Knaur, München, 1981.
Der Volks Brockhaus, F. A. Brockhaus, Wiesbaden, 1981.

ITALIANO

Enciclopedia Garzanti della letteratura, Garzanti Editore, Milano, 1979.
Enciclopedia Garzanti Universale, Garzanti Editore, Milano, 1969.
Enciclopedia Italiana di Scienze, Lettere ed Arti, Istituto Giovanni Treccani, Milano, 1929.

Grande Dizionario Enciclopedico Utet, Unione Tipografico-Editrice Torinese, Torino, 1966.
La nuova enciclopedia universale Garzanti, Garzanti Editore, Milano, 1982.

ESPAÑOL

Díaz-Plaja, Guillermo, *La Literatura universal*, Ediciones Danae, Barcelona, 1977.
Diccionario Enciclopédico Labor, Editorial Labor, Barcelona, 1967.
Diccionario Enciclopédico Salvat Universal, Salvat Editores, Barcelona, 1969.
Enciclopedia Universal Ilustrada Europeo–Americana, José Espasa, Barcelona, 1907–30.
García-Pelayo y Gross, Ramón, *Pequeño Larousse en color*, Ediciones Larousse, Paris, 1972.

РУССКИЙ

Агеенко, Ф. Л., Зарва, М. В. Словарь ударений для работников радио и телевидения ('Dictionary of Stresses for Radio and Television Staffs'). М., Русский язык, 1984.
Большая советская энциклопедия ('Large Soviet Encyclopedia'). М., Советская Энциклопедия, 1970–81.
Вайнкоп, Ю. Я., Гусин, И. Л. Краткий биографический словарь композиторов ('Concise Biographical Dictionary of Musical Composers'). Л., Музыка, 1979.
Географический энциклопедический словарь ('Geographical Encyclopedic Dictionary'). М., Советская Энциклопедия, 1983.
Гиляревский, Р. С., Старостин, Б. А. Иностранные имена и названия в русском тексте ('Foreign Names Titles in a Russian Text'). М., Международные отношения, 1969.
Названия СССР, союзных республик и зарубежных стран на 20 языках ('Names of the USSR, Union Republics, and Foreign Countries in 20 Languages'). М., ВИНИТИ, 1974.
Новиков, М. П. (общ. ред.). Атеистический словарь ('Atheist Dictionary'). М., Политиздат, 1983.
Петровский, Н. А. Словарь русских личных имён ('Dictionary of Russian Personal Names'). М., Советская Энциклопедия, 1966.
Рыбакин, А. И. (сост.). Словарь английских личных имён ('Dictionary of English Personal Names'). М., Советская Энциклопедия, 1973.
Словарь географических названий зарубежных стран ('Dictionary of Geographical Names of Foreign Countries'). М., Недра, 1965.
Советский энциклопедический словарь ('Soviet Encyclopedic Dictionary'). М., Советская Энциклопедия, 1980.

II BILINGUAL DICTIONARIES

(F)   Mansion, J. E., *Harrap's New Standard French and English Dictionary*, Harrap, London, 1980.
(D)   Cassell's *German–English English–German Dictionary*, completely revised by Harold T. Betteridge, Cassell, London, 1978.
(I)   Hazon, Mario, *Grande Dizionario Inglese–Italiano Italiano–Inglese*, Garzanti Editore, Milano, 1981.
(E)   Smith, Colin and Bermejo Marcos, Manuel and Chang-Rodríguez, Euginio, *Collins Spanish–English English–Spanish Dictionary*, Collins, London and Glasgow, 1981.
(SU) Galperin, Prof. I. R. (ed.), *New English–Russian Dictionary*, Soviet Encyclopaedia Publishing House, Moscow, 1972.
        Falla, P. S. (ed.), *The Oxford English–Russian Dictionary*, Clarendon Press, Oxford, 1984.